RELIGION AND FOREIGN AFFAIRS

RELIGION AND FOREIGN AFFAIRS
Essential Readings

Dennis R. Hoover and Douglas M. Johnston
Editors

This work is published in association with
The Review of Faith & International Affairs,
which is published quarterly at the Institute for Global Engagement.

BAYLOR UNIVERSITY PRESS

Cover Design by Martyn Schmoll
Cover Image © Getty Images/Richard Newstead

Library of Congress Cataloging-in-Publication Data

Religion and foreign affairs : essential readings / Dennis R. Hoover and Douglas M. Johnston, editors.
    p. cm.
  Includes bibliographical references.
  ISBN 978-1-60258-242-2 (pbk. : alk. paper)
  1. Religion and international relations. 2. Religion and politics. I. Hoover, Dennis. II. Johnston, Douglas, 1938–
  BL65.I55R44 2012
  201'.727--dc23

                         2011032154

BAYLOR
UNIVERSITY

Printed in the United States of America on acid-free paper with a minimum of 30% PCW recycled content.

To all those
past, present, and future
who labor to transform religious conflict and
discrimination into sustainable peace and freedom.

TABLE OF CONTENTS

SECTION IV
Religion and Conflict

SECTION V
Religion and Peacemaking

ACKNOWLEDGMENTS

Many thanks to Carey Newman at Baylor University Press for proposing this book project as a collaboration between the Press and *The Review of Faith & International Affairs* and for the encouragement, advice, patience, and professionalism that he and all the staff at the Press gave us throughout this compendium's long gestation. We are grateful as well for the advice that Ruth Melkonian-Hoover, Chris Seiple, and Paul Brink provided on various dimensions of the table of contents at critical junctures. We gratefully acknowledge the Institute for Global Engagement (IGE), which underwrote the project and which, along with the International Center for Religion & Diplomacy (ICRD), provided us with the time and staff support necessary to put together such an ambitious, wide-ranging anthology. Assistance came from numerous colleagues, including Karin Christianson, Judd Birdsall, Brittany Ceaser, Victoria Barrett, Nathan Hitchen, Lacey Jenkins, Ramah Kudaimi, Sarah McKinley, Michael B. Schoenleber, Annalise Thompson—and, above all, Anna Carrington (IGE) and Patrick Moore (ICRD), who provided invaluable assistance in research, editing, and running a marathon gauntlet of reprint permissions.

—Introduction—

RELIGION AND THE GLOBAL AGENDA
From the Margins to the Mainstream?

—Dennis R. Hoover and Douglas M. Johnston

OVER THE LAST decade there has been a marked increase in interest among scholars, practitioners, and policymakers in the role of religion in world politics and global affairs. Indeed, the literature in the interdisciplinary field of religion and international affairs has grown to such an extent that it is now possible to publish a wide-ranging compendium of excellent articles—such as the present reader, which is designed as a broad survey.

The bad news, however, is that the field should have reached this level of maturation long ago. One of the earliest articulations of the factors inhibiting the field's development was Edward Luttwak's 1994 essay "The Missing Dimension."[1] Luttwak eloquently explained that the intellectual bias against taking religion seriously can be traced historically to a certain Enlightenment overreaction against the constraints imposed by premodern Christendom.

> Astonishingly persistent, Enlightenment prejudice has remained amply manifest in the contemporary professional analysis of foreign affairs. Policymakers, diplomats, journalists, and scholars who are ready to over-interpret economic causality, who are apt to dissect social differentiations most finely, and who will minutely categorize political affiliations, are still in the habit of disregarding the role of religion, religious institutions, and religious motivations in explaining politics and conflict. . . . One is therefore confronted with a learned repugnance to contend intellectually with all that is religion or belongs to it.[2]

This prejudice has been animated by both secularization *theory* and an anti-religious secular*ism*.[3] Secularization theory holds that as modernization advances, religion recedes. The retreat of religion is said to entail the growth of the avowedly secular portion of the population and the privatization of religious belief and practice among those who continue to maintain some kind of religious identity. In a strictly empirical sense, secularization theory does not necessarily have any normative content: it is simply a testable hypothesis about what happens to religion under conditions of modernity. If it is a valid theory—and until recently a great many assumed it was—it feeds the cycle of ignoring or at least sidelining religion in academia and public policy analysis.

Anti-religious secular*ism*, by contrast, is more than an academic theory. It is a normative disposition—one found frequently among the Western (and Westernized) intelligentsia, including many foreign affairs professionals. It assumes not only that modernization is likely to have certain functionally subversive effects on religion but also that secularity is the *correct* direction of history. Religion is thought to be a regressive and irrational force, and individuals would be better off if they left it behind entirely. If they insist on clinging to religiosity, then legally and culturally religion should be strictly a private matter cordoned off from public life.

But many religious believers have doggedly refused to cooperate with the change forecast by secularization theory and advocated by apostles of secularism. Manifestations of religious persistence and even resurgence have been obvious, both in the United States and internationally. Yet specialists in international affairs have been slower to shed their blinders than have specialists in American culture and politics. Consider by way of example the scholarly responses to two cases of "fundamentalist" mobilization that date from 1979.

First, in American politics there was the founding of the Moral Majority. Led by Jerry Falwell, a prominent pastor and activist in the fundamentalist stream of American evangelicalism, the Moral Majority quickly became the flagship organization of the religious right. The various battles over abortion and cultural issues that had been flaring since the 1960s merged into a larger "culture war" by the 1980s. Domestic social sciences were not particularly well prepared to study and understand resurgent religion, but a sufficiently large cadre of scholars did respond to realities on the ground, pushing their disciplines to develop new analytical capacities and to make room for religious studies. Within a few years, studies of religion and American public life were proliferating.

The other big religion story of 1979 was from the foreign desk—namely, the Islamic revolution in Iran. Professionals in international affairs were not any better prepared than professionals elsewhere to anticipate and respond to such developments. Luttwak recounts a memorable anecdote of how the CIA reacted to a recommendation, given prior to the revolution, that Iran's religious situation should be monitored. The recommendation was dismissed "on the grounds that it would amount to mere 'sociology,' a term used in intelligence circles to mean the time-wasting study of factors deemed politically irrelevant."[4]

What was surprising was how durable the "mere sociology" attitude vis-à-vis religion and international affairs proved to be, and not just in intelligence circles. By and large the disciplines that address international affairs continued to give religion short shrift. This accusation of neglect is not just special pleading for religious studies, for as Daniel Philpott has shown, the analytical absence of religion in the field is empirically verifiable. A survey of 1,600 articles in four leading international relations journals over the period 1980–1999 found that only a handful treated religion as a significant variable.[5] Likewise, as Jack Snyder has observed, religion was dealt with superficially or not at all in the literature of the major schools of international relations theory—realism, liberalism, and even constructivism (which in principle should have more room for religion).[6]

To be sure, there were some exceptions to the general pattern of ignoring religion, and the frequency of these exceptions increased after the end of the Cold War. The most famous exception, however, is one that proves the rule. This was Samuel P. Huntington's 1993

Foreign Affairs article "The Clash of Civilizations?" The Cold War had provided a clear paradigm for understanding international relations and the principal sources of international conflict. Huntington's bold thesis was that differences between civilizations would now be the primary force shaping global conflict. Religion was deeply implicated in such conflict because Huntington defined "civilizations" almost entirely along religious lines, drawing particular attention to conflict between "Islamic civilization" and "the West."[7]

"The Clash of Civilizations?" was the article that launched a thousand other articles—a cottage industry debating the merits of the paradigm conceptually, empirically, strategically, and morally. In that sense it was helpful in catalyzing a revival of scholarship related to religion in international affairs. But it also did a disservice in that it framed the relevance of religion largely in negative and reductionist terms. In reality, religion is part of the problem—often in very complex and contingent ways—in many more issues than just the conflicts that erupt along civilization borders. However, religion—especially in cultural and legal environments of responsible religious liberty—can also be a key part of the solution to a wide range of concerns on the global agenda. As a theory, then, the clash of civilizations managed to both overstate and understate the relevance of religion.

Beyond the "clash" discourse, the 1990s also saw a revival of interest in the relevance of religion to a few specific areas of policy/practice, such as conflict resolution and human rights.[8] In the field of conflict resolution, for example, the Center for Strategic & International Studies launched a Religion and Conflict Resolution Project, which later produced the seminal 1994 work *Religion, the Missing Dimension of Statecraft*, edited by Douglas M. Johnston and Cynthia Sampson.[9] Building on these foundations, five years later Johnston founded the International Center for Religion and Diplomacy.[10]

In human rights, one of the most notable examples was the mid-1990s mobilization of a grassroots campaign focused on international religious freedom. The campaign led to passage of the International Religious Freedom Act (IRFA) in 1998, which created an Office of International Religious Freedom within the State Department, a U.S. Commission on International Religious Freedom, and a new position of Ambassador-at-Large for International Religious Freedom. The movement also helped energize private sector efforts to study and promote the conditions necessary for sustainable religious freedom. Prominent among these was the Institute for Global Engagement.[11] The Institute was first established in 1997 as a center within World Vision.[12] Then in 2000 Robert and Margaret Ann Seiple incorporated the Institute as an independent nonprofit organization. (Robert Seiple was president of World Vision from 1987 to 1998 and U.S. Ambassador-at-Large for International Religious Freedom from 1998 to 2000.)

It was not until after 9/11, however, that the foreign affairs establishment as a whole began to wake up to the significance of religion's role. The shock of the terrorist attacks created a sudden consensus that "religion matters." As Dwight D. Eisenhower once said, "Being shot at focuses the mind wonderfully."

Fortunately, a "clash of civilizations" interpretation of the attacks did not become the reigning paradigm (perhaps because the thesis had already been assiduously dissected and disputed over the previous eight years). Today, if anything reigns in the field, it is confusion—but at least there is now widespread determination to sort through the complexities and make progress in matters both theoretical and practical. Indeed, recent years have witnessed a remarkable surge in new publications, centers, and programs in the field.[13]

Thus, the time is ripe for publication of a general reader on religion and global affairs. To that end, Baylor University Press and *The Review of Faith & International Affairs* partnered to produce this first-of-its-kind compendium, which features a diverse sample of learned yet accessible essays by distinguished scholars and practitioners. Our objective for this collection is to provide significant entreé into this young field, stimulating discussion and whetting appetites for further study, research, policy debate, curricular development, and practical engagement. Here it is important to note three disclaimers. First, we do not pretend that this collection is exhaustive; the public role of religion is too vast and variegated to cover in a single volume. Second, in making the assertion that "religion matters" we are by no means suggesting that the definition of "religion" is self-evident or uncomplicated; in some contexts religion is primarily a matter of propositional beliefs held by individuals, in others it is more of a comprehensive and communal way of life. Broadly speaking, we concur with the definition used by Daniel Philpott (see page 34 of this reader): "Religion is a set of beliefs about the ultimate ground of existence, that which is unconditioned, not itself created or caused, and the communities and practices that form around these beliefs."[14] Third, we compiled these articles not because we necessarily agree with all the points they make, but rather to provide a unique resource convenient for use as a textbook, reference work, and/or primer.

The authors featured in this collection include influential scholars such as Samuel P. Huntington, David Little, José Casanova, Katherine Marshall, Scott M. Thomas, Philip Jenkins, Peter L. Berger, Vali Nasr, Rosalind I. J. Hackett, and many others. The expanding nature of the field, however, warrants the inclusion of voices beyond academia as well—for example, former Secretary of State Madeleine Albright, Archbishop of Canterbury Rowan Williams, and journalists Robert D. Kaplan and David Brooks.

The reader is divided into ten thematic sections, which correspond to the kinds of themes that tend to figure prominently in (among other places) survey courses on global affairs/international relations.

Section I: Secularization, Desecularization, and the Disciplines of International Affairs

The implications of religious resurgence in public life are today exceedingly difficult to ignore. Especially since 9/11, secularization theory has lost influence; true believers in the theory are harder to come by. Still, it has cast a long shadow intellectually—and in any case, secular*ism* remains common. Section I provides an overview, not so much as a stand-alone segment of the reader, but rather as a framework for understanding the rest of the book. Our first selection from the eminent theorist Charles Taylor discusses what it means for a regime to be "secular." Peter L. Berger then explores factors that had, already in the 1990s, led some scholars to declare that the world was "desecularizing" rather than secularizing. Daniel Philpott then examines 9/11's impact specifically on secularism in international relations. An article by Rosalind I. J. Hackett looks at desecularization's impact on nation-states and the public sphere, with the American example as a case study. The final piece in this section, David Brooks' *Atlantic Monthly* essay "Kicking the Secularist Habit," illustrates how critiques of secularization theory and secularism have come to the fore not just in certain quarters of academia, but at a more popular level, too.

Section II: Theoretical Foundations from Antiquity

Section II begins with an excerpt from Thucydides' *Peloponnesian War*, followed by two contrasting perspectives on the wisdom of ancient "pagan realist" principles for contemporary international relations. An article by Robert D. Kaplan provides a concise summary of an argument he presents in his 2001 book, *Warrior Politics: Why Leadership Demands a Pagan Ethos*. Kaplan's article is coupled here with an essay by Dennis R. Hoover responding to the *Warrior Politics* thesis. Hoover challenges Kaplan's interpretation of pagan ethics and his assumption that a morality based on religious principles is inappropriate in world affairs today. This section then presents excerpts from Augustine's *City of God*, followed by an essay from Reinhold Niebuhr reflecting on Augustine's biblically informed realism. John A. Rees then provides some broader context for the use of various sacred texts in international affairs. Finally, Scott M. Thomas suggests lessons from the prophet Isaiah's theology of international relations, arguing that this theology upended ancient Israel's reliance on *realpolitik* and that it can inform a postpositivist understanding of contemporary "human security."

Section III: Ethics of Force

A subject that has been particularly prominent in both ancient and modern thought on the affairs of nations is the ethics of force, which is the focus of section III. Because the most influential tradition of ethical reasoning about the use of force is just war theory, this section begins with a classic excerpt on the subject by Thomas Aquinas. This is followed by a selection from one of the modern era's most formidable pacifist theologians, John Howard Yoder. Yoder's essay was written in the context of the Persian Gulf War (1990–1991), which many have considered less morally problematic than the Iraq War (2003). The Iraq War is the context of the next selections in the reader—an exchange between George Weigel and Rowan Williams. An article by James Turner Johnson then applies classical just war theory's guidelines to questions about the use of torture in the contemporary "war on terrorism." The section concludes with an article by John Kelsay examining Islamic ethics of violence through the lens of jihad and the ongoing debate within Islam over the meaning of jihad.

Section IV: Religion and Conflict

As the headlines about nontraditional warfare remind us every day, religion is indeed part of the problem in global conflict. Section IV begins with an article by Mark Juergensmeyer, who explains that "militant religious activists often interject religious mythology into real-life political struggles, and find in religion a legitimization and a support for acts of violence as if they were mandated by God." This is followed by a pair of articles that illustrate some of the main contours of the debate over religion and conflict: Samuel P. Huntington's essay "The Clash of Civilizations?" and an article by Richard E. Rubenstein and Jarle Crocker critiquing Huntington's thesis. Also in this section, Chris Seiple suggests that in national security a "new framework is needed, one that facilitates the positive social contributions of faith so that the negative side-effects of repressed religion can be avoided." Philip Jenkins' chapter explores historical examples of how repression of religion in the name of "security" often backfires. Brian J. Grim then summarizes contemporary empirical studies of the social ramifications of restricting/repressing religion. According to Grim, the statistical evidence suggests strongly that religious freedom is "good for what ails us" because it promotes security—both directly and indirectly. In the final piece in this section, John D. Carlson and Matt Correa take a step back and survey the field of religion and conflict and discuss key challenges and questions for the future.

Section V: Religion and Peacemaking

Religion's potential to be part of the solution is perhaps seen most evidently in the peacemaking and reconciliation efforts that section V explores. R. Scott Appleby catalogues a variety of peacemaking efforts and laments how the habit of professional hyperspecialization often separates those who study extremists from those who study nonviolent religious actors. Brian Cox and Daniel Philpott note how themes of reconciliation can be found in all of the world's major religions, and they describe how "faith-based diplomacy" works in practice. Douglas M. Johnston discusses the potential for military chaplains to be agents of peacemaking and conflict prevention through their expanding role as "religious leader liaisons" in theaters of operation. Marc Gopin explores religion and peacemaking in an especially difficult, high-stakes case: the Israeli-Palestinian conflict. He argues that religion can help "provide creative middle positions of trust building, evidence of transformation, and interim pro-social measures that will grease the wheels of rational diplomacy." Drew Christiansen looks at Catholic approaches to peacemaking, and in particular the peacemaking legacy of Pope John Paul II. Finally, Hisham Soliman examines Islamic texts to present a distinctly Islamic foundation for peacemaking, one that includes a recentered definition of jihad, a respect for historical tradition, and an appeal to religious duty.

Section VI: Religion, Globalization, and Transnationalism

Religious beliefs know no state boundaries, as section VI makes clear. In the first selection, "Jihad vs. McWorld," Benjamin Barber discusses some of the complexities and contradictions of globalization. James Kurth then outlines modernist, postmodernist, and premodernist paradigms regarding the role of religion in the globalization process. He argues that the Protestant tradition rejected hierarchy and community and therefore helped foment a globalization that has now evolved to become more secular and selfish in nature. Essays from Jeffrey Haynes and from Robert Wuthnow and Stephen Offutt explore the impact that transnational religious actors have on world affairs. Haynes focuses in particular on the Roman Catholic Church and the Organization of the Islamic Conference, arguing that organizations like these should not be seen as threats to state sovereignty. Wuthnow and Offutt observe that transnational religious connections (seen in the flow of both people and resources) are nothing new, but the scholarship regarding these connections is still lacking. In the final essay in this section, Timothy A. Byrnes considers the impact of recent migrations on European identity and transnational politics.

Section VII: Religion and Economic Development

The global resurgence of religion has also had a considerable impact on foreign aid and the relief and development community. In fact, one could argue that religion was present in development all along; religion has always affected economic cultures and development dynamics. Section VII begins with an essay by Peter L. Berger, who argues that the historic affinity between the Protestant ethic and economic development is alive and well today, especially in the growing Pentecostal movement. He also discusses analogues to the Protestant ethic in other religious traditions. Seth Kaplan examines faith-based organizations' critical role in development, arguing that this role has been underestimated and underappreciated in Western development philosophies. Sallie McFague then examines religion's role in addressing environmental concerns and sustainable development, arguing that Christianity has "implicitly and sometimes explicitly supported a neoclassical economic paradigm and a consumer culture that has devastated the planet and widened the gap between the rich and the poor." Marcus Noland and Howard Pack provide a nuanced perspective on the Middle East's relative underdevelopment and demographic challenges, arguing that religion and culture are two significant but not determining factors for attitudes toward globalization and economic development. A selection by Katherine Marshall then surveys how the intersection of religion and development presents challenges and opportunities for the roles, rights, and wellbeing of women.

Section VIII: Religion, Democracy, and the State

Some of the most controversial questions in the field of religion and international affairs are whether deeply religious (especially Muslim) populations have an inherent bias against liberal democracy, and the extent to which religion and state can become enmeshed without fundamentally undermining democracy. Section VIII begins with Jonathan Fox and Shmuel Sandler's large-scale comparative analysis of different degrees and types of separation of religion and state. They demonstrate how most Western democracies do not insist on full separation of religion and state. The next selection is from Steven V. Mazie, who parses linkages between religion and state in the case of Israel, arguing that, within appropriate limits, it is possible for it to be both Jewish and liberal democratic. An article by Robert D. Woodberry and Timothy S. Shah then reminds us that though the link between Protestant Christianity and democracy is strong historically, "opposing hierarchy and liberating individual consciences in religion does not automatically make one a foe of authoritarianism and a friend of liberty in politics." This is followed by an article from Vali Nasr, who explores the rise of Muslim democratic parties in countries like Turkey, Pakistan, and Malaysia. He concludes that the forces most likely to succeed in the "strategic middle" of the political spectrum are those that "integrate Muslim values and moderate Islamic politics into broader right-of-center platforms that go beyond exclusively religious concerns." Max L. Stackhouse then discusses "public theology" and democracy, arguing that democracies need more than the right to vote for elected representatives; they need a flourishing civil society that fosters an "inner moral fiber" in the country's citizens. The section concludes with an essay by Thomas F. Farr arguing that U.S. promotion of democracy abroad is hamstrung by a failure of both the political left and right to understand "public religion," particularly in Muslim-majority societies.

Section IX: Religious Freedom and Human Rights

Section IX begins with an article by Paul A. Brink, who contends that a working consensus on the definition of human rights can be attained despite the deep cultural and religious pluralism of the global public square. This is paired with an article by Kevin J. Hasson, who compares the United Nations' Universal Declaration of Human Rights to Vatican II's declaration on religious freedom, *Dignitatis Humanae*; he argues that the anthropology of human dignity articulated in the latter provides a firmer philosophical footing for human rights. The next essay, by Allen D. Hertzke, discusses some of the practical effects of the Catholic Church's embrace of religious freedom, particularly in the context of the American social movement for international religious freedom and human rights that formed in the mid-1990s; the movement was energized by evangelical Protestants, but its successes also depended on Catholic support. Paul Marshall tracks global trends of religious repression and describes four common contexts where it occurs: radical Islam, communism/postcommunism, South Asian religious/ethnic nationalism, and intrareligious conflict. David Little explains why religious freedom should be granted special status but notes how it is part of a "bundle" of human rights. José Casanova explores religious freedom in light of the cultural challenges presented by globalization. And John Witte, Jr. rounds out this section with an article discussing international law on the right to convert and charting a path for appropriate evangelism in a diverse world.

Section X: Religion and the Future of U.S. Foreign Policy

This section presents a collection of essays taking stock of the role religion has played and could play in U.S. foreign policy. The section begins with a prescient article by Barry Rubin first published in 1990. Rubin surveys several key regions around the world where U.S. foreign policy would benefit greatly from a better understanding of religion. This is followed by an excerpt from Madeleine Albright's 2006 book, *The Mighty and the Almighty: Reflections on America, God, and World Affairs*. Albright explores the potential for a faith-based diplomacy that complements, not replaces, traditional diplomacy. An article by Jack Miles then critiques the way U.S. foreign policy has dealt with religion intellectually and practically. In the final selection, Robert A. Seiple applies similar critiques in the specific context of religious freedom diplomacy, arguing that the U.S. government can and should collaborate with nongovernmental organizations in practical strategies for promoting human rights.

* * *

The world is ever more complicated and interconnected. This presents exciting opportunities for creative innovations and problem solving, but also many threats—including existential ones. Religion is relevant at multiple levels to all of these dynamics. Though long neglected, religion is now on the research and discussion agendas of scholars and practitioners alike. But it is not enough to "pay attention" to religion. Indeed, in some cases the only thing worse than ignoring religion is to approach it in an ill-informed way, with assumptions that are either overly positive or overly negative. The current and rising generations of leaders in international affairs need to be equipped with in-depth knowledge and critical thinking skills to deal with the role that religion plays. This compendium is designed specifically to help meet this need. As Madeleine Albright argues in her chapter, the task at hand is to "think more expansively about the role of religion" and "take fully into account the immense power of religion to influence how people think, feel, and act."

— Section I —

SECULARIZATION, DESECULARIZATION, AND THE DISCIPLINES OF INTERNATIONAL AFFAIRS

THE MEANING OF SECULARISM

—Charles Taylor

1

It is generally agreed that modern democracies have to be "secular."[1] There is perhaps a problem, a certain ethnocentricity, involved in this term. But even in the Western context the term is not limpid and may in fact be misleading. What in fact does it mean? There are at least two models of what constitutes a secular regime. Both involve some kind of separation of church and state. The state can't be officially linked to some religious confession, except in a vestigial and largely symbolic sense, as in England or Scandinavia. But secularism requires more than this. The pluralism of society requires that there be some kind of neutrality, or "principled distance," to use Rajeev Bhargava's term.[2]

If we examine it further, secularism involves in fact a complex requirement. There is more than one good sought here. We can single out three, which we can classify in the categories of the French Revolution trinity: liberty, equality, fraternity. First, no one must be forced in the domain of religion, or basic belief. This is what is often defined as religious liberty, including of course, the freedom not to believe. This is what is also described as the "free exercise" of religion, in the terms of the U.S. First Amendment. Second, there must be equality between people of different faiths or basic beliefs; no religious outlook or (religious or areligious) *Weltanschauung* can enjoy a privileged status, let alone be adopted as the official view of the state. Third, all spiritual families must be heard, included in the ongoing process of determining what the society is about (its political identity) and how it is going to realize these goals (the exact regime of rights and privileges). This (stretching the point a little) is what corresponds to "fraternity."

These goals can, of course, conflict; sometimes we have to balance the goods involved. Moreover, we might add a fourth goal: that we try as much as possible to maintain relations of harmony and comity between the supporters of different religions and *Weltanschauungen*. (Maybe this is what really deserves to be called "fraternity," but I am still attached to the neatness of the above schema, with only the three traditional goods.)

* *The Hedgehog Review* 12, no. 3 (Fall 2010): 23–34.

Sometimes the claim seems to be made, on behalf of one or another definition of secularism, that it can resolve the question of how to realize these goals in the domain of timeless principles, and that no further input or negotiation is required to define them for our society now. The basis for these principles can be found in reason alone, or in some outlook which is itself free from religion, purely *laïque*. Jacobins are on this wavelength, as was the early John Rawls.

The problem with this is that there is no such set of timeless principles that can be determined, at least in the detail they must be for a given political system, by pure reason alone, and situations differ very much and require different kinds of concrete realization of agreed general principles, so that some degree of working out is necessary in each situation. It follows that dictating the principles from some supposedly higher authority above the fray violates the good of fraternity, that is, the idea that all spiritual families must be heard. It deprives certain spiritual families of a voice in this working out. And, therefore, this leaves us very often with difficult conflicts and dilemmas between our basic goals.

The issues concerning secularism have evolved in different Western societies in recent decades because the faiths represented in those societies have changed. We need to alter the way in which we proceed when the range of religions or basic philosophies expands: for example, the arrival of substantive communities of Muslims in contemporary Europe and the U.S. and the recent legislation in France against wearing the *hijab* in schools. Normally, this kind of thing needs to be negotiated. Of course, sometimes this is not possible; certain basic laws have to be observed. But the general principle is that religious groups must be seen as much as interlocutors and as little as menace as the situation allows.

These groups also evolve if they're in a process of redefinition of this kind in a democratic, liberal context. José Casanova has pointed out how American Catholicism was originally targeted in the nineteenth century as inassimilable to democratic mores, in ways very analogous to the suspicions that nag people over Islam today. The subsequent history has shown how American Catholicism evolved, and in the process changed world Catholicism in significant ways. There is no reason written into the essence of things why a similar evolution cannot take place in Muslim communities.[3] If this doesn't happen, it will in all likelihood be because of prejudice and bad management.

One of our basic difficulties in dealing with these problems is that we have the wrong model, which has a continuing hold on our minds. We think that secularism (or *laïcité*) has to do with the relation of the state and religion, whereas in fact it has to do with the (correct) response of the democratic state to diversity. If we look at the three goals above, they have in common that they are concerned with protecting people in their belonging and/or practice of whatever outlook they choose or find themselves in; treating people equally whatever their option; and giving them all a hearing. There is no reason to single out religious (as against nonreligious), "secular" (in another widely used sense), or atheist viewpoints. Indeed, the point of state neutrality is precisely to avoid favoring or disfavoring not just religious positions, but any basic position, religious or nonreligious. We can't favor Christianity over Islam, but also we can't favor religion over against nonbelief in religion, or vice versa.

The late-Rawlsian formulation for a secular state cleaves very strongly to certain political principles: human rights, equality, the rule of law, democracy. These are the very basis of the state, which must support them. But this political ethic can be and is shared by people of very different basic outlooks (what Rawls calls "comprehensive views of the good"). A Kantian will justify the rights to life and freedom by pointing to the dignity of rational agency; a Utilitarian will speak of the necessity to treat beings who can experience joy and suffering in such a way as to maximize the first and minimize the second; and a Christian will speak of humans as made in the image of God. They concur on the principles, but differ on the deeper reasons for holding to this ethic. The state must uphold the ethic, but must refrain from favoring any of the deeper reasons.

2

The idea that secularism makes a special case of religion arises from the history of its coming to be in the West (as does, indeed, the name). To put it briefly, there are two important founding contexts for this kind of regime, the U.S. and France. In the U.S. case, the whole range of comprehensive views, or deeper reasons, were in the original case variants of (Protestant) Christianity, stretching to a smattering of Deists. Subsequent history has widened the palette of views beyond Christianity, and then beyond religion. But in the original case, the positions between which the state was to be neutral were all religious. Hence the First Amendment: Congress shall pass no law establishing religion or impeding the free exercise thereof.

The word "secularism" didn't appear in the early decades of American public life, but this was the sign that a basic problem had not yet been faced. Because the First Amendment concerned the separation of church and state, it opened the possibility of giving a place to religion that no one would accept today. Thus in the 1830s, a judge of the Supreme Court could argue that while the First Amendment forbade the identification of the federal government with any church, since all the churches were Christian (and in effect Protestant), one could invoke the principles of Christianity in interpreting the law. For Judge Joseph Story, the goal of the First Amendment was "to exclude all rivalry among Christian sects," but nevertheless "Christianity ought to receive encouragement from the state." Christianity was essential to the state because the belief in "a future state of rewards and punishments" is "indispensable to the administration of justice." What is more, "it is impossible for those who believe in the truth of Christianity, as a divine revelation, to doubt, that it is a special duty of government to foster, and encourage it among the citizens."[4]

This primacy of Christianity was upheld even later in the nineteenth century. As late as 1890, 37 of the 42 existing states recognized the authority of God in the preambles or texts of their constitutions. A unanimous judgment of the Supreme Court of 1892 declared that if one wanted to describe "American life as expressed by its laws, its business, its customs and its society, we find everywhere a clear recognition of the same truth . . . that this is a Christian nation."[5] In the latter part of the century, resistance began to build to this conception, but a National Reform Association (NRA) was founded in 1863 with the following goal:

> The object of this Society shall be to maintain existing Christian features in the American Government . . . to secure such an amendment to the Constitution of the United States as will declare the nation's allegiance to Jesus Christ and its acceptance of the moral laws of the Christian religion, and so indicate that this is a Christian nation, and place all the Christian laws, institutions and usages of our government on an undeniable legal basis in the fundamental law of the land.[6]

After 1870, the battle was joined between the supporters of this narrow view, on one hand, and those who wanted a real opening to all other religions and also to nonreligion. The latter included not only Jews, but also Catholics who (rightly) saw the "Christianity" of the NRA as excluding them. It was in this battle that the word "secular" first appeared on the American scene as a key term, and very often in its polemical sense of non- or antireligious.[7]

In the French case, *laïcité* came about in a struggle *against* a powerful church. The strong temptation was for the state itself to stand on a moral basis independent from religion. Marcel Gauchet shows how Charles Renouvier laid the grounds for the outlook of the Third Republic radicals in their battle against the church. The state has to be "*moral et enseignant*" (moral and instructive). It has "*charge d'âmes aussi bien que toute Église ou communauté, mais à titre plus universel*" (responsibility for souls as well as the whole church and community, but with a more universal scope). Morality is the key criterion. In order not to be under the church, the state must have "*une morale indépendante de toute religion*" (a morality independent of all religion) and enjoy a "*suprématie morale*" (moral supremacy) in relation to all religions. The basis of this morality is liberty. In order to hold its own before religion, the morality underlying the state has to be based on more than just utility or feeling; it needs a real "*théologie rationnelle*" (rational theology) like that of Kant.[8] The wisdom of Jules Ferry, and later of Aristide Briand and Jean Jaurez, saved France at the time of the Separation (1905) from such a lopsided regime, but the notion stuck that *laïcité* was all about controlling and managing religion.

If we move, however, beyond such originating contexts and look at the kinds of societies in which we are now living in the West, the first feature that strikes us is the wide diversity, not only of religious views, but also of those which involve no religion, not to speak of those which are unclassifiable in this dichotomy. The goals of liberty, equality, and fraternity require that we treat all of these even-handedly.

3

This fixation on religion is complex, and it is bound up with two other features we often find in the debates on secularism: the first is the tendency to define secularism or *laïcité* in terms of some institutional arrangement, rather than starting from the goals I proposed above. And so you hear mantra-type formulae, like "the separation of church and state," or the necessity of removing religion from public space ("*les espaces de la République*" [the spaces of the Republic] as in the recent French debate). The second follows from the first, or may easily seem to. If the whole matter is defined by one institutional formula, then one must just determine which arrangement of things best meets this formula, and there is no need to think further. One cannot find oneself in a dilemma, as will easily happen if one is pursuing more than one goal, because here there is just one master formula.

Hence one often hears these mantras employed as argument-stoppers, the ultimate decisive response which annuls all objections. In the U.S., people invoke the "Wall of Separation" as the ultimate criterion, and hyper-Republicans in France cite *laïcité* as the final word. (Of course, if one consulted the First Amendment of the U.S. Constitution, one would find two goals mentioned, the rejection of establishment and the assurance of "free exercise." It is not inconceivable that these could conflict.)

This kind of move amounts, from the standpoint I am adopting here, to a fetishization of the favored institutional arrangements, whereas one should start from the goals and derive the concrete arrangements from these. It is not that some separation of church and state, some mutual autonomy of governing and religious institutions, will not be an inescapable feature of any secularist regime, and the same goes for the neutrality of the public institutions. These are both indispensable, but what these requirements mean in practice ought to be determined by how we can maximize our three (or four) basic goals.

Take for example the wearing of the *hijab* by Muslim women in public schools, which has been a hot issue in a number of Western democracies. In France, pupils in public schools were famously forbidden the headscarf, seen as a "*signe religieux ostentatoire*" (an ostentatious religious sign) according to the notorious Loi Stasi of 2004. In certain German states, pupils can wear it, but not teachers. In the UK and other countries, there is no general interdict, but the individual schools can decide.

What are the reasons for this variation? Plainly in all these cases, legislators and administrators were trying to balance two goals. One was the maintenance of neutrality in public institutions seen (rightly) as an essential entailment of equality between all basic beliefs. The other was ensuring the maximum possible religious liberty, or in its most general form, liberty of conscience. The goal of equality seems to push us towards permitting the *hijab* anywhere. But various arguments were made to override this in the French and German cases. For the Germans, what was disturbing was that someone in authority in a public institution should be religiously marked, as it were. In the French case, an attempt was made to cast doubt on the proposition that wearing the *hijab* was a free act. There were dark suggestions that the girls were being forced by their families, or by their male peers, to adopt this dress code. That argument was frequently used, however dubious it might appear in the light of the sociological research carried out among the pupils themselves, but the Stasi Commission largely ignored it.

The other main argument was that wearing the headscarf in school was less an act of piety than a statement of hostility against the Republic and its essential institution of *laïcité*. This was the meaning behind the introduction of the concept of "*signe ostentatoire*" (ostentatious sign). A smaller discrete sign would be no problem argued the Stasi Commission, but these attention-grabbing features of dress were meant to make a highly controversial statement. It was in vain that Muslim women protested that "*le foulard n'est pas un signe*" ("the headscarf is not a sign").

On one level, these different national answers to the same question reflect different takes on how to balance the two main goals of a secular regime. But on another level, the dilemma and its resolution remain hidden under the illusion that there is only one principle here, say, *laïcité* and its corollary of the neutrality of public institutions or spaces, that it's just a matter of applying an essential feature of our republican regime, and that there is no need or place for choice or the weighing of different aims.

Perhaps the most pernicious feature of this fetishization is that it tends to hide from view the real dilemmas that we encounter in this realm, and that leap into view once we recognize the plurality of principles at stake.

4

This fetishization reflects a deep feature of life in modern democracies. We can see why as soon as we ponder what is involved in self-government, what is implied in the basic mode of legitimation of states that are founded on popular sovereignty. For the people to be sovereign, they need to form an entity and have a personality.

The revolutions that ushered in regimes of popular sovereignty transferred the ruling power from a king onto a "nation," or a "people." In the process, they invented a new kind of collective agency. These terms existed before, but the thing they now indicated, this new kind of agency, was something unprecedented, at least in the immediate context of early modern Europe. Thus the notion "people" could certainly be applied to the ensemble of subjects of the kingdom, or to the nonelite strata of society, but prior to the turnover, it hadn't indicated an entity that could decide and act together, to whom one could attribute a will.

But for people to act together, in other words, to deliberate in order to form a common will on which they will act, requires a high degree of common commitment, a sense of common identification. A society of this kind presupposes trust, the basic trust that members and constituent groups have to have, the confidence that they are really part of the process, that they will be listened to and their views taken account of by the others. Without this mutual commitment, this trust will be fatally eroded.

And so we have in the modern age a new kind of collective agency. It is one with which its members identify, typically as the realization/bulwark of their freedom and/or the locus of their national/cultural expression (or most often, some combination of the two). Of course, in premodern societies, too, people often "identified" with the regime, sacred kings, or hierarchical orders; they were often willing subjects. But in the democratic age, we identify as free agents. That is why the notion of popular will plays a crucial role in the legitimating idea.

This means that the modern democratic state has generally accepted common purposes, or reference points, the features whereby it can lay claim to being the bulwark of freedom and locus of expression of its citizens. Whether or not these claims are actually founded, the state must be so imagined by its citizens if it is to be legitimate.

So questions can arise for the modern state for which there are no analogues in most premodern forms: what/whom is this state for? whose freedom? whose expression? These questions seem to make no sense applied to, say, the Austrian or Turkish Empires—unless one answered the "whom for?" question by referring to the Habsburg or Ottoman dynasties, and this would hardly give you their legitimating ideas.

This is the sense in which a modern state has what I want to call a political identity, defined as the generally accepted answer to the "what/whom for?" question. This is distinct from the identities of its members, that is, from the reference points, many and varied, that define for each of them what is important in their lives. There better be some overlap, of course, if these members are to feel strongly identified with the state, but the identities of individuals and constituent groups will generally be richer and more complex, and often quite different from each other.[9]

In other words, a modern democratic state demands a "people" with a strong collective identity. Democracy obliges us to show much more solidarity and much more commitment to one another in our joint political project than was demanded by the hierarchical and authoritarian societies of yesteryear. In the good old days of the Austro-Hungarian

Empire, the Polish peasant in Galicia could be altogether oblivious of the Hungarian country squire, the bourgeois of Prague, or the Viennese worker, without this in the slightest threatening the stability of the state. On the contrary, this condition of things only becomes untenable when ideas about popular government start to circulate. This is the moment when subgroups that will not, or cannot, be bound together, start to demand their own states. This is the era of nationalism, of the break up of empires.

I have been discussing the political necessity of a strong common identity for modern democratic states in terms of the requirement of forming a people, a deliberative unit. But this is also evident in a number of other ways. Thinkers in the civic humanist tradition, from Aristotle to Arendt, have noted that free societies require a higher level of commitment and participation than despotic or authoritarian ones. Citizens have to do for themselves, as it were, what otherwise the rulers do for them. But this will only happen if these citizens feel a strong bond of identification with their political community, and hence with those who share with them in this.

From another angle again, because these societies require strong commitment to do the common work, and because a situation in which some carry the burdens of participation and others just enjoy the benefits would be intolerable, free societies require a high level of mutual trust. In other words, they are extremely vulnerable to mistrust on the part of some citizens in relation to others, that the latter are not really assuming their commitments—for example, that others are not paying their taxes, or are cheating on welfare, or are benefitting as employers from a good labor market without assuming any of the social costs. This kind of mistrust creates extreme tension and threatens to unravel the whole skein of the mores of commitment that democratic societies need to operate. A continuing and constantly renewed mutual commitment is an essential basis for taking the measures needed to renew this trust.

The relation between nation and state is often considered from a unilateral point of view, as if it were always the nation that sought to provide itself with a state, but there is also the opposite process. In order to remain viable, states sometimes seek to create a feeling of common belonging. This is an important theme in the history of Canada, for example. To form a state, in the democratic era, a society is forced to undertake the difficult and never to be completed task of defining its collective identity.

Thus what I have been calling political identity is extremely important in modern democratic states. And this identity is usually defined partly in terms of certain basic principles (democracy, human rights, equality), and partly in terms of their historical, or linguistic, or religious traditions. It is understandable that features of this identity can take on a quasi-sacred status, for to alter or undermine them can seem to threaten the very basis of unity without which a democratic state cannot function.

It is in this context that certain historical institutional arrangements can appear as untouchable. They may appear as an essential part of the basic principles of the regime, but they will also come to be seen as a key component of its historic identity. This is what one sees with *laïcité* as invoked by many French *républicains*. The irony is that in the face of a modern politics of (multicultural) identity, they invoke this principle as a crucial feature of (French) identity. This is unfortunate, but very understandable. It is one illustration of a general truth: that contemporary democracies as they progressively diversify will have to undergo redefinitions of their historical identities, which may be far-reaching and painful.

5

We should see this in the context of the modern understanding of political society. The crucial move that we see in the modern West from the seventeenth century, the move that takes us out of the cosmic religious conceptions of order, establishes a new "bottom-up" view of society, as existing for the protection and mutual benefit of its (equal) members. There is a strong normative view attached to this new conception, which I have called the "modern moral order."[10] It enshrines basically three principles: (1) the rights and liberties of the members, (2) the equality among them (which has of course been variously interpreted, and has mutated towards more radical conceptions over time), and (3) the principle that rule is based on consent (which has also been defended in more and less radical forms).

These basic norms have been worked out in a host of different philosophical anthropologies, and according to very different concepts of human sociability. It very soon transcended the atomism that narrowed the vision of its early formulators, like Locke and Hobbes. But the basic norms remain and are more or less inseparable from modern liberal democracies.

The rejection of cosmic-religious embedding thus was accomplished by a new conception of "the political," a new basic norm, which, as Claude Lefort suggests, involved its own representation of political authority, but one in which the central spot remained paradoxically empty. If the notion of sovereignty is retained, no one person or group can be identified with it.

Democratic societies are organized not necessarily around a "civil religion," as Jean-Jacques Rousseau claimed, but certainly around a strong "philosophy of civility," enshrining the three norms, which in contemporary societies are often expressed as (1) human rights, (2) equality and nondiscrimination, and (3) democracy.

But in certain cases, there can be a civil religion: a religious view incorporating and justifying the philosophy of civility. This was arguably so for the young American republic. It was adopting a form that was clearly part of God's providential plan for mankind ("We hold these truths to be self-evident, that all men are created equal . . ."). Or it can alternatively be part of a non- or even antireligious ideology, as with the First French Republic. One can even argue that all-englobing views of this kind seem more "natural" to many of our contemporaries. After all, the principles of our civil philosophy seem to call for deeper grounding. If it's very important that we agree on the principles, then surely things are much more stable if we also accept a common grounding. Or so it may appear, and the centuries-long tradition of political life seems to testify for this idea.

For indeed the overlapping consensus between different founding views on a common philosophy of civility is something quite new in history, and relatively untried. It is consequently hazardous. And besides, we often suspect that those with different basic views can't really subscribe to these principles, not the way we do (because, as "we" know, "atheists can't have principles," or as another "we" knows, "religions are all against liberty and or equality").

The problem is that a really diverse democracy can't revert to a civil religion, or antireligion, however comforting this might be, without betraying its own principles. We are condemned to live in an overlapping consensus.

6

We have seen how this strongly motivated move to fetishize our historical arrangements can prevent us from seeing our secular regime in a more fruitful light, which foregrounds the basic goals we are seeking, and which allows us to recognize and reason about the dilemmas which we face. But this connects to the other main cause of confusion I cited above, our fixation on religion as the problem. In fact, we have moved in many Western countries from an original phase in which secularism was a hard-won achievement warding off some form of religious domination, to a phase of such widespread diversity of basic beliefs, religious and areligious, that only clear focus on the need to balance freedom of conscience and equality of respect can allow us to take the measure of the situation. Otherwise we risk needlessly limiting the religious freedom of immigrant minorities, on the strength of our historic institutional arrangements, while sending a message to these same minorities that they by no means enjoy equal status with the long-established mainstream.

This whole matter deserves much further consideration, more than I can give it here, but I am convinced that this further examination would lend even more credibility to the revisionary ideal I am proposing here, which amounts to this: what deserve to be called "secularist" regimes in contemporary democracy have to be conceived not primarily as bulwarks against religion but as good faith attempts to secure the three (or four) basic goals I outlined above. And this means that they attempt to shape their institutional arrangements, not to remain true to hallowed tradition, but to maximize the basic goals of liberty and equality between basic beliefs.

THE DESECULARIZATION OF THE WORLD
A Global Overview

—Peter L. Berger

A few years ago the first volume coming out of the so-called Fundamentalism Project landed on my desk. The Fundamentalism Project was very generously funded by the MacArthur Foundation and chaired by Martin Marty, the distinguished church historian at the University of Chicago. A number of very reputable scholars took part in it, and the published results are of generally excellent quality. But my contemplation of this first volume gave me what has been called an "*aha!* experience." The book was very big, sitting there on my desk—a "book-weapon," the kind that could do serious injury. So I asked myself, why would the MacArthur Foundation shell out several million dollars to support an international study of religious fundamentalists?

Two answers came to mind. The first was obvious and not very interesting. The MacArthur Foundation is a very progressive outfit; it understands fundamentalists to be anti-progressive; the Project, then, was a matter of knowing one's enemies. But there was also a more interesting answer. "Fundamentalism" is considered a strange, hard-to-understand phenomenon; the purpose of the Project was to delve into this alien world and make it more understandable. But to whom? *Who* finds this world strange? Well, the answer to *that* question was easy: people to whom the officials of the MacArthur Foundation normally talk, such as professors at elite American universities. And with this came the *aha!* experience. The concern that must have led to this Project was based on an upside-down perception of the world, according to which "fundamentalism" (which, when all is said and done, usually refers to any sort of passionate religious movement) is a rare, hard-to-explain thing. But a look either at history or at the contemporary world reveals that what is rare is not the phenomenon itself but knowledge of it. The difficult-to-understand phenomenon is not Iranian mullahs but American university professors—it might be worth a multi-million-dollar project to try to explain that!

* Peter L. Berger, ed., *The Desecularization of the World: Resurgent Religion and World Politics* (Grand Rapids: Wm. B. Eerdmans, 1999), 1–18.

Mistakes of Secularization Theory

My point is that the assumption that we live in a secularized world is false. The world today, with some exceptions to which I will come presently, is as furiously religious as it ever was, and in some places more so than ever. This means that a whole body of literature by historians and social scientists loosely labeled "secularization theory" is essentially mistaken. In my early work I contributed to this literature. I was in good company—most sociologists of religion had similar views, and we had good reasons for holding them. Some of the writings we produced still stand up. (As I like to tell my students, one advantage of being a social scientist, as against being, say, a philosopher or a theologian, is that you can have as much fun when your theories are falsified as when they are verified!)

Although the term "secularization theory" refers to works from the 1950s and 1960s, the key idea of the theory can indeed be traced to the Enlightenment. That idea is simple: Modernization necessarily leads to a decline of religion, both in society and in the minds of individuals. And it is precisely this key idea that has turned out to be wrong. To be sure, modernization has had some secularizing effects, more in some places than in others. But it has also provoked powerful movements of counter-secularization. Also, secularization on the societal level is not necessarily linked to secularization on the level of individual consciousness. Certain religious institutions have lost power and influence in many societies, but both old and new religious beliefs and practices have nevertheless continued in the lives of individuals, sometimes taking new institutional forms and sometimes leading to great explosions of religious fervor. Conversely, religiously identified institutions can play social or political roles even when very few people believe or practice the religion that the institutions represent. To say the least, the relation between religion and modernity is rather complicated.

The proposition that modernity necessarily leads to a decline of religion is, in principle, "value free." That is, it can be affirmed both by people who think it is good news and by people who think it is very bad news. Most Enlightenment thinkers and most progressive-minded people ever since have tended toward the idea that secularization is a good thing, at least insofar as it does away with religious phenomena that are "backward," "superstitious," or "reactionary" (a religious residue purged of these negative characteristics may still be deemed acceptable). But religious people, including those with very traditional or orthodox beliefs, have also affirmed the modernity/secularity linkage, and have greatly bemoaned it. Some have then defined modernity as the enemy, to be fought whenever possible. Others have, on the contrary, seen modernity as some kind of invincible worldview to which religious beliefs and practices should adapt themselves. In other words, *rejection* and *adaptation* are two strategies open to religious communities in a world understood to be secularized. As is always the case when strategies are based on mistaken perceptions of the terrain, both strategies have had very doubtful results.

It is possible, of course, to reject any number of modern ideas and values theoretically, but making this rejection stick in the lives of people is much harder. To do that requires one of two strategies. The first is *religious revolution*: one tries to take over society as a whole and make one's counter-modern religion obligatory for everyone—a difficult enterprise in most countries in the contemporary world. (Franco tried in Spain and failed; the mullahs are still at it in Iran and a couple of other places.) And this *does* have to do with modernization, which brings about very heterogeneous societies and a quantum leap in intercultural communication, two factors favoring pluralism and *not* favoring the establishment (or reestablishment) of religious monopolies. The other possible way of getting people to reject modern ideas and values in their lives is to create *religious subcultures* designed to keep out the influences of the outside society. That is a somewhat more promising exercise than religious revolution, but it too is fraught with difficulty. Modern culture is a very powerful force, and an immense effort is required to maintain enclaves with an airtight defense system. Ask the Amish in eastern Pennsylvania. Or ask a Hasidic rabbi in the Williamsburg section of Brooklyn.

Interestingly, secularization theory has also been falsified by the results of adaptation strategies by religious institutions. If we really lived in a highly secularized world, then religious institutions could be expected to survive to the degree that they manage to adapt to secularity. That has been the empirical assumption of adaptation strategies. What has in fact occurred is that, by and large, religious communities have survived and even flourished to the degree that they have *not* tried to adapt themselves to the alleged requirements of a secularized world. To put it simply, experiments with secularized religion have generally failed; religious movements with beliefs and practices dripping with reactionary supernaturalism (the kind utterly beyond the pale at self-respecting faculty parties) have widely succeeded.

The Catholic Church vs. Modernity

The struggle with modernity in the Roman Catholic Church nicely illustrates the difficulties of various strategies. In the wake of the Enlightenment and its multiple revolutions, the initial response by the Church was militant and then defiant rejection. Perhaps the most magnificent moment of that defiance came in 1870, when the First Vatican Council solemnly proclaimed the infallibility of the Pope and the immaculate conception of Mary, literally in the face of the Enlightenment about to occupy Rome in the shape of the army of Victor Emmanuel I. (The disdain was mutual. If you have ever visited the Roman monument to the Bersaglieri, the elite army units that occupied the Eternal City in the name of the Italian *Risorgimento*, you may have noticed the placement of the heroic figure in his Bersaglieri uniform—he is positioned so that his behind points exactly toward the Vatican.)

The Second Vatican Council, almost a hundred years later, considerably modified this rejectionist stance, guided as it was by the notion of *aggiornamento*, bringing the Church up to date—that is, up to date with the modern world. (I remember asking a Protestant theologian what he thought would happen at the Council—this was before it had convened; he replied that he didn't know but he was sure they would not read the minutes of the last meeting!) The Second Vatican Council was supposed to open windows, specifically the windows of the Catholic subculture that had been constructed when it became clear that the overall society could not be reconquered. In the United States, this Catholic subculture has been quite impressive right up to the very recent past. The trouble with opening windows is that you can't control what comes in, and a lot has come in—indeed, the whole turbulent world of modern culture—that has been very troubling to the Church. Under the current pontificate the Church has been steering a nuanced course between rejection and adaptation, with mixed results in different countries.

This is as good a point as any to mention that all my observations here are intended to be "value free"; that is, I am trying to look at the current religious scene objectively. For the duration of this exercise I have put aside my own religious beliefs. As a sociologist of religion, I find it probable that Rome had to do some reining in on the level of both doctrine and practice, in the wake of the institutional disturbances that followed Vatican II. To say this, however, in no way implies my theological agreement with what has been happening in the Roman Catholic Church under the present pontificate. Indeed, if I were Roman Catholic, I would have considerable misgivings about these developments. But I am a liberal Protestant (the adjective refers to my religious position and not to my politics), and I have no immediate existential stake in what is happening within the Roman community. I am speaking here as a sociologist, in which capacity I can claim a certain competence; I have no theological credentials.

The Global Religious Scene

On the international religious scene, it is conservative or orthodox or traditionalist movements that are on the rise almost everywhere. These movements are precisely the ones that rejected an *aggiornamento* with modernity as defined by progressive intellectuals. Conversely, religious movements and institutions that have made great efforts to conform to a perceived modernity are almost everywhere on the decline. In the United States this has been a much commented upon fact, exemplified by the decline of so-called mainline Protestantism and the concomitant rise of Evangelicalism; but the United States is by no means unusual in this.

Nor is Protestantism. The conservative thrust in the Roman Catholic Church under John Paul II has borne fruit in both number of converts and renewed enthusiasm among native Catholics, especially in non-Western countries. Following the collapse of the Soviet Union there occurred a remarkable revival of the Orthodox Church in Russia. The most rapidly growing Jewish groups, both in Israel and in the Diaspora, are Orthodox. There have been similarly vigorous upsurges of conservative religion in all the other major religious communities—Islam, Hinduism, Buddhism—as well as revival movements in smaller communities (such as Shinto in Japan and Sikhism in India). These developments differ greatly in their social and political implications. What they have in common is their unambiguously *religious* inspiration. Consequently, taken together they provide a massive falsification of the idea that modernization and secularization are cognate phenomena. At the very least they show that *counter*-secularization is at least as important a phenomenon in the contemporary world as secularization.

Both in the media and in scholarly publications, these movements are often subsumed under the category of "fundamentalism." This is not a felicitous term, not only because it carries a pejorative undertone but also because it derives from the history of American Protestantism, where it has a specific reference that is distortive if extended to other religious traditions. All the same, the term has some suggestive use if one wishes to explain the aforementioned developments. It suggests a combination of several features—great religious passion, a defiance of what others have defined as the *Zeitgeist*, and a return to traditional sources of religious authority. These are indeed common features across cultural boundaries. And they do reflect the presence of secularizing forces, since they must be understood as a reaction *against* those forces. (In that sense, at least, something of the old secularization theory may be said to hold up, in a rather back-handed way.) This interplay of secularizing and counter-secularizing forces is, I would contend, one of the most important topics for a sociology of contemporary religion, but far too large to consider here. I can only drop a hint: Modernity, for fully understandable reasons, undermines all the old certainties; uncertainty is a condition that many people find very hard to bear; therefore, any movement (not only a religious one) that promises to provide or to renew certainty has a ready market.

Differences among Thriving Movements

While the aforementioned common features are important, an analysis of the social and political impact of the various religious upsurges must also take full account of their differences. This becomes clear when one looks at what are arguably the two most dynamic religious upsurges in the world today, the Islamic and the Evangelical; the comparison also underlines the weakness of the category of "fundamentalism" as applied to both.

The Islamic upsurge, because of its more immediately obvious political ramifications, is better known. Yet it would be a serious error to see it only through a political lens. It is an impressive revival of emphatically *religious* commitments. And it is of vast geographical scope, affecting every single Muslim country from North Africa to Southeast Asia. It continues to gain converts, especially in sub-Saharan Africa (where it is often in head-on competition with Christianity). It is becoming very visible in the burgeoning Muslim communities in Europe and, to a much lesser extent, in North America. Everywhere it is bringing about a restoration, not only of Islamic beliefs but of distinctively Islamic lifestyles, which in many ways directly contradict modern ideas—such as ideas about the relation of religion and the state, the role of women, moral codes of everyday behavior, and the boundaries of religious and moral tolerance. The Islamic revival is by no means restricted to the less modernized or "backward" sectors of society, as progressive intellectuals still like to think. On the contrary, it is very strong in cities with a high degree of modernization, and in a number of countries it is particularly visible among people with Western-style higher education—in Egypt and Turkey, for example, many daughters of secularized professionals are putting on the veil and other accoutrements of Islamic modesty.

Yet there are also great differences within the movement. Even within the Middle East, the Islamic heartland, there are both religiously and politically important differences between Sunni and Shi'ite revivals—Islamic conservatism means very different things in, say, Saudi Arabia and Iran. Away from the Middle East, the differences become even greater. Thus in Indonesia, the most populous Muslim country in the world, a very powerful revival movement, the Nudhat'ul-Ulama, is avowedly pro-democracy and pro-pluralism, the very opposite of what is commonly viewed as Muslim "fundamentalism." Where the political circumstances allow this, there is in many places a lively discussion about the relation of Islam to various modern realities, and there are sharp disagreements among individuals who are equally committed to a revitalized Islam. Still, for reasons deeply grounded in the core of the tradition, it is probably fair to say that, on the whole, Islam has had a difficult time coming to terms with key modern institutions, such as pluralism, democracy, and the market economy.

The Evangelical upsurge is just as breathtaking in scope. Geographically that scope is even wider. It has gained huge numbers of converts in East Asia—in all the Chinese communities (including, despite severe persecution, mainland China) and in South Korea, the Philippines, across the South Pacific, throughout sub-Saharan Africa (where it is often synthesized with elements of traditional African religion), apparently in parts of ex-Communist Europe. But the most remarkable success has occurred in Latin America; there are now thought to be between forty and fifty million Evangelical Protestants south of the U.S. border, the great majority of them first-generation Protestants. The most numerous component within the Evangelical upsurge is Pentecostalism, which combines biblical orthodoxy and a rigorous morality with an ecstatic form of worship and an emphasis on spiritual healing. Especially in Latin America, conversion to Protestantism brings about a cultural transformation—new attitudes toward work and consumption, a new educational ethos, and a violent rejection of traditional *machismo* (women play a key role in the Evangelical churches).

The origins of this worldwide Evangelical upsurge are in the United States, from which the missionaries first went out. But it is very important to understand that, virtually everywhere and emphatically in Latin America, this new Evangelicalism is thoroughly indigenous and no longer dependent on support from U.S. fellow believers—indeed, Latin American Evangelicals have been sending missionaries to the Hispanic community in this country, where there has been a comparable flurry of conversions.

Needless to say, the religious contents of the Islamic and Evangelical revivals are totally different. So are the social and political consequences (of which I will say more later). But the two developments also differ in another very important respect: The Islamic movement is occurring primarily in countries that are already Muslim or among Muslim emigrants (as in Europe), while the Evangelical movement is growing dramatically throughout the world in countries where this type of religion was previously unknown or very marginal.

Exceptions to the Desecularization Thesis

Let me, then, repeat what I said a while back: The world today is massively religious, is *anything but* the secularized world that had been predicted (whether joyfully or despondently) by so many analysts of modernity. There are, however, two exceptions to this proposition, one somewhat unclear, the other very clear.

The first apparent exception is Europe—more specifically, Europe west of what used to be called the Iron Curtain (the developments in the formerly Communist countries are as yet very under-researched and unclear). In Western Europe, if nowhere else, the old secularization theory would seem to hold. With increasing modernization there has been an increase in key indicators of secularization, both on the level of expressed beliefs (especially those that could be called orthodox in Protestant or Catholic terms) and, dramatically, on the level of church-related behavior—attendance at services of worship, adherence to church-dictated codes of personal behavior (especially with regard to sexuality, reproduction, and marriage), recruitment to the clergy. These phenomena, long observed in the northern countries of the continent, have since World War II rapidly engulfed the south. Thus Italy and Spain have experienced a rapid decline in church-related religion. So has Greece, thereby undercutting the claim of Catholic conservatives that Vatican II is to be blamed for the decline. There is now a massively secular Euro-culture, and what has happened in the south can be simply described (though not thereby explained) by that culture's invasion of these countries. It is not fanciful to predict that there will be similar developments in Eastern Europe, precisely to the degree that these countries too will be integrated into the new Europe.

While these facts are not in dispute, a number of recent works in the sociology of religion, notably in France, Britain, and Scandinavia, have questioned the term "secularization" as applied to these developments. A body of data indicates strong survivals of religion, most of it generally Christian in nature, despite the widespread alienation from the organized churches. A shift in the institutional location of religion, then, rather than secularization, would be a more accurate description of the European situation. All the same, Europe stands out as quite different from other parts of the world, and certainly from the United States. One of the most interesting puzzles in the sociology of religion is why Americans are so much more religious *as well as* more churchly than Europeans.

The other exception to the desecularization thesis is less ambiguous. There exists an international subculture composed of people with Western-type higher education, especially in the humanities and social sciences, that is indeed secularized. This subculture is the principal "carrier" of progressive, Enlightened beliefs and values. While its members are relatively thin on the ground, they are very influential, as they control the institutions that provide the "official" definitions of reality, notably the educational system, the media of mass communication, and the higher reaches of the legal system. They are remarkably similar all over the world today, as they have been for a long time (though, as we have seen, there are also defectors from this subculture, especially in the Muslim countries). Again, regrettably, I cannot speculate here as to why people with this type of education should be so prone to secularization. I can only point out that what we have here is a globalized *elite* culture.

In country after country, then, religious upsurges have a strongly populist character. Over and beyond the purely religious motives, these are movements of protest and resistance *against* a secular elite. The so-called culture war in the United States emphatically shares this feature. I may observe in passing that the plausibility of secularization theory owes much to this international subculture. When intellectuals travel, they usually touch down in intellectual circles—that is, among people much like themselves. They can easily fall into the misconception that these people reflect the overall visited society, which, of course, is a big mistake. Picture a secular intellectual from Western Europe socializing with colleagues at the faculty club of the University of Texas. He may think he is back home. But then picture him trying to drive through the traffic jam on Sunday morning in downtown Austin—or, heaven help him, turning on his car radio! What happens then is a severe jolt of what anthropologists call culture shock.

Resurgent Religion: Origins and Prospects

After this somewhat breathless *tour d'horizon* of the global religious scene, let me turn to some questions posed for discussion. . . . *First, what are the origins of the worldwide resurgence of religion?* Two possible answers have already been mentioned. One: Modernity tends to undermine the taken-for-granted certainties by which people lived through most of history. This is an uncomfortable state of affairs, for many an intolerable one, and religious movements that claim to give certainty have great appeal. Two: A purely secular view of reality has its principal social location in an elite culture that, not surprisingly, is resented by large numbers of people who are not part of it but who feel its influence (most troublingly, as their children are subjected to an education that ignores or even directly attacks their own beliefs and values). Religious movements with a strongly anti-secular bent can therefore appeal to people with resentments that sometimes have quite non-religious sources.

But I would refer once more to the little story with which I began, about American foundation officials worried about "fundamentalism." In one sense, there is nothing to explain here. Strongly felt religion has always been around; what needs explanation is its absence rather than its presence. Modern secularity is a much more puzzling phenomenon than all these religious explosions—if you will, the University of Chicago is a more interesting topic for the sociology of religion than the Islamic schools of Qom. In other words, the phenomena under consideration here on one level simply serve to demonstrate continuity in the place of religion in human experience.

Second, what is the likely future course of this religious resurgence? Given the considerable variety of important religious movements in the contemporary world, it would make little sense to venture a global prognosis. Predictions, if one dares to make them at all, will be more useful if applied to much narrower situations. One prediction, though, can be made with some assurance: There is no reason to think the world of the twenty-first century will be any less religious than the world is today. A minority of sociologists of religion have been trying to salvage the old secularization theory by what I would call the last-ditch thesis: Modernization *does* secularize, and movements like the Islamic and the Evangelical ones represent last-ditch defenses by religion that cannot last; eventually, secularity will triumph—or, to put it less respectfully, eventually Iranian mullahs, Pentecostal preachers, and Tibetan lamas will all think and act like professors of literature at American universities. I find this thesis singularly unpersuasive.

Having made this general prediction—that the world of the next century will not be less religious than the world of today—I will have to speculate very differently regarding different sectors of the religious scene. For example, I think that the most militant Islamic movements will find it hard to maintain their present stance *vis-à-vis* modernity once they succeed in taking over the governments of their countries (this, it seems, is already happening in Iran). I also think that Pentecostalism, as it exists today among mostly poor and uneducated people, is unlikely to retain its present religious and moral characteristics unchanged, as many of these people experience upward social mobility (this has already been observed extensively in the United States). Generally, many of these religious movements are linked to non-religious forces of one sort or another, and the future course of the former will be at least partially determined by the course of the latter. In the United States, for instance, militant Evangelicalism will have a different future course if some of its causes succeed in the political and legal arenas than if it continues to be frustrated in these arenas. Also, in religion as in every other area of human endeavor, individual personalities play a much larger role than most social scientists and historians are willing to concede. There might have been an Islamic revolution in Iran without the Ayatollah Khomeini, but it would probably have looked quite different. No one can predict the appearance of charismatic figures who will launch powerful religious movements in unexpected places. Who knows—perhaps the next religious upsurge in America will occur among disenchanted post-modernist academics!

Third, do the resurgent religions differ in their critique of the secular order? Yes, of course they do, depending on their particular belief systems. Cardinal Ratzinger and the Dalai Lama will be troubled by different aspects of contemporary secular culture. What both will agree upon, however, is the shallowness of a culture that tries to get along without any transcendent points of reference. And they will have good reasons to support this view. The religious impulse, the quest for meaning that transcends the restricted space of empirical existence in this world, has been a perennial feature of humanity. (This is not a theological statement but an anthropological one—an agnostic or even an atheist philosopher may well agree with it.) It would require something close to a mutation of the species to extinguish this impulse for good. The more radical thinkers of the Enlightenment and their more recent intellectual descendants hoped for something like this, of course. So far it has not happened, and as I have argued, it is unlikely to happen in the foreseeable future. The critique of secularity common to all the resurgent movements is that human existence bereft of transcendence is an impoverished and finally untenable condition.

To the extent that secularity today has a specifically modern form (there were earlier forms in, for example, versions of Confucianism and Hellenistic culture), the critique of secularity also entails a critique of at least these aspects of modernity. Beyond that, however, different religious movements differ in their relation to modernity. As I have said, an argument can be made that the Islamic resurgence strongly tends toward a negative view of modernity; in places it is downright anti-modern or counter-modernizing, as in its view of the role of women. By contrast, I think it can be shown that the Evangelical resurgence is positively modernizing in most places where it occurs, clearly so in Latin America. The new Evangelicals throw aside many of the traditions that have been obstacles to modernization—*machismo*, for one, and also the subservience to hierarchy that has been endemic to Iberian Catholicism. Their churches encourage values and behavior patterns that contribute to modernization. To take just one important case in point: In order to participate fully in the life of their congregations, Evangelicals will want to read the Bible; this desire to read the Bible encourages literacy and, beyond this, a positive attitude toward education and self-improvement. They also will want to be able to join in the discussion of congregational affairs, since those matters are largely in the hands of laypersons (indeed, largely in the hands of women); this lay operation of churches necessitates training in administrative skills, including the conduct of public meetings and the keeping of financial accounts. It is not fanciful to suggest that in this way Evangelical congregations serve—inadvertently, to be sure—as schools for democracy and for social mobility.

Religious Resurgence and World Affairs

Other questions . . . concern the relation of the religious resurgence to a number of issues not linked to religion.

First, international politics. Here one comes up head-on against the thesis, eloquently proposed not long ago by Samuel Huntington, that, with the end of the Cold War, international affairs will be affected by a "clash of civilizations" rather than by ideological conflicts. There is something to be said for this thesis. The great ideological conflict that animated the Cold War is certainly dormant for the moment, but I, for one, would not bet on its final demise. Nor can we be sure that new ideological conflicts may not arise in the future. To the extent that nationalism is an ideology (more accurately, each nationalism has its *own* ideology), ideology is alive and well in a long list of countries.

It is also plausible that, in the absence of the overarching confrontation between Soviet Communism and the American-led West, cultural animosities suppressed during the Cold War period are surfacing. Some of these animosities have themselves taken on an ideological form, as in the assertion of a distinctive Asian identity by a number of governments and intellectual groups in East and Southeast Asia. This ideology has become especially visible in debates over the allegedly ethnocentric/Eurocentric character of human rights as propagated by the United States and other Western governments and governmental organizations. But it would probably be an exaggeration to see these debates as signaling a clash of civilizations. The situation closest to a religiously defined clash of civilizations would come about if the worldview of the most radical branches of the Islamic resurgence came to be established within a wider spectrum of countries and became the basis of the foreign policies of these countries. As yet this has not happened.

To assess the role of religion in international politics, it would be useful to distinguish between political movements that are genuinely inspired by religion and those that use religion as a convenient legitimation for political agendas based on quite non-religious interests. Such a distinction is difficult but not impossible. Thus there is no reason to doubt that the suicide bombers of the Islamic Haws movement truly believe in the religious motives they avow. By contrast, there is good reason to doubt that the three parties involved in the Bosnian conflict, commonly represented as a clash between religions, are really inspired by religious ideas. I think it was P. J. O'Rourke who observed that these three parties are of the same race, speak the same language, and are distinguished only by their religion, which none of them believe. The same skepticism about the religious nature of an allegedly religious conflict is expressed in the following joke from Northern Ireland: As a man walks down a dark street in Belfast, a gunman jumps out of a doorway, holds a gun to his head, and asks, "Are you Protestant or Catholic?" The man stutters, "Well, actually, I'm an atheist." "Ah yes," says the gunman, "but are you a Protestant or a Catholic atheist?"

Second, war and peace. It would be nice to be able to say that religion is everywhere a force for peace. Unfortunately, it is not. Very probably religion in the modern world more often fosters war, both between and within nations. Religious institutions and movements are fanning wars and civil wars on the Indian subcontinent, in the Balkans, in the Middle East, and in Africa, to mention only the most obvious cases. Occasionally, indeed, religious institutions try to resist warlike policies or to mediate between conflicting parties. The Vatican mediated successfully in some international disputes in Latin America. There have been religiously inspired peace movements in several countries (including the United States, during the Vietnam War). Both Protestant and Catholic clergy have tried to mediate the conflict in Northern Ireland, though with notable lack of success.

But it is probably a mistake to look here simply at the actions of formal religious institutions or groups. There may be a diffusion of religious values in a society that could have peace-prone consequences even in the absence of formal actions by church bodies. For example, some analysts have argued that the wide diffusion of Christian values played a mediating role in the process that ended the apartheid regime in South Africa, even though the churches were mostly polarized between the two sides of the conflict, at least until the last few years of the regime, when the Dutch Reformed Church reversed its position on apartheid.

Third, economic development. The basic text on the relation of religion and economic development is, of course, the German sociologist Max Weber's 1905 work *The Protestant Ethic and the Spirit of Capitalism.* Scholars have been arguing over the thesis of this book for over ninety years. However one comes out on this (I happen to be an unreconstructed Weberian), it is clear that some values foster modern economic development more than others. Something *like* Weber's "Protestant ethic" is probably functional in an early phase of capitalist growth—an ethic, whether religiously inspired or not, that values personal discipline, hard work, frugality, and a respect for learning. The new Evangelicalism in Latin America exhibits these values in virtually crystalline purity, so that my own mental subtitle for the research project on this topic conducted by the center I direct at Boston University has been, "Max Weber is alive and well and living in Guatemala." Conversely, Iberian Catholicism, as it was established in Latin America, clearly does *not* foster such values.

But religious traditions can change. Spain experienced a remarkably successful period of economic development beginning in the waning years of the Franco regime, and one of the important factors was the influence of Opus Dei, which combined rigorous theological orthodoxy with a market-friendly openness in economic matters. I have suggested that Islam, by and large, has difficulties with a modern market economy; yet Muslim emigrants have done remarkably well in a number of countries (for instance, in sub-Saharan Africa), and there is a powerful Islamic movement in Indonesia that might yet play a role analogous to that of Opus Dei in the Catholic world. I should add that for years now there has been an extended debate over the part played by Confucian-inspired values in the economic success stories of East Asia; if one is to credit the "post-Confucian thesis" and also to allow that Confucianism is a religion, then here would be a very important religious contribution to economic development.

One morally troubling aspect of this matter is that values functional at one period of economic development may not be functional at another. The values of the "Protestant ethic" or a functional equivalent thereof are probably essential during the phase that Walt Rostow called "the take-off," but may not be so in a later phase. Much less austere values may be more functional in the so-called post-industrial economies of Europe, North America, and East Asia. For example, frugality, however admirable from a moral viewpoint, may actually be a vice economically speaking. Although undisciplined hedonists have a hard time climbing out of primitive poverty, they can do well in the high-tech, knowledge-driven economies of the advanced societies.

Finally, human rights and social justice. Religious institutions have, of course, made many statements on human rights and social justice. Some of these have had important political consequences, as in the civil-rights struggle in the United States and the collapse of Communist regimes in Europe. But, as mentioned previously, there are different religiously articulated views about the nature of human rights. The same goes for ideas about social justice: what is justice to some groups is gross injustice to others. Sometimes it is very clear that positions taken by religious groups on such matters are based on a religious rationale; the principled opposition to abortion and contraception by the Roman Catholic Church is such a clear case. At other times, though, positions on social justice, even if legitimated by religious rhetoric, reflect the location of the religious functionaries in this or that network of non-religious social classes and interests. To stay with the same example, I think that this is the case with most of the positions taken by American Catholic institutions on social-justice issues other than those relating to sexuality and reproduction.

I have dealt very briefly with immensely complex matters. I was asked to give a global overview, and that is what I have tried to do. There is no way that I can end this with some sort of uplifting sermon. Both those who have great hopes for the role of religion in the affairs of this world and those who *fear* this role must be disappointed by the factual evidence. In assessing this role, there is no alternative to a nuanced, case-by-case approach. But one statement can be made with great confidence: Those who neglect religion in their analyses of contemporary affairs do so at great peril.

4

THE CHALLENGE OF SEPTEMBER 11 TO SECULARISM IN INTERNATIONAL RELATIONS

—Daniel Philpott

The greatest assault on the United States since the end of the Cold War, perhaps since its very founding, had little plausible origin in the dynamics of alliances and polarity, in the rise and fall of great powers, in any state's quest for security, or even in the actions of any state at all. For this reason, it eludes the emphases of realism, traditionally the dominant school in international relations scholarship. Neither was it accomplished by a parliament or a voting public, a multinational corporation, labor union, or farm lobby, or by any of the other agents that liberals believe influence foreign policy. The attack had little to do with international organizations or international institutions or with trade, finance, or investment; it involved international development indirectly at best. Only in the loosest sense of the term was the attacker a nongovernmental organization, still less one with an address near the United Nations. It was not an epistemic community. It was perhaps a transnational actor, but manifestly not a human rights organization or one of the issue networks familiar in the literature. It was motivated by ideas, but not economic, strategic, or politically liberal ones. It did not use nuclear weapons or biological or chemical ones—indeed it used nothing more sophisticated than box cutters, flying lessons, and some elaborate planning. Rather, those involved in crashing planes into the World Trade Center and the Pentagon on September 11, 2001, were animated by a kind of conception, were organized around a kind of idea, and appraised the international system according to a kind of notion to which international relations scholars have paid relatively little attention: religion.

With few exceptions, international relations scholars have long assumed the absence of religion among the factors that influence states. Their inattention is not without its reasons. Like a watchman who nods off as the creature he surveils himself falls asleep, these scholars have been describing a structure of political authority that was forged centuries ago by a sharply secularizing set of events and that has endured in its secular guise ever since. This authority structure can be called the Westphalian synthesis. On September 11 the synthesis was shaken by the fitful rumblings of a Rip Van Winkle awakening from

* *World Politics* 55, no. 1 (October 2002): 66–95.

long centuries of slumber, a figure whose identity is public religion—religion that is not privatized within the cocoon of the individual or the family but that dares to refashion secular politics and culture. Of all the fits and starts in the arousal of public religion over the past generation, the most radical and volatile is a political theology—radical Islamic revivalism, it can be called—that directly challenges the authority structure of the international system. This radical revivalism is the tradition behind al-Qaeda's attacks. The attacks and the broader resurgence of public religion ought, then, to sound the alarm clock for international relations scholars, as a call to direct far more energy to understanding the impetuses behind movements across the globe that are reorienting purposes and policies, alignments and dilemmas.

The Secularization of International Relations

The very term *religion* must be used provisionally and with care. Some scholars doubt whether it is even a meaningful concept, that is, an essential phenomenon of which there are different forms, a genus with different species. In the Middle Ages Christians used the term *religio*, but not very often and then usually to refer to the communal life of monastics. The medieval philosopher Thomas Aquinas used *religio* to mean the activity of giving proper reverence to God through worship. By contrast, the familiar, contemporary usage of religion, appearing first in early modern Europe, refers to a universal interior impulse toward God or to a system of propositional beliefs about the transcendent. It is this thinner concept of which there can be a plurality of forms, as infinite as the variety of propositions about God and gods.[1]

A resulting problem is that the modern usage of the term religion, denoting private, propositional beliefs, fails to encompass traditional faiths. Practiced communally through worship and devotion, they regulate all realms of life and make no easy distinction between mundane and spiritual. Is a more embracing, open-ended definition of religion available? The difficulty then becomes finding one that includes Hinduism, Christianity, Buddhism, and other instances of what scholars mean by world religions but that excludes what they usually do not mean—Marxism, Nazism, nationalism, and witchcraft, all of which, after all, have also inspired feverish belief, ritual, and devotion. There is a provisional response, if not a resolution, to these dilemmas, a definition that brings attention to those religions that are newly relevant to international politics: religion is a set of beliefs about the ultimate ground of existence, that which is unconditioned, not itself created or caused, and the communities and practices that form around these beliefs.[2] The nation and Marxist political ideology, though they surely inspire people to worship, kill, die, idolize, and genuflect, do not in their essential forms encompass beliefs about the ultimate ground of existence.

If this is religion, secularization is the decline of it. The decline occurs in different forms and degrees, corresponding to the different valences of religious commitment.[3] The first, most thorough form of secularization is the erosion of subjective belief in an ultimate ground of existence, a deity, God. In ceasing to believe in religious claims, people usually also cease to worship and pray in community, in churches, synagogues, mosques, and temples. They reject religion altogether. It is both possible and common, though, for people to drop community but retain their beliefs. This second form of secularization, captured in sociologist Grace Davie's phrase, "believing without belonging," is more partial.[4] A third form, most pertinent here, is the one most distinctive to politics. It is sociologist

David Martin's influential concept of secularization as "differentiation," which "denotes the process whereby each social sector becomes specialized."[5] In the political realm religion interacts far less intimately with governing institutions than it once did, whether through its legitimizing influence, through the overlapping prerogatives of religious and political authorities, or through its receipt of the state's direct and active support. Constitutions cease explicitly to direct the loyalties of citizens to God. Political ideologies—Marxism, liberalism, fascism, nationalism, and liberalism—channel loyalties toward an object other than God. International laws, institutions, and organizations advance purposes having little to do with religion. So do the parties, unions, lobbies, and armies through which people urge, advocate, and rebel against the state. The temporal is distinguished from the spiritual, politics from religion.

Secularization is not an ethical claim, for scholars can agree on its presence or absence or some gradation of either, while separately celebrating it, lamenting it, or expressing some gradation of either. Whether religious commitments are compatible with any secularly expressed political end is complex and contingent. Many religious believers, for instance, applaud the Western separation of church and state. Secularization is a rather descriptive statement, holding that the political ends of citizens, organizations, and societies themselves are no longer as explicitly religious as they once were or are no longer explicitly religious at all.

The discipline of political science and the field of international relations in turn become secularized when its scholars describe politics as secularized, that is, as if states, nations, international organizations, and the parties, lobbies, and businesses which seek to influence them pursue ends that include power, security, wealth, peace, stability, economic development, robust international law, a cleaner environment, and the alleviation of humanitarian disaster, but do not include the spread or promotion of a religion, or any of these other ends out of a religious motivation. By this definition, international relations scholarship is indeed secularized. A survey of articles in four leading international relations journals over the period 1980–99 finds that only six or so out of a total of about sixteen hundred featured religion as an important influence.[6] There are important exceptions. *Orbis* and *Millennium* have each published special issues on religion and international organization within the last four years, the latter theorizing innovatively about the role of religion.[7] More famously, Samuel Huntington's "clash of civilizations" thesis, forecasting that the major armed conflicts in the post–Cold War era will be fought between representatives of religiously defined civilizations, has arguably become the most widely cited and debated thesis of the past decade on the character of contemporary international relations.[8] Yet few international relations scholars, either in sympathy or criticism of Huntington's thesis, have joined him in asserting religion's role in relations between states. Journals and university presses in the field treat religion in scant proportion to its expanding space in newspaper headlines over the past few decades. Meanwhile, an accumulating group of historians, sociologists, and journalists are corroborating this increasing influence through claims about the "revenge of God," the "desecularization of the world," and the resurgence of "public religion in the modern world."[9] Inattention to these trends on the part of political scientists can have yielded only their deep surprise at September 11, not only in the predictive sense (who *did* predict it after all?), but also in the conceptual sense. Their concepts gave them little reason to think that an event like this could happen.

The Roots of Secularization in the Practice of International Relations

The secularized mien of international relations scholarship is unsurprising. Deeply embedded in the international system itself is a secularized authority structure whose origins lie in calamitous strife over the relationship between spiritual and temporal authority. The structure arises from a resolution to this strife that sharply differentiated the two kinds of authority and that subsequently expanded the terms of this resolution to a global dominion that still endures. In plumbing its workings, scholars readily and naturally assume the commitments embedded in it. The phenomenon shapes the thought.

This authority structure is the Westphalian synthesis, which weaves together four component norms of authority, all emblematic of the Peace of Westphalia of 1648. The norms did not emerge then and there ex nihilo. Some had begun to take shape centuries earlier only to be consolidated at Westphalia; some worked themselves out decades afterward. What is important is that they embodied the secularizing spirit of this settlement of the Thirty Years War, nay, of the previous century of strife over spiritual and temporal authority. Each strand of the synthesis arose from the struggles ignited by the Protestant Reformation, itself entailing a new set of ideas about authority. Each revolved around the rise and consolidation of the system of sovereign states. Each articulates aspects of an answer to the most fundamental question about political authority—its relationship to the ground of existence. Just as a dweller moving about his house takes for granted its architecture, so scholars, statespersons, or anyone else immersed in war, commerce, or other business among nations often take for granted the international authority structure. Take it for granted, that is, until the day that it is formidably defied.

The Peace of Westphalia marked a victory of the sovereign state as a form of political authority. This was the first strand of the Westphalian synthesis—a kind of political organization where a single locus of authority—a prince or, later, a junta or a people ruling through a constitution—is supreme within a territory. The sovereign state became virtually the only form of polity within Europe to practice substantive, not merely formal, constitutional authority. A continent of sovereign states—fighting, allying, trading, forming pacts and protocols over scores of matters—then formed a system characterized by anarchy, the defining feature of international relations.

The victory of a sovereign state system signaled at the same time the defeat of another scheme for organizing international authority, one in which religion had played a far more significant role. In this sense, the first strand of the Westphalian synthesis is a secularizing one. Westphalia was the culmination of a centuries-long metamorphosis, a gradual supplanting of one political order by another, that began with Europe in the High Middle Ages. In the Respublica Christiania there existed no sovereignty, no supreme authority within a territory. From the pope and the Holy Roman Emperor, down through kings to barons, bishops, dukes, counts, and peasants, authorities were united together in a single social entity, reflecting the unity of the church as the Body of Christ. With the exception of patches of Europe during short stretches of the Middle Ages, none of these authorities enjoyed supremacy within a territory; none enjoyed sovereignty. The vast majority were limited in their prerogatives by an outside authority or ruled over a vassal who had external fealties. Politics and religion were profoundly mingled, too, with the church exercising manifold prerogatives that were, by any modern definition, civil. Bishops and archbishops held large amounts of land, exercised legitimate coercive force, levied taxes, and served nobles, princes, and kings as chancellors, regents, and other officers. The pope exercised legislative, executive, and judicial powers.[10]

This portrait captured Europe best at the apogee of the Middle Ages, roughly between the eleventh and thirteenth centuries. But even as late as the sixteenth and early seventeenth centuries, much of Europe was still under the authority of a vast quasi-medieval conglomerate that linked together the Holy Roman Empire, the Habsburg monarchy, the Spanish king, and the Catholic Church. Within this expanse, ecclesiasts continued to exercise civil functions. Most importantly, the emperor enforced religious uniformity. It was not until 1648 that these privileges would effectively disappear. By that time, ecclesiastical authorities held scant temporal powers within Europe's sovereign states and the emperor commanded virtually no authority within the territories of princes, particularly the authority to enforce the confessional character of the realm.[11]

With the rise of the state system came the end of a political practice that had dominated European politics for 130 years—authorities' enforcement of religion outside their territory. This proscription of intervention is the second strand of the Westphalian synthesis. It was yet another restriction on what temporal authority would do on behalf of religion, another sense in which temporal and religious authority became differentiated. Since the Protestant Reformation had begun in Germany in 1517, princes, kings, nobles, the emperor, and the pope had striven to extend or preserve their faith with little respect for territorial limits, an armed contest that expanded eventually into the Thirty Years War. In 1555 it appeared that a settlement had been reached within the empire at the Peace of Augsburg. Its formula, *cuius regio, eius religio* (whose the region, his the religion), established sovereignty in matters of faith. But Augsburg did not last. The settlement's endless arcane clauses were symptomatic of the burning desire of political and ecclesiastical authorities alike to continue the fight to spread their faith. As late as 1629, riding the momentum of a political victory in the Thirty Years War, the emperor Ferdinand decreed the Edict of Restitution, calling for the restoration of Catholicism in all the lands that had become Protestant since Augsburg. Only with Westphalia did such contests end and did religion largely cease to be a casus belli in Europe—at least until the late twentieth century, when it became an issue in Northern Ireland and Yugoslavia. Kalevi Holsti notes that during the period 1648–1713, immediately following Westphalia, religion was a major issue in only three wars, all between Europeans and Muslims.[12]

The result of these trends for Europe was pluralism, though pluralism of a certain sort. Sovereign authorities, respecting one another's rights to govern religion in their territory as they please, would no longer take up arms to change it. Within the state, however, religious freedom for the individual was still rare; at best, a state might allow more than one sect or faith to exist, but only in certain regions and proportions as dictated by detailed provisions of the peace. Most importantly, states would refrain from seeking to define the relationship between politics and religion within other states' borders. Noninterference in matters of religion would prove to be the prototype for a more generalized norm of nonintervention, one of the keystones of international society, the set of norms that states share in common.[13]

It was the Protestant Reformation that sparked the protracted conflict over religion and that led ultimately to the end of intervention for religion at Westphalia. Such conflict raged in Germany, the Netherlands, France, and Sweden, culminating in the continent-wide Thirty Years War, a conflagration that killed more than one-fourth of the German population alone. Westphalia served as a truce of exhaustion, a peace that would end the fighting of decades.

The Reformation's religious pluralism amounted to nothing deeper than a modus vivendi. Though it would persist in practice, a widely shared principled acceptance was long in coming. In particular, the Catholic church continued to hold that in principle the polity ought to promote the Catholic faith as the single religion of the realm. Upon hearing of the settlement at Westphalia, Pope Innocent X issued a bull, *Zel Domus*, that condemned the treaties as "null, void, invalid, iniquitous, unjust, damnable, reprobate, inane, empty of meaning and effect for all time."[14] As late as the nineteenth century the Vatican continued to condemn international law as a Protestant science. Nonetheless, it was powerless to force any change in the Westphalian settlement, for a clause in the treaties had declared preemptively that papal protests would not nullify the treaties. The pope could do little more than lament its temporal impotence, which later came to be symbolized by the absurdity of the Vatican owning a submarine in the nineteenth century.

The third strand of the Westphalian synthesis complements the separation entailed in the first two. Not only would state authorities refrain from intervening abroad to shape the relationship between politics and religion, but they would increasingly refrain altogether from seeking actively to promote the work and welfare of churches and religion, even in their own realm. The most dramatic form of this differentiation was religious freedom.

At the time of Westphalia, religious freedom was largely a concept in the minds of European philosophers, as it had been already for more than a century. These thinkers offered different rationales for why an individual ought to have the right to choose his faith. The weakest form of the argument was voiced by the *politiques*, Catholics who persistently held to the ideal of a uniform faith in the political realm but who did not consider its sustenance worth a civil war. Other philosophers rooted religious freedom in deep or partial skepticism—the cloudiness of knowledge of religion yielded the individual's right to decide it for himself. The most robust form of the argument, though, was the claim that religious freedom is grounded in truth—the deliverance either of reason or of New Testament scriptures. Many of these proponents also held that aside from being a right, religious freedom would promote the health of religion itself. For them, secularization, at least this type of differentiation, did not constitute a setback for faith.

The practice of religious freedom came gradually, in pieces, in places. The American and French Revolutions declared it a fundamental "right of man," even though the latter sought to suppress the structure of the Catholic Church. In places like England religious freedom developed more gradually and always in partnership with a nationally established church. Catholic states like Spain, by contrast, sought to safeguard a confessional state where Catholic belief was espoused uniformly. Configurations of religious freedom and of relationships between church and state have been remarkably diverse. It was not until the Second Vatican Council of 1965 that the Catholic church embraced religious freedom, resting it on deep philosophical and theological foundations.[15] Of course, the differentiation by which the state did not directly promote religion also found far more excessive—and brutal—forms. Especially in the twentieth century, states have actively sought to expunge religions, or even religion altogether—the most extreme cases being the Nazi genocide against the Jews and the attempts of communist regimes in the Soviet Union and elsewhere to cleanse religion entirely from their midst. It was religious freedom, though, that most characteristically extended the state's restraint in promoting religious practice and belief, deepening the differentiation that Westphalia had expanded.

Just as states came to promote religion less actively and directly, so religious authorities in Europe came to exercise ever fewer temporal prerogatives—holding temporal office, raising taxes, wielding control over large tracts of land. This fourth strand mirrors the third. It, too, was strongly influenced by the Protestant Reformation. The Reformation's influence was not exclusive. As demonstrated by an extensive literature, changes in economic organization, military technology and organization, and the ability of state bureaucracies to raise taxes and troops—all contributed to the gradual victory of the state over rival authorities, an evolution that long predated Protestantism.[16] For its part, the Reformation had three broad effects that diminished the temporal power of prelates. First, its very doctrines held that such powers were corrupting and that they had little basis in Christian belief. Rather, these powers should be concentrated in the hands of princes and kings and legislatures, who, though still under obligation to rule according to Christian principles, were better suited to exercise them. Martin Luther's famous doctrine of Two Kingdoms was a call for the separation of spheres. Second, in their very removal of themselves from the authority of Catholic officials, Protestants diminished the influence of this authority considerably. Third, more indirectly, the concentration of temporal powers in the hands of state rulers was brought on by Protestants' need for protection from the enforcement efforts of the Holy Roman Emperor. To avoid being stamped out, Protestants placed their safety and, to a significant degree, the governance of their churches under the authority of princes.[17] Through its very propositions and the effects of these propositions on their need for security, the Reformation elicited the transfer of temporal powers from ecclesiasts to secular rulers.

The relationship between spiritual and temporal authority known as the Westphalian synthesis remains robust to this day. The norms of authority entailed in each strand amount to a political theology, a doctrine of religion's role in society. States are the legitimate polity in the international system; states refrain from seeking to alter the relationship between religion and politics in other states; religious authorities exercise few if any temporal functions, still less any on a transnational level; and states seek far less vigorously to promote the welfare of religions than they did prior to Westphalia. These are its four strands, defining essential features of the authority structure of the modern international system.

Over the ensuing centuries, the synthesis would deepen in all of its strands. The purposes of many states strayed more than ever, coming to include fascism, communism, Marxism, nationalism, secular versions of liberalism, and social democracy. The synthesis would also widen. In the generation after Westphalia its chief theological competitor, Islam, began to experience the long, slow decline of its political power. At the same time, European sovereign states continued the long slow division of the rest of the world into colonies that they had begun in the sixteenth century. Over the three centuries following Westphalia, Africa, Asia, the Middle East, and Latin America would be colonized. Then, in a reversal of momentum, the colonized gradually revolted against this domination and achieved independence, first in the Americas during the nineteenth century, then across the globe, as virtually every remaining empire crumbled during the twentieth century. Typically, their leaders acted out of nationalism, an idea inherited from their European rulers. The result was the global expansion of the Westphalian synthesis, making the sovereign state the only form of political authority ever to occupy the entire globe.

Like the Westphalian system in Europe, the global Westphalian system could accommodate a variety of relationships between religion and politics within states, some of which allow religion to play a much stronger, more public, more interventionist role than it does in the West. But prior to the past generation most states have respected the Westphalian synthesis—by virtue of the very fact that they are states, by their respect of other states' configuration of temporal and religious authority, and in terms of the relatively differentiated roles of religion and state. Of course, states have often violated the Westphalian rules of authority, too. During the Cold War both the liberal democratic capitalist world and the communist world tried to extend their models of governance into other states, sometimes through military intervention. Yet most states on both sides continued to insist on nonintervention as the general rule, even as—toward their own infractions—they temporized, equivocated, and argued the legitimacy of exceptions.[18]

Though theological developments helped to bring about the Westphalian synthesis, it, like Max Weber's "iron cage," far outlasted these originating ideas. Plausibly, a challenge to this synthesis would require an organization motivated by a political theology that calls into question its tenets of authority. An organization like al-Qaeda.

The Roots of Secularization in International Relations Thought

The scholarship follows the phenomenon. Some early modern philosophers sought to understand the new set of institutions through old commitments. Theologians like Victoria, Suarez, Gentili, and Grotius tried to discover how a system of sovereign states could be placed on a theologically valid foundation. Another set of philosophers left theology largely behind. In depicting states as bereft of religious purposes, they thus adopted contemporary secularizing trends into their thought. Here were the beginnings of a tradition that rose quickly to prominence and that would in later centuries come to dominate international relations thought—the realist tradition. Its early modern articulators, Niccolò Machiavelli, Cardinal Richelieu, and Thomas Hobbes, all described the political changes of their day as a departure from classical Christianity and from its political embodiment in medieval Christendom. They held instead that states would flourish by affirming this departure in their actions. Realist voices perpetuated these commitments. At the beginning of the Cold War, a fertile moment for the tradition, American realists deployed their forebears' ideas in laying the foundation for international relations as a social science and helping the United States forge a response to the challenge of Soviet power.[19]

Central to realism, both then and now, is the concept of the state as a distinct political entity with distinct interests—its own logic, its own reason, in Cardinal Richelieu's famous formulation, *raison d'état*.[20] The concept arose as kings evolved from regionally prominent rulers of private "estates" to sovereigns of "states," where they ruled supreme within a set of territorial borders. An understanding of the state as a discrete body politic also assumed its declaration of independence from the authority of Christendom, the encompassing body of emperor and ecclesiasts that constrained the authority of kings.

If the state had its own "reason," its own interests, then of what did these consist? Its telos was no longer Thomas Aquinas's "common good," a state of justice and peace in which a whole array of virtues were safeguarded. Rather, it was now the mere security of the body.

As Hobbes described the situation, in a milieu of anarchy, where the state was now one of many bodies politic with no common Leviathan, security was precarious, often threatened by war. Closely following Hobbes, Kenneth Waltz would later call this condition one of "self-help."[21] Here, states could afford to attend to little else but to preserve themselves.

And to preserve their security, states must make it their primary pursuit to possess relative military power—military forces and the population, technology, wealth, and taxation structure to support them. States' fundamental interest in the pursuit of power is another key tenet of realism, what Hans Morgenthau called one if its six "signposts." For realists like Hobbes, it was international anarchy that necessitated the drive for power. For other realists, like Machiavelli and Morgenthau, whom Michael Doyle calls "fundamentalists," the will to power is rooted in human nature and pervades politics at all levels.[22] Morgenthau's intellectual *Bildung* involved an encounter—almost religious in fervor, but secularizing in substance—with the writings of Friedrich Nietzsche, whom he would later call a "kindred soul," "the god of my youth." From Nietzsche, Morgenthau learned that all social "reality" emanates from the person's consuming urge to gain pleasure and avoid pain, resulting in a ubiquitous struggle for power. By contrast, all ideas and normative principles are limited, relative, and contingent. These commitments later shaped Morgenthau's most famous books, *Scientific Man and Power Politics*, his excoriation of Anglo-American liberalism, and *Politics among Nations*, his classic of international politics. Here, he finds objective, empirically verifiable behavior in the realm of the political, where the struggle for power is all. Implied in Morgenthau's Nietzscheanism is the death of religion, metaphysics, and the ability of reason to grasp objective, transcendent truth.[23] In international relations these would no longer be considered the ends of states.

It is not surprising, then, that theorists for whom power is primary also counsel statespersons to violate "Christian morality" if the interests of the state require it. Machiavelli notoriously considered Christian morality enfeebling and counseled the prince to be prepared not to be good.[24] As a churchman, Cardinal Richelieu could not renounce Christian morality outright, but he certainly thought that kings should not be restricted by absolute norms in their pursuit of interests. Even twentieth-century "Christian realists" like Reinhold Niebuhr were skeptical that state action could be properly understood as motivated by deep religious concerns: in a world of power any attempt by states to pursue seriously a religious or transcendent ideal would ironically come to naught. He counseled leaders to act according to a calculation of the lesser of two evils.[25] Almost every realist in the tradition echoes this point, that states should place their own security and survival over compliance with any absolute moral obligation, even when such obligation is rooted in a rationally discernible common morality.[26]

All of the above tenets of realism are now found in the thought of the tradition's leading contemporary theorist, Kenneth Waltz, whose 1979 *Theories of International Politics* seeks to anchor realism in a more rigorous social scientific foundation and is the central reference point in contemporary realist discourse.[27] Realism's essential secularism, it follows, is also found there. Waltz takes states to be motivated by power, the vital ingredient of security in an environment of anarchy—leaving little room for them to be motivated by anything else.

The major competition for realism over the last two centuries has come from liberalism. Liberals from Kant onward through the Anglo-American tradition have been united in their belief in the rational possibility that states could escape the iron grip of the competition for power and cooperate in pursuing peace and prosperity.[28] Cooperation occurs when certain conditions are present—democratic regimes, liberal ideas, economic interdependence, and effective international institutions. But rarely do liberals consider religion as a shaper of states' ends. Rooted in the Enlightenment, most describe international politics as an almost wholly secular world, where states are consumed with the pursuit of stability, peace, and economic growth. Continuing the trend are contemporary liberal institutionalists, who, even in their criticism of realism, retain its rationalist assumptions that states are distinct unitary bodies whose primary pursuit is material power. Liberalism, whether classical or contemporary, has deservedly come to enjoy great prestige, as has realism, as an explanation of war, trade, and diverse forms of conflict and cooperation. But it does not help us to understand events seemingly wrought by religion.

Of course, there are other international relations scholars who dissent from realism and liberalism altogether—Marxists, constructivists, postmodernists. But they, too, deviate little from the secularist assumption. Constructivists, whose assertion of the malleability and plurality of state identities would seem to create the most room for religious purposes, rarely give them attention.[29]

Broader trends in the social sciences over the past generation have further reinforced the secularism of international relations scholarship. Most important is the secularization thesis of the 1950s and 1960s. Rooted in the modernization narrative that grew out of the Enlightenment, the thesis held, quite simply, that as industrialization, urbanization, rationalization, and science marched forward, religion would correspondingly find itself in retreat. Proponents held that secularization would occur in all of its forms—in private belief, in outward practice, and in public expressions of religion. It would be irreversible, absorbing, and global, eviscerating beliefs in Jehovah, Allah, Christ, and the Hindu gods alike. Though entailing a far wider sociological enterprise than the description of international relations, the secularization thesis nicely corroborated the commitments of realism and liberalism.[30] Similarly, the behavioral revolution of the 1950s gave prestige and impetus to a form of social science that rarely took religious motivations seriously. Its emphasis on purely empirical explanation and its spare assumptions about motivation are quite compatible with the assumptions of Waltz. Together, all of these trends created the intellectual milieu in which commercial airplanes driven into the towers of the World Trade Center came as an utter conceptual surprise.

The Desecularization of International Relations

Today, a growing number of analysts are finding that, in fact, religious beliefs, practices, and political ends are not in decline. One of secularism's original proponents during the 1960s, leading sociologist of religion Peter Berger, now writes:

> [T]he assumption that we live in a secularized world is false. The world today, with some exceptions to which I will come presently, is as furiously religious as it ever was, and in some places more so than ever. This means that a whole body of literature by historians and social scientists loosely labeled "secularization theory" is essentially mistaken. In my early work I contributed to this literature. I was in good company—most sociologists of religion had similar views, and we had good reasons for holding them. Some of the

writings we produced still stand up. (As I like to tell my students, one advantage of being a social scientist, as against being, say, a philosopher or a theologian, is that you can have as much fun when your theories are falsified as when they are verified!)[31]

Another sociologist of religion, Rodney Stark, documents Berger's claim through a broad survey of empirical trends found in recent writings on secularization. Most strikingly, in Western Europe, where secularization was argued to be strongest, no demonstrable decline in religious participation has taken place. Generally, participation rates remain low compared with America and elsewhere, while subjective religiosity remains high. But these trends have persisted for centuries. Stark questions the "myth of past piety," drawing upon a body of scholarship to show that medieval and early modern Europe, widely thought to be a place and time of wide and thick religion, was characterized by low rates of participation and a surprising variety of beliefs. "As for the ordinary people," he writes, "during the middle ages and during the Renaissance, the masses rarely entered a church, and their private worship was directed toward an array of spirits and supernatural agencies, only some of them Christian." In America, little evidence of religious decline exists. Over the past century and a half the rate of church membership has increased by more than three times, while a range of other measures of commitment have either held steady or have risen modestly. In formerly communist Eastern Europe and Russia, Stark reports, church attendance has risen steadily during the 1980s and 1990s. Claimants of secularization have asserted their thesis less vigorously toward the non-Western world. Stark confirms that there, too, the case against secularization is strong. In Islam, he argues, "there is a profound compatibility of the Islamic faith and modernization." Studies of Java, Pakistan, and Turkey show a positive correlation of Islamic faith and educational and occupational prestige, contrary to the predictions of modernization theory. In Taiwan, Hong Kong, Japan, and Chinese Malaysia, traditional folk religions are flourishing among the young. Although careful sociological studies capture only portions of a vast landscape of continents, the aggregate of these studies, along with more impressionistic perspectives, calls into question the core claims of the secularization thesis.[32]

Most pertinently for the argument at hand, scholars have documented a rise in the influence of religion on politics. Three separate trends have been identified. First, religious organizations are growing in their power to shape public debate and the policies of governments.[33] The Hindu nationalist parties in India, Muslim movements in Turkey, Orthodox Christians in Russia, conservative Christians in America, ultra-Orthodox Jews and Orthodox Jewish nationalists in Israel, and evangelicals in Latin America have all come to exercise increasing influence over laws governing marriage, education, foreign policy toward favored groups and states, religious minorities, and the relationship between religion and the institutions of the state. Second, religious organizations exercise a transnational influence upon the politics of outside states. Since its embrace of human rights and democracy at the Second Vatican Council, for instance, the Catholic Church has fostered democratization in Poland, Spain, Portugal, the Philippines, and throughout Latin America. Jews in America provide strong direct support to Israel. Worldwide Islamic organizations like the Muslim Brotherhood provide social services in many nations, building loyal followings who then articulate Islamic politics, sometimes through violence. Third, even more powerfully, religion shapes not only the policies of states but also their very constitutions, thus becoming "the law of the land." This is most dramatic in the Muslim world, where, in an "Islamic resurgence" over the past couple of decades, shari'a has become public law in Iran, Sudan, Saudi Arabia, Pakistan, Malaysia, and twelve of Nigeria's thirty-six states. In its own way, each of these trends challenges secularization as differentiation. Some challenge the Westphalian synthesis, especially the norms that prescribe state restraint in matters of religion and its reverse. Most radical of all, religiously motivated groups are questioning the very legitimacy of the international order, the Westphalian synthesis, in all of its stands. The most influential of these are networks of Muslims who act on behalf of the unity of the *umma*, or the people of Islam. Like al-Qaeda.

The Challenge of Radical Islamic Revivalism to Secularized International Relations

The assault on the World Trade Center and the Pentagon, the killing of some three thousand civilians on September 11, 2001, was motivated by a political theology that regards the Westphalian synthesis as despicably secularized. This political theology, which we can call "radical Islamic revivalism," began in the early twentieth century as an internal moral critique of Islamic civilization, one that regards it as having decayed to a state of barbarism. Over decades the most ardent proponents of radical Islamic revivalism began to identify the sources of decline on the outside, too, and to advocate a violent antidote.

Popular misconceptions underline the importance of striving for clarity about what Islamic revivalism is not. Though theologically rooted, it represents only a small niche in the spectrum of Islamic views of political theology. Its beliefs and its actions fly in the face of doctrines of warfare that run widely and deeply in the Islamic tradition: a prohibition of the direct, intentional killing of innocents; the requirement of justly constituted authority; a restrictive understanding of who is an aggressor that would thoroughly reject Osama bin Laden's assessment of the United States; and strong restraint toward enlisting Muslim civilians in warfare, a practice to be confined to cases of extreme emergency attack.[34] The Organization of the Islamic Conference unanimously condemned the attacks of September 11. Though anecdotal evidence exists of a more diffuse popular hostility to the West among Muslims, only a narrow minority of Muslims subscribes to the specific tenets of radical Islamic revivalism.[35] Its impact far outweighs its numbers.

Nor should the object of radical Islamic revivalism's ire be misunderstood. It is not Christianity or the historic traditions of Western civilization that the movement rejects, though it may not be particularly friendly to either (and it is far more hostile to Judaism). What it primarily scorns, rather, is a secularized political order that challenges its own political theology of authority, along with the particular offenses perpetrated against Islam by the United States, the most powerful representative of this order. Part and parcel of this secularized order is the Westphalian synthesis.

Radical Islamic revivalism challenges every element of that synthesis. Against the norm that in the modern international system the legitimate polity is the sovereign state stands Osama bin Laden's fatwa of February 1998:

> In compliance with God's order, we issue the following fatwa to all Muslims: the ruling to kill the Americans and their allies—civilians and military—is an individual duty for every Muslim who can do it in any country in which it is possible to do it, in order to liberate the Al-Aqsa Mosque [Jerusalem] and the holy mosque [Mecca] from their grip, and in

order for their armies to move out of the lands of Islam. . . . This is in accordance with the words of Almighty God, "and fight the pagans all together as they fight you all together," and "fight them until there is no more tumult or oppression, and there prevail justice and faith in God."

Unlike the state, radical revivalists like bin Laden are religiously constituted actors, bound together by a common political-theological outlook that claims authority to act on behalf of the *umma*—that is, all Muslims, in whatever state they may live—and even to order them into battle.[36] They are not a state themselves and they exercise authority in the name of a group that extends far beyond the confines of any state.

In the Westphalian order nonintervention is an ensconced norm of international society, and the tradition of noninterference in other states' governance of religion dates back to the days of *cuius regio, eius religio*. Radical Islamic revivalism is dedicated precisely to the opposite position—crossing borders in order to influence how states treat religion. Revivalists aim to bring Islamic societies under the authority of divine law, shari'a. All over the world they wage what they regard as defensive wars against defilements of Islam—on Palestinians at the hands of Israel, on Iraqi civilians at the hands of the United States, on holy ground in Saudi Arabia that is violated by the United States.

Against the trend of the decades surrounding Westphalia, when religious authorities, especially ones outside the state, ceased to exercise temporal powers, Islamic revivalists aim to have religious authorities play a far more powerful role than in secular states. Under shari'a they would influence state officials far more, through their teachings, their directives, and their direct advice; in Shi'ite interpretations they would actually be the state officials, as are imams in Iran.

In the modern state system of the Westphalian model, state officials create and protect spheres where religious authority and norms do not govern strongly or are allowed to be chosen freely; sometimes they seek to suppress religion altogether. Radical Islamic revivalists, by contrast, envision government officials promoting shari'a in every sector of society, with little concern for the religious freedom of non-Muslims. In all of these ways, Islamic revivalists unravel the Westphalian synthesis. Their blueprint for the relationship of religion to politics is reminiscent of medieval Europe; their methods and organization evoke those of transnational movements of Protestants and Catholics in early modern Europe.

What are the intellectual roots of such thinking? What is the substance of its critique of modern politics? How does this critique translate into violence against outsiders? How did al-Qaeda in particular emerge from this critique?

Again, radical revivalists are but a small minority of Muslims and hold a minority position along the spectrum of Muslim political theology. Sohail Hashmi describes this spectrum as entailing three general competing Muslim views of the legitimacy of the international system. First, there are "statists," who wholly accept the territorial state. They regard Islam as one important source of national identity in states where the vast majority of the population is Muslim but otherwise view it as an impediment to modernization and national integration. For statists, Islam is instrumental to the state-building enterprise. This view, he says, "remain[s] peripheral to the Islamic discourse." Second, the broad middle is occupied by "Islamic internationalists," who accept separate Muslim states, but assert pan-Islamic obligations that transcend the interests of individual states. Third, there are "Islamic cosmopolitans" for whom territorially delimited sovereign states are an illegitimate remnant of European imperialism, designed to weaken the Muslim world, who perpetuate the violation of Islamic tenets of universality and solidarity. Emblematic is Ayatollah Khomeini, who supported the spread of Islamic revolution far beyond Iran's borders. He and the like-minded are the equivalent of what are here called radical revivalists.[37]

How did radical revivalists come to their position? At the core of the tradition stands a theologically based view of Islam's current historical condition, namely, that it is one of corruption and decrepitude or, more precisely, *jahiliyyah*, the state of barbarism and ignorance that characterized the period prior to Muhammad. The critique is mainly an internal one, based on the view that Islam has veered alarmingly from its true meaning.[38] *Jahiliyyah* even more strongly characterizes the Western world, whose superior power enables it to impose its corruption on Islam. State governments and the international order alike have fallen into secularism, where shari'a governs only insufficiently and religion is wrongly confined to a private sphere. Against these evils, there is a need for intensive jihad, a holy struggle. This was the view of the first articulators of radical revivalism in the Sunni tradition, who began to write and organize in the first half of the twentieth century. Generally, their perspective goes under the name *Salafiyya*, a word derived from *al-Salaf al-Salih*, meaning the "venerable forefathers" and referring to the generation of the Prophet.[39] They emerged in the wake of the abolition of the caliphate in 1924, this centuries-old entity of Muslims united under one political head. Until the late 1970s they exercised little systematic political influence, and were overshadowed by the more secularized and dominant pan-Arab nationalism.

Three articulators of the critique make it more vivid. Abu Ala Al-Mawdudi was one of the earliest voices of the radical revivalist critique and the founder of the Jama'at-i Islami Party in Pakistan. Just as the Prophet had fought the *jahiliyyah* of his time, Al-Mawdudi thought, so Muslims must now use all means at their disposal to resist the modern *jahiliyyah* spread by the West. Arguing that states are a Westernized corruption, Al-Mawdudi actively campaigned against the creation of Pakistan, a position for which he received broad support among conservative Muslims in India.[40] Though he would later come to terms with reality and participate in Pakistani politics for three decades, he never became a nationalist or a strong supporter of the concept of the state. During the Cold War he called for a universal jihad, though not a military or violent one, against the imperialist powers of the West and the Soviet Union.[41]

A second key figure in the rise of radical revivalism was Hasan Al-Banna, who as a young schoolteacher founded the Muslim Brotherhood in 1928. For Al-Banna, as for Al-Mawdudi, secularism was unacceptable. Islam is a total way of life, he insisted, and could not be confined to the private sphere. A charismatic leader, he mobilized throngs of people to bring an Islamic solution to the ills of modernity. The Brotherhood ran night schools, established hospitals and clinics, built factories, and taught Muslims modern labor laws. At the same time, a "secret apparatus" of the Brotherhood began to organize violent operations against declared enemies of Islam. Al-Banna formally denounced the operations, but there is evidence to suggest that he knew of them. Today, the bulk of the party continues to fight its battles in the political arena, but its radical fringe persists in violence, targeting tourist buses and riverboats.[42]

A third figure, the Egyptian Sayyid Qutb, expanded on Al-Mawdudi's critique of secular modernity to become the most prominent voice of Sunni radical revivalism after World

War II. "Every significant Sunni fundamentalist movement had been influenced by Qutb," writes Karen Armstrong.[43] When Qutb first joined the Muslim Brotherhood (of which he would later become a leader), he was still a reformer who wanted to give Western democracy an Islamic dimension. He came to endorse violent military action only after he was imprisoned for his membership in the Brotherhood by Egyptian president Gamal Abdel Nasser in 1956. It was in a concentration camp that he became convinced that religious and secular people could not coexist in peace. He took from the writings of Al-Mawdudi that *jahiliyyah* was relevant to modern conditions. In his last published work, *Milestones* (1964), Qutb "openly declared that the existing order in all countries, including so called 'Muslim' ones, was anti-Islamic, and called on Islamic activists to prepare themselves to replace the present *Jahili* (that is, barbaric and ignorant) order."[44] He was the first to extend Al-Mawdudi's use of the term *jahiliyyah* to societies of nominal Muslims not governed entirely by Islam. For him, non-Muslim Westerners and communists were not the only enemy; so, too, were "apostate" Muslims like Egypt's Nasser. Despite Islam's prohibition of Muslims taking up arms against one another, Qutb pronounced secular Muslims to be "corrupters of the faith" and thereby legitimate targets of a military form of jihad. "For Qutb, the modern *jahiliyyah* in both Egypt and the West was even worse than the *jahiliyyah* of the Prophet's time, because it was not based on 'ignorance' but was a principled rebellion against God," writes Armstrong.[45] The faithful must reject "all man-made laws and governments which are the foundations of the new paganism. The true believers, the elect, must organize themselves into vanguard groups apart from the new society of ignorance and repeat the original establishment of Islam through withdrawal/migration, jihad, and conquest of power."[46] Nasser's government executed Qutb in 1966.[47]

How does this theologically based critique of modernity translate into a view of the international political order? The ultimate goal of radical revivalists is the Islamization of this order, replacing secular order with divine order, the nation-state with an Islamic system, democracy with an Islamic notion of consultation, positive law and human legislation with shari'a and government of the people and by the people with God's rule.[48] Exactly what form of polity is supposed to emerge is ambiguous and varies among revivalists. After extensively analyzing the literature of contemporary radical revivalists, Bassam Tibi concludes that a restoration of the caliphate, the unity of Islam under a single head, the caliph, is no longer a widely shared goal.[49] Tibi writes that "although the current revival of political Islam" is an

> expression of Islamic revolt against the prevailing international order of nation-states and its local configurations, it is not a revival of traditional Islamic political thought. Islamic fundamentalists do not speak about the restoration of the traditional Islamic order of the caliphate, but rather of the *nizam Islami*/Islamic order, with clearly modern implications.

He cites one major pamphlet that argues for the primary importance of shari'a as the basis for political legitimacy, with the form of polity being a secondary issue.[50] The unity of the entire Muslim people, or the *umma*, is still a powerful concept in Islam. As long as the possibility of such unity in political form remains remote, it fails to translate into anything but a vague notion of polity. But this ambiguity does not detract from radical Islamic revivalism's challenge to the Westphalian synthesis. It is embodied by nonstate groups that claim authority for a people that is not itself confined to a state; its proponents engage in

violence and other means of suasion across borders to change the temporal-spiritual ordering of authority within states; they advocate a greatly strengthened influence of religious
authorities on state institutions; and they look to state institutions to promote Islam.

Revivalists' resistance to the Westphalian synthesis often takes the form of violence.
"Islam's image of itself is to be the religion of peace," writes Tibi.[51] But, he tells us, non-
Muslims are seen as hindrances to this mission. Although in the classical doctrine, jihad
is not to take the form of aggression, revivalists interpret the need to promote the spread
of Islam in ways that can incorporate offensive revolutionary violence, as well as defensive
combat.[52] It was the second generation of revivalists, impatient with the lack of success of
their moral revivalist fathers, who began to advocate violence. Qutb, the hinge of this turn,
imagined an "Islamic world revolution." In a pamphlet inspired by Qutb, Egyptian radical
revivalist M.A.S. Faraj declared that "the idols of the world can only be made to disappear
through the power of the sword." Since the abolition of the caliphate in 1924, according to
revivalists, Muslim rulers have replaced Islamic law with the laws of the infidels and forced
believers to live under these laws, as the Mongols had done. Since they are apostates, they
must suffer the punishment for apostasy—death.[53] Describing an example of the transformation of jihad from a defensive concept to an offensive one, Olivier Roy notes that in
the war in Afghanistan, jihad was used by the traditional clerics (*ulama*) quite differently
from how it was used by the lay religious radicals of the mujahadeen. "For the ulama it
was understood as a defensive action designed to protect a threatened region from foreign
encroachments or from secularization initiated by the state," he explains, but "for the new
fundamentalists it was interpreted as an offensive action designed to topple an illegitimate
secular state, whatever its policy toward religion might be."[54]

Radical Islamic revivalists have in recent decades begun to turn their doctrines of violence toward outsiders, particularly the United States. *Salafi* writings portray the United
States as an instrument of Satan, oppressing Muslims and threatening Islamic civilization
with its secular culture and power. The U.S. is considered the leader of a "Zionist-Crusader"
alliance dedicated to destroying Islam. More than just a pact between the United States
and Israel, the alliance is seen to have oppressed Muslims not only in Palestine but also in
Bosnia, Chechnya, Lebanon, and Iraq. Qutb, bin Laden, and many other radical revivalists have portrayed the United States as a sworn enemy of Islam that must be resisted by
force. Drawing on the thirteenth-century philosopher ibn Taymiyya, the radical revivalists
often analogize the United States to the Mongol barbarians who invaded the Islamic world
during the Middle Ages.[55]

A theologically based critique of the modern world, a call for violent attacks on the
modern international political order, a focus on America as the primary enemy—all of
these strands are woven together by the al-Qaeda movement. The son of a billionaire Saudi
owner of a construction company, Osama bin Laden underwent a conversion to theological radicalism in the early 1970s. It was in the war against the Soviet Union in Afghanistan that he honed his skills and developed his reputation as a military leader. Indeed,
the war was a profound unifying event for radical revivalists all over the world, as they
arrived to resist the imperialist invasion of 1979. In Afghanistan, bin Laden worked closely
with Abdullah Azzam, a Palestinian member of the Muslim Brotherhood, helping him to
recruit young Muslims for the Afghan front and to prevent outbursts of factional violence
between Sunni and Shi'ite volunteers. Toward the end of the war, however, a rift grew

between the two leaders over the proper way to carry out Islamic revival. While Azzam preferred to concentrate on building an Islamic state in Afghanistan, bin Laden and the Egyptians sought to conduct a fight against several *kafir* (infidel) countries at once, including apostate Muslim countries and Western nations such as the United States. Eventually bin Laden and the Egyptians parted company. In the late 1980s bin Laden established the al-Qaeda network to bring together and train Sunni Arab Muslims who had fought in Afghanistan against the Soviet invasion. Now they could expand outward to take on a broader array of enemies. Stripped of his Saudi citizenship for his advocacy of extremist views, he set up his operation in Afghanistan in the early 1990s.[56]

In forming the ideology of the al-Qaeda movement, bin Laden drew from radical revivalist themes in both Qutb's thought and Saudi Wahabbism. Al-Qaeda is exceptional among revivalists in proclaiming the goal of establishing a pan-Islamic caliphate throughout the world. This only deepens its challenge to the Westphalian synthesis. It proposes to accomplish its goal by working with allied Islamic extremist groups to overthrow regimes it deems "non-Islamic" and expelling Westerners and non-Muslims from Muslim countries. In February 1998 it issued a statement under the banner of "The World Islamic Front for Jihad against the Jew and Crusaders," proclaiming it the duty of all Muslims to kill U.S. citizens—including civilians—and their allies everywhere. Al-Qaeda, then, translates radical Islamic revivalism into a notion of jihad that is more ambitious and more violent than that of almost any other radical revivalist group. On the basis of this notion, it has operated in Sudan, Egypt, Saudi Arabia, Yemen, Somalia, Afghanistan, Indonesia, Malaysia, Singapore, Bangladesh, Pakistan, Bosnia, Croatia, Albania, Algeria, Tunisia, Lebanon, the Philippines, Tajikistan, Azerbaijan, Kenya, Tanzania, Indian Kashmir, and Chechnya.[57] It was acting on this concept of the international system when it bombed the World Trade Center in 1993, American embassies in Kenya and Tanzania in August 1998, and the *U.S.S. Cole* in 2000, and when it sent planes crashing into the World Trade Center and Pentagon on September 11, 2001.

Rediscovering Religion in International Relations Scholarship

If international relations scholars are to understand the violence of September 11, then they must come to understand how religious movements like radical Islamic revivalism, acting on their political theology, challenge the Westphalian synthesis, the fundamental authority structure of the international order. In fact, the field is not bereft of concepts that can assist the project. Constructivists show us that simply assuming state interests to be power will prevent us from understanding a whole variety of international phenomena.[58] Only a grasp of the variability of identity can help us to begin to understand acts motivated by radical Islamic revivalism. Margaret Keck and Kathryn Sikkink's concept of transnational issue networks identifies nongovernmental groups whose members extend across borders, are held together by common ideas about justice, and seek to influence the politics of states accordingly.[59] Organizationally, radical Islamic revivalism fits this general definition. The concept of international society, from the English school, asserts the existence of common values and norms that are held across states.[60] It is rules of international society that radical revivalist groups protest; it is their own alternative set of rules that they propose to substitute. The clash between radical Islamic revivalism and Westphalian international society can be understood as dueling international societies.

But each of these concepts must be significantly extended if we are to understand the actions of radical revivalists. Most importantly, we must come to understand that these groups are defined, constituted, and motivated by religious beliefs, beliefs about the ultimate ground of existence. Out of these beliefs, they then construct a political theology as well as a social critique that measures the distance between that theology and contemporary social conditions and prescribes action accordingly. That such beliefs constitute influential global networks and motivate their actions call into question the secularization of international relations, in both practice and theory.

The argument here, of course, is open to challenge. The strongest skeptic would doubt the independent role claimed here for political theological ideas, their vital influence in forming radical Islamic revivalism and in sustaining it over generations. In the spirit of modernist secularism, this critic's doubt would lie either in a reductionist view that ideas are nothing more than the product of underlying economic, organizational, technological, or other material forces and structures or that they are at best "focal points" that gather, channel, and coordinate independent ends, usually political or economic advancement.[61]

The debate is an old one, with many episodes, dating back at least as far as Max Weber and Karl Marx. What kind of alternative explanations might the skeptic muster? One is poverty. Economic hardships and a diagnosis of them as caused by international structures motivate ideologies that identify and urge attacks on these structures, the argument runs. A more sophisticated variant points not simply to poverty but to deprived expectations. It is those poor who have been educated or exposed to the world of wealth, power, and sophisticated culture but have no opportunity for advancement or enjoyment of it who are most likely to adopt radical religious ideologies. It is in locales where economic or political advancement is limited that such ideologies will be most prevalent. Other explanations would point to colonialism or Western influence: it is where these are or have been strongest that radical revivalism arises in reaction. Others might point to rapid social change or modernization as a cause.

Only careful research can sort out these causes. It is not clear at the outset that radical Islamic revivalism will reduce to any other factor or that it will prove a mere coordinator of separate preferences. Initial suspicion of a "deprived expectations alone" explanation, for instance, arises from the observation that out of tens of poor countries in the world where these expectations are likely to exist, radical political theology develops only in a few. Something else must be at work in these locales. The best explanations of radical Islamic revivalism are likely to identify complex patterns of causation. Some causes will consist of historical circumstances that are not independent of radical ideas but that reinforce their propositions. The decline of the caliph and the collapse of political forms of Islam by the 1920s suggest that revivalism would develop. The failure of the first generation to achieve major reforms would suggest that a more radical second generation would arise. Broadly material factors may prove an important part of the story, too. Perhaps radical revivalists are most likely to arise from particular social or economic strata or to come from a particular political environment. Again, though, only careful empirical research can begin to sort out explanations, better and worse.

A new exploration of religion would formulate broad general questions that gauge religion's influence. What role do circumstantial factors play? To what extent does the development of political theology have an autonomous logic of its own? Are certain forms of ideas, certain propositions most likely to persuade? What are they? How influential is the historical embeddedness of religious ideas? Do traditional ones have a better chance of flourishing? Are religious identities largely the manipulations of political elites, as some theorists of nationalism would claim? What is the role of intellectuals and religious authorities? What factors determine the form that religious identities will take? And under what conditions does a radical Islamic revivalist movement turn from peaceful means to violence? The interesting questions will be not only causal but also descriptively empirical. How widely held are certain political theologies, of which radical Islamic revivalism is one? There is evidence, for instance, that the ill feelings toward the U.S. that motivated the attack are broadly articulated in newspapers throughout the Muslim world. Other interesting questions will call for an interpretation of doctrines themselves. Exactly what conception of international society is espoused by radical Islamic revivalists? As has been shown, al-Qaeda is exceptional for its advocacy of restoration of the caliphate. Other revivalists are content to expand governance by shari'a within the framework of the existing system of sovereign states. How do theological conceptions inform political ones?

Over the past generation international relations scholars have devoted great effort and have achieved impressive successes in explaining how and whether states attain various goods for their citizens, including security, sometimes conquest, economic growth, sometimes great wealth, human rights, sometimes high levels of justice, environmental purity, and a world in which they can freely express themselves. They do all of this along with explaining states' pursuit or denial of goods for other states' citizens: security from weapons of mass destruction, prosperity, development out of poverty, and the alleviation of genocide and humanitarian disasters. But people across the globe seek other ends, too: to worship and submit to their God, to protect and defend their mosques, temples, shrines, synagogues, and churches, to convert others to their faith, to reside in a realm governed by shari'a, to live under a government that promotes morality in many spheres of society, to draw on their faith to extend civil rights to minorities and women, and to practice forgiveness and reconciliation in the wake of decades of injustices. Is it any surprise that such ends spill into the realm of international politics? International relations scholars must become more aware of these sorts of ends if they are to plumb international politics today, particularly the poignant and surprising politics of September 11.

5

RETHINKING THE ROLE OF RELIGION IN CHANGING PUBLIC SPHERES
Some Comparative Perspectives

—Rosalind I. J. Hackett

I. Introduction

Until the early 1990s, there was a clear disparity between the growing significance of religion on the world stage and the literature one could read on this score in either scholarly or popular publications. Historian Scott Appleby stated candidly that "Western myopia on this subject of religious power has been astounding."[1] Former ambassador Robert A. Seiple, the first-ever U.S. Ambassador-at-Large for International Religious Freedom, criticizes the academic disciplines that address international affairs for giving religion "short shrift."[2] For a long time, scholars assumed that religions were the carriers of tradition and predicted that they would enter into decline because of secularization and privatization.[3] The recent increase in claims for the recognition and implementation of religious ideas, identities, values, practices, and institutions in the governance of nation-states and the lives of their citizens, however, indicates that these predictions were wrong.[4] In the words of Talal Asad, "a straightforward narrative of progress from the religious to the secular is no longer acceptable."[5]

Spurred by globalization, democratization, and the rise of modern media, this remarkable religious resurgence is evident in a variety of places—from scholarly work and popular interest to the increased awareness of the importance of religion in diplomacy and peace-building.[6] Debates and publications regarding the appropriate role of religion in both emergent and longstanding democracies increasingly inform political will and public policy.

However, religious resurgence brings new problems for both emergent and established nation-states. This Article contends that nation-states can achieve successful governance only through careful management of religious and cultural differences and through respect for religious minorities and non-conventional religious groups in increasingly multi-religious and multicultural national contexts.[7]

Part II of this Article discusses the heightened role of religion, and the concomitant recognition of this role, in the public sphere. Part III addresses the new prominence of

* *Brigham Young University Law Review* 2005, no. 3: 659–82.

religion in American public life and the critical role religious activism is now playing in contested social issues. Part IV deals with the tension between secularism and religion and offers a glimpse of some of the problems associated with religious diversity and competition. Part V offers a brief conclusion.

II. Background: The Increased Recognition of Religion in the Public Sphere

A. Academic Recognition of Religion in the Public Sphere

Prior to the early 1990s, literature had been lacking in the area of religion in the public sphere, notably at the international level. This lack of recognition of religion caused scholars and observers to downplay the significance of religion in domestic and global affairs.[8] The early 1990s marked an upsurge in literature recognizing the role of religion in the public sphere.

One of the most influential and controversial of these writings was Samuel Huntington's piece, *The Clash of Civilizations?*[9] Huntington argued that the world would be shaped, in large measure, by the interactions among seven or eight major civilizations, namely, Western, Confucian, Japanese, Islamic, Hindu, Slavic-Orthodox, Latin American, and possibly African. The article provoked criticism by suggesting that the most important differentiating feature was religion and that post–Cold War optimism would be shattered by dangerous and deep-rooted cultural conflict.[10] Many scholars felt that Huntington oversimplified the mapping of the contemporary world by declaring that "[t]he fault lines between civilizations will be the battle lines of the future."[11]

Prescient or not, Huntington's work stimulated a flood of long overdue studies on the role of religion in international affairs. It sent die-hard secular political scientists and social critics into a tailspin, as evidenced by the flurry of publications more attentive to the influence of religion in the last decade.[12] A landmark study entitled *Religion, the Missing Dimension of Statecraft*[13] demonstrates that religion has been absent from the analysis of many international conflicts and their resolutions. This study advocates the reconsideration of religion as an important factor in international diplomacy.

Other published works have also helped focus attention on the growing importance of religion on the international scene. One of these publications was José Casanova's influential study, *Public Religions in the Modern World*.[14] This book reconsiders the relationship between religion and modernity and argues that many religious traditions have been making their way, sometimes forcefully, out of the private sphere and into public life at an increasingly transnational level.[15] This movement of religion into the public sphere, notes Hent de Vries, is also facilitated by the radical transformation of "the functions ascribed to modern subjectivity, to the political, the economy, the nation, the state, the public sphere, [and] privacy."[16]

Moreover, the mass media dimension of these developments has been well articulated by sociologist Manuel Castells, who argues that we have passed from Giddens's era of "late modernity" into the age of the "network society."[17] The information technology revolution and the restructuring of capitalist economies have generated this new form of society. In Castells's opinion, these societal changes have led to a disjunction between the local and the global, as well as a disjunction between power and experience for most individuals and social groups.[18] Consequently, he states, "[t]he search for meaning takes place . . . in the reconstruction of defensive identities around communal principles."[19] These new forms of communal resistance or "cultural communes," as Castells terms them, are at the base of the new primacy of identity politics in today's network society and information age.[20] He sees the resurgence of religious fundamentalism as reflecting the contestations of the new global order.[21] Given their reactive nature, these movements constitute a social barometer aiming to construct "social and personal identity on the basis of images of the past and projecting them into a utopian future, to overcome unbearable present times."[22]

With that background, the September 11th terrorist attacks spectacularly demonstrated the effects of religious ideology on the public sphere. In the words of Philip Jenkins, a prominent academic commentator on contemporary religious affairs, "the twenty-first century will almost certainly be regarded by future historians as a century in which religion replaced ideology as the prime animating and destructive force in human affairs, guiding attitudes to political liberty and obligation, concepts of nationhood, and, of course, conflicts and wars."[23] The production of works on Islam, on religion and violence generally, and on peace and tolerance has escalated exponentially since September 11th. Additionally, September 11th brought home to many not only the need to know more about other religious interpretations of the world, but also a stronger sense of the ambivalence of the sacred[24] and our global connectedness. One human rights scholar poignantly calls this "our shared vulnerability."[25]

B. Popular Recognition of Religion in the Public Sphere

Interestingly, while journalists and academic analysts have rushed to catch up with global religious resurgences, books promoting religion, more religion, or better religion are bestsellers in many parts of the world. Books on religion or spirituality now feature regularly on *The New York Times* bestseller list, ranging from religious reflections and spiritual guides to modern interpretations of ancient, sacred wisdom.[26] One can also find histories and contemporary accounts of religious traditions, concepts, and holy places written for the general reader, such as *A History of God* and *The Battle for God* by popular British author Karen Armstrong.[27]

Once President Bill Clinton started singing the praises of Yale law professor Stephen Carter's works, such as *The Culture of Disbelief: How American Law and Politics Trivialize Religious Devotion*,[28] sales went up exponentially.[29] Explaining how preserving a special role for religious communities can strengthen democracy, Carter criticizes contemporary American law and politics for marginalizing religious faith such that it cannot be a resource for political action.[30] In his more recent book, *God's Name in Vain: The Wrongs and Rights of Religion in Politics*,[31] Carter expresses his concerns about the risks and limitations of political involvement for religious people and communities. He writes,

> We must never become a nation that propounds an official religion or suggests that some religions are more American than others. At the same time, one of the official religions we must never propound is the religion of secularism, the suggestion that there is something un-American about trying to live life in a way that puts God first. Quite the contrary: Preserving the ability of the faithful to put God first is precisely the purpose for which freedom of religion must exist.[32]

Carter worries about religious voices losing their prophetic edge by being co-opted by political forces and about the antireligious politics of the political elite. He suggests that without an independent religious conscience there might never have been an abolitionist movement, a movement for the rights of industrial workers, or the civil rights movement.[33] In the book, he lays out what he considers to be the basis of "principled and prophetic religious activism."[34] Incidentally, Carter has been criticized for propagating a version of religion which is "self-evidently personalistic, moralistic, and experiential, and most definitely of the monotheistic variety"; which sustains the misleading dichotomy of "church-state"; and which prevents people from seeing how values may be cultivated in the "secular" realm.[35] Another critic describes Carter's book as "a product of the very culture it purports to criticize," saying that it advances a view of religion as legitimate only when in service of democracy.[36] Even this criticism indicates the stakes of the debate about religion's role in the public sphere.

C. Diplomatic Recognition of Religion in the Public Sphere

As an extension of the greater recognition of the role of religion on the international stage, a number of new initiatives to extend the scope of faith-based organizations to the diplomatic realm are notable. A number of recently published works realistically address the religious dimension of specific diplomatic efforts such as conflict transformation and peacebuilding.[37] A new book, *Faith-Based Diplomacy: Trumping Realpolitik*,[38] gives shape to this emerging field. The editor, Douglas Johnston, calls for religious imperatives to be "incorporated as a major consideration in U.S. foreign policy,"[39] and for greater consideration to be given to the peacebuilding capacity of religion at the diplomatic level.[40] Additionally, a new journal, *The Review of Faith & International Affairs*, encourages interfaith dialogue, provides resources for those wanting "to build bridges of understanding within faith and international affairs," and a forum for analysis and opinion that "sharpens both spiritual and political discernment."[41] In a recent article in this journal, for example, one can read about the rituals of prayer and fasting that led to a breakthrough in difficult peace negotiations in the Kashmir region.[42]

Along with practical analysis in journals and books, new organizations are sprouting up to encourage a place for religion in diplomacy. For instance, the International Center for Religion and Diplomacy in Washington, D.C., works "[t]o address identity-based conflicts that exceed the reach of traditional diplomacy by incorporating religion as part of the solution."[43]

The Center's mission statement says:

> Regardless of one's spiritual persuasion, there are two compelling reasons why the Center's work is important: (1) the need for more effective preventive measures to minimize the occasions in which we have to send our sons and daughters in harm's way and (2) the need for a stable global environment to support continued economic growth that can benefit an expanding percentage of the world's population.

By linking religious reconciliation with official diplomacy, the ICRD is creating a new synergy for peacemaking that serves both of these needs. It also provides a more fruitful approach for dealing with ethnic conflict, tribal warfare, and religious hostilities.[44]

Other organizations with a specific focus on peacebuilding through religious understanding include the program on Religion and Conflict Resolution at the Tanenbaum Center for Interreligious Understanding,[45] PeaceMakers International,[46] and the Program on Religion, Conflict and Peacebuilding at the Joan B. Kroc Institute for International Peace Studies at the University of Notre Dame,[47] which seeks to strengthen the potential for peacebuilding within religious traditions in addition to exploring the complex roles of religion in contemporary conflicts.[48]

While the burgeoning of organizations that treat seriously the religious dimensions of domestic and foreign policy clearly indicates a trend, there is no obvious consensus at this early stage regarding the merits or outcomes of this trend.

III. Religion in U.S. Public Policy

The increased presence of religious belief and practice in the public arena is due in part to the evolution of the Supreme Court's Establishment Clause and Free Exercise Clause jurisprudence, as well as the growing intervention of religious communities in contested social policy debates. What remains unclear is exactly what role religion should take in policymaking and how these new manifestations of religious activism may contravene First Amendment doctrine.

John Witte, legal scholar and director of the Interdisciplinary Study of Religion at Emory Law School, sees the shift to more public religion in the United States as both inevitable and necessary. He notes that over the last fifteen years the U.S. Supreme Court has abandoned much of its earlier separationism.[49] The metaphorical "wall of separation between church and state," envisaged by Jefferson,[50] no longer looms large in the Court's opinions, and privatization of religion is no longer the bargain that must be struck in order to attain religious freedom.[51] According to Witte, there are two principles that emanate from the recent cases. First, public manifestations of religion must be as free as private religious practice because religious groups, in his words, "provide leaven and leverage for the polity to improve."[52] Second, the freedom of public religion sometimes requires the support of the state because it is impossible for religious bodies to avoid contact with today's modern welfare state and all its ramifications in the educational, welfare, legal, social, and health care sectors.[53]

Such developments, in part, explain the rise of what Dennis R. Hoover calls "an activist religious center in American public life."[54] The new mobilization of predominantly conservative Christians exemplifies this resurgence of an active, religious public sphere. The activism of conservative Christians has manifested itself in two principal ways: first, they have called on certain politicians and writers for religion to assume a more prominent role in public life; and second, they have advocated the "charitable choice" provision of the welfare reform law, whereby government support is provided for faith-based organizations to address social problems.[55] In addition, conservative Christians played a major role in persuading the U.S. government to make religious freedom a central aspect of its foreign policy with the International Religious Freedom Act of 1998.[56] As a result of this law, there is now an Ambassador-at-Large for International Religious Freedom, an office in the State Department, an Advisory Commission, and an annual report on the state of religious freedom worldwide.[57] In addition, the President is required to resort to a range of disciplinary actions against countries that are major violators of religious freedom.[58]

Moreover, President George W. Bush has talked openly about the influence of his religious faith, particularly in the aftermath of September 11th.[59] This has occasioned numerous articles in leading news magazines and newspapers regarding the President's personal religious beliefs and practices.[60] While statistics show that the majority of Americans like their leader to be God-fearing, they are not so keen about public professions of faith.[61] Some journalists have criticized statements by politicians that there could be no morality without religion.[62]

Religion's influence in U.S. politics is obvious in recent debates about school prayer, abortion, and homosexuality, as well as in the success of grassroots religious organizations in mobilizing voters.[63] Many liberal secularists decry this trend, rejecting any interaction between politics and religion. But in *Why I Am Not a Secularist*,[64] political theorist William E. Connolly argues that secularism needs refashioning to be more inclusive of the complex range of viewpoints now active in public life, including those predicated on religious belief.[65] Through its narrow and intolerant understandings of public reason, secularism draws fire from its mainly Christian critics for not recognizing "the sources of morality most citizens endorse."[66]

Along similar lines, philosopher and ethicist Jeffrey Stout, in his latest book, *Democracy and Tradition*,[67] makes a cogent case for greater inclusion of religious voices in a multicultural democratic context. Indeed, he begins his book with an epigraph from John Dewey: "Democracy is a form of government only because it is a form of moral and spiritual association."[68] Seeking to negotiate a way beyond the current impasse between secular liberalism and the new traditionalism, Stout examines the roots of modern democracy. Drawing on American pragmatist philosophy, he argues that democracy's achievements are predicated upon a vision of allowing a multitude of claims to be heard.[69]

For political philosopher Paul Weithman, any questions regarding the role religion may play in citizens' decision making are essentially moral questions because a society's commitment to liberal democracy necessarily entails certain moral and normative commitments for its citizens. Weithman has produced two well-argued books on this subject, *Religion and the Obligations of Citizenship*, and an earlier, edited volume, *Religion and Contemporary Liberalism*.[70] He identifies two main sets of questions that arise with regard to the proper role of religion in democratic politics. The first set asks how religion may affect political outcomes and how those outcomes square with the commitments of liberal democracy. In other words, he asks whether state support for a religion, all religions, or religious codes of conduct can be consistent with liberal democracy.

In exploring this first set of questions, Weithman demonstrates how attention to political outcomes can illuminate what he calls the "puzzles" that arise in a liberal democracy.[71] For example, in the much debated case of whether prayer should be permitted in public schools, he demonstrates that if prayer is permitted because the majority favors it, the liberty of the minority is compromised in the name of a democratic commitment to majoritarianism.[72] But if prayer is not permitted, he explains, the liberal commitment to freedom of religion and the protection of minorities can thwart measures the majority would like to enact. In another example, Weithman explores whether some citizens should be allowed to make ritual use of drugs that are generally proscribed. If so, he argues, the commitment to the equal treatment of all before the law can, under some circumstances, cede to religious liberty. If not, he states, it is rather that "religious liberty can be restricted in the name of treating all as equals before a law that the state has an interest in enforcing."[73] Such are the dilemmas of a liberal democracy.

The second set of questions highlighted by Weithman pertains to religious political inputs. This line of inquiry concerns the use of religious arguments in the political sphere either as a basis for voting, for political preferences, or for policymaking. As he rightly notes, "[l]iberal democratic commitments to religious toleration and church-state separation are sometimes thought to be incompatible with citizens' taking their religiously based political views as the basis of important political decisions."[74] He asks whether there is a difference between religious and political leaders and ordinary citizens, or between fora, in terms of the appropriateness of religious political inputs.[75]

Weithman's contentions force citizens to think more critically and more deeply about the nature of citizenship. Because voting and advocacy are collective enterprises, they must be conducted responsibly and reasonably. He notes that citizens in liberal democracies, such as the United States, are deeply divided on the nature and demands of citizenship.[76] Sometimes these disagreements stem from the political activities of religious organizations; in those societies where the political role of such organizations is more valued however, this is less of an issue. Weithman feels that religious organizations may be instrumental in facilitating people's political participation and in developing their sense of citizenship; they may also generate debate regarding the conditions of participation and the goods that should be conferred by various levels of participation. Consequently, he argues that "citizens may offer exclusively religious arguments in public debate and that they may rely on religious reasons when they cast their votes."[77] Importantly, Weithman underscores the need to distinguish between those who violate the obligations of citizenship and those whose politics we dislike. In other words, restrictions on religious political argument are sometimes based on assumptions about what religious citizens stand for, when in reality there may be considerable diversity of opinion. Weithman employs empirical data and contextual differences to query presumptions and to assess what he calls the "reasonability of deep disagreement."[78]

Thus, the current debate over the proper role of religion in the public sphere indicates a reexamination of the traditional conception of a proverbial wall between church and state. This debate indicates that religion should play a new, yet still undetermined, part in public policy.

IV. Management of Religious and Cultural Difference and the Treatment of Minorities

A. Tension between Religion and Secularism

While some writers have sought ways to popularize religion for the Western consumer or have tried to find cogent historical and theoretical arguments for a greater public role for religion, other observers approach these issues by addressing the tensions, and as will be shown, the misunderstandings, between secularism and religion. They see growing antagonism in modern democratic states between secularism, with its focus on individual rights, and the resurgence of religion, with its communitarian emphasis. As a case in point, the summer 2003 issue of the prestigious journal *Daedalus: Journal of the American Academy of Arts and Sciences* is devoted to the topic of secularism and religion.[79] Several of the writers address the possibilities of religious pluralism and freedom in various national and regional contexts. Others, such as renowned religion analyst Martin Marty, search for new paradigms, such as a "religio-secular world," to represent these changing global dynamics.[80]

One of the best scholarly approaches to the contested place of religion in the public sphere is anthropologist Talal Asad's latest book, *Formations of the Secular: Christianity, Islam, Modernity.*[81] In keeping with his understanding of modern anthropology, he explores the phenomenon of secularism across different time periods, cultures, and regions. By so doing, Asad shows how embedded concepts, such as religion and secularism, are supported or challenged by a variety of "sensibilities, attitudes, assumptions, and behaviors."[82] Asad contends that the modern idea of a secular society involves a "distinctive relation between state law and personal morality, such that religion became essentially a matter of private belief."[83] Translating the individual's ability to freely express and practice his or her beliefs into a legal right brings religion back into the public domain.[84]

One of Asad's most important conclusions is that a "secular state is not one characterized by religious indifference, or rational ethics—or political toleration. It is a complex arrangement of legal reasoning, moral practice, and political authority. This arrangement is not the simple outcome of the struggle of secular reason against the despotism of religious authority."[85] To get beyond the notion that religion and secularism are competing ideologies, Asad avers that it behooves us to look at "what people do with and to ideas and practices,"[86] and why meanings and concepts change. He also argues that religion has always been a factor in the world of power, and that "the categories of 'politics' and 'religion' turn out to implicate each other more profoundly than we thought."[87] In other words, modern state power is highly pervasive, and it seeks to regulate all aspects of individual and social life, including religion.[88]

Similarly nuanced analysis of the concept of the secular is provided by historian Nikki Keddie, who emphasizes the fact that the word secular has had a far greater variety of meanings than current usage may suggest.[89] For centuries in Europe, it referred to the change in clerical status whereby a monk became a secular priest.[90] It was only in the nineteenth century that secularism became known as the independent doctrine that religious institutions and values should play no role in the affairs of the state.[91]

Keddie compares the rise and fall of secular and religious politics in various parts of the world and notes the contextual factors that influence these trends.[92] For example, Muslim countries have negative views of secularism because they associate it with autocratic rule and Western influence.[93] This is well evidenced in the case of Nigeria, where Nigerian Muslims commonly critique the purported neutrality of the secular state as a Western Christian conspiracy to undermine Islam.[94] By comparison, Islam as a force for mobilization still seems relatively untainted. Yet somewhat paradoxically, Keddie notes, the Islamic country where anti-clerical feelings run highest and secularist reforms have been successful is present-day Iran.[95]

Keddie contends that constant battles in South Asia—namely in India and Sri Lanka—between religious nationalism and secular movements serve to weaken support for secularism in the region.[96] So too does the imposition of secularist ideas from the top down, without ensuring support for them at the popular level or from religious leaders.[97] Since Western political hegemony is less of an issue in India than it is in the Muslim world, there are many Indian intellectuals who defend secularism even if they may criticize its application.[98] In fact, Keddie states that contemporary India has probably produced the largest body of writing in the modern world debating the merits of secularism.[99] With the controversial efforts of the previous Indian government (the Bharatiya Janata Party or BJP) to promote Hindu nationalism to the detriment of religious minorities,[100] a number of recent publications advocate the need to move beyond current understandings of secularism in order to effectively protect minority interests.[101]

The writings of scholars like Asad and Keddie teach that there is a need to put the concepts of secularism and religion in their appropriate historical and cultural contexts. Seen in context, these concepts are not always as unequivocal or as polarized as is commonly assumed.[102] Furthermore, secularization has been in progress around the world for far longer, and its success has been far more partial, than is often known. This comparative and historical knowledge could help mitigate some of the current tensions and misunderstandings over secularism, notably in states such as Nigeria.[103]

B. Religious Pluralism

Accompanying the increased role of religion in the public sphere is the challenge and opportunity of religious diversity. In some parts of the world, such as Latin America, the concern is less about secularization and the marginalization of religion and more about the rise of new religious groups competing for power, recognition, and resources. Disestablishing state religions and dismantling the complicities between dominant religions and state power have changed the stakes of coexistence between religious communities. Against the backdrop of the forces of democratization, mediatization, and the global market, religious groups are compelled to justify their existence to the state and consumers alike. These processes are clearly visible in many Latin American countries, where the powerful Roman Catholic Church now has to compete in the marketplace along with burgeoning evangelical groups and indigenous revival movements.

Political scientist Dan Levine, who has been conducting research on religion and politics in this region for many years, observes:

> Latin America is now approaching a state of pluralism (among Christian groups) for the first time in its history. This religious pluralism entails not only a multiplicity of voices speaking "in the name of religion" but also a conflict for voice within specific groups. The spread of literacy and the access to mass media have diffused the tools of religious expertise into many hands.[104]

Local and international scholars are working to interpret this new plurality of religious identities and formations. Levine offers a positive reading of the politicization of religion in Latin America:

> A story that not long ago could be told with confidence about how Catholicism supported and reflected the established order became a story in which religion (Protestant as well as Catholic) has become a source of new ideas about how to organize society and politics, and how to lead the good life. It is no exaggeration to say that many of the region's most significant movements for change would have been unthinkable without religious participation and legitimation.[105]

Levine also points out that the pluralization of religious voices, leading to greater religious activism and public presence, has immediate consequences for democracy.[106] He states that "in a plural environment, it is to everyone's interest to maintain open civil society with guarantees of free speech and equal access to institutions and to public spaces."[107] This is especially important as these societies leave behind the dictatorships and religious monopolies which characterized the Latin American scene up until the late 1980s. Levine points to the emergence of discourses on the human and civil rights of the person, which have been helpful in modernizing the state.[108]

Efforts to accommodate religious and cultural diversity in transitional states and new democratic dispensations are naturally subject to extensive scrutiny. South African law withstands this scrutiny because of its explicit recognition of religious and cultural minorities and celebration of the country's diverse heritage after decades of neo-colonial repression. South Africa has implemented these changes primarily through its constitution,[109] religious broadcasting,[110] and religious education.[111] The new government has, for the most part, resisted efforts to continue to privilege South Africa's Christian majority (over seventy percent of South Africans are Christians according to the most recent census).[112] Many of the religious leaders who fought for liberation from the brutal apartheid regime have become officials of the new government.

Interestingly, many European countries seem regressive in terms of honoring the rights of minority religious groups in their territories. Alarmed at the growth of immigrant populations, particularly Muslims (there are now an estimated four to five million Muslims in France, for example),[113] some European governments have taken draconian measures to curb the activities of non-conventional and unpopular religious groups.[114] Sects are feared for their purported negative psychological effects and undue American influence.[115] The wearing of the Muslim veil in the workplace and schools has been fiercely contested in France and Germany.[116] French President Jacques Chirac contends that the veil or scarf is a sign of "aggressive proselytism" and has introduced controversial new legislation banning the wearing of religious symbols in public schools.[117] In eastern Europe, Russia, and central Asia more generally, there are similar patterns of cultural preservation and animosity toward competing religious options.[118]

The rise of religion among immigrant and diasporic communities and in the public debates about multiculturalism has given culture, particularly cultural practice, a new prominence in regional, national, and international politics. Frequently the disputes over symbols, resources, recognition, and access are resolved in the legal sphere.[119]

This ongoing controversy over religious identity is manifest in the possible inclusion of references to God or Europe's Christian heritage in the new constitution of the European Union.[120] Another pertinent example is the battle in international politics over family values.[121] Similarly, women often find themselves at the center of conflicts over the public expression of identity, as Martha Nussbaum has cogently demonstrated in her writings.[122] As these examples illustrate, religious symbols can become flashpoints for the problems of religious pluralism.

Bill Moyers, a respected and popular commentator, asks what possibilities exist for new and more equitable conversations about religious difference and conceptions of the good life.[123] Moyers wants to learn from difference but not be alienated by it nor expect it to be glossed over by liberal common denominators.[124] Similarly, a team of renowned North American legal and cultural experts has recently published their extensive deliberations on how to balance communitarian demands (of which religious identity is a dimension) with the standards of modern liberal democracies.[125] Others rightly point to the challenges of moving from a "rampant diversity to a culture of pluralism,"[126] and balancing the alternatives of homogeneity and heterogeneity.[127]

Negotiating multiculturalism has ceased to be a trivial issue, particularly when now associated with security questions.[128] It is further compounded by what Talal Asad terms the collision of "overlapping patterns of territory, authority, and time . . . with the idea of the imagined national community"—in other words, the difficulty of allowing "multiple ways of life" to flourish in ever-complex space and time.[129] Harmonious pluralism will require rethinking on a number of levels and an honest dialogue among all parties involved in each particular context, informed by constitutional and international human rights standards as well as a judicious sense of history. Academics should not be forgotten in these processes, as there is good evidence that their intervention in France and Germany, for example, has served to lessen the moral panic over so-called sects and cults.[130]

V. Conclusion

The eruption of religion into changing political landscapes the world over indicates two important findings. First, the management of religious and cultural difference and the treatment of minorities have emerged as key elements of successful governance. Second, these issues necessitate public debate and dialogue, with educational and media sites emerging as significant popular locations for this purpose, supplementing initiatives by political and religious leaders.

It is heartening to learn that the awareness of heightened risks of religious conflict, or the threats to peace posed by extremist religious groups, has engendered an upsurge in inter-religious dialogue in many parts of the world. However, we must be vigilant concerning the forces of deregulation and liberalization that inevitably accompany democratization and globalization. While the new opportunities afforded religious individuals and communities to represent themselves and to participate in the public sphere are undeniable, and indeed long overdue in many instances, they can equally lead to new forms of separatism and demonization of religious others.[131] The development of civil society values of tolerance, cooperation, and civility can easily be subordinated to the logic of the market or to the pressures of religious and political fundamentalism.[132] It therefore behooves us to play our humble parts, whether as religious or political leaders, educators, lawyers, or media professionals, human rights activists or ordinary laypersons, liberals or conservatives, in ensuring that the call for more public expressions of religion is met in the most equitable way possible.

6

KICKING THE SECULARIST HABIT
A Six-Step Program

—David Brooks

Like a lot of people these days, I'm a recovering secularist. Until September 11 I accepted the notion that as the world becomes richer and better educated, it becomes less religious. Extrapolating from a tiny and unrepresentative sample of humanity (in Western Europe and parts of North America), this theory holds that as history moves forward, science displaces dogma and reason replaces unthinking obedience. A region that has not yet had a reformation and an enlightenment, such as the Arab world, sooner or later will.

It's now clear that the secularization theory is untrue. The human race does not necessarily get less religious as it grows richer and better educated. We are living through one of the great periods of scientific progress and the creation of wealth. At the same time, we are in the midst of a religious boom.

Islam is surging. Orthodox Judaism is growing among young people, and Israel has gotten more religious as it has become more affluent. The growth of Christianity surpasses that of all other faiths. In 1942 this magazine published an essay called "Will the Christian Church Survive?" Sixty years later there are two billion Christians in the world; by 2050, according to some estimates, there will be three billion. As Philip Jenkins, a Distinguished Professor of History and Religious Studies at Pennsylvania State University, has observed, perhaps the most successful social movement of our age is Pentecostalism (see "The Next Christianity," October [2002] *Atlantic*). Having gotten its start in Los Angeles about a century ago, it now embraces 400 million people—a number that, according to Jenkins, could reach a billion or more by the half-century mark.

Moreover, it is the denominations that refuse to adapt to secularism that are growing the fastest, while those that try to be "modern" and "relevant" are withering. Ecstatic forms of Christianity and "anti-modern" Islam are thriving. The Christian population in Africa, which was about 10 million in 1900 and is currently about 360 million, is expected to grow to 633 million by 2025, with conservative, evangelical, and syncretistic groups dominating. In Africa churches are becoming more influential than many nations, with both good and bad effects.

* *The Atlantic Monthly* 291, no. 2 (March 2003): 27–28.

Secularism is not the future; it is yesterday's incorrect vision of the future. This realization sends us recovering secularists to the bookstore or the library in a desperate attempt to figure out what is going on in the world. I suspect I am not the only one who since September 11 has found himself reading a paperback edition of the Koran that was bought a few years ago in a fit of high-mindedness but was never actually opened. I'm probably not the only one boning up on the teachings of Ahmad ibn Taymiyyah, Sayyid Qutb, and Muhammad ibn Abd al-Wahhab.

There are six steps in the recovery process.

First you have to accept the fact that you are not the norm. Western foundations and universities send out squads of researchers to study and explain religious movements. But as the sociologist Peter Berger has pointed out, the phenomenon that really needs explaining is the habits of the American professoriat: religious groups should be sending out researchers to try to understand why there are pockets of people in the world who do not feel the constant presence of God in their lives, who do not fill their days with rituals and prayers and garments that bring them into contact with the divine, and who do not believe that God's will should shape their public lives. Once you accept this (which is like understanding that the earth revolves around the sun, not vice-versa) you can begin to see things in a new way.

The *second* step toward recovery involves confronting fear. For a few years it seemed that we were all heading toward a benign end of history, one in which our biggest worry would be boredom. Liberal democracy had won the day. Yes, we had to contend with globalization and inequality, but these were material and measurable concepts. Now we are looking at fundamental clashes of belief and a truly scary situation (at least in the Southern Hemisphere) that brings to mind the Middle Ages, with weak governments, missionary armies, and rampant religious conflict.

The *third* step is getting angry. I now get extremely annoyed by the secular fundamentalists who are content to remain smugly ignorant of enormous shifts occurring all around them. They haven't learned anything about religion, at home or abroad. They don't know who Tim LaHaye and Jerry B. Jenkins are, even though those co-authors have sold 42 million copies of their books. They still don't know what makes a Pentecostal a Pentecostal (you could walk through an American newsroom and ask that question, and the only people who might be able to answer would be the secretaries and the janitorial staff). They still don't know about Michel Aflaq, the mystical Arab nationalist who served as a guru to Saddam Hussein. A great Niagara of religious fervor is cascading down around them while they stand obtuse and dry in the little cave of their own parochialism; and many of them are journalists and policy analysts, who are paid to keep up with these things.

The *fourth* step toward recovery is to resist the impulse to find a materialistic explanation for everything. During the centuries when secularism seemed the wave of the future, Western intellectuals developed social-science models of extraordinary persuasiveness. Marx explained history through class struggle, other economists explained it through profit maximization. Professors of international affairs used conflict-of-interest doctrines and game theory to predict the dynamics between nation-states. All these models are seductive and partly true. This country has built powerful institutions, such as the State Department and the CIA, that use them to try to develop sound policies. But none of the models can adequately account for religious ideas, impulses, and actions, because religious fervor can't be quantified and standardized. Religious motivations can't be explained by cost-benefit analysis.

Over the past twenty years domestic-policy analysts have thought hard about the roles that religion and character play in public life. Our foreign-policy elites are at least two decades behind. They go for months ignoring the force of religion; then, when confronted with something inescapably religious, such as the Iranian revolution or the Taliban, they begin talking of religious zealotry and fanaticism, which suddenly explains everything. After a few days of shaking their heads over the fanatics, they revert to their usual secular analyses. We do not yet have, and sorely need, a mode of analysis that attempts to merge the spiritual and the material.

The recovering secularist has to resist the temptation to treat religion as a mere conduit for thwarted economic impulses. For example, we often say that young Arab men who have no decent prospects turn to radical Islam. There's obviously some truth to this observation. But it's not the whole story: neither Mohammed Atta nor Osama bin Laden, for example, was poor or oppressed. And although it's possible to construct theories that explain their radicalism as the result of alienation or some other secular factor, it makes more sense to acknowledge that faith is its own force, independent of and perhaps greater than economic resentment.

Human beings yearn for righteous rule, for a just world or a world that reflects God's will—in many cases at least as strongly as they yearn for money or success. Thinking about that yearning means moving away from scientific analysis and into the realm of moral judgment. The crucial question is not What incentives does this yearning respond to? but Do individuals pursue a moral vision of righteous rule? And do they do so in virtuous ways, or are they, like Saddam Hussein and Osama bin Laden, evil in their vision and methods?

Fifth, the recovering secularist must acknowledge that he has been too easy on religion. Because he assumed that it was playing a diminishing role in public affairs, he patronized it. He condescendingly decided not to judge other creeds. They are all valid ways of approaching God, he told himself, and ultimately they fuse into one. After all, why stir up trouble by judging another's beliefs? It's not polite. The better option, when confronted by some nasty practice performed in the name of religion, is simply to avert one's eyes. Is Wahhabism a vicious sect that perverts Islam? Don't talk about it.

But in a world in which religion plays an ever larger role, this approach is no longer acceptable. One has to try to separate right from wrong. The problem is that once we start doing that, it's hard to say where we will end up. Consider Pim Fortuyn, a left-leaning Dutch politician and gay-rights advocate who criticized Muslim immigrants for their attitudes toward women and gays. When he was assassinated, last year, the press described him, on the basis of those criticisms, as a rightist in the manner of Jean-Marie Le Pen, which was far from the truth. In the post-secular world, today's categories of left and right will become inapt and obsolete.

The *sixth* and final step for recovering secularists is to understand that this country was never very secular anyway. We Americans long for righteous rule as fervently as anybody else. We are inculcated with the notion that, in Abraham Lincoln's words, we represent the "last, best hope of earth." Many Americans have always sensed that we have a transcendent mission, although, fortunately, it is not a theological one. We instinctively feel, in ways that people from other places do not, that history is unfulfilled as long as there are nations in which people are not free. It is this instinctive belief that has led George W. Bush to respond so ambitiously to the events of September 11, and that has led most Americans to support him.

Americans are as active as anyone else in the clash of eschatologies. Saddam Hussein sees history as ending with a united Arab nation globally dominant and with himself revered as the creator of a just world order. Osama bin Laden sees history as ending with the global imposition of shari'a. Many Europeans see history as ending with the establishment of secular global institutions under which nationalism and religious passions will be quieted and nation-states will give way to international law and multilateral cooperation. Many Americans see history as ending in the triumph of freedom and constitutionalism, with religion not abandoned or suppressed but enriching democratic life.

We are inescapably caught in a world of conflicting visions of historical destiny. This is not the same as saying that we are caught in a world of conflicting religions. But understanding this world means beating the secularist prejudices out of our minds every day.

— Section II —

THEORETICAL FOUNDATIONS FROM ANTIQUITY

"MELIAN DIALOGUE"
History of the Peloponnesian War

—Thucydides

Chapter XVII

Sixteenth Year of the War—The Melian Conference—Fate of Melos

The next summer Alcibiades sailed with twenty ships to Argos and seized the suspected persons still left of the Lacedaemonian faction to the number of three hundred, whom the Athenians forthwith lodged in the neighboring islands of their empire. The Athenians also made an expedition against the isle of Melos with thirty ships of their own, six Chian, and two Lesbian vessels, sixteen hundred heavy infantry, three hundred archers, and twenty mounted archers from Athens, and about fifteen hundred heavy infantry from the allies and the islanders. The Melians are a colony of Lacedaemon that would not submit to the Athenians like the other islanders, and at first remained neutral and took no part in the struggle, but afterwards upon the Athenians using violence and plundering their territory, assumed an attitude of open hostility. Cleomedes, son of Lycomedes, and Tisias, son of Tisimachus, the generals, encamping in their territory with the above armament, before doing any harm to their land, sent envoys to negotiate. These the Melians did not bring before the people, but bade them state the object of their mission to the magistrates and the few; upon which the Athenian envoys spoke as follows:

> Athenians: Since the negotiations are not to go on before the people, in order that we may not be able to speak straight on without interruption, and deceive the ears of the multitude by seductive arguments which would pass without refutation (for we know that this is the meaning of our being brought before the few), what if you who sit there were to pursue a method more cautious still? Make no set speech yourselves, but take us up at whatever you do not like, and settle that before going any farther. And first tell us if this proposition of ours suits you.

The Melian commissioners answered,

> Melians: To the fairness of quietly instructing each other as you propose there is nothing to object; but your military preparations are too far advanced to agree with

what you say, as we see you are come to be judges in your own cause, and that all we can reasonably expect from this negotiation is war, if we prove to have right on our side and refuse to submit, and in the contrary case, slavery.

Athenians: If you have met to reason about presentiments of the future, or for anything else than to consult for the safety of your state upon the facts that you see before you, we will give over; otherwise we will go on.

Melians: It is natural and excusable for men in our position to turn more ways than one both in thought and utterance. However, the question in this conference is, as you say, the safety of our country; and the discussion, if you please, can proceed in the way which you propose.

Athenians: For ourselves, we shall not trouble you with specious pretences—either of how we have a right to our empire because we overthrew the Mede, or are now attacking you because of wrong that you have done us—and make a long speech which would not be believed; and in return we hope that you, instead of thinking to influence us by saying that you did not join the Lacedaemonians, although their colonists, or that you have done us no wrong, will aim at what is feasible, holding in view the real sentiments of us both; since you know as well as we do that right, as the world goes, is only in question between equals in power, while the strong do what they can and the weak suffer what they must.

Melians: As we think, at any rate, it is expedient—we speak as we are obliged, since you enjoin us to let right alone and talk only of interest—that you should not destroy what is our common protection, the privilege of being allowed in danger to invoke what is fair and right, and even to profit by arguments not strictly valid if they can be got to pass current. And you are as much interested in this as any, as your fall would be a signal for the heaviest vengeance and an example for the world to meditate upon.

Athenians: The end of our empire, if end it should, does not frighten us: a rival empire like Lacedaemon, even if Lacedaemon was our real antagonist, is not so terrible to the vanquished as subjects who by themselves attack and overpower their rulers. This, however, is a risk that we are content to take. We will now proceed to show you that we are come here in the interest of our empire, and that we shall say what we are now going to say, for the preservation of your country; as we would fain exercise that empire over you without trouble, and see you preserved for the good of us both.

Melians: And how, pray, could it turn out as good for us to serve as for you to rule?

Athenians: Because you would have the advantage of submitting before suffering the worst, and we should gain by not destroying you.

Melians: So that you would not consent to our being neutral, friends instead of enemies, but allies of neither side.

Athenians: No; for your hostility cannot so much hurt us as your friendship will be an argument to our subjects of our weakness, and your enmity of our power.

Melians: Is that your subjects' idea of equity, to put those who have nothing to do with you in the same category with peoples that are most of them your own colonists, and some conquered rebels?

Athenians: As far as right goes they think one has as much of it as the other, and that if any maintain their independence it is because they are strong, and that if we do not molest them it is because we are afraid; so that besides extending our empire we should gain in security by your subjection; the fact that you are islanders and weaker than others rendering it all the more important that you should not succeed in baffling the masters of the sea.

Melians: But do you consider that there is no security in the policy which we indicate? For here again if you debar us from talking about justice and invite us to obey your interest, we also must explain ours, and try to persuade you, if the two happen to coincide. How can you avoid making enemies of all existing neutrals who shall look at case from it that one day or another you will attack them? And what is this but to make greater the enemies that you have already, and to force others to become so who would otherwise have never thought of it?

Athenians: Why, the fact is that continentals generally give us but little alarm; the liberty which they enjoy will long prevent their taking precautions against us; it is rather islanders like yourselves, outside our empire, and subjects smarting under the yoke, who would be the most likely to take a rash step and lead themselves and us into obvious danger.

Melians: Well then, if you risk so much to retain your empire, and your subjects to get rid of it, it were surely great baseness and cowardice in us who are still free not to try everything that can be tried, before submitting to your yoke.

Athenians: Not if you are well advised, the contest not being an equal one, with honor as the prize and shame as the penalty, but a question of self-preservation and of not resisting those who are far stronger than you are.

Melians: But we know that the fortune of war is sometimes more impartial than the disproportion of numbers might lead one to suppose; to submit is to give ourselves over to despair, while action still preserves for us a hope that we may stand erect.

Athenians: Hope, danger's comforter, may be indulged in by those who have abundant resources, if not without loss at all events without ruin; but its nature is to be extravagant, and those who go so far as to put their all upon the venture see it in its true colors only when they are ruined; but so long as the discovery would enable them to guard against it, it is never found wanting. Let not this be the case with you, who are weak and hang on a single turn of the scale; nor be like the vulgar, who, abandoning such security as human means may still afford, when visible hopes fail them in extremity, turn to invisible, to prophecies and oracles, and other such inventions that delude men with hopes to their destruction.

Melians: You may be sure that we are as well aware as you of the difficulty of contending against your power and fortune, unless the terms be equal. But we trust that the gods may grant us fortune as good as yours, since we are just men fighting against unjust, and that what we want in power will be made up by the alliance of the Lacedaemonians, who are bound, if only for very shame, to come to the aid of their kindred. Our confidence, therefore, after all is not so utterly irrational.

Athenians: When you speak of the favor of the gods, we may as fairly hope for that as yourselves; neither our pretensions nor our conduct being in any way contrary to what men believe of the gods, or practice among themselves. Of the gods we believe, and of men we know, that by a necessary law of their nature they rule wherever they can. And it is not as if we were the first to make this law, or to act upon it when made: we found it existing before us, and shall leave it to exist for ever after us; all we do is to make use of it, knowing that you and everybody else, having the same power as we have, would do the same as we do. Thus, as far as the gods are concerned, we have no fear and no reason to fear that we shall be at a disadvantage. But when we come to your notion about the Lacedaemonians, which leads you to believe that shame will make them help you, here we bless your simplicity but do not envy your folly. The Lacedaemonians, when their own interests or their country's laws are in question, are the worthiest men alive; of their conduct towards others much might be said, but no clearer idea of it could be given than by shortly saying that of all the men we know they are most conspicuous in considering what is agreeable honorable, and what is expedient just. Such a way of thinking does not promise much for the safety which you now unreasonably count upon.

Melians: But it is for this very reason that we now trust to their respect for expediency to prevent them from betraying the Melians, their colonists, and thereby losing the confidence of their friends in Hellas and helping their enemies.

Athenians: Then you do not adopt the view that expediency goes with security, while justice and honor cannot be followed without danger; and danger the Lacedaemonians generally court as little as possible.

Melians: But we believe that they would be more likely to face even danger for our sake, and with more confidence than for others, as our nearness to Peloponnese makes it easier for them to act, and our common blood ensures our fidelity.

Athenians: Yes, but what an intending ally trusts to is not the goodwill of those who ask his aid, but a decided superiority of power for action; and the Lacedaemonians look to this even more than others. At least, such is their distrust of their home resources that it is only with numerous allies that they attack a neighbor; now is it likely that while we are masters of the sea they will cross over to an island?

Melians: But they would have others to send. The Cretan Sea is a wide one, and it is more difficult for those who command it to intercept others, than for those who wish to elude them to do so safely. And should the Lacedaemonians miscarry in this, they would fall upon your land, and upon those left of your allies whom Brasidas did not reach; and instead of places which are not yours, you will have to fight for your own country and your own confederacy.

Athenians: Some diversion of the kind you speak of you may one day experience, only to learn, as others have done, that the Athenians never once yet withdrew from a siege for fear of any. But we are struck by the fact that, after saying you would consult for the safety of your country, in all this discussion you have mentioned nothing which men might trust in and think to be saved by. Your strongest arguments depend upon hope and the future, and your actual resources are too scanty, as compared with those arrayed against you, for you to come out victorious. You will therefore show great blindness of judgment, unless, after allowing us to retire, you can find some counsel more prudent than this. You will surely not be caught by that idea of disgrace, which in dangers that are disgraceful, and at the same time too plain to be mistaken, proves so fatal to mankind; since in too many cases the very men that have their eyes perfectly open to what they are rushing into, let the thing called disgrace, by the mere influence of a seductive name, lead them on to a point at which they become so enslaved by the phrase as in fact to fall willfully into hopeless disaster, and incur disgrace more disgraceful as the companion of error, than when it comes as the result of misfortune. This, if you are well advised, you will guard against; and you will not think it dishonorable to submit to the greatest city in Hellas, when it makes you the moderate offer of becoming its tributary ally, without ceasing to enjoy the country that belongs to you; nor when you have the choice given you between war and security, will you be so blinded as to choose the worse. And it is certain that those who do not yield to their equals, who keep terms with their superiors, and are moderate towards their inferiors, on the whole succeed best. Think over the matter, therefore, after our withdrawal, and reflect once and again that it is for your country that you are consulting, that you have not more than one, and that upon this one deliberation depends its prosperity or ruin.

The Athenians now withdrew from the conference; and the Melians, left to themselves, came to a decision corresponding with what they had maintained in the discussion, and answered, "Our resolution, Athenians, is the same as it was at first. We will not in a moment deprive of freedom a city that has been inhabited these seven hundred years; but we put our trust in the fortune by which the gods have preserved it until now, and in the help of men, that is, of the Lacedaemonians; and so we will try and save ourselves. Meanwhile we invite you to allow us to be friends to you and foes to neither party, and to retire from our country after making such a treaty as shall seem fit to us both."

Such was the answer of the Melians. The Athenians now departing from the conference said, "Well, you alone, as it seems to us, judging from these resolutions, regard what is future as more certain than what is before your eyes, and what is out of sight, in your eagerness, as already coming to pass; and as you have staked most on, and trusted most in, the Lacedaemonians, your fortune, and your hopes, so will you be most completely deceived."

The Athenian envoys now returned to the army; and the Melians showing no signs of yielding, the generals at once betook themselves to hostilities, and drew a line of circumvallation round the Melians, dividing the work among the different states. Subsequently the Athenians returned with most of their army, leaving behind them a certain number of their own citizens and of the allies to keep guard by land and sea. The force thus left stayed on and besieged the place.

About the same time the Argives invaded the territory of Phlius and lost eighty men cut off in an ambush by the Phliasians and Argive exiles. Meanwhile the Athenians at Pylos took so much plunder from the Lacedaemonians that the latter, although they still refrained from breaking off the treaty and going to war with Athens, yet proclaimed that any of their people that chose might plunder the Athenians. The Corinthians also commenced hostilities with the Athenians for private quarrels of their own; but the rest of the Peloponnesians stayed quiet. Meanwhile the Melians attacked by night and took the part of the Athenian lines over against the market, and killed some of the men, and brought in corn and all else that they could find useful to them, and so returned and kept quiet, while the Athenians took measures to keep better guard in future.

Summer was now over. The next winter the Lacedaemonians intended to invade the Argive territory, but arriving at the frontier found the sacrifices for crossing unfavorable, and went back again. This intention of theirs gave the Argives suspicions of certain of their fellow citizens, some of whom they arrested; others, however, escaped them. About the same time the Melians again took another part of the Athenian lines which were but feebly garrisoned. Reinforcements afterwards arriving from Athens in consequence, under the command of Philocrates, son of Demeas, the siege was now pressed vigorously; and some treachery taking place inside, the Melians surrendered at discretion to the Athenians, who put to death all the grown men whom they took, and sold the women and children for slaves, and subsequently sent out five hundred colonists and inhabited the place themselves.

8

THE RETURN OF ANCIENT TIMES
Why the Warrior Politics of the Twenty-First Century Will Demand a Pagan Ethos

—Robert D. Kaplan

In 1988, during the Palestinian intifada, the Israeli Defense Minister, Yitzhak Rabin, referring to Palestinian protesters, reportedly told Israeli soldiers to "go in and break their bones." Rabin's standing with the public began to rise thereafter. In 1992 hard-line Israeli voters switched to the Labor Party, only because Rabin headed the ticket. As Prime Minister, Rabin used his new power to start peace talks with the Palestinians and the Jordanians. Rabin, who was assassinated in 1995, is now judged a hero by enlightened public opinion the world over.

In 1970 and again in the 1980s King Hussein of Jordan cracked down brutally on the Palestinians. Had Hussein been subject to Western judicial procedures, he might have been implicated in mistreating considerable numbers of people through his security services. Yet Hussein's crackdown saved his kingdom from those who would have been less just in office than he was.

Western admirers of Rabin and Hussein prefer to forget their ruthlessness. But Niccolò Machiavelli would have understood that such tactics were central to their virtue. In an imperfect world, Machiavelli wrote, good men bent on doing good must learn how to be bad. And in this world virtue has much less to do with individual perfection than with political results.

By substituting pagan for Christian virtue, Machiavelli explained better than any political scientist today how Rabin and Hussein could become what they were. There is nothing amoral about Machiavelli's pagan virtue either. The late Oxford philosopher Isaiah Berlin observed that Machiavelli's values may not be Christian but they are moral. Berlin implied that they are the Periclean and Aristotelian values of the ancient *polis*—values that secure a stable political community. (If you want to act strictly according to Christian ethics, Berlin suggested in explaining Machiavelli, that's fine—so long as you don't assume political responsibility for the lives of too many others.) But even Machiavelli has his limits. By his standards, Rabin and Hussein are moral, because they used only the minimum degree of

* *Atlantic Monthly* 285, no. 6 (June 2000): 14–18.

cruelty required to further a virtuous cause. Augusto Pinochet is not. His cruelty was excessive and his cause was questionable, so he lacks virtue.

Machiavelli's emphasis on political necessity rather than moral perfection framed his philosophical attack on the Church. By in effect leaving the Church, he left the medieval world and kindled the political Renaissance, renewing links with Thucydides, Polybius, Livy, Tacitus, Seneca, Sallust, and other classical thinkers.

A tenet of classical philosophy states that primitive necessity and self-interest drive politics—all to the good, because competing self-interests allow for compromise, whereas rigid moral arguments lead to war, which is rarely the better option. Explaining Machiavelli brilliantly, the Harvard professor Harvey Mansfield writes in *Machiavelli's Virtue* (1966) that primitive necessity is irresistible, because human affairs are always "in motion": "A man or a country may be able to afford generosity today, but what of tomorrow?" (Today we may be able to intervene in East Timor, but what if we have to fight China over the Taiwan Strait tomorrow?) "Anxious foresight" must therefore be the centerpiece of any prudent policy.

In recent decades, however, such verities have sometimes been disdained by American foreign-policy makers, journalists, academics, and intellectuals. The uncomfortable classical truths enunciated in the fifth century B.C. by the historian Thucydides, revived by Machiavelli, and imbibed by Alexander Hamilton and James Madison—truths such as *Morality and patriotism can best be obtained through self-interest; Conflict is inherent in the human condition; The law of nature precludes a republic of perfect virtue and demands instead a balance of forces among men and groups*—are often forgotten. The American elite has come to believe that the solution for humanity is to adopt a few universally applicable remedies, such as democracy, respect for minority rights, and free-market capitalism. Whether liberals or neoconservatives, many of those who came of age in the 1960s have trouble dealing with such facts as national characteristics ingrained by historical and geographic circumstance, and violence for its own sake.

The 1994–1996 war in Chechnya illustrates ancient verities to which policymakers and intellectuals often cannot admit. Chechen fighters pulled rockets out of the pods of downed Russian helicopters and refitted them in order to shoot down low-flying Russian planes, and wore fur masks to keep their faces from being burned by the backfire. The Chechens fought with a ferocity and an ingenuity unusual even by the standards of the Caucasus, which can be explained by a nineteenth-century Muslim warrior tradition against Russian colonialism. But nowadays thinking in terms of group character is often dismissed as deterministic: to think of Chechens as Chechens is to stereotype, denying each Chechen his individuality. Any reference to tragic histories anywhere—the Balkans, sub-Saharan Africa—is similarly tagged deterministic and therefore invalid.

Seeing the future purely in terms of group characteristics and historical experience can certainly immobilize policy. But it is also true that outlawing generalizations about peoples and regions immobilizes meaningful discussion about them. Denying such factors as history and culture and geography, and denying the effects of these factors on group behavior, would end the work of intelligence services and others who try to forestall crises through anxious foresight. Seneca, the first-century Roman stoic, wrote that foresight based on probability is all we ever have to go by, and probability need not mean inevitability.

Statements regarding Kosovo by the Clinton Administration in the spring of last year are another example of an inability to confront difficult truths. Because the Administration insufficiently acknowledged the historical hatred between Serbs and Albanians in Kosovo, it seemed ill prepared for both the ethnic-cleansing campaign the Serbs perpetrated against Albanians in response to the NATO bombing and the retributive attacks by Albanians against Serbs. The Serbian leader, Slobodan Milosevic, bears responsibility for the atrocities, but he also had historical memory with which to work. The Administration sold the war as a moral crusade against Milosevic; because the American public would tolerate significant casualties only for reasons of national interest, the Administration limited itself to a low-risk air campaign. The air war eventually succeeded, but by the time it did, thousands of Albanian Kosovars had died. Just as good men must learn how to be bad in order to do good, moral goals often require "amoral" arguments, or, rather, arguments using an ancient morality—arguments the Administration failed to make convincingly.

* * *

Nothing demonstrates the gulf between our lofty goals and the reality of the human condition better than the refrain "No more Bosnias." In fact there were several Bosnias in the Caucasus of the early 1990s, to which the American media and intellectual community paid scant attention. Abkhazia, Ossetia, and Nagorno-Karabakh all suffered ethnic killings and expulsions involving more than a million people combined. The American elite yearns for singularity: if atrocities are rare, then they are preventable. But the truth is that sectarian killing in poor parts of the world may for the foreseeable future overwhelm our appetite for armed intervention. Thus triage, rather than wish fulfillment ("No more Bosnias"), will define American foreign policy.

Preventing even selected Bosnias will depend on our use of anxious foresight based on models of historical and geographical circumstance, national characteristics, and the like, reinforced by strong intelligence agencies and conflict-resolution teams. We must remember that human progress has often been made in the space between idealism and savagery: idealism, by idealizing, ignores difficult facts, however well-intentioned it is.

Indeed, the more modern and technological we become—the more our lives become a mechanized routine against instinct—the more the most instinctual forces within us rebel. And in those places that fail to compete technologically, many young men may become ancient warriors, raping and pillaging and wearing tribal insignia rather than uniforms— as we have already seen in the Balkans, sub-Saharan Africa, and elsewhere. We will learn that there is no modern or postmodern anymore. There is only the continuation of the ancient—a world that, however technological and united by global institutions, the Greek and Roman philosophers would recognize and be able to cope with.

* * *

The outlines of the post–Cold War world have now emerged. The evils of the twentieth century—Nazism, fascism, communism—were caused by populist mass movements in Europe whose powers were magnified by industrialization; likewise, the terrors of the next century will be caused by populist movements (themselves an aspect of worldwide democratization), this time empowered by post-industrialization. Because industrialization depended on scale, it concentrated power in the hands of state rulers; the evils of Hitler and Stalin were consequently enormous. Post-industrialization, with its miniaturization, puts power in the hands of anyone with a laptop and a pocketful of plastic explosives. So we will have new evils and chronic instability. The world will truly be ancient.

The thinkers who will guide us through these troubling but by no means apocalyptic times will be those who teach us how to discern unpleasant truths in the midst of crises and how to act with both caution and cunning. The United States requires a generation of policymakers armed with a classical education.

The curriculum should consist of ancient historians and philosophers and those who have carried on their tradition: Machiavelli, Burke, Hobbes, Gibbon, Kant, Madison, Hamilton, Tocqueville, Mill, and, in the twentieth century, Berlin, Raymond Aron, Arnold Toynbee, Reinhold Niebuhr, and George Kennan. These are only examples, and a range of opinions exists within this group. (Berlin, for instance, opposes the determinism implicit in Gibbon's and Toynbee's grand sweep of history.)

What most of these men have in common is skepticism and a constructive realism. Machiavelli and the eighteenth-century Briton Edmund Burke both thought that conscience was a pretense to cover self-interest. Hobbes instructed that faith must be excluded from philosophy, because it is not supported by reason; reason concerns cause and effect, and so philosophy ultimately concerns the resolution of forces; and in politics this leads to the balance of power and a search for order. As distasteful as the ideas of Machiavelli and Hobbes may seem to the contemporary mind, those two philosophers invented the modern state. They saw that all men needed security in order to acquire material possessions, and that a bureaucratic organ was required to regulate the struggle for acquisition peacefully and impartially. The aim of such an organ was never to seek the highest good, only the common good.

The Founding Fathers departed from Machiavelli in placing more faith in ordinary people, but they did adhere to his ideas of pagan virtue. Recognizing that faction and struggle are basic to the human condition, they substituted the arenas of party politics and the marketplace for actual battlefields.

The same principles have also governed the relationships between states, which shift constantly for advantage and frequently take the law into their own hands. In such a world, the theologian Niebuhr cautioned, America's very dominance would ultimately ensnarl its destiny with those of many other nations; thus our democratic vision would be weakened by a vast web of history. Kennan, the statesman, warned that the more underdeveloped the country, the more ruthless we must be toward its inhabitants to improve their society. Such unsavory truths, all descending ultimately from Thucydides' *The Peloponnesian War*, are too rarely taught. Our elites are less like Renaissance pragmatists than like medieval churchmen, sanctimoniously dividing the world into good and evil.

Ancient wisdom is certainly not a cure for the foreign-policy challenges ahead. It is merely a way of reintroducing a kind of thinking, long pilloried, that will be useful in a world where—for some decades, at least—the sheer number and complexity of crises will test our moralistic certainties. Ancient morality need not undermine Judeo-Christian ethics. Rather, the sophisticated use of the one in foreign policy may help to advance the other.

9

UNREALISTIC REALISM
A Reflection on Robert D. Kaplan's "Warrior Politics"

—Dennis R. Hoover

Those who follow international affairs—specialists and spectators alike—are frequently in search of a paradigmatic holy grail, the One Big Thing that will provide both descriptive and prescriptive direction in an always-complex world. Little more than a decade ago, the dominant paradigm was one of a (seemingly) permanent struggle between the capitalist West and the communist East. After the Cold War, the roaring Nineties saw many tempted by a more idealistic paradigm—worldwide dominance of liberal democracy, economic globalization, international law . . . the end of history.

But to Robert D. Kaplan, this was all irrational exuberance. As a correspondent for *The Atlantic Monthly* and author of several books, including such titles as *Balkan Ghosts*, *To the Ends of the Earth*, and *The Coming Anarchy*, Kaplan earned a reputation as one of America's premier prophets of pessimism. His writing is a combination of political reportage, commentary, and what Michael Ignatieff once called "travel writing from Hell." He has, in short, earned the right to warn the over-comfortable West that things might get worse before they get better—and they might not get better at all.

In his latest book, *Warrior Politics: Why Leadership Demands a Pagan Ethos* (New York: Random House, 2002), Kaplan breaks with his pattern of travel-based writing and stays home to read some very old books. Kaplan trolls for insights in works of pre-Christian antiquity from the likes of Thucydides, Livy, and Sun Tzu, as well as a clutch of moderns that Kaplan sees as emulating, in one way or another, this "pagan" ethos—primarily Hobbes, Machiavelli, Churchill, and Malthus. And while his methodology is new, Kaplan's paradigm is the same as it has always been, "realism."

In light of September 11, there is much to be said for looking reality square in the eye. Completed months before the terrorist attacks, some of the warnings issued in *Warrior Politics* about the rise of barbarism now seem prescient. Still, realism has to have a foundation. It is one thing to observe that the reality of international affairs is often driven by nothing more than naked aggression, self-interest, power politics, and imperial ambition. It is quite another to elevate these observations into an "ism."

* *The Brandywine Review of Faith & International Affairs* 1, no. 1 (Spring 2003): 48–56.

In *Warrior Politics*, Kaplan repeatedly asserts that his version of realism is not amoral—it's just that it reflects "pagan" rather than "Christian" virtue. Taking inspiration from Machiavelli, Kaplan's is an "ethic of consequence" rather than an "ethic of intent." This metric of virtue is not affected by sordid motivations, nor even by cruelty of means (though Kaplan somehow draws the line, without specifying criteria for recognizing it, at "excessive" cruelty). What matters are results.

It's why Kaplan's conclusion unabashedly endorses the goal of creating a global American imperium. "Alas, our prize for winning the Cold War," Kaplan writes, "is not merely the opportunity to expand NATO, or to hold democratic elections in places that never had them, but something far broader: *We and nobody else will write the terms for international society*. . . . A century of disastrous utopian hopes has brought us back to imperialism, that most ordinary and dependable form of protection for ethnic minorities and others under violent assault" (pp. 146–47, emphasis in original).

And where should leaders in the new imperium look for guidance? "True bravery and independence of thought are best anchored by examples from the past, culled from the pages of the great books," says Kaplan (p. 150). No books of scripture make Kaplan's recommended reading list. Indeed, he is nothing if not clear about the gauntlet he is throwing down—people of religious faith, Christians especially, should not use their religiously-grounded ethics to impose any serious moral limits on the conduct of international affairs, nor should secular policy elites listen to them if they try. "[I]f there is such a thing as progress in politics," Kaplan avers, "it has been the evolution of religious virtue to secular self-interest" (p. 115).

Notwithstanding the honest differences that divide them, "Christian realists" and "Christian idealists" alike should resist the idea that the One Big Thing for our times is Kaplan's pagan imperialism.

The Importance of Being Gloomiest

In some respects it is tempting to dismiss this book as insignificant by the standards of political philosophy. It is a brief (of actual text there are only 155 pages), peripatetic set of musings from a seasoned journalist who has ventured out of area. Kaplan is the first to admit, as he does in the preface, that he is an armchair analyst of the classics. Yet he suggests there are advantages in amateurism: "A layman encountering the classics could be compared to a traveler during his first days in a strange country: there are things he will misinterpret, but he will also spot things that longtime residents have ceased to notice" (p. xx). We never learn exactly what things professionals in classics and philosophy have stopped noticing.

He is also strikingly candid on the very first page about his own selectivity. After lamenting the problem of writers "selecting facts and insights to defend a particular vision," Kaplan simply shrugs it off: "To this dilemma there may be no solution" (p. ix). "[I]n the essay that follows I am still a journalist," Kaplan adds on p. xxi. "I report on the classics and the views of contemporary scholars, integrating them into a story much as any journalist would with disparate material at hand."

Kaplan prides himself on his talents as a provocateur, and several reviewers of *Warrior Politics* rose to the bait. "The book is a confused sequence of historical observations, from which Mr. Kaplan makes undisciplined extrapolations and arrives, for the most part, at embarrassingly banal conclusions" (*The Economist*).[1] Kaplan taps out "a mishmash of conventional pieties (e.g. Churchill is good; Chamberlain, bad), term-paperism, and futurist hokum" (*Business Week*).[2] The book offers "a few shrewd, but unoriginal, observations delivered in an intellectually bullying style. . . . After Sept. 11, we have little need for Chicken Little with a college library card" (*Denver Post*).[3]

Still, Kaplan is a gifted wordsmith. And an influential one. President Bush reportedly read Kaplan's *Eastward to Tartary* (2000), and was so impressed that he invited him to the White House for a chat about foreign affairs. Like some of his other books, *Warrior Politics* has made the bestseller lists. Kaplan has also been in high demand as a speaker at conferences, military bases, even the Joint Chiefs of Staff.[4] In short, Kaplan is a journalist to be reckoned with.

Self-Interest

Warrior Politics is dripping with contempt for any actor in international affairs whom Kaplan thinks is guilty of "moralism" or "sanctimony." "To listen to public discourse in America, one would think that morality is entirely a Judeo-Christian invention" (p. 29). "[T]he concern of the Republican Right with 'values' and that of liberals with 'humanitarian intervention' may be less a sign of a higher morality than of the luxury afforded by domestic peace and prosperity" (p. 99).

One target of Kaplan's ire is the media. He takes fellow journalists to task for their naive overemphasis on human rights, "the highest level of altruism" (p. 125). (Never mind that human rights are merely the beginning of justice, not the highest morality.) But Kaplan does not stop there, as he wishes to indict religious actors in international affairs, too. In a section in which he admiringly discusses Machiavelli and the "problem with faith," Kaplan writes, "It is not that religion is bad, Machiavelli explains, but that religion leads to extremism when its otherworldliness impinges too much on worldly affairs" (pp. 114–15).

Yet Kaplan is only willing to pit his pagan ethos against a straw man. For instance, Christianity, according to Kaplan, "is about the moral conquest of the world, while Greek tragedy is about the clash of irreconcilable elements. . . . [W]e will have to recognize that while virtue is good, outstanding virtue can be dangerous" (p. 77).

As an alternative to a faith-based virtue that "impinges too much" on international affairs, Kaplan submits power—power in service of self-interest and order. "[T]he acceptance of a world governed by a pagan notion of self-interest exemplified by Thucydides makes statesmanship likelier to succeed: it curtails illusions, reducing the scope for miscalculation. Historically grounded liberalism recognizes that liberty did not arise from abstract reflection, moral or otherwise, but from difficult political choices made by rulers acting in their own self-interest. As the Danish classicist and historian David Gress notes, liberty grew in the West mainly because it served the interest of power" (p. 51).

Again, Kaplan does not mean to endorse thoroughgoing immorality. He describes his realism as seeking to "combine tough tactics with long-range Kantian goals" (p. x). Kaplan insists that, "The strategic pursuit of self-interest is not a cold and amoral pseudo-science, but a moral act of those who know the horrors of battle and seek to avoid them" (p. 42). The attempted fusion is ultimately unsuccessful, however, because he does not define moral limits on self-interest and tries to de-legitimize those who would.

He romanticizes the power of self-interest "to shape and improve the world" (p. 60) without explaining how it can be relied upon to have this effect in the violent, Hobbesian arena of international affairs. He also ignores the extent to which moral choice and national self-interest are intertwined. National interests don't just "happen." For instance, Kaplan is keen to support U.S. decisions to ally with repressive regimes if doing so seems strategically necessary (a form of power politics Kaplan sees as unfortunate yet "virtuous"—on the pagan definition). But where does "strategic necessity" come from in, say, the U.S.-Saudi Arabia alliance? While oil is not the sum total of this relationship, U.S. consumption of oil is a choice—one for which Americans are morally responsible.

Kaplan also argues that rapid democratization can be counterproductive in some cases, which is certainly a valid point. But repressive governance can also breed terrorism, which is hardly in American self-interest.

And then there are Kaplan's views of relief and development groups. "Values, however universal in principle, will always require muscle and self-interest to enforce," Kaplan concludes on p. 101, adding, "To expect human beings and organizations to think about the interests of others before their own is to ask them to deny their own instincts for self-preservation. Even with relief charities and other nongovernmental organizations, self-interest comes first: they lobby for intervention in areas where they are active, rather than in others where they are less so."

In this Kaplan is inexcusably uncharitable to charities (many of which are, of course, religious). And, more than that, he is flatly wrong to ignore the positive influence of NGOs—most of which act not out of a pinched conception of self-interest but in accordance with their moral vision of the greater good. Kaplan may be right that some NGOs show lobbying bias toward areas where they are active. But often such areas are chosen precisely because they are the areas of greatest need. Kaplan's blanket indictment also rests on a flawed conception of the way lobbying works. For instance, while he is quick to dismiss the social sciences, the relevant literature demonstrates that the effectiveness of religious groups in lobbying for international aid is often a function of on-the-ground expertise (valued highly by public officials), not of self-interest.[5]

Furthermore, recent years have witnessed a renewed appreciation of the potential of NGOs, especially faith-based NGOs, to make tangible, empirically significant contributions to the preventive and restorative dimensions of diplomacy. Far from some utopian scheme, it reflects a surge of interest in practical peacemaking.

Douglas Johnston and Cynthia Sampson's widely cited *Religion, the Missing Dimension of Statecraft* pointed to the emerging reality nearly a decade ago.[6] More recently, programs such as the Religion and Peacemaking Initiative at the U.S. Institute of Peace have highlighted some manifestations of this work:

- The Community of Sant'Egidio in Italy has mediated between factions in many conflicts, including negotiations to end Mozambique's civil war.
- The Plowshares Institute and leaders in the Mennonite community have developed educational resources in peacebuilding, and have trained some 1,400 grassroots leaders in South Africa.
- World Vision has introduced peacebuilding components into its international relief and development projects, while on the home front it has helped shape U.S. foreign policy on "conflict diamonds" in Angola and Sierra Leone.

- In the American Jewish Joint Distribution Committee's work in Kosovo, as well as in Catholic Relief Services' work in the Philippines, members of conflicting groups have been brought together to jointly plan and operate development projects.

The list of examples could easily be expanded.[7]

What's more, the state of thinking on such matters is moving beyond mere anecdote. Indeed, a diverse group of ethicists, theologians, international relations scholars, and conflict resolution practitioners (a group including both pacifists and "just war" theorists) has been promoting a new paradigm of proactive peace building under the banner "just peacemaking."

In the introduction of the 1998 book by that title, three leaders of the group, Glen Stassen (Baptist), John Langan (Roman Catholic), and Duane Friesen (Mennonite), explain that their paradigm "encourages pacifists to fulfill what their name (derived from the Latin *pacemfacere*) means, 'peacemakers.' And it calls just war theorists to fill in the contents of their underdeveloped principles of last resort and just intention—to spell out what resorts must be tried before trying the last resort of war, and what intention there is to restore a just and lasting peace."[8] It's a perspective that doesn't settle (nor does it claim to settle) the serious differences between the pacifist and just war traditions, but it does underscore the still-considerable room for points of consensus regarding normative peacemaking practices.

Empire

A key tenet of Kaplanism is that the meek shall not inherit the earth. He receives reassurance in this view from Machiavelli, who "believed that because Christianity glorified the meek, it allowed the world to be dominated by the wicked: he preferred a pagan ethic that elevated self-preservation over the Christian ethic of sacrifice" (p. 52). This is the foundation of Kaplan's apologia for American imperium: if we wish to see a world in which moral ideals have a chance of flourishing, we must set those ideals aside and use sheer force (ruthlessly, if need be) to maintain and expand national power.

"Values—good or bad—Machiavelli says, are useless without arms to back them up," Kaplan writes. "Therefore, for policymakers, projecting power comes first; values come second" (p. 62).

Kaplan thinks Americans can and should take inspiration from ancient empires, such as the Han dynasty of China, whose "global equivalent can now only be achieved by the United States" (p. 145). What we could really use these days, he argues, is the "organizing mechanism of a great hegemon." To be sure, Kaplan is not calling for outright territorial conquest. The empire he has in mind is held together mainly via soft power, with only occasional use of brute force (when self-interest and/or necessity dictate). But it is an empire nonetheless.

As empires go, Kaplan is particularly impressed with the British. In fact, his "pagan" ethos is not, strictly speaking, very pagan at all, as it appears to be based mainly on nineteenth-century European *realpolitik* and colonialism, Exhibit A being the British Empire. For example, Kaplan swoons over Winston Churchill, endorsing his rationalizations for colonial adventures and defending him against the charge that racism helped motivate his imperialism.

Kaplan's primary reference is Churchill's *The River War* (1899), a history of British conquest of the Sudan. Kaplan writes that, "For Churchill, glory is rooted in a morality of consequence: of actual results rather than good intentions. The British military enterprise in the Nile Valley was admirable only because it was followed by 'the marvelous work of creating good government and prosperity.'. . . [I]t is difficult to condemn Churchill for having supported colonialist interventions that provided stability and a better material life for the local inhabitants" (pp. 22–23).

Kaplan barely acknowledges centuries of Judeo-Christian reflection about "just war," which would not sanction this ends-justifies-the-means ethos. In the single page that Kaplan devotes to just war theory, he argues that, historically, the notion of a just war presupposed

> the existence of a Leviathan—the pope or the Holy Roman emperor—to enforce the moral code. But in a world without a universal arbiter of justice, discussions of war as "just" or "unjust" carry little meaning beyond the intellectual and legal circles in which such discussions take place. . . . Ho Chi Minh killed at least 10,000 of his own civilians prior to the entry of American troops into Vietnam. Did this make our intervention in Vietnam just? Perhaps, but it was still a mistake. The Mexican War was probably unjust— motivated as it was by sheer territorial aggression. But it was a war worth fighting: the United States acquired Texas and the entire Southwest, including California. (p. 130)

Especially troublesome is that Kaplan thinks the state of war can have positive benefits over the state of peace, regardless of the particular territory at stake. On Kaplan's reading, ancient history "teaches that without struggle—and the sense of insecurity that motivates it—there is decadence" (p. 26). His commitment to this view leads him to cite a Churchillian chain of reasoning in *The River War* that verges on the bizarre: "For, as in the Roman State, when there are no more worlds to conquer and no rivals to destroy, nations exchange the desire for power for the love of art, and so by a gradual, yet continual, enervation and decline turn from the vigorous beauties of the nude to the more subtle allurements of the draped, and then sink to actual eroticism and ultimate decay" (quoted on p. 26).

In places Kaplan seems to think that a simplistic machismo is the mark of a true leader. His phraseology in praising Churchill's leadership is emblematic: "toughness," "manhood," "heroic outlook" (p. 26). Later, he uses the phrase "manly vigor" in a section describing Machiavellian virtue (p. 55).

Kaplan goes out of his way to make sure that such "vigor" is defined so as to include the use of ruthless violence. "As Machiavelli says," Kaplan emphasizes on p. 113, "in an imperfect world men bent on doing good—and who have responsibility for the welfare of a great many others—must know occasionally how to be bad, and to savor it." On p. 128, Kaplan argues against the use of new, non-lethal technologies in warfare thusly: "Bullets that don't kill and sonic waves that immobilize a crowd by causing a sensation of nausea and diarrhea may facilitate an individual commando operation, but warriors will interpret such an aversion to violence as weakness." On p. 61, Kaplan argues that a measure of the pagan virtue of Abraham Lincoln is that he was "sufficiently ruthless to target the farms, homes, and factories of Southern civilians in the latter phase of the Civil War."

Writing in the February 25, 2002 *National Review*, Brian Anderson rightly asked, "Why should a leader 'savor' getting his hands dirty? Did Lincoln relish the steps he took to win the Civil War? Shouldn't the proper attitude toward killing civilians or using deceit during wartime be one of haunted necessity? Two of the great Machiavellians of the 20th century, after all, were Stalin and Hitler; surely Kaplan doesn't want to elevate such monsters into moral exemplars."[9]

Character

Kaplan's only answer to the question of limits on leaders is to appeal to "character":

- "In the future, do not expect wartime justice to depend on international law; as in ancient times, this justice will depend upon the moral fiber of military commanders themselves" (p. 118).
- "The moral basis of our foreign policy will depend upon the character of our nation and its leaders, not upon the absolutes of international law" (p. 131).
- "Effective leadership will always reside within the mystery of character" (p. 150).

Kaplan under-specifies, to say the least, the origins and nature of the "character" that stands between a Lincoln and a Hitler. Kaplan never considers whether Lincoln imbibed virtues from the Judeo-Christian tradition in a way that Hitler did not. The appeal to character, furthermore, is not consistent with what Kaplan sees as "realist" assumptions about the nature of humanity. If mankind's state of nature is nasty and brutish, why should we endorse Kaplan's highly elitist view of international relations? *Warrior Politics* rarely passes over a chance to warn of the dangers of "mass" opinion and "populist movements." But who will watch the watchman?

That these points appear to be lost on Kaplan is especially evident in the range of historical figures he claims as allies. The American Founders, for instance, are said to have had "an overriding fear of anarchy" (p. 85) and to have "adhered to the idea of pagan virtue" (p. 87). The Federalist Papers, on Kaplan's view, "could be defined as an elaboration of Hobbesian truth" (p. 86). The core of James Madison's wisdom is said to be the assumption that "primitive necessity and self-interest drive politics, and that this can be good in itself, because competing self-interests are the basis for compromise, while stiff moral arguments lead to war and civil conflict, rarely the better options" (p. 63).

But the genius of the founding was not its fidelity to Old World pessimism, but rather the creative tension it embraced between pessimism and optimism. *Warrior Politics* is not the first book in which Kaplan has tried to press the Founders into service of his flawed agenda, as the same argument appeared in *The Coming Anarchy*. Kaplan had plenty of time to learn from his critics on this score, had he been so inclined. For instance, in the April 10, 2000 issue of *The New Republic*, Robert Kagan noted rightly that:

> If it was an enlightened despotism that the Founders wanted, how did they manage to establish a democratic republic? . . . Kaplan appears to believe that realists have a monopoly on the appreciation of tragedy, that believers in progress cannot acknowledge the enduring "reality of human evil." This is a self-serving and inaccurate conceit. Those who seek to improve the human condition may be as aware of the darker sides of life as any realist. Idealism is not a variety of innocence. The Founders were not tragic realists, they

were tragic idealists. Indeed, tragic idealism may have been their particular contribution to the political imagination.[10]

The Founders aimed to build political institutions strong enough to govern effectively, yet simultaneously checked and balanced against the ever-present threat of tyranny. Their assumptions about the dangers of large concentrations of power were shaped by experience and the Judeo-Christian tradition within which they stood. And the same principles apply to international affairs.[11] Unchecked power invites corruption, yet Kaplan has no qualms recommending just such an absolute concentration in the hands of an American hegemon.

Whether or not the label "idealist" is used, the American experiment is predicated on certain truths held as self-evident and universal—justice, equality, liberty, rule of law. In seeking a "more perfect" union, the Founders chose balanced institutions and distributions of power. Likewise, in international affairs today Americans should aspire to balance, and not insist on an American exceptionalism that scoffs at international law and shows no decent respect for the opinion of allies.

"Global institutions like the war crimes tribunal are an outgrowth of Western power, not a replacement for it," Kaplan argues on p. 146. This is a false dichotomy; a realistic Christian approach to international institutions, for example, does not demand that Western power be "replaced," just that it seek more than its own preservation, and that it recognize legitimate limits.[12]

Faith-Based Foreign Affairs

Just as Kaplan misappropriates the Founders, he also makes dubious claims of intellectual fealty with "Christian realists." On p. 109 Kaplan allows as how "Some versions of Christianity are quite compatible with foreign policy realism." He drops a few names thought to be representative of this "version" of Christianity, such as Reinhold Niebuhr, and suggests that Christian realism seeks "a way to use pagan, public morality to advance—albeit indirectly—private, Judeo-Christian morality. Put in our own terms, human rights are ultimately and most assuredly promoted by the preservation and augmentation of American power."

While a global Leviathan run by the United States would obviously be better for human rights, relatively speaking, than one run by an authoritarian regime, "Christian realism" does not provide a blank check for the acquisition of power by the U.S., or any other state for that matter. Alongside his reading of ancient classics, Kaplan should have read the May, 1959 issue of his own magazine, *The Atlantic Monthly*. There he would have found "Foreign Policy and Christian Conscience," in which the eminently realistic George F. Kennan wrote:

> The sovereign national state, to which so much reverent devotion is paid in the various gradations of patriotism and chauvinism that make up national feelings, has no foundation in Christian principle, whatever its secular justification. Nowhere in Christ's teachings was it suggested that mankind ought to be divided into political families of this nature, each a law unto itself, each recognizing no higher authority than its own national ego, each assuming its interest to be more worthy of service than any other with which it might come into conflict. Surely this whole theory is an absurdity from the Christian standpoint. Before we could achieve a Christian foreign policy we would have to

overcome this unlimited egotism of the sovereign national state and find a higher interest which all of us could recognize and serve.[13]

By "higher interest," Kennan did not mean the United Nations in its present form, flawed and feckless as it often is. Still, he stressed that "the UN does represent the germ of something immensely necessary and immensely hopeful for this endangered world: namely, a sense of conscience higher than the national one, a sense of the fellowship of fate by which we are all increasingly bound together."

Kaplan says we must prepare to wage warrior politics, but does not lift a finger to explain how we might also wage a politics of peace. The Kaplanian pose is to express regret that international law and international institutions are still so weak, and then argue that because they are weak they should be ignored. Likewise, he scolds those who push liberal democracy on countries that are not ready for it, and then expends no effort arguing for the kind of investments that would make countries ready for it—economic development, institutional reform, religious freedom and civil society promotion, education and health care . . . all of which would require that a respectable percentage of GNP be earmarked for international aid and administered effectively.

The priority on security in the post-9/11 world makes Kaplan's vision of a power politics divorced from morality tempting. As he predicts on p. 102 of *Warrior Politics*, "a variant of European-style pragmatism may encroach upon the American public and its policymakers. Wilsonian morality is attractive only so long as Americans think they are invulnerable."

Yet Americans—religious and secular alike—should think twice about abandoning their sense of idealism entirely. As Thomas Friedman has recently argued:

> If I've learned anything from living abroad, it's that while other nations often make fun of or scoff at America's naïve optimism, deep down they envy that optimism and rue the day we would give it up and adopt the tragic European view of history. Because our optimism about human nature and its commitment to the rule of law, not just power, is the engine of the modern West. . . . "Never forget," a top German official said to me, "that it was the combination of American hard power and soft power that defeated the Soviet Union. [Europe's] so-called realism is really a deep pessimism that came out of all our religious wars. If you become like us, America will lose its very power and attraction for others— the reason that even people who hate you are attracted to you.". . . No doubt after 9/11 we can't be naïve optimists anymore. But optimists we must remain. We have to find a way of defending ourselves from others' weapons of mass destruction without losing our own weapon of mass attraction.[14]

To the extent that people of faith have, in fact, made naïve nuisances of themselves, issuing moral proclamations without confronting practical questions about how power is to be organized and wielded, *Warrior Politics* is a sobering corrective. Kaplan is onto something when, on p. 88, he notes that, "Because so many states in the developing world have flimsy institutions, the paramount question in world politics in the early twenty-first century will be the re-establishment of order." But a "realism" that expects men and women to pledge their lives and sacred honor for "order" alone, without also aspiring to justice, is unrealistic indeed.

10

EXCERPTS FROM BOOK 19
City of God

—Augustine

Excerpt from Chapter 5
*Of the Social Life, Which, Though Most Desirable,
Is Frequently Disturbed by Many Distresses*

On all hands we experience these slights, suspicions, quarrels, war, all of which are undoubted evils; while, on the other hand, peace is a doubtful good, because we do not know the heart of our friend, and though we did know it today, we should be as ignorant of what it might be tomorrow. Who ought to be, or who are more friendly than those who live in the same family? And yet who can rely even upon this friendship, seeing that secret treachery has often broken it up, and produced enmity as bitter as the amity was sweet, or seemed sweet by the most perfect dissimulation? It is on this account that the words of Cicero so move the heart of every one, and provoke a sigh: "There are no snares more dangerous than those which lurk under the guise of duty or the name of relationship. For the man who is your declared foe you can easily baffle by precaution; but this hidden, intestine, and domestic danger not merely exists, but overwhelms you before you can foresee and examine it" (*In Verrem*, ii, 1.15). It is also to this that allusion is made by the divine saying, "A man's foes are those of his own household" (Matt 10:36)—words which one cannot hear without pain; for though a man have sufficient fortitude to endure it with equanimity, and sufficient sagacity to baffle the malice of a pretended friend, yet if he himself is a good man, he cannot but be greatly pained at the discovery of the perfidy of wicked men, whether they have always been wicked and merely feigned goodness, or have fallen from a better to a malicious disposition. If, then, home, the natural refuge from the ills of life, is itself not safe, what shall we say of the city, which, as it is larger, is so much the more filled with lawsuits civil and criminal, and is never free from the fear, if sometimes from the actual outbreak, of disturbing and bloody insurrections and civil wars?

Chapter 7
*Of the Diversity of Languages, by Which the Intercourse of Men
Is Prevented; And of the Misery of Wars, Even of Those Called Just*

After the state or city comes the world, the third circle of human society—the first being the house, and the second the city. And the world, as it is larger, so it is fuller of dangers, as the greater sea is the more dangerous. And here, in the first place, man is separated from man by the difference of languages. For if two men, each ignorant of the other's language, meet, and are not compelled to pass, but, on the contrary, to remain in company, dumb animals, though of different species, would more easily hold intercourse than they, human beings though they be. For their common nature is no help to friendliness when they are prevented by diversity of language from conveying their sentiments to one another; so that a man would more readily hold intercourse with his dog than with a foreigner. But the imperial city has endeavored to impose on subject nations not only her yoke, but her language, as a bond of peace, so that interpreters, far from being scarce, are numberless. This is true; but how many great wars, how much slaughter and bloodshed, have provided this unity! And though these are past, the end of these miseries has not yet come. For though there have never been wanting, nor are yet wanting, hostile nations beyond the empire, against whom wars have been and are waged, yet, supposing there were no such nations, the very extent of the empire itself has produced wars of a more obnoxious description— social and civil wars—and with these the whole race has been agitated, either by the actual conflict or the fear of a renewed outbreak. If I attempted to give an adequate description of these manifold disasters, these stern and lasting necessities, though I am quite unequal to the task, what limit could I set? But, say they, the wise man will wage just wars. As if he would not all the rather lament the necessity of just wars, if he remembers that he is a man; for if they were not just he would not wage them, and would therefore be delivered from all wars. For it is the wrongdoing of the opposing party which compels the wise man to wage just wars; and this wrongdoing, even though it gave rise to no war, would still be matter of grief to man because it is man's wrongdoing. Let every one, then, who thinks with pain on all these great evils, so horrible, so ruthless, acknowledge that this is misery. And if any one either endures or thinks of them without mental pain, this is a more miserable plight still, for he thinks himself happy because he has lost human feeling.

Chapter 15
*Of the Liberty Proper to Man's Nature, and the Servitude Introduced by Sin,
a Servitude in Which the Man Whose Will Is Wicked Is the Slave of His Own Lust,
Though He Is Free So Far as Regards Other Men*

This is prescribed by the order of nature: it is thus that God has created man. For "let them," He says, "have dominion over the fish of the sea, and over the fowl of the air, and over every creeping thing which creepeth on the earth" (Gen 1:26). He did not intend that His rational creature, who was made in His image, should have dominion over anything but the irrational creation—not man over man, but man over the beasts. And hence the righteous men in primitive times were made shepherds of cattle rather than kings of men, God intending thus to teach us what the relative position of the creatures is, and what the desert of sin; for it is with justice, we believe, that the condition of slavery is the result of sin. And this is why we do not find the word "slave" in any part of Scripture until righteous

Noah branded the sin of his son with this name. It is a name, therefore, introduced by sin and not by nature. The origin of the Latin word for slave is supposed to be found in the circumstance that those who by the law of war were liable to be killed were sometimes preserved by their victors, and were hence called servants (*servus*, "a slave," from *servare*, "to preserve"). And these circumstances could never have arisen save through sin. For even when we wage a just war, our adversaries must be sinning; and every victory, even though gained by wicked men, is a result of the first judgment of God, who humbles the vanquished either for the sake of removing or of punishing their sins. Witness that man of God, Daniel, who, when he was in captivity, confessed to God his own sins and the sins of his people, and declares with pious grief that these were the cause of the captivity (Dan 9). The prime cause, then, of slavery is sin, which brings man under the dominion of his fellow—that which does not happen save by the judgment of God, with whom is no unrighteousness, and who knows how to award fit punishments to every variety of offence. But our Master in heaven says, "Every one who doeth sin is the servant of sin" (John 8:34). And thus there are many wicked masters who have religious men as their slaves, and who are yet themselves in bondage; "for of whom a man is overcome, of the same is he brought in bondage" (2 Pet 2:19). And beyond question it is a happier thing to be the slave of a man than of a lust; for even this very lust of ruling, to mention no others, lays waste men's hearts with the most ruthless dominion. Moreover, when men are subjected to one another in a peaceful order, the lowly position does as much good to the servant as the proud position does harm to the master. But by nature, as God first created us, no one is the slave either of man or of sin. This servitude is, however, penal, and is appointed by that law which enjoins the preservation of the natural order and forbids its disturbance; for if nothing had been done in violation of that law, there would have been nothing to restrain by penal servitude. And therefore the apostle admonishes slaves to be subject to their masters, and to serve them heartily and with goodwill, so that, if they cannot be freed by their masters, they may themselves make their slavery in some sort free, by serving not in crafty fear, but in faithful love, until all unrighteousness pass away, and all principality and every human power be brought to nothing, and God be all in all.

Chapter 16
Of Equitable Rule

And therefore, although our righteous fathers (the patriarchs) had slaves, and administered their domestic affairs so as to distinguish between the condition of slaves and the heirship of sons in regard to the blessings of this life, yet in regard to the worship of God, in whom we hope for eternal blessings, they took an equally loving oversight of all the members of their household. And this is so much in accordance with the natural order, that the head of the household was called *paterfamilias*; and this name has been so generally accepted, that even those whose rule is unrighteous are glad to apply it to themselves. But those who are true fathers of their households desire and endeavor that all the members of their household, equally with their own children, should worship and win God, and should come to that heavenly home in which the duty of ruling men is no longer necessary, because the duty of caring for their everlasting happiness has also ceased; but, until they reach that home, masters ought to feel their position of authority a greater burden than servants their service. And if any member of the family interrupts the domestic peace by disobedience, he is corrected either by word or blow, or some kind of just and legitimate punishment, such as society permits, that he may himself be the better for it, and be readjusted to the family harmony from which he had dislocated himself. For as it is not benevolent to give a man help at the expense of some greater benefit he might receive, so it is not innocent to spare a man at the risk of his falling into graver sin. To be innocent, we must not only do harm to no man, but also restrain him from sin or punish his sin, so that either the man himself who is punished may profit by his experience, or others be warned by his example. Since, then, the house ought to be the beginning or element of the city, and every beginning bears reference to some end of its own kind, and every element to the integrity of the whole of which it is an element, it follows plainly enough that domestic peace has a relation to civic peace—in other words, that the well-ordered concord of domestic obedience and domestic rule has a relation to the well-ordered concord of civic obedience and civic rule. And therefore it follows, further, that the father of the family ought to frame his domestic rule in accordance with the law of the city, so that the household may be in harmony with the civic order.

Chapter 17
What Produces Peace, and What Discord, Between the Heavenly and Earthly Cities

But the families which do not live by faith seek their peace in the earthly advantages of this life; while the families which live by faith look for those eternal blessings which are promised, and use as pilgrims such advantages of time and of earth as do not fascinate and divert them from God, but rather aid them to endure with greater ease, and to keep down the number of those burdens of the corruptible body which weigh upon the soul. Thus the things necessary for this mortal life are used by both kinds of men and families alike, but each has its own peculiar and widely different aim in using them. The earthly city, which does not live by faith, seeks an earthly peace, and the end it proposes, in the well-ordered concord of civic obedience and rule, is the combination of men's wills to attain the things which are helpful to this life. The heavenly city, or rather the part of it which sojourns on earth and lives by faith, makes use of this peace only because it must, until this mortal condition which necessitates it shall pass away. Consequently, so long as it lives like a captive and a stranger in the earthly city, though it has already received the promise of redemption, and the gift of the Spirit as the earnest of it, it makes no scruple to obey the laws of the earthly city, whereby the things necessary for the maintenance of this mortal life are administered; and thus, as this life is common to both cities, so there is a harmony between them in regard to what belongs to it. But, as the earthly city has had some philosophers whose doctrine is condemned by the divine teaching, and who, being deceived either by their own conjectures or by demons, supposed that many gods must be invited to take an interest in human affairs, and assigned to each a separate function and a separate department—to one the body, to another the soul; and in the body itself, to one the head, to another the neck, and each of the other members to one of the gods; and in like manner, in the soul, to one god the natural capacity was assigned, to another education, to another anger, to another lust; and so the various affairs of life were assigned—cattle to one, corn to another, wine to another, oil to another, the woods to another, money to another, navigation to another, wars and victories to another, marriages to another, births and fecundity to another, and other things to other gods: and as the celestial city, on the other hand, knew that one God only was to be worshipped, and that to Him alone was due that service which the Greeks call λατρεία, and which can be given only to a god, it has come to pass that the two cities could not have common laws of religion, and that the heavenly city has been compelled in this matter to dissent, and to become obnoxious to those who think differently, and to stand the brunt of their anger and hatred and persecutions, except insofar as the minds of their enemies have been alarmed by the multitude of the Christians and quelled by the manifest protection of God accorded to them. This heavenly city, then, while it sojourns on earth, calls citizens out of all nations, and gathers together a society of pilgrims of all languages, not scrupling about diversities in the manners, laws, and institutions whereby earthly peace is secured and maintained, but recognizing that, however various these are, they all tend to one and the same end of earthly peace. It therefore is so far from rescinding and abolishing these diversities, that it even preserves and adopts them, so long only as no hindrance to the worship of the one supreme and true God is thus introduced. Even the heavenly city, therefore, while in its state of pilgrimage, avails itself of the peace of earth, and, so far as it can without injuring faith and godliness, desires and maintains a common agreement among men regarding the acquisition of the necessaries of life, and makes this earthly peace bear upon the peace of heaven; for this alone can be truly called and esteemed the peace of the reasonable creatures, consisting as it does in the perfectly ordered and harmonious enjoyment of God and of one another in God. When we shall have reached that peace, this mortal life shall give place to one that is eternal, and our body shall be no more this animal body which by its corruption weighs down the soul, but a spiritual body feeling no want, and in all its members subjected to the will. In its pilgrim state the heavenly city possesses this peace by faith; and by this faith it lives righteously when it refers to the attainment of that peace every good action toward God and man; for the life of the city is a social life.

11

AUGUSTINE'S POLITICAL REALISM

—Reinhold Niebuhr

The terms "idealism" and "realism" are not analogous in political and in metaphysical theory; and they are certainly not as precise in political, as in metaphysical, theory. In political and moral theory "realism" denotes the disposition to take all factors in a social and political situation, which offer resistance to established norms, into account, particularly the factors of self-interest and power. In the words of a notorious "realist," Machiavelli, the purpose of the realist is "to follow the truth of the matter rather than the imagination of it; for many have pictures of republics and principalities which have never been seen." This definition of realism implies that idealists are subject to illusions about social realities, which indeed they are.

"Idealism" is, in the esteem of its proponents, characterized by loyalty to moral norms and ideals, rather than to self-interest, whether individual or collective. It is, in the opinion of its critics, characterized by a disposition to ignore or be indifferent to the forces in human life which offer resistance to universally valid ideals and norms. This disposition, to which Machiavelli refers, is general whenever men are inclined to take the moral pretensions of themselves or their fellowmen at face value; for the disposition to hide self-interest behind the façade of pretended devotion to values, transcending self-interest, is well-nigh universal. It is, moreover, an interesting human characteristic, proving that the concept of "total depravity," as it is advanced by some Christian realists, is erroneous. Man is a curious creature with so strong a sense of obligation to his fellows that he cannot pursue his own interests without pretending to serve his fellowmen.

The definitions of "realists" and "idealists" emphasize disposition, rather than doctrines; and they are therefore bound to be inexact. It must remain a matter of opinion whether or not a man takes adequate account of all the various factors and forces in a social situation. Was Plato a realist, for instance, because he tried to guard against the self-interest of the "guardians" of his ideal state by divesting them of property and reducing their family responsibilities to a minimum? Does this bit of "realism" cancel out the essential

* Reinhold Niebuhr, *Christian Realism and Political Problems* (New York: Scribner's, 1953), 119–48.

unrealism, inherent in ascribing to the "lusts of the body" the force of recalcitrance against the moral norm; or in attributing pure virtue to pure mind?

The Distinctive Nature of Augustine's Realism

Augustine was, by general consent, the first great "realist" in Western history. He deserves this distinction because his picture of social reality in his *Civitas Dei* gives an adequate account of the social factions, tensions, and competitions which we know to be well-nigh universal on every level of community; while the classical age conceived the order and justice of its polis to be a comparatively simple achievement, which would be accomplished when reason had brought all subrational forces under its dominion.

This difference in the viewpoints of Augustine and the classical philosophers lies in Augustine's biblical, rather than rationalistic, conception of human selfhood, with the ancillary conception of the seat of evil being in the self. Augustine broke with classical rationalism in his conception of the human self, according to which the self is composed of mind and body; the mind being the seat of virtue because it has the capacity to bring all impulses into order; and the body, from which come the "lusts and ambitions," being the cause of evil. According to Augustine, the self is an integral unity of mind and body. It is something more than mind and is able to use mind for its purposes. The self has, in fact, a mysterious identity and integrity transcending its functions of mind, memory, and will. "These three things, memory, understanding, and love are mine and not their own," he declares, "for they do what they do not for themselves but for me; or rather I do it by them. For it is I who remember by memory and understand by understanding and love by love."[1] It must be observed that the transcendent freedom of self, including its capacity to defy any rational or natural system into which someone may seek to coordinate it (its capacity for evil), makes it difficult for any philosophy, whether ancient or modern, to comprehend its true dimension. That is why the classical wise men obscured it by fitting its mind into a system of universal mind, and the body into the system of nature; and that is also why the modern wise men, for all their rhetoric about the "dignity" of the individual, try to cut down the dimension of human selfhood so that it will seem to fit into a system of nature.

This conception of selfhood is drawn from the Bible, rather than from philosophy, because the transcendent self which is present in, though it transcends, all of the functions and effects of the self, is comprehensible only in the dramatic-historical mode of apprehension which characterizes biblical faith. Augustine draws on the insights of neo-Platonism to illustrate the self's power of self-transcendence; but he rejects Plotinus' mystic doctrine, in which the particular self, both human and divine, is lost in a vast realm of undifferentiated being.

Augustine's conception of the evil which threatens the human community on every level is a corollary of his doctrine of selfhood. "Self-love" is the source of evil rather than some residual natural impulse which mind has not yet completely mastered. This excessive love of self, sometimes also defined as pride or *superbia*, is explained as the consequence of the self's abandonment of God as its true end and of making itself "a kind of end." It is this powerful self-love or, in a modern term, "egocentricity," this tendency of the self to make itself its own end or even to make itself the false center of whatever community it inhabits, which sows confusion into every human community. The power of self-love is more spiritual than the "lusts of the body," of which Plato speaks; and it corrupts the processes of the mind more than Plato or Aristotle knew. That is why Augustine could refute the classical theory with the affirmation that "it is not the bad body which causes the good soul to sin but the bad soul which causes the good body to sin." At other times Augustine defines the evil in man as the "evil will," but with the understanding that it is the self which is evil in the manifestation of its will. "For he who extols the whole nature of the soul as the chief good and condemns the nature of the flesh as if it were evil, assuredly is fleshly both in the love of the soul and in the hatred of the flesh."[2] This concise statement of the Christian position surely refutes the absurd charge of moderns that the Christian faith is "dualistic" and generates contempt for the body. It also establishes the only real basis for a realistic estimate of the forces of recalcitrance which we must face on all levels of the human community, particularly for a realistic estimate of the spiritual dimension of these forces and of the comparative impotence of "pure reason" against them.

Compared with a Christian realism, which is based on Augustine's interpretation of biblical faith, a great many modern social and psychological theories, which fancy themselves anti-Platonic or even anti-Aristotelian and which make much of their pretended "realism," are in fact no more realistic than the classical philosophers. Thus modern social and psychological scientists are forever seeking to isolate some natural impulse such as "aggressiveness" and to manage it; with equal vanity they are trying to find a surrogate for Plato's and Aristotle's disinterested "reason" in a so-called "scientific method." Their inability to discover the corruption of self-interest in reason or in man's rational pursuits, and to measure the spiritual dimensions of man's inhumanity and cruelty, gives an air of sentimentality to the learning of our whole liberal culture. Thus we have no guidance amid the intricacies of modern power politics, except as the older disciplines, less enamored of the "methods of natural science," and the common sense of the man in the street, supply the necessary insights.

The "City of This World"

Augustine's description of the social effects of human egocentricity or self-love is contained in his definition of the life of the "city of this world," the *civitas terrena*, which he sees as commingled with the *civitas dei*. The "city of this world" is dominated by self-love to the point of contempt of God; and is distinguished from the *civitas dei* which is actuated by the "love of God" to the point of contempt of self. This "city" is not some little city-state, as it is conceived in classical thought. It is the whole human community on its three levels of the family, the commonwealth, and the world.

A potential world community is therefore envisaged in Augustine's thought. But, unlike the Stoic and modern "idealists," he does not believe that a common humanity or a common reason gives promise of an easy actualization of community on the global level. The world community, declares Augustine, is "fuller of dangers as the greater sea is more dangerous."[3] Augustine is a consistent realist in calling attention to the fact that the potential world community may have a common human reason, but it speaks in different languages and "Two men, each ignorant of each other's language" will find that "dumb animals, though of a different species, could more easily hold intercourse than they, human beings though they be."[4] This realistic reminder that common linguistic and ethnic cultural forces, which bind the community together on one level, are divisive on the ultimate level, is a lesson which our modern proponents of world government have not yet learned.

Augustine's description of the *civitas terrena* includes an emphasis on the tensions, frictions, competitions of interest, and overt conflicts to which every human community is exposed. Even in the family, one cannot rely on friendship "seeing that secret treachery has often broken it up."[5] This bit of realism will seem excessive until we remember that our own generation has as much difficulty in preserving the peace and integrity in the smallest and most primordial community, the family, as in integrating community on the highest global level.

The *civitas terrena* is described as constantly subject to an uneasy armistice between contending forces, with the danger that factional disputes may result in "bloody insurrection" at any time. Augustine's realism prompts him to challenge Cicero's conception of a commonwealth as rooted in a "compact of justice." Not so, declares Augustine. Commonwealths are bound together by a common love, or collective interest, rather than by a sense of justice; and they could not maintain themselves without the imposition of power. "Without injustice the republic would neither increase nor subsist. The imperial city to which the republic belongs could not rule over provinces without recourse to injustice. For it is unjust for some men to rule over others."[6]

This realism has the merit of describing the power realities which underlie all large-scale social integrations whether in Egypt or Babylon or Rome, where a dominant city-state furnished the organizing power for the Empire. It also describes the power realities of national states, even democratic ones, in which a group, holding the dominant form of social power, achieves oligarchic rule, no matter how much modern democracy may bring such power under social control. This realism in regard to the facts which underlie the organizing or governing power refutes the charge of modern liberals that a realistic analysis of social forces makes for state absolutism; so that a mild illusion in regard to human virtue is necessary to validate democracy. Realistic pessimism did indeed prompt both Hobbes and Luther to an unqualified endorsement of state power; but that is only because they were not realistic enough. They saw the dangers of anarchy in the egotism of the citizens but failed to perceive the dangers of tyranny in the selfishness of the ruler. Therefore they obscured the consequent necessity of placing checks upon the ruler's self-will.

Augustine's realism was indeed excessive. On the basis of his principles he could not distinguish between government and slavery, both of which were supposedly the rule over man by man and were a consequence of, and remedy for, sin; nor could he distinguish between a commonwealth and a robber band, for both were bound together by collective interest; "For even thieves must hold together or they cannot effect what they intend." The realism fails to do justice to the sense of justice in the constitution of the Roman Empire; or, for that matter, to the sense of justice in a robber band. For even thieves will fall out if they cannot trust each other to divide the loot, which is their common aim, equitably. But the excessive emphasis upon the factors of power and interest, a wholesome corrective to Cicero's and modern Ciceronian moralistic illusions, is not fatal to the establishment of justice so long as the dangers of tyranny are weighed as realistically as the dangers of anarchy.

Augustine's realistic attitude toward government rests partly upon the shrewd observation that social peace and order are established by a dominant group within some level of community; and that this group is not exempt from the corruption of self-interest merely because the peace of society has been entrusted to it. (One thinks, incidentally, how accurately the Augustinian analysis fits both the creative and the ambiguous character of the American hegemony in the social cohesion of the free world.)

The realism is partly determined by his conception of a "natural order" which he inherited from the early Christian fathers, who in turn took it from that part of the Stoic theory which emphasized the primordial or primitive as the natural. This Stoic and Christian primitivism has the merit of escaping the errors of those natural law theories which claim to find a normative moral order amid the wide variety of historic forms or even among the most universal of these forms. The freedom of man makes these Stoic conceptions of the "natural" impossible. But it has the weakness which characterizes all primitivism, whether Stoic, Christian, or Romantic, for it makes primitive social forms normative. A primitive norm, whether of communal property relations or unorganized social cohesion, may serve provisionally as an occasion for the criticism of the institutions of an advancing civilization, more particularly the institutions of property and government; but it has the disadvantage of prompting indiscriminate criticism. This lack of discrimination is obvious in primitivistic Stoicism, in early Christianity, in seventeenth-century Cromwellian sectarianism, in Romanticism, and in Marxism and anarchism.

Augustine expressed this idea of a primitive social norm as follows:

> This is the prescribed order of nature. It is thus that God created man. For "let them," He says, "have dominion over the fish of the sea and the fowl of the air and over every creeping thing, which creepeth on the earth." He did not intend that His rational creature, made in His image, should have dominion over anything but irrational creation—not man over man but man over beasts. And hence the righteous men of primitive times were made shepherds of cattle rather than kings of men.[7]

This primitivism avoids the later error of the absolute sanctification of government. But its indiscriminate character is apparent by his failure to recognize the difference between legitimate and illegitimate, between ordinate and inordinate subordination of man to man. Without some form of such subordination the institutions of civilization could not exist.

The Commingling of the Two Cities

If Augustine's realism is contained in his analysis of the *civitas terrena*, his refutation of the idea that realism must lead to cynicism or relativism is contained in his definition of the *civitas dei*, which he declares to be "commingled" with the "city of this world" and which has the "love of God" rather than the "love of self" as its guiding principle. The tension between the two cities is occasioned by the fact that, while egotism is "natural" in the sense that it is universal, it is not natural in the sense that it does not conform to man's nature as one who transcends himself indeterminately and can only have God rather than self for his end. A realism becomes morally cynical or nihilistic when it assumes that the universal characteristic in human behavior must also be regarded as normative. The biblical account of human behavior, upon which Augustine bases his thought, can escape both illusion and cynicism because it recognizes that the corruption of human freedom may make a behavior pattern universal without making it normative. Good and evil are not determined by some fixed structure of human existence. Man, according to the biblical view, may use his freedom to make himself falsely the center of existence; but this does not change the fact that love rather than self-love is the law of his existence, in the sense that man can only be healthy, and his communities at peace, if man is drawn out of himself and saved from the self-defeating consequences of self-love.

There are several grave errors in Augustine's account of love and of the relation of love to self-love; but before considering them we might well first pay tribute to his approach to political problems. The virtue of making love, rather than justice, into the norm for the community may seem, at first blush, to be dubious. The idea of justice seems much more relevant than the idea of love, particularly for the collective relationships of men. The medieval tradition, which makes the justice of a rational "natural law" normative even for Christians when they consider the necessities of a sinful world, seems much more realistic than modern forms of sentimental Protestantism which regards love as a simple alternative to self-love which could be achieved if only we could preach the idea persuasively enough to beguile men from the one to the other.

Augustine's doctrine of love as the final norm must be distinguished from modern sentimental versions of Christianity which regard love as a simple possibility, and which think it significant to assert the obvious proposition that all conflicts in the community would be avoided if only people and nations would love one another. Augustine's approach differs from modern forms of sentimental perfectionism in the fact that he takes account of the power and persistence of egotism, both individual and collective, and seeks to establish the most tolerable form of peace and justice under conditions set by human sin. He inherited the tradition of monastic perfection; and he allows it as a vent for the Christian impulse toward individual perfection, without however changing the emphasis upon the duty of the Christian to perfect the peace of the city of this world. Furthermore, he raises questions about monastic perfection which, when driven home by the Reformation, were to undermine the whole system.

> I venture to say [he writes] that it is good for those who observe continence and are proud of it, to fall that they may be humbled. For what benefit is it to anyone in whom is the virtue of continence, if pride holds sway? He is but despising that by which man is born in striving after that which led to satan's fall . . . holy virginity is better than conjugal chastity . . . but if we add two other things, pride and humility . . . which is better, pride or humility? . . . I have no doubt that a humble married woman is to be preferred to a proud virgin. . . . A mother will hold a lesser place in the Kingdom of Heaven, because she has been married, than the daughter, seeing that she is a virgin. . . . But if thy mother has been humble and thou proud, she will have some sort of place, but thou none.[8]

While Augustine's doctrine of love is thus not to be confused with modern sentimentalities which do not take the power of self-love seriously, one may well wonder whether an approach to politics which does not avail itself of the calculations of justice may be deemed realistic. We have already noted that Augustine avails himself of the theory of the "natural law," only in the primordial version of the theory. If primordial conditions of a "natural order" are not to be defined as normative, the only alternative is to assume a "rational order" to which the whole of historical life conforms. Aquinas, in fact, constructed his theory of the natural law upon classical, and primarily Aristotelian, foundations. It was the weakness of both classical and medieval theories that they assumed an order in history, conforming to the uniformities of nature. Aristotle was aware of deviations in history, greater than those in nature; but he believed that there was nevertheless one form "which was marked by nature as the best." There is, in other words, no place in this theory of natural law for the endlessly unique social configurations which human beings, in their freedom over natural necessity, construct. The proponents of "natural law" therefore invariably introduce some historically contingent norm or social structure into what they regard as God's inflexible norm. That was the weakness of both classical and medieval social theory; and for that matter of the natural law theories of the bourgeois parties of the eighteenth century, who had found what they regarded as a more empirically perceived "natural law." But the modern empirical intelligence was no more able than the deductive rational processes of classical and medieval times to construct a social norm not colored by the interests of the constructor, thus introducing the taint of ideology into the supposed sanctities of the law.

We must conclude, therefore, that Augustine was wise in avoiding the alleged solution of a natural law theory, which was the basis of so much lack of realism in both the classical and the medieval period, and which can persist today, long after the Aristotelian idea of fixed form for historical events has been overcome, as the dogma of a religious system which makes its supposed sanctities into an article of faith. Augustine's conception of the radical freedom of man, derived from the biblical view, made it impossible accept the idea of fixed forms of human behavior and of social organization, analogous to those of nature, even as he opposed the classical theory of historical cycles. Furthermore, his conception of human selfhood, and of the transcendence of the self over its mind, made it impossible to assume the identity of the individual reason with a universal reason, which lies at the foundation of the classical and medieval natural law theories. It is in fact something of a mystery how the Christian insights into human nature and history, expressed by Augustine, could have been subordinated to classical thought with so little sense of the conflict between them in the formulations of Thomas Aquinas; and how they should have become so authoritative in Roman Catholicism without more debate between Augustinian and Thomistic emphases.

Augustine's formula for leavening the city of this world with the love of the city of God is more adequate than classical and medieval thought, both in doing justice to the endless varieties of historical occasions and configurations and in drawing upon the resources of love rather than law in modifying human behavior. Every "earthly peace," declares Augustine, is good as far as it goes. "But they will not have it long for they used it not well while they had it." That is, unless some larger love or loyalty qualifies the self-interest of the various groups, this collective self-interest will expose the community to either an overt conflict of competing groups or to the injustice of a dominant group which "when it is victorious . . . will become vice's slave."

Let us use some examples from current national and international problems to illustrate the Augustinian thesis.

There is, or was, a marked social tension between the middle classes of industrial owners and the industrial workers in all modern industrial nations. In some of them, for instance in Germany and France, this tension led to overt forms of the class conflict. In others such as Britain, the smaller European nations, and America, this tension was progressively resolved by various accommodations of interest. Wherein lay the difference? It did not lie in the possession of more adequate formulae of justice in some nations than in others. The difference lay in the fact that in some nations the various interest groups had, in addition to their collective interest, a "sense of justice," a disposition to "give each man his due" and a loyalty to the national community which qualified the interest struggle. Now, that spirit of justice is identical with the spirit of love, except at the highest level of the spirit of love, where it becomes purely sacrificial and engages in no calculation of what the due of each man may be. Two forms of love, the love of the other and the love of the community, were potent, in short, in modifying the acerbites and injustices of the class struggle. The two forms of love availed themselves of various calculations of justice in arriving at and defining their ad hoc agreements. But the factors in each nation and in each particular issue were too variable to allow for the application of any general rules or formulas of justice. Agreements were easier, in fact, if too much was not claimed for these formulas. Certain "principles" of justice, as distinguished from formulas or prescriptions, were indeed operative, such as liberty, equality, and loyalty to covenants; but these principles will be recognized as no more than the law of love in its various facets.

In the same manner, the international community is exposed to exactly the tensions and competitions of interest which Augustine describes. There are no formulas of justice or laws which will prevent these tensions from reaching overt conflict, if the collective interest of each nation is not modified by its loyalty to a higher value, such as the common civilization of the free nations. Where this common loyalty is lacking, as in our relation with Russia, no formula can save us from the uneasy peace in which we live. The character of this peace is just as tentative as Augustine described it. Whenever common loves or loyalties, or even common fears, lay the foundation for community, it must of course be our business to perfect it by calculations of justice which define our mutual responsibilities as exactly as possible.

It must be noted that the Augustinian formula for the leavening influence of a higher upon a lower loyalty or love, is effective in preventing the lower loyalty from involving itself in self-defeat. It corrects the "realism" of those who are myopically realistic by seeing only their own interests and failing thereby to do justice to their interests where they are involved with the interests of others. There are modern realists, for instance, who, in their reaction to abstract and vague forms of international idealism, counsel the nation to consult only its own interests. In a sense, collective self-interest is so consistent that it is superfluous to advise it. But a consistent self-interest on the part of a nation will work against its interests, because it will fail to do justice to the broader and longer interests, which are involved with the interests of other nations. A narrow national loyalty on our part, for instance, will obscure our long-range interests where they are involved with those of a whole alliance of free nations. Thus the loyalty of a leavening portion of a nation's citizens to a value transcending national interest will save a "realistic" nation from defining its interests in such narrow and short-range terms as to defeat the real interests of the nation.

Critique of Augustine's Realism

We have acknowledged some weaknesses in the Augustinian approach to the political order which we must now define and examine more carefully.

1. Non-Catholics commonly criticize Augustine's alleged identification of the *civitas dei* with the visible Church. But we must absolve him of this charge or insist on a qualification of the criticism. He does indeed accept the Catholic doctrine, which had grown up before his day; and he defines the visible Church as the only perfect society. There are

passages in which he seems to assume that it is possible to claim for the members of the Church that they are solely actuated by the *amor dei*. But he introduces so many reservations to this assertion that he may well be defined in this, as in other instances, as the father of both Catholicism and the Reformation. Of the Church, Augustine declared, "by faith she is a virgin. In the flesh she has few holy virgins."[9] Or again: "God will judge the wicked and the good. The evil cannot now be separated from the good but must be suffered for a season. The wicked may be with us on the threshing floor . . . in the barn they cannot be."[10] The reservations which he made upon the identification of the Church and the kingdom laid the foundations for the later Reformation position.

2. But these reservations about the sinners who might be present in the visible Church cannot obscure a graver error in his thought. This error is probably related to his conception of grace which does not allow for the phenomenon, emphasized by the Reformation, that men may be redeemed in the sense that they consciously turn from self to Christ as their end, and yet they are not redeemed from the corruption of egotism which expresses itself, even in the lives of the saints. This insight is most succinctly expressed in Luther's phrase *simul justus et peccator* (both justified and a sinner). When Augustine distinguished between the "two loves" which characterize the "two cities," the love of God and the love of self, and when he pictured the world as a commingling of the two cities, he does not recognize that the commingling is due not to the fact that two types of people dwell together, but because the conflict between love and self-love is in every soul. It is particularly important to recognize this in political analyses; for nothing is more obvious than that personal dedication is no guarantee against the involvement of the dedicated individual in some form of collective egotism.

3. We have frequently referred to Augustine's definition of the "two loves" which inform the "two cities" of which "the one is selfish and the other social," the one loving self to the point of contempt of God and the other loving God to the point of contempt of self. The question is whether Anders Nygren is right in *Agape and Eros* in defining the Augustinian concept of *amor dei* as rooted in a classical rather than a biblical concept.

In defense of Augustine it must be said that he is not insensible to the two facets of the love commandment and therefore does not define the *amor dei* in purely mystical terms as a flight from this world. He insists on the contrary that the *amor dei* is "social" and he offers the concord among brethren as a proof of the love of God. But nevertheless Nygren is right in suggesting that the thought of Plotinus has colored Augustine's conceptions sufficiently so that the *agape* of the New Testament is misinterpreted by Augustine's conception of *caritas* and *amor dei*. The *agape* form of love in the New Testament fails to be appreciated particularly in two of its facets:

First, the equality of the "two loves," the love of God and the love of the neighbor (enforced in the Scripture by the words "the second is like unto [the first]"), is violated by Augustine under the influence of Plotinus, even as a later medieval Catholic mystic, St. John of the Cross, violated it when he regarded the love of the creature as a ladder which might lead us to the love of God, but must be subordinated to the latter. Augustine wants us to love the neighbor for the sake of God, which may be a correct formulation; but he wants us to prove the genuineness of our love of God in the love of the neighbor, or by leading him to God. Thus the meeting of the neighbor's need without regard to any ultimate religious intention is emptied of meaning. The love of neighbor is for him not part of a double love commandment, but merely the instrument of a single love commandment which bids us flee all mortality, including the neighbor, in favor of the immutable good.

The second facet of the *agape* concept of the New Testament which tends to be obscured by Augustine is the notion of sacrificial love, the absurd principle of the cross, the insistence that the self must sacrifice itself for the other. It is not fair to Augustine to say that he neglects this facet of meaning, for he seems to emphasize it so constantly. He comes closest to its meaning when he deals with the relation of humility to love. Yet it seems fair to say that he was sufficiently imbued by classical mystical thought forms so that the emphasis lies always upon the worthiness or unworthiness of the object of our love; the insistence is that only God and not some mutable "good" or person is worthy of our love. This is a safeguard against all forms of idolatry. But it does not answer another important question: when I love a person or a community do I love myself in them or do I truly love them? Is my love a form of alteregoism? The Augustinian *amor dei* assumes that the self in its smallness cannot contain itself within itself, and therefore it is challenged to go out from itself to the most ultimate end. But it hardly reveals the full paradox of self-realization through self-giving, which is a scandal in the field of rational ethics as the cross is a scandal in the field of rational religion. Yet it is the source of ultimate wisdom. For the kind of self-giving which has self-realization as its result must not have self-realization as its conscious end; otherwise the self by calculating its enlargement will not escape from itself completely enough to be enlarged.

The weakness of Augustine in obscuring these facets of the *agape* principle may be illustrated, without unfairness I hope, by referring to his treatment of family love. He questions the love of mate or children as the final form of love, but not for New Testament reasons. He does not say: "When you love your wife and children are you maybe really loving yourself in them and using them as the instruments of your self-aggrandizements?" He declares instead, in effect: "You must not love your family too unreservedly because your wife and children are mortal. They also belong to the rivers of Babylon, and, if you give them absolute devotion, the hour of bereavement will leave you desolate." Of course, Augustine is too much the Christian to engage in a consistent mystic depreciation of the responsibilities and joys of this earthly life. After all, his whole strategy for the "commingling" of the two cities revolves around the acceptance of the ordinary responsibilities of home and state, but in performing these tasks for the ultimate, rather than the immediate end. He asks:

> What then? Shall all perish who marry and are given in marriage, who till the fields and build houses? No, but those who put their trust in these things, who prefer them to God, who for the sake of these things are quick to offend God, these will perish. But those who either do not use these things or who use them as though they used them not, trusting more in Him who gave them than in the things given, understanding in them His consolation and mercy, and who are not absorbed in these gifts lest they fall away from the giver, these are they whom the day will not overtake as a thief unprepared.[11]

Modern Illusions and "The River of Babylon"

We must not, in criticizing Augustine for neo-Platonic elements in his thought, obscure the Christian elements which will be equally an offense to modern men who regard the world as self-sufficing and self-explanatory, who reject as absurd the Christian faith that there is not only a mystery behind and above the world of observed phenomena and intelligible meanings, but that it is a mystery whose meaning has been disclosed as a love which elicits our answering love. This modern generation, with its confidence in a world without mystery, and without meaning beyond simple intelligibility, will not be beguiled from its unbelief by a reminder that its emancipation from God has betrayed it into precisely those idolatries—the worship of false gods, the dedication to finite values as if they were ultimate—of which Augustine spoke. But it must be recorded nevertheless as a significant fact of modern history. While it is an offense to regard communism as the inevitable end-product of secularism, as some Christians would have us believe, it is only fair to point out that the vast evils of modern communism come ironically to a generation which thought it would be easy to invest all the spiritual capital of men, who mysteriously transcend the historical process, in some value or end within that process; and communism is merely the most pathetic and cruel of the idolatrous illusions of this generation.

We must be clear about the fact that all the illusions about man's character and history, which made it so difficult for either the classical or the modern age to come to terms with the vexing problems of our togetherness, seem to stem from efforts to understand man in both his grandeur and his misery by "integrating" him into some natural or rational system of coherence. Thereby they denied the mystery of his transcendence over every process which points to another mystery beyond himself, without which man is not only a mystery to himself but a misunderstood being.

We cannot deny that from a Christian standpoint the world is like a "river of Babylon," to use Augustine's symbol; and that Augustine is right in suggesting that ultimately we cannot find peace if we are merely tossed down the river of time. We must find security in that which is not carried down the river. "Observe however," declares Augustine (in a simile which will seem strange to generations which have made the "rivers of Babylon," the stream of temporal events, into forces of redemption, but which will not seem so strange as the modern experience proves history as such to be less redemptive than we had believed):

> The rivers of Babylon are all things which are here loved, and pass away.
>
> For example, one man loves to practice husbandry, to grow rich by it, to employ his mind on it, to get his pleasure from it. Let him observe the issue and see that what he has loved is not a foundation of Jerusalem, but a river of Babylon.
>
> Another says, it is a grand thing to be a soldier; all farmers fear those who are soldiers, are subservient to them, tremble at them. If I am a farmer, I shall fear soldiers; if a soldier, farmers will fear me. Madman! thou has cast thyself headlong into another river of Babylon, and that still more turbulent and sweeping. Thou wishest to be feared by thy inferior; fear Him Who is greater than thou. He who fears thee may on a sudden become greater than thou, but He Whom thou oughtest to fear will never become less.
>
> To be an advocate, says another, is a grand thing; eloquence is most powerful; always to have clients hanging on the lips of their eloquent advocate, and from his words looking for loss or gain, death or life, ruin or security. Thou knowest not whither thou has cast

thyself. This too is another river of Babylon, and its roaring sound is the din of the waters dashing against the rocks. Mark that it flows, that it glides on; beware, for it carries things away with it.

To sail the seas, says another, and to trade is a grand thing—to know many lands, to make gains from every quarter, never to be answerable to any powerful man in thy country, to be always travelling, and to feed thy mind with the diversity of the nations and the business met with, and to return enriched by the increase of thy gains. This too is a river of Babylon. When will the gains stop? When wilt thou have confidence and be secure in the gains thou makest? The richer thou art, the more fearful wilt thou be. Once shipwrecked, thou wilt come forth stripped of all, and rightly wilt bewail thy fate *in* the rivers of Babylon, because thou wouldest not sit down and weep *upon* the rivers of Babylon.

But there are other citizens of the holy Jerusalem, understanding their captivity, who mark how human wishes and the diverse lusts of men hurry and drag them hither and thither, and drive them into the sea. They see this, and do not throw themselves into the rivers of Babylon, but sit down upon the rivers of Babylon and upon the rivers of Babylon weep, either for those who are being carried away by them, or for themselves whose deserts have placed them in Babylon.[12]

Whatever the defects of the Augustine approach may be, we must acknowledge his immense superiority both over those who preceded him and who came after him. A part of that superiority was due to his reliance upon biblical rather than idealistic or naturalistic conceptions of selfhood. But that could not have been the only cause, else Christian systems before and after him would not have been so inferior. Or were they inferior either because they subordinated the biblical-dramatic conception of human selfhood too much to the rationalistic scheme, as was the case with medieval Christianity culminating in the thought of Thomas Aquinas, or because they did not understand that the corruption of human freedom could not destroy the original dignity of man, as was the case with the Reformation with its doctrines of sin, bordering on total depravity and resulting in Luther's too pessimistic approach to political problems?

As for secular thought, it has difficulty in approaching Augustine's realism without falling into cynicism, or in avoiding nihilism without falling into sentimentality. Hobbes' realism was based on an insight which he shared with Augustine, namely, that in all historical encounters, the mind is the servant and not the master of the self. But he failed to recognize that the self which thus made the mind its instrument was a corrupted and not a "normal" self. Modern "realists" know the power of collective self-interest as Augustine did; but they do not understand its blindness. Modern pragmatists understand the irrelevance of fixed and detailed norms; but they do not understand that love must take the place as the final norm for these inadequate norms. Modern liberal Christians know that love is the final norm for man; but they fall into sentimentality because they fail to measure the power and persistence of self-love.

Thus Augustine, whatever may be the defects of his approach to political reality, and whatever may be the dangers of a too slavish devotion to his insights, nevertheless proves himself a more reliable guide than any known thinker. A generation which finds its communities imperiled and in decay from the smallest and most primordial community, the family, to the largest and most recent, the potential world community, might well take counsel of Augustine in solving its perplexities.

12

"REALLY EXISTING" SCRIPTURES
On the Use of Sacred Text in International Affairs

—John A. Rees

As is often quoted, Andre Malraux (may have) once said, "The twenty-first century will be religious or it will not be at all." If this sentiment is even partly true, then the reading of scriptures will once again become as important for diplomacy as it is for devotion. Yet as anyone with a sense of history knows, political claims of biblical proportion have almost always failed to satisfy temporal aspirations, let alone eternal ones. So how do we avoid manipulating scripture for opportunistic political ends and still allow the voices of sacred text to have a constructive role in political discussion? This, I believe, is one of the central questions to address if Malraux's new post-secular century is to turn out better rather than worse.

The Ideological Manipulation of Scripture

An introductory example illustrates the saliency of the issue. U.S. President George W. Bush has lavished the U.S. mission in Iraq with the ancient words of Isaiah 61, "to the captives come out, and to those in darkness be free."[1] Whether the second Iraq War is justifiable or not, many would intuit that the president is simply "proof-texting" from the Bible to support the American campaign. They are well-known words, and most commonly read in the president's own religion of Christianity as a messianic text, as the universal promise of peace with justice fulfilled in the life of Jesus of Nazareth (see Luke 4:14-21). And therein lies the problem: to attribute the American presence in Iraq with a messianic quality is to equate, however inadvertently, the enforced peace brought by U.S. troops with the *pax Christi* (peace of Christ), a Christianization of the Jewish notion of shalom, when from every angle it appears more like the ancient *pax Romana*—an empire managing lesser powers for its own self-interest.[2] Richard Bauckham warns of "the ideological manipulation of Scripture" in political religion,[3] and the president's exegesis may illustrate the problematic use of sacred text in what Clifford Geertz similarly terms the "rising tendency to ideologize faith" in international affairs today.[4]

* *The Brandywine Review of Faith & International Affairs* 2, no. 1 (Spring 2004): 17–26.

Yet the recognition that sacred text, Christian or otherwise, can be *abused* for ideological ends does not negate the possibility that these same scriptures can also be *used* to achieve positive political goals in international affairs. Such a possibility, it seems to me, depends upon the saliency of three principles: (1) scriptures "*really exist*" as a political resource; (2) scriptures contain a *diversity of political ideas*, not a single political agenda; and (3) scriptural texts can contribute to *open political discussion* and the development of *open political systems*.

"Really Existing" Scriptures

Understanding the increased profile of religion in international affairs raises what Scott Thomas calls the need to "take cultural and religious pluralism seriously."[5] At the frontline of any faith-based diplomatic activity lies an age-old problem: how does my *particular* religious tradition contribute to a *universal* agreement on matters of human conduct and political community? The problem of "the other" has always been a contentious one for any pluralist society, whether the Roman Empire of the ancient world or the civil societies and global villages of today. It is also the central challenge for a functioning democracy. Amartya Sen argues that meeting this challenge into the future requires a notion of democracy, broadly understood as "open public discussion," that is sourced in the history of cultures the world over. He writes,

> The championing of pluralism, diversity, and basic liberties can be found in the history of many societies. The long tradition of encouraging and protecting public debates on political, social, and cultural matters in, say, India, China, Japan, Korea, Iran, Turkey, the Arab world, and many parts of Africa, demand much fuller recognition in the history of democratic ideas.[6]

If we take seriously Sen's argument for the global roots of democracy, then researching how global democratic development can occur in what the late Edward Said called "the bewildering interdependence of our time"[7] requires the (re)inclusion of cultural traditions, many of which have been formed by religious texts, beliefs, and practices.

One acclaimed effort at imagining the future of international political culture is Andrew Linklater's study *The Transformation of Political Community*.[8] Central aspects of Linklater's work are described as the pursuit of "greater moral and economic equality whilst remaining sensitive to cultural difference" and "the idea of an inclusive intercultural dialogue" which will "provide a foundation for a new cosmopolitan community of humankind."[9] There is much to be commended in Linklater's book. However, as in the work of most theorists of international relations, it has been observed that religion remains the missing dimension in his thesis.[10] In a powerful critique, political scholar Jean Bethke Elshtain observes that Linklater's study neglects entirely "the *already extant* international communities that command transnational attachment, namely, those grounded in universal religions."[11] To counter this oversight Elshtain characterizes issues of identity and loyalty in "really existing" religious communities as follows: "A plurality of forms of membership, loyalty, and identity are recognized. At times, commitment to a particular community may take precedence. But one is also a member of an international, plural body consisting of trans-national forms of membership."[12] An example of this trans-national community is carried in the Islamic concept of *umma*, defined by Hasan Hanafi as "a nation without boundaries, a community of believers . . . [an] ideal community irrespective of geography."[13]

In the same way that Elshtain appeals to the "really existing communities" of religion as a vital element in international affairs, I wish to argue for the existence of "really existing" sacred texts as an important and under-utilized resource in open political discussion. Those who practice or observe faith-based politics know instinctively that religious texts do function in this way. For instance, in reference to the Abrahamic religions, Brian Cox and Daniel Philpott acknowledge that "God reveals his vision for how his people are to live together through scriptural texts" and that these texts "emanate principles that prescribe the nature and purpose of government . . . the duties of citizens . . . the distribution of economic wealth, the treatment of the poor, punishment, war, and other matters."[14] Beyond stand-alone ethical principles, scriptures have long provided what Thomas sums as "narratives that shape the identity of a community."[15] These narratives are not simply retold for posterity's sake, but rather, to adopt the words of Stanley Hauerwas, have been remembered in a way that has "formed the soul and determined future direction" of local and international communities of faith.[16]

Hauerwas would insist that because different faiths tell different stories, they therefore produce particular (i.e., unique) community dynamics.[17] True enough, but the faster one asserts this point the sooner one bumps into an important universal: through the process of interpretation and tradition building, *all* sacred texts help generate community narratives of potential political consequence. It is not until we experience the doing of those narratives—what Brazilian theologian Clodovis Boff calls the "imperative that praxis addresses"[18]—that really existing political commonalities and differences *between* religious narratives may be truly understood.

I am not arguing for the replacement or usurping of the secular texts of international relations, such as Western-style constitutions or international charters, by religious texts. Rather, I am arguing that sacred texts be read *alongside* their textual "others" as really existing sources of ethics for the building of real political outcomes.

Texts create institutional regimes. Texts constrain and recreate political behavior. Texts are read as sources of moral authority in the rough realities of international conflict. Texts give content to dialogues regarding human values and rights. While this understanding of texts is a given in respect to the constitutions of nation-states and charters of international law, religious texts have been reduced to function only as sources of ethical principle. It is certainly true that sacred scriptures shape some of the highest (and lowest) principles of human conduct, however I would argue they also help satisfy what Elshtain sees as the need to focus on "concrete structures and institutions of political power."[19]

And the need is real. At the time of this writing there is a potentially explosive standoff over whether the new Iraqi constitution should be influenced by Islamic or secular principles. Also, only weeks ago the French government passed laws to inhibit religious freedom for the sake of upholding the secular foundations of the Republic.[20] Finding ways to include scriptural resources, and the cultural traditions that these texts have helped form, as part of global political discussion is fast becoming one of our central challenges: how can we conceive political religion as a positive force in international affairs?

Of course, behind such a project exists a complex, longstanding tension in human political experience, namely, the degree to which we can, and should or should not, separate the "sacred" from the "secular" when promoting ethics and building institutions that can govern us all. As a way of approaching this challenge I wish to apply the words of Jonathan Sacks that "sometimes it is helpful to simplify, to draw a diagram rather than a map, in order to understand what may be at stake in a social transition."[21] What follows is an attempt to draw two diagrams, to introduce two basic principles, that outline how "really existing scriptures" might begin to function in the open public discussions of world politics.

The Plurality of Scripture

The political theorist and biographer John Keane claims there is a need in modern political theory to break the "bad monist habit" of constantly referring back to a "grounding principle" in order to validate a theoretical idea.[22] He argues, for instance, that the concept of civil society is a "signifier of plurality" and therefore has a "polysemic" rather than a singular or fixed quality.[23] Keane's "monist habit" is of particular relevance to political theorists from monotheistic religions such as Judaism, Christianity, and Islam. After all, it is an axiom of any monotheistic worldview that all truth emanates from One God. It would therefore appear a maxim of monist logic to also believe that the scriptures of each monotheistic faith promote a singular coherent view on matters of temporal authority and political life. But they do not. In the same way that Keane understands political theories to be "signifiers of plurality," monotheistic scriptures contain a diversity of political ideas, not a single political agenda. I wish to illustrate this point from the Christian and Islamic traditions, and begin with a simple, if not simplistic, survey of New Testament ideas about political authority.

Example 1: A Plural View of the State

The text of Romans 13:1-7, written in the reign of the Emperor Nero, commands Christians to "diligently obey the governing authorities" because such authorities are "servants of God." In radical contrast, the text of Revelation 13, written in the reign of Domitian, envisions the persecuting imperial power of Rome as a beast lurching out of the primordial sea. In between these extremes lies the famous words of Jesus, who seems to take a middle road between eternal and temporal authority when he commands a deputation of Pharisees to "render unto Caesar what is Caesar's, and render unto God what is God's" (Mark 12:17).

So what is the New Testament position on the role of temporal political authority? While there exists a plurality of interpretations for each of these texts,[24] when taken together it also seems that notions of political/state authority in the New Testament vary according to context and author. One might assume from this that scripture is self-contradictory on the issue, or that one of those texts must act to override the others in the interests of canonical or ideological unity. However, against these options a third alternative is possible: when taken together, the diversity of views about governing authority constitutes a *dynamic* understanding of state power that reflects the full spectrum of state behaviors: states can provide order and so should be obeyed (Romans 13); states can act with malicious intent and so should be vilified (Revelation 13); state power is temporal in relation to our eternal hopes and so should be relativized (Mark 12). This plural, "polysemic" view of state authority reflects what Walter Wink has described as a dynamic theology of the spiritual "powers" that exists behind political reality:

Temporally: the powers *were* created, they *are* fallen, and they *shall be* redeemed. This can be asserted as a belief in the final triumph of God over the forces of evil. But this schema is also simultaneous: God at one and the same time *upholds* a given political or economic system, since some such system is required to support human life; *condemns* that system insofar as it is destructive of fully human life; and *presses for its transformation* into a more humane order. Conservatives stress the first, revolutionaries the second, reformers the third. The Christian is expected to hold together all three.[25]

The politico-legal philosopher Martin Krygier likewise argues for a dynamic understanding of the concept of the state when he writes, "States differ. . . . Since 'the state' is not one thing, indiscriminate opposition to 'it' is as foolish as it is in some quarters popular."[26] Notice how Wink's dynamic view of political power in relation to both God's activity and human participation resonates with Krygier's perspective below on the power of states and our rightful response toward such power:

> States protect us from terrible evils and so they should be valued. They have potential to do special evils of their own, so they must be restrained. And there are goods that only they can do, and these should be encouraged. None of these propositions is inconsistent with the others, so one can respect them all.[27]

Both Wink and Krygier break the "monist habit" of needing to justify state power via one immovable definition, and opt instead for a "polysemic" perspective that helps shape political action across the full range of state behaviors, from the open and free to the despotic and authoritarian. That one of these views is sourced in the reading of sacred text illustrates the potential for scripture to be used in open political discussion.

Example 2: Interpretation and Political Evolution

Whatever the variable nature of biblical perspectives on political issues, one might assume, given stereotypes about the inflexibility of Islamic political regimes, that the Qur'an is more likely to contain a singular and explicit political theory or agenda. Not so, according to international relations scholar Sohail Hashmi who criticizes the notion of Islamic political unity in the same way others have attacked the "civilizational" division of world politics:

> As critics of the "clash of civilizations" thesis have pointed out, the greatest danger of such an emphasis on civilizations is to make them into holistic, nonporous units. There is nothing, of course, more porous than the boundaries of civilizations. Islamic civilization is no exception. . . . It is utterly meaningless today to speak of an Islamic "tradition" or "civilization" as a monolithic force operating in international politics.[28]

The ethics of Islam are diverse. Hashmi in part traces this diversity back to differences between the early schools of Islamic jurisprudence, one of which emphasized that "revelation could be supplemented by reason," the other that "ethical value was derived entirely from God's command."[29] The former approach (Mu'tazilite) seeks to open Qur'anic interpretation to "human reason guided by principles of equity and public interest."[30] The latter approach (Ash'arite) emphasizes "the literal interpretation of the Qur'an and predeterminism."[31] Both ethical approaches "can be derived from the Qur'an"[32] thereby emphasizing the diversity of political ideas and practice that could potentially stem from devout Islamic interpretation.

The importance of Hashmi's views, echoed in the work of other theorists such as Hanafi's "reflective Islamic approach" to the notion of civil society,[33] is that the political views that are read out of sacred texts are dependent upon traditahs of interpretation. In this sense, no text can generate its own fixed and unchallengeable political reality. This is an important point, because it addresses perhaps the gravest fear concerning the role of sacred text in international affairs, namely, that it will inevitably encourage a closed and backward-looking political system.

By way of an illustration, consider the Iranian political situation. Iran is often held up as proof that Islamic theocratic politics are retrograde, a point re-emphasized by the recent elections which seemed far more fixed than free. In fact, the closer one looks at the politics of Iran, the more one sees not the fixed fundamentalism of religious political control, but rather, a very dynamic process of political evolution within the interpretive tradition of Shi'a Islam.

The stereotype of fundamentalism implies rigidity and a disengagement from contemporary culture. And, if the erroneous judgments and oppressive eccentricity of the Iranian regime were our only focus, there is plenty of rigidity to be found. Just ask Iranian women forced to wear the veil under threat of violence including death, or children sent into the battlefield against Iraq, or Salman Rushdie, himself a foreign symbol of the oppression against Iranian poets, playwrights, and journalists. Yet it was Rushdie who, on another subject, wrote, "These are hurried, sloganizing times, and we don't have the time or worse, the inclination to assimilate many-sided truths."[34] So it is that Iranian political religion is a many-sided phenomenon, and Qur'anic interpretations and religious traditions play a central role in the unfolding of events. Let us consider five aspects of the drama.

Firstly, the religious foundations of the revolution in Iran can be understood as undergirding an indigenous political uprising against an imperial power. The popular support for the 1978 revolution was the direct result of oppression under the Shah, a puppet to Western interests in the region, installed through a CIA coup that the U.S. no longer even bothers to deny. It was under this oppression that the Qur'anic scholar Ruhollah Khomeini expressed dissent and was eventually sent into exile. In the consciousness of ordinary Iranians Khomeini therefore became like the Hidden Imam of the Shi'ite tradition who would one day return and restore justice. A political expectation was thus born from a grassroots religious tradition.

Secondly, Khomeini was not a traditionalist in Shi'ite religion, but an innovator. His interpretive theory of *Velayat-i-Faqih* (Mandate of the Islamic Jurist) controversially called for Shi'ite involvement in government as a means of upholding God's Infinite Justice in the face of tyranny. This doctrine was opposed by conservative mullahs who took the more traditional approach of quietism and withdrawal from politics. Khomeini's nationalism was also different from the pan-Islamic polity implicit in the concept of *umma* where the faith community is not organized within the fences of any state. "In an Islamic context," writes religious scholar Karen Armstrong, "Khomeini's message was modern."[35]

Thirdly, French researcher Olivier Roy claims that Iranian political institutions and law are influenced by, but not controlled by, Islamic principles. "It is clear that Islam is not the basis of the whole system. In fact it is the constitution which defines the place of Islam. It is more the law which defines Islam than Islam defines the law."[36] The implication here is that even in a so-called fundamentalist state, influences additional to religious text and interpretation are necessary for any political system to function. (Indeed one might argue that religious fundamentalism can only occur once an external ideological influence, such as nationalism or racism, is imposed upon religious texts.)

Fourthly, the 1997 election of moderate president Mohammad Khatami reflected the scope for a democratic process of political change *within* the "Islamic" system, not against it. As Armstrong astutely observes, "President Khatami is seeking a more democratic and liberal interpretation of Islam. . . . But Khatami is not reneging on Khomeini or his revolution: Iranians want to come to modernity on their own terms."[37] Similarly, the Iranian lawyer and human rights activist Shirin Ebadi, winner of the 2003 Nobel Peace Prize, has called for reform by using the interpretations of Islamic tradition as her starting point.

Fifthly, Khatami's inability to wrest power from the conservatives, and the recent shut-out of reformers from the parliamentary system, does not imply a victory for purer or truer political religion. Akbar Rafsanjani and the Council of Guardians may destroy the democratic process but this may only mean they have stopped the natural political evolution seeded in the modern and innovative interpretations of the revolution for the age-old reasons of power and wealth.[38]

Political scholar H. E. Chehabi wrote in 1991, "[F]or better or worse, change will come from within the regime."[39] Time will tell which one—better or worse—it is. We can hope, indeed pray, for an eventual victory of moderate Islamic forces. The interpretation and reinterpretation of Islamic political ethics will play a crucial role in keeping open public discussion alive during this ongoing crisis. The re-imposition of some sort of secularism upon Iran would itself be retrograde.

Scripture in Open Political Discussion and Systems

As the hopes of the reformers in Iran illustrate, part of believing that sacred text can play a constructive role in open public discussion is the degree to which it can be employed in the creation of open political systems. What follows are two examples of scripture informing open pluralistic political visions, one from the Hebrew Bible, the other from the Qur'an.

Example 1: Scripture in Open Political Discussion

The political writer Michael Ignatieff once praised a book by the Israeli philosopher Avishai Margalit as "a model of how philosophers, using only a fine attention to distinctions between similar sounding moral terms, can help to clarify . . . our moral language."[40] A similar recommendation could be given regarding Rabbi Jonathan Sacks' astute study of the origins of "political and civil society" in Western thought.[41] Sacks seeks to distinguish each "society" by contrasting Greek from Hebrew understandings of what it is that "leads individuals to form associations and sustain them."[42]

Of particular interest is the foundational role Sacks gives to two understandings "both implicit in the Bible, but quite different in their application."[43] The first is seen in Thomas Hobbes' *Leviathan*, which seeks to describe the "state of nature" in a way that "closely resembles the biblical description of the era of the Flood."[44] In this world where Hobbes famously described human existence as "solitary, poor, nasty, brutish, and short," it is the social contract that makes human togetherness function: "This, the social contract, brings into being the 'great Leviathan' of the state, and thus is born *political society*—the central repository of power to bring about a social order."[45] The second understanding is illustrated by the union of Adam and Eve in the garden—another "state of nature"—but one held together by a *covenant* not a contract, by a marriage not by the state. It is the story of *civil society*.

> What kind of bond is this? Clearly, given the way the Hebrew Bible describes it, it is not a Hobbesian contract between two independent individuals, each seeking their own interests. It is instead—in a key word of Jewish thought—a covenant (*brit* in Hebrew), and this is neither an alliance of interests nor, strictly speaking, an emotional state. It is a bond of identity, as if to say: "This is part of *who I am*.". . . How then does this narrative differ from that of Hobbes? Its central figure is not "I" but the "We" of which I am a part. . . . On this account, our affiliations and attachments are not irrelevant, but essential, to the structure of the obligations we form. We owe duties to others because they are a part of who we are.[46]

Sacks' contrast between the contract of political society and the covenant of civil society is powerful, particularly for those whose social and political commitment grows out of biblical narratives read among Jewish and Judeo-Christian communities the world over. Yet rather than use this distinction in a triumphalistic way, as if to trumpet the moral ascendency of covenant over contract, of the civil over the political, Sacks instead affirms the complementarity and interdependence between these elements. In this way, he resists the temptation to pit secular and religious perspectives, as well as realist and liberal ones, against each other in a zero-sum fashion but instead strives to tell an integrated story where each element remains important.

> So there are two stories about human associations, one told in our political classics, the other in our great religious texts. Clearly they are not mutually exclusive. Civil society requires the institutions of politics for the resolution of its conflicts and the maintenance of peace and defense. Political society, according to most of its theorists, needs the undergirding of civil virtue. Both stories represent enduring truths about the human situation and both need to be told if people are to live together peaceably for any length of time.[47]

Thus we have cast before us a combined vision of the real and ideal, of security and aspiration, of organization and relation, each in an open dialogue with the other, and all grounded with definitional precision in a sacred text considered to be "one of the great meta-narratives of Western civilization."[48] It is a fine example of how to employ sacred text in a way that informs and encourages the open political discussion necessary for the achievement of democratization in a post-secular global order.

Example 2: Scripture and the Development of Open Political Systems

J. R. Gibbins and B. Reimer describe the current state of international affairs as one where "postmodernization and globalization processes are changing the nature of the territorial nation state as well as changing the values of institutions."[49] For various scholars and public thinkers this is producing new visions of *civil society*, that realm of free association independent of (and in partnership with) state power that also reaches across international borders. It is not surprising, therefore, especially in light of Elshtain's "really existing" international religious communities, that Keane observes the global trend of "Muslim actors intent on developing and redefining civil society."[50] Keane argues that in some contexts fledgling civil societies "are best nurtured and protected by renewing religious faith" and that "these emergent post-secular civil societies not only pose a challenge to political despotism," they also promise the transition towards the rule of law. Keane cites the "path-breaking" work of Tunisian Qur'anic scholar Sheikh Rachid al-Ghannouchi in the following way:

> Just as the followers of the Prophet lived the relationship between *ad-dini* (the religious) and *as-siyasi* (the political), so Ghannouchi insists that the laws and institutions of a modern political community should nurture and honor the dignity of its citizens. . . . He insists that Muslims must also use their human capacity for reason (*'aql*) and *ijtihad* [context bound judgments] and work to create, renew, and nurture civil society institutions (*al-mujtama' al-ahli*).[51]

Not all commentators consider Ghannouchi to be as progressive as Keane suggests. In a conversation with journalist and author Robin Wright, Moroccan scholar Abdou Filali-Ansary contrasts the work of Ghannouchi with Iranian philosopher Abdul Karim Soroush: "Ghannouchi is a main representative of Islamist attitudes and thought (and faces persecution for that); Soroush is a formidable intellectual opponent of Islamism (for which he, too, faces persecution from his government)."[52] Filali-Ansary sees Soroush as the "true reformer" of the two because his views "are closer to modern humanism" in the cause of "open religion" and not simply "radical innovation." Filali-Ansary doubts the reformist credentials of Ghannouchi because "the community [of faith]—not the individual—remains the ultimate reality and objective" of his work.

But a politics shaped by religious texts and interpretive traditions need not lose itself, as Filali-Ansary seems to suggest it must, to the universal story of "modern humanism" (or any other contemporary narrative) in order to function as a constructive democratic influence in international affairs. If politics and democracy can be drawn from cultural traditions (as Sen argues) and narratives of identity (as Thomas argues), then Ghannouchi's explicit and particular use of Qur'anic interpretation might in fact save Islamic post-secular politics from forcing itself into an alien (and imperial?) story of modern individualism. In concert with the work of Soroush, it might also help Islamic political ethics reclaim its own humanistic narrative in the process.

Conclusion

In this article, I have drawn on examples from the Abrahamic faiths and on the work of leading theologians and philosophers to sketch some starting principles for thinking about how religious scripture can contribute positively to international affairs. Scriptures "really exist" as a political resource, they contain a diversity of political ideas (not a single political agenda), and they can contribute constructively to open political discussion and the development of open political systems.

The great challenges that we now face in global affairs demand more than conventional thinking and resources; one vital resource is religious scripture. Indeed, without community text-based approaches—like that of Ghannouchi, and indeed many others across different religious traditions—there may be nothing to mediate between reactionary traditionalism (the seedbed of religious fundamentalism) and tradition-less individualism (the seedbed of economic exploitation). There is therefore much at stake over this issue in the post-secular century that awaits.

13

ISAIAH'S VISION OF HUMAN SECURITY
Virtue-Ethics and International Politics

—Scott M. Thomas

> God . . . is just as much present in the remorseless economic trends and in the oscilla-
> tions of the balance of power as he is in the fall of a sparrow (Matthew 10:29-39); and
> we see that he is indeed sovereign in history, the peripeties of the historical process are
> properly understood as judgments and that all history is ultimately Sacred history.[1]
>
> —*Martin Wight*

For scholars and practitioners in international affairs it should be both sobering and inspiring to realize that the ideals of the United Nations, as far as the organization's founders were concerned, are summarized by the vision of the prophet Isaiah.[2] His key prophecy (Isaiah 2:4-6), on "nations hammering their swords into plowshares and their spears into sickles," is now written on the granite, curved wall, called the Isaiah Wall, in the plaza in front of the United Nations building in New York. Indeed, the Book of Isaiah with its visions of peace and the restoration of Israel has loomed larger in the Western theo-political imagination than almost any book of the Hebrew Bible.

It has contributed to various types of messianic ideas and schemes, Zionism as well as anti-Semitism, Catholic liberation theology, such as that of Daniel and his brother Philip Berrigan,[3] as well as to feminist, environmentalist, and inter-faith theologies.[4] Isaiah's vision of the "peaceable kingdom" (Isaiah 11:6-9) was one of the passages most often used by the Anabaptists and the historic "peace churches" of the Radical Reformation in their writings on international relations. William Penn famously used it in a practical way, in his "Essay Towards the Present and Future Peace of Europe" (1693).[5]

In the Book of Isaiah we find a narrative of the rise and decline of nations and empires, Assyria, Babylonia, and Persia, and the search for peace and security through war, alliances, and the balance of power. It is the stuff of classic *realpolitik*—all of which the prophet Isaiah roundly criticizes, and in a way that resonates strongly with what we today call the "virtue-ethics" tradition. What, according to Isaiah, does the virtue-ethics approach mean for faith, social life, and foreign policy? Isaiah, contrary to the realist narrative of power

* *The Review of Faith & International Affairs* 4, no. 3 (Winter 2006): 21–30.

politics, presents a holistic vision of sustainable peace and security for international relations. He calls Israel back to Yahweh's alternative understanding of wellbeing, authenticity, and development—what can be called his global vision of *human security*, a concept that is increasingly prominent in the discourse and practice of the United Nations.

An Ancient Clash of Civilizations

In the Book of Isaiah we see that Yahweh reveals himself as a personal God through his words and his specific acts rather than as a distant deity. His revelation is always mediated through specific settings in time and place. While this can cause problems of interpretation, we are best able to grasp the truth of Isaiah's message when it is put into the concrete forms of daily life.[6] This is equally true of his understanding of international relations, expressed in real-world terms. Sadly, too many modern-day interpreters (including many conservative American evangelicals) often step back from this approach to Isaiah, making one of two common mistakes. Either they use the book to promote an obscure understanding of eschatology that legitimates U.S. hegemony and militarism, or they argue that the book is mainly for personal moral application, and do not emphasize the relevance of Isaiah's message to foreign policy.[7]

However, what is so remarkable from the perspective of international relations is how often in the prophetic tradition theology and international relations are interrelated. In fact, a great deal of the revelation of Yahweh is mediated through the types of events that scholars identify with international relations—wars, alliances, and the balance of power. What we vividly confront in the Book of Isaiah is the meaning of trust and faithfulness to Yahweh *in the context of international relations*. Isaiah's prophesying took place amidst a series of actual crises in foreign policy, and his visions illustrate the perennial problems of power, justice, and security in the world of nations; this is what gives the Book of Isaiah a timeless quality for scholars of international relations.

Isaiah's prophetic ministry was overshadowed by Assyria's plans for world empire and the threat that this posed to the security of small or weak states on the eastern coast of the Mediterranean Sea, such as Israel, Judah, and Syria (Aram). In a few years Assyria conquered the whole of the Near East up to the borders of Egypt. Its local vassals paid tribute, forming a suzerain international system (a type of international system in which a powerful state dominates and subordinates its neighbors without directly taking them over).[8] An unstable or negative peace came into being, enforced and maintained by the realist's this-worldly tools of power politics and statecraft. Military force, alliances, arms races, the balance of power, and spheres of influence generated a structure of stability underpinned by fear and uncertainty.[9]

Israel and Judah's national security dilemmas were not those of an empire or great power, but rather those of any other small state living next to hostile great powers.[10] Indeed, an important part of their status as a "chosen nation," a nation picked out by Yahweh to be a light unto all nations, was their status as weak and insignificant actors in the ancient Near Eastern international system. Thus, their foreign policy dilemmas were similar to those of modern Israel or Jordan in relation to its Arab neighbors.[11] They can equally be compared to those of Mexico, Brazil, or Nicaragua in relation to the United States; Sri Lanka in relation to India; the Baltic states or the Caucasus in relation to Russia; East Asia in relation to China; or East Timor in relation to Indonesia.

The diplomatic and political problems facing Judah and Israel as small or weak states can be easily translated into international relations terms. Many of Isaiah's prophecies relate to the way the rulers of Judah and Israel tried to resolve their country's "security dilemma" using the mechanisms of power politics and negative peace. Theirs was the basic problem of international order faced by all political communities given the anarchical structure of the international system. King Ahaz is depicted as preferring an alliance *with* Assyria over a coalition of small states, led by Syria and Israel, directed against that power (2 Kings 16–18; Isaiah 7–8). Some 30 years later, under King Hezekiah, there was another foreign policy debate over whether Judah should form an opposing alliance, siding this time with Egypt *against* Assyria (Isaiah 28–31, 36–38; 2 Kings 18–20). The switch illustrates the realist maxim of statecraft, that states have no permanent allies, only permanent interests.

Why does the Isaiah tradition depict Ahaz, based on his decisions in foreign policy, as the "bad king," the faithless ruler who did not trust in Yahweh for Judah's security, and Hezekiah as the "good king" who did trust Yahweh?[12] Most troubling for the realists among us, Ahaz and Hezekiah seem to be judged on the basis of whether or not they relied on power politics to maintain Judah's security rather than on quiet confidence in the actions of Yahweh.[13]

In 733–734 Israel and Syria (Aram) tried to persuade Ahaz to bring Judah into an anti-Assyrian alliance (2 Kings 16:5-9). In balance of power diplomacy this was a classic attempt to form an alignment against a great power. When Ahaz refused, they attacked him in order to overthrow him and put a more pliant candidate on the throne (Isaiah 7:6). Ahaz, against the warnings of Isaiah, appealed to Assyria for assistance (Isaiah 7:4-7). In other words, Isaiah's famous counsel for Ahaz to trust in Yahweh, to "be firm and calm" (Isaiah 7:4), and his strong opposition to Ahaz's advisors who backed the anti-Assyrian coalition (Isaiah 8:6, 12), were evoked by a concrete foreign policy dilemma.

Ahaz's refusal to join the anti-Assyrian alliance resulted in the Syro-Ephraimite War in 733 fought by Judah against Syria (Aram) and the Northern Kingdom of Israel, symbolized by "Ephraim," its dominant tribe (Isaiah 7–8). The use of the term "Ephraim" to designate the Northern Kingdom, rather than "Israel," suggests that the country had already begun to lose territory to Assyria and in desperation aligned with a non-brother to the northeast (Aram) against a brother to the south (Judah). In this section we see that "Israel is slowly becoming one of 'the nations.'"[14] Crucially, the *identity* of Judah, and not only state survival, is what concerned the prophet Isaiah.

Assyria ended up annexing the northern and eastern provinces of the Northern Kingdom of Israel, while Judah became a vassal state (2 Kings 16:10-18), paying tribute to Assyria, and adopting some of its religious practices, such as acknowledging the deities of Assyria's state religion (Isaiah 7:2). In Isaiah, in the aftermath of the Syro-Ephraimite War, we can see the almost inevitable spread of Assyria's cultural and religious hegemony throughout its suzerain international system.

Judah's foreign policy dilemma was stark: should it choose a pro- or anti-Assyrian orientation? This was a more difficult strategic choice than what we might imagine. Given its size, military weakness, and vulnerability, it did not really have any good foreign policy options. Given Ahaz's military and political constraints, an alliance with Assyria was an understandable move—at the level of *realpolitik*.

Despite what Isaiah says, Ahaz shows great political skill and acumen. As Adam Watson points out, by making an alliance with Assyria, he was trying to remove Judah from the destructive politics of the region. In fact, the pro-Assyrian option was presumably attractive to Ahaz for a variety of reasons, such as regional stability, trade, and economic development. It might be argued that Ahaz's foreign policy contradicts any notion of an ancient clash of civilizations, since it seems that culture for Ahaz was trumped by power politics. However, as we shall see, this was exactly Isaiah's problem. Isaiah recognized that there *was* a clash of civilizations, and he called on Ahaz to trust in Yahweh's covenantal relationship with Judah for the country's security rather than on alliances and the balance of power (Isaiah 7–12). He opposed Judah's foreign policy because he knew that power politics would neither resolve the clash of civilizations nor promote human security.

Engaging Yahweh's World

The revival of the virtue-ethics tradition was probably the most important development in moral philosophy and Christian ethics in the late 20th century. The early virtue-ethics tradition goes back to Aristotle and Aquinas. Its resurgence in our day is part of the story of how many people have become disillusioned with part of the Enlightenment heritage. There is growing skepticism that realists' or liberal internationalists' appeals to reason, self-interest, or even the common good are sufficient to produce the good society or a more peaceful world.[15]

Isaiah saw Judah's foreign policy choices in a counter-intuitive way because he had a vision or theology of international relations, which he saw as Yahweh's domain.[16] What might the virtue-ethics tradition tell us about this foreign policy vision, and how might it be made intelligible to scholars of international relations today?[17] Virtue-ethics, with its narrative conceptions of identity and social action, is concerned with the long-term consequences of decisions in foreign policy, not only their immediate effects. Put in contemporary terms, it is relevant to avoiding "blowback" from foreign policy entanglements.[18]

Yahweh's admonitions through Isaiah's oracles are not only to do the right thing—to act with faithfulness, justice, and righteousness. Isaiah does not look at discrete foreign policy decisions as if they were simply puzzles in what virtue-ethicists call "quandary ethics." He is not just interested in what the ruler should do in a particular situation, such as whether to go to war as part of an anti-Assyrian coalition or promote regional stability by joining with Assyria as the great regional power.[19] Isaiah looked at decision-making in foreign policy from a broader narrative approach emphasizing Judah's identity. This means that for Isaiah, unlike for Ahaz, identity, culture, and the national interest go together. The primary question for ethics as well as foreign policy is what kind of community the Israelites were meant to become in the international society of the ancient Near East, given that they were a chosen people covenanted to bless the nations of the world.[20]

Social constructivists argue that international society is concerned as much with identity as with interests, indeed that larger questions of identity frame narrow questions of national interest.[21] What sort of community does a people want to be? What kind of world do they want to live in? The survival of the state is not a self-evident value or categorical imperative. In 1940 General Pétain wanted to preserve an independent core state, Vichy France, in the midst of Nazi-occupied Europe, but General de Gaulle was ready to envisage a government-in-exile and a retreat to London. Why were both men patriots? Pétain, a hero of World War I, saw himself as the savior of France in the sense of the French state. de Gaulle sought to save France not only as a territory, but also as an idea about how the French people should live in the world. These are the central questions of foreign policy. Therefore, as Robert Cooper has argued, analytical theory and normative theory inextricably go together.[22]

Isaiah could not have agreed more. Isaiah calls Ahaz not only by his name, but also formally as "The House of David" (Isaiah 7:2), suggesting that this "narrative is concerned not only with this specific military crisis, but also with the long-term reality of the Davidic dynasty."[23] More than Judah's survival as a geographic entity or independent state was involved, given that Israel was already occupied. At stake, too, was its identity as the royal house of David, and Yahweh's covenant going back to the prophet Nathan. These promises, which were recalled at the coronation of the kings of Judah and at the annual harvest festivals, declared that the house and throne of David would endure forever (1 Samuel 25:28; 2 Samuel 7:11-16; 2 Samuel 23:5; Psalm 132:11).

Thus, for King Ahaz, what seemed to be politically astute "was not thereby justified in the eyes of faith." [24] A faithful foreign policy for Isaiah, hard as this is for realists to accept, flies in the face of balance of power diplomacy. Isaiah interpreted world politics through his theology of international relations. Seen in this light, the king stood "in total antithesis to the radical form of wellbeing voiced and offered by the prophet," a form of wellbeing that could not be brought about by the realist's tools of statecraft.[25] Isaiah's vision of human security encompassed this radical form of wellbeing, cultural authenticity, and economic development.

From a virtue-ethics perspective Isaiah argues that Judah's rulers (and hence the people of Judah) cannot grasp what is going on in the social world of international relations because they have not been trained to interpret the world in a particular way. It is not by chance that for Isaiah one of the key issues in his irenic prophecy is proper instruction in the word of the Lord so that one can see clearly what is going on in domestic society and in international relations. The nations come to learn from Yahweh, and the form of instruction is the Torah and the word of the Lord, which comes forth from Jerusalem.

Torah encompasses a wide range of meanings including law, teaching, and instruction, and can be associated with the revealed Law of Moses in the Pentateuch. This is why the Book of Isaiah was interpreted in the Jewish tradition as a commentary on the Mosaic Torah. However, this perspective should not relegate to a secondary position either prophetic teaching or the prophetic polemic against legalism. "Both law and prophetic proclamation were expounded in terms of a deepening grasp of God's reality," what we can call a deepening grasp of Yahweh's theology of international relations.[26]

In Isaiah positive peace is part of the true worship of God, Torah obedience, and faithfulness to Yahweh in the world. In Yahweh's new dispensation the cult and rituals are constitutive of the faith community, meant to train its members in Torah, so as to build the kind of society that *interprets the world in a particular way* (Isaiah 1:10-17). Such a society is concerned with what happens to the widow, the orphan, the poor, and the oppressed, and accordingly acts with justice, righteousness, and peace both at home and toward the neighboring nations.[27]

Isaiah criticized the rulers of Judah for lacking the kind of knowledge and discernment that comes with being trained in the correct path of Torah (Isaiah 1:3, 10-17). Ritual is worthless when the courts, which should pursue justice and champion the rights of the oppressed and weakest members of society, fail to do so (Isaiah 1:10-17). Israel is supposed to become a model and a blessing to its neighbors, for "when thy laws prevail in the land, the inhabitants of the world learn justice" (Isaiah 26:9).

Human Security

In recent years a variety of scholars, research institutes, and international organizations have developed a more holistic and integrative understanding of peace and security than that which prevailed during the Cold War. They have envisaged a people-centered rather than state-centered concept of security, one focused on the safety of communities and individuals rather than the security of states in the international system.[28] They began by recognizing that the security of states does not necessarily lead to the safety of peoples, and so while national security focuses on the defense of the state from external attack, human security is about protecting individuals and communities from *any* form of political violence.[29]

One of the concerns of human security is public safety and the protection of civilians in war-torn or failed states. We can see this phenomenon of social disintegration among some of the states of the ancient Near East, whether Judah or Egypt, with its civil disorder and a failed economy (Isaiah 19:1-15). Isaiah's explanation for the rise of failed states is simple: In the case of Judah, the collapse of the state has been engendered by the breakdown of justice (Isaiah 1:21-28; 5:7) as well as the threat of war and foreign invasion by Syria and Israel (Isaiah 7–8).

The New Jerusalem Bible titles this section "Anarchy in Jerusalem" (Isaiah 3:1-7).[30] Otto Kaiser, interestingly, writes of this passage of Isaiah in terms of "the total collapse of the state," drawing on his own wartime experiences: "Anyone who remembers the months that followed May 1945 in Germany will have the sensation in reading this passage of being carried right back to those days."[31] We could equally add the contemporary examples of Somalia, Ethiopia, Liberia, the Ivory Coast, and Sierra Leone.[32]

What does Isaiah have to say about all this? He argues that Jerusalem was a fortress for justice at the beginning of Yahweh's dealings with his people, in which the covenant's ordinances were genuinely in force. But the city lost its noble title under the rule of unfaithful judges, and fell into wrong ways. The prophet is not deceived by outward appearances—sacrifices and offerings. What is decisive in passing judgment on Jerusalem, the city of God, is not its apparent sense of national security or level of economic development. It is not only arms and strong defenses that provide security, for any ruler and his national security advisors can boast, "We have a strong city, whose walls and ramparts are our deliverance" (Isaiah 26:1; cf. 7:3-9; 22:8-14; 28:14-18). What is decisive is the attitude of its inhabitants, especially the ruling elite or social class, toward Yahweh's demand for justice and righteousness, since prosperity spawned moral, economic, and political corruption (Isaiah 1:21-28).

The problem is that the very people who should be concerned about keeping law and order in their capacity as royal officials, the judges and princes, seek only their own advantage (Isaiah 1:23), and sell their support to the highest bidder.[33] Many political scientists now argue that in the West the pluralist, interest group conception of liberal democracy has paralyzed the best-intentioned public officials, stifling attempts to cut or improve government programs, and distorting policy outcomes. The greatest goodies (in Robert Putnam's words) go to the rich, the well connected, or the best organized.[34] Isaiah said very much the same thing (Isaiah 1:17; 10:2, 3:121-15). As Kaiser surmises, what concerns Isaiah is "the easy way in which the ruling and property-owning classes accept the practical acts of unfaithfulness, which are evident in their daily life."[35]

Another aspect of human security is what writers in peace studies call "positive peace," "stable peace," or "sustainable peace." Sustainable peace is defined as not just the absence of war or its expectation. It requires more than a cease-fire, the laying down of arms, or a peace treaty.[36] The idea of stable peace is an inherent part of the Hebrew concept of *shalom*, signifying wellbeing and wholeness: restoring or reuniting what has been divided. It is synonymous with prosperity and security (Psalm 122:6-7), both of which are the product of justice (Psalm 122:5). *Shalom* designates a state of affairs or a relationship in which things are balanced out, where rightful claims are satisfied. This can only happen in a society governed by justice. Thus, the modern concept of positive or sustainable peace involves a return to the original, more holistic concept of peace with justice and safety implicit in the original Hebrew.[37] Injustice and oppression lead inevitably to anxiety and turmoil, with little chance of wellbeing (Isaiah 48:22; 57:21).[38]

Once we stop reading Greco-Roman or Western presuppositions about justice as legal equity into the Hebrew Bible, a more holistic concept of justice emerges in Isaiah, one consistent with the concept of positive peace. The Western concept of justice as a person's proper conduct over against an absolute ethic of justice can be contrasted with the Hebrew notion of justice as the divine order by which all things are rightly governed. We have to recognize that in ancient Israel and in the Hebrew Bible justice was always a more inclusive concept, concerning people and relationships rather than abstract ideas or norms. Thus, *shalom* and the Hebrew conception of justice represent in a partial, provisional way what we have now come to call human security and sustainable human development.

Sustainable peace also requires what we now call "good governance"—political accountability, respect for human rights, public safety, and the protection of civilians. And, beyond all these things, scholars and practitioners are beginning to acknowledge that sustainable peace requires something even more difficult: a profound sense of repentance, forgiveness, and reconciliation between states, social groups, communities, and individuals.[39] We can see this exemplified in a variety of "truth commissions," not only in South Africa, but also after civil wars, with their related atrocities, in a wide array of countries, including Bolivia, Guatemala, Ethiopia, and Sierra Leone.[40]

Still, what makes the concern for peace and social justice, as part of the countervailing narrative of a holistic concept of positive peace, different in Isaiah from similar concerns expressed in the contemporary peace studies literature is that it is embedded in an explicitly *religious* narrative. Isaiah calls Judah the "house of Jacob" (Isaiah 2:5-6), referring to the country's covenant with Yahweh, its requirements and promises, in the Genesis narratives. Isaiah is effectively saying that Judah's security and wellbeing depend on cultural and religious authenticity—its linkage to Yahweh.

Thus, Isaiah's famous oracle (Isaiah 2:4-6) is embedded in a religious narrative that expresses Isaiah's theology of international relations. This theology shows how cultural and religious authenticity is related to peace, security, and economic development. Isaiah's narrative is about the decay of Israel's religious life, not the absence of a religious life as in a modern secular society. Isaiah is concerned about the decay, corruption, and distortion of genuine religion by a people who think they are being religious and fulfilling the demands of worship and Torah obedience (Isaiah 1:2-6; 2:6-22; 3:1–4:1; 5:1-7, 8-30). Yahweh's judgment of their disobedience through Isaiah's oracles focuses on the paradox of how an outwardly "religious" nation in terms of ritual and public worship can be, from Yahweh's perspective, a godless nation. Dramatically, Isaiah asks, how can a people truly worship Yahweh when they have blood on their hands? They lack knowledge, discernment, or understanding of what is really going on in domestic and international politics because they are no longer trained by the Torah to interpret the world in this way (Isaiah 1:16; cf. 10:6; 29:13-14).

Conclusion

For scholars and practitioners reading Isaiah, it would be easy to try to separate facts from values, morality from causality, or explanatory from interpretive theory. But a post-positivist approach to biblical interpretation as well as to international relations reveals the larger, underlying relationships in society and politics that underpin human security in Isaiah's day as well as our own. If we resist this normative level of intellectual engagement we multiply the risks of unintended, negative consequences—blowback—in foreign policy.

What is Judah or Israel (for)? This is the question underlying Isaiah's prophesying. By analogy today we might ask, what is the United States (for)? or the European Union? or any modern political entity that wields power? These are questions of identity and significance, and social constructivists have shown us that choices in foreign policy cannot be reduced to problems in quandary ethics. A state has to have a national self before it can have a national interest. What kind of polity does a people seek for itself in the world, and what kind of world does it seek for its polity? Questions of meaning, identity, and foreign policy are inextricably bound up.

Isaiah's criticism of Judah's foreign policy occurs because its rulers have a narrow conception of national security that underplays the importance of cultural authenticity for genuine human development. They sell out their birthright and abandon their responsibility to promote *shalom*, settling for the immediate gratification of idolatry, political stability, and material prosperity. All this occurs in a society that while it claims to be living by the Torah and truly worshipping Yahweh, is really based on injustice and economic oppression.

— Section III —

ETHICS OF FORCE

14

OF WAR (FOUR ARTICLES)
Summa Theologica

—Thomas Aquinas

We must now consider war, under which head there are four points of inquiry:

(1) Whether some kind of war is lawful?
(2) Whether it is lawful for clerics to fight?
(3) Whether it is lawful for belligerents to lay ambushes?
(4) Whether it is lawful to fight on holy days?

Whether it is always sinful to wage war?

Objection 1: It would seem that it is always sinful to wage war. Because punishment is not inflicted except for sin. Now those who wage war are threatened by Our Lord with punishment, according to Mt. 26:52: "All that take the sword shall perish with the sword." Therefore all wars are unlawful.

Objection 2: Further, whatever is contrary to a Divine precept is a sin. But war is contrary to a Divine precept, for it is written (Mt. 5:39): "But I say to you not to resist evil"; and (Rm. 12:19): "Not revenging yourselves, my dearly beloved, but give place unto wrath." Therefore war is always sinful.

Objection 3: Further, nothing, except sin, is contrary to an act of virtue. But war is contrary to peace. Therefore war is always a sin.

Objection 4: Further, the exercise of a lawful thing is itself lawful, as is evident in scientific exercises. But warlike exercises which take place in tournaments are forbidden by the Church, since those who are slain in these trials are deprived of ecclesiastical burial. Therefore it seems that war is a sin in itself.

On the contrary, Augustine says in a sermon on the son of the centurion [*Ep. ad Marcel. cxxxviii]: "If the Christian Religion forbade war altogether, those who sought salutary advice in the Gospel would rather have been counselled to cast aside their arms, and to give up soldiering altogether. On the contrary, they were told: 'Do violence to no man . . . and be content with your pay' [*Lk. 3:14]. If he commanded them to be content with their pay, he did not forbid soldiering."

I answer that, In order for a war to be just, three things are necessary. First, the authority of the sovereign by whose command the war is to be waged. For it is not the business of a private individual to declare war, because he can seek for redress of his rights from the tribunal of his superior. Moreover it is not the business of a private individual to summon together the people, which has to be done in wartime. And as the care of the common weal is committed to those who are in authority, it is their business to watch over the common weal of the city, kingdom, or province subject to them. And just as it is lawful for them to have recourse to the sword in defending that common weal against internal disturbances, when they punish evil-doers, according to the words of the Apostle (Rm. 13:4): "He beareth not the sword in vain: for he is God's minister, an avenger to execute wrath upon him that doth evil"; so too, it is their business to have recourse to the sword of war in defending the common weal against external enemies. Hence it is said to those who are in authority (Ps. 81:4): "Rescue the poor: and deliver the needy out of the hand of the sinner"; and for this reason Augustine says (Contra Faust. xxii, 75): "The natural order conducive to peace among mortals demands that the power to declare and counsel war should be in the hands of those who hold the supreme authority."

Secondly, a just cause is required, namely that those who are attacked, should be attacked because they deserve it on account of some fault. Wherefore Augustine says (Questions. in Hept., qu. x, super Jos.): "A just war is wont to be described as one that avenges wrongs, when a nation or state has to be punished, for refusing to make amends for the wrongs inflicted by its subjects, or to restore what it has seized unjustly."

Thirdly, it is necessary that the belligerents should have a rightful intention, so that they intend the advancement of good, or the avoidance of evil. Hence Augustine says (De Verb. Dom. [*The words quoted are to be found not in St. Augustine's works, but Can. Apud. Caus. xxiii, qu. 1]): "True religion looks upon as peaceful those wars that are waged not for motives of aggrandizement, or cruelty, but with the object of securing peace, of punishing evil-doers, and of uplifting the good." For it may happen that the war is declared by the legitimate authority, and for a just cause, and yet be rendered unlawful through a wicked intention. Hence Augustine says (Contra Faust. xxii, 74): "The passion for inflicting harm, the cruel thirst for vengeance, an unpacific and relentless spirit, the fever of revolt, the lust of power, and such like things, all these are rightly condemned in war."

Reply to Objection 1: As Augustine says (Contra Faust. xxii, 70): "To take the sword is to arm oneself in order to take the life of anyone, without the command or permission of superior or lawful authority." On the other hand, to have recourse to the sword (as a private person) by the authority of the sovereign or judge, or (as a public person) through zeal for justice, and by the authority, so to speak, of God, is not to "take the sword," but to use it as commissioned by another, wherefore it does not deserve punishment. And yet even those who make sinful use of the sword are not always slain with the sword, yet they always perish with their own sword, because, unless they repent, they are punished eternally for their sinful use of the sword.

Reply to Objection 2: Such like precepts, as Augustine observes (De Serm. Dom. in Monte i, 19), should always be borne in readiness of mind, so that we be ready to obey them, and, if necessary, to refrain from resistance or self-defense. Nevertheless it is necessary sometimes for a man to act otherwise for the common good, or for the good of those with whom he is fighting. Hence Augustine says (Ep. ad Marcellin. cxxxviii): "Those whom we have to punish with a kindly severity, it is necessary to handle in many ways against their will. For when we are stripping a man of the lawlessness of sin, it is good for him to be vanquished, since nothing is more hopeless than the happiness of sinners, whence arises a guilty impunity, and an evil will, like an internal enemy."

Reply to Objection 3: Those who wage war justly aim at peace, and so they are not opposed to peace, except to the evil peace, which Our Lord "came not to send upon earth" (Mt. 10:34). Hence Augustine says (Ep. ad Bonif. clxxxix): "We do not seek peace in order to be at war, but we go to war that we may have peace. Be peaceful, therefore, in warring, so that you may vanquish those whom you war against, and bring them to the prosperity of peace."

Reply to Objection 4: Manly exercises in warlike feats of arms are not all forbidden, but those which are inordinate and perilous, and end in slaying or plundering. In olden times warlike exercises presented no such danger, and hence they were called "exercises of arms" or "bloodless wars," as Jerome states in an epistle [*Reference incorrect: cf. Veget., De Re Milit. i].

Whether it is lawful for clerics and bishops to fight?

Objection 1: It would seem lawful for clerics and bishops to fight. For, as stated above (Article [1]), wars are lawful and just in so far as they protect the poor and the entire common weal from suffering at the hands of the foe. Now this seems to be above all the duty of prelates, for Gregory says (Hom. in Ev. xiv): "The wolf comes upon the sheep, when any unjust and rapacious man oppresses those who are faithful and humble. But he who was thought to be the shepherd, and was not, leaveth the sheep, and flieth, for he fears lest the wolf hurt him, and dares not stand up against his injustice." Therefore it is lawful for prelates and clerics to fight.

Objection 2: Further, Pope Leo IV writes (xxiii, qu. 8, can. Igitur): "As untoward tidings had frequently come from the Saracen side, some said that the Saracens would come to the port of Rome secretly and covertly; for which reason we commanded our people to gather together, and ordered them to go down to the seashore." Therefore it is lawful for bishops to fight.

Objection 3: Further, apparently, it comes to the same whether a man does a thing himself, or consents to its being done by another, according to Rm. 1:32: "They who do such things, are worthy of death, and not only they that do them, but they also that consent to them that do them." Now those, above all, seem to consent to a thing, who induce others to do it. But it is lawful for bishops and clerics to induce others to fight: for it is written (xxiii, qu. 8, can. Hortatu) that Charles went to war with the Lombards at the instance and entreaty of Adrian, bishop of Rome. Therefore they also are allowed to fight.

Objection 4: Further, whatever is right and meritorious in itself, is lawful for prelates and clerics. Now it is sometimes right and meritorious to make war, for it is written (xxiii, qu. 8, can. Omni timore) that if "a man die for the true faith, or to save his country, or in defense of Christians, God will give him a heavenly reward." Therefore it is lawful for bishops and clerics to fight.

On the contrary, It was said to Peter as representing bishops and clerics (Mt. 16:52): "Put up again thy sword into the scabbard [Vulg.: 'its place'] [*'Scabbard' is the reading in Jn. 18:11]." Therefore it is not lawful for them to fight.

I answer that, Several things are requisite for the good of a human society: and a number of things are done better and quicker by a number of persons than by one, as the Philosopher observes (Polit. i, 1), while certain occupations are so inconsistent with one another, that they cannot be fittingly exercised at the same time; wherefore those who are deputed to important duties are forbidden to occupy themselves with things of small importance. Thus according to human laws, soldiers who are deputed to warlike pursuits are forbidden to engage in commerce [*Cod. xii, 35, De Re Milit.].

Now warlike pursuits are altogether incompatible with the duties of a bishop and a cleric, for two reasons. The first reason is a general one, because, to wit, warlike pursuits are full of unrest, so that they hinder the mind very much from the contemplation of Divine things, the praise of God, and prayers for the people, which belong to the duties of a cleric. Wherefore just as commercial enterprises are forbidden to clerics, because they unsettle the mind too much, so too are warlike pursuits, according to 2 Tim. 2:4: "No man being a soldier to God, entangleth himself with secular business." The second reason is a special one, because, to wit, all the clerical Orders are directed to the ministry of the altar, on which the Passion of Christ is represented sacramentally, according to 1 Cor. 11:26: "As often as you shall eat this bread, and drink the chalice, you shall show the death of the Lord, until He come." Wherefore it is unbecoming for them to slay or shed blood, and it is more fitting that they should be ready to shed their own blood for Christ, so as to imitate in deed what they portray in their ministry. For this reason it has been decreed that those who shed blood, even without sin, become irregular. Now no man who has a certain duty to perform, can lawfully do that which renders him unfit for that duty. Wherefore it is altogether unlawful for clerics to fight, because war is directed to the shedding of blood.

Reply to Objection 1: Prelates ought to withstand not only the wolf who brings spiritual death upon the flock, but also the pillager and the oppressor who work bodily harm; not, however, by having recourse themselves to material arms, but by means of spiritual weapons, according to the saying of the Apostle (2 Cor. 10:4): "The weapons of our warfare are not carnal, but mighty through God." Such are salutary warnings, devout prayers, and, for those who are obstinate, the sentence of excommunication.

Reply to Objection 2: Prelates and clerics may, by the authority of their superiors, take part in wars, not indeed by taking up arms themselves, but by affording spiritual help to those who fight justly, by exhorting and absolving them, and by other like spiritual helps. Thus in the Old Testament (Joshua 6:4) the priests were commanded to sound the sacred trumpets in the battle. It was for this purpose that bishops or clerics were first allowed to go to the front: and it is an abuse of this permission, if any of them take up arms themselves.

Reply to Objection 3: As stated above (Question [23], Article [4], ad 2) every power, art or virtue that regards the end, has to dispose that which is directed to the end. Now, among the faithful, carnal wars should be considered as having for their end the Divine spiritual good to which clerics are deputed. Wherefore it is the duty of clerics to dispose and counsel other men to engage in just wars. For they are forbidden to take up arms, not as though it were a sin, but because such an occupation is unbecoming their personality.

Reply to Objection 4: Although it is meritorious to wage a just war, nevertheless it is rendered unlawful for clerics, by reason of their being deputed to works more meritorious still. Thus the marriage act may be meritorious; and yet it becomes reprehensible in those who have vowed virginity, because they are bound to a yet greater good.

Whether it is lawful to lay ambushes in war?

Objection 1: It would seem that it is unlawful to lay ambushes in war. For it is written (Dt. 16:20): "Thou shalt follow justly after that which is just." But ambushes, since they are a kind of deception, seem to pertain to injustice. Therefore it is unlawful to lay ambushes even in a just war.

Objection 2: Further, ambushes and deception seem to be opposed to faithfulness even as lies are. But since we are bound to keep faith with all men, it is wrong to lie to anyone, as Augustine states (Contra Mend. xv). Therefore, as one is bound to keep faith with one's enemy, as Augustine states (Ep. ad Bonif. clxxxix), it seems that it is unlawful to lay ambushes for one's enemies.

Objection 3: Further, it is written (Mt. 7:12): "Whatsoever you would that men should do to you, do you also to them": and we ought to observe this in all our dealings with our neighbor. Now our enemy is our neighbor. Therefore, since no man wishes ambushes or deceptions to be prepared for himself, it seems that no one ought to carry on war by laying ambushes.

On the contrary, Augustine says (Questions. in Hept. qu. x super Jos): "Provided the war be just, it is no concern of justice whether it be carried on openly or by ambushes": and he proves this by the authority of the Lord, Who commanded Joshua to lay ambushes for the city of Hai (Joshua 8:2).

I answer that, The object of laying ambushes is in order to deceive the enemy. Now a man may be deceived by another's word or deed in two ways. First, through being told something false, or through the breaking of a promise, and this is always unlawful. No one ought to deceive the enemy in this way, for there are certain "rights of war and covenants, which ought to be observed even among enemies," as Ambrose states (De Officiis i).

Secondly, a man may be deceived by what we say or do, because we do not declare our purpose or meaning to him. Now we are not always bound to do this, since even in the Sacred Doctrine many things have to be concealed, especially from unbelievers, lest they deride it, according to Mt. 7:6: "Give not that which is holy, to dogs." Wherefore much more ought the plan of campaign to be hidden from the enemy. For this reason among other things that a soldier has to learn is the art of concealing his purpose lest it come to the enemy's knowledge, as stated in the Book on Strategy [*Stratagematum i, 1] by Frontinus. Such like concealment is what is meant by an ambush which may be lawfully employed in a just war.

Nor can these ambushes be properly called deceptions, nor are they contrary to justice or to a well-ordered will. For a man would have an inordinate will if he were unwilling that others should hide anything from him.

This suffices for the Replies to the Objections.

Whether it is lawful to fight on holy days?

Objection 1: It would seem unlawful to fight on holy days. For holy days are instituted that we may give our time to the things of God. Hence they are included in the keeping of the Sabbath prescribed Ex. 20:8: for "sabbath" is interpreted "rest." But wars are full of unrest. Therefore by no means is it lawful to fight on holy days.

Objection 2: Further, certain persons are reproached (Is. 58:3) because on fast-days they exacted what was owing to them, were guilty of strife, and of smiting with the fist. Much more, therefore, is it unlawful to fight on holy days.

Objection 3: Further, no ill deed should be done to avoid temporal harm. But fighting on a holy day seems in itself to be an ill deed. Therefore no one should fight on a holy day even through the need of avoiding temporal harm.

On the contrary, It is written (1 Machab 2:41): The Jews rightly determined . . . saying: "Whosoever shall come up against us to fight on the Sabbath-day, we will fight against him."

I answer that, The observance of holy days is no hindrance to those things which are ordained to man's safety, even that of his body. Hence Our Lord argued with the Jews, saying (Jn. 7:23): "Are you angry at Me because I have healed the whole man on the Sabbath-day?" Hence physicians may lawfully attend to their patients on holy days. Now there is much more reason for safeguarding the common weal (whereby many are saved from being slain, and innumerable evils both temporal and spiritual prevented), than the bodily safety of an individual. Therefore, for the purpose of safeguarding the common weal of the faithful, it is lawful to carry on a war on holy days, provided there be need for doing so: because it would be to tempt God, if notwithstanding such a need, one were to choose to refrain from fighting.

However, as soon as the need ceases, it is no longer lawful to fight on a holy day, for the reasons given: wherefore this suffices for the Replies to the Objections.

JUST WAR TRADITION
Is It Credible?

—John Howard Yoder

Public dialogue in the U.S. about the Persian Gulf War has drawn heavily on the language of the just war tradition—more so than has been the case with any war since at least the 1860s. The tradition has been appealed to by journalists and politicians, as if it were common knowledge, as a basis for making (or denying) the claim that the war in the Persian Gulf should go on.

Most of the time, the just war tradition is used to test a particular war (or a strategy or a weapon) for its moral and legal acceptability. That was done recently in the *Christian Century* by James Turner Johnson and Alan Geyer (February 6–13 [1991]). The reciprocal approach is also needed: the tradition can be tested by a war. Does the tradition in fact facilitate shared moral and legal decisions by so labeling issues that they can be adjudicated?

Johnson is right that the just war tradition is "deeply rooted in both Christian tradition and international law." He is also right, in the several books he has written on the theme, in reporting that it has never been universally accepted or applied by Christian moralists or statesmen. It has never been promulgated *ex cathedra* by Rome, though it is in the Anglican, Lutheran, and Reformed confessions. Deep rootage does not make the tradition morally true; but it does set the stage for giving it a fair test. The Gulf War, both in the ways it is like all wars and in the ways it is unique, makes the testing both concrete and urgent, while also heightening the chances that the "facts" available when this text is drafted will have been changed by the time it reaches readers.

There is no reason for me to survey the current debate as concerns the substance of the arguments, nor to suggest my own verdict on each of the contested points, as I would do in a setting where time and structure would permit a serious debate in just war terms. What I want to do is to view the debate as a test of whether the entire just war mode of moral discourse is adequate to guide the responsible citizenship of people who claim that their first moral obligation is to the God whom Jesus taught them to praise and obey, and their second to the neighbor, *including the enemy*, whom Jesus taught them to love.

* *Christian Century*, March 13, 1991, 295–98.

The just war tradition does serve, some of the time, as an agenda, a checklist of questions which it is fitting to ask in considering war. If your concern is not on that list (for example, if you think "love your enemy" is itself an adequate moral guide), it will be denied standing in the debate. If on the other hand you ask about "last resort" or "innocent immunity," others will grant your fight to put the question. That being the system's intention, there are three questions we obviously can pursue: a) Does the system as system have integrity in that its concepts are so defined as really to serve as criteria? b) Do the people claiming to use the system have moral integrity in that they will renounce the strategies and actions which the system rejects? c) Is the system compatible with the other elements of Christian moral commitment which it does not expressly include? The first of these questions is our first concern here. My more basic concern as a Christian pacifist would of course be with the third.

Does the just war tradition work? Let's consider some instances.

1. The Facts of the Case

As distinguished from people holding to pacifism or the "holy war," people holding to the just war tradition claim to make decisions on the empirically knowable facts of the case. It is assumed that these facts are knowable in principle and known in fact: Has there been naked aggression? Is the belligerent government legitimate? Has everything else been tried? Moralists have assumed that these facts could be ascertained. In our present experience that is not so easy. The control of information is a science and an art (known in the trade—in the language of billiards—as "spin"). In early February this reached a new level of brazenness. Margaret Tutwiler informed us that when the President had told conservative Protestant broadcasters that the U.S. wanted unconditional surrender and a war crimes trial, he was expressing his emotions, not policy; that when Secretary of State James Baker and his Soviet colleague Alexander Bessmertnykh said that the coalition would accept a ceasefire and would promise a regional peace conference, that was inoperative because it had not been checked. For "spin" purposes, it helps to have several different statements, each supposed to please somebody or send some message, with none of them binding and no call for consistency among them. From mid-January to mid-February we were told almost daily both that there is no schedule and that the war is proceeding on schedule. On February 13–14, Generals Kelly, Schwarzkopf, and Neal gave significantly different readings as to whether the tragedy of the bunker bombing in Baghdad would lead to changes in targeting policy. All the media commentaries interpret these discrepancies more in terms of spin control than of truth.

2. Who in Fact Does Decide?

The just war tradition was not originally intended to be used in democracies. It was originally assumed that decisions about war belong to sovereigns. The democratic vision which makes the citizenry "sovereign" changes how the system has to work. Disinformation and spin control invalidate the administrators' claim to legitimacy. Civilian and military administrators are not trained to distinguish dissent from disloyalty, secrecy from security. They thus can refuse to provide "the people" with the wherewithal for evaluating the claimed justifications.

This change makes the availability of usable nonsectarian language like that of the just war tradition all the more necessary, because there must be debate. Yet in the sovereign's eyes the debate seems to be unfair and disloyal. Both George Bush and Margaret Tutwiler would rather that we not all consider ourselves entitled to share in moral decisions about the killing done in our name. This phenomenon is not new, however. Ferdinand and Isabella did not appreciate the questions Francisco de Vitoria was asking about their treatment of Native Americans.

I do not propose to side simply with the media in their complaints about access and censorship. Yet it is clear that without reliable sources of information there is no basis for evaluating most of the claims on which a just war decision is based. When the head of the Joint Chiefs parries a factual question with "trust me," I don't.

3. Reality Is Deep and Wide

The just war paradigm for decision, like much of the rest of ethical casuistry, assumes a punctual conception of legal-moral decision. The decision to go to war, or to use such and such a strategy, it is assumed, is made at one time, not before or after that instant. What is either right or wrong is that punctual decision, based upon the facts of the case at just that instant, and the just war tradition delivers the criteria for adjudicating that decision. This procedure undervalues the longitudinal dimensions of the conflict. Here Geyer's reading is truer to the facts than Johnson's, as he takes account of what he calls "the burdens of history." During the first Reagan-Bush decade, other cases of "naked aggression" somehow did not need to be punished so rigorously. Iraq was textually told in July that the U.S. would not intervene; the classical distinction between "moral" just cause and "material" just cause becomes pertinent at this point.

In real life most decisions are not punctual. They have longitude—they were prepared for by a lot that went before. Setting mid-January as a firm deadline, counter to most of the wisdom of ancient diplomacy and the modern social science of conflict resolution, was done weeks before. As the date approached, Bush's definition of its degree of firmness escalated to the point that by the 15th he in fact had no freedom to do otherwise. Yet the just war paradigm had not illuminated the weeks spent painting the U.S. and Iraq into their respective corners in the way it looked on January 15. Even less did it take account of the still longer predisposing factors for which the U.S. is more to blame than Saddam Hussein: the decade spent competing with the U.S.S.R. in building up Hussein's forces, and the explicit statements made in July to the effect that what Hussein might choose to do with border problems was not our concern. The full amplitude of the just war tradition would be capable of considering such components of complicity and even entrapment as part of the definition of just cause, but our public discourse has consistently described the case as if the history of Mesopotamia began in August.

The claim that the UN resolutions suffice to assure "just authority" is belied by destruction in Iraq unrelated to freeing Kuwait (bridges, roads, municipal water and sewage systems) and by restatements of war aims (asking Iraqis to replace Saddam Hussein, demanding unconditional surrender and a war crimes trial) which go far beyond the UN objective (note as well the elements of bad faith in the UN appeal to which Geyer pointed).

Does a vote in which despite enormous pressures 47 senators opposed the resort to military force (and some of the "yea" voters said the president had acted wrongly throughout the fall but now they would rally 'round the flag) constitute a moral mandate? One can grant that this consultation of Congress is better than stonewalling completely the right of Congress to be consulted, and that the UN actions constitute more backing than we ever even thought about requesting for Panama or Grenada. Thus the criterion of "legitimate authority" is more nearly met than at some other times. Yet the scale of the air war has gone far beyond the UN authorization, as did the continuing escalation of the war aims so that by February 15 Pentagon projections were assuming the demand for unconditional surrender rather than withdrawal, and by February 25 flanking actions were undertaken to prevent withdrawal.

4. Shared Definitions?

The public is deceived by the tacit assumption that because the "criteria" can be listed in common-sense language there must be a shared definition of most of the operational terms, as there is in a natural science or even in law. A criterion is something you can measure with; that can be done only if its meaning is shared by the several parties. In real use, however, most of the just war "criteria" are so subject to bias that they do not serve to adjudicate with any semblance of objectivity. The words like "legitimate authority" and "just cause" provide a common language, but they serve only to talk past each other. The contrast between my esteemed colleagues and good friends Geyer and Johnson exemplifies this brilliantly; the words are the same, but they use them to describe two different worlds.

5. What Is the Alternative?

In most cases we are deceived by the tacit assumption that *if and when* the criteria are *not* met, one does not go to war. The doctrine can (theoretically) have teeth at several points: refusal to obey an unjust order, "selective conscientious objection" when called to serve an unjust cause, suing for peace when one cannot win without using unjust means, prosecuting a war crime. Yet no nonpacifist church has prepared its members for such hard choices. No independent information sources assure the availability of the facts that would demand or enable such resistance.

6. The Rubbery Claim of Discrimination

The hopeless debate over the Ash Wednesday bunker attack demonstrates how rubbery is the claim of discrimination. Johnson is right that "smarter" weapons can be discriminating; yet the exponential escalation of the number of sorties throws away much of that gain. More is abandoned when the concept of "military target" is expanded to include the main highway between Baghdad and Amman, so that when Jordanian refugee buses and fuel trucks are destroyed it is the drivers' fault. When antiaircraft artillery is placed on the roof of a home it is the householders' fault. When scores of women and children take overnight refuge in a bunker it is Saddam's fault. Assigning blame is not the same as moral discernment. Such reallocation of "fault" may have some pertinence for the sacrament of absolution (where "intention" matters in a particular way), or as mitigation in a war-crimes procedure, but it does not protect innocent lives. When General H. Norman Schwarzkopf said the next day that "all Saddam Hussein needs to do to stop our killing civilians is to surrender," he replaced a restraint *in bello* with an accusation *ad bellum*.

Discussion is radically distorted by assuming that the only "legitimate means" question is civilian immunity. There are many more treaty commitments, all the way to the October 1980 conventions on "excessive use of conventional weapons" (certainly a fair description of the scale of the air war since mid-January).

7. How Does One Measure "Proportionality"?

We must weigh the devastation of Iraq (even if there were no civilian deaths) and the promise of decades of future trouble in the region against the evil of failing to reverse promptly the August 2 annexation. By what coefficients do we do that weighing?

What then is the tradition good for? The current debate, and the Johnson-Geyer exchange as one instance, suffices (other evidences, other hard-to-apply criteria, could be added) to demonstrate the incapacity of the system to yield a clear and commonly accessible adjudication of contested cases. What the just war tradition is really good for is that together with pacifism it can identify and denounce the less restrained views which in fact dominate public discourse and decision-making. These views are in principle three:

1. Many people think that since war consists by definition in the breakdown of civility, it is not only counterfactual but also counterproductive to try to retrieve the notion of moral accountability within the struggle. A maximum effort subject to minimal scruples will best end the anarchy and the suffering. Michael Walzer calls this stance "realism," emphasizing by the quotes that its claim to self-evidence is spurious. Reinhold Niebuhr espoused the term with less restraint, though his view of the moral issue was highly nuanced. Charles Clayton Morrison called war "hell"; hell is where there are no moral decisions, only the outworking of earlier sins. Against this, the just war tradition maintains that moral accountability and the possibility of restraint do not end when war looms. The a priori presumption against recourse to war needs to be overridden by fact-based warrants (*jus ad bellum*); once hostilities are undertaken the means must be legitimate and proportionate (*jus in bello*).

2. Many people think that what justifies war is a transcendent cause, discerned by a prophetic person. Overlapping with the "just" alternative in early medieval thought, "holy" war or the Crusade differs from the just war (properly so-called) as to cause, last resort, and probable success, and usually with regard to the human dignity of the enemy/ infidel. Against this view, the just war tradition maintains that even wrong belief does not deprive humans of their rights, and even a religious rationale does not justify wrong means.

3. Many people think that war frees its actors from moral restraints by offering a unique setting for the proof of the virility of a political elite, of military personnel, or of a nation. The conflictual activities delicately referred to by some of our rulers as "ass-kicking" must be understood not so much ethically as ritually. The adversary is not a fellow human with dignity (before God and the law) equal to one's own, but an opportunity to prove one's manly qualities by facing danger and shedding blood.

When held to honestly, the just war tradition agrees with pacifism in rejecting these three views. It is these three views, however, which in fact dominate real politics. The fundamental deception imposed on our public discourse is that despite the use of just war categories by sincere people, the overall shape of the macro decisions is determined by the other three kinds of dynamism.

Sometimes this deception may be intentional and cynical; but that is not my present claim. More prevalent and more insidious is the fact that just war discourse deceives sincere people by the very nature of its claim to base moral discernment upon the facts of the case and on universally accessible rational principles. It lets them think that their morality is somehow less provincial and more accessible to others than if it referred explicitly to the data of Christian faith, including the words and the work of Jesus.

"Has there ever been a just war?" Cynics ask this because they think that their disregard for restraint is thereby validated. Pacifists ask it because they wonder how seriously to take the just war thinkers' claim not to have sold out morally. The question is wrong. The basis of moral obligation is not the record of past successes in doing right. Has there ever been a perfectly monogamous spouse? A faithful Christian church? The fitting question is whether *in the current case* those who claim that heritage are *in fact* letting it set the limits of their action. On that question the jury is still out. The claim of my nonpacifist colleagues that the system they are using is more socially responsible, more understandable to ordinary people, more culturally accessible to people of other value communities, more able to manage with discrimination the factual data of political decisions, than is my testimony to Jesus' words and work, still has the burden of proof.

MORAL CLARITY IN A TIME OF WAR

—George Weigel

In Book Three of Tolstoy's epic, *War and Peace*, the hero, Pierre Bezukhov, arrives at the battlefield of Borodino to find that the fog of war has descended, obscuring everything he had expected to be clear. There is no order, there are no familiar patterns of action, all is contingency. He could not, Count Bezukhov admits, "even distinguish our troops from the enemy's." And the worst is yet to come, for once the real fighting begins, chaos takes over in full.

From the *Iliad* to Tolstoy and beyond, that familiar trope, "the fog of war," has been used to evoke the millennia-old experience of the radical uncertainty of combat. The gut-wrenching opening scenes of *Saving Private Ryan* brought this ancient truth home to a new generation of Americans: in even the most brilliantly planned military campaign, such as the Allied invasion of Normandy, contingency is soon king, and overcoming it draws on a man's deepest reserves of courage and wit.

Some analysts, however, take the trope of "the fog of war" a philosophical step further and suggest that warfare takes place beyond the reach of moral reason, in a realm of interest and necessity where moral argument is a pious diversion at best and, at worst, a lethal distraction from the deadly serious business at hand.

To which men and women formed by biblical religion, by the great tradition of Western moral philosophy, or by the encounter between biblical religion and moral philosophy that we call moral theology must say: "No, that is a serious mistake." Nothing human takes place outside the realm or beyond the reach of moral reason. Every human action takes place within the purview of moral judgment.

Thus moral muteness in a time of war *is* a moral stance: it can be a stance born of fear; it can be a stance born of indifference; it can be a stance born of cynicism about the human capacity to promote justice, freedom, and order, all of which are moral goods. But whatever its psychological, spiritual, or intellectual origins, moral muteness in wartime is a form of moral judgment—a deficient and dangerous form of moral judgment.

* *First Things* 128 (December 2002): 20–27.

That is why the venerable just war tradition—a form of moral reasoning that traces its origins to St. Augustine in fifth-century North Africa—is such an important *public* resource. For fifteen hundred years, as it has been developed amidst the historical white water of political, technological, and military change, the just war tradition has allowed men and women to avoid the trap of moral muteness, to think through the tangle of problems involved in the decision to go to war and in the conduct of war itself—and to do all that in a way that recognizes the distinctive realities of war. Indeed, in the national debate launched by the war against terrorism and the threat of outlaw states armed with weapons of mass destruction, we can hear echoes of the moral reasoning of Augustine and his successors:

- What is the just cause that would justify putting our armed forces, and the American homeland, in harm's way?
- Who has the authority to wage war? The President? The President and Congress? The United States acting alone? The United States with a sufficient number of allies? The United Nations?
- Is it ever right to use armed force first? Can going first ever be, not just morally permissible, but morally imperative?
- How can the use of armed force contribute to the pursuit of justice, freedom, and order in world affairs?

That these are the questions that instinctively emerge in the American national debate suggests that the just war tradition remains alive in our national cultural memory. And that is a very good thing. But it is also a somewhat surprising thing, for the past thirty years have witnessed a great forgetting of the classic just war tradition among those who had long been assumed to be its primary intellectual custodians: the nation's religious leaders, moral philosophers, and moral theologians. That forgetting has been painfully evident in much of the recent commentary from religious leaders in the matter of U.S. policy toward Iraq, commentary that is often far more dependent on political and strategic intuitions of dubious merit than on solid moral reasoning. The fact of the matter today is that the just war tradition, as a historically informed method of rigorous moral reasoning, is far more alive in our service academies than in our divinity schools and faculties of theology; the just war tradition "lives" more vigorously in the officer corps, in the Uniform Code of Military Justice, and at the higher levels of the Pentagon than it does at the National Council of Churches, in certain offices at the United States Conference of Catholic Bishops, or on the Princeton faculty. (There are different degrees of forgetfulness here, of course, and recent statements by the U.S. Catholic bishops on the question of Iraq were of a higher degree of intellectual seriousness than the effusions of other national religious bodies. But the bishops' statements did, I would argue, continue a pattern of just war forgetfulness whose origins I shall discuss below.)

This "forgetting" in the places where the just war tradition has been nurtured for centuries has led to confusions about the tradition itself. Those confusions have, in turn, led to distorted and, in some cases, irresponsible analyses from the quarters to which Americans usually look for moral guidance. That is why it is imperative that the just war tradition be retrieved and developed in these first perilous years of the twenty-first century. At issue is the public moral hygiene of the Republic—and our national capacity to think with moral rigor about some very threatening realities of today's world.

* * *

In one of last year's most celebrated books, *Warrior Politics*, veteran foreign correspondent Robert Kaplan suggested that only a "pagan ethos" can provide us with the kind of leadership capable of safely traversing the global disorder of the twenty-first century. Kaplan's "pagan ethos" has several interlocking parts. It is shaped by a tragic sense of life, one that recognizes the ubiquity, indeed inevitability, of conflict. It teaches a heroic concept of history: fate is not all, and wise statecraft can lead to better futures. It promotes a realistic appreciation of the boundaries of the possible. It celebrates patriotism as a virtue. And it is shaped by a grim determination to avoid "moralism," which Kaplan (following Machiavelli, the Chinese sage Sun Tzu, and Max Weber) identifies with a morality of intentions, oblivious to the peril of unintended or unanticipated consequences. For Kaplan, exemplars of this "pagan ethos" in the past century include Theodore Roosevelt, Winston Churchill, and Franklin Roosevelt.

Reading *Warrior Politics*, and reflecting on the concept of morality that informs it, reminded me of an old story related by Father John Courtney Murray, S.J. During the Korean War, the proudly Protestant Henry Luce, son of China missionaries, found himself confused by the debate over "morality and foreign policy" that Harry Truman's "police action" had stirred up. What, Luce asked Fr. Murray, did foreign policy have to do with the Sermon on the Mount? "What," Fr. Murray replied, "makes you think that morality is identical with the Sermon on the Mount?" Kaplan, a contemporary exponent of foreign policy realism, seems to share Henry Luce's misimpression that in the classic tradition of the West the moral life is reducible to the ethics of personal probity and interpersonal relationships, the implication being that issues of statecraft exist somewhere "outside" the moral universe. The just war tradition takes a very different view.

As indicated above, the classic tradition insists that no aspect of the human condition falls outside the purview of moral reasoning and judgment—including politics. Politics is a human enterprise. Because human beings are creatures of intelligence and free will—because human beings are inescapably *moral* actors—every human activity, including politics, is subject to moral scrutiny. There is no Archimedean point outside the moral universe from which even the wisest "pagan" statesman can leverage world politics.

Indeed, what Kaplan proposes as a "pagan ethos" is a form of moral reasoning that would be enriched by a serious encounter with the classic just war tradition. One need not be a "pagan," as Kaplan proposes, to understand the enduring impact of original sin on the world and its affairs; Genesis 1–3 and a good dose of Augustine's *City of God* will do the job just as well, and arguably better. One need not be a "pagan" to be persuaded that moral conviction, human ingenuity, and wise statecraft can bend history's course in a more humane direction; one need only reflect on the achievement of Pope John Paul II and the church-based human rights resistance in Central and Eastern Europe in helping rid the world of the plague of communism.

A realistic sense of the boundaries of the humanly possible in given situations is not foreign to the classic moral tradition of the West; prudence, after all, is one of the cardinal virtues. Nor is patriotism necessarily "pagan"; indeed, in a country culturally configured like the United States, patriotism is far more likely to be sustained by biblical rather than "pagan" moral warrants. As for "moralism" and its emphasis on good intentions, I hope I shall not be thought unecumenical if I observe that that is a Protestant problem, and that Catholic moral theology in the Thomistic stream is very dubious about voluntaristic theories of the moral life and their reduction of morality to a contest between the divine will and my will. (See "A Better Concept of Freedom," *First Things*, March 2002.)

Kaplan notwithstanding, we can get to an ethic appropriate for leadership in world politics without declaring ourselves "pagans." And, as Brian Anderson has argued in a thoughtful review of Kaplan's book in *National Review*, we can get there while retaining "a crucial place for a transcendent *ought* that limits the evil governments can do." An ethic for world politics can be built against an ampler moral horizon than Kaplan suggests.

As a tradition of statecraft, the just war argument recognizes that there are circumstances in which the first and most urgent obligation in the face of evil is to stop it. Which means that there are times when waging war is morally necessary to defend the innocent and to promote the minimum conditions of international order. This, I suggest, is one of those times. Grasping that does not require us to be "pagans." It only requires us to be morally serious and politically responsible. Moral seriousness and political responsibility require us to make the effort to "connect the dots" between means and ends.

Thus the just war tradition is best understood as a sustained and disciplined intellectual attempt to relate the morally legitimate use of proportionate and discriminate military force to morally worthy political ends. In this sense, the just war tradition shares Clausewitz's view of the relationship between war and politics: unless war is an extension of politics, it is simply wickedness. For Robert Kaplan, Clausewitz may be an archetypal "pagan." But on this crucial point, at least, Clausewitz was articulating a thoroughly classic just war view of the matter. Good ends do not justify any means. But as Fr. Murray liked to say, in his gently provocative way, "If the end doesn't justify the means, what does?" In the classic just war tradition of statecraft, what "justifies" the resort to proportionate and discriminate armed force—what makes war make moral sense—is precisely the morally worthy political ends being defended and/or advanced.

That is why the just war tradition is a theory of statecraft, not simply a method of casuistry. And that intellectual fact is the first thing about the just war tradition that must be retrieved today if we seek a public moral culture capable of informing the national and international debate about war, peace, and international order.

* * *

The second crucial idea to be retrieved in the contemporary renewal of the just war tradition is the distinction between *bellum* and *duellum*, between warring and "duelling," so to speak. As intellectual historian and just war theorist James Turner Johnson has demonstrated in a number of seminal works, this distinction is the crux of the matter in moral analysis. *Bellum* is the use of armed force for *public* ends by *public* authorities who have an *obligation* to defend the security of those for whom they have assumed responsibility. *Duellum*, on the other hand, is the use of armed force for *private* ends by *private* individuals. To grasp this essential distinction is to understand that, in the just war tradition, "war" is a moral category. Moreover, in the classic just war tradition, armed force is not inherently suspect morally. Rather, as Johnson insists, the classic tradition views armed force as something that can be used for good or evil, depending on who is using it, why, to what ends, and how.

Thus those scholars, activists, and religious leaders who claim that the just war tradition "begins" with a "presumption against war" or a "presumption against violence" are quite simply mistaken. It does not begin there, and it never did begin there. To suggest otherwise is not merely a matter of misreading intellectual history (although it is surely that). To suggest that the just war tradition begins with a "presumption against violence" inverts the structure of moral analysis in ways that inevitably lead to dubious moral judgments and distorted perceptions of political reality.

The classic tradition, as I have indicated, begins with the presumption—better, the moral judgment—that rightly constituted public authority is under a strict moral obligation to defend the security of those for whom it has assumed responsibility, even if this puts the magistrate's own life in jeopardy. That is why Thomas Aquinas locates his discussion of *bellum iustum* within the treatise on charity in the *Summa Theologica* (II-II, 40.1). That is why the late Paul Ramsey, who revivified Protestant just war thinking in America after World War II, described the just war tradition as an explication of the public implications of the Great Commandment of love-of-neighbor (even as he argued that the commandment sets limits to the use of armed force).

If the just war tradition is a theory of statecraft, to reduce it to a casuistry of means-tests that begins with a "presumption against violence" is to begin at the wrong place. The just war tradition begins by defining the moral responsibilities of governments, continues with the definition of morally appropriate political ends, and only then takes up the question of means. By reversing the analysis of means and ends, the "presumption against violence" starting point collapses *bellum* into *duellum* and ends up conflating the ideas of "violence" and "war." The net result is that warfare is stripped of its distinctive moral texture. Indeed, among many American religious leaders today, the very notion of warfare as having a "moral texture" seems to have been forgotten.

The "presumption against violence" starting point is not only fraught with historical and methodological difficulties. It is also theologically dubious. Its effect in moral analysis is to turn the tradition inside-out, such that war-conduct (*in bello*) questions of proportionality and discrimination take theological precedence over what were traditionally assumed to be the prior war-decision (*ad bellum*) questions: just cause, right intention, competent authority, reasonable chance of success, proportionality of ends, and last resort. This inversion explains why, in much of the religious commentary after the terrorist attacks of September 11, 2001, considerable attention was paid to the necessity of avoiding indiscriminate noncombatant casualties in the war against terrorism, while little attention was paid to the prior question of the moral obligation of government to pursue national security and world order, both of which were directly threatened by the terrorist networks.

This inversion is also theologically problematic because it places the heaviest burden of moral analysis on what are inevitably contingent judgments. There is nothing wrong, per se, with contingent judgments; but they are *contingent*. In the nature of the case, we can have less surety about *in bello* proportion and discrimination than we can about the *ad bellum* questions. As I hope I have shown above, the tradition logically starts with *ad bellum* questions because the just war tradition is a tradition of statecraft: a tradition that attempts to define morally worthy political ends. But there is also a theo-logic—a theo-logical logic—that gives priority to the *ad bellum* questions, for these are the questions on which we can have some measure of moral clarity.

The "presumption against violence" and its distortion of the just war way of thinking can also lead to serious misreadings of world politics. One such misreading, precisely from this intellectual source, may be found in the 1983 U.S. bishops' pastoral letter, "The Challenge of Peace" (TCOP). TCOP was deeply influenced by the emphasis laid on questions of *in bello* proportionality and discrimination because of the threat of nuclear war. No doubt these were important issues. But when that emphasis drove the moral analysis, as it did in TCOP, the result was a distorted picture of reality and a set of moral judgments that contributed little to wise statecraft. Rather than recognizing that nuclear weapons were one (extremely dangerous) manifestation of a prior conflict with profound moral roots, the bishops' letter seemed to suggest that nuclear weapons could, somehow, be factored out of the conflict between the West and the Soviet Union by arms control. And in order to achieve arms control agreements with a nervous, even paranoid, foe like the Soviet Union, it might be necessary to downplay the moral and ideological dimensions of the Cold War. That, at least, was the policy implication of the claim that the greatest threat to peace (identified as such because *in bello* considerations and the "presumption against violence" trumped everything else) was the mere possession of nuclear weapons.

The opposite, of course, turned out to be true. Nuclear weapons were not the primary threat to peace; communism was. When communism went, so did the threat posed by the weapons. As the human rights resistance in Central and Eastern Europe brought massive regime change inside the Warsaw Pact, creating dynamics that eventually led to the demise of the USSR itself, the risks of nuclear war were greatly diminished and real disarmament (not "arms control") began. The "presumption against violence" starting point, as manifest in TCOP, produced a serious misreading of the political realities and possibilities.

The claim that a "presumption against violence" is at the root of the just war tradition cannot be sustained historically, methodologically, or theologically. If the just war tradition is a tradition of statecraft, and if the crucial distinction that undergirds it is the distinction between *bellum* and *duellum*, then the just war tradition cannot be reduced, as too many religious leaders reduce it today, to a series of means tests that begins with a "presumption against violence." To begin here—to imagine that the role of moral reason is to set a series of hurdles (primarily having to do with *in bello* questions of proportionality and discrimination) that statesmen must overcome before the resort to armed force is given moral sanction—is to begin at the wrong place. And beginning at the wrong place almost always means arriving at the wrong destination.

*   *   *

Fifteen years ago, before I had learned something about literary marketing, I published a book entitled *Tranquillitas Ordinis: The Present Failure and Future Promise of American Catholic Thought on War and Peace*. There I argued that, as a theory of statecraft, the just war tradition contained within itself a *ius ad pacem*, in addition to the classic *ius ad bellum* (the moral rules governing the decision to go to war) and *ius in bello* (the rules governing the use of armed force in combat). By coining the phrase *ius ad pacem*, I was trying to prize out of the just war way of thinking a concept of the peace that could and should be sought through the instruments of politics—including, if necessary, the use of armed force. Like the just war tradition itself, this concept of peace finds its roots in Augustine: in *The City of God*, peace is *tranquillitas ordinis*, the "tranquillity of order," or as I preferred to render it in more contemporary terms, the peace of "dynamic and rightly ordered political community."

In Augustine's discussion of peace as a *public* or political issue, "peace" is not a matter of the individual's right relationship with God, nor is it a matter of seeking a world without conflict. The former is a question of interior conversion (which by definition has nothing to do with politics), and the latter is impossible in a world forever marked, even after its redemption, by the *mysterium iniquitatis*. In the appropriate *political* sense of the term, peace is, rather, *tranquillitas ordinis*: the order created by just political community and mediated through law.

This is, admittedly, a humbler sort of peace. It coexists with broken hearts and wounded souls. It is to be built in a world in which swords have not been beaten into plowshares, but remain swords: sheathed, but ready to be unsheathed in the defense of innocents. Its advantage, as Augustine understood, is that it is the form of peace that can be built through the instruments of politics.

This peace of *tranquillitas ordinis*, this peace of order, is composed of justice and freedom. The peace of order is not the eerily quiet and sullen "peace" of a well-run authoritarian regime; it is a peace built on foundations of constitutional, commutative, and social justice. It is a peace in which freedom, especially religious freedom, flourishes. The defense of basic human rights is thus an integral component of "work for peace."

This is the peace that has been achieved in and among the developed democracies. It is the peace that has been built in recent decades between such traditional antagonists as France and Germany. It is the peace that we defend within the richly diverse political community of the United States, and between ourselves and our neighbors and allies. It is the peace that we are now defending in the war against global terrorism and against aggressor states seeking weapons of mass destruction.

International terrorism of the sort we have seen since the late 1960s, and of which we had a direct national experience on September 11, 2001, is a deliberate assault, through the murder of innocents, on the very possibility of order in world affairs. That is why the terror networks must be dismantled or destroyed. The peace of order is also under grave threat when vicious, aggressive regimes acquire weapons of mass destruction—weapons that we must assume, on the basis of their treatment of their own citizens, these regimes will not hesitate to use against others. That is why there is a moral *obligation* to ensure that this lethal combination of irrational and aggressive regimes, weapons of mass destruction, and credible delivery systems does not go unchallenged. That is why there is a moral *obligation* to rid the world of this threat to the peace and security of all. Peace, rightly understood, demands it.

This concept of peace-as-order can also enrich our understanding of that much-bruited term, the "national interest." The irreducible core of the "national interest" is composed of those basic security concerns to which any responsible democratic statesman must attend. But those security concerns are related to a larger sense of national purpose and international responsibility: we defend America because America is worth defending, on its own terms and because of what it means for the world. Thus the security concerns that make up the core of the "national interest" should be understood as the necessary inner dynamic of the exercise of America's international responsibilities. And those responsibilities include the obligation to contribute, as best we can, to the long, hard, never-to-be-finally-accomplished "domestication" of international public life: to the quest for ordered liberty in an evolving structure of international public life capable of advancing the classic goals of politics—justice, freedom, order, the general welfare, and peace. Empirically and morally, the United States cannot adequately defend its "national interest" without concurrently seeking to advance those goals in the world. Empirically and morally, those goals will not be advanced if they are pursued in ways that gravely threaten the basic security of the United States.

In eradicating global terrorism and denying aggressive regimes weapons of mass destruction, the United States and those who walk this road with us are addressing the most threatening problems of global *dis*-order that must be resolved if the peace of order, the peace of *tranquillitas ordinis*, is to be secured in as wide a part of the world as possible in the twenty-first century. Here, national interest and international responsibility coincide.

* * *

Moral clarity in a time of war requires us to retrieve the idea of the just war tradition as a tradition of statecraft, the classic structure of just war analysis, and the concept of peace as *tranquillitas ordinis*. Moral clarity in *this* time of war also requires us to develop and extend the just war tradition to meet the political exigencies of a new century, and to address the international security issues posed by new weapons technologies. Permit me to sketch briefly three areas in which the *ad bellum* ("war-decision") criteria of the just war tradition require development, even as I suggest what the policy implications of these developments might be in today's circumstances.

Just Cause

In the classic just war tradition, "just cause" was understood as defense against aggression, the recovery of something wrongfully taken, or the punishment of evil. As the tradition has developed since World War II, the latter two notions have been largely displaced, and "defense against aggression" has become the primary, even sole, meaning of "just cause." This theological evolution has parallels in international law: the "defense against aggression" concept of just cause shapes Articles 2 and 51 of the Charter of the United Nations. In light of twenty-first-century international security realities, it is imperative to reopen this discussion and to develop the concept of just cause.

As recently as the Korean War (and, some would argue, the Vietnam War), "defense against aggression" could reasonably be taken to mean a defensive military response to a cross-border military aggression already underway. New weapons capabilities and outlaw or "rogue" states require a development of the concept of "defense against aggression." To take an obvious current example: it makes little moral sense to suggest that the United States must wait until a North Korea or Iraq or Iran actually launches a ballistic missile tipped with a nuclear, biological, or chemical weapon of mass destruction before we can legitimately do something about it. Can we not say that, in the hands of certain kinds of states, the mere possession of weapons of mass destruction constitutes an aggression—or, at the very least, an aggression waiting to happen?

This "regime factor" is crucial in the moral analysis, for weapons of mass destruction are clearly not aggressions waiting to happen when they are possessed by stable, law-abiding states. No Frenchman goes to bed nervous about Great Britain's nuclear weapons, and no sane Mexican or Canadian worries about a preemptive nuclear attack from the United States. Every sane Israeli, Turk, or Bahraini, on the other hand, is deeply concerned about the possibility of an Iraq or Iran with nuclear weapons and medium-range ballistic missiles. If the "regime factor" is crucial in the moral analysis, then preemptive military action to deny the rogue state that kind of destructive capacity would not, in my judgment, contravene the "defense against aggression" concept of just cause. Indeed, it would do precisely the opposite, by giving the concept of "defense against aggression" real traction in the world we must live in and transform.

Some will argue that this violates the principle of sovereignty and risks a global descent into chaos. To that, I would reply that the post-Westphalian notions of state equality and sovereign immunity assume at least a minimum of acquiescence to minimal international norms of order. Today's rogue states cannot, on the basis of their behavior, be granted that assumption. Therefore, they have forfeited that immunity. The "regime factor" is determinative, in these extreme instances.

To deny rogue states the capacity to create lethal disorder, precisely because their possession of weapons of mass destruction threatens the minimum conditions of order in international public life, strengthens the cause of world order; it does not undermine it. Surely the lessons of the 1930s are pertinent here.

On the matter of just cause, the tradition also needs development in terms of its concept of the relevant actors in world politics. Since September 11, some analysts have objected to describing our response to the international terrorist networks as "war" because, they argue, al-Qaeda and similar networks are not states, and only states can, or should, wage "war," properly understood. There is an important point at stake here, but the critics misapply it.

Limiting the legitimate use of armed force to those international actors who are recognized in international law and custom as exercising "sovereignty" has been one of the principle accomplishments of just war thinking as it has shaped world political culture and law; over a period of centuries, the classic distinction between *bellum* and *duellum* has been established in international law. At the same time, however, it does not fudge or blur this crucial distinction to recognize that al-Qaeda and similar networks function like states, even if they lack certain of the attributes and trappings of sovereignty traditionally understood. Indeed, terrorist organizations provide a less ambiguous example of a legitimate military target, because, unlike conventional states (which are always admixtures of good and evil, against whom military action sometimes threatens the good as well as the evil), the "parasite states" that are international terrorist organizations are unmitigated evils whose only purpose is wickedness—the slaughter of innocents for ignoble political ends. Thus the exigencies of the current situation require us to think outside the Westphalian box, so to speak, but to do so in such a way as to avoid dismantling de facto the distinction between *bellum* and *duellum*.

Competent Authority

Two questions involving the *ad bellum* criterion of "competent authority" have been raised since September 11: the question of the relationship between a government's domestic and foreign policy and its legitimacy as a belligerent, and the question of whether "competent authority" now resides in the United Nations only.

One of the more distasteful forms of post-September 11 commentary can be found in suggestions that there were "root causes" to terrorism—root causes that not only explained the resort to mass violence against innocents, but made the use of such violence humanly plausible, if not morally justifiable. The corollary to this was the suggestion that the United States had somehow brought the attacks on itself, by reasons of its dominant economic and cultural position in the world, its Middle East policy, or some combination thereof. The moral-political implication was that such a misguided government lacked the moral authority to respond to terrorism through the use of armed force.

The root causes school blithely ignores the extant literature on the phenomenon of contemporary terrorism, which is emphatically not a case of the wretched of the earth rising up to throw off their chains. But it is the moral-political implication the root causes school draws that I want to address. Here, Lutheran scholar David Yeago has been a wise guide. Writing in the ecumenical journal *Pro Ecclesia*, Yeago clarified an essential point:

> The authority of the government to protect the law-abiding and impose penalties on evildoers is not a reward for the government's virtue or good conduct. . . . The protection of citizens and the execution of penalty on peace-breakers is the commission which constitutes government, not a contingent right which it must somehow earn. In the mystery of God's providence, many or indeed most of the institutional bearers of governmental authority are unworthy of it, often flagrantly so, themselves stained with crime. But this does not make it any less the vocation of government to protect the innocent and punish evildoers. A government which refused to safeguard citizens and exercise judgment on wrong out of a sense of the guilt of past crime would only add the further crime of dereliction of duty to its catalog of offenses.

The question of alliances and international organizations must also be addressed in the development of just war thinking about competent authority. Must any legitimate military action be sanctioned by the UN Security Council? Or, if not that, then is the United States obliged, not simply as a matter of political prudence but as a matter of moral principle, to gain the agreement of allies (or, more broadly, "coalition partners") to any use of armed force in response to terrorism, or any military action against aggressive regimes with weapons of mass destruction?

That the UN Charter itself recognizes an inalienable national right to self-defense suggests that the Charter does not claim sole authority to legitimate the use of armed force for the Security Council; if you are under attack, according to the Charter, you don't have to wait for the permission of China, France, Russia, or others of the veto-wielding powers to defend yourself. Moreover, the manifest inability of the UN to handle large-scale international security questions suggests that assigning a moral veto over U.S. military action on these fronts to the Security Council would be a mistake. Then there is the question of what we might call "the neighborhood" on the Security Council: What kind of moral logic is it to claim that the U.S. government must assuage the interests of the French foreign ministry and the strategic aims of the repressive Chinese government—both of which are in full play in the Security Council—in order to gain international moral authority for the war against terrorism and the defense of world order against outlaw states with weapons of mass destruction? A very peculiar moral logic, indeed, I should think.

Building coalitions of support for dismantling the international terror networks and denying rogue states lethal weapons capacities is politically desirable (and in some instances militarily essential). But I very much doubt that it is morally imperative from a classic just war point of view. The United States has a unique responsibility for leadership in the war against terrorism and the struggle for world order; that is not a statement of hubris but of empirical fact. That responsibility may have to be exercised unilaterally on occasion. Defining the boundaries of unilateral action while defending its legitimacy under certain circumstances is one crucial task for a developing just war tradition.

Last Resort

Among those who have forgotten the just war tradition while retaining its language, the classic *ad bellum* criterion of last resort is usually understood in simplistically mathematical terms: the use of proportionate and discriminate armed force is the last point in a series of options, and prior, nonmilitary options (legal, diplomatic, economic, etc.) must be serially exhausted before the criterion of last resort is satisfied. This is both an excessively mechanistic understanding of last resort and a prescription for danger.

The case of international terrorism again compels a development of this *ad bellum* criterion. For what does it mean to say that all nonmilitary options have been tried and found wanting when we are confronted with a new and lethal type of international actor, one that recognizes no other form of power except the use of violence and that is largely immune (unlike a conventional state) to international legal, diplomatic, or economic pressures? The charge that U.S. military action after September 11 was morally dubious because all other possible means of redress had not been tried and found wanting misreads the nature of terrorist organizations and networks. The "last" in last resort can mean "only," in circumstances where there is plausible reason to believe that nonmilitary actions are unavailable or unavailing.

As for rogue states developing or deploying weapons of mass destruction, a developed just war tradition would recognize that here, too, last resort cannot be understood mathematically, as the terminal point of a lengthy series of nonmilitary alternatives. Can we not say that last resort has been satisfied in those cases when a rogue state has made plain, by its conduct, that it holds international law in contempt and that no diplomatic solution to the threat it poses is likely, and when it can be demonstrated that the threat the rogue state poses is intensifying? I think we can. Indeed, I think we must.

Some states, because of the regime's aggressive intent and the lack of effective internal political controls on giving lethal effect to that intent, cannot be permitted to acquire weapons of mass destruction. Denying them those weapons through proportionate and discriminate armed force—even displacing those regimes—can be an exercise in the defense of the peace of order, within the boundaries of a developed just war tradition. Until such point as the international political community has evolved to the degree that international organizations can effectively disarm such regimes, the responsibility for the defense of order in these extreme circumstances will lie elsewhere.

*   *   *

Finally, moral clarity in this time of war requires a developed understanding of the "location" of the just war tradition in our public discourse and in responsible governance.

If the just war tradition is indeed a tradition of statecraft, then the proper role of religious leaders and public intellectuals is to do everything possible to clarify the moral issues at stake in a time of war, while recognizing that what we might call the "charism of responsibility" lies elsewhere—with duly constituted public authorities, who are more fully informed about the relevant facts and who must bear the weight of responsible decision-making and governance. It is simply clericalism to suggest that religious leaders and public intellectuals "own" the just war tradition in a singular way.

As I have argued above, many of today's religious leaders and public intellectuals have suffered severe amnesia about core components of the tradition, and can hardly be said to own it in any serious intellectual sense of ownership. But even if today's religious leaders and public intellectuals were fully in possession of the tradition, the burden of decision-making would still lie elsewhere. Religious leaders and public intellectuals are called to nurture and develop the moral-philosophical riches of the just war tradition. The tradition itself, however, exists to serve statesmen.

There is a charism of political discernment that is unique to the vocation of public service. That charism is not shared by bishops, stated clerks, rabbis, imams, or ecumenical and interreligious agencies. Moral clarity in a time of war demands moral seriousness from public officials. It also demands a measure of political modesty from religious leaders and public intellectuals, in the give-and-take of democratic deliberation.

Some have suggested, in recent months, that the just war tradition is obsolete. To which I would reply: to suggest that the just war tradition is obsolete is to suggest that politics—the organization of human life into purposeful political communities—is obsolete. To reduce the just war tradition to an algebraic casuistry is to deny the tradition its capacity to shed light on the irreducible moral component of all political action. What we must do, in this generation, is to retrieve and develop the just war tradition to take account of the new political and technological realities of the twenty-first century. September 11, what has followed, and what lies ahead, have demonstrated just how urgent that task is.

WAR AND STATECRAFT
An Exchange

—Rowan Williams and George Weigel

Rowan Williams

In October 2002, George Weigel of the Ethics and Public Policy Center in Washington, D.C., delivered a lecture on "Moral Clarity in a Time of War" [see *First Things*, December 2002]. The lecture was a response to various statements from religious leaders in the run-up to the conflict in Iraq, most of which, in Weigel's judgment, exhibited a deplorable ignorance or misunderstanding of the just war tradition. Weigel sets out not only to dust off what he believes is the authentic heart of the tradition, but also to defend a reading of that tradition which would offer secure moral grounding for a preemptive U.S. action against Iraq, or any comparable "rogue state."

It is a formidable and sophisticated essay, building upon the author's earlier work on the theological definitions of peace and order and upon the extensive work over several decades of James Turner Johnson on just war in the modern age. With much of Weigel's critique I am in sympathy. I believe, however, that his account of the tradition is in one respect seriously questionable, and that his defense of preemptive action cannot be accommodated as easily as he thinks within the terms of classical just war theory.

First, though, my points of agreement. Weigel refers to recent work in the U.S. on the need for a "warrior" ethos of a fundamentally pagan kind to sustain us through the trials of late modern international politics; we need—so this style of argument maintains—heroism, ruthlessness, patriotic fervor, and a profound suspicion of moralistic or idealistic rhetoric that clouds our sense of what is possible in tragically constrained circumstances. As Weigel notes, this is effectively to say that morality has no public voice, that what he calls "statecraft" is beyond the reach of moral, especially religiously moral, principle; and he rightly rejects this as an unsustainable view for any religious person. Just war theory is a form of statecraft (i.e., it is an aspect of political ethics, which concerns how to do right in the conduct of ordered community life); it is a way of saying that war is not some monstrous aberration in human life, for which all standing orders are suspended, but is a

* First Things 141 (March 2004): 14–22.

set of actions requiring the same virtues as political life in general. As Weigel writes, "The just war tradition is best understood as a sustained and disciplined intellectual attempt to relate the morally legitimate use of proportionate and discriminate military force to morally worthy political ends." Interestingly, Weigel here echoes, without mentioning, the argument of Oliver O'Donovan in *Peace and Certainty* (1989) about certain justifications of nuclear deterrence—that the Cold War advocates of massive deterrence involving indiscriminate targeting were, like pacifists, refusing to see war as an activity among others with a possible ethical structure. The apologist for deterrence of this kind assumes a sort of Manichaean view that war is of its nature irrational and apocalyptic, avoidable only by threats of total annihilation.

Against this mythology, Weigel rightly claims that we must think about war in moral categories and treat it as essentially a *public* enterprise, as opposed to private violence. But here my doubts begin. Weigel accuses recent writers on the subject of presenting the tradition as having a "presumption against violence" and thus making it a "casuistry of means-tests," a set of hoops to be jumped through; and he says that one result of this is to focus attention unduly on what are usually called the *ius in bello* issues of restraint on the methods to be used in conflict. He claims that, in fact, the tradition has no such presumption and must be understood as beginning from questions about just cause, which are directly related to the defense of the political good of a society against aggression, the punishment of aggression against another, or of some other flagrant evil. Such aggression, Weigel suggests, doesn't have to be an actual event of military violence: the mere possession of weapons of mass destruction by a state whose regime may properly be mistrusted as an enemy of justice constitutes some sort of sufficient cause for intervention. Weigel finds terrorist networks to be enough like states to present even more obviously legitimate targets for preemptive action. At the same time, such networks are unlike states (even very bad states) in being not a mixture of good and bad, but "unmitigated evils whose only purpose is wickedness—the slaughter of innocents for ignoble political ends."

So to my first caveat. Weigel denies any presumption against violence in the tradition. But this is an odd reading of, say, St. Thomas Aquinas' discussion in the *Summa Theologiae* (II-II.40). Formally, this is a consideration of those conditions under which what would otherwise be gravely sinful would not be so. It is true to say that there is no specific discussion here of violence (to which I shall return in a moment); the focus is on the scriptural warnings about warfare, the sinfulness of disturbing peace, and so on. But it would be quite fair to say that St. Thomas is granting that there is a prima facie case against war, which is only resolved by appeal to the duty of the ruler to preserve peace internally and externally by the literal use of the sword (something explicitly allowed in Scripture). Private use of violence is wrong because a private person always has the alternative of resorting to law to seek redress; but if (as we might say) law itself is threatened, and the public good undermined, there is no higher court to look to.

Some of this is illuminated if we turn to Aquinas' discussions of violence (I-II.6.4; II-II.66.8 and 175.1). Violence is an external force compelling certain sorts of action; as such, it is bound to appear as against nature or against justice (since it takes from someone or some group what is theirs, intrudes on their territory, restricts the exercise of their freedom of choice, and so on). External acts may be subject to violence, though the freedom of the will can never be affected in itself. There is, however, a recognition that external force is sometimes used to accelerate a natural movement; in which case it is not exactly violence in the pure sense. The implication is that action which intends what is natural to human beings, even if formally coercive, is legitimate; so that action which employs violence of some sort for the restoration of a broken or threatened social order does not have the nature of sin. This is the basis on which a large part of Aquinas' discussion of legal penalties rests (II-II.64-65).

Public good is what is natural to human beings, the context in which they may exercise their freedom to realize the image of God. Confronted with action that is inimical to order, action that is "inordinate" in respect of public goods, the restraint on the freedom of others, the intrusion into what is theirs, and the privation of their personal resources that we normally call violence is not sinful. But in the nature of the case, only those charged with preserving the public good are competent and legitimate judges of the public good. An act of private redress, private vengeance, vigilantism, or whatever, may purport to punish inordinate behavior but it only deals with the offense to the individual, not the offense to the social body; thus it fails to heal the social body and even makes the wound worse. The private person must never use the violence that the ruler can rightly use, as a private person has the right of redress by legal due process.

The point of this long excursus into somewhat technical matters is to establish that Weigel's claim that there is no presumption against violence in classical just war theory needs a good deal of refining. The ruler who administers the law may use coercion for the sake of the common good in domestic policing and in international affairs. But such coercion will always need publicly available justification in terms of the common good, since otherwise it will appear as an arbitrary infringement of natural justice. The whole point is that there is precisely a presumption against violence, which can be overcome only by a very clear account of the needs of the common good and of what constitutes a "natural" life for human beings.

Now Weigel is clear about some of these wider considerations: he writes of "the long, hard, never-to-be-finally-accomplished 'domestication' of international public life." Likewise, he states that "the quest for ordered liberty in an evolving structure of international public life capable of advancing the classic goals of politics—justice, freedom, order, the general welfare, and peace" must serve as the "inner dynamic" of any pursuit of the national interest by the U.S. in order for it to be described as "just." My problem is that by denying that there is a presumption against violence in the tradition, Weigel denies himself the most significant touchstone in the tradition for discerning the rationale of using force: external constraint on human liberty is normally a bad thing, but it is not so when human liberty is exercised against the liberty of others or indeed against one's own dignity as a social and moral being. The point is that coercion is simply not to be justified unless it is answerable to a clear account of common *human* good. Even the security of a specific state has to be seen in the light of this broader framework. So to provide an account of coercion as a moral tool, we need to have a robust account of the balance of liberties in an ordered society, just as Weigel wants—but one, I suggest, in which it is understood that violence, as an external limit on the freedom of another, is essentially anomalous because the essence of healthy social life is the *voluntary* restriction of any one agent's liberty in the corporate act of social life. More specifically still, Christian doctrine, in describing the optimal human community as the Body of Christ, with all its biblical associations, considers the social unit as an exchange of free gift before it is a community ruled by coercion. If and when coercion is exercised, it is in response to situations in which certain citizens or subgroups are prevented from proper social action by the arbitrary violence of others. This is intrinsic to the exercise of law in our world, where voluntary self-gift is not exactly automatic.

This begins to suggest that the active reconstruction of justice in a society is not an optional extra to military engagement; but it also reinforces the point about which I agree most earnestly with Weigel, that war as a moral option is a tool for the promotion of specific social goods. As such, however, it is subject to the usual criteria by which means towards an end are to be judged—to considerations of "prudence." In the language of scholastic ethics, we must judge the fitness of means to ends. Or, more plainly, military options have to be weighed against other ways of securing or restoring justice. Weigel seems to assume that we have already gotten to the point where such a discernment has happened; not only coercion in general but military coercion has emerged as the only pos-sible course. In what he says about terrorism, Weigel makes this assumption explicit: there is no point in asking what responses are appropriate to terrorism. "In circumstances where there is plausible reason to believe that nonmilitary actions are unavailable or unavailing," Weigel claims, "the 'last' in 'last resort' can mean 'only.'"

This suggests, uncomfortably, that there are circumstances in which you will know almost automatically when it is a waste of time to consider nonmilitary options; and the implication of earlier comments is that where terrorism is concerned this can be taken for granted, since terrorists have no recognizable political aims, or are devoid of political rationality. The assumption that an enemy can be regarded as devoid of political rational-ity is briefly but effectively discussed by Oliver O'Donovan in the essay mentioned above. There he argues that the principle of "total" deterrence (the nuclear threat) is presented as the only realistic option by assuming "an enemy . . . who cannot be made susceptible to the codes of honor and rational political interest"; but this, he points out, is to locate original sin or radical evil outside oneself (corporate or individual)—to assume that it is unproblematic to identify political rationality with one's own agenda. But such a view is the opposite of "realism."

Which brings us to an awkwardness in Weigel's position. The terrorist, he says, has no aims that can be taken seriously as political or moral. But this is a sweeping state-ment, instantly challengeable. The terrorist is objectively wicked, no dispute about that, in exercising the most appalling form of blackmail by menacing the lives of the innocent. Nothing should qualify this judgment. But this does not mean that the terrorist has no serious moral goals. It is possible to use unspeakably wicked means to pursue an aim that is shared by those who would not dream of acting in the same way, an aim that is intel-ligible or desirable. The risk in claiming so unproblematic a right to define what counts as politics and so to dismiss certain sorts of political calculation in combating terrorism is that the threatened state (the U.S. in this instance) loses the power of self-criticism and becomes trapped in a self-referential morality which creates even deeper difficulties in the application of just war theory.

I noted earlier the need for a ruler or government to be exposed to assessment by larger standards of the human good than national interest. Weigel is clear that the U.S. is de facto the only power capable of taking the lead in the struggle for world order, and he is skepti-cal of an international tribunal in which "the interests of the French foreign ministry and the strategic aims of the repressive Chinese government" dictate the determinations of the Security Council. The point is not without substance; but who is to adjudicate the interests of the U.S. government and its strategic aims, which cannot automatically be assumed to be identical with the detached promotion of "world order"?

This is by no means an anti-American argument, as the same could be said about any specific government assuming the identity of its interests with "world order." Weigel is unconvinced that any kind of international consensus is imperative for just war theory to be applicable to a U.S. intervention against rogue states or terrorist networks. But, granting the weakness of international legal institutions and the practical difficulties entailed in activating them credibly, it is important to allow that no government can simply be a judge in its own case in this respect. Indeed, this issue takes us back to one of the absolute fundamentals of just war theory: violence is not to be undertaken by private persons. If a state or administration acts without due and visible attention to agreed international process, it acts in a way analogous to a private person.

The private person has redress in a higher court; do states? Aquinas and later just war theorists were writing in a context where what we understand as international legal structures did not exist (outside the Church, whose standing in such matters was a matter of complex dispute in the Middle Ages). There is a principle which allows the lower jurisdiction to act if the higher is absent or negligent. Does this apply in the modern context? I do not seek to settle these questions here, only to note that their significance for restating anything like a just war theory seems to be underrated by Weigel. Even if the international structures do not exist or lack credibility, the challenge remains as to how any one nation can express its accountability to the substantial concerns of international law.

As to the appropriate structures for this in the middle to long term, that too is a question I cannot seek to settle here. But if I may make a suggestion which I have outlined elsewhere, there is surely a case for a Standing Commission on Security within the UN structure, incorporating legal and other professionals, capable of taking expert evidence, which could advise on these questions and recommend UN intervention where necessary—instead of complete reliance on the present Security Council framework, which suffers from all the problems Weigel and others have identified. This is one way of recognizing that in the present world of global economic interdependence, colonial and postcolonial relationships, instant communications, and so forth, it is more essential than ever to have institutions that express and activate some commitment to a common good that is not nationally defined. A significant part of what I have been arguing is that the just war tradition in fact demands this kind of internationalism, in the sense that it makes a strong challenge to violence as the tool of private interest or private redress; and "privacy" of this kind is most definitely something that can be ascribed to states as well as individuals.

Weigel concludes his argument by appealing for a recognition of where just war theory should fit into the processes of democratic decision making. He rightly says that it represents an ethic designed to serve statesmen; but then he proposes a really startling theological novelty. He writes that "a charism of political discernment is unique to the vocation of public service," and he claims that this is a gift denied to church leaders and other religious spokespersons, so that a measure of modesty is appropriate in such persons when they participate in public argument.

This is related to, though not identical with, the more prosaic point that religious leaders don't know what governments know and therefore have no privileged extra information that would enable them to make more morally secure judgments than their rulers. But this requires further thought. First of all, there is no such thing in moral theology as a "charism of political discernment." A charism is a gift of the Holy Spirit bestowed for the building up of the Body of Christ, and wisdom is undoubtedly a gift of the Holy Spirit. But there is no charism that goes automatically with political leadership. A political leader may or may not be open to the gifts of the Spirit; democracy itself assumes, though, that the professed wisdom of any leader or any party is challengeable.

What we can properly expect in political leaders is not charism but virtue—the virtue of political prudence, which involves, once again, understanding what means are appropriate to agreed ends. Like all virtues, this one requires good habits that are formed by appropriate teaching and learning and that do not simply reach a plateau of excellence but need daily renewal and exercise. Of course governments know things that citizens don't (it would be a bit worrying if they didn't); but it needs to be said, with appropriate modesty, that others know things that the government sometimes does not. Lawyers, NGOs, linguists, anthropologists, religious communities, journalists, strategists, military and diplomatic historians—all know some things that may not instantly appear on the radar screen of any government, and the democratic process is about making sure that government hears what it may not know. This is not a claim to superior expertise overall, but simply to a voice in the debate and a freedom to exercise discernment on the basis of what is publicly available for judgment. Any appeal to universally superior knowledge, let alone some sort of charism of office, risks preempting real political or, indeed, theological debate in this area.

In the end, my unease with Weigel's otherwise welcome and excellent essay is that it encourages a weakening of the freedom of moral theology to sustain the self-critical habit in a nation and its political classes. By sidestepping the subtleties of the analysis of violence in the traditional theory it ends by leaving the solitary nation-state battling terror or aggression morally exposed to an uncomfortable degree; and it attempts to avoid this problem by appealing to a not-very-plausible theological innovation in the shape of the "charism of responsibility." If the just war theory is to be properly reconsidered—not as a checklist of moral requirements but as part of a wide-ranging theory of political good and political coercion—it needs to be replanted in a greater depth of soil. And it needs to see itself, as Weigel correctly says, as part of a protracted argument about statecraft. In that argument, many voices have a proper place, more at times than governments might find comfortable.[1]

George Weigel

Rowan Williams' lecture makes abundantly clear that a formidable theological intelligence is now resident at Lambeth Palace. That is a development of prime importance in refining the public moral debate in this time of war, and I welcome it wholeheartedly. I am also grateful to the Archbishop for identifying the significant points of agreement between us—although, as I hope to demonstrate, I have a rather different reading of the implications of several of those agreements.

In order to foster the further clarification of thought for which Dr. Williams calls, let me begin with some context-setting. In writing "Moral Clarity in a Time of War," my first intention was not to promote a reading of the just war tradition that would provide a secure moral rationale for preemptive U.S.-led military action against the regime of Saddam Hussein, similar outlaw states, or international terrorism; it was to propose a revitalization of the just war way of thinking as the basis of morally serious statecraft in the Western democracies in the circumstances of a post–September 11 world. To be sure, Iraq was an urgent test case for the just war tradition in this new and dangerous situation; and it is no secret that, in my judgment, a just war case for military action against the Saddam Hussein regime could be mounted. Still, I trust that my essay did not put the policy cart before the theological horse.

For the essay's first purpose was to address a grave theological and ecclesial problem: over more than a quarter century, religious intellectuals and pastoral leaders had distorted, and were continuing to distort, the just war tradition by disengaging it from its proper context within a theory of statecraft. And it seemed to me that the only way to bring the tools of moral reasoning to bear on the distinctive circumstances of this particular time of war, this post–September 11 world, was to restore just war thinking to its proper location within Christian moral reflection on the distinctive ends of public life. Thus I take it as a very good sign for the future of the discussion that Dr. Williams agrees with me on four crucial points: that the just war tradition is not a free-floating casuistry of means tests; that just war thinking must function within a normative understanding of the political task; that, in this very specific sense, "war" is a moral category—it is the use of proportionate and discriminate armed force for public ends by publicly accountable public authorities who have a moral obligation to defend those for whom they have assumed responsibility; and that "war" (*bellum*) must be rigorously distinguished from brigandage, piracy, terrorism, and other forms of *duellum*, the use of armed force by private persons for private ends.

These points of agreement bring us to the first significant disagreement—one that involves the starting point for just war reflection. Does the just war way of thinking begin with a "presumption against war," or does it begin elsewhere?

This entire discussion has been confused by the tendency of "presumption against war" proponents to fudge the language, so that in some instances we are told that the tradition begins with a presumption against war, whereas on other occasions the tradition is said to begin with a presumption against violence. While I quoted both these formulations in "Moral Clarity," the real issue is the so-called presumption against war, as the *terminus a quo* for just war thinking. Thus the Archbishop's interesting observations on the Aristotelian-Thomistic understanding of "violence" do not quite get us to the heart of the argument.

In thinking about these matters, I rely on the historical research of James Turner Johnson, who insists that there is simply no warrant in the tradition—in its Augustinian, medieval, or early modern forms—for starting just war thinking with a presumption against war. Rather, as I wrote with emphasis in my essay, the tradition "*begins somewhere else.*" If the just war tradition is theologically and historically embedded within a more comprehensive theory of statecraft—a theory which stresses the prior obligation of public authority to advance and defend the peace of right order (*tranquillitas ordinis*), which is composed of freedom, justice, and security—then just war thinking "begins" not with presumptions for or against war but with a context-setting moral judgment about the obligation of public authority to pursue the peace of right order—which includes the obligation of providing for the security of one's people against aggression. That, and nothing other than that, is the "starting point" for just war thinking. Questions of how—can the peace of right order be defended and advanced through nonmilitary means, or must proportionate and discriminate armed force be deployed?—come into focus only when the what and the why of morally defensible political ends have been established. Dr. Williams' reference to Aquinas' discussion of just war in the *Summa* demonstrates this (even as it undermines his historically and theologically questionable claim that Aquinas, too, shares the presumption against war). Why can a sovereign ruler override what Dr. Williams calls Aquinas' "prima facie case against war"? Because, I suggest, the ruler is under a prior moral obligation, a responsibility to defend the peace of right order. That prior obligation is the beginning of all morally serious thinking about the use of armed force for morally serious ends.

Thus just war thinking, in Aquinas and elsewhere, has to be located within a given theologian's more comprehensive understanding of the normative character of statecraft, its ends, and the means appropriate to securing those ends—a point I could have made clearer in my essay.

What does this have to do with today's arguments? A lot, actually. For the net result of the presumption against war has not been to reinforce the obvious—namely, that public authority has to make a moral case that the use of armed force in defending the peace of right order is the only responsible option in this instance, because other nonmilitary means have failed or have been reasonably judged to be unavailing, given the threat and the aggressor. Rather, the presumption against war has smuggled into the just war discussion a pacifist premise—armed force is wicked—that classic just war thinking rejects. As I suggested in "Moral Clarity," the classic just war tradition does not regard armed force as inherently suspect morally; rather, classic just war thinking treats armed force as an instrument that can be used for good or for evil, depending on who is using it, for what ends, and how.

That smuggled pacifist premise has made a hash of theological method, inverting the tradition by putting *ius in bello* questions ahead of the determinations that give those questions moral sense—the determinations of the *ius ad bellum*. It has also distorted the prudential judgments of many religious leaders as they have tried to read the signs of the times through the filter of the presumption against war. Time and again in recent years religious leaders have been proven wrong in their predictions about the likely consequences of various uses of armed force. There is certainly an ideological element to these failures of prognostication, as more and more of the world's established Christian leadership has adopted, from the international left, a functional pacifism whose primary objection to the use of armed force has to do with who is using it—that is, the West, understood as an oppressor culture. But ideological predispositions don't explain every facet of this global clerical lurch *à gauche*; something else is also going on here. And that something else is, I think, the presumption against war, which functions like a badly manufactured pair of eyeglasses, distorting the vision of the observer. To return, once again, to the most obvious example of this artificial myopia: in their 1983 pastoral letter, "The Challenge of Peace," the Catholic bishops of the United States seriously misread the moral and political dynamics of the last decade of the Cold War (insisting that nuclear arms control was the key to peace, not regime change in the Soviet Union and its satellites), not because the (complex) facts of the case were not there to be seen and understood, but because the presumption against war blurred their perception of what they were seeing. The same, I suggest, holds true for the many warnings of catastrophe from religious leaders that preceded the Gulf War of 1991 and the most recent Iraq War.

Dr. Williams once jocularly referred to himself as a "hairy lefty," and while his article here rises far above the standards of analysis and judgment typically found in religious activist circles, there are several points in his essay at which, I respectfully suggest, portside-tilting politics are getting the better of empirically informed theological analysis.

The first of these has to do with terrorism and outlaw states. The Archbishop's claim that today's terror networks are motivated by some form of political rationality is, at the very least, misleading, for it seems to ignore the powerful currents of nihilism at work in the Taliban, al-Qaeda, and other contemporary terrorist organizations and networks. Anarchic nihilism has been a prominent feature of modern terrorism since its origins in nineteenth-century Russia. When that form of nihilism is married to a distorted conception of monotheism, it yields a goal that I am sure Dr. Williams rejects on moral grounds (i.e., the coercive imposition of politicized Islam on a national and international scale) and a method—mass murder—that he rightly deplores. As for outlaw states, it would strain credulity to suggest that Kim Jong Il's aims for North Korea are either "intelligible" or "desirable," so I cannot imagine that the Archbishop's (entirely appropriate) counsel to be careful in defining "what counts as politics" applies here. Moreover, to deny that a rogue state or terrorist organization lacks morally defensible goals is not to conclude, without further analytic ado, that military action is the most appropriate means for dealing with the threat posed by, say, North Korea. As classic just war thinking would affirm, there is no one-size-fits-all strategic prescription for dealing with the world's madmen.

The Archbishop is right to caution against nations acting as judges in their own cases. But is that really what happened in the U.S. government's decision-making prior to the recent Iraq War? The U.S.-led action in Iraq was supported by allies, most notably the government of Dr. Williams' own country. After strenuous efforts to secure Security Council approval for the use of armed force to vindicate Security Council resolutions, the Bush administration, its judgment confirmed by the governments involved in a coalition of the willing, did not decide to act as its own judge; it decided, again with allies, that some of the judges in this instance—in particular, France, Germany, and Russia—could not be taken seriously as moral or political arbiters of the case in question. The administration's judgment, supported by Great Britain, Spain, Italy, Poland, Australia, and others, was not unilateralist; and that judgment was reached after vigorous public and governmental debate within the states involved in the U.S.-led coalition. For that reason (and many others), the suggestion that the United States government was acting, in the case of Saddam Hussein's regime, as a "private person" strikes me as unpersuasive.

The Archbishop is quite right in arguing that the just war tradition demands a form of internationalism. The question for prudential judgment is whether the current UN system is in fact a form of internationalism that commands moral respect. Dr. Williams and I are quite agreed that the UN is in need of serious reform. The difference between us seems to involve a disagreement about whether the present UN is in fact a political and moral entity independent of states and a genuinely disinterested internationalist force in world politics. In my view, the recent debacle in the Security Council with respect to Iraq demonstrates that, in dealing with international security issues, today's UN is entirely the tool of states, many of the most important of which—again, France, Germany, and Russia—are certainly not making their policy calculations on genuinely internationalist grounds, or on grounds of moral reason rightly understood. Perhaps this could change; but until it does, the moral obligations of national leaders will remain what they have always been.

This fact of life leads to the important question of the international accountability of a powerful country such as the United States. Serious moral reasoning about that question does not begin by assuming that the present UN system is the only, or perhaps even the primary, locus for measuring that accountability. The development of morally and politically worthy international institutions of conflict resolution—which is demanded both by the just war tradition (as the Archbishop suggests) and by Catholic social doctrine from Pius XII through John Paul II—must begin with a frank assessment of the corruptions of the present UN system, not with the assumption that the UN has achieved any sort of monopoly on the moral legitimation of the use of armed force in defense of the peace of right order.

I gladly accept Dr. Williams' proposal that "virtue" (with specific reference to the virtue of prudence) is the apt word for getting at the distinctive habitus to be desired in public authorities, while assuring him that, in using "charism," I was not suggesting that the presidential oath of office (or its British parliamentary equivalent) involves an infusion of any particular gift of the Holy Spirit. And we are quite agreed that public authorities ought to consult widely in developing their own moral clarity in this time of war. It is certainly true that those outside the halls of power can sometimes see things that those inside have difficulty discerning. From my own experience with the present U.S. administration, I can say with some assurance that this point is well understood in the White House, the National Security Council, and the Department of Defense.

These things happen differently in the United States than in Great Britain, where the policy debate (at least as I observe it) is conducted within far more confined circles; the Archbishop rightly cautions against drawing that circle of consultation too narrowly. By the same token, as a distinguished theologian, he surely agrees that public authorities will be more willing to learn from theology's distinctive perspective on national and international security issues when theologians and clergymen demonstrate that their perceptions are informed by a clear view of the just war tradition as part of a responsible Christian theory of statecraft.

Having written early and at length that a revolution of conscience preceded and made possible the Revolution of 1989 in Central and Eastern Europe, I am not unaware of the imperative of sustaining what Dr. Williams nicely describes as "the freedom of moral theology to sustain the self-critical habit in a nation and its political classes." Perhaps the aforementioned difference between the United States and Great Britain as political cultures leads me to be somewhat less concerned about the possibility of a weakening of theology's critical voice in the foreign policy debates of the early twenty-first century. My confidence that the debate will continue to be morally informed here in America may also have something to do with the relative culture-forming capacities of Christian communities here and in Britain. (It would be interesting, for example, to learn if the just war tradition is as alive in the British defense and military establishment, or at Sandhurst and Dartmouth, as it is in the American officer corps, and at West Point and Annapolis.)

In any event, and to return to the beginning, I take Dr. Williams' lecture—and our basic agreement on the intrinsic relationship of the just war tradition to a morally informed Christian theory of statecraft—as a hopeful sign that what I termed the "forgetting" of the just war tradition may be remedied by the kind of forthright, critical, and ecumenical conversation to which the Archbishop and I are both committed.

18

TORTURE
A Just War Perspective

—James Turner Johnson

I have been asked to bring a just war perspective to the contemporary debate over torture. I do not believe I have seen any effort to do this in the various sorts of discussions of the problem of torture I have read over the past several years. Rather, the discourse has been framed largely in terms of the "war on terrorism"—arguments over how to combat terrorism, how to protect the lives of those threatened by terrorist attacks, how to preserve United States national security in the face of the threat posed by terrorism, and so on. More specifically, what I have seen—in abundance—is various forms of consequentialist argumentation, including the balancing of lesser and greater evils and debates over whether torture actually works or not to produce useful intelligence.

By contrast, the classic just war tradition is not, *pace* so many contemporary philosophers and ethicists, rooted in consequentialist reasoning. *Pace* also the United States Conference of Catholic Bishops, whose spokesmen since the bishops' adoption of a revised, untraditional form of just war theory in *The Challenge of Peace* in 1983, have regularly given priority to the consequentialist criteria of last resort, proportionality, and reasonable hope of success. These have figured prominently in all their public statements against the use of armed force by the United States.

The classic form of just war reasoning found in the historical tradition is something quite different. All the consequentialist criteria just mentioned have been added to just war reasoning quite recently, dating back no more than about forty years. This is not to say that they do not have their uses in moral argument, only that they are not part of the idea of just war found in the classic just war tradition, as this took shape from the twelfth- and thirteenth-century canonists through Aquinas, theorists of the Chivalric Code, and later theologians like Vitoria, Suarez, Grotius, and the English Puritan William Ames. This classic conception remained intact in the moral tradition until recently and, in a development tracing to Grotius, also provides the moral base for the law of armed conflict in international law. Properly to bring a just war perspective to the problem of torture means looking back into the formal provisions of the classic idea of just war and the moral

* *The Review of Faith & International Affairs* 5, no. 2 (Summer 2007): 29–31.

logic underlying it, then asking what moral wisdom can be drawn from this for thinking about torture.

Formally, the just war idea by the beginning of the modern period included requirements defining both when resort to force is just and imposing limits on how force might be used—the two aspects of just war reasoning later called the *jus ad bellum* and the *jus in bello*. The former included the requirements that use of force be undertaken only on sovereign authority (that is, by a person or persons with final responsibility for the common good of a political community); that it be undertaken only for a just cause (punishing evildoing, retaking things wrongly taken by others, or in other ways defending the common good of the community in question); and that it be undertaken only with a right intention (understood negatively as avoidance of certain specified wrong intentions, positively as the intention of establishing or reestablishing peace). The limits on how force might be used were defined in two ways: by lists of classes of persons (and their property) not to be made the object of direct, intended attack, and by prohibitions against certain types of weapons and uses of weapons deemed *mala in se*. These formal provisions were conceived deontologically; that is, they established binding moral duties on those involved in the decisions about whether to use force and how to use it, if the former decision were that force is justified in the case at issue.

But underlying this deontological structure of the formal just war rules lay a conception of the moral agent in terms of a virtue theory of ethics. The sovereign, for example, was not conceived simply as whoever happened to be head of a political community, but as one who needed to possess the virtues necessary to exercise political leadership and serve the common good. Similarly, the soldier was not simply anyone who happened to carry arms but one who had had the virtues of the profession of arms inculcated in him. These two forms of moral logic supported each other: a ruler who misused the armed power at his command was understood as a tyrant, not a sovereign, and a soldier was reminded of what his professional virtue required by the just war lists of wrong intentions, illicit targets, and wrongful means.

To my knowledge none of the major theorists and jurists who gave shape to just war tradition in its classic form ever discussed torture. But they never discussed counter-city bombing or the use of poison gas, or many other specific matters, either. One may work forward from what they did say, and the moral logics behind that, to issues before us today. What we know as terrorism can never be just, by classic just war standards, because the people who authorize terrorist attacks do not have the moral right to do so and because the direct, intended objects of those attacks are noncombatants. Similarly, a response to a terrorist attack, even if undertaken in the name of sovereign responsibility for the common good, can never morally involve an attack on whole populations of persons among whom terrorists live and take shelter. Such judgments follow straightforwardly and simply from understanding the meaning embodied in classic just war thinking.

For the case of torture two elements of the classic idea of just war apply, and perhaps three: what the tradition says on wrong intention, what it says on those not to be directly and intentionally attacked, and perhaps also the limits on morally permissible means.

First to the matter of wrong intention. For classic just war thinkers this was defined by a passage from Augustine they often quoted:

What is evil in war? It is not the deaths of some who will soon die anyway. The passion for inflicting harm, the cruel thirst for vengeance, an unpacific and relentless spirit, the fever of revolt, the lust of power, and such like things; all these are rightly condemned in war. (*Contra Faust.* xxii, 74)

For an extended period in the eleventh and twelfth centuries a series of church councils in Western Europe imposed penances on warriors who had taken part in battle, assuming that in the heat of combat they might likely have been motivated by one or more of these wrong intentions and giving them the opportunity to repent and seek to atone for this. For the case of torture, this concept of wrong intention bears directly on any person or persons who inflict it: can they do so without one or more of the wrong intentions Augustine listed, or other similarly wrong intentions? Unless such persons have no moral sense at all (in criminal cases they are understood as psychopathic personalities), I think not, for torture not only harms the person who is its object, but it corrupts and damages the person who does it as well. In itself this is a strong reason why we should not, as a society, endorse torture.

Second, what about the matter of doing no direct, intended harm to noncombatants? Traditional just war thought, as well as the law of armed conflict in international law, approaches this matter by listing classes of persons who normally do not take a direct part in the fighting or in close support of those who do, and prohibiting direct, intended harm to them. The earliest lists include classes of people who normally did not bear arms: women, children, the aged and infirm, clergy and monks, peasants working their land, merchants and pilgrims on the road, ordinary townspeople. In the latter part of the Middle Ages this list expanded to include warriors who had been captured or rendered incapable of fighting by wounds. The most recent formulation in the law of armed conflicts renders all the former—and more—under the term "civilians," while specifically naming prisoners of war and the wounded as not to be made the object of further attack. This limitation applies to all persons involved in armed conflict of any kind, including those involving terrorism.

As to the matter of means, the classic prohibition of certain means as *mala in se* serves as a reminder that some means simply ought not to be used in war. The lists that could be compiled of weapons bans and limits in both the moral and international legal traditions quite obviously do not include every single means that ought not to be used. Sometimes the moral repugnance of a given means is itself reason not to have to name it explicitly as wrong to employ. I suggest the distinctive means of torture are of this sort: they are so morally repugnant no second thought should be needed to know that they ought not to be used.

In sum, reflecting on just war tradition yields two very basic and important pieces of moral wisdom, corresponding to the deontological and virtue-ethics aspects of the tradition, respectively. First, there are some things that are never to be done; the rules prohibiting direct, intended attacks on those not taking part in the use of force extend to the prohibition of torture of prisoners. Second, there are some things that a good person may never do; torturing involves intentions that are directly contrary to what it means to be a good human person. Torture is wrong in both these ways. In addition, the means distinctive to torture violate both these concerns. Together, these implications of just war tradition tell us that torture should never be morally allowed.

19

THE NEW JIHAD AND ISLAMIC TRADITION

—John Kelsay

On October 21, 2001, Osama bin Laden issued a statement via Al Jazeera television. With U.S.-led military action underway in Afghanistan, bin Laden spoke about the September 11 attacks in New York and Washington, D.C.

> God Almighty hit the United States at its most vulnerable spot. Here is the United States. It was filled with terror from its north to its south and from its east to its west. Praise be to God. What the United States tastes today is a very small thing compared to what we have tasted for tens of years. Our nation has been tasting this humiliation and contempt for more than eighty years. Its sons are being killed, its blood is being shed, its holy places are being attacked, and it is not being ruled according to what God has decreed.

Bin Laden speaks of those carrying out the September 11 attacks as God's convoy, the vanguard of Islam. He prays for them, asking God to "elevate their status and grant them Paradise."

These comments set the context for a discussion of "the new jihad and the Islamic tradition." By the "new jihad," I mean bin Laden's or al-Qaeda's commitment to armed struggle against the United States and its allies. This jihad is "new," in the sense that it is "up to date" or recent. That is how bin Laden and other al-Qaeda spokespersons present their efforts. For them, this jihad is the latest chapter in a struggle as old as humanity. It is the most recent instantiation of the conflict between Islam, that submission to the will of God which constitutes the natural religion of humanity, and the attitude of heedlessness towards God's will.

From bin Laden's point of view, the new jihad is thus a consistent expression of historic Islamic tradition. I want to question this. I will suggest that bin Laden's jihad is new, not so much in the sense of "up to date," as in the sense of a departure from tradition, an innovation.

Many people argued something like this in the wake of the September 11 attacks. Representatives of American Muslim groups, for example, issued statements disassociating

---

* Templeton Lectures on Religion and World Affairs, FPRI Wire, October 2003.

Islam from the attacks, and quoting Qur'an 5:32, which indicates that if anyone kills another unjustly, it is as though he or she killed the entire world. If one is looking for texts, it's a simple matter to show that there is a gap between jihad as envisioned by Osama bin Laden and jihad in Islamic tradition.

In the end, however, citing such texts does not settle much. It ignores bin Laden's arguments, for example concerning when killing is justified, and which persons are legitimate as targets of military activity.

I am going to take a more difficult road. Islamic tradition on matters of war is really a kind of extended conversation about God's law, the shari'a. In this conversation, one reads the texts of the Qur'an, reports of the example of the Prophet, the recorded judgments of great scholars, and then argues about how these relate to current circumstances. In these comments, I shall display an argument between Muslims. In particular, I want to show how some, who actually agree with al-Qaeda on many issues of import, nonetheless find reason to criticize some aspects of the new jihad as inconsistent with Islamic tradition. I begin with a review of some classic themes of Islamic tradition. I then provide a brief summary of the modern career of those themes. Then follows the heart of my remarks, which is a discussion of an argument among Islamists regarding the new jihad. Finally, I advance a brief conclusion.

Themes in the History of Islamic Political Thought

Over the course of 14 centuries, Islamic political thought centers on two great themes. The first of these emphasizes the importance of establishing a just public order, while the second focuses on notions of honorable combat.

Historically speaking, Muslim scholars held that the establishment of a just public order is an obligation. Some said it was so by God's command; others said this was a dictate of reason. In either case, they usually thought of the phrase "just public order" in terms of a state defined by an Islamic establishment. We would put it this way: a just public order is one in which Islam is the established religion; where the ruler is a Muslim, and consults with recognized Islamic authorities on matters of policy; finally, where groups committed to other religions could live in safety, because they are "protected" by the Islamic establishment. This pattern held for many Muslim thinkers from the time of the early Islamic conquests (in the seventh century C.E.) through the demise of the Ottoman caliphate (in 1924).

Notions of honorable combat developed in connection with reflection on the duty to establish a just public order. The idea was that, under certain conditions, the establishment, maintenance, and defense of justice would require armed force. When such conditions occurred, armed force or combat was to be conducted in accord with norms of honor. For example, resort to combat needed authorization by publicly recognized authorities. Such authorities should make sure that fighting occurred in connection with a just cause, and with the intention of building, maintaining, or protecting public order. The same authorities should consider whether or not fighting would be a proportionate response to perceived injustice, whether Muslim forces were likely to succeed, and whether fighting would serve the end of building the kind of public order that serves peace. Finally, they were to consider whether combat is the most fitting way to pursue justice, considering the circumstances—in other words, are there alternative ways to seek justice that might be more appropriate in a given case?

In addition to these considerations, those fighting for justice were to be governed by the saying attributed to the Prophet Muhammad: "Do not cheat or commit treachery. Do not mutilate anyone, nor should you kill children." Other reports indicate that Muhammad further prohibited the direct and intentional killing of women, the very old, those physically or mentally handicapped, monks, and others. The idea was that honorable combat involved soldiers fighting soldiers and those noncombatants are never to be the direct target of military action. Of course, there are times when combat involves taking aim at a military target, knowing that there is a strong likelihood of indirect harm to civilians (that is, "collateral damage"). In such cases, Muslim scholars debated many issues related to the use of particular weaponry: Should a fighting force make use of mangonels or hurling machines, for example? The concern in these cases was that certain weapons might cause disproportionate or excessive damage to civilians, even though the direct target of the weapon was military in nature.

Modern Tensions

For the last 80 years, the tradition of Islamic political thought has been under stress or under dispute. In itself, this is not unique. Traditions are always susceptible of dispute. That is, they are so for as long as they are living traditions. One generation bequeaths to the next a framework for discussion; the new generation tries to establish a "fit" between that which is handed down and its own set of circumstances. When people stop arguing about a tradition, that is a sign it is no longer viable.

Thus, Muslim argument is nothing new. Nevertheless, one could say that the last 80 years mark a period of particular stress, in which the most contentious point has been the question "What constitutes a just public order?" In 1924 the new Turkish Republic withdrew support for the Ottoman ruler. This effectively abolished the last remaining symbol of the great empires of the Middle Period, as well as of the older notions of a universal state governed by an Islamic establishment. In the years following, and indeed for much of the 20th century, Muslim intellectuals argued about the shape a modern Islamic political order might take. One part of that argument focused (and still focuses) on the sort of legal regime such an order should have. Must a properly Islamic state be governed by divine law only, in the sense that its laws and policies are derived directly from the Qur'an, the example of the Prophet, and interpretive precedents established by the consensus of recognized scholars? Or can such a state form its laws and policies based on a more diverse set of sources? For example, can an Islamic State shape its policies based on contemporary international practice? Those holding that an Islamic State must be governed by divine law only are sometimes called "fundamentalists" or "radicals." Those arguing for a more diverse set of sources are sometimes called "moderates." None of these terms is entirely adequate, but they are the terms of contemporary discussion, and thus I employ them here.

The focus on the meaning of the phrase "Islamic State" means, in effect, that most modern Islamic political thought is concerned with how one might fulfill the obligation to establish a just public order. More recently, however, attention has turned to the historic notion of honorable combat. We are familiar by now with the "moderate" side of this debate. Post-9/11, many moderate Muslims argue that, even if fundamentalists are right, and that the current state of political order is unjust, there are nevertheless limits on what one may do to effect change. There are some tactics, people say, that violate the

Muslim conscience. This is especially true of tactics that make noncombatants or civilians into direct targets of military or para-military attacks. The conduct of martyrdom operations in Palestinian resistance to Israel is of concern in this regard. Even more is the use of indiscriminate tactics by al-Qaeda.

Critiques of the New Jihad

Moderate Muslims have been very clear in condemning al-Qaeda's tactics as a violation of Islamic tradition. Less well-covered in American or European media is the fact that some fundamentalists have also been vigorous in this regard. That is, there are those who share with al-Qaeda a sense that a just public order must be governed by divine law only, yet who think al-Qaeda's tactics are problematic, on Islamic grounds.

For example, on July 10, 2002, the Al Jazeera network interviewed a well-known Saudi dissident, Shaykh Muhsin al-'Awaji.[1] Two others joined by telephone. All three had served time in prison for criticisms of the royal family and its policies of cooperation with the United States. All hold for government by divine law, in the strong sense. All have on other occasions expressed support for armed resistance by Muslims.

During the interview, the conversation turned to Osama bin Laden. The three scholars indicated that, after initial approval of bin Laden, they and many others have changed their opinion. Shaykh al-'Awaji commented that,

> In the past, when he was fighting the Russians in Afghanistan, bin Laden was the greatest of jihad warriors, in the eyes of the Saudi people and in the eyes of the Saudi government. He and the others went to Afghanistan with official support, and the support of the learned [the "ulama" or religious scholars].

In some ways, this positive assessment of bin Laden still holds. Given all the facts, however, al-'Awaji and his colleagues revised their estimate. Bin Laden, they said, is guilty of spreading discord among Muslims. He labels people heretics without proof, and some operations sponsored by al-Qaeda bring harm to Muslims. Most critically, al-Qaeda's tactics violate the norms of honorable combat. "He and those with him target innocent people, and I refer to the innocents on the face of the entire earth, of every religion and color, and in every region."

The immediate background of al-'Awaji's remarks is formed by the June 7, 2002 publication of Sulayman abu Ghayth's internet article "In the Shadow of the Lances." There, an al-Qaeda spokesman argued vigorously that the norms of reciprocal justice indicate that Muslims "have the right to kill four million Americans, two million of them children." al-'Awaji's arguments would seem a direct rebuke to this kind of reasoning. For him, it appears, Muslims are to fight with honor, which means (among other things) that they are not to engage in direct attacks on noncombatants. Similarly, consider the arguments offered by Shaykh 'Umar Bakri Muhammad of al-Muhajiroun, a fundamentalist group based in the United Kingdom. Shaykh 'Umar's tract, *Jihad: The Method for Khilafah?* appeared at www.almuhajiroun.com in September 2002. This tract attempted to evaluate the place of armed struggle in the attempt to found a state governed by divine law. The author then discussed the nature and place of armed resistance in contemporary contexts.

According to Shaykh 'Umar, jihad, in the sense of "armed struggle," is a term reserved for fighting authorized by an established Islamic government. This is the sense of the reference to khilafah in his title. Literally, the term suggests "succession" to the Prophet Muhammad. Shaykh 'Umar uses the term as a designation for Islamic government. His discussion reiterates one of the great themes of Islamic political thought, that is, the necessity that justice be embodied in a political order. And, as he indicates, when this political order is in place, it should seek to extend its influence by appropriate means. These can and should include honorable combat.

For the last 80 years, the kind of authority indicated by the term khilafah has been absent from political life. This fact sets the context for the rest of Shaykh 'Umar's argument. Muslims are required to work to change this situation, and to establish khilafah. To that end, may or should they engage in jihad? The answer is no, first of all because of the nature of the concept. Jihad designates fighting that occurs under the auspices of an established government. By definition, then, fighting that takes place apart from such a government's authorization cannot be jihad. To this definitional "no" Shaykh 'Umar adds a second reason: Islamic political thought requires that authority be legitimate, in the sense of established through a process of consultation and assent. The submission of Muslims to an authority thus ought not to be compelled. Islamic government should be established through persuasion.

Shaykh 'Umar indicates that the process of consultation and assent may be conducted in a number of ways. He then moves to a discussion of contemporary resistance among Muslims. In his view, the Muslim community is in a kind of political twilight zone. Without a duly constituted khilafah, there can be no fighting worthy of the title jihad. Yet Muslims are in need of defense, in Chechnya, Kashmir, and other locations. What are they to do?

As Shaykh 'Umar has it, Islam recognizes a right of extended self-defense. Everyone has the right to defend his/her own life, liberty, and property. Everyone also has the right, and in some sense the duty, to defend the lives, liberties, and properties of others who are victims of aggression. This kind of fighting is called qital, a word that quite literally indicates "fighting" or "killing." Where Muslims are under attack, their co-religionists around the globe may and should come to their defense. When they do, however, they should understand that fighting is delimited, first in terms of its goals. Qital is not a proper means of establishing Islamic government. Second, qital is limited in its means. Interestingly, in this qital and jihad are similar, since both are governed by norms of honorable combat, or as Shaykh 'Umar puts it, by the "pro-life" values of the Prophet Muhammad: "not killing women and children, not killing the elderly or monks." Tactics that involve direct attacks on noncombatants are ruled out.

Given the type of criticism voiced by al-'Awaji, Shaykh 'Umar, and others, it's not surprising that the leadership of al-Qaeda would respond. Thus, in November 2002, a "Letter to America" bearing the name of Osama bin Laden appeared.[2]

The first part of the "Letter" is a list of reasons for fighting against the U.S. and its allies. The second part of the text moves to the question of tactics. "You may then dispute that all the above does not justify aggression against civilians, for crimes they did not commit and offenses in which they did not partake."

The concern here is clearly with arguments that al-Qaeda tactics violate norms of honorable combat. The author of "Letter" does not accept these. Two counterarguments are cited in justification of a policy of attacking civilians as well as soldiers.

First, the United States claims to be a democracy. "The American people have the ability and choice to refuse the policies of their government and even to change it if they want."

Second (and in a way reminiscent of abu Ghayth's argument), the author cites the *lex talionis*. "God, the Almighty, legislated the permission and the option to take revenge . . . whoever has killed our civilians, then we have the right to kill theirs." Harm suffered may be avenged by the infliction of damage proportionate to the original harm. Muslims have the right to kill U.S. and other "enemy" civilians, because the U.S. and its allies engage in actions that kill civilians on the Muslim side.

Concluding Remarks

What are we to make of this exchange? Primarily, I think it is important to know that such conversations take place. The post-9/11 discussion of Islam and fighting has tended to swing between two assertions: Either Islam has nothing to do with fighting of this type, or it has everything to do with it. Neither of these assertions is accurate. Neither catches the sense of Islamic tradition as a living reality, in which people try to discern God's will in particular circumstances by reading agreed-upon texts and reasoning according to established rules. In that light, it is important to get a sense of the conversations Muslims have about political justice and honorable combat. In these remarks, I have tried to show that these include conversations between "allied" groups of fundamentalists or radicals, as well as between moderates and fundamentalists. This fact seems important in itself. Among other things, the post-9/11 Muslim discussion of al-Qaeda tactics suggests the power of certain ideas; for example, that there are limits on what one can do, even when one is fighting for justice. In this sense, the post-9/11 conversation among Muslims goes back to the Qur'an itself, which at 2:190 indicates to Muslims:

> Fight against those who are fighting you but do not violate the limits. God does not approve those who violate the limits.[3]

I believe this verse contains a proposition of interest to Muslims and non-Muslims, religious people of all faiths as well as those who profess no faith, as we try to respond to the demands of justice.

— Section IV —

RELIGION AND CONFLICT

20

TERROR MANDATED BY GOD

—Mark Juergensmeyer

Shortly after Noam Friedman, an off-duty Israeli soldier, lay down on the ground in a crowded market in Hebron on 1 January 1997 and sprayed M16 automatic rifle fire at Arab shoppers, wounding seven, he claimed that he had been on a mission from God. "Abraham bought the Cave of the Patriarchs for four hundred shekels of silver," Friedman said, referring to the Hebron shrine that is holy to all three Abrahamic faiths—Judaism, Christianity, and Islam. "And," he added, "nobody will give it back."[1]

Friedman's actions, eerily similar to the 1994 attack on Arab worshippers at the Cave of the Patriarchs by Dr. Baruch Goldstein, a Jewish settler who was also garbed in uniform at the time, and to the 1995 assassination of Prime Minister Yitzhak Rabin by Yigal Amir, are characteristic of a new face of terrorism. These are terrorist acts committed not just for a strategic political objective but as part of a religious mission. In many such cases, including the attacks of Friedman and Goldstein, the perpetrators see themselves as soldiers in a spiritual army, engaged in a great cosmic war. These religious warriors hope that their victory will usher in a new epoch and a new religious kingdom on earth.

In an earlier book, I looked at this extraordinary longing for religious kingdoms that has fueled new movements for religious nationalism around the world.[2] I am now working on a follow-up volume that deals specifically with the violent aspects of this confrontation between religion and the secular state: religious terrorism. For this new project I have conducted case studies and held interviews in the Middle East, India, Japan, and the United States. I have focused on the Aum Shinrikyo's nerve gas attack in the Tokyo subways; the World Trade Center bombing and the Bojinka plot to blow up a series of airplanes by a group of Muslims associated with Sheik Omar Abd al-Rahman; the Sikh Khalistani movement's airplane highjacking, car bombings, and political assassinations in India; the Hamas suicide bus bombings in Jerusalem; the attacks by members of Kach and other extreme Jewish groups in Hebron; and assaults by Christian militia and the killing of abortion clinic staff by other militant Christians in the United States.

* *Terrorism and Political Violence* 9, no. 2 (Summer 1997): 16–23.

In studying these cases, I regard terrorism as "the public performance of violent power." By that I mean acts that are meant to demonstrate the strength of a movement and its ideas in the public sphere. For that reason, I view acts of religious terrorism as cultural constructions that have a broad public audience.[3] In looking at these cases, I have tried to answer two basic questions: why do religious groups seek public power, and why do they seek it now?

Why Religion?

The Japanese case of religious terrorism provides some interesting clues, in part because the violence of the 1994 nerve gas attack in the Tokyo subways was so unexpected. Like Europe, America, and much of the rest of the world, Japanese society has witnessed an explosive growth of new religious movements, so there was nothing unusual in Japan about the emergence of a new religion like Aum Shinrikyo and its eclectic religious philosophy that blends Mahayana and Tibetan Buddhism with new age mysticism, a self-help philosophy, and Christian visions of the apocalyptic end of the millennium. There was nothing unusual about Aum's tight, secretive organization, its cathartic initiation process, and the subservience it required to its almost god-like and dominating leader. There was nothing unusual about the movement's paranoia, its Manichaean black-and-white view of the world. What was unusual about Aum Shinrikyo was the projection of these religious ideas onto a political plane, and its attempt to make the secular Japanese state into a satanic foe.

What is distinctive about the international terrorism of the 1980s and 1990s is this combination of politics and religion. By politics I mean the awareness of, and challenge to, the prevailing social order and its recognized authorities. By religion I mean not just an ethnic religious identity—such as Irish Catholic or Tamil Hindu—but the appropriation of an ideology of transformative significance, the sort of religious and political vision that transformed Iran after the Islamic revolution of 1978–79.[4] Such an ideology is usually couched in the rhetoric of traditional religion and touches on a great many aspects of daily life. It provides the vision and commitment that propels an activist into scenes of violence, and it supplies the ideological glue that makes that activist's community of support cohere.

As in the case of the Aum Shinrikyo, militant religious activists often interject religious mythology into real-life political struggles, and find in religion a legitimization and a support for acts of violence as if they were mandated by God. In their vision of a world gone bad, what most of us regard as ordinary politics—the secular politics of modern civil societies—is viewed as the enemy of religion.

In the view of the leader of Aum Shinrikyo, for example, the Japanese government was in collusion with the United States in a global plot to destroy religion. Similarly, Rabbi Meir Kahane regarded the secular politics of the Israelis—backed by the United States—as a greater enemy than the Arabs, and Sheik Omar Abd al-Rahman aimed at attacking the American government's support for Egypt's nominally Islamic but basically secular government in Cairo, which the Sheik saw as a satanic enemy of Islam.

In the Japanese case, Aum's leader, Shoko Asahara, envisioned a new political order to be led by its members after a colossally destructive World War III, which he predicted would occur around the year 2000. The nerve gas attack in the Tokyo subways in 1995 was meant to be an indication of the cosmic confrontation to come. One of the members of the movement told me that when he heard about the attack he was convinced that Shoko Asahara's prophecies were being fulfilled, and that "the weird time has come."[5]

Inside the Aum Shinrikyo movement's headquarters in Tokyo, those members of the movement who were not involved in the plot quickly came to the conclusion that the nerve gas assault on the subways was indeed an attack on the Japanese government, albeit a deceptive one undertaken by the government itself in order to deflect the public's attention from what the Aum members thought had really occurred: the Third World War had broken out, and the Japanese government had been secretly captured by America. The use of nerve gas seemed to confirm this theory, since the Aum members assumed that in Japan only American army bases possessed such a weapon.[6]

Prophetic statements made by the leader of the movement, Shoko Asahara, scarcely months before the subway attack indicate another reason for doing it, and also indicate why Asahara and his colleagues chose the Kasumigaseki station of the subways as the prime location. Asahara prophesied that in the coming great conflagration at the end of the twentieth century, the most devious of weapons, including nerve gas, would be used against the populace. Sarin was mentioned by name. Asahara urged the public to join movements such as Aum that were protecting themselves against such an attack, since the Japanese government could not sufficiently protect them; it had prepared "a poor defense for the coming war," Asahara said.[7] He went on to say that the government had constructed only one subway station of sufficient depth and security to be used as a haven in time of nuclear or poisonous gas attack. "Only the Kasumigaseki subway station, which is near the Diet Building," Asahara explained, "can be used as a shelter."[8]

In Asahara's mind, then, the Kasumigaseki station was not only a symbol of government activity, but of governmental power: it symbolized the government's attempts to protect its citizens in time of crisis. When he unleashed nerve gas in this location, Asahara showed that that power and that protection were vulnerable, for the government could not guard its people even in Tokyo's safest place. By implication only Aum, with its spiritual and physical forms of defense, could offer a true haven. The attack on the Kasumigaseki station, then, was intended as an assault on the Japanese public's sense of security. The enormous public response to the event amply demonstrated that the public interpreted the attack in precisely that way.

In virtually every other recent example of terrorism, the building, vehicle, structure, or locale where the assault has taken place has had a symbolic significance. In some cases the symbolism of the locale was specific: the abortion clinics in the United States, for example, that were bombed by religious pro-life activists; or the tourist boats and hotels in Egypt that were attacked by Islamic activists who regarded them as impositions from a foreign culture. Sheik Abd al-Rahman had proclaimed such tourists sites as "sinful" and insisted that "the lands of Muslims will not become bordellos for sinners of every race and color."[9] The shrine of the Cave of the Patriarchs in Hebron, where Dr. Goldstein killed scores of praying Muslims, also had specific symbolic significance, for Goldstein and his group regarded the shrine as emblematic of the Muslim occupation of Jewish territory.

The symbolism of other locations has been more general: the locations were emblematic of the power and stability of society itself. Buildings such as the World Trade Center and Oklahoma City federal building, along with airplanes, subways, and public buses, are examples of such general symbols. One group—the Islamic al Fuqra ("the impoverished") movement based in upstate New York—is accused of hatching a plot to disable Colorado's electrical system.[10] In showing the vulnerability of a nation's most stable and powerful entities, movements that undertake these acts of sabotage touch virtually everyone in a nation's society. Any person in the United States could have been riding the elevator in the World Trade Center, visiting the Oklahoma City federal building, or taking a trip on Air India flight 182 when the bombs exploded; and everyone in the United States will look differently at the stability of public buildings and transportation systems as a result of these violent incidents.

What is significant about these symbolically central things, including subways and airplanes, is that they represent power. They are cultural centers in Clifford Geertz's use of the term: "concentrated loci of serious acts."[11] What makes them centers is that they are the "arenas" in a society, "where its leading ideas come together with its leading institutions" and where "momentous events" are thought to occur.[12] When one attacks such a place, be it an airport or the World Trade Center or the Kasumigaseki subway station in central Tokyo, one challenges the power and legitimacy of society itself.

The Post-Modern Terrorism of Religion

It is clear, then, that the use of violence allows a religious group to assert not only its power but also its legitimacy. Challenging the notion that the state holds the monopoly on morally sanctioned violence, as Max Weber once averred, religious groups can show their moral superiority by sanctioning violence on their own.

But why would religious activists want to demonstrate this power over secular authority now? In looking for answers to this question, I have sought clues in the common temporal context of all recent acts of religious terrorism: namely, this particular period of late twentieth-century modernity. What was significant about the Enlightenment three centuries ago was its proclamation of the death of religion; what is significant about the present period is the perception of the death of secularism. By that I mean the widespread impression that secular culture and its forms of nationalism are unable to provide the moral fiber that unites national communities, or offer the ideological strength to sustain states that have been buffeted by economic and military failures. In other words, there is the widespread perception that politics is immoral and public life desperately needs the sacred cleansing that religion can offer it.

The shifts in economic and political power that have occurred following the break-up of the Soviet Union and the sudden rise of Japanese and other Asian economies in the last twenty years of the twentieth century have had significant social repercussions. The public sense of insecurity that has come in the wake of these changes is felt not only in the societies of those nations that are economically devastated by them—especially countries in the former Soviet Union—but also in economically stronger areas. The United States, for example, has seen a remarkable degree of disaffection with its political leaders and witnessed the rise of right-wing religious movements that feed on the public's perception of the immorality of government.

At the extreme end of this religious rejection are members of Defensive Action, a violent anti-abortion group; the Christian Identity movement, such as the Freemen Community in Montana; the Christian militia that supported Timothy McVeigh, the convicted bomber of the Oklahoma Federal Building; and isolated groups such as the Branch

Davidian sect headquartered in Waco, Texas. Similar movements have emerged in Israel— Rabbi Meir Kahane's Kach party was an extreme example—and in Japan, which is also experiencing disillusionment regarding its national purpose and destiny. As in America, the critique and sectarian experiments with Japan's political alternatives often take religious forms. New religious movements in Japan that have attempted to play a political and social role in society include the Soka Gakkai, Agon Shu, and the now infamous Aum Shinrikyo.

The global shifts that have led to a crisis of national purpose in developed countries have, in a somewhat different way, affected the less developed nations. Leaders such as India's Jawaharlal Nehru, Egypt's Gamal Abdel Nasser, and Iran's Reza Shah Pahlavi once were committed to creating versions of America—or a kind of cross between America and the Soviet Union—in their own countries. But a new generation of leaders has emerged in areas that were formerly European colonies who no longer believe in the Westernized vision of a Nehru, a Nasser, or the Shah. Rather, they are eager to complete the process of de-colonialization.

The former colonies have seen a resurgence of religious activists such as Sheik Ahmed Yassin in Palestine, Sayyid Qutb and his disciple, Sheik Omar Abd al-Rahman, in Egypt, L. K. Advani in India, Sant Jarnail Singh Bhindranwale in India's Punjab, and the Ayatollah Khomeini in Iran (a country which was never colonized but fell under Western influence under the Shah). These leaders have asserted the legitimacy of their countries' own traditional values in the public sphere, and built a postcolonial national identity based on indigenous culture. This determination was made all the more keen when confronted with the media assault of Western music, videos, and films that satellite television has beamed around the world, and which has threatened to obliterate local and traditional forms of cultural expression.

The result of this disaffection with the culture of the modern West has been what I have called a "loss of faith" in the political form of that culture, secular nationalism.[13] Although a few years ago it would have been a startling notion, the idea has now become virtually commonplace that nationalism as we know it in the modern West is in crisis, in large part because it is seen as a cultural construction closely linked with what Jürgen Habermas has called "the project of modernity."[14] Increasingly we live in a multicultural world where a variety of views of nationhood are in competition. In a world that verges on cultural anarchism, religious answers to the questions of identity and meaning have extraordinary popular appeal.

The Future of Religious Terrorism

These trends that have given rise to movements of religious nationalism around the world will not soon abate. Since violence has been the way that many of these movements express their power and lay claims to their legitimacy, it is unlikely that the world has seen the end of acts of religious terrorism. In fact, the symbolic importance of the year 2000 as a convergence point in history may propel Christian movements especially into a greater activism and a greater propensity for violent confrontation.

Although acts of violence will most likely continue to be conducted by small rogue bands, it is important to take seriously not only their potential for destruction, but their broad bases of support within society at large. In most cases, the postmodern religious rebels who have promoted religious solutions to society's problems are neither anomalies nor anachronisms. From Algeria to Idaho, the small but potent groups of violent activists represent masses of supporters, and they exemplify currents of thinking and cultures of commitment that have risen to counter the prevailing modernism—the ideology of individualism and skepticism—that in the past three centuries has emerged from the European Enlightenment and spread throughout the world.

Religious activists like Yigal Amir, Sheik Omar Abd al-Rahman, and Shoko Asahara have come to hate secular governments with an almost transcendent passion and dream of revolutionary changes that will establish a godly social order in the rubble of what the citizens of most secular societies regard as modern, egalitarian democracies. Their enemies seem to most of us to be both benign and banal: modern, secular leaders like Yitzhak Rabin or Anwar Sadat, and such symbols of prosperity and authority as the international airlines, the World Trade Center, and the Japanese subway system. The logic of their ideological religious view is, although difficult to comprehend, profound, for it contains a fundamental critique of the world's post-Enlightenment secular culture and politics.

In the wake of secularism, and after years of waiting in history's wings, religion has made its re-appearance as an ideology of public order in a dramatic fashion: violently. Religion's renewed political presence is accompanied by violence in part because of the nature of religion and its claims for power over life in death. In part it is due to the nature of secular politics, which places its own legitimacy on the currency of weapons and can only be challenged successfully on a military level. And in part it is due to the nature of violence itself. Violence is a destructive display of power, and in a time when competing groups are attempting to assert their strength, the power of violence becomes a valuable political commodity. At the very least the proponents of a religious ideology of social control such as the leaders of the Aum Shinrikyo have to remind the populace of the godly power that makes their ideology potent; at their destructive worst, religious activists try to create man-made incidents of terror on God's behalf.

21

THE CLASH OF CIVILIZATIONS?

—Samuel P. Huntington

The Next Pattern of Conflict

World politics is entering a new phase, and intellectuals have not hesitated to prolifer- ate visions of what it will be—the end of history, the return of traditional rivalries between nation states, and the decline of the nation state from the conflicting pulls of trib- alism and globalism, among others. Each of these visions catches aspects of the emerging reality. Yet they all miss a crucial, indeed a central, aspect of what global politics is likely to be in the coming years.

It is my hypothesis that the fundamental source of conflict in this new world will not be primarily ideological or primarily economic. The great divisions among humankind and the dominating source of conflict will be cultural. Nation states will remain the most pow- erful actors in world affairs, but the principal conflicts of global politics will occur between nations and groups of different civilizations. The clash of civilizations will dominate global politics. The fault lines between civilizations will be the battle lines of the future.

Conflict between civilizations will be the latest phase of the evolution of conflict in the modern world. For a century and a half after the emergence of the modern interna- tional system with the Peace of Westphalia, the conflicts of the Western world were largely among princes—emperors, absolute monarchs, and constitutional monarchs attempting to expand their bureaucracies, their armies, their mercantilist economic strength, and, most important, the territory they ruled. In the process they created nation states, and beginning with the French Revolution the principal lines of conflict were between nations rather than princes. In 1793, as R. R. Palmer put it, "The wars of kings were over; the wars of peoples had begun." This nineteenth-century pattern lasted until the end of World War I. Then, as a result of the Russian Revolution and the reaction against it, the con- flict of nations yielded to the conflict of ideologies, first among communism, fascism- Nazism, and liberal democracy, and then between communism and liberal democracy. During the Cold War, this latter conflict became embodied in the struggle between the

* *Foreign Affairs* 72, no. 3 (Summer 1993): 22–49.

two superpowers, neither of which was a nation state in the classical European sense and each of which defined its identity in terms of its ideology.

These conflicts between princes, nation states, and ideologies were primarily conflicts within Western civilization, "Western civil wars," as William Lind has labeled them. This was as true of the Cold War as it was of the world wars and the earlier wars of the seventeenth, eighteenth, and nineteenth centuries. With the end of the Cold War, international politics moves out of its Western phase, and its centerpiece becomes the interaction between the West and non-Western civilizations and among non-Western civilizations. In the politics of civilizations, the people and governments of non-Western civilizations no longer remain the objects of history as targets of Western colonialism but join the West as movers and shapers of history.

The Nature of Civilizations

During the Cold War the world was divided into the First, Second, and Third Worlds. Those divisions are no longer relevant. It is far more meaningful now to group countries not in terms of their political or economic systems or in terms of their level of economic development but rather in terms of their culture and civilization.

What do we mean when we talk of a civilization? A civilization is a cultural entity. Villages, regions, ethnic groups, nationalities, religious groups, all have distinct cultures at different levels of cultural heterogeneity. The culture of a village in southern Italy may be different from that of a village in northern Italy, but both will share in a common Italian culture that distinguishes them from German villages. European communities, in turn, will share cultural features that distinguish them from Arab or Chinese communities. Arabs, Chinese, and Westerners, however, are not part of any broader cultural entity. They constitute civilizations. A civilization is thus the highest cultural grouping of people and the broadest level of cultural identity people have short of that which distinguishes humans from other species. It is defined both by common objective elements, such as language, history, religion, customs, institutions, and by the subjective self-identification of people. People have levels of identity: a resident of Rome may define himself with varying degrees of intensity as a Roman, an Italian, a Catholic, a Christian, a European, a Westerner. The civilization to which he belongs is the broadest level of identification with which he intensely identifies. People can and do redefine their identities and, as a result, the composition and boundaries of civilizations change.

Civilizations may involve a large number of people, as with China ("a civilization pretending to be a state," as Lucian Pye put it), or a very small number of people, such as the Anglophone Caribbean. A civilization may include several nation states, as is the case with Western, Latin American, and Arab civilizations, or only one, as is the case with Japanese civilization. Civilizations obviously blend and overlap, and may include subcivilizations. Western civilization has two major variants, European and North American, and Islam has its Arab, Turkic, and Malay subdivisions. Civilizations are nonetheless meaningful entities, and while the lines between them are seldom sharp, they are real. Civilizations are dynamic; they rise and fall; they divide and merge. And, as any student of history knows, civilizations disappear and are buried in the sands of time.

Westerners tend to think of nation states as the principal actors in global affairs. They have been that, however, for only a few centuries. The broader reaches of human history have been the history of civilizations. In *A Study of History*, Arnold Toynbee identified 21 major civilizations; only six of them exist in the contemporary world.

Why Civilizations Will Clash

Civilization identity will be increasingly important in the future, and the world will be shaped in large measure by the interactions among seven or eight major civilizations. These include Western, Confucian, Japanese, Islamic, Hindu, Slavic-Orthodox, Latin American, and possibly African civilization. The most important conflicts of the future will occur along the cultural fault lines separating these civilizations from one another.

Why will this be the case?

First, differences among civilizations are not only real; they are basic. Civilizations are differentiated from each other by history, language, culture, tradition, and, most important, religion. The people of different civilizations have different views on the relations between God and man, the individual and the group, the citizen and the state, parents and children, husband and wife, as well as differing views of the relative importance of rights and responsibilities, liberty and authority, equality and hierarchy. These differences are the product of centuries. They will not soon disappear. They are far more fundamental than differences among political ideologies and political regimes. Differences do not necessarily mean conflict, and conflict does not necessarily mean violence. Over the centuries, however, differences among civilizations have generated the most prolonged and the most violent conflicts.

Second, the world is becoming a smaller place. The interactions between peoples of different civilizations are increasing; these increasing interactions intensify civilization consciousness and awareness of differences between civilizations and commonalities within civilizations. North African immigration to France generates hostility among Frenchmen and at the same time increased receptivity to immigration by "good" European Catholic Poles. Americans react far more negatively to Japanese investment than to larger investments from Canada and European countries. Similarly, as Donald Horowitz has pointed out, "An Ibo may be . . . an Owerri Ibo or an Onitsha Ibo in what was the Eastern region of Nigeria. In Lagos, he is simply an Ibo. In London, he is a Nigerian. In New York, he is an African." The interactions among peoples of different civilizations enhance the civilization-consciousness of people that, in turn, invigorates differences and animosities stretching or thought to stretch back deep into history.

Third, the processes of economic modernization and social change throughout the world are separating people from longstanding local identities. They also weaken the nation state as a source of identity. In much of the world religion has moved in to fill this gap, often in the form of movements that are labeled "fundamentalist." Such movements are found in Western Christianity, Judaism, Buddhism, and Hinduism, as well as in Islam. In most countries and most religions the people active in fundamentalist movements are young, college-educated, middle-class technicians, professionals, and business persons. The "unsecularization of the world," George Weigel has remarked, "is one of the dominant social facts of life in the late twentieth century." The revival of religion, "la revanche de Dieu," as Gilles Kepel labeled it, provides a basis for identity and commitment that transcends national boundaries and unites civilizations.

Fourth, the growth of civilization-consciousness is enhanced by the dual role of the West. On the one hand, the West is at a peak of power. At the same time, however, and perhaps as a result, a return to the roots phenomenon is occurring among non-Western civilizations. Increasingly one hears references to trends toward a turning inward and "Asianization" in Japan, the end of the Nehru legacy and the "Hinduization" of India, the failure of Western ideas of socialism and nationalism and hence "re-Islamization" of the Middle East, and now a debate over Westernization versus Russianization in Boris Yeltsin's country. A West at the peak of its power confronts non-Wests that increasingly have the desire, the will, and the resources to shape the world in non-Western ways.

In the past, the elites of non-Western societies were usually the people who were most involved with the West, had been educated at Oxford, the Sorbonne, or Sandhurst, and had absorbed Western attitudes and values. At the same time, the populace in non-Western countries often remained deeply imbued with the indigenous culture. Now, however, these relationships are being reversed. A de-Westernization and indigenization of elites is occurring in many non-Western countries at the same time that Western, usually American, cultures, styles, and habits become more popular among the mass of the people.

Fifth, cultural characteristics and differences are less mutable and hence less easily compromised and resolved than political and economic ones. In the former Soviet Union, communists can become democrats, the rich can become poor and the poor rich, but Russians cannot become Estonians and Azeris cannot become Armenians. In class and ideological conflicts, the key question was "Which side are you on?" and people could and did choose sides and change sides. In conflicts between civilizations, the question is "What are you?" That is a given that cannot be changed. And as we know, from Bosnia to the Caucasus to the Sudan, the wrong answer to that question can mean a bullet in the head. Even more than ethnicity, religion discriminates sharply and exclusively among people. A person can be half-French and half-Arab and simultaneously even a citizen of two countries. It is more difficult to be half-Catholic and half-Muslim.

Finally, economic regionalism is increasing. The proportions of total trade that were intraregional rose between 1980 and 1989 from 51 percent to 59 percent in Europe, 33 percent to 37 percent in East Asia, and 32 percent to 36 percent in North America. The importance of regional economic blocs is likely to continue to increase in the future. On the one hand, successful economic regionalism will reinforce civilization-consciousness. On the other hand, economic regionalism may succeed only when it is rooted in a common civilization. The European Community rests on the shared foundation of European culture and Western Christianity. The success of the North American Free Trade Area depends on the convergence now underway of Mexican, Canadian, and American cultures. Japan, in contrast, faces difficulties in creating a comparable economic entity in East Asia because Japan is a society and civilization unique to itself. However strong the trade and investment links Japan may develop with other East Asian countries, its cultural differences with those countries inhibit and perhaps preclude its promoting regional economic integration like that in Europe and North America.

Common culture, in contrast, is clearly facilitating the rapid expansion of the economic relations between the People's Republic of China and Hong Kong, Taiwan, Singapore, and the overseas Chinese communities in other Asian countries. With the Cold War over, cultural commonalities increasingly overcome ideological differences, and mainland China and Taiwan move closer together. If cultural commonality is a prerequisite for economic integration, the principal East Asian economic bloc of the future is likely to be centered on China. This bloc is, in fact, already coming into existence. As Murray Weidenbaum has observed,

> Despite the current Japanese dominance of the region, the Chinese-based economy of Asia is rapidly emerging as a new epicenter for industry, commerce, and finance. This strategic area contains substantial amounts of technology and manufacturing capability (Taiwan), outstanding entrepreneurial, marketing, and services acumen (Hong Kong), a fine communications network (Singapore), a tremendous pool of financial capital (all three), and very large endowments of land, resources, and labor (mainland China). . . . From Guangzhou to Singapore, from Kuala Lumpur to Manila, this influential network—often based on extensions of the traditional clans—has been described as the backbone of the East Asian economy.[1]

Culture and religion also form the basis of the Economic Cooperation Organization, which brings together ten non-Arab Muslim countries: Iran, Pakistan, Turkey, Azerbaijan, Kazakhstan, Kyrgyzstan, Turkmenistan, Tajikistan, Uzbekistan, and Afghanistan. One impetus to the revival and expansion of this organization, founded originally in the 1960s by Turkey, Pakistan, and Iran, is the realization by the leaders of several of these countries that they had no chance of admission to the European Community. Similarly, Caricom, the Central American Common Market, and Mercosur rest on common cultural foundations. Efforts to build a broader Caribbean-Central American economic entity bridging the Anglo-Latin divide, however, have to date failed.

As people define their identity in ethnic and religious terms, they are likely to see an "us" versus "them" relation existing between themselves and people of different ethnicity or religion. The end of ideologically defined states in Eastern Europe and the former Soviet Union permits traditional ethnic identities and animosities to come to the fore. Differences in culture and religion create differences over policy issues, ranging from human rights to immigration to trade and commerce to the environment. Geographical propinquity gives rise to conflicting territorial claims from Bosnia to Mindanao. Most important, the efforts of the West to promote its values of democracy and liberalism to universal values, to maintain its military predominance, and to advance its economic interests engender countering responses from other civilizations. Decreasingly able to mobilize support and form coalitions on the basis of ideology, governments and groups will increasingly attempt to mobilize support by appealing to common religion and civilization identity.

The clash of civilizations thus occurs at two levels. At the micro-level, adjacent groups along the fault lines between civilizations struggle, often violently, over the control of territory and each other. At the macro-level, states from different civilizations compete for relative military and economic power, struggle over the control of international institutions and third parties, and competitively promote their particular political and religious values.

The Fault Lines between Civilizations

The fault lines between civilizations are replacing the political and ideological boundaries of the Cold War as the flash points for crisis and bloodshed. The Cold War began when

Western Christianity circa 1500

Orthodox Christianity and Islam

RUSSIA

FINLAND

SWEDEN

ESTONIA

LATVIA

LITHUANIA

BELA-RUSSIA

POLAND

CZECH REP.

SLOVAKIA

UKRAINE

SLOVENIA

HUNG.

MOLD.

CROATIA

ROMANIA

BOSNIA

SERBIA

Black Sea

MONTE-NEGRO

MACEDONIA

BULGARIA

ALB.

ITALY

GREECE

TURKEY

N

0 ——— 200
MILES

Source: W. Wallace, THE TRANSFORMATION OF WESTERN EUROPE. London: Pinter, 1990.
Map by Ib Ohlsson for FOREIGN AFFAIRS.

the Iron Curtain divided Europe politically and ideologically. The Cold War ended with the end of the Iron Curtain. As the ideological division of Europe has disappeared, the cultural division of Europe between Western Christianity, on the one hand, and Orthodox Christianity and Islam, on the other, has reemerged. The most significant dividing line in Europe, as William Wallace has suggested, may well be the eastern boundary of Western Christianity in the year 1500. This line runs along what are now the boundaries between Finland and Russia and between the Baltic states and Russia, cuts through Belarus and Ukraine separating the more Catholic western Ukraine from Orthodox eastern Ukraine, swings westward separating Transylvania from the rest of Romania, and then goes through Yugoslavia almost exactly along the line now separating Croatia and Slovenia from the rest of Yugoslavia. In the Balkans this line, of course, coincides with the historic boundary between the Hapsburg and Ottoman empires. The peoples to the north and west of this line are Protestant or Catholic; they shared the common experiences of European history—feudalism, the Renaissance, the Reformation, the Enlightenment, the French Revolution, the Industrial Revolution; they are generally economically better off than the peoples to the east; and they may now look forward to increasing involvement in a common European economy and to the consolidation of democratic political systems. The peoples to the east and south of this line are Orthodox or Muslim; they historically belonged to the Ottoman or Tsarist empires and were only lightly touched by the shaping events in the rest of Europe; they are generally less advanced economically; they seem much less likely to develop stable democratic political systems. The Velvet Curtain of culture has replaced the Iron Curtain of ideology as the most significant dividing line in Europe. As the events in Yugoslavia show, it is not only a line of difference; it is also at times a line of bloody conflict.

Conflict along the fault line between Western and Islamic civilizations has been going on for 1,300 years. After the founding of Islam, the Arab and Moorish surge west and north only ended at Tours in 732. From the eleventh to the thirteenth century the Crusaders attempted with temporary success to bring Christianity and Christian rule to the Holy Land. From the fourteenth to the seventeenth century, the Ottoman Turks reversed the balance, extended their sway over the Middle East and the Balkans, captured Constantinople, and twice laid siege to Vienna. In the nineteenth and early twentieth centuries as Ottoman power declined Britain, France, and Italy established Western control over most of North Africa and the Middle East.

After World War II, the West, in turn, began to retreat; the colonial empires disappeared; first Arab nationalism and then Islamic fundamentalism manifested themselves; the West became heavily dependent on the Persian Gulf countries for its energy; the oil-rich Muslim countries became money-rich and, when they wished to, weapons-rich. Several wars occurred between Arabs and Israel (created by the West). France fought a bloody and ruthless war in Algeria for most of the 1950s; British and French forces invaded Egypt in 1956; American forces returned to Lebanon, attacked Libya, and engaged in various military encounters with Iran; Arab and Islamic terrorists, supported by at least three Middle Eastern governments, employed the weapon of the weak and bombed Western planes and installations and seized Western hostages. This warfare between Arabs and the West culminated in 1990, when the United States sent a massive army to the Persian Gulf to defend some Arab countries against aggression by another. In its aftermath NATO planning is increasingly directed to potential threats and instability along its "southern tier."

This centuries-old military interaction between the West and Islam is unlikely to decline. It could become more virulent. The Gulf War left some Arabs feeling proud that Saddam Hussein had attacked Israel and stood up to the West. It also left many feeling humiliated and resentful of the West's military presence in the Persian Gulf, the West's overwhelming military dominance, and their apparent inability to shape their own destiny. Many Arab countries, in addition to the oil exporters, are reaching levels of economic and social development where autocratic forms of government become inappropriate and efforts to introduce democracy become stronger. Some openings in Arab political systems have already occurred. The principal beneficiaries of these openings have been Islamist movements. In the Arab world, in short, Western democracy strengthens anti-Western political forces. This may be a passing phenomenon, but it surely complicates relations between Islamic countries and the West.

Those relations are also complicated by demography. The spectacular population growth in Arab countries, particularly in North Africa, has led to increased migration to Western Europe. The movement within Western Europe toward minimizing internal boundaries has sharpened political sensitivities with respect to this development. In Italy, France, and Germany, racism is increasingly open, and political reactions and violence against Arab and Turkish migrants have become more intense and more widespread since 1990.

On both sides the interaction between Islam and the West is seen as a clash of civilizations. The West's "next confrontation," observes M. J. Akbar, an Indian Muslim author, "is definitely going to come from the Muslim world. It is in the sweep of the Islamic nations from the Maghreb to Pakistan that the struggle for a new world order will begin." Bernard Lewis comes to a similar conclusion:

We are facing a mood and a movement far transcending the level of issues and policies and the governments that pursue them. This is no less than a clash of civilizations—the perhaps irrational but surely historic reaction of an ancient rival against our Judeo-Christian heritage, our secular present, and the worldwide expansion of both.[2]

Historically, the other great antagonistic interaction of Arab Islamic civilization has been with the pagan, animist, and now increasingly Christian black peoples to the south. In the past, this antagonism was epitomized in the image of Arab slave dealers and black slaves. It has been reflected in the on-going civil war in the Sudan between Arabs and blacks, the fighting in Chad between Libyan-supported insurgents and the government, the tensions between Orthodox Christians and Muslims in the Horn of Africa, and the political conflicts, recurring riots, and communal violence between Muslims and Christians in Nigeria. The modernization of Africa and the spread of Christianity are likely to enhance the probability of violence along this fault line. Symptomatic of the intensification of this conflict was Pope John Paul II's speech in Khartoum in February 1993 attacking the actions of the Sudan's Islamist government against the Christian minority there.

On the northern border of Islam, conflict has increasingly erupted between Orthodox and Muslim peoples, including the carnage of Bosnia and Sarajevo, the simmering violence between Serb and Albanian, the tenuous relation between Bulgarians and their Turkish minority, the violence between Ossetians and Ingush, the unremitting slaughter of each other by Armenians and Azeris, the tense relations between Russians and Muslims in Central Asia, and the deployment of Russian troops to protect Russian interests in the Caucasus and Central Asia. Religion reinforces the revival of ethnic identities and restimulates Russian fears about the security of their southern borders. This concern is well captured by Archie Roosevelt:

> Much of Russian history concerns the struggle between Slavs and the Turkish peoples on their borders, which dates back to the foundation of the Russian state more than a thousand years ago. In the Slavs' millennium-long confrontation with their eastern neighbors lies the key to an understanding not only of Russian history, but Russian character. To understand Russian realities today one has to have a concept of the great Turkic ethnic group that has preoccupied Russians through the centuries.[3]

The conflict of civilizations is deeply rooted elsewhere in Asia. The historic clash between Muslim and Hindu in the subcontinent manifests itself now not only in the rivalry between Pakistan and India but also in intensifying religious strife within India between increasingly militant Hindu groups and India's substantial Muslim minority. The destruction of the Ayodhya mosque in December 1992 brought to the fore the issue of whether India will remain a secular democratic state or become a Hindu one. In East Asia, China has outstanding territorial disputes with most of its neighbors. It has pursued a ruthless policy toward the Buddhist people of Tibet, and it is pursuing an increasingly ruthless policy toward its Turkic-Muslim minority. With the Cold War over, the underlying differences between China and the United States have reasserted themselves in areas such as human rights, trade, and weapons proliferation. These differences are unlikely to moderate. A "new cold war," Deng Xiaoping reportedly asserted in 1991, is under way between China and America.

The same phrase has been applied to the increasingly difficult relations between Japan and the United States. Here cultural difference exacerbates economic conflict. People on each side allege racism on the other, but at least on the American side the antipathies are not racial but cultural. The basic values, attitudes, and behavioral patterns of the two societies could hardly be more different. The economic issues between the United States and Europe are no less serious than those between the United States and Japan, but they do not have the same political salience and emotional intensity because the differences between American culture and European culture are so much less than those between American civilization and Japanese civilization.

The interactions between civilizations vary greatly in the extent to which they are likely to be characterized by violence. Economic competition clearly predominates between the American and European subcivilizations of the West and between both of them and Japan. On the Eurasian continent, however, the proliferation of ethnic conflict, epitomized at the extreme in "ethnic cleansing," has not been totally random. It has been most frequent and most violent between groups belonging to different civilizations. In Eurasia the great historic fault lines between civilizations are once more aflame. This is particularly true along the boundaries of the crescent-shaped Islamic bloc of nations from the bulge of Africa to central Asia. Violence also occurs between Muslims, on the one hand, and Orthodox Serbs in the Balkans, Jews in Israel, Hindus in India, Buddhists in Burma, and Catholics in the Philippines. Islam has bloody borders.

Civilization Rallying: The Kin-Country Syndrome

Groups or states belonging to one civilization that become involved in war with people from a different civilization naturally try to rally support from other members of their own civilization. As the post–Cold War world evolves, civilization commonality, what H. D. S. Greenway has termed the "kin-country" syndrome, is replacing political ideology and traditional balance of power considerations as the principal basis for cooperation and coalitions. It can be seen gradually emerging in the post–Cold War conflicts in the Persian Gulf, the Caucasus, and Bosnia. None of these was a full-scale war between civilizations, but each involved some elements of civilizational rallying, which seemed to become more important as the conflict continued and which may provide a foretaste of the future.

First, in the Gulf War one Arab state invaded another and then fought a coalition of Arab, Western, and other states. While only a few Muslim governments overtly supported Saddam Hussein, many Arab elites privately cheered him on, and he was highly popular among large sections of the Arab publics. Islamic fundamentalist movements universally supported Iraq rather than the Western-backed governments of Kuwait and Saudi Arabia. Forswearing Arab nationalism, Saddam Hussein explicitly invoked an Islamic appeal. He and his supporters attempted to define the war as a war between civilizations. "It is not the world against Iraq," as Safar Al-Hawali, dean of Islamic Studies at the Umm Al-Qura University in Mecca, put it in a widely circulated tape. "It is the West against Islam." Ignoring the rivalry between Iran and Iraq, the chief Iranian religious leader, Ayatollah Ali Khamenei, called for a holy war against the West: "The struggle against American aggression, greed, plans, and policies will be counted as a jihad, and anybody who is killed on that path is a martyr." "This is a war," King Hussein of Jordan argued, "against all Arabs and all Muslims and not against Iraq alone."

The rallying of substantial sections of Arab elites and publics behind Saddam Hussein called those Arab governments in the anti-Iraq coalition to moderate their activities and temper their public statements. Arab governments opposed or distanced themselves from subsequent Western efforts to apply pressure on Iraq, including enforcement of a no-fly zone in the summer of 1992 and the bombing of Iraq in January 1993. The Western-Soviet-Turkish-Arab anti-Iraq coalition of 1990 had by 1993 become a coalition of almost only the West and Kuwait against Iraq.

Muslims contrasted Western actions against Iraq with the West's failure to protect Bosnians against Serbs and to impose sanctions on Israel for violating U.N. resolutions. The West, they allege, was using a double standard. A world of clashing civilizations, however, is inevitably a world of double standards: people apply one standard to their kin-countries and a different standard to others.

Second, the kin-country syndrome also appeared in conflicts in the former Soviet Union. Armenian military successes in 1992 and 1993 stimulated Turkey to become increasingly supportive of its religious, ethnic, and linguistic brethren in Azerbaijan. "We have a Turkish nation feeling the same sentiments as the Azerbaijanis," said one Turkish official in 1992. "We are under pressure. Our newspapers are full of the photos of atrocities and are asking us if we are still serious about pursuing our neutral policy. Maybe we should show Armenia that there's a big Turkey in the region." President Turgut Özal agreed, remarking that Turkey should at least "scare the Armenians a little bit." Turkey, Özal threatened again in 1993, would "show its fangs." Turkey Air Force jets flew reconnaissance flights along the Armenian border; Turkey suspended food shipments and air flights to Armenia; and Turkey and Iran announced they would not accept dismemberment of Azerbaijan. In the last years of its existence, the Soviet government supported Azerbaijan because its government was dominated by former communists. With the end of the Soviet Union, however, political considerations gave way to religious ones. Russian troops fought on the side of the Armenians, and Azerbaijan accused the "Russian government of turning 180 degrees" toward support for Christian Armenia.

Third, with respect to the fighting in the former Yugoslavia, Western publics manifested sympathy and support for the Bosnian Muslims and the horrors they suffered at the hands of the Serbs. Relatively little concern was expressed, however, over Croatian attacks on Muslims and participation in the dismemberment of Bosnia-Herzegovina. In the early stages of the Yugoslav breakup, Germany, in an unusual display of diplomatic initiative and muscle, induced the other 11 members of the European Community to follow its lead in recognizing Slovenia and Croatia. As a result of the pope's determination to provide strong backing to the two Catholic countries, the Vatican extended recognition even before the Community did. The United States followed the European lead. Thus the leading actors in Western civilization rallied behind its coreligionists. Subsequently Croatia was reported to be receiving substantial quantities of arms from Central European and other Western countries. Boris Yeltsin's government, on the other hand, attempted to pursue a middle course that would be sympathetic to the Orthodox Serbs but not alienate Russia from the West. Russian conservative and nationalist groups, however, including many legislators, attacked the government for not being more forthcoming in its support for the Serbs. By early 1993 several hundred Russians apparently were serving with the Serbian forces, and reports circulated of Russian arms being supplied to Serbia.

Islamic governments and groups, on the other hand, castigated the West for not coming to the defense of the Bosnians. Iranian leaders urged Muslims from all countries to provide help to Bosnia; in violation of the U.N. arms embargo, Iran supplied weapons and men for the Bosnians; Iranian-supported Lebanese groups sent guerrillas to train and organize the Bosnian forces. In 1993 up to 4,000 Muslims from over two dozen Islamic countries were reported to be fighting in Bosnia. The governments of Saudi Arabia and other countries felt under increasing pressure from fundamentalist groups in their own societies to provide more vigorous support for the Bosnians. By the end of 1992, Saudi Arabia had reportedly supplied substantial funding for weapons and supplies for the Bosnians, which significantly increased their military capabilities vis-à-vis the Serbs.

In the 1930s the Spanish Civil War provoked intervention from countries that politically were fascist, communist, and democratic. In the 1990s the Yugoslav conflict is provoking intervention from countries that are Muslim, Orthodox, and Western Christian. The parallel has not gone unnoticed. "The war in Bosnia-Herzegovina has become the emotional equivalent of the fight against fascism in the Spanish Civil War," one Saudi editor observed. "Those who died there are regarded as martyrs who tried to save their fellow Muslims."

Conflicts and violence will also occur between states and groups within the same civilization. Such conflicts, however, are likely to be less intense and less likely to expand than conflicts between civilizations. Common membership in a civilization reduces the probability of violence in situations where it might otherwise occur. In 1991 and 1992 many people were alarmed by the possibility of violent conflict between Russia and Ukraine over territory, particularly Crimea, the Black Sea fleet, nuclear weapons, and economic issues. If civilization is what counts, however, the likelihood of violence between Ukrainians and Russians should be low. They are two Slavic, primarily Orthodox peoples who have had close relationships with each other for centuries. As of early 1993, despite all the reasons for conflict, the leaders of the two countries were effectively negotiating and defusing the issues between the two countries. While there has been serious fighting between Muslims and Christians elsewhere in the former Soviet Union and much tension and some fighting between Western and Orthodox Christians in the Baltic states, there has been virtually no violence between Russians and Ukrainians.

Civilization rallying to date has been limited, but it has been growing, and it clearly has the potential to spread much further. As the conflicts in the Persian Gulf, the Caucasus, and Bosnia continued, the positions of nations and the cleavages between them increasingly were along civilizational lines. Populist politicians, religious leaders, and the media have found it a potential means of arousing mass support and of pressuring hesitant governments. In the coming years, the local conflicts most likely to escalate into major wars will be those, as in Bosnia and the Caucasus, along the fault lines between civilizations. The next world war, if there is one, will be a war between civilizations.

The West versus the Rest

The West is now at an extraordinary peak of power in relation to other civilizations. Its superpower opponent has disappeared from the map. Military conflict among Western states is unthinkable, and Western military power is unrivaled. Apart from Japan, the West faces no economic challenge. It dominates international political and security institutions and with Japan international economic institutions. Global political and security issues are effectively settled by a directorate of the United States, Britain, and France, world economic issues by a directorate of the United States, Germany, and Japan, all of which maintain extraordinarily close relations with each other to the exclusion of lesser and largely non-Western countries. Decisions made at the U.N. Security Council or in the International Monetary Fund that reflect the interests of the West are presented to the world as reflecting the desires of the world community. The very phrase "the world community" has become the euphemistic collective noun (replacing "the Free World") to give global legitimacy to actions reflecting the interests of the United States and other Western powers.[4] Through the IMF and other international economic institutions, the West promotes its economic interests and imposes on other nations the economic policies it thinks appropriate. In any poll of non-Western peoples, the IMF undoubtedly would win the support of finance ministers and a few others, but get an overwhelmingly unfavorable rating from just about everyone else, who would agree with Georgy Arbatov's characterization of IMF officials as "neo-Bolsheviks who love expropriating other people's money, imposing undemocratic and alien rules of economic and political conduct, and stifling economic freedom."

Western domination of the U.N. Security Council and its decisions, tempered only by occasional abstention by China, produced U.N. legitimation of the West's use of force to drive Iraq out of Kuwait and its elimination of Iraq's sophisticated weapons and capacity to produce such weapons. It also produced the quite unprecedented action by the United States, Britain, and France in getting the Security Council to demand that Libya hand over the Pan Am 103 bombing suspects and then to impose sanctions when Libya refused. After defeating the largest Arab army, the West did not hesitate to throw its weight around in the Arab world. The West in effect is using international institutions, military power, and economic resources to run the world in ways that will maintain Western predominance, protect Western interests, and promote Western political and economic values.

That at least is the way in which non-Westerners see the new world, and there is a significant element of truth in their view. Differences in power and struggles for military, economic, and institutional power are thus one source of conflict between the West and other civilizations. Differences in culture, that is basic values and beliefs, are a second source of conflict. V. S. Naipaul has argued that Western civilization is the "universal civilization" that "fits all men." At a superficial level much of Western culture has indeed permeated the rest of the world. At a more basic level, however, Western concepts differ fundamentally from those prevalent in other civilizations. Western ideas of individualism, liberalism, constitutionalism, human rights, equality, liberty, the rule of law, democracy, free markets, and the separation of church and state often have little resonance in Islamic, Confucian, Japanese, Hindu, Buddhist, or Orthodox cultures. Western efforts to propagate such ideas produce instead a reaction against "human rights imperialism" and a reaffirmation of indigenous values, as can be seen in the support for religious fundamentalism by the younger generation in non-Western cultures. The very notion that there could be a "universal civilization" is a Western idea, directly at odds with the particularism of most Asian societies and their emphasis on what distinguishes one people from another. Indeed, the author of a review of 100 comparative studies of values in different societies concluded that "the values that are most important in the West are least important worldwide."[5] In the political realm, of course, these differences are most manifest in the efforts of the

United States and other Western powers to induce other peoples to adopt Western ideas concerning democracy and human rights. Modern democratic government originated in the West. When it has developed in non-Western societies it has usually been the product of Western colonialism or imposition.

The central axis of world politics in the future is likely to be, in Kishore Mahbubani's phrase, the conflict between "the West and the Rest" and the responses of non-Western civilizations to Western power and values.[6] Those responses generally take one or a combination of three forms. At one extreme, non-Western states can, like Burma and North Korea, attempt to pursue a course of isolation, to insulate their societies from penetration or "corruption" by the West, and, in effect, to opt out of participation in the Western-dominated global community. The costs of this course, however, are high, and few states have pursued it exclusively. A second alternative, the equivalent of "bandwagoning" in international relations theory, is to attempt to join the West and accept its values and institutions. The third alternative is to attempt to "balance" the West by developing economic and military power and cooperating with other non-Western societies against the West, while preserving indigenous values and institutions; in short, to modernize but not to Westernize.

The Torn Countries

In the future, as people differentiate themselves by civilization, countries with large numbers of people of different civilizations, such as the Soviet Union and Yugoslavia, are candidates for dismemberment. Some other countries have a fair degree of cultural homogeneity but are divided over whether their society belongs to one civilization or another. These are torn countries. Their leaders typically wish to pursue a bandwagoning strategy and to make their countries members of the West, but the history, culture and traditions of their countries are non-Western. The most obvious and prototypical torn country is Turkey. The late twentieth-century leaders of Turkey have followed in the Attatürk tradition and defined Turkey as a modern, secular, Western nation state. They allied Turkey with the West in NATO and in the Gulf War; they applied for membership in the European Community. At the same time, however, elements in Turkish society have supported an Islamic revival and have argued that Turkey is basically a Middle Eastern Muslim society. In addition, while the elite of Turkey has defined Turkey as a Western society, the elite of the West refuses to accept Turkey as such. Turkey will not become a member of the European Community, and the real reason, as President Özal said, "is that we are Muslim and they are Christian and they don't say that." Having rejected Mecca, and then being rejected by Brussels, where does Turkey look? Tashkent may be the answer. The end of the Soviet Union gives Turkey the opportunity to become the leader of a revived Turkic civilization involving seven countries from the borders of Greece to those of China. Encouraged by the West, Turkey is making strenuous efforts to carve out this new identity for itself.

During the past decade Mexico has assumed a position somewhat similar to that of Turkey. Just as Turkey abandoned its historic opposition to Europe and attempted to join Europe, Mexico has stopped defining itself by its opposition to the United States and is instead attempting to imitate the United States and to join it in the North American Free Trade Area. Mexican leaders are engaged in the great task of redefining Mexican identity and have introduced fundamental economic reforms that eventually will lead to fundamental political change. In 1991 a top adviser to President Carlos Salinas de Gortari described at length to me all the changes the Salinas government was making. When he finished, I remarked: "That's most impressive. It seems to me that basically you want to change Mexico from a Latin American country into a North American country." He looked at me with surprise and exclaimed: "Exactly! That's precisely what we are trying to do, but of course we could never say so publicly." As his remark indicates, in Mexico as in Turkey, significant elements in society resist the redefinition of their country's identity. In Turkey, European-oriented leaders have to make gestures to Islam (Özal's pilgrimage to Mecca); so also Mexico's North American–oriented leaders have to make gestures to those who hold Mexico to be a Latin American country (Salinas' Ibero-American Guadalajara summit).

Historically Turkey has been the most profoundly torn country. For the United States, Mexico is the most immediate torn country. Globally the most important torn country is Russia. The question of whether Russia is part of the West or the leader of the Slavic-Orthodox civilization has been a recurring one in Russian history. That issue was obscured by the communist victory in Russia, which imported a Western ideology, adapted it to Russian conditions, and then challenged the West in the name of that ideology. The dominance of communism shut off the historic debate over Westernization versus Russification. With communism discredited Russians once again face that question.

President Yeltsin is adopting Western principles and goals and seeking to make Russia a "normal" country and a part of the West. Yet both the Russian elite and the Russian public are divided on this issue. Among the more moderate dissenters, Sergei Stankevich argues that Russia should reject the "Atlanticist" course, which would lead it "to become European, to become a part of the world economy in rapid and organized fashion, to become the eighth member of the Seven, and to put particular emphasis on Germany and the United States as the two dominant members of the Atlantic alliance." While also rejecting an exclusively Eurasian policy, Stankevich nonetheless argues that Russia should give priority to the protection of Russians in other countries, emphasize its Turkic and Muslim connections, and promote "an appreciable redistribution of our resources, our options, our ties, and our interests in favor of Asia, of the eastern direction." People of this persuasion criticize Yeltsin for subordinating Russia's interests to those of the West, for reducing Russian military strength, for failing to support traditional friends such as Serbia, and for pushing economic and political reform in ways injurious to the Russian people. Indicative of this trend is the new popularity of the ideas of Petr Savitsky, who in the 1920s argued that Russia was a unique Eurasian civilization.[7] More extreme dissidents voice much more blatantly nationalist, anti-Western, and anti-Semitic views, and urge Russia to redevelop its military strength and to establish closer ties with China and Muslim countries. The people of Russia are as divided as the elite. An opinion survey in European Russia in the spring of 1992 revealed that 40 percent of the public had positive attitudes toward the West and 36 percent had negative attitudes. As it has been for much of its history, Russia in the early 1990s is truly a torn country.

To redefine its civilization identity, a torn country must meet three requirements. First, its political and economic elite has to be generally supportive of and enthusiastic about the move. Second, its public has to be willing to acquiesce in the redefinition. Third, the dominant groups in the recipient civilization have to be willing to embrace the convert. All three requirements in large part exist with respect to Mexico. The first two in large part exist with respect to Turkey. It is not clear that any of them exist with respect to Russia's joining the West. The conflict between liberal democracy and Marxism-Leninism was between ideologies which, despite their major differences, ostensibly shared ultimate goals of freedom, equality, and prosperity. A traditional, authoritarian, nationalist Russia could have quite different goals. A Western democrat could carry on an intellectual debate with a Soviet Marxist. It would be virtually impossible for him to do that with a Russian traditionalist. If, as the Russians stop behaving like Marxists, they reject liberal democracy and begin behaving like Russians but not like Westerners, the relations between Russia and the West could again become distant and conflictual.[8]

The Confucian-Islamic Connection

The obstacles to non-Western countries joining the West vary considerably. They are least for Latin American and East European countries. They are greater for the Orthodox countries of the former Soviet Union. They are still greater for Muslim, Confucian, Hindu, and Buddhist societies. Japan has established a unique position for itself as an associate member of the West: it is in the West in some respects but clearly not of the West in important dimensions. Those countries that for reason of culture and power do not wish to, or cannot, join the West compete with the West by developing their own economic, military, and political power. They do this by promoting their internal development and by cooperating with other non-Western countries. The most prominent form of this cooperation is the Confucian-Islamic connection that has emerged to challenge Western interests, values, and power.

Almost without exception, Western countries are reducing their military power; under Yeltsin's leadership so also is Russia. China, North Korea, and several Middle Eastern states, however, are significantly expanding their military capabilities. They are doing this by the import of arms from Western and non-Western sources and by the development of indigenous arms industries. One result is the emergence of what Charles Krauthammer has called "Weapon States," and the Weapon States are not Western states. Another result is the redefinition of arms control, which is a Western concept and a Western goal. During the Cold War the primary purpose of arms control was to establish a stable military balance between the United States and its allies and the Soviet Union and its allies. In the post–Cold War world the primary objective of arms control is to prevent the development by non-Western societies of military capabilities that could threaten Western interests. The West attempts to do this through international agreements, economic pressure, and controls on the transfer of arms and weapons technologies.

The conflict between the West and the Confucian-Islamic states focuses largely, although not exclusively, on nuclear, chemical, and biological weapons, ballistic missiles and other sophisticated means for delivering them, and the guidance, intelligence, and other electronic capabilities for achieving that goal. The West promotes nonproliferation as a universal norm and nonproliferation treaties and inspections as means of realizing that norm. It also threatens a variety of sanctions against those who promote the spread of sophisticated weapons and proposes some benefits for those who do not. The attention of the West focuses, naturally, on nations that are actually or potentially hostile to the West.

The non-Western nations, on the other hand, assert their right to acquire and to deploy whatever weapons they think necessary for their security. They also have absorbed, to the full, the truth of the response of the Indian defense minister when asked what lesson he learned from the Gulf War: "Don't fight the United States unless you have nuclear weapons." Nuclear weapons, chemical weapons, and missiles are viewed, probably erroneously, as the potential equalizer of superior Western conventional power. China, of course, already has nuclear weapons; Pakistan and India have the capability to deploy them. North Korea, Iran, Iraq, Libya, and Algeria appear to be attempting to acquire them. A top Iranian official has declared that all Muslim states should acquire nuclear weapons, and in 1988 the president of Iran reportedly issued a directive calling for development of "offensive and defensive chemical, biological, and radiological weapons."

Centrally important to the development of counter-West military capabilities is the sustained expansion of China's military power and its means to create military power. Buoyed by spectacular economic development, China is rapidly increasing its military spending and vigorously moving forward with the modernization of its armed forces. It is purchasing weapons from the former Soviet states; it is developing long-range missiles; in 1992 it tested a one-megaton nuclear device. It is developing power-projection capabilities, acquiring aerial refueling technology, and trying to purchase an aircraft carrier. Its military buildup and assertion of sovereignty over the South China Sea are provoking a multilateral regional arms race in East Asia. China is also a major exporter of arms and weapons technology. It has exported materials to Libya and Iraq that could be used to manufacture nuclear weapons and nerve gas. It has helped Algeria build a reactor suitable for nuclear weapons research and production. China has sold to Iran nuclear technology that American officials believe could only be used to create weapons and apparently has shipped components of 300-mile-range missiles to Pakistan. North Korea has had a nuclear weapons program under way for some while and has sold advanced missiles and missile technology to Syria and Iran. The flow of weapons and weapons technology is generally from East Asia to the Middle East. There is, however, some movement in the reverse direction; China has received Stinger missiles from Pakistan.

A Confucian-Islamic military connection has thus come into being, designed to promote acquisition by its members of the weapons and weapons technologies needed to counter the military powers of the West. It may or may not last. At present, however, it is, as Dave McCurdy has said, "a renegades' mutual support pact, run by the proliferators and their backers." A new form of arms competition is thus occurring between Islamic-Confucian states and the West. In an old-fashioned arms race, each side developed its own arms to balance or to achieve superiority against the other side. In this new form of arms competition, one side is developing its arms and the other side is attempting not to balance but to limit and prevent that arms build-up while at the same time reducing its own military capabilities.

Implications for the West

This article does not argue that civilization identities will replace all other identities, that nation states will disappear, that each civilization will become a single coherent political entity, that groups within a civilization will not conflict with and even fight each other. This paper does set forth the hypotheses that differences between civilizations are real and important; civilization-consciousness is increasing; conflict between civilizations will supplant ideological and other forms of conflict as the dominant global form of conflict;

international relations, historically a game played out within Western civilization, will increasingly be de-Westernized and become a game in which non-Western civilizations are actors and not simply objects; successful political, security, and economic international institutions are more likely to develop within civilizations than across civilizations; conflicts between groups in different civilizations will be more frequent, more sustained, and more violent than conflicts between groups in the same civilization; violent conflicts between groups in different civilizations are the most likely and most dangerous source of escalation that could lead to global wars; the paramount axis of world politics will be the relations between "the West and the Rest"; the elites in some torn non-Western countries will try to make their countries part of the West, but in most cases face major obstacles to accomplishing this; a central focus of conflict for the immediate future will be between the West and several Islamic-Confucian states.

This is not to advocate the desirability of conflicts between civilizations. It is to set forth descriptive hypotheses as to what the future may be like. If these are plausible hypotheses, however, it is necessary to consider their implications for Western policy. These implications should be divided between short-term advantage and long-term accommodation. In the short term it is clearly in the interest of the West to promote greater cooperation and unity within its own civilization, particularly between its European and North American components; to incorporate into the West societies in Eastern Europe and Latin America whose cultures are close to those of the West; to promote and maintain cooperative relations with Russia and Japan; to prevent escalation of local inter-civilization conflicts into major inter-civilization wars; to limit the expansion of the military strength of Confucian and Islamic states; to moderate the reduction of counter military capabilities and maintain military superiority in East and Southwest Asia; to exploit differences and conflicts among Confucian and Islamic states; to support in other civilizations groups sympathetic to Western values and interests; to strengthen international institutions that reflect and legitimate Western interests and values and to promote the involvement of non-Western states in those institutions.

In the longer term other measures would be called for. Western civilization is both Western and modern. Non-Western civilizations have attempted to become modern without becoming Western. To date only Japan has fully succeeded in this quest. Non-Western civilization will continue to attempt to acquire the wealth, technology, skills, machines, and weapons that are part of being modern. They will also attempt to reconcile this modernity with their traditional culture and values. Their economic and military strength relative to the West will increase. Hence the West will increasingly have to accommodate these non-Western modern civilizations whose power approaches that of the West but whose values and interests differ significantly from those of the West. This will require the West to maintain the economic and military power necessary to protect its interests in relation to these civilizations. It will also, however, require the West to develop a more profound understanding of the basic religious and philosophical assumptions underlying other civilizations and the ways in which people in those civilizations see their interests. It will require an effort to identify elements of commonality between Western and other civilizations. For the relevant future, there will be no universal civilization, but instead a world of different civilizations, each of which will have to learn to coexist with the others.

22

CHALLENGING HUNTINGTON

—Richard E. Rubenstein and Jarle Crocker

With the end of the Cold War, scholars and policymakers face a daunting task: how to craft a new paradigm capable of revealing the principal sources of conflict and collaboration in a rapidly changing international system. In "The Clash of Civilizations?"[1] Samuel Huntington boldly offers to fill that theoretical vacancy. Huntington's model of competing civilizations seeks to provide an analysis of current international conflicts, a method of predicting future strife, and a solid theoretical foundation for constructing foreign policy. While considerably in vogue abroad, the "clashing civilizations" thesis has encountered substantial resistance at home. Even so, few critics appear to have examined the theory's underlying assumptions and long-range implications or accepted the author's challenge to suggest a more comprehensive and useful paradigm.

This essay takes up Huntington's challenge. Its purpose is to answer three questions critical to an evaluation of his theory:

- Is the model of "clashing civilizations" a new paradigm?
- How well does it account for the causes of conflict in the post–Cold War world?
- Is it the best paradigm for the job, or are there more promising theories in view?

Huntington's thesis is simply stated: The international system, formerly based on major Soviet, American, and Third World power blocs, is in transition to a new system composed of eight major civilizations. They are the Western, Japanese, Confucian, Hindu, Islamic, Slavic-Orthodox, Latin American, and—"possibly," says the theorist—African. "Civilization," in his lexicon (as in that of his predecessors, Oswald Spengler and Arnold Toynbee), denotes the broadest practical basis for human cultural affiliation short of species consciousness. Culture, not class, ideology, or even nationality, will differentiate the contending power blocs of the future. The trend in each bloc is toward greater civilizational "consciousness." The major wars of the future will be fought along civilizational "fault lines," like those separating Western Croatia and Slovenia from Muslim Bosnia and

* *Foreign Policy* 96 (Fall 1994): 113–28.

Slavic-Orthodox Serbia, or Muslim Pakistan from Hindu India. Western policy, in the context of the new order, will necessarily be directed toward maintaining world hegemony by destabilizing hostile civilizations militarily and diplomatically, playing them off against each other in the "balance of power" mode, and learning to live with global diversity.

Assuming, for the moment, that there are eight (and only eight) civilizations, why must their future relations be oriented toward conflict? On the one hand, says Huntington, "differences do not necessarily mean conflict." But civilizations will clash because they embody incompatible political and moral values; for example, Western ideas of individualism and democracy run counter to the beliefs of many non-Western civilizations. Even so, one might ask, why not live and let live? Why should clashing values generate political and military confrontation? Huntington does not answer that question directly. He assumes that politicized civilizations are power blocs, each of which naturally struggles for survival, influence, and, where necessary, domination. Fortunately, the West is now on top, but other civilizations are finally developing the economic, military, and cultural capacities to challenge Western hegemony and reshape the world through the lens of non-Western values and beliefs. (It is that vision of non-Western ascendancy that makes Professor Huntington's essay so appealing to many politicians in the Third World.) "The West against the Rest" therefore describes the most likely fault line of future civilizational relations.

Is this a new paradigm or a mere modification of the Cold War model that Huntington claims to have discarded? Certain differences seem obvious: The primary units of international conflict are now said to be civilizations, not states; the world of clashing civilizations is multipolar, not bipolar; and the major players are united by cultural affinity rather than by class or ideology. But beneath the surface of the new world-picture, familiar mechanisms are at work. Huntington's thinking remains bounded by the assumptions of political realism, the dominant philosophy of the Cold War period. For him, as for earlier realists, international politics is, above all, a struggle for power between coherent but essentially isolated units, each of which seeks to advance its own interests in an anarchic setting. Huntington has replaced the nation-state, the primary playing piece in the old game of realist politics, with a larger counter: the civilization. But in crucial respects, the game itself goes on as always.

The results of that continuity are peculiar. It is as if Galileo had explained his telescopic observations by recourse to Aristotelian physics. Huntington's civilizations are essentially super-states motivated by the same imperatives of insecurity and self-aggrandizement as were their Cold War and historical predecessors. As a result, the policies generated by his new paradigm are not easily distinguished from those inspired by the old order of competitive states and ideological blocs. For example, since the safest place in an anarchical system is on top or in alliance with a hegemon, Huntington counsels Westerners to be wary of disarmament, lest other civilizations take advantage of Western demilitarization to alter the fundamental balance of power. He also advises the West to develop "a more profound understanding" of other civilizations, to identify "elements of commonality," and to learn to coexist with others. But "peaceful coexistence" of that sort was a basic principle of Cold War strategy. Its context was a ceaseless struggle for power in which diplomacy was, in effect, a continuation of war by other means. Huntington's advice—coexist, but keep your powder dry—remains firmly within the power-struggle paradigm.

What is new, given the triumphalism of much post–Cold War writing, is Huntington's pessimism. In an interview with *New Perspectives Quarterly*, he said the West must now face a world in which, "despite its current preponderance in economic and military power, the balance of power is shifting into the hands of others." That Spenglerian pessimism has Social Darwinist as well as realist roots; in the struggle for survival and supremacy, victory belongs to the civilization most culturally unified, most determined, and best adapted to the pursuit of global power. Therefore, Huntington sees multiculturalism—"the de-Westernization of the United States"—as a grave threat to U.S. and Western interests.

> If . . . Americans cease to adhere to their liberal democratic and European-rooted political ideology, the United States as we have known it will cease to exist and will follow the other ideologically defined superpower onto the ash heap of history.[2]

The theorist insists that affirmative action and policies favoring multiculturalism threaten "the underlying principles that have been the basis of American political unity." But the issue, for the moment, is not whether he is promoting nativism. It is whether he is offering us a new dish or warmed-over Cold War pie.

Unfortunately, the answer seems plain. Although Huntington's defense of 100 percent Americanism is made in the context of an alien civilizational (as opposed to alien communist) plot, both the alleged threat and the recommended responses are depressingly familiar. The Soviet menace may have vanished, but new enemies—in particular, the dreaded "Confucian-Islamic connection"—now endanger America's global interest. Two responses are therefore required: a movement of cultural unification and revitalization, and a renewed commitment to military, political, and cultural collective security. First, we must deal with the enemy within, already defined by the theorist as unassimilated nonwhite immigrant groups. Second, seeing that "the West against the Rest" is a recipe for disaster, Westerners will have no choice but to contract defensive alliances with more *simpatico* or compliant civilizations against the more ambitious and alien powers. Huntington advises the West to "incorporate" East European and Latin American cultures, to "maintain cooperative relations" with Russia and Japan, and to "strengthen international institutions that reflect and legitimate Western interests and values." He offers us no reason to expect his civilizational system to remain multipolar—and there is no reason at all that it should. The old Cold War is dead, he loudly declares. Then—*sotto voce*—Long live the new Cold War!

In responding to Huntington's vision, we do not maintain that cultural differences themselves are politically meaningless. Cultural similarities or differences can become the basis for massive political mobilization—but only in response to exogenous factors that the theorist has not considered. It is a mistake to dismiss Huntington's vision of global civilizational strife as fantastic: Its realization is all too possible. But it is essential to provide a better explanation of the conditions that could generate a violent clash of civilizations.

Culture and Ideology: A Misunderstanding

Ultimately, Huntington's claim to have produced a new paradigm depends upon his ability to defend the distinction between political ideology, the basis for the old world order, and cultural values, the foundation of "civilization." The theorist puts it clearly in a response to his critics entitled, "If Not Civilizations, What?" maintaining that what ultimately counts for people is not political ideology or economic interest. Faith and family, blood and belief, are what people identify with and what they will fight and die for. And that is why the clash of civilizations is replacing the Cold War as the central phenomenon of global politics.

Distinct cultures, in his view, create differences of value that are far more difficult to reconcile than mere conflicts of interest or ideology. Huntington appears to consider such cultural commitments primordial. He would have us believe, for example, that even if the Chinese decide to take the capitalist road, their "Confucian" values will forever remain alien to those of the West. Moreover, by associating "faith" with "family" and "belief" with "blood," he suggests that cultural values are inextricably bound up with ethnic identity. Finally, he conflates ethnicity with civilization, assuming that all Muslims, for example, are part of a vast ethnic group whose primordial values lead them inevitably to persecute heretics, veil women, and establish theocratic regimes.

Each link in that chain of assumptions raises questions that Huntington does not appear to have considered, much less answered. Are his eight civilizations ethnic groups writ large, or are they unstable, multiethnic formations unified (if at all) as much by elite coercion, economic interest, and ideology as by a common culture? Are the "values" that he discusses ancient and highly resistant to change, or are they rather ideological constructions of relatively recent vintage—shifting syntheses capable of rapid alteration in response to changing events? It seems that Huntington has misunderstood the process of cultural change and value-formation. He seems wholly unaware that, as anthropologist Nigel Harris put it in his *Beliefs in Society*, "culture is not some external strait-jacket, but rather multiple suits of clothes, some of which we can and do discard because they impede our movements." Nor does he recognize the extent to which modern anthropological theory has undermined the distinction between cultural tradition and ideology. As anthropologist Kevin Avruch notes in the October 1992 issue of *Ethnic and Racial Studies*:

> "Traditions" . . . and "nations" . . . are recent and modern because they are continually caught up in processes of social and cultural construction. They are invented and reinvented, produced and reproduced, according to complex, interactive, and temporally shifting contingencies of material conditions and historical practice. They are products of struggle and conflict, of material interests and of competing conceptions of authenticity and identity. They are rooted in structures of inequality. The apparently requisite patina of antiquity is somehow connected . . . to the need for authentic identity.

Huntington's civilizations, it seems clear, are ideological constructs as "recent and modern" as nations, and equally rooted in "structures of inequality." The cultural materials available to define a politicized "civilization" are so rich, varied, and contradictory that any political definition reflects choices made by modern leaders in response to modern problems. For example, the tendency to characterize Indian culture as exclusively Hindu fails to reflect the current problems of upper-caste Indians besieged by lower-caste and lower-class demands.

Similarly, modern Islamism is very much a product of the twentieth century. No doubt, some of the raw materials used in its construction date back to the time of the Prophet. Other materials, from oil revenues and electronic communications to the economic theories of Ayatollah Ruhollah Khomeini, are quite new. But even the older traditions do not represent imperishable values so much as attitudes and customs themselves the products of earlier change. The survival of those customs reflects their plasticity—their capacity to participate in the creation of *new* culture. And which customs are chosen for continuation or revival by twentieth-century Islamicists depends on their conception of "relevance," not on the dictates of unalterable tradition. The veiled Muslim woman who watches television at home, goes shopping in public, attends political rallies, or works in an office is neither the "emancipated" woman of the West nor the secluded woman of Islamic tradition. Indeed, the extent to which older gender roles and attitudes can be or should be preserved is continually debated, even in fundamentalist circles.

The raw materials of tradition can be used to create an extremely wide range of alternative "civilizations." What chiefly conditions the creative process is not tradition so much as the local and global environments in which culture develops. But Huntington would have us believe that the range of civilizational choices is strictly bounded by given traditional "values."

The effect of that cultural determinism is to revive that peculiar strain of Western thinking which saw the Cold War itself as a *kulturkampf*: a clash of civilizations. In American anticommunism there was always a split, cross-cutting the division separating conservatives from liberals, between rational/voluntarist and irrational/determinist interpretations of communist behavior. While the former pictured communism as a chosen belief system subject to change or abandonment under certain conditions, the latter emphasized the force of cultural determinism—that ineffable and immutable "something" in Russian, Chinese, or Vietnamese culture that inclined those peoples toward aggressive totalitarianism.

The logical implication, then and now, was not merely that the Other was different, but that he was inferior. If each civilization is the product (and prisoner) of its unique traditions, no basis for supracultural judgment or action exists. Near the end of his essay, Huntington pictures "a world of different civilizations, each of which will have to learn to coexist with others." But his own extreme relativism undermines that pious hope. If "the West against the Rest" truly describes the future of international conflict, what choice is there but to defend "Our" inherited values against "Theirs"?

States, Nations, and Civilizations

Old or new, a paradigm stands or falls according to its ability to describe, predict, and make sense of events. How well does Huntington's theory account for the causes of conflict in the emerging international system? According to "The Clash of Civilizations?" the history of militarized disputes in the modern international system began with wars between princes during the century and a half following the 1648 Peace of Westphalia. The nation-states that emerged out of that period molded the nature of conflict in the next phase—the era of interstate warfare. The 1917 Russian Revolution heralded the third era, a period of ideological conflict, which has now come to a close. It is to be succeeded, according to Huntington, by a period of civilizational conflict, as individuals and nations confronted by the obsolescence of earlier structures are compelled to construct their identities around larger and more encompassing politico-cultural entities.

A neat progression, but does it describe what is happening in the post–Cold War world? Does it predict the likely course of future international conflict? Many of Huntington's critics upbraid him for relegating the state to a secondary (if still important) status in the system of the future. However, he is correct to perceive a long-term trend away from states as the primary actors in international politics. He is also correct to note attempts to form new pan-national blocs on the basis of alleged cultural commonalities. But two mistakes lead the theorist to overschematize, overstate, and otherwise misconceive those developments. First, he fails to recognize that ethnic nations may be as resistant to incorporation in multinational civilizational blocs as they were to absorption by colonialist empires. Second, in order to reassert the importance of cultural factors in international politics, he turns liberal and Marxist reductionism on its head, arguing that cultural differences have become the primary facilitator of international conflict rather than one basis (among others) for conflict mobilization.

Huntington has little to say about the remarkable proliferation and increase of ethnic or national conflicts that predated the collapse of the Soviet empire by at least two decades. For purposes of proving his thesis, he selects, out of the various ethno-national conflicts now raging, those that seem to pit one "civilization" against another. But that selectivity will not wash. Huntington wants to talk about Islamic-Western conflict in Iraq, for example, but not about the struggles between Iraq's Muslim peoples: Sunnis, Shi'ites, and Kurds. (Indeed, the last thing he wants to discuss is the insistence by Arabs, Persians, and Kurds that they each constitute separate historical civilizations!) Similarly, while citing the fighting in Africa between Muslims and Christians or animists, he is silent about the type of inter-ethnic struggles now rending Rwanda, Liberia, and other African countries. In fact, out of the dozens of current ethnic conflicts, at least as many are conflicts *within* civilizations as conflicts between them. Further, even where they are nationally inter-civilizational, most of those conflicts remain localized and do not involve what Huntington calls "civilization rallying."

That should not surprise us. For reasons unexplored by Huntington, the ethnic nation, not the multiethnic civilization, has become the primary matrix for the construction of political identity and a fertile source of global conflict. Violent struggles today are just as likely to pit ethnic nation against ethnic nation, religious group against religious group, or ethnic nation against multinational state, as they are civilization against civilization. Of the roughly 180 states that compose the current world system, 15 at most can be called nations in the sense that a vast majority of people believe that they share a common ancestry and cultural identity. The norm for states is multinationality, with 40 percent containing people from five or more distinct nations. In slightly less than one-third of the cases overall, the largest national group does not even compose a majority of the state. And if such diversity is characteristic of mere states, how much more characteristic is it of multinational or civilizational empires!

As a result, many conflicts continue to be intra- as well as inter-civilizational. Even where nations at war do belong to different civilizations, it generally makes more sense to consider their conflicts national rather than civilizational. For example, Huntington presents the warfare between Muslims, Serbs, and Croats in former Yugoslavia as a prototypical clash of civilizations. But in no relevant way do those struggles differ from those between interpenetrated ethnic "families" *within* alleged civilizational boundaries: Pushtuns and

Baluchis vs. Punjabis in Pakistan; Catholics vs. Protestants in Northern Ireland; Hutus vs. Tutsis in Rwanda and Burundi; and so forth. The key to inter-civilizational struggle, according to Huntington, is "civilizational rallying" by "kin-countries." But the evidence suggests, first, that ethnic rallying is at least as common as rallying of the civilizational variety; and, second, that "kin countries" cannot be counted on to provide their civilizational brethren with more than verbal support, if that.

Huntington cannot have it both ways. If "rallying" proves the trend toward a clash of civilizations, does not the failure to rally disprove his thesis? His answer, no doubt, would be, "Wait and see." For the present, however, the primary cultural unit in international politics remains the nation—be it ethnic, tribal, religious, or political—not the civilization.

Problems of Causation and Prediction

Of course, this is not to say that ethnic nations are eternal or that they may not at some point be superseded by civilizations. Anything "constructed" can be reconstructed, and civilization-consciousness can be conceived of (and sometimes "sold") as an expanded ethnic consciousness. Suppose, then, that Huntington were to abandon the jejune notion that modern civilizations are homogenous nations sharing primordial cultural values. Suppose that he were to recognize them as ideological constructs designed to permit mobilization of diverse ethnic groups. Imagine, finally, that he were to face frankly the problem of the relativity of ethnicity, admitting that "Islamic civilization," for example, might well turn out to be a hopeless project, given the existence of separate Turkish, Persian, Arab, Kurdish, and Malay cultures, and that civilizations he has not named (Buddhist, Polynesian, Latin American Indian, etc.) could become the foci for new movements of unification. The theorist might still insist that the destiny of the nation is to be subsumed by larger civilizational units capable of offering their various ethnic components the satisfactions of membership in a greatly extended, more powerful "family." And he might still predict that the fate of those larger units, once organized, is to struggle for global power.

But what should one make of such predictions? *Will* new pan-national empires based on ideologized "tribal" identities arise to challenge the West and reorganize the international system? History tells us that it is possible. The rise of the reactionary European "pan movements" of the late-nineteenth and early twentieth centuries seems quite similar to the development Huntington prophesies. But what conditions favor the development of new pan movements? What would make the merely possible probable?

Those questions reveal the existence of a theoretical hole in Huntington's model. Since he provides little evidence of the direct causes of civilizational conflicts, Huntington is unable to specifically predict when or where they will occur. In fact, no primordialist theory can tell us when cultural similarities will become the raw material for ideological mobilization. The factors generating the current Islamic and Hindu revivals, like those that enabled Hitler to mobilize pan-Germanic sentiment in the interests of National Socialism, lie almost entirely off Huntington's theoretical map. Having declared that difference between nations, classes, and ideologies will not be the primary source of conflict, he is unable to connect the rise of radical Islamism, for example, with the collapse of world oil prices, Western support for corrupt local regimes, the failure of secular elites to extend the benefits of modernization to local workers and peasants, massive unemployment among

Arab youth, the persistence of internal ethnic and class divisions, the collapse of social-ist alternatives, and so forth. Nor can he explain why so many middle-class Indians now see Hindu revivalism as a solution to their problems, or what drives many contemporary Russians to endorse through popular vote the neo-fascist policies of Vladimir Zhirinovsky.

That same gap in causal explanation leads the theorist to make dubious predictions about the future of Western civilization. On the one hand, Huntington wishes us to believe that since Germany and the United States are both members of the Western "family," seri-ous conflict between the two powers (or between any other Western states) is no longer conceivable. On the other hand, since Japan is, by definition, non-Western, economic conflict between that nation and the United States has been cast in civilizational terms. But a moment's reflection will reveal that Westernism is as much an ideological construct as was communism or the "Free World." Under the pressure of a serious economic crisis, intensified global competition, or radical political change in one country or the other, Germans and Americans could easily rediscover their "essential" differences. Conversely, socioeconomic and political developments could accelerate (or decelerate) the convergence between the Japanese and Western civilizations.

Basic Human Needs

Huntington's cultural determinism leads him not only to obscure the conditions that sometimes produce pan-national movements, but also to view differences between civiliza-tions as largely fundamental. That is, at least, logical. For if each civilization is the product and advocate of its own unique, primordial values, no common value-base exists that will permit conflict resolution. Among civilizational strangers, the best that one can expect is a truce. But the relativist trap is not inescapable. Huntington himself refers obliquely to unspecified cultural "commonalities." As soon as one recognizes destructive social conflict as the result of unsatisfied basic needs—needs common to all humans, whatever their cultural heritage—the questions of causation and of conflict resolution can be demystified and answered.

By specifying the commonalities hinted at by Huntington, the paradigm of basic human needs challenges realist assumptions at their source. Conflict specialists John Bur-ton, Paul Sites, and others argue that serious social conflict is not generated by individual aggressiveness or international lawlessness as much as by the failure of existing systems to satisfy people's basic needs.[3] Certain needs (e.g., identity, bonding, security, meaning, and development) are shared by all human beings. Unlike interests, they are not bargainable; people will not trade their identities or belief-systems for money or surrender them even at gunpoint. And unlike values, they are not specific to particular cultures or civiliza-tions. Local cultures, or the state of a society's development, define the satisfiers of basic needs, but the needs themselves are universal. Moreover, they are irrepressible, demanding satisfaction no matter how a society's leaders may seek to suppress or manipulate them. If adherence to a street gang, a nation, or a civilization is a way of attempting to satisfy unfulfilled needs for identity, bonding, and security, neither coercion nor persuasion will alter that behavior. On the other hand, the conflicts generated by unsatisfied needs can be resolved (not just managed) by altering existing social and political arrangements to the extent necessary to satisfy them. The problem, ordinarily, is not a shortage of satisfiers; it is the unwillingness of elites to make the necessary system changes.

In that light, what *are* the circumstances that could generate pan-national or civilizational conflicts in the post–Cold War era? In modern times, at least, culture is unlikely to function as a political rallying-point unless at least three conditions are met:

First, the participants must feel that their identities, liberties, and livelihoods are seriously and immediately threatened by powerful, culturally distinguishable outsiders, often supported by local allies—an "enemy within." The degree of perceived threat is far more salient, in that regard, than the degree of perceived cultural difference.

Second, participants' other methods of satisfying their basic needs for identity, development, meaning, and security must be discredited or currently unavailable. The merger of one's class or nation with others in some pan-national entity is unlikely to occur unless class- and ethnic-based organizations have already proven ineffectual.

Third, some regional hegemon must be capable of persuading or forcing weaker nations to accept its "representation" of their cultural and political interests. Even Huntington would probably find it hard to conceive of a Slavic-Orthodox civilization without Russia, a Hindu civilization without India, or a Confucian civilization without China. In fact, where no contender for hegemony exists, as in the case of the Buddhist nations, Huntington does not count the civilization as a "player" at all.

Pan-nationalist militancy, in other words, is not a spontaneous growth but a response to political subordination, cultural humiliation, and blocked economic development. The case of Germany illustrates that process. It took Napoleon's conquests to provoke the construction of a Germanic political identity, and Prussian hegemony to give that identity institutional expression. It took British and French imperialism to convince Germans that, as the German nationalist Ernst Hasse wrote in his work *Deutsche Politik*, they "had the same right to expand as other great peoples, and that if not granted this possibility overseas, [they would] be forced to do it in Europe." And it took a combination of the Versailles system, the Great Depression, and the collapse of liberal and socialist alternatives to convert pan-German nationalism into Nazi racial supremacy. By the same token, if the Islamic-Confucian alliance so feared by Huntington should materialize to challenge Western power, or if Slavic-Orthodox peoples should reunite around a hegemonic Russia, cultural values and the "will to power" will have far less to do with such developments than with the inability of Western-dominated peoples to satisfy their basic needs for identity, security, and development.

Why, indeed, unless basic human needs are unfulfilled, should those who participate in different cultures fight? While human history surely provides examples of violent cultural and civilizational conflict, more prevalent still are stories of culture-groups avoiding, tolerating, or accommodating each other; merging with other groups to form new entities; or absorbing or being absorbed by others. In fact, from the perspective of conflict resolution, Huntington has got things exactly backwards. Struggles between social classes and between different levels of the power-knowledge hierarchy can be very difficult to resolve. Conflicts based primarily on cultural differences alone are easier to settle. That is because the parties to intercultural conflicts generally seek goods such as identity and mutual recognition, which are *not* in short supply, and because the clash of cultural values or worldviews is not nearly as absolute as Huntington implies. Hindus and Muslims in India do not generally make war on each other simply because one group loves cows and the other eats them. One can imagine any number of sociopolitical systems that would permit cow-lovers and cow-eaters, those who worship in temples and those who worship in mosques, to recognize each other's identities and interact without massacring each other. The principal obstacles to Hindu-Muslim peace in India are not incompatible cultural values but social and political conditions that allow each group to believe that it can survive only at another's expense. Without altering the conditions that make it impossible to satisfy basic human needs, conflicts like that one cannot be resolved. Huntington's pessimism with regard to resolving civilizational conflict is evidently based not only on his cultural relativism, but on the silent assumption that, in the brave new post–Cold War world, this sort of system-change is impossible.

We disagree. In response to Huntington's dark vision of civilizational struggle, we answer: Destructive conflict between identity groups, including pan-nationalist or civilizational groupings, can be averted and can be resolved if they do occur. But a violent clash of civilizations could well result from our continuing failure to transform the systems of inequality that make social life around the globe a struggle for individual and group survival—systems that feed the illusion that either one civilization or another must be dominant. Pan-national movements remain, as they have been in the past, misguided responses to foreign domination and native misgovernment. In our view, Huntington's call for the global defense of Western interests against competing civilizations therefore represents the worst sort of self-fulfilling prophecy. Nevertheless, his rhetorical question, "If not civilizations, what?" deserves an answer. Satisfying basic human needs on a global basis will require a powerful movement for social change—a movement waiting to be born.

23

MEMO TO THE STATE
Religion and Security

—Chris Seiple

If a government does not understand how easy it is to turn religion into an enemy of the state, then it might do just that. Indeed, even though the role of religion in international relations is now a hot topic among policymakers and in the academy, this dimension of the issue has been left relatively under-investigated.

Religious adherents worship something that is not only greater than themselves but also greater than their governments. The state's natural policy question is therefore simple: How can government reliably believe in their citizens when their citizens believe in something greater than the government?

In authoritarian and totalitarian regimes, the governmental reaction to this problem is most often to repress religion, with predictably counterproductive results. However, sometimes democratic societies also needlessly create or exacerbate problems because their governments have not adequately understood religion's relationship with security. A new framework is needed, one that facilitates the positive social contributions of faith so that the negative side-effects of repressed religion can be avoided. To that end, here are five recommendations for governments as they deal with religion in public life.

Religion: Problem & Solution

Understanding the promise and peril of religion is difficult, especially for the West's secular societies. Since the European Enlightenment, with its pivotal turn in philosophy away from tradition and toward rationalism and science, the Western world has attempted to separate matters of the state from matters of religion in the name of good governance. This principle, the separation of Church and State, has become a founding premise of most Western countries, and in many ways, the results have been positive.

However, too often the casualty of this division has been proper analysis. Failing to address the role of religion in public and political life can lead to a profound misunderstanding of global trends, events, and societies, including our own. By neglecting to factor

* *The Review of Faith & International Affairs* 5, no. 1 (Spring 2007): 39–42.

religion into political analysis, secular democracies can "repress" religion through ignoring it or granting it mere tolerance rather than showing it respect.

The irony for the West, and especially the United States, is that this lesson has been learned before. Many of the first Europeans to migrate to America were minorities fleeing persecution for their beliefs. Yet some of these same people established colonies wherein they persecuted anyone who did not believe as they did. Fortunately this pattern was recognized and broken early on, when Roger Williams fled the theocracy of Massachusetts to establish the colony of Rhode Island. Here liberty was defined not as the opposite of religious fundamentalism, namely secularist fundamentalism, but rather as *religious pluralism*. This robust form of religious freedom was later institutionalized through the leadership of other Founders such as William Penn, James Madison, and Thomas Jefferson. These American forefathers recognized the danger of not allowing religion a proper place in public discourse.

If governments cannot understand religion, then Samuel Huntington will be proven right—stereotypes will settle in as the clash of civilizations becomes inevitable. On the other hand, if governments and their citizens allow for the possibility that religion, and religious people, can play a positive role in preventing and resolving conflicts, then they are much closer to protecting national security through a dialogue about civilization. In many ways, however, the secular governments of the West are still collectively unequipped to engage religiously-based worldviews—such that we can work with and promote their best in order to help them defeat their worst.

A Seat at the Table for Religion

Too many international relations experts worship at the wailing wall of "church-state separation"—often ignoring religion altogether—to the detriment of themselves and the policymakers they advise. The result is that religion is overlooked as a legitimate component of *realpolitik*.

Consider the example of the war in Iraq. In April 2003, as U.S. interagency teams waited in Kuwait before going in to advise the various Iraqi ministries, there was debate about what to do with Iraq's Ministry for Religion. One official simply stated: "We don't do religion."

Not surprisingly, when Grand Ayatollah Sistani, the leader of Iraq's Shi'a majority, later issued a religious edict on 28 June 2003 regarding American plans for a transition to Iraqi rule, it was ignored. When the senior U.S. official in Iraq, Paul Bremer, was called home for emergency consultations in November 2003 to discuss the transition, one Iraqi leader, who had been installed by the U.S. immediately after the invasion, said: "We waited four months, thanks to Bremer. We could have organized [this transition] by now had we started when Sistani issued his fatwa. But the Americans were in denial."

It is no wonder that long-time national security writer Sydney J. Freedberg would observe in the 21 November 2003 issue of *National Journal*: "Americans are baffled by Iraq because we have spent three and a half centuries in a post-Westphalian world where state trumps faith and tribe. . . . Before we can understand our enemies, or our allies, in the Middle East, we have 350 years of assumptions to unlearn." In retrospect, it is now clear that between June and November of 2003 the various sectarian groups organized—in part because the U.S. did not know how to address religion as a part of *realpolitik*, let alone take seriously the senior Shi'a leader and the majority population that he represented.

If they seek sustainable stability, secular governments need people and organizations who operate at the intersection of religion and *realpolitik*. These "bilingual" ambassadors exist, and the world needs them more than ever before.

Good Faith vs. Bad Religion

Consider another American illustration: U.S. engagement of Muslim-majority societies since 9/11. The United States has primarily responded to 9/11 these past five years by focusing on gates, guns, and guards. Naturally enough after suffering a horrific attack, the explicit purpose has been keeping "them" out and "us" protected.

The problem with this approach, however, is that it remains all about "us." We have made no sustained effort to understand "them." And if we cannot begin to grasp the Muslim worldview—including its historical and cultural manifestations in particular places around the world—then we will never be able to communicate.

In order to communicate, Americans and their government must understand that the Muslim worldview is inherently rooted in faith. Islam is, of course, on the agenda of every security expert, but almost always in a way that is limited to the ideological dimensions of militant Islam. For example, the new term of reference is "Islamo-Fascism." Somehow, by invoking a 20th century concept rooted in the extreme nationalism and totalitarianism of the state, we are supposed to understand the theological roots of a non-state group that thinks of itself as religious.

Likewise vis-à-vis the word "jihad." Jihad is a sacred concept to Muslims who regard it first as an internal struggle of purification. By describing terrorists as "jihadis," American journalists and government officials validate the terrorists' perception of themselves as religious, and in the process they needlessly insult pious Muslims.

If a government has no ability to understand the theology associated with the citizens of its various religious groups—and their co-religionists around the world—it will only heighten tension by misnaming and mischaracterizing motivations and actions. Instead, it should be the responsibility of governments to understand the faith systems of their citizens, if only to encourage them to police their own ranks in the name of their own faith. More specifically, governments need to encourage emerging authentic voices through theological training. The more broadly trained religious leaders there are—that is, the more clerics who understand the very best of their faith and the diversity of its cultural expressions—the less likely it is that the faith will be manipulated by political entrepreneurs. It is imperative to the stability and development of societies worldwide that governments encourage and facilitate religious leaders literate in their faith and culture. "Seminary" is security.

Engagement on Common Ground

It is too often the case that people of one culture and region assume that people from another think the same way they do. This phenomenon is frequently manifested in the West's promotion of universal human rights. While their premise and articulation make perfect sense to Westerners, their blunt, moralistic promulgation is often viewed as cultural imperialism by non-Westerners. Fair enough; the manner in which a message is conveyed is usually more important than the message when engaging a culture other than ones own.

That said, there are indeed common principles that every culture shares. It is imperative for each of us—no matter our culture—to seek the tie that binds, to find ways to love and respect each other in a language and logic that the other understands.

By way of example, consider the Institute for Global Engagement's current efforts in relational diplomacy in Pakistan's Northwest Frontier Province, a part of the world that serves as a hideout for the Taliban, al-Qaeda, and probably Osama bin Laden. Over the last year the Institute has been working carefully and in a principled way with the Chief Minister of the province to promote justice and mercy—concepts common to Christianity and Islam—by enabling educational and socio-economic opportunity for people of all faiths. In short, in this geo-strategically important and largely closed region, taking the time to find common ground is what provided the Institute with a place to stand.

Responsible Religious Liberty & Counterterrorism

There are times, of course, when giving certain militant religious groups too much freedom can create serious security risks. One need only recall the case of Aum Shinrikyo in Japan, where, because of its religious cult status, it was constitutionally protected from investigation before its 20 March 1995 sarin gas attack on the Tokyo subways. We saw a similar thing with last year's "7/7" bombers in London, among whom was a former disciple of the Islamist group Hizb ut-Tahrir (HT). HT is banned in Germany, where they have historic experience with hate speech, but not banned in the UK.

However, governments should not respond in simplistic ways to the risk of religious radicalism. It is not enough for a government to grant wide freedom to religious groups it deems non-threatening and to suppress those it deems threatening. Religious groups are not static entities that can be assigned permanently to "good" and "bad" categories. Instead, they must be engaged holistically and preemptively, and with the objective of cultivating not just "tolerance" but rather *respect*—mutual respect between religious groups and between religions and the government. This will often be a matter of simply tapping the reservoirs of respect that already exist, rather than attempting to impose the value through indoctrination. Indeed, every society has religio-cultural mores that support hospitality and respect for guests and minorities. If the government encourages these cultural mechanisms it will likely enjoy the approval of its people, minimizing the chances of religious groups becoming dangerously radicalized, and maximizing the chances of retaining nonviolent engagement options if a religious group does slip into extremism.

Conclusion

"Civil society" is only characterized by civility when there is a balance between the "freedom to" something (liberty) and the "freedom from" something (security). The fulcrum will vary according to historical and cultural context, but the true test of the civility of any society will always be how it respects the minority in its midst. If this balance can be found, then security and stability will result. In such a context, religion will contribute to the development of society as people of faith practice the best of their values by serving their community.

As Gerard Powers once said: "The best way to counter religious extremism or manipulation of religion is with strengthened, more authentic religion, not weakened religion. The challenge for religious leaders . . . is to show that religion can be a counter to extreme nationalism and a source of peace because of, not in spite of, its close link with culture and national identity."[1]

24

THE POLITICS OF PERSECUTED RELIGIOUS MINORITIES

—Philip Jenkins

> History teaches us that men and nations only behave wisely
> once they've exhausted all other alternatives.

—Abba Eban

Debates about the free expression and practice of religion are usually framed in philosophical terms. Virtually no one questions that this freedom is, in principle, a desirable end, though controversy might arise over the precise limitations necessary for public order. Even those least sympathetic in practice to religious freedom tend to praise it in theory. The debate, then, revolves around the best means of securing the maximum degree of religious freedom possible in the circumstances of a given society.[1]

But let us ask a question rarely heard, namely, if a society fails to respect religion, what are the real-world sociopolitical consequences for that society? We may of course stipulate that the "letter of the law"—human rights covenants and international treaties—will be offended. But what practical harm might follow? Based on a historical and comparative perspective, I want to suggest that a society that limits the religious rights of its subjects might suffer grave and extremely damaging consequences, injuries that may go far beyond those to international prestige or diplomatic favor. Indeed, the experience of religious minorities under persecution constitutes a major, if under-explored, element of the explanation of why some processes of nation-building fail. The politics of persecuted minorities is a topic with far-reaching consequences for national and international security.[2]

We must begin by defining the concept of persecution in the most direct and physical sense, namely an effort by government to repress major activities by a given religious group, commonly with the goal of eliminating that group in the long or short term, or at least reducing its significance to nothing. Naturally, it is often difficult to separate religious persecution from other forms of repression based for instance on ethnicity, race, or political factors. Can one properly describe the Nazi attack on the European Jews as religious

---

* Robert A. Seiple and Dennis R. Hoover, eds., *Religion & Security: The New Nexus in International Relations* (Lanham, Md.: Rowman & Littlefield, 2004), 25–36.

in nature? Presumably not, since Jews could not save themselves by converting to another religion, even the religion of the majority of Germans. In that case, we should properly speak of racial rather than religious conflict.

In other conflicts, religious motives might not be wholly explicit, though most observers would agree that they predominated. In early modern England, the persecution of Roman Catholics that prevailed with varying degrees of severity from 1558 to the end of the seventeenth century was never explicitly religious. Rather, Catholics and especially clergy were tortured and executed for their denial of the legitimacy of the state, namely for treason or sedition. The consequence of this policy was, however, explicitly religious, so that whoever said Mass was guilty of treason. By the same standard, we might say that the repression of Shi'ite Islam in a modern nation like Ba'athist Iraq reflected no religious prejudice, but rather a hostility to the rival political claims of the Shi'ite clergy.[3] As in early modern England, the consequence was still a massive religious and anti-clerical persecution. Though a certain leeway must be granted in terms of definition, we will not generally encounter too many difficulties arriving at a reasonable consensus definition.

It should be said at the outset that religious persecution can succeed. If anyone believes that "you can't kill an idea," I would ask that optimistic person to produce a living representative of traditions like the medieval French Cathars or Albigensians, annihilated in wars and successive persecutions during the thirteenth and fourteenth centuries. Or equally, what was the story of Judaism in England during the 360 years following the total expulsion commanded by King Edward I in 1290? There might be isolated instances of crypto-Jews in England, but essentially, a long and significant communal history was snuffed out almost overnight.

But assume that persecution is not so totally successful, that it continues for decades or centuries. Based on numerous examples past and present, a number of themes can be identified that link religious persecution closely to political unrest and instability.

Going Underground

First, and perhaps most significant, persecuted communities are forced to operate clandestinely, where they learn traditions of conspiracy and secret organization. These traditions may not be overtly radical or insurrectionary, but they can create a substantial and potentially dangerous framework that can be exploited by enemies of a state in the long term. Think for instance of some of the underground networks that survived the most devastating persecutions in early modern Europe, groups like the Family of Love and the Anabaptists, and the elaborate informal networks they developed.[4] Neither provided the core of any kind of armed resistance. On the other hand, we think of the modern story of religion under Soviet rule, which especially in the Stalinist era inflicted the most savage persecution upon believers of all kinds. In the Soviet puppet state of Mongolia, for instance, the Buddhist clergy was all but annihilated.

The Muslims proved a much tougher target. While clergy could be killed or compromised, the Soviets found their deadliest enemies in the great Sufi brotherhoods that had done so much to spread Islam across Central Asia. The Soviets condemned the Sufis as the *zikristi*, those who said the *dhikr*, the sacred chant of the name of God that Sufis employ to induce a mystic state. Zikrists were savagely persecuted, but never uprooted, because of their powerful underground networks. These alone proved able to survive Soviet totalitarianism, and the Sufi orders were able to reemerge with amazing success in the post-Soviet era.[5] Their underground survival must recall that of other suppressed religious networks, like those of early modern Europe: we may think of the Catholic clergy in Protestant-dominated England or Ireland, or the Protestants in seventeenth century France.

Orders like the Naqshbandi are critical to understanding the modern politics of Central Asia. The Sufi orders were and also are the core of the Chechen resistance in the Caucasus region, naturally enough since like many Muslims through Central and Western Asia, the Chechens were converted to Islam by the Sufi orders. It is astounding how many accounts of the Chechen/Russian conflicts fail to pay due attention to this Sufi context; and equally, how the U.S. has failed to exploit the massive ideological divisions that separate Sufi Islam from the intolerant puritanical traditions of the Wahhabists. Traditions like the Naqshbandi Order have proved so resilient, so skilled at clandestine survival, that we must doubt any claims by repressive Islamic states like Saudi Arabia that they have suppressed or eliminated Sufi practices. Driven them underground, perhaps, but eliminated, probably not. As in the former Soviet Union, they are rather lying dormant, ready to re-emerge. Persecution may actually strengthen clandestine networks, not to mention the loyalty of ordinary believers. Sociologists of religion are very familiar with the idea that people value most that for which they suffer most.[6]

Holy Warriors

Second, if persecuted religious groups do survive, they often do so by developing quite active and effective military traditions. A simple Darwinian principle may be at work here. Groups that do not so adapt are largely doomed, unless the persecution ends spontaneously, or they find some favorable refuge: I think of the Amish and the Mennonites on American soil. But if such refuges are not available, persecuted groups often become highly effective warriors, and some of the world's toughest fighters owe their origins to the need to defend religious dissidence. Examples are quite numerous. We may think of the Sikhs, originally founded in sixteenth-century India as a tolerant and peaceful order pledged to achieve reconciliation between Islam and Hinduism. Over time they were persecuted more and more savagely by India's Mughal rulers, until by the eighteenth century, extinction seemed imminent. The solution was found in transformation into a military brotherhood, the *khalsa*, in which every man was a lion, a *singh*. The Sikhs survived and flourished in independence, and their fighting qualities deeply impressed the British Raj. Wise governments of India have respected the Sikhs' right to be left alone, a principle violated in the 1980s by Prime Minister Indira Gandhi, who attacked their Golden Temple. She of course perished soon afterwards at the hands of her Sikh bodyguards.[7]

Such stories of dissident warriors are by no means rare. In late medieval Europe, the persecuted Hussites of Bohemia formed the most formidable fighting machine of their day, and used pioneering mobile armor formations, early "tanks." Britain's religious wars of the seventeenth century produced several separate groupings subjected to appalling persecution, who responded by forming Sikh-like traditions and structures. In Scotland, the Covenanters were radical Calvinists who rejected the existing church and state as illegitimate and diabolical, and suffered terribly for it. When their allies came to power in 1689, they joined the military establishment as the Cameronian Regiment, a legendary force within the British army, and one that long retained its religious character: "It was essentially an armed congregation, and was the only unit in the British Army to carry their weapons into church. Each company elected an elder, each man carried a Bible, and no church services were held without armed pickets being posted to defend it."[8]

No sophisticated theory is needed to understand the religious or political dynamic here. In a threatening environment, enemies of the state must often develop a strong military tradition if they are to survive. This is the story of the Sikhs, the Cameronians, and also of Middle Eastern groupings like the Druzes and the Maronite Christians of Lebanon and Syria. The Druze people are a classic example both of militarization and of the emphasis on the clandestine that we noted earlier. The fact that they hold views that are absolute anathema to orthodox Islam meant that they were forced to become very tough warriors, as the U.S. Marines found in their encounter with Lebanon in 1983. The Druze also practice a principle of secrecy. Followers of the Druze religion are allowed, and even encouraged, to deny their religion and to pretend that they are members of whatever the official religion may be at a particular time and place. Great value is placed on silence, secrecy, occultation—the essential tools of survival in a very dangerous environment.[9] Clearly, as Indira Gandhi was forced to realize in her country, the existence of such independent and well-armed minorities can pose real problems for state formation and the assertion of national unity.

People of Blood

Third, groups that resist and survive persecution often develop or cultivate ideologies that make sense of their suffering, and that promise rewards for themselves, and punishment for persecutors. These ideologies can in turn provide justification for resistance, and in some cases, for warfare. In practical terms, this means that persecuted groups are prone to apocalyptic ideas and to martyrdom. In approaching this, we face something of a chicken-and-egg situation. Do persecuted movements develop such ideologies as a consequence of their sufferings, or it is that groups that already possess these ideas are more likely to survive under repression, and to leave us a record of their ideas? Perhaps both processes are at work.

The popularity of Christian apocalyptic is not difficult to understand, since the most famous book that bears that name, the Revelation of Saint John, was almost certainly composed as a direct response to Roman persecution, so its mindset appeals immediately to modern counterparts in that situation. The book offers an analysis of the secular world as under the power of demonic forces, which find their seat above all in cities, and which are pledged to destroy the tiny righteous remnant of God's chosen. Persecution and martyrdom are inevitable consequences of faithfulness to God, while deceit and treachery threaten to entrap the saints at every stage. Suffering and bloodshed are not just meaningful, but perhaps essential to salvation. The only solution is a rigid rejection of the world and its evil ways, and faith in God who will shortly intervene to annihilate evil and proclaim justice. It is scarcely surprising that such ideas appealed so mightily to Christians under persecution through history. We think for instance of the Huguenots of France in the late seventeenth century. As they were persecuted and expelled, their extremists developed ever more apocalyptic and fanatical ideas, through revolutionary sects like the Camisards. Associates of the movement developed ideas of prophetic inspiration, like the notorious French Prophets whose outbursts did so much to discredit religious extremism in early eighteenth-century England.[10]

Ideas of martyrdom need not be rooted in apocalyptic or explicit scriptural warrant. We find another classic example of a cult of martyrdom among the persecuted English Catholics of the early modern period, for whom official repression was such a standard expectation. In turn, ideas of sacrifice, martyrdom, and sacrificial bloodshed became integrated into the religious schema, and left a long historical inheritance. One of the most popular nineteenth-century Catholic hymns commemorated the "Faith of our fathers living still in spite of dungeon, fire, and sword." As one of the supreme historical ironies, this hymn has now become popular among Protestants, the descendants of those who once commanded the fire and sword.[11]

In more contemporary terms, we think of the Shi'a tradition in Islam, a group that for a millennium has often known persecution and exclusion, and that has developed its ideas of sacrificial bloodshed and innocent suffering, focused on the martyr Imam Hussain and his death at Karbala. These acts are in turn commemorated by rituals that are fundamental to the lived experience of the faith, namely the Ashura festivities that provide such a close Muslim counterpart to the Christian Easter. Shi'ism is also messianic in its expectation of the return of the twelfth imam, and apocalyptic in looking to the end times.[12] None of these ideas necessarily leads to violent or subversive behavior: even if they deploy the most hair-raising rhetoric, apocalyptic groups through history commonly tend to be quietist, accepting their own bloodshed in the cause of religion, dying rather than killing. But the existence of these religious strands can potentially serve as the foundation for activities that disrupt or even destroy a state.

In practical terms, a group whose religion revolves around relics, blood, and a cult of death is commonly difficult to overawe and difficult to incorporate into a state: ask the Irish, or rather, ask the British who tried to oppress them. Often too, recalcitrance in one area, political resistance, spills over into other social areas, so that Catholic Ireland became progressively more ungovernable during the nineteenth century, as the common people rejected the legitimacy not just of the official church but of the state, its laws, and its economic order. A persecuted people is hard to govern—an obvious point, but one that is often neglected. It is easy for activists to manipulate that kind of sentiment, to manipulate the idea of the blood of the martyrs, in order to generate opposition to the state. In one of the most famous speeches in modern Irish history, Padraig Pearse proclaimed that:

> Our foes are strong and wise and wary; but, strong and wise and wary as they are, they cannot undo the miracles of God who ripens in the hearts of young men the seeds sown by the young men of a former generation. . . . Rulers and Defenders of Realms had need to be wary if they would guard against such processes. Life springs from death; and from the graves of patriot men and women spring living nations. The Defenders of this Realm have worked well in secret and in the open. They think that they have pacified Ireland. They think that they have purchased half of us and intimidated the other half. They think that they have foreseen everything, think that they have provided against everything; but the fools, the fools, the fools!—they have left us our Fenian dead, and while Ireland holds these graves, Ireland unfree shall never be at peace.[13]

Besides the Irish, we might also think of the ordinary people of Iran, Iraq, or Lebanon, extremely long-suffering, until their patience is finally exhausted. And though the Shi'ites did not invent suicide bombings, they have since the 1980s popularized the notion of "martyrdom operations," the devastating attack by a *shahid* martyr, an idea that fits so well into their traditions of virtuous sacrifice. These ideas have of course subsequently been assimilated into Sunni Islam.[14]

Men of God

Persecution often tends to change the internal dynamic of a movement, to concentrate power and prestige in the hands of a clerical elite. The most important example of this may be the early Christian movement itself, which developed such a powerful focus on martyrdom and sacrificial bloodshed, and which came to be personified in the figure of the bishops, who were so often the successors and heirs of martyrs. They were in a sense descended from a primal act of blood-offering. Elaine Pagels has argued that it was precisely the orthodox focus on martyrdom and episcopacy that gave the Orthodox/Catholic church its edge over rival and competing sects like the Gnostics, which were ultimately stigmatized as heretics, and eventually vanished.[15] The early Church father Tertullian declared, famously, that the blood of martyrs is the seed of the church. Similar processes can be discerned in more recent historical eras, especially in the Catholic Church of early modern and modern times. In Great Britain and Ireland, the association with martyrdom and persecution gave an enormous cachet to the Catholic priesthood, which lasted long after the actual age of rack and rope had faded into historical memory.[16] This element did much to create the powerful clericalism of Irish Catholicism in the United States, which largely survived into our own day.

These ideas of mysticism and martyrdom were much in evidence once more during the 1950s, when the persecution of the Catholic Church under Communist regimes struck such a chord among American believers, who were such enthusiastic advocates of confrontation with the Soviet Union. Catholic anti-Communism was also closely linked to ideas of apocalypse, to the Antichrist (who was commonly identified with Stalin) and with mystical revelation, through the figure of the Virgin Mary. These ideas have been powerful in our own time through the global influence of Pope John Paul II, another scion of a persecuted church, namely in Poland. Such ideas can be reinterpreted in secular terms, so that both Ireland and Poland have been presented as "martyr nations," and their heroes viewed as martyrs. It is impossible to understand the great heroes of secular Irish nationalism like Padraig Pearse except in this sub-Catholic context of this mystical theme of secular martyrdom: the great event of the Irish nationalist calendar is of course Easter, and its symbol the Easter lily of Resurrection. Those ideas then permeate ostensibly secular nationalist guerrilla movements like the Irish Republican Army.[17]

Of course, these ideas are not confined to Christianity, since they find such powerful parallels especially in Shi'ite Islam. Shi'ism—that apocalyptic creed—is also the section of Islam most dominated by clergy, and most prone to attribute messianic hopes to specific living clergy, imams and ayatollahs. The story of modern politics in Iran, Iraq, and Lebanon can be told through the collective biographies of leading clerics and ayatollahs, whose charisma is often linked to specific families and bloodlines. As in the Catholic instance, the more a state seeks to curb these traditions through violence, the more the official violence and repression is interpreted through the language of martyrdom, and the more awe and loyalty is attached to the martyr and his heirs and spiritual successors. We think of the experience of the Shi'ite clergy in Iran, or the massive disaffection of the Shi'ites in Ba'athist Iraq.

As in the Catholic context, the view of a hostile outside world tends to support ideas of separation and withdrawal, and the creation of a whole alternative subculture of clerically dominated institutions. This process is especially evident in education. In turn, the existence of alternative schools and colleges can further generate conflicts with the established order, since they directly challenge theories of national unity and homogenization.

Brothers Across the Seas

Assume that a state has repressed, but failed to destroy, a religious minority that has developed some or all of the characteristics that have been outlined above. The minority largely rejects the legitimacy of the state, which it views in terms of evil or demonic forces; it sees its own sufferings as part of a divine plan; it might explore ideas of apocalyptic, messianic, and redemptive violence; its cohesion and discipline are constantly reinforced by reference to the pressing dangers from the threatening outside world. Such a community is obviously deeply dangerous to the internal stability of a nation. A self-reinforcing process might also be at work. The more a community declares its opposition to the established order, the less likely it is that members of that community will be absorbed into the establishment. The more they are excluded, the more they will devote their loyalties and efforts to the religious subculture, and the more they will be seen as clannish, separatist, or subversive.

But these internal conflicts are not necessarily the worst danger faced by a persecuting state. Very few religions exist entirely within the defined boundaries of one state or nation. Some may spread over a subcontinent, or might indeed be global. A religious tradition persecuted in one nation might represent the dominant order in another, or at least might command more power and respect. People who are persecuted in one jurisdiction therefore have natural friends and allies and sympathizers in other regions. The political and diplomatic consequences are obvious. The persecuted Catholics of Tudor and Stuart England naturally found common cause with the powerful Catholic regimes of European states, especially imperial Spain. Though most ordinary English Catholics rejected treason and conspiracy, enough activists were prepared to share these schemes to create a permanent danger of subversion. And even those who rejected overt treason were sufficiently influenced by the ideologies of clericalism and martyrdom that they would be loath to betray a priest on the run. The Catholic subculture became, in effect, a ready-made nationwide resistance network, complete with safe houses.[18] A large part of the history of the Middle East in early modern times consists of the struggle between Shi'ite Iran and the Sunni Ottoman Empire, and the Shi'ites and minorities often served as an unstable factor in this relationship.

A persecuted minority can thus become an ideal fifth column, which in the correct circumstances might support an invasion or an armed incursion. It is impossible to understand the extraordinary repressive apparatus of Ba'athist Iraq except in terms of the pervasive danger posed by its domestic fifth column, that 60 percent of Iraqis who espoused Shi'ism, and who looked for support and sympathy to the neighboring Shi'ite state of Iran. Such fears naturally reached new heights during the open war between the two nations between 1980 and 1988. Apart from its potential as a fifth column, a persecuted minority can provide an intelligence service, and even a *casus belli*: "We" will not stand idly by and tolerate "your" persecution of our brothers and sisters.

In another area too, that of exile, the politics of persecution endanger security. Whether we are dealing with Catholics or Protestants in the early modern era, or radical Muslims today, official repression commonly drives activists and dissidents to seek exile beyond the reach of the state apparatus. Commonly, those driven from their homelands are religious leaders and exiles. Exile communities can serve many functions. They are notoriously vulnerable to the machinations of rival governments and intelligence services, who might even find in them the nucleus of an alternative government for the persecuting nation. An exile center—be it a cleric's retreat, a court, or a college—can also become a center for conspiracy and intelligence in its own right. We think of the Jesuit colleges in early modern Europe, or the household of the Ayatollah Khomeini in the 1970s, prior to the Iranian revolution. Also, exiles are free of the need to compromise with the practical realities of their homelands, and commonly drift to the most radical and extreme positions, violently opposed to the nations that drive them away. When the Spanish expelled their Jewish communities in the fifteenth and sixteenth centuries, those Jews did not simply fade into obscurity, but often found homes in Protestant nations like the Netherlands, where they served as powerful activists for radically anti-Spanish policies. The Irish Catholics forced into exile by the British state became the "Wild Geese," whose flight took them into the military service of many European Catholic states. In the wars of the eighteenth century, the Wild Geese were commonly the deadliest military enemies of the emerging British Empire.

Conclusion

Religious persecution can thus provide massive obstacles to nation-building, and to creating a stable, just, and secure international order. It also produces a vicious cycle, in which violence itself breeds theories and structures conducive to violence. And yet we know that the pattern can ultimately be ended. Apart from Northern Ireland, it has been a great many years since Protestants and Catholics have killed each other in Europe. Can anything be learned from this experience that might be applied to the contemporary world?

Ultimately, a kind of exhaustion set in. During the late seventeenth century, after decades of warfare and persecution, rival factions wearied of the cycle in which one faction would strike at another, only to be persecuted by them in turn. Gradually, people came to realize that it was in their own interests to limit the power of the state to penalize any religious interest whatever. If Baptists could force Catholics to take an unpopular oath of loyalty, then Catholics could impose their ideas when they were in the ascendant. Far better, then, to eliminate religious tests as far as possible—though the process was not complete until Victorian times. The history of civil and political rights in England and America is the story of how all factions came to this common realization.

I also think of the seventeenth-century founder of international law, the great Dutch scholar Hugo Grotius. He made one of the most important intellectual leaps in human history. He wanted to write a book on international law but not in terms of revelation, of what God said, what the Bible said. Yet he wanted to avoid charges of religious unorthodoxy. So, he used an argument rather like this—I paraphrase shamelessly—"Now, of course, God exists. Everyone knows this. But just suppose for the sake of argument, as in a mathematical proof, just suppose God was not a given—*etsi Deus non daretur*. Just suppose that. Now, what are the intellectual consequences?" The Enlightenment can be described as the extrapolation of that principle.

That enormous principle might yet be liberating in an Islamic context. If a society could be persuaded to believe, not that God is not there, not that God does not act, but that we should look at politics and culture *etsi Deus non daretur*. Just suppose God is not a given. What follows? In the context of Europe, that proviso was a major source of the Enlightenment. Might it yet ignite future Enlightenments? And might it yet help end modern cycles of religious intolerance and violence?

25

RELIGIOUS FREEDOM
Good for What Ails Us?

—Brian J. Grim

To judge from international survey data, people the world over want to be able to practice their religion freely. In the 2007 Pew Global Attitudes Survey, publics in 34 countries covering five different regions were asked about the importance of practicing their religion freely.[1] The response was extremely high, ranging from 84 percent in Eastern Europe to 98 percent in Africa. On average across the 34 countries, 93 percent indicated that it is important to be able to live in a country where they can practice their religion freely, with less than 2 percent indicating that it wasn't important at all.

Yet at the same time, religion is implicated in many of today's most urgent security problems. Millions have been killed or displaced due to religion-related conflicts in the first years of the twenty-first century alone.[2] Such conflicts lead to political instability, prevent the consolidation of democracy, and feed terrorism.

FIGURE 1
Living in a country where I can freely practice my religion is important

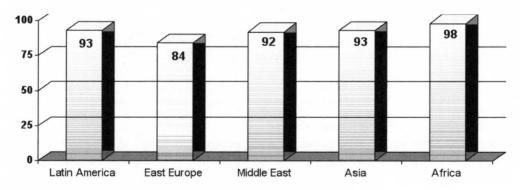

Average of country percentages in each region (2007 Global Attitudes Survey, 34 countries)

* *The Review of Faith & International Affairs* 6, no. 2 (Summer 2008): 3–7.

This raises a critical question: While the global public may want religious freedom, is it risky to give it to them?[3] Or alternatively, could religious freedom in fact be an essential part of the solution to socio-political problems? In what follows, I explore the global relationship between religious freedom and social wellbeing (or lack thereof), drawing from extensive international data on religious freedom and various social and political indicators.

Is Religious Freedom *Correlated* with Socio-economic Wellbeing?

At an anecdotal level, my own international observations while living abroad lead me to hypothesize that religious freedom should correlate strongly with positive social indicators. For example, I have lived in both the Kingdom of Saudi Arabia and the United Arab Emirates. In the Emirates, where my Catholic faith was legal, I had many ways to contribute to society, both through the church as well as through other avenues. I felt motivated to work hard and contribute to society. In Saudi Arabia, however, where my Catholic faith was illegal, I had much less enthusiasm for work and no real desire to contribute to society outside of work. If my feelings were representative, it could be part of the explanation for the fact that the per capita income in the Emirates is $55,200, while in Saudi Arabia it is only $20,700.[4]

Are there multinational statistical data that confirm these impressions? According to a recent study of 101 countries conducted by the Hudson Institute's Center for Religious Freedom, the answer is yes (see figure 2). The presence of religious freedom in a country mathematically correlates with the presence of other fundamental, responsible freedoms[5] (including civil and political liberty, press freedom, and economic freedom) and with the longevity of democracy.[6]

Harvard Economist and Nobel Laureate Amartya Sen[7] argues, however, that human freedom is not just the *general* opportunity for such freedoms, but also the *specific* processes within a country that result in better lives. Thus, if religious freedom is an integral part of the "bundled commodity" of human freedoms, religious freedom should be closely associated with the general betterment of people's lives. The Hudson Institute data again confirm just such a correlation. The study found that wherever religious freedom is high, there tends to be fewer incidents of armed conflict, better health outcomes, higher levels of earned income, and better educational opportunities for women. Moreover, religious freedom is associated with higher overall human development, as measured by the human development index.[8]

Does Religious Freedom *Lead to* Socio-economic Wellbeing?

Religious freedom, then, is *associated* with better social outcomes, but can we say there is a causal relationship? More advanced statistical tests suggest that there is indeed a critical independent contribution that religious freedom is making. A growing body of research supports the proposition that the religious competition inherent in religious freedom results in increased religious participation;[9] and religious participation in turn can lead to a wide range of positive social and political outcomes, as discussed below. Furthermore, as religious groups make contributions to society and become an accepted part of the fabric of society, religious freedom is consolidated. This can be conceptualized as a *religious freedom cycle* (see figure 3).

FIGURE 2
Fundamental, Responsible Human Freedoms—A Bundled Commodity

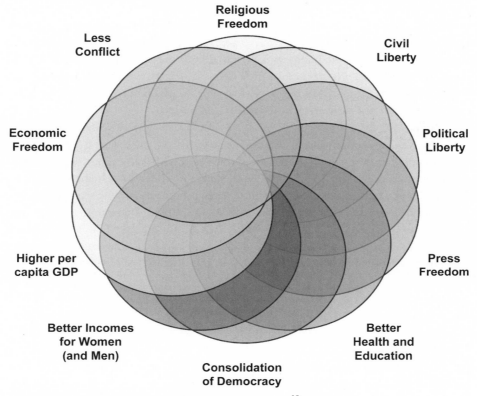

Statistically significant correlations found in the 2007 Hudson Institute study[10] *(101 countries)*

FIGURE 3
The Religious Freedom Cycle

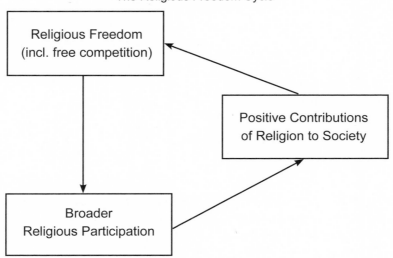

Theoretical model based on review of existing research

In recent years, many studies have looked at the benefits of the social capital and spiritual capital generated through active civic and religious involvement.[11] As more people actively participate in religion, religious groups increasingly bring tangible benefits such as literacy, vocational, and health training; marital and bereavement counseling; poverty relief; and more. Faith-based organizations, for example, are the major providers of care and support services to people living with HIV/AIDS in the developing world,[12] and there is growing scientific evidence of the health benefits associated with religious participation itself.[13] Some studies suggest that the advent of new religious forms can help to improve the lives of women[14] and activate greater civic participation.[15]

Established religions, however, often act to curtail competition from new religious groups by preventing proselytism,[16] restricting conversion, and putting up barriers that make it difficult for new religions to gain a foothold.[17] My colleague Roger Finke and I recently published a study in the *American Sociological Review* which found that the attempt to restrict fair religious competition results in more violence and conflict, not less. Specifically, we found that social restrictions on religious freedom lead to government restrictions on religious freedom, and the two act in tandem to increase the level of violence related to religion—which in turn cycles back and leads to even higher social and government restrictions on religion. This creates what we call the *religious violence cycle* (see figure 4).

FIGURE 4
The Religious Violence Cycle

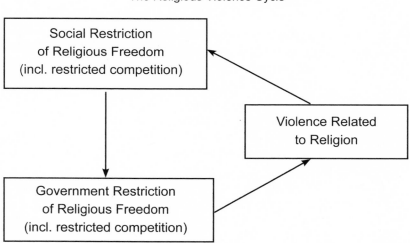

Structural Equation Model, 143 countries, populations > 2 million.
Grim and Finke, "Religious Persecution in Cross-National Context," American Sociological Review *72, no. 4 (2007): 649.*[23]

Our research on 143 countries finds that when governments and religious groups in society do not erect barriers to religious competition but respect and protect such activities as conversion and proselytism, religious violence is less. A further analysis of the data shows that countries with no restrictions on conversion, in particular, tend to have higher levels of fundamental freedoms, better lives for women, and less overall armed conflict.[18]

These results offer a different perspective than the "clash of civilizations" theory, in that, rather than religious competition automatically leading to violence, the protection of fair religious competition actually leads to *less* religious violence.

One unique aspect of these findings is that *social* restriction of religious freedom (or social religious intolerance) drives government restrictions.[19] Examples include the social pressures in India for anti-conversion laws, calls for shari'a law in northern Nigeria and parts of Indonesia, expulsions of evangelicals in Chiapas, Mexico,[20] and numerous religious rebellions from China's long history.[21] One of the clearest historical examples of the way social restrictions of religious freedom can feed into the religious violence cycle is the Holocaust. Research has shown that the Nazi government's violence toward Jewish people reinforced pre-existing social prejudices, creating a cycle of violence that was banally carried out with the support of many in German society.[22]

A clear current example of the religious violence cycle can be seen in Iraq. The U.S. State Department concluded in 2007 that the religious freedom situation has dramatically deteriorated. In pre-invasion Iraq, life for many religious and ethnic communities was certainly dire, especially for Shi'ites and Kurds. However, in the years after the invasion, the Shi'a, who were previously targeted for violence, acquired the political reins, and with their newfound power, religiously oriented Shi'a parties successfully lobbied for the insertion of the so-called repugnancy clause in the recent Iraqi constitution, which requires that no law can contradict Islam. It essentially gives Islam, and advocates of Shi'a Islam in particular, veto power over any law in Iraq, lessening the power of any other religious group in the political process. This new political environment has exacerbated religious sectarian violence. In the process, minority religious groups ranging from Christians to Yazedis have been targeted. Now, the economy cannot get on its feet, democracy is not functioning, and women, especially in Baghdad by the account of many, have become virtual prisoners in their own homes for fear of unmentionable violence.

Conclusion

To quote sociologist Peter Berger, we are in an "age of explosive, pervasive religiosity."[24] Thus, it is essential to understand how the affairs of nations and peoples are affected by religious freedom—in both its social and governmental aspects. The empirical data are clear on two points. First, religious freedom is part of the "bundled commodity" of human freedoms that energize broader productive participation in civil society by all religious groups, which is conducive to the consolidation of democracy and to socio-economic progress. Secondly, religious freedom reduces conflict and increases security by, among other things, removing grievances religious groups have toward governments and their fellow citizens.

In sum, religious freedom promotes stability, helps to consolidate democracy, and lessens religious violence. Based on an analysis of the data, it is clear that religious freedom is much more than an American pet project; rather, religious freedom is a universal aspiration. As another sociologist, N. J. Demerath, has said, the challenge for governments is to "set the rules for cultural conflict and assure an equitable framework for religious diversity."[25]

26

HOW SHALL WE STUDY RELIGION AND CONFLICT?
Challenges and Opportunities in the Early Twenty-First Century

—John D. Carlson and Matt Correa

When a major international publication like *The Economist* publishes an eighteen-page special report dedicated to "the new wars of religion," as it did it in its November 3, 2007 issue, scholars of religion and an array of disciplines sit up and take notice. The eye-catching cover certainly helps—an ominous hand descends from foreboding grey clouds, index finger slightly extended, suggesting a menacing, presumably monotheistic deity delivering orders to his followers below. The image vividly captures religion's notoriously explosive potential, for clasped within the heavenly hand is a grenade, the pin still in place.

What was striking to some of us who study religion, particularly its political and conflictual dimensions, is that, overall, the articles within are laced with the nuance and subtlety often found wanting in many journalistic treatments of religion and conflict.[1] The frequent lament among scholars of religion—that the mainstream media peddles patchy stereotypes because it just "doesn't 'get' religion"—may not hold in the case of *The Economist*'s special report. One possible explanation for this development is that in the wake of the events of September 11, 2001, religion—at least religion's relation to war, violence, and large-scale public conflict—has ceased to be the province of specialists. More than ever, religion seems to impact other fields and disciplines outside the formal study of religion. Perhaps, it is now, crudely put, everyone's concern.

This article explores this development by examining the interdisciplinary state of scholarship on issues and themes falling under the broad rubric of "religion and conflict," a term which we discuss in greater detail below. We sketch out a framework of what may be an emerging interdisciplinary "field" or, at least, a shared set of enquiries formed by the overlap of established, new, or reinvigorated areas of study. Our thesis is straightforward—the study of "religion and conflict" is best conceived as an interdisciplinary enterprise, and its successful pursuit requires the collective energies and diverse insights of scholars of religion as well as historians, political scientists, sociologists, and others.

* *St. Antony's International Review* 3, no. 2 (2008): 13–30.

We begin with a narrative that seeks to make sense of our current moment. We consider warrants for an interdisciplinary approach by taking stock of institutions on the frontlines of some particularly complex challenges faced in the early part of the twenty-first century. We then briefly outline some contours of a potentially emerging field of religion and conflict. As scholars of religion, we discuss the resources our discipline contributes to such scholarship as well as its limitations, both of which reinforce the need to join efforts with other fields that approach matters of religion differently.

A "New" Post-secular Moment?

The refrain "everything has changed" was uttered with such frequency and conviction following September 11 that it came to annunciate a new era in global political life. One defining feature of the new century, it was widely held, would be the dramatic capacity of religion to shape the social and political universe. One emerging lesson was that for too long the West had ignored the violent impact religion can have in world affairs, and scholars from many disciplines took notice of these concerns.

Looking back at this ostensibly liminal moment, however, there may be other ways to interpret the state of world affairs. One response holds that we have not learned much at all from September 11. If anything, the events of that dreadful day only entrenched the conviction that when religion and politics converge, violence readily ensues. Recent examples range from terrorists' commitments to radical Islamism to religiously charged conflicts in Kashmir, Northern Ireland, Afghanistan, Iraq, Lebanon, and Israel and the Palestinian territories. A cottage industry of scholarship affirming the "religion can be violent" thesis has cropped up.[2] For many, the public faces of religion remain Osama bin Laden and other epitomes of religiously inspired violence, rather than the Dalai Lama or Pope John Paul II. Some particularly strident voices began warning about the intolerant dangers of religion, calling us back to our secularist ideals.[3]

However others, including many who study religion, saw in the events of September 11 more continuity in historical patterns than a significant shift in paradigms. Well before religiously-justified acts of terrorism became a leitmotif of the twenty-first century, they pointed out that religion has long been a force of often dramatic social transformation and political influence, and, at times, violence.[4] Such scholarship is marked by differences over religion's valences—whether religion more often serves forces for good or for ill. There is a consensus among these scholars, though, that religion's linkage to violence is real even if understudied or overstated.

One need not be a religion scholar to appreciate the importance of such events as the Crusades, the Reformation, or the explosive growth of Christianity and Islam around the world that has begun to overshadow the secularization of Western Europe.[5] But scholars of religion may have been less surprised by what has been called the "post-secular" turn and religious corrections to, or backlashes against, secularization.

But does all this mean that nothing really has changed in how we understand religion and public conflicts in the twenty-first century? While it is true that assumptions about secularization were being challenged long before 2001, whether looking to the influence of the religious right on politics in the United States, the Iranian Revolution, religious nationalism in India, or ethno-religious fracturing in the Balkans, September 11 concretized the dangers of religious violence with unprecedented force. It also opened or reopened our eyes to a longer history and wider global view of religion's public resurgence, this time drawing more people in. Unconverted secularists quickly grasped religion's public import.[6]

The State of Our Institutions

Since September 11, the public has been seeking greater knowledge about religion and its role in violence and political conflict. Yet, some of the most vital institutions of public life, at least from a U.S.-based perspective, are still lagging behind. Institutional culture in the U.S. is steeped in the assumptions of secularization theory. The paucity of instruction about religion in public schools—basic literacy is essential for citizens to understand the religious features of our world and its history—has been noted with concern by some scholars.[7] Early failures to distinguish teaching religion (i.e., religious instruction) from teaching *about* religion have put children and citizens behind in understanding how religion shapes human identity, history, and global society.

Institutionally, religion is treated as a private matter. For those serving in government, traditional training in the social sciences has often marginalized religion's public importance. This comes at great cost to those who serve as government officials, Foreign Service officers, and policymakers. The legal principle of separation of church and state does not relieve us from understanding the multifaceted relationships between religion and politics. Many religion scholars have described the challenge of being taken seriously by those on the political scene about the varied roles religion plays in international conflict. Peacebuilders attest that religious nongovernmental organizations (NGOs) offer crucial knowledge, contacts, and skills for which secular diplomats are no substitute. The secularist two-stage strategy of "avoid and contain" still prevails across too many government sectors, as attested by the Federal Bureau of Investigation's inadequate handling of the Branch Davidian raid. Religion's influence cannot be ignored and simply contained once deemed a threat.[8]

Military service academies and war colleges have yet to provide sufficient curricular space for the study of religion despite the obvious ways in which the armed forces have been implicated in ethno-religious and sectarian conflicts. If during the Cold War, thriving Soviet studies programs were developed to help understand "the adversary," why ignore the religious dimensions of the most important security dynamics today? Fortunately, more attention is paid to "culture" than has been the case, and religion seems to be working its way into this context.[9] However, one wonders whether earlier *education* about religion might provide a more solid foundation for *training* about specific religious customs and practices.

There are, however, indications that the disregard of religion in politics is changing. Many political scientists are engaging religion, sometimes even theology.[10] Prominent figures such as Madeleine Albright have begun arguing for the need to take religion seriously as part of state diplomacy.[11] Scholarship by those who appreciate the significant role religious leaders can play in fomenting or resolving political conflicts is ongoing.[12] Religion experts have been placed in pivotal government agencies like the Central Intelligence Agency. New programs are sprouting up, such as the Council on Foreign Relations' Religion and Foreign Policy program,[13] and among U.S. universities, there is now a bevy of research centers devoted to religion's importance in political and cultural issues.[14] Nevertheless, many public institutions still have not fully positioned themselves to engage the complex religious challenges of our day, which stands to have corrosive effects unless corrected.

Post-secular Challenges

Several observations, trends, and problems confronting us in the early twenty-first century call for greater attention to the ways we conceive and study religion and conflict. These challenges are sufficiently complex to warrant significant mobilization of diverse intellectual resources and interdisciplinary scholarship. In particular, the convergence of normative and empirical analysis offers a constructive path forward.

One prevailing challenge involves the now faltering theory of secularization, which presumed that the ascent of human reason toward new heights would force religion's retreat into private life, desacralizing the public pursuits of citizens and polities. Followed to its logical conclusion, this theory suggests that the irresistible tide of secularization may one day wash away individual faith altogether. Secularization narratives also have included, implicitly if not explicitly, a normative component claiming that religion's privatization and dwindling influence are situated within a broader teleology.

Whether or not the empirical strand of the secularization thesis *is* fraying, we are still left with a trenchant question—what *ought* to be the role of religion in national and international political life, given that certain secular assumptions are still in place? The answer does not follow inevitably from either the empirical claims of secularization theory or from more recent evidence that undermines it. Scholars who see their primary task to think normatively must be part of a common venture informed by empirical accounts of what is happening in the world. Traditional divisions in the academy, however—within religious studies as well—have not postured us well to confront this problem. Interdisciplinary scholarship could help provide a needed correction. The brief history of the twenty-first century thus far urges us to consider some other questions, too, involving the intersections of religion, politics, and culture. For example:

(1)   What, if any, overarching relationships can be discerned between the public resurgence of religion and its propensity for pernicious conflict? What are the factors, institutions, commitments, and mores that prevent public conflict from turning violent? What are the causes that give way to religious factionalism and religion's alliances with tribalism or nationalism? Are secularization and democracy universal antidotes?

(2)   Democracy's relationship to religion has often been complex but is becoming no simpler. Religion has been rooted in many young democracies and democratic movements from the United States to Poland and other nations around the world. But many established democracies increasingly feel threatened by emerging and struggling popular democratic movements in places where religion or "religious extremism" challenges certain secular democratic presuppositions. Must proponents of democracy be committed to the value of a secular realm? And which, if any, theological beliefs must underwrite such religious commitments to secular life?

(3)   Many people worry that violent forms of fundamentalism comprise the greatest security threat to religious and non-religious communities alike. Many states, however, do not appreciate the reactionary nature of fundamentalism and what has been seen to be its parasitic relationship upon secularization.[15] Assuming this is true, how can secular governments offer a tenable path for defeating violent forms of religious

extremism? Could it be that some problems with religion can only be resolved by granting more—not less—space to religion?

(4) It is often claimed that religion is an important cause or factor in violence and war. Yet others will note that distinctively a-religious movements and ideas lay behind the worst atrocities and bloodiest struggles in the twentieth century. Are secular forms of violence under-examined compared to religious violence? How shall we assess the religious and non-religious sources and dynamics of violence or war such that each receives the scrutiny that is due? Such a question, however, raises other concerns over how we define religion or distinguish religious facets from other economic, political, or cultural facets of human life. For that matter, how is violence defined, and how, if at all, should it be distinguished from the state's use of force? These are not simple empirical questions, as we show below, but call for normative evaluation as well.

(5) Given the historic specter of the Crusades and Europe's wars of religion, those in the West are loath to invoke religion to justify the use of force. Yet, the influential just war tradition, with its longstanding religious roots, provides guidance for when force may be morally justifiable if not required. Certain Islamic notions of defensive jihad argue similarly. Can or should such religious beliefs be called upon to justify coercion or force? Or can religious believers only repair to their faiths when calling for non-violence? Similarly, while some religious peacebuilders resist the notion that military force is a justifiable means for ending conflict, just war advocates often over-look the impact of religious peacebuilders in political conflicts. Can deeper insight be achieved by bringing together these different approaches?

(6) National political scenes are being transformed by religious forces. Turkey's recent election placed a religious party at the helm of its secular state. The American religious scene also contains contradictions—a recent poll indicates that a majority of Americans felt that religion held either too much or too little influence over their respective parties.[16] How can religious citizens, across many countries, both support and withstand the principles of secular government? How might comparative study of these questions yield insight about the boundaries where religion ends and secular begins? Or, do these categories no longer yield the clarity they once did?[17]

These are far-ranging questions that signal distinctive challenges for our age. As no single academic discipline possesses the wisdom, methods, or resources for resolving these daunting issues, the energies, talents, and insights of many minds and disciplinary methods will be required. There are indications that such an incipient venture may be underway already.

Signs of an Emerging Field? Outlining the Study of Religion and Conflict

Across an array of fields—history, religious studies, ethics, theology, peace studies, political science, governmental studies, sociology, international studies, and others—there are many scholars who, in profound and intriguing ways, are addressing *religion and conflict*—that is, dimensions of violence or other significant forms of public conflict.[18] Many were hard at work long before global jihadism or the "war on terrorism" dominated the headlines. Together, they point the way toward what may be an emerging field that explores how religion is involved in multiple forms of conflict. Many areas of study in which religion and conflict are central themes overlap, so the research interests of many scholars and their audiences flow simultaneously into several disciplinary tributaries. Thus, what follows is more of an effort to chart the waters than to "map out" the terrain that defines a field, fencing in certain approaches, fencing out others. We aim to point out some of the emerging contours in order to elicit discussion about the warrants of further scholarly transit across these various regions of study. We offer one way to describe the several areas—at different stages of development—in which the study of religion and conflict is pursued. Due to constraints of space, works cited should not be seen as exhaustive.

One body of literature is devoted to *religious and ethical perspectives on conflict*, including numerous theological and moral traditions that reflect upon war and peace. The just war tradition, particularly, has burgeoned in the last fifty years, with continuing controversy over its relationship to pacifism, another formidable tradition of ethical reflection.[19] There also has been renewed interest in Christian realism and the work of Reinhold Niebuhr.[20] More recently, Islamic perspectives on war and peace have become acutely germane.[21] Important comparative projects examine different perspectives on war and peace across religious traditions and between secular and religious frameworks.[22]

The study of *religion in international politics and international relations* has surged with recent activity.[23] New classes devoted to these themes appear in both religion and political science departments. Among the "religion and" sub-themes being explored are "religion and security,"[24] "religion and diplomacy,"[25] and "religion and democracy."[26] The issues addressed include religion's relationship to sovereignty, statecraft, foreign policy, and non-state political movements, terrorism, and counter-terrorism.

A third area of concerted focus is *religion and violence*. Foci within this field include defining, conceptualizing, and cataloguing religious and non-religious forms of violence; assessing the causes and dynamics of religious conflict; understanding religion's role in conflict escalation and other forms of violence in which religion is involved; and finally, examining the psychology and sociology of religion and violence.[27] We discuss the challenges presented by this category of scholarship in greater detail below.

The study of *religion and national public life* in Asia, Africa, Europe, and the Americas has also blossomed in recent years. In the context we know best, the U.S., the debates brought on by the publications of such landmark books as *The Naked Public Square*, *Habits of the Heart*, and *Culture Wars* are cases in point.[28] Major works by Rawls, Rorty, and others have issued challenges to the ways in which religious language and ideas are deployed in the discourse of public conflicts,[29] which themselves have sparked a range of religious and secular critiques.[30] A steady stream of legislative initiatives, cultural events, and cases coming before the U.S. Supreme Court, not to mention electoral politics and the 2000 election of another evangelical Christian to the presidency, have flooded U.S. political life with questions about the public role of religion. From fields of law, religion, politics, journalism, public policy, and sociology—many are contributing to and expanding this lively conversation. Interestingly, the conflicts at the border of religion and science have become increasingly fraught in American public life, often shaping, or shaped by, binary categories like religion and secular, reason and faith.

Another area of study that has attracted the attention of scholars and practitioners alike has been the area of *religion and peacebuilding*.[31] The locus of this region of enquiry and practice has involved the study and application of religious principles to prevent violent conflicts from occurring (conflict prevention), to limit their escalation (conflict management), to resolve existing conflicts (conflict resolution) and to seek justice and ensure "resolved" conflicts do not lapse back into violence (reconciliation). From the preponderance of disputed territories (e.g., Kashmir) to the scourge of war and violent conflicts (e.g., in the Balkans, Rwanda, and Iraq), to the need for post-conflict reconciliation measures such as war crimes tribunals and truth and reconciliation commissions in nations recovering from violent conflict (e.g., South Africa, Chile, and, again, Rwanda and Iraq), there is no shortage of work for scholars and practitioners active in peacebuilding, peacemaking, or inter-religious dialogue movements. Theologians and others seeking to bring forgiveness to bear on political life also contribute vitally to this area.[32]

These recent trends in scholarship indicate that a significant body of literature has amassed, which points toward shared areas of scholarly investigation that we might refer to collectively as "religion and conflict." The existence of pre–September 11 scholarship suggests this form of enquiry has been present inchoately for some time and has grown further since then. No doubt the divisions here entail problematic presuppositions as well. The attempt, however, is to provide a working framework that allows one to explore untapped possibilities for further scholarly investigations, particularly those that bring together distinctive areas of study as part of a larger research enterprise. As the works cited make clear, religion and conflict can be approached from numerous existing disciplines such as religious studies, ethics, and theology; political science, international relations, and foreign affairs; history, sociology, and psychology; and others. The interdisciplinary character of religion and conflict scholarship is something we urge to continue so as to enhance intellectual richness, pool together disparate bodies of knowledge, and sharpen collective insight. The reality is that scholars studying religion and conflict may have more in common with people in other disciplines than in their own. As a further warrant for interdisciplinary approaches, we consider the contributions and limitations of our own field, the study of religion, for thinking about religion and conflict.

Problems with "Religion," "Conflict," and "Religion and Conflict"

Returning briefly to *The Economist* cover described above is instructive, for it represents visually a problem to which scholars of religion often are attentive: the hazards of defining and deploying the category of "religion." The stakes are nowhere higher than when religion is associated with violence. The image of the divine hand and grenade suggests that "religion" is a tangible thing—like some cosmic entity descending from the heavens reifying itself to alter earthly political affairs. Conceiving religion as such a distinct, ahistorical intervention from above gives lie to the reality that, in spite of humanity's connection to the sacred or beliefs about the divine, religion is, and always has been, an earthly phenomenon.

Some scholars of religion claim the academic category of religion—as distinct from other social, ethnic, economic, political, and cultural features of life—is a fiction, created by those who study religion and who believe it can be isolated from other features of human life.[33] Some might go so far as to say that there is no such "thing" or "object" as religion; there are only people who hold and act upon beliefs that many understand as religious. Such beliefs are themselves diverse, conflicting, and contested even within traditions. This approach to religion breeds caution and restraint about making broader generalizations about the role religion does or should play in politics, culture, and all matters of violent or non-violent forms of conflict. The effort to categorize religion and religious violence—often followed by the effort to remove or contain religion so as to minimize violence—overlooks the deeper reality that conflict and violence are, foremost, part of the human condition, not religion or secular life. These issues, raised most directly in the discipline of religious studies, invite us to question basic assumptions about "religious violence" that not only permeate popular and academic discourse but that also underwrite existing systems and practices.

Interestingly, both popular and scholarly studies of religion tend to offer a relatively narrow range of perspectives about religion's relationship to conflict or violence. Two common approaches point up the different valences attached to religion. The "blame" position involves an anti-religious thrust in which religion is deemed the cause or root of violence. Religious violence, according to this view, is particularly pernicious—more so than non-secular violence.[34] Religion is seen, fundamentally, as a problem (if not *the* problem), and it would be best if religion simply went away. Such anti-religious voices seek to roll back the tide of "post-secular" forces in the world. In the "exonerate" category, others seek to demonstrate how acts of so-called "religious violence" are not essentially religious at all. For these apologists, religious violence occurs when religion is "hijacked" or corrupted for political, ideological, or non-religious reasons. From this standpoint, true or authentic religion is peaceful and constructive. Violent religion is false or heretical.

The picture is certainly more complex than either the blame or exonerate positions can explain. Some religious studies scholars have tried to locate themselves between the anti-religious and exculpatory poles. In this "middle position," the concept of *religious violence* is useful, since it explains how violence can be authentically religious without arguing that religion is inherently prone to violence and intolerance.[35] Surely there are types of violence that are most accurately described as religious, even if that label inevitably also permits some distortion. The medieval Crusades serve as an apt illustration given the deep religious justifications for those conflicts. As historians of the Crusades note, however, there were mutually entangling political dimensions we ought not overlook.[36] Likewise, exclusive attention to Islamist terrorists' religious ideologies can limit awareness of their deep detestation of many U.S. foreign policies.[37] One should also be clear that those who justify violence on religious grounds are often critiqued by others who hold a different interpretation of the same faith. This is the reality of religious pluralism internal to any particular religious tradition or faith. Furthermore, different appeals to religion, whether calling for violence or extolling peace, reveal different levels of religious literacy.[38] In short, to dismiss the place of religious ideas for those who wage violence in religion's name is just as problematic as ignoring those who argue from within their faith against such violence.

Other scholars of religion, however, ask: what is signified and obscured when a discrete concept of religious violence is used to frame a wide range of fierce conflicts across the globe and throughout history? William T. Cavanaugh considers how an Enlightenment definition of religion and a bias against religious violence obscure our evaluation of secular violence carried out by the state.[39] Over-reliance on religious categories of violence could, for example, shroud consideration of the United States' use of atomic weapons in World War II, which were far more devastating than any terrorist actions have been.

But religion may not be the most problematic category either. Perhaps we need to think more carefully about "violence." Here, other forms of religious and moral reflection must be brought to bear. In certain religious (and secular) accounts of the just war tradition, the use of atomic weapons is just as abhorrent since it violates *jus in bello* principles of non-combatant immunity that prohibit targeting cities and population centers. Religiously grounded just war theorists, however, also might invite greater distinctions between violence and justifiable use of force—a distinction the critics above do not discuss.[40] Just war considerations of "right authority" and "just cause" that permit and may require state use of force to protect citizens from harm introduce moral questions of legitimacy alongside empirical discussions of violence and destruction. As Hannah Arendt reminds us, illegitimacy—whether exercised by the state or its opponents—is the salient feature of violence.[41] Just as we ought not take the importance of "religion" for granted, we should scrutinize more thoroughly such apparently intuitive categories as "violence," not all forms of which may be equally condemnable.

Finally, a focus on religion and conflict may obscure the reality that not all conflict is bad. However true it may be that religious movements and actors have spurred odious forms of conflict, they also have served some of the noblest struggles in modern times. Religious actors and ideas have played indispensable roles challenging oppressive governments, as we saw recently in Burma; ending morally corrupt, authoritarian regimes in South Africa and Eastern Europe; and witnessing to justice, human rights, and the cessation of violence in other parts of the world. Major progressive and social reforms in the West—abolitionism and the Civil Rights movement—entailed crucial forms of conflict that could not have succeeded without their religious dimensions. President Eisenhower's show of force in sending in the U.S. Army to enforce desegregation of public schools also exemplifies that some displays of force may be a necessary dimension of conflict. Violence and conflict exist on a continuum. Empirically speaking, there is a spectrum of power and coercion that exists in any conflict, from the force of non-violent demonstrations to the barrel of the policeman's gun. Questions of legitimacy must be situated and evaluated along a separate, intersecting axis, because sometimes those who stand for "peace" and "order" perform the greatest violence of all.[42]

This discussion suggests that if we are to think further about problems involving "religion and conflict," we shall need to scrutinize carefully our categories and terms. Collectively, scholars who study religion often puzzle over such matters, though they must be joined by scholars from other fields. Sorting out crucial distinctions—between religion and secular, violence and power, illegitimacy and legitimacy—requires the work of empirical study, critical analysis, *and* constructive ethical thinking across a range of scholarship on religion.

While current theories of religion provide a crucial critical lens for examining religion and conflict, the humanities, including fields of religion or religious studies, often have suffered from their own institutional and disciplinary shortcomings. Within religious studies, scholars sometimes have focused on discrete traditions with relatively little reference to their larger interactions. The study of religion can presuppose theoretical models of abstraction and detachment, which do not attend sufficiently to the lived religious beliefs of real people. Yet, the forms of religion most in need of engagement are very much alive, vigorously interacting and shaping global public life. Some religion scholars have begun to enliven their own research agendas by engaging these forces head on; others might do well to follow.

Furthermore, serious discussion of the political realm is too often neglected in religious studies, ceded to the domain of political science. Power usually affords a lens for critique—those who have power are critiqued. Within religious studies circles, one often finds assumptions about government and politics that resist certain basic truths about power, coercion, and other inescapable features of human life. Appreciation of such realities, however, permits more modest proposals to emerge from within these inevitably imperfect constraints. The risk of not engaging political thinking more concertedly is the perception of utopianism or disengagement from the polis. Interdisciplinary engagement invites assessment of the strengths and insights brought to bear by various fields and disciplines. It also calls for modesty about their limitations, in the hope of offsetting them through further intellectual and disciplinary cross-pollination.

Future Directions

Military and intelligence communities speak of "stovepipes" to represent the image of numerous people working on a common problem in which each party possesses only a partial, tubular view of the overall picture. This article has argued for the value of bringing different disciplines into common conversation about the study of religion and conflict in hopes of breaking down disciplinary barriers, offering a more comprehensive view and cultivating deeper forms of discernment.

Warrants for further cultivating such an interdisciplinary "field" include public accessibility, comprehensiveness, and the sheer exigency of the challenges we face in the early twenty-first century. Research that incorporates materials, techniques, and approaches on religion and conflict from a range of disciplines across the humanities and social sciences stands to yield more fecund, balanced, and sharpened scholarship. There are more resources, methodologies, and points of view available to those who share common interests with others outside their own methodological discipline. There is particular need to integrate empirical work with normative analysis and reflection. Working with scholars and writing for readers outside one's immediate discipline also challenges scholars to be more precise and explicit and less wedded to disciplinary jargon and assumptions. In turn, those outside of one's own field, in which certain assumptions may not be shared, may demand more rigorous forms of evidence and argumentation than would otherwise be required. Finally, interdisciplinary engagement serves to make scholarship more interesting and accessible to general readers and, by extension, to those outside the academy and within public institutions working on "real world" issues of religion and conflict, expanding the tangible impact of academic studies. The problems of a global era, in the end, are simply too great and multisided to encourage forging ahead in narrow and insular ways. An interdisciplinary approach irreducible to one area, methodology, or discipline stands a better chance of understanding and resolving problems of religion and conflict in this complex age.

— Section V —

RELIGION AND PEACEMAKING

27

RELIGION AND GLOBAL AFFAIRS
Religious "Militants for Peace"

—R. Scott Appleby

Symposia like this one are welcome signs that a growing chorus of leaders are recognizing that it is high time to examine "the other side" of religion in international affairs. The burden of this essay is to argue that "the other side" is not "the lighter side," as in "the well-intentioned but ineffective do-gooder" side: religious militants dedicated to conflict mediation, the nonviolent promotion of human rights, and other elements of long-term peacebuilding have proven themselves to be no less resilient, no less "zealous" than their violent counterparts. They are, however, less organized, less funded, less publicized, and less well understood.

Violent, exclusivist, anti-pluralist "true believers" need no introduction. In recent years, extremist violence in Northern Ireland, France, the Balkans, Iran, Sudan, Algeria, Egypt, Pakistan, India, and Sri Lanka has been cloaked, in whole or in part, in religious garb. Secular militants, who fear little else, fear religious extremism as a particularly ruthless and unpredictable de-stabilizing force. Religion's unique ability to sustain cycles of violence beyond the point of rational calculation and enlightened self-interest was not lost on PLO chairman Yasser Arafat and the late Israeli Prime Minister Yitzhak Rabin, for example. During the final fury of the intifada, as the death toll among both Israelis and Palestinian Arabs mounted from massacres, suicide bombings, and other acts of religious violence, bitter enemies chose to attempt reconciliation in the face of the unrelenting threat posed by religious extremism, the one anarchic political force neither side seemed able to contain.

Meanwhile, new technologically enhanced acts of religious terrorism have achieved a prominence and political salience disproportionate to the actual number of perpetrators or their sympathizers. Today a tiny minority of violent religious actors might command the attention of an entire nation, as was the case in the United States following the 1993 bombing of the World Trade Center in New York City by Muslim extremists.

* *The SAIS Review* 18, no. 2 (1998): 38–44.

Religious Peacebuilding

The dreadful record of religiously inspired violence and intolerance notwithstanding, history paints a more complicated picture of religious agency. Religious radicals of the Christian Reformation were prominent among the early modern proponents of religious liberty and freedom of speech; Baptists, the original advocates of religious autonomy, were champions of church-state separation. Hindu and Christian religious leaders, including martyrs for peace Mohandas K. Gandhi and Martin Luther King, Jr., were influential pioneers of nonviolence as both a spiritual practice and a political strategy. Islam, Judaism, Sikhism, and Buddhism have also produced champions of nonviolent religious militancy.

The contemporary inheritors of this legacy of religious peacemaking include Christian ethicists who refine just war and pacifist traditions in light of contemporary military and political circumstances as well as Muslim jurists and theologians who defend the integrity and priority of Islamic law while demonstrating its adaptability in the building of just and stable Muslim societies. Meanwhile, Jewish, Buddhist, Hindu, Islamic, and Christian scholars and religious leaders plumb and "translate" their respective traditions of wisdom and cultural values in the effort to establish cross-cultural norms of religious human rights. Finally, transnational religious communities, such as the lay Roman Catholic Community of Sant'Egidio, engage in conflict transformation through the provision of good offices, mediation, and social services in nations gripped by civil or regional wars, while local religious leaders work for genuine reconciliation among aggrieved parties.

Related to these efforts and operating on a global level are a host of religious nongovernmental organizations (NGOs), some hailing from the early years of the United Nations and working under its auspices, others active as independent agents of peace and development. Such organizations and agencies as the Mennonite Central Committee, the World Conference on Religion and Peace, Malaysia's JUST World Trust, the Society of Engaged Buddhists, and Catholic Relief Services foster ecumenical cooperation in communities riven by ethnic and religious violence, conduct workshops and courses in religious resources for conflict transformation, and facilitate communication and dialogue between communities historically divided over competing ethnic and/or religious claims. Other NGOs such as the Appeal of Conscience Foundation, led by Rabbi Arthur Schneier, depend on the international status of individual religious leaders whose personal prestige and integrity gain them access to high government officials.

Finally, the major religious traditions of the world themselves continue to evolve; one finds evidence, for example, of the internal transformation of international religious communities such as the Roman Catholic Church, which has reevaluated the purposes and methods of its missions and relief work in light of the imperatives of dialogue and inculturation rather than proselytizing. In the 1990s, several denominations and religious or multireligious bodies have been preparing themselves for, and assuming, proactive peacemaking roles. The expanded range of institutionally affiliated religious actors include lay and clerical human rights advocates, development and relief workers, missionaries, denominational structures, ad hoc commissions and delegations, and interdenominational and multireligious bodies such as the World Council of Churches.

The term religious peacebuilding encompasses the full range of efforts by these various actors. Their work has followed several patterns, tracked by Cynthia Sampson, John

Paul Lederach, and Douglas Johnston, among others. The social location of the religious actors varies. In helping resolve conflicts in Nicaragua and Nigeria, peacemakers worked within the political process, while in the Philippines, South Africa, and Israel/Palestine they remained external to it. In East Germany at the end of the Cold War, Christians operated on the margins during the initial stages of the revolution but later assumed key roles in the political transition. Multiple religious actors participated in Rhodesia where the Quakers and the religious NGO Moral Re-Armament worked within the political process, while the Roman Catholic Church exerted influence from the outside.

The religious actors played varying roles as well. In East Germany and the Philippines, church leaders articulated a critique of existing injustices and helped opposition groups develop a compelling social vision. Muslim and Jewish activists in the Holy Land established centers for cross-cultural dialogue and rapprochement. In South Africa, resistance churches provided a forum for political expression where alternatives did not exist. In Northern Ireland, Catholic and Protestant church leaders such as Cardinal Cahal Daly and Reverend John Dunlop challenge the complacency and prejudice of their respective faith communities, while parachurch and ecumenical movements such as Corrymeela bring Catholics and Protestants together to address social needs and to collaborate on economic projects.

Demonstrating the effectiveness of such groups is akin to proving a negative: no one knows exactly how many lives have been saved by their efforts, however, most observers agree that the level of intercommunal violence and the death toll would be far greater in the absence of their efforts.

Several constructive aspects of religious peacemaking need not be taken on faith alone. Fairly well documented are the cases in which religious actors have operated as third party intermediaries, either with the formal or informal sponsorship of a religious body or ecumenical organization, or as an independent NGO. Moral Re-Armament, for example, an independently funded network of spiritually motivated individuals without organizational ties to any specific church, worked in Rhodesia alongside Quakers, who counted on the financial support of their co-religionists. In Mozambique, the members of Sant'Egidio exploited their contacts with Italian government officials, as well as with the Vatican and with leaders on both sides of the country's civil war. Their involvement as social service providers in Mozambique garnered special insight into the warring parties, influenced the attitudes and actions of political leaders, and helped to monitor and shape succeeding developments.

Where religion was welcomed as an important ingredient in statecraft, it was one actor among many, of course, and depended on other players' expertise in the political, economic, and security dimensions of the conflict; nonetheless, religious peacebuilders can point to a modest but solid record of success in what seems to be merely the first phase of their involvement in conflict transformation. Indeed, religiously based conflict resolution may be the most rapidly expanding sector in the international field of conflict analysis and transformation.

It is clear that the religious communities who take on a peacemaking role often enjoy the considerable advantages of popular credibility. They exist as widespread organizations and networks at every level of society and have the ability to mobilize significant elements of the larger community, including international funding and moral support. In several settings, the church or mosque is the only major institution over which the state is not able to exercise complete control, and it serves as an alternative moral authority to a corrupt regime.

Complicating Matters

In light of the dual role of religion as both instigator of violence and agent of reconciliation, the increasing prominence of religious actors in the post–Cold War world raises complex questions and problems. The spectre of religious violence plays into the hands of the opponents of religious liberty. Regimes clinging to power without a popular base of legitimacy exploit the fear of "fundamentalism" in order to suppress any form of religious expression, public or private, and to legitimate their own gross human rights violations. Further undermining religion's credibility as peacemaker is the fact that its "constructive" side is not always so constructive. In many settings it is the established religious leaders—not only the fundamentalists—who oppose the notion as well as the practice of universal religious human rights.

The ambiguity of religion's role extends to the issue of religious freedom. The persecution of Christians, Muslims, Jews, Baha'is, and others is neither an illusion nor a propaganda tool of spiritually-minded, empire-building evangelicals. On the other hand, there are evangelical sects that take full advantage of the borderless freedoms of NGO-status and the support of multinationals seeking a low-cost, low-expectation labor force. Such organizations move into developing regions like the southern Philippines preaching a name-it-and-claim-it gospel of wealth, prosperity, and the Western way; many times these groups are impervious to local customs and the turf claims of indigenous religions and tend to foment or exacerbate conflict.

The argument here, then, is not that religion is an uncomplicated or entirely benevolent presence in international relations, but that evidence exists to warrant a serious and comprehensive testing of the following claim: As advocates of justice and architects of the social conditions necessary for the cessation of hostilities and the sustaining of peaceful relations among peoples, religious actors represent a powerful source of political stability and economic prosperity in the post–Cold War world.

Opposing Extremism

Contrary to the misconceptions popular in some academic and political circles, religious actors play this critical and positive role in world affairs not when they moderate their religion or marginalize their deeply held, vividly symbolized, and often highly particular beliefs in a higher order of love and justice. Religious actors make a difference when they remain religious actors. The skeptic immediately answers: yes, these organizations make a difference when they are religious—they kill, extort, take hostages, and oppress women. Yet religious extremists, despite the recruiting boost they receive from unjust social and political conditions in many states, are a minority within every religious community. The purveyors of violence fail to attract a majority of believers precisely because they transgress against core affirmations of the religious tradition. The religious tradition is a vast and complex body of wisdom built up over many generations. Its foundational sources—sacred scriptures and/or oral teachings—express and interpret the experiences of the sacred which led to the formation of the religious community. A religious tradition is no less than these sources, but it is always more. The deeper meaning and significance of their foundational sources continues to be revealed throughout history. Thus tradition, in its fullness, encompasses the range of interpretations that have accumulated over time and achieved authoritative status because its supporters have probed, clarified, and developed the insights and teachings contained in their primary texts.

To be traditional, then, is to take seriously not only the foundational sources of the religion, but also the various authoritative interpretations of those sources. Such interpretations enable the religion to evolve practices in support of peace rather than war, reconciliation rather than retaliation. Their adherents might be said to be "militant"—zealous, disciplined, and self-sacrificing—but they are not violent: their passion in the service of truth takes on the character of a nonviolent spiritual "crusade." Ironically, the violence-prone "extremists," though they claim to be upholding the "fundamentals" of the religion, are in fact anti-traditional or selectively traditional. In order to gain allegiance beyond a small cadre of ultra-orthodox "true believers," they must convince their co-religionists to deviate from the traditional path of healing and peacemaking. It is not secular propagandists but fellow religious leaders who are best situated to counter the arguments of the advocates of religious violence. Both "types" of religious leaders, the violence-legitimating extremist and the violence-renouncing militant, draw upon traditional religious sources. Understanding the nature of the difference between their approach to and uses of these sources is essential to the task of undermining the former and promoting the latter.

While the religious extremist is often integrated into a well-organized movement, armed to the teeth, expertly trained, lavishly funded, ideologically disciplined, and involved in a kind of "ecumenical" collaboration with other violence-prone organizations, the local religious peacemaker (in waiting) is, with some promising and notable recent exceptions, relatively isolated, underfunded, unskilled in the proven techniques of peacebuilding, and overlooked. Prior to the recent benign intervention of religious and cultural NGOs, the success stories largely depended on heroic individuals who relied on their own inner strength, charisma, and courage in opposing dominative violence and state-sponsored forms of oppression. We remain far from reaping the benefits of organized, adequately funded programs of education and training in religious peacebuilding in most conflict settings around the world. Such programs, if they are to be successful, must draw on the resources, wisdom, and local practitioners of the religious traditions themselves.

Hindering development in this direction is the fragmented character of the nascent field of religion and international relations. On one side are the scholars and analysts who study the extremists, the radical fundamentalists and religious terrorists. On the other side are scholars and activists who emphasize and strive to develop the overlooked capacities of nonviolent religious actors as mediators and reconcilers. With a few notable exceptions, these two groups are isolated from one another, working in separate institutions with different and uncoordinated agendas. Unfortunately, they also tend to work at cross-purposes.

This is particularly unfortunate in light of the post–Cold War tendency of the major powers to formulate foreign policy around moral concerns such as peacekeeping, humanitarian assistance, human rights, and the prevention of genocide. For those who hope to see religion's potential for peacebuilding put to the test, the post–Cold War period is therefore a moment of promise. Latent or lingering attitudes confining religion to a disruptive role are both inaccurate and unimaginative; they should not prevent policymakers from exploring the vast untapped potential of benevolent religious "militants for peace."

28

FAITH-BASED DIPLOMACY
An Ancient Idea Newly Emergent

—Brian Cox and Daniel Philpott

Since the attacks of September 11, 2001, a chorus of scholars and analysts has been sing-ing heartily about what only a few had spoken of for many decades: the influence of reli-gion in international affairs.[1] But their dominant melody is agonistic—religion, they say, has provoked a clash of civilizations, communal conflict in Bosnia, Kosovo, Kashmir, and the Sudan, and terrorist attacks against the United States. Audible, too, however, is a discor-dant strain, one that tells of churches and synagogues, imams and pastors, religious com-munities, organizations, and networks who have worked to bring peace to Sudan, Kashmir, Nicaragua, and Mozambique; nonviolent transitions to democracy in Poland, Portugal, the Philippines, South Africa, and across Latin America; and truth commissions to South Africa, Chile, and El Salvador. This strain cries out for amplification. Irenic, restorative, and constructive, it holds realistic promise for those who seek to quell violent conflict, effect reconciliation, and elicit justice in the wake of evil.

What begs to be amplified, in fact, is a whole family of initiatives that may be sum-marized as "faith-based diplomacy." In the parlance of diplomats, faith-based diplomacy is "track two," that is, diplomacy practiced by non-state actors, officials of nongovern-mental organizations (NGOs), religious leaders, and private citizens.[2] Most distinctively, it is rooted in religions—their texts, their practices, their traditions, and the two-vectored spiritual orientation around which all of them revolve: first, the proper orientation of politics to the transcendent, and second, the active role of the divine in human affairs. Practitioners of faith-based diplomacy will, to be sure, draw upon secular expertise in conflict resolution and analysis, political science and philosophy, experience in national security, diplomacy, community development, and the like. But their central, orienting compass is their faith.

Here, we seek to describe these principles and practices in the hope that with a keener understanding of them, practitioners can better integrate their faith and their expertise and become what Scott Appleby has called "militants for peace."[3] From what sources do we draw such principles and practices? One is our own experience. Between us, we have

* *The Brandywine Review of Faith & International Affairs* 1, no. 2 (Fall 2003): 31–40.

practiced faith-based diplomacy in the Czech Republic, Slovakia, Hungary, Croatia, Serbia, Bosnia, Kosovo, Sudan, Burundi, and Kashmir (India and Pakistan). Currently, under the auspices of the International Center for Religion and Diplomacy in Washington, D.C., we are working together on a project in Kashmir that seeks to develop a movement of faith-based reconciliation among the younger generation of Kashmiris, a movement that serves as a means to a political settlement, a framework of sociopolitical healing, and a moral vision that shapes the political order and civil society.

We have also learned much from the experiences of other scholars and practitioners working along similar lines, including John Paul Lederach, Rabbi Marc Gopin, Scott Appleby, Mohammed Abu-Nimer, and the Community of Sant'Egidio.[4] Most recently, Douglas Johnston has edited a book on faith-based diplomacy that presents the insights of prominent scholars and activists on the subject.[5]

Finally, our understanding of faith-based diplomacy arises from our own faith perspective, particularly from our reflection upon the political implications of the life and teachings of Jesus of Nazareth. In profound respects, the principles and practices of faith-based diplomacy are embedded in other faith traditions, too. In Kashmir, we have witnessed them effect reconciliation between Hindus and Muslims. To recognize such commonality is not to assert a universalistic or syncretic convergence of religions, but only to seek out their mutual potential for fruitful diplomacy. What principles and practices of diplomacy, then, do religions yield?

Principles

Faith-based diplomacy is oriented towards the divine. That is its most central and distinctive principle. Its motivating vision of politics, its assumptions about human nature and the political order, and the norms that govern its conduct all arise from an understanding of the nature and activity of the divine—understood in some traditions as a personal God and in other traditions as the source of meaning and existence.

Expressing crucially this divine orientation is a vision of the political order that serves as the lodestar of the faith-based diplomat. As the Abrahamic faiths understand it, God reveals his vision for how his people are to live together through scriptural texts. The Jewish Torah, for instance, describes this vision as shalom, a harmony that amounts to far more than a negative peace in which people refrain from harming one another, but implies a condition of active love for each person consistent with his God-given dignity. Many faiths also look to "natural law," divinely instilled moral precepts understood through reason, for guidance in governance.

From these sources emanate principles that prescribe the nature and purpose of government and temporal authority, the duties and entitlements of citizens, the respective roles of temporal and spiritual authority, the distribution of economic wealth, the treatment of the poor, punishment, war, and other matters. Of course, a multiplicity of interpretations of these texts and principles has proliferated down through the centuries, and some principles will overlap with secular conceptions. What is important for the faith-based diplomat is that the political order is shaped by a divinely grounded vision. In any such vision, the "horizontal" relationships among members and between members and outsiders will reflect their "vertical" relationship with the divine. The Abrahamic faiths hold that a recognition of God's sovereignty is the basis of community among God's followers. The very meaning of Islam is submission to God, a concept that is the basis of shari'a, the divine law. For Jews, God's covenant with the people of Israel and the laws revealed in it are the basis of their common community. Christians view society as ordered around God's self-revelation in Jesus of Nazareth.

When Pope John Paul II proposed forgiveness as a principle for the nations in his address on the World Day of Peace, 2002, he understood this to be a direct response to God's mercy towards humanity. So, too, the faith-based diplomat—whether she is helping to construct a truth commission, imparting a moral vision to a divided village, building networks of relationship between political and religious leaders, working for a peace settlement, or seeking to build a movement for reconciliation within a civil society—will base her work on what she understands to be a divine plan for humanity. Though her immersion in the darkest corners of human suffering will frequently remind her of the distance between this vision and the world as it is, it will yet be this vision that motivates her and makes her work intelligible.

An orientation towards the divine, though, involves more than a vision for the political order. Faith-based diplomacy is also premised upon divine agency in human affairs. Reconciliation between enemies, solidarity with the poor, and the overturning of unjust structures, along with the practices through which the faith-based diplomat contributes to them—prayer, fasting, religiously based conflict resolution, love for enemies, spiritual friendship—are understood to be the work of the divine.

Such an understanding helps to make sense out of events that may seem surprising on their own terms. Our work in Kashmir, for instance, features a four-day seminar that imparts a moral vision of reconciliation to activists and leaders in civil society, both Hindu and Muslim. At the start of one seminar, an angry Hindu stood before the participants and issued a bitter diatribe against the Kashmiri Muslim community—surely an inauspicious beginning of a vision of reconciliation. But over the subsequent days, through the prayer of the seminar leaders, through spiritual conversations between him and several Muslims that extended into the wee hours of the night, through Muslim expressions of repentance towards him, his spirit was gradually changed. On the final day, he stood up again before the group and apologized for Hindu insensitivity towards Muslim suffering and forgave Muslims for their oppression of Hindus. It was an instance of what we understand to be the work of the divine.

History's more famous faith-based social movements were conducted with a similar understanding. The American civil rights movement of the 1950s was famous for its commitment to overturning unjust laws and its spirit of reconciliation and love of enemies. What is less often recognized is that the movement's signature activities of marching, imprisonment, and verbal protest were ensconced in prayer, worship, the seeking of the guidance of God, and the life of the Christian community. Individual and community sought God; God shaped the movement's unique and astonishing politics. Spiritual practice shaped political practice similarly in the Indian movement against British colonialism led by Mahatma Gandhi and in important parts of the anti-apartheid movement against South Africa.

Faith-based diplomacy's orientation to the divine is found, too, in its view of human nature. It understands first that people matter. A trivial statement? Not when one recalls that leading views of international politics view diplomacy as the outworking of colossal forces—the international balance of power, the global economic system, the class structure, and technology. In such theories human nature tends to be either ignored, underestimated, or misconstrued.

In faith-based diplomacy, human nature matters in general, as does the vision and leadership of certain humans in particular. In humans is found a spiritual hunger, an alienation that is fulfilled in a living relationship with the divine. Faith-based diplomacy also recognizes the evil in the human soul. Taking the form of the *animus dominandi*, envy, anger, hatred, and spite, evil is a living, efficacious, spiritual reality, not a mere dysfunction or a byproduct of social conditions. Its eradication and defeat are, in turn, accomplished not through human agency, whether the work of psychology or arms, but through divine intervention. Alienated and susceptible to evil, fulfilled through the divine, the person is the site of potential spiritual transformation. It is with this potential in mind that faith-based diplomacy is conducted.

Flowing out of its orientation towards the divine is a second broad theme in faith-based diplomacy: reconciliation. "Reconciliation" is now a familiar term in public discourse, a buzzword today in America, and a common phrase elsewhere. Yet it can also arouse deep passions. In the July 2002 opening of the Institute for Reconciliation in Srinagar, Kashmir, one prominent Kashmiri journalist challenged the very idea of reconciliation. In a moment of passionate anger he shouted out, "Does reconciliation mean submitting lamely to a rapist when you are being raped as we are here in Kashmir?"

Reconciliation, though, is neither a recent trend nor a Western importation. The ancient religions express it most deeply, defining it as the restoration of relationship. In Hebrew, reconciliation is expressed as *tikkun olam*, meaning "to heal, to repair, to transform." Its Greek derivatives are *katallage, apokatallasso, and diallasso*, meaning "to bring forces together that would naturally repel each other," "to break down walls or barriers," and "to heal or change the nature of a relationship." In Latin, the word *concilium*, meaning a deliberative process by which adversaries work out their differences "in council," expresses the concept, while Arabic denotes reconciliation as *salima*, meaning peace, safety, security, and freedom, and *salaha*, meaning to be righteous, to do right, settlement, compromise, restoration, and restitution. In Sanskrit the word *dhynan* (zen) means awakening or enlightenment leading to liberation, reconciliation, and atonement. *Yoga* means "union, integration."

To be sure, differences abound among and within faith traditions about the meaning of reconciliation and about the relative roles of punishment, forgiveness, apology, atonement, and the practice of these concepts in public law. Still, reconciliation is important in each tradition. It pervades Judaism, in which atonement, central to the Torah, infuses halakhah, the Jewish law, wherein punishment, repentance, and restitution are all arrayed towards restoration. Christianity extends the logic of atonement to God's mercy toward sinners on the cross. In Islam, the Qur'an's repeated references to Allah's mercy and injunctions to forgiveness imply a restorative logic, one indeed practiced in Arabic rituals of *sulh*, designed to bring reconciliation between offenders and victims. In Hinduism the conception of dharma, or human obligations, found in the Laws of Manu, appears to stress retributive punishment, but speaks also of repentance and penance through which an offender is restored in his soul and returned to his rightful place in the social order. Reconciliation reached its height in Hinduism through the life and thought of Mahatma

Gandhi, though he drew upon other faiths as well. He once exemplified his vision by counseling a Hindu murderer of a Muslim to find an orphan Muslim boy and raise him as Muslim. The Buddhist faith is epitomized by the restoration of the offender's soul and of relationships among the estranged. Both its compendium of ethics, the Vinaya, and the judicial practice of traditional Tibetan culture stress reconciliation as a response to evil.

If restoration of relationship is found in faith traditions, then so, too, the restoration of political orders wounded by war and injustice is a natural principle for faith-based diplomacy. When armies are squared off and guns are firing, reconciliation demands first a political settlement among leaders. But a settlement is not enough. Reconciliation involves a far greater breadth of participants and depth of transformation. Absent this breadth and depth, a political settlement itself may not succeed.

Six years after Israeli Prime Minister Yitzhak Rabin and Palestinian leader Yasser Arafat achieved an apparent breakthrough for peace in the Oslo Accords, the two sides descended into a war of suicide bombings and harsh Israeli reprisals. When asked why Oslo had collapsed, the lead U.S. negotiator of the agreement, Dennis Ross, commented that whereas political leaders had come to an agreement, far too much hatred and far too little sympathy for peace persisted between the Israeli and Palestinian people. What was needed was a change of hearts and minds at the grassroots and middle levels of society. Such reconciliation on the ground can exert upward pressure on political leadership, eliciting new possibilities for a lasting peace.

The deeper, broader reconciliation of faith-based diplomacy is in fact a family of interwoven ideas. Together, they propose reconciliation as a moral vision for wounded societies. The first of these ideas is the healing of historical wounds. Prominent contemporary theories hold that bitter memories of past injustices are only illusory causes of racial, ethnic, and religious conflicts, conflicts whose true causes are cynical elites who manipulate popular identities, globalization, and dysfunctional demographic patterns, and the trauma of economic and political transition. A faith-based perspective demurs. Such factors contribute to conflict, but so do memories of past crimes against one's parents, grandparents, great grandparents, and one's historic community, dormant resentments that may ever erupt into atrocities. Left unhealed, historical wounds fester endlessly. "That which is forgotten cannot be healed and that which is unhealed becomes the cause of greater evil in the future," as the Jewish author Elie Wiesel once wrote.

If the power of memories is not illusory, neither is the power of healing. Crucially, healing is not forgetting. It begins with the members of a community examining their suffering at the hands of their enemy. The next, more dramatic step is their acknowledgment of their enemy's suffering. This recognition can, often to surprising degrees, lead to the change of heart, the repentance, and the embrace of the other in which healing begins. As the religious traditions—and faith-based diplomacy—understand it, this occurs before, through, and with the assistance of divine power.

The second idea, flowing from the first, is apology and forgiveness, practiced with respect to misdeeds perpetrated in the name of the political order. Apology is the acknowledgment of one's misdeeds and the expression of sorrow to one's victim; forgiveness is the victim's foregoing of all claims to anger, resentment, and payment against the offender. Such practices are usually not the first inclination of doers and sufferers of evil; the change in heart that comes from examination and acknowledgment are usually prerequisites.

Apology and forgiveness, though, are essential to the restoration of wounded communities. It is not surprising that most religious traditions give prominent place to these practices. The Abrahamic faiths understand them as direct responses to God's mercy.

In our seminars in Kashmir, we have often found that we could not talk about apology and forgiveness until we had first addressed yet a third aspect of reconciliation—social justice. The participants could not acknowledge or forego anger, they insisted, until the seminar addressed such issues as self-determination, human rights, colonialism, racism, democracy, economic justice, and restitution for past evils. So we discovered the important interrelationship between justice and forgiveness. Forgiveness does not mean giving up the pursuit of justice. But without forgiveness, "justice" becomes angry, hostile revenge—an escalation, not a solution.

Like visions for the political order and reconciliation, social justice has a contested history of thought in virtually all of the faith traditions. But a few threads are broadly common. First, accountability for injustices on the part of offenders is essential. Reconciliation without it is cheap. Second, most religions propose a healthy pluralism and inclusion where people of varying ethnicities, races, and religions not only tolerate one another's rights, but also value differences and affirm the richness of complementarity. Surah 49:13 in the Qur'an expresses just such inclusivity: "O mankind! We created / You from a single (pair) / Of a male and a female, / And made you into / Nations and tribes, that / Ye may know each other / Not that ye may despise / (Each other)." Third, virtually all faith traditions advocate an economics of compassion that gives special emphasis to the dignity of the poor.[6]

Reconciliation and a divinely grounded vision of the political order, then, are foundational principles of faith-based diplomacy. To articulate them is not to deny the complex differences in how religions understand them or the "internal pluralism" within religions.[7] Nor is it to deny the overlap in many matters between faith-based principles and ones that do not require faith to grasp—traditional Western criteria for the justice of war, for instance. Rather, to set forth these broad principles it is to point to distinctive ideas that religious traditions have to offer about statecraft in the hope that in their application, new political possibilities will emerge.

Practices

How, then, is faith-based diplomacy conducted? Into what courses of action does a divinely grounded vision of the political order and reconciliation translate? At least six practices emerge.

Impartation of Moral Vision

One method is simply the inculcation of principles of faith-based diplomacy in people who are likely to be agents of change in their society. Such is the aim of our seminars in faith-based reconciliation. They impart to participants a moral vision—a set of foundational values—centered upon reconciliation and informed by a divinely grounded understanding of politics. We communicate this vision through eight principles, taught through lecture and considered in small group discussions: pluralism, inclusion, peacemaking through conflict resolution, social justice, forgiveness, healing collective wounds, sovereignty, and atonement. The participants are challenged to comprehend these principles, but also, through examining their own suffering and their community's suffering, and then, through a "learning conversation," come to embrace the principles as relevant ones for their world. Many participants then make the decisive, activating commitment to carry this embrace into Kashmiri society as agents of reconciliation. The result is a nascent cadre of foot soldiers committed to reconciliation.

Civil Society at Work

A cadre of foot soldiers—working outside government, and often comprising leaders of NGOs, universities, religious bodies, and various professions—evokes the concept of civil society, a favorite theme of political philosophers dating back to Alexis de Tocqueville and G. W. F. Hegel in the nineteenth century. Associations, clubs, religious bodies, sundry organizations—this "middle layer" of society, the theory runs, is a vital source of democratic participation and a limit to the power of the state. In the democratic revolutions of 1989 in East Germany, Poland, Hungary, and Czechoslovakia, civil society, alloyed heavily with religious bodies, evidenced this claim in catalyzing non-violent political change.

So, too, civil society is a strategic site for faith-based diplomacy. John Paul Lederach, a contemporary practitioner of reconciliation hailing from the Mennonite tradition, argues for the practical importance of the middle layers of society in bringing "sustainable peace."[8] Compared to top officials, whose responsibility for the whole creates confining political pressure, the middle rungs enjoy more flexibility to envision and practice creative ideas. Yet, unlike people at the grassroots, they also have the influence and contact with leaders above them to urge reconciliation upon them effectively. Both flexible and efficacious, they are positioned to be conduits of new ideas.

If the members of a civil society were to embrace a moral vision of reconciliation, they could then speak about it in universities, at religious gatherings, in newspapers, on television, and at public forums, and urge it more privately upon leaders of warring factions in a conflict. This is the premise of our seminars in Kashmir, which bring together religious leaders, civil servants, officials of NGOs, student leaders, and professionals including lawyers, doctors, business people, academics, journalists, and writers. This whole group, comprising both Hindus and Muslims, males and females, usually numbers about 80 participants. They range in age, though a significant portion are likely future leaders who are now in their 20s and 30s. Over the past three years, the seminars have graduated over 300 participants, many of whom have formed the ranks of a movement committed to advocating reconciliation in Kashmir. Thus is civil society at work, propelled by faith.

Personal Relationships

A movement of reconciliation needs a special ingredient both to hold it together and to gain the cooperation of political and military leaders. It is personal relationships that accomplish these tasks. Only naturally are they central to faith-based reconciliation, given its emphases on the activity of God, personal transformation, and the role of healing and apology. The faith-based diplomat forms and encourages friendships.

One of the dramatic success stories of faith-based diplomacy is the work of the Sant'Egidio Community, a Catholic lay organization that in 1992 facilitated the settlement of a 16-year-long war in Mozambique that took over one million lives. The Community began in 1968 among high school students in Rome who began to pray together and to live simple lives of friendship, especially with the poorest of the poor. Over subsequent decades, these friendships expanded throughout the globe, coming to include countries like Mozambique, where friendships extended to leaders of both major factions in the war as well as to local Catholic bishops and other civil society figures. In the late 1980s, when the factions showed signs of a willingness to explore peace, the Community drew upon its deep network of friendships to bring both sides to its headquarters in Rome, where it sponsored nine rounds of negotiations over two years. It practiced sound diplomacy by keeping the parties away from the international media, but also ordinary friendship, even taking one negotiator with a toothache to a dentist for treatment. In such an atmosphere, the Community negotiated a settlement that has remained peaceful ever since.

Our work in Kashmir likewise depends crucially upon personal relationships. It began in September 2000 with a meeting with a young Muslim man who had trod his own path of reconciliation. Once a top leader of the underground Kashmiri separatist struggle who had both wielded the gun and suffered imprisonment, he had experienced a change of heart that led him to become a leading spokesman for peace. Hearing the message of reconciliation, he was moved to embrace it and to become the key Kashmiri leader of our work. Over time, our deep commitment to one another's welfare and to encouraging one another in our mutual work has become essential for the trust that allows us to take risks together. The resulting movement for reconciliation is also bound together by friendships, these sustained though a network of cell groups, where committed alumni of the seminars meet regularly to encourage one another and grow deeper in their understanding of the work.

Spiritual Conversations

Arising from personal relationships is the practice of spiritual conversations. It is in track two diplomacy that such dialogues usually take place, that is, in meetings between unofficial emissaries and official political and military leaders. But spiritual conversations are hardly a traditional tool of statecraft, even in unofficial settings. Such discussions engage leaders in "conversations of the heart" in which they share what they have suffered: the friends, loved ones, career hopes, and property that they have lost; their hatred or resignation or hopefulness about these losses; their dreams for the future; and the place of the divine in all of these matters.

We often find political and military leaders to be surprised by these conversations—not only that they take place, but that they elicit sympathy and lead to friendships. On one occasion when we brought up forgiveness in a conversation with a prominent Kashmiri separatist leader, he responded with a 45-minute screed cataloging his suffering. Upon finishing, he looked up at us and we thanked him for trusting us enough to share deeply personal affairs. He responded that we were the first people who seemed to care enough to listen to his suffering. He later acknowledged that both he and his people would need to practice forgiveness if Kashmir was to have any future. It was a spiritual change wrought by a spiritual conversation.

Prayer and Fasting

Devout believers of virtually all faiths pray and fast. Should not prayer and fasting also infuse faith-based diplomacy? Expressing the believer's submission to the divine, prayer and fasting usher a spiritual power into the site of a violent conflict, one that effects personal transformation. Our work in Kashmir commonly involves a team of people who pray and fast during seminars, diplomatic meetings, and public forums. Certain episodes of transformation, typically instances where an embittered person comes to express profound words of healing, apology, or forgiveness, bear the marks of the sort of divine assistance that can come as a response to prayer and fasting.

Our seminar of July 2002 was the first one to bring together Kashmiri Muslims with Pandits, a Hindu ethnic group that Muslims had expelled from the Kashmir Valley in the early 1990s and who are now living in refugee camps in Jammu, a southern, Hindu-majority region of the state of Jammu and Kashmir.[9] It was a risky proposition from the outset. We held the seminar in Gulmarg, a high mountain village in Kashmir, to which many of the Pandits were returning for the first time since their expulsion. The prayer and fasting team was, in our view, essential to our prospects for success.

Two days later, we witnessed a poignant outbreak of healing when several Islamic clerics and scholars stood up during a service of reconciliation, acknowledged the role of the Muslims in driving out the Pandits, repented, asked forgiveness, and vowed to work for the repatriation of the Pandit community to the Kashmir Valley. Days later, when the Pandits returned home to the refugee camps in Jammu, their stories of changed Muslim hearts reverberated through the refugee community, stirring up new interest in reconciliation.

Rituals for Reconciliation

Like prayer and fasting, rituals and ceremonies that are normally directed towards worship, celebration, mourning, petition, and healing can be potently redirected towards the resolution of conflicts and the transformation of people wounded by political violence. The reading of sacred texts, common prayer, liturgy, and rites of healing can all become tools of faith-based diplomacy.

The most powerful moments of our work in Kashmir come in a reconciliation service at the close of the seminar. With the participants seated in a circle, sacred scriptures about reconciliation are read. Participants then take the opportunity to inscribe on a slip of paper any memories of which they want to unburden themselves, whether through apology, forgiveness, or general healing. Next, while the group is carrying out prayer and meditation, some of the participants will rise and speak words of healing. Often, a member of the opposing community will then reciprocate with an acknowledgment and further words of healing. Together, members of each community also practice rituals of coming together with members of the other community. At the end—surprising us the first time we saw it—the participants typically close the ritual with songs of peace, even including "We Shall Overcome," sung in Urdu.

At one seminar, words of healing were spoken by a Kashmiri Muslim man who had lost his father, a politician, to the guns of Muslim militants eight years earlier. Militants then came to his house one night, murdered his brother, and shot him many times. He survived his wounds, after nine surgeries. He had vowed to seek revenge, and for the past eight years had been seeking to find and kill the gunman. But in the service of reconciliation, following three days of intense reflection on reconciliation, flanked by the prayers of his fellow participants, he stood and announced emotionally that he had experienced a transformation of heart and publicly forgave his perpetrator, renouncing all revenge. In a meeting nine months later, he recounted the story of his transformation, showing me pictures of himself before and after he had been shot: "You see, I used to be handsome!" He spoke emotionally of the freedom he had discovered, and of his renewed commitment to working with other victims of violence, widows, and orphans.

Rabbi Marc Gopin has proposed that rituals of grieving can also be used to heal conflict between communities. The Jewish practice of *aveilus*—the mourning of a loved one through acknowledgment, burial, remembering, and then healing and recovery—could, he argues, be used by Arabs and Jews in the Middle East to address and heal memories of lost loved ones, homes, and land dating back one hundred years.[10] Similarly, Arab Islamic communities have developed rituals of *sulh* for settling conflicts between community members that could be practiced on a larger scale. Conceived of as alternatives to cycles of vengeance, they involve entire families and even village leaders in the hearing of grievances, mutual mourning, restitution, forgiveness, and restoration of normal friendship. As with the other practices of faith-based diplomacy, rituals for reconciliation emanate from faith and draw from the wells of healing.

Contexts

The practical, the worldly, the skeptical, surely every diplomat of the traditional sort will want to know: what difference does faith-based diplomacy make? With all the equanimity of a divine grounding, the faith-based diplomat might respond with Mother Teresa's quip that faithfulness, not success, is what matters. True, the most important virtue of faith-based diplomacy is doubtless faith itself, the belief that one's actions will, through divine assistance, bear munificent fruit. Still, even the least worldly-minded faith-based diplomat must interest himself in whether his work effects good or ill, succeeds or backfires.

An interest in effects of the work begets an interest in the contexts in which the work is most likely to occur. Of these there are at least four. First, there are conflicts whose parties define themselves by their religion and perhaps even fight over religion: Sudan, the Israeli-Palestinian conflict, and, in important ways, the conflicts of the 1990s in Yugoslavia. Kashmir is ever more such a conflict as militant groups come increasingly to seek not merely self-determination but the spread of Dar al Islam. In such conflicts, an approach that resonates with the religious worldview of the factions may well achieve successes that purely secular approaches will not. As a former militant leader told us, "it is not enough to take the gun out of the militant's hand. One must deal with the ideas that compel him to pick up the gun in the first place. To do that, one must present a more compelling idea."

The second situation favorable to faith-based diplomacy is one in which, regardless of the identities of the parties, certain religious leaders enjoy a charisma that they may exercise for settlement and reconciliation. Gandhi's ability to halt rioting through fasting during the partition of India is exemplary, explainable only through his own concept of "soul force."

The third situation is civilizational dialogue. Conflict, at least of the broad ideological sort, occurs even among the broadest religious collectivities—Islamic and Western civilizations, for example, between whom popular tensions have escalated as of late. In response, both President Mohamed Khatami of Iran and Pope John Paul have proposed a "dialogue between civilizations" that involves spiritual conversations among religious leaders. People of faith are indeed equipped well to foster such dialogue as they understand the complexities of the theologies that define worldviews, and are able to avoid shallow forms of "consensus" that seek only a lowest common denominator that few devout religious believers can endorse.

Fourth are situations in which faith-based diplomats are well positioned to become trusted envoys. This position may arise from their links within a society—witness Sant'Egidio's network of friendships in Mozambique. Or, it may come from a leader's prestige. The role that Reverend Jesse Jackson played in negotiating for hostages in Yugoslavia and Lebanon is such a case. In both situations, parties were more willing to accord respect to faith-based diplomats because of their religious calling.

All told, then, in any of these situations, what difference might the principles and practices of faith-based diplomacy make? Dramatic results abound on the personal level—in the bitter partisan who comes to embrace forgiveness and healing, in the cadres of committed friends and activists who willingly put themselves in danger by coming to urge reconciliation, in transformations and healings and renewals. We have seen such results in Kashmir.

But faith-based diplomacy might well effect social change, too. It takes inspiration from religious movements that have, over the last twenty years, altered the history of nations: toppling authoritarianism in Poland, the Philippines, East Germany, Brazil, South Africa, and elsewhere; bringing reconciliation in the wake of political transitions in South Africa and Chile; and brokering peace settlements in Mozambique, Nicaragua, and between Chile and Argentina. Claims of efficaciousness should not, of course, be overstated. Few of the changes in Eastern Europe or South Africa, for example, would have occurred apart from new environments created by the end of the Cold War; in every case, economic, political, and social circumstances and leadership on many fronts helped to produce the outcome. These many layers of causality warrant humility. Still, the same episodes also ought to inspire boldness for our contemporary diplomacy. Large in significance, concentrated in time, each bearing the unmistakable influence of faith, they together suggest that faith-based diplomacy is, in the words of Victor Hugo, "an idea whose time has come."

29

MILITARY CHAPLAINS
Bridging Church and State

—Douglas M. Johnston

There is only one radical means of sanctifying human lives. Not armored plating, or
tanks, or planes, concrete fortifications. The one radical solution is peace.

—*Yitzhak Rabin*

In early 2001, the U.S. Navy initiated a training program in religion and statecraft for
all Navy, Marine Corps, and Coast Guard Chaplains. The purpose of this training,
which took place under the sponsorship of the Chief of Navy Chaplains, was to enhance
the conflict-prevention capabilities of the sea-service commands, which are typically at
the forefront of our country's overseas involvements. Among other avenues of inquiry,
this training explored in considerable depth the benefits that would accrue from military
chaplains (1) establishing relationships of trust with local religious leaders, and (2) serving
as advisors to their military commanders on the religious (and cultural) implications of
command decisions that were either being contemplated or implemented.

The training, which was conducted around the world by a four-person team of religion and conflict resolution experts,[1] was well-received by the chaplains, with about a third
of them enthusiastic about the possibility of an expanded mandate, another third quite
willing to give it a try, and the remainder protesting that this wasn't why they had "signed
up." Based on their performance during the program, it became obvious that with the
right kind of training, the two-thirds who were supportive represented a formidable capability that could be brought to bear to good effect, especially in situations where religion
was a significant ingredient in the security equation. Capitalizing on this capability, however, was going to require two important steps. First, the line officer community[2] would
need to expand the rules of engagement (ROE) for its military chaplains to include these
new functions. Second, the Chaplain Corps would have to adjust its personnel policies
to support the new ROE by providing chaplains who want to participate in this manner

---

* Douglas M. Johnston, *Religion, Terror, and Error: U.S. Foreign Policy and the Challenge of Spiritual Engagement* (Westport, Conn.: Praeger, 2011), 127–36.

the opportunity to do so, perhaps through development of an appropriate training sub-specialty within the corps.[3]

Although the stakes skyrocketed with the attacks of 9/11, neither of the above measures has proven easy to address. During the course of the 2001 training program, for example, it became clear during visits to various military commands that even if the chaplains were willing to take on the added functions, the line community was going to take further convincing. Illustrative of this challenge was one Marine General's response to the idea of expanding the chaplain's functions in which he slammed his fist on the table and said, "The role of my military chaplains is to attend to the spiritual needs of the men and women of my command. Period!"

With the line community in mind, an article was published in the *U.S. Naval Institute Proceedings* which described the training that had taken place and made a strong case for capitalizing on the formidable potential of military chaplains in addressing the nation's preventive agenda.[4] Although the article had no apparent effect at the time, it is encouraging to note the progress that has taken place during the intervening years. Much of that progress, however, has been ad hoc in nature, and there is still a great deal to be done. As a review of history will make clear, though, changing the role of military chaplains is neither unprecedented nor a particularly novel idea.

Historic Background

The first evidence of using military chaplains dates back to the Roman Army in the 5th century C.E.[5] From scant evidence, it appears that their likely role at that point was to provide divine endorsement of the righteousness of the war in which they were engaged and to provide reassurance that those who paid the ultimate price would be accorded favorable treatment in the Hereafter.

The modern chaplaincy, however, traces its roots to medieval Catholicism three centuries later when the Council of Ratisbon in 742 C.E., authorized the use of church officials to perform church rituals in a military setting:

> We prohibit the servant of God in every way from bearing arms or fighting in the army or going against the enemy, except those alone who because of their sacred office, namely, for the celebrating of mass and caring for the relics of the saints, have been designated for this office; this is to say, the leader may have with him one or two bishops with their priest chaplains, and each captain may have one priest, in order to hear the confessions of the men and impose upon them proper penance.[6]

During the reign of Charlemagne from 768 to 814 C.E., the chaplain's role expanded from merely attending to the spiritual needs of the troops to providing divine endorsement of the righteousness of the cause for which they were fighting.

In 1095 Pope Urban II assigned Bishop Adhémar of Le Puy to be his personal representative in the First Crusade. As the Papal Legate, Adhémar not only acted as spiritual leader of the Crusade, he also organized relief for poor pilgrims, and appealed to the West for more Crusaders.[7] Until his death from disease at the siege of Antioch, he also played a key role in maintaining the cohesiveness of the Crusade, settling numerous disputes that arose between the various Christian generals involved.[8] Later Pope Innocent III (1198–1216) and Pope Gregory IX (1227–1241) refined the spiritual duties to (1) encourage proper Christian behavior on the battlefield and in camp, and (2) promote the fighting spirit of the soldiers through inspiring sermons.[9] In the mid 1600s, the duties shifted according to the changing dynamics of the Reformation and even went so far in colonial America as to include the role of "soldier-priest" when fighting against the Indians.[10]

American Realities

The American experience included a similar ebb and flow with respect to the scope of chaplain activities. Even before the formation of America and its army, one finds their use in colonial militias like that headed by Captain John Mason, a British Army Major who immigrated to New England in 1632 and who led an expedition from the colony of Connecticut against the Pequot Indians in the wake of some prior skirmishes. Since Mason's force was responsible for the "Mystic Massacre" in 1637, which led to the death of nearly every man, woman, and child of the Pequot tribe, it would appear that mercy was not high on the agenda. Later in 1725, Captain Henry Dwight, a Massachusetts militia leader, enlisted a chaplain to provide moral authority in matters of discipline, drunkenness, and general fitness for duty (in addition to performing church services for the soldiers and their families).

During the Revolutionary War, George Washington's First Order to his Army reflected his religious leanings:

> The General most earnestly requires and expects a due observance of those articles of war established for the government of the army, which forbid profane cursing, swearing, and drunkenness. And in like manner, he requires and expects of all officers and soldiers, not engaged in actual duty, a punctual attendance of Divine service, to implore the blessing of Heaven upon the means used for our safety and defense.[11]

These views were reconfirmed during his Farewell Address from the presidency when he stated that "reason and experience both forbid us to expect that National Morality can prevail in exclusion of religious principle."[12] On July 29, 1775, the Second Continental Congress authorized the assignment of chaplains to the U.S. Army.[13]

From then until the present, there has been constant change both in the total number of chaplains (including going out of business altogether on at least two occasions) and in their duties. Over time, the latter ranged from the normal clerical functions to those of teacher (of non-religious subjects), doctor, psychologist, and morale builder.

Following World War II and into the Cold War, chaplains became increasingly involved in civic action and humanitarian assistance projects.[14] During the Vietnam War, the role further evolved from morale builder to moral advisor, especially with respect to combating drugs, alcohol abuse, and racism. The later "pacification efforts" even led to chaplains ministering beyond the boundaries of their flocks. The roots of the newly recommended role of religious liaison (in which chaplains interact with local religious leaders) can largely be seen as tracing their origins to this Vietnam experience.[15] Thus, as the geographic reach of the United States has grown over time, so too has the scope of the chaplain's mission.

Today's Challenge

The chaplain's role became even more expansive following 9/11, as some chaplains took creative license in advancing humanitarian projects and others even began interacting with indigenous religious leaders and/or serving as cultural advisors to their commanders. However, the pendulum soon swung back to a more cautionary stance in response to concerns within the chaplain community about the possibility of being perceived as intelligence agents in religious garb, a perception that could clearly compromise their non-combatant status. There was also concern that the parent religious organizations, which endorse their clergy for service as chaplains within the armed forces (and retain a degree of control over their conduct once assigned), might oppose this expanded role.

Each of the above concerns has been carefully addressed in the latest revision to Joint Publication 1-05, which provides doctrinal guidance for the religious support of joint military operations. Among other things, JP 1-05 stipulates the parameters that are to govern the chaplain's roles as principal advisor to the joint force commander on religious affairs, and as a key advisor to the commander on the impact of religious factors on military operations. It specifically prohibits any activities that might compromise the chaplain's non-combatant status such as functioning as intelligence collectors, engaging in manipulation or deception operations, identifying targets for combat operations, serving as lead negotiators for the command in given situations,[16] or even removing one's chaplain insignia. These prohibitions, however, do not preclude chaplains from participating in operational planning or in providing command and staff with religious insights that can contribute to an enhanced situational awareness. The latter, which is particularly important when it comes to deterring conflict, will often derive from the relationships of trust that chaplains establish through their networking with local religious leaders, NGOs, private voluntary organizations, international organizations, and the interagency community (e.g., Embassy country teams, USAID officials, and Provincial Reconstruction Teams, among others).

Of paramount importance, military chaplains can contribute to preventing conflict and mediating differences thanks to the religious legitimacy they bring to communications with other clerics. These channels are often preferred over others by indigenous religious leaders and typically represent the only avenue available for conducting religious engagement.[17] With one foot in the religious world as a member of the clergy and the other in the secular as a military officer, chaplains are well-suited to serve as intermediaries between the military and religious leaders in zones of conflict and during post-conflict stabilization. Nonetheless, chaplains should always approach this task cautiously, not only out of concern for their own safety, but for the safety of the religious leaders with whom they meet. The risks are real and must be anticipated.

"Chaplain Liaison in Support of Military Engagement" is defined in JP 1-05 as "any command-directed contact or interaction where the chaplain, as the command's religious representative, meets with a leader on matters of religion to ameliorate suffering and to promote peace and the benevolent expression of religion."[18] The overriding requirement that governs this kind of engagement is that it be directed by the commander and that it be in concert with strategic intent.

Tomorrow's Challenge

There have been any number of instances in which U.S. military chaplains have engaged with local religious leaders in Iraq and Afghanistan in projects ranging from organizing and celebrating community religious services to coordinating mosque renovation projects and forming religious councils. The list goes on; but suffice it to say that almost all of these efforts have contributed to improved dialogue, increased trust, or a reduction in violence.[19] Quite apart from any policy or doctrinal considerations, it seems clear that chaplain liaison has already become a living reality. Moreover, the liaison function itself may become a stepping stone to an even more expansive mission statement in the future, as implied by the theme of a 2009 international conference on "The Role of the Chaplain in Reconciliation and Healing in Post-Conflict Reconstruction."[20]

In some respects, a future move in this direction would actually represent a revisiting of the past. During a time of tremendous chaos immediately following World War II, U.S. Army Chaplains played an instrumental role in stabilizing and rebuilding shattered societies in both Germany and Japan. They did this through addressing the immediate and potential long-term effects of the conflict by recognizing loss, promoting reconciliation, facilitating the rebuilding of institutions, and working toward social transformation.[21] Certainly, the dual functions of bridge-building and serving as agents of reconciliation seem tailor-made for today's chaplain operating in today's environment.

One consideration that should be taken into account when assessing the liaison function is the fact that chaplains rotate assignments rather frequently. In the Navy, there is the added complication of abbreviated port visits, which do not provide much opportunity for developing relationships with religious leaders ashore. Trust takes time, so it is important that chaplains record whatever progress they make in developing it so their successors can build upon what has gone before. A secure website could facilitate this kind of information transfer and provide an effective vehicle for recording "lessons learned" and "best practices" for the benefit of others. Such measures notwithstanding, the quality of relationships inevitably relates to personal chemistry, which also takes time to develop. Hence, the desirability of the more permanent presence that religion attachés would provide.

The enlightened use of military chaplains is a function of the military commander's discretion. Yet, little religious education is provided to prospective or current military commanders either at the Service Academies, the Command and Staff Colleges, or the various War Colleges. As a consequence, U.S. military commanders in the field are essentially "winging it."[22] In the absence of a formal requirement to engage religious leaders, a military unit's interaction with them—and the chaplain's role in this activity—has basically been a function of the instincts and judgment of the unit commander. The stakes in this process were expressed rather bluntly in an issue of the *Naval War College Review* in 1996:

> An operational commander, however well-trained in the military issues, who is ignorant of or discounts the importance of religious belief can strengthen his enemy, offend his allies, alienate his own forces, and antagonize public opinion. Religious belief is a factor he must consider in evaluating the relationship with allies, and his courses of action.[23]

To gain the full benefits of a broadened mandate for military chaplains, the commanders for whom they work must have a basic (if not nuanced) familiarity with the religious imperatives at play within his or her AOR. Because an enlightened understanding of the underlying religious environment can make the difference between failure and success, it is important that military commands understand and be able to deal with this aspect of any conflict in which they become involved. In short, the same kind of energy, commitment, and investment should be devoted to Islamic and Middle Eastern regional studies as was applied to Soviet studies during the Cold War.

Pentagon planners should review the current training requirements for military officers, with an eye toward determining what additional training in religion should be added at each stage in the officer's development to ensure that military commanders can think both strategically and tactically about the influence of religious factors in their decision making. Some cultural and religious instruction is already provided for most military units prior to deploying overseas. Although this training includes strategic as well as tactical aspects, it varies in quality and timeliness and often suffers from its "once-over-lightly" nature.

Related training for military chaplains, although further along, is still a work in progress. As a result of the Base Realignment and Closure process, the services have co-located their training for chaplains at the Armed Forces Chaplain Center (AFCC) at Fort Jackson, South Carolina. There, the Army, which is strongly committed to the expanded role for military chaplains, has created a new Center for World Religions that will eventually provide its chaplains with training on the impact of religion on joint, interagency, intergovernmental, and multinational operations. It will also develop strategies and capabilities for conducting chaplain liaison in support of military engagements.[24] The Air Force and Navy (including the Marine Corps) do not have a similar program, but it is probably only a matter of time before the Army's Center provides such training for all of the services (including, at some point, members of the line officer communities).

Although some chaplains will not be well-suited to perform these added responsibilities, consideration should be given by the military services to creating a religion and culture sub-specialty for those chaplains who are willing (and able) to serve in the expanded capacity.[25] A challenging curriculum for those who are so motivated would clearly enhance the conflict prevention capabilities of their military commands.[26] As things currently stand, however, service-wide acceptance of the religious-diplomatic function is still ad hoc in nature owing to the absence of an institutionalized selection process and the training regime to support it. There is a long way to go before the desired level of effectiveness will be reached. Just how far is reflected in the following observations of a recognized expert in this area based on recent conversations with combatant commanders and military chaplains:[27]

- Not all of the chaplains serving in Iraq and Afghanistan who provided "advice" to commanders or conducted religious leader liaison were successful.
- Some commanders commented that their chaplains knew less about the religion of their Area of Operations than they did.
- Some chaplains who had no previous war experience suffered from war shock to the point where they weren't able to adequately address the spiritual needs of the troops.
- Some chaplains commented that they disliked Muslims and would not deal with them unless so ordered.

Other challenges related to using chaplains in the suggested liaison and advisory roles include the fact that: (1) some religious groups that sponsor (endorse) chaplains do not view interfaith dialogue as an appropriate function, (2) the chaplain's short time in theater may limit his or her ability to follow-through in meeting the expectations of local populations, (3) chaplains typically have limited language skills and cultural understanding, and (4) some chaplains may not have the maturity, knowledge, or personal disposition to work closely with religious leaders of other cultures and faiths. All of these considerations give added credence to the corresponding need for religion attachés (or their equivalent) in the U.S. Missions of those countries where chaplains could become involved on this basis.

In contrast to the combat-related failings of some chaplains in Iraq and Afghanistan, other chaplains have been responsible for a number of highly effective interventions in these same theaters of operation. Most of these have resulted from the chaplains taking the initiative, securing their commanders' approval, and then following through.[28]

On some occasions, it has been the commanders themselves who have initiated the intervention. In one instance, Army Lieutenant General Karl Eikenberry, then Commanding General, Combined Forces Command–Afghanistan (and later Ambassador to Afghanistan), asked the Navy chaplain assigned to his command to serve as the liaison between the command and the Afghan Ministry of Religious Affairs in addressing a problem that had arisen with a campaign to inoculate Afghans against polio. Some Taliban-sympathizing mullahs had spread the word that this was actually a sinister ploy to convert Afghans to Christianity "by injection," and several World Health Organization (WHO) staff had been killed as a result. The Navy chaplain not only secured the cooperation of the Ministry, but also communicated quietly with the subversives and was able to turn the situation around.[29]

On another occasion, a U.S. Army truck had lost its brakes in downtown Kabul and plowed into a crowd, killing several Afghan civilians. A tense atmosphere prevailed, as all U.S. personnel were ordered off the streets. The same Commanding General again sent his chaplain to meet with the Minister of Religious Affairs to deal with the problem. The chaplain was able to calm the situation, helped initiate an investigation of the incident, and followed through by leading subsequent discussions relating to remuneration.[30]

In Iraq, command support for chaplain engagements with key Muslim clerics was instrumental in securing their support for a concerned Local Citizens Program that matured into the Sons of Iraq program and the turning point in the war known as the Anwar Awakening.[31]

It has been said that chaplains are only as good as the training they receive and that the training is only as good as the policy and doctrine that supports and directs it. To the extent this is so, the new JP 1-05 gives strong reason to hope.

Inspiration from Afar

How other countries have made use of their military chaplains can also be instructive. For example, Canada—a country that stands out in terms of its peacemaking initiatives around the world—is placing an increasing emphasis on how chaplains can assist their commands to become more aware of, and thus prepared for, cultural, psychological, and religious factors that significantly impact military operations. Canadian chaplains have also been quite active in engaging local religious leaders. As noted by a Major in the Canadian Chaplain Corps:

> As Canadians, deployed chaplains will discover among local religious and community leaders genuine intrigue and curiosity with respect to Western thinking, beliefs and values. A desire to engage in some form of dialogue, reference the existing conflict and/or its residual effects, is also not uncommon.[32]

In 2008 the Canadian government Chief of the Defense Staff authorized the chaplaincy to "provide Canadian Forces (CF) leadership with perspective and guidance on religious, spiritual, and ethical matters in garrison and in the field." It also explicitly endorsed a role in conflict resolution:

> Chaplains will require increased levels of training, education, and experience in religious understanding and reconciliation in order to contribute effectively to the conflict resolution processes internal to the CF and in operational settings.[33]

It is noteworthy that Canadian Force chaplains are already trained for and actively engaged in developing indigenous religious leader support for stability operations.[34]

Norway also makes expansive use of its chaplains, including the mandate to participate in conflict resolution activities. Norwegian chaplains in peacekeeping operations maintain constant contact with religious leaders (both Christian and other traditions), "as a way of contributing constructively to conflict resolution."[35]

Going back in time, one finds other examples of using chaplains in expansive roles. During the Spanish-American War in the Philippines (April to August 1898), for example, U.S. Army General John (Black Jack) Pershing used his chaplain as a liaison with Catholic clergy in the north and Muslim leaders in the south to temper the hostilities.[36] Sixty-five years later, when French commanders found themselves in tight predicaments during the Algerian War for Independence, it was their military chaplains who they often sent out to negotiate with the Muslim insurgents.[37] Implicit in this action was French recognition of the unique role that chaplains can play in mitigating or preventing conflict (in addition to dealing with the human casualties after it has erupted).

Conclusion

In both the Philippine and Algerian examples, military chaplains played roles that extend beyond the current, evolving expansion of duties. The lesson of historical examples like these for the modern chaplaincy is this: Rather than confining the chaplain's liaison role within rigidly circumscribed boundaries, we would do well to provide greater latitude to those chaplains who are well-educated and seasoned practitioners in this arena. Even the French—the authors of secularism—understood the need to deal creatively with religious imperatives. With so much at stake, can we afford to do any less?

30

RELIGION AS DESTROYER AND CREATOR OF PEACE
A Postmortem on Failed Peace Processes

—Marc Gopin

Religion and conflict are sufficiently intertwined at this stage of the Arab/Israeli conflict that it behooves us to reflect on what went wrong with peace processes that ignored the vital role of religion. We should pursue this analysis both in terms of diagnosis of a conflict situation as well as in terms of recommendations for management and resolution.

The pervasive support of the settlements and its effect on Israeli policy is clearly driven in strong measure by religious constituencies. By contrast, Islamicist impact on the continuing demand for all of historic Palestine is plainly apparent, as is cultural and religious permission to pursue ever deadlier forms of assault on innocent civilians. Both sides' religious communities have contributed to making the Temple Mount a central crux of the conflict. Thus, religion is not the only factor of the conflict but it has definitely contributed in no small measure to its perpetuation and escalation.

What the study of religion had to teach us and what the Oslo process needed was a much deeper understanding of religious negotiables and non-negotiables. Religion, especially in monotheistic cultures, carries ancient instincts and values. Those who orchestrated the Oslo process on all sides tended to hold these ancient instincts and values in disdain. That is why they wanted issues of Jerusalem and the Temple Mount to be left for last, as if they could be swept into a done deal at the last minute. And that is one of the reasons that they were so roundly defeated by this issue in those last tragic months of negotiation. There is no question that the issue of refugees and the right of return played an equally important role at Camp David.

The destructive impact of religious symbols was two-fold: (1) Religiously contested spaces and symbols are inherently connected to the deepest of human emotions, even very often for members of a cultural or ethnic group who are not otherwise religious; and (2) The deliberate covering up of these issues until the last months implied a disdain of religious values that already encouraged rejectionism on the part of religious constituencies. In an insidious way, unresolved and un-addressed emotional symbols, such as contested

* Center for World Religions, Diplomacy, & Conflict Resolution, George Mason University, http://crdcgmu. wordpress.com/research, January 26, 2002.

religious spaces, are accidents waiting to happen. They are there to be exploited by anyone who wants to destroy a peacemaking process.

That is what happened. I remember speaking on the phone with someone who was intimately familiar with the Camp David talks in the summer months before the Intifada started. He never said much, but, uncharacteristically, he said to me curtly, "Does someone know how to explain to them that there actually was a Jewish presence on this Temple Mount thousands of years ago?" I sensed in that phone call the exasperation, the sad unpreparedness for this most delicate and hurtful phase of the negotiations. Later I would learn that Arafat had hardly said anything for two weeks, despite the honest hard work and rather pitiful enthusiasm of his advisors. But Arafat did manage to pointedly remark that there was never a Jewish temple on the Temple Mount, the most holy site of the Jewish community for two thousand years. What better torpedo?

I cannot help but wonder whether, in addition to the parochial political motivations of Sharon to stroll on the Temple Mount later in that fateful year of the beginning of the Al-Aqsa Intifada, that he did not also consider his walk on the Temple Mount, with dozens of police, as a reply to Arafat. In many ways both acted characteristically, one with feigned ignorance and denial, and the other with overwhelming force.

There is another piece to the story that is less commonly known. Arafat, as some have recounted recently, is a man of split personality, able to orchestrate two conversations and two intentionalities simultaneously. That dishonesty has been his favorite mode of survival, but it has also been the deepest source of his alienation from most American administrations. American leaders understand men of violence, and anyone familiar with American foreign policy knows that they are willing to work with them. But they cannot abide perpetual liars. It seems to drive them crazy, especially the current President Bush. Seasoned diplomats are used to dealing with deception, but Arafat takes this to a level that has alienated him from most leaders.

But what of this other side of Arafat, the side that deals amicably with rabbis and many other Jews? Why did he waste political capital putting me and other rabbis on Palestinian television, for example, right in the middle of the Intifada? He volunteered to me, after a powerful session of inter-religious exchanges, in the presence of many people—Jews, Christians, and Muslims—that he used to pray as a child with the old Jewish men at the Western Wall, thus implicitly honoring and acknowledging it as a Jewish holy site. Why did he say this to us in April and then in August at Camp David deny any Jewish sacred presence on the Temple Mount? Arafat had said these things to us at the same time that his Mufti in Jerusalem was denying any historic Jewish existence on the Temple Mount. The entire issue is absurd in light of Islamic sources themselves that refer to the Temple Mount as Bais al-Miqdas in numerous *hadith*, as we will outline below. These are enigmas that devolve into questions of split personality, as well as political and emotional manipulation. But it is the manipulation of religion that is important.

We see several political strains of behavior that pave the way for the cynical manipulation of religious emotions in the absence of a serious attempt to treat religion as a part of the conflict and a part of its resolution. Damage to honor, humiliation, denial of existence, are key weapons of war, especially civil wars. Just as Jewish attachment to Israel has been denied in the Arab world for over a century, the attachment relegated to the manipulation of European Zionists, so too the very existence of the Palestinian people as such is denied by much right wing Jewish propaganda.

The heart of the heart of these denials comes to full fruition on the Temple Mount. It is the locus of ultimate denial and injury. It always will be until the religions involved and the history of the peoples molded by those religions are given their due position of honor and respect in processes of resolution.

I should not be misinterpreted in this regard. I do not speak of empowering religious political parties, terror groups, or manipulative religious leaders and political appointees. Clergy can be part of the solution but it will only be worsened by privileging reactionary parties or religious leaders. The key is for the sensibilities of religious people to be heard. The voice of the people is what was missing from the peace process as a whole. The projection of that voice, negatively speaking, could have prognosticated the dangers and inadequacies of Oslo formulae on both sides. Positively, the voice of the people could have been instrumental in devising steps that would actually have been effective in combating extremism and empowering moderates, secular and religious alike. The goal would not have been to supplant secular, progressive elites with religious elites in peace processes. That could have been equally disastrous. The key was for peace processes to be based on authentic methods of listening to all of the ugliness in popular attitudes as well as their basic human needs—for protection, for dignity, for jobs, for the preservation of their religious lives and sacred spaces. We would have known what we were up against, but also how to engage a much broader process of peace and justice making.

Many had blamed this course of events that shifted the conflict to central religious symbols on Ariel Sharon's visit with hundreds of troops to the Temple Mount. It is true that it was the match that lit the Al-Aqsa Intifada. But many others argue it was the killing of the stone throwers by Israeli riot police on the holy ground the day afterward.

This ignores completely, however, the deeper reason that the Temple Mount came to embody the struggle. As of January 2001, the major rabbis of Israel were declaring that Israel could not give up sovereignty on the Temple Mount. *The New York Times* reported that the rabbis had said that "the Temple Mount is the holiest place to the Jewish people," and that there is ". . . a religious, sovereign, moral and historical right of the Jewish people to this mount" that predates the birth of other religions.[1]

Note the principal need of the rabbis to emphasize the earlier date of Judaism, because a major source of Jewish collective injury that is unstated is the building of the mosques on top of the holiest site in Jewish life, which embodies messianic dreams of the future.

For their part, the key Islamic leaders had echoed parallel viewpoints. Sheikh Sabri, the Mufti of Jerusalem, declared, "We cannot permit any non-Muslim sovereignty over the entire area of Al Aksa, either above or below ground."[2] But the same article went on to inform that over 100 rabbis had expressed their interest in *shared sovereignty*. Indeed there were more and more rabbinic voices in the Jewish community for shared sovereignty, including my own.

There was no parallel movement in the Islamic community. Furthermore, the Sheikh's comments were meant to specifically disallow one compromise that negotiators had worked on, namely, Jewish sovereignty below ground, where the sacred ruins of the Jewish temples lie, and Palestinian sovereignty above, where the mosques had been built on top of the ruins.

All of these positions of intransigence, reflecting a willingness to perpetuate and provoke the bloodiest stage of Israeli-Arab relations, all for the sake of this piece of land, are actually bitter fruits. They are the fruits of the complete diplomatic, secular neglect of religious communities and religious leaders in the decades of the Oslo peace process. The Temple Mount/Haram was a symbol waiting to be plucked for use by rejectionists.

This was a startling testimony to the consequences of exclusion from peacemaking of those on all sides. This includes the American negotiators who uttered the word "peace" so often and did not make an iota of effort to create parallel religious processes of negotiation, trust building, acknowledgment of the past, apologies, healing, and a shared understanding of history.

It reached the absurd level of countless indications from the negotiators that no one had even been prepared to understand that this Temple Mount actually housed the oldest core of Jewish identity, or that the Noble Sanctuary would become the core issue of rejectionism in the rest of the Arab world. The Palestinian negotiators seemed to not have a clue of its importance for Jews, and that seemed to be both a result of no shared understanding of history, a delusional denial, and also a willful neglect of this subject for years by third parties and by secular, Israeli peacemakers who had never faced their own ambivalent identities as Jews—until, of course, it mattered, and came out at the worst possible moment for peace. I was astonished to learn from unofficial but very senior Palestinian intellectuals who met for years with Jews, even rabbis, and were led to believe that because traditional Jewish law forbids going on to the Temple Mount that its sovereignty would not be a major stumbling block. This was serious miscommunication over many years that was a complicated combination of denial and neglect of the central importance of ancient religious symbols and sacred spaces.

There were so many foolish mistakes that ignited the Al-Aqsa Intifada, but this willful disregard of religious and cultural identity was an important factor. In general, the misunderstanding of the deep cultural contest over space, defined in ethno-nationalist terms or in religious terms, or both, was a principal deterrent to any peace deal, especially because the ceaseless building of settlements was designed to scuttle a deal over space, in fact to make a separate Palestinian space impossible.

At the same time the lack of cultural preparedness on the Arab/Islamic side for even the notion of shared sovereignty over space that was sacred to both religions for millennia is an essential part of this tragedy. There is no other way to say it. Islamic sources *themselves* refer repeatedly to this spot as *bait al maqdis*,[3] the Hebrew name used for thousands of years by ancient Judaism for Jewish Temples that are buried beneath this spot. Mohammed himself referred to it this way, and prayed towards it for a considerable time, according to Islam's own stories.

To deny in the contemporary framework the sacredness of the Temple Mount to Jews suggests a desperate need to deny history, even Islam's own sacred historical records. It is to deny the need to right historical wrongs. It cannot be separated from the Palestinians' own sense of betrayal and disappointment at not being able to right the historical wrongs perpetrated on them. Sacred history and mythology becomes a football of competing injuries.

Sharing the Temple Mount was (and perhaps still is) an opportunity to heal history. Sacred places built on the ruins of other people's sacred spaces, as a sign of victory, is one of the great and intractable tragedies of religious history, one of the most important ways in which religions are responsible for bloodshed. This is certainly true in India with mosques built on top of Hindu holy sites. In point of fact, Jerusalem embodies one long history of this kind of conquest, going back to the Canaanites.

But Camp David was the opportunity to right a historical wrong, to develop a new stage of sharing sacred space that was lost due to lack of preparation and to psychological denial. The future of diplomacy cannot repeat this. Sharing is the only possible answer for descendants, for those who have inherited the bad decisions of previous generations of believers.

Some will argue that this was impossible in the hermeneutics of each tradition. It is and was possible. I spoke to many religious people on both sides, quite knowledgeable, who felt it was eminently possible. But many were afraid of extremists in their midst. The most important point is that all of this intransigence could have been mollified and attenuated with years of careful relationship building, the righting of other social wrongs, and with leaders who felt that their people were ready, had been made ready, for some compromises. Then the compromise, the carefully considered, hermeneutically developed religious solutions, would have fallen to the earth like a ripe apple. But it was not to be.

Let us continue, however, with the concrete hermeneutic ways in which this compromise must ultimately occur. And it involves, among other paths that we have discussed, a prioritizing of moral behavior over ownership in the definition of sacredness, in the conceptualization of what it means to occupy sacred space.

There is no question that each religious community deserves its own independent spaces of sacredness on these holy spots, such as the Temple Mount or the Cave of the Patriarchs and Matriarchs in Hebron.[4] Some spaces on the Temple Mount need to be exclusive. There can and should be ways in which all of those spaces, however, collectively come under the rubric of moral rules that all agree should govern sacred space. This would bind everyone together ethically and mythically even as it recognizes separate spaces.

How could we accomplish this feat? One way involves a return to that original home of sacralization in the monotheistic prophets, namely the moral pre-conditions governing the entrance to sacred ground.[5] In other words, all groups would, for example, participate in the aid to the poor, to those who suffer, as a part of the occupation of sacred ground. All would agree in that space to respectful and honorable modes of greeting and to moral/spiritual etiquette that has roots in all three Abrahamic traditions. All would agree to special treatment of animal and plant life in the sacred spaces, rules that all the religions have embedded, and that could be utilized as the basis of healing cooperation. All would have attitudes of respect for property of the other, and especially lost property, fundamental contractual and legal assumptions of Exodus, as well as the other Books of Moses.

There were specific ancient psalms specifically governing entry rights to the Temple Mount, which asked the rhetorical question, "Who is allowed to go up to the mountain of God?"[6] Honesty is one of the primary characteristics of such a person, and therefore agreed upon rules of honesty in speech and practice would also become a part of the sacralization of space in the Old City and especially the Temple Mount. There are also laws governing respectful speech, and, last but not least, the respectful treatment of elders.

Muslims have in their cultural repertoire the notion of *dar al-Islam* which, as I have just noted about sacred space, can be interpreted exclusively in terms of ownership and domination. Or it can be defined ethically in terms of agreed upon ethical practices, and agreed upon systems of respect for the religion. Similarly, the Jewish concept of *eretz ha-kodesh*, the Holy Land, can be interpreted exclusively, even racially, in terms of who will own what, and who is allowed to be there. This is the holiness of space defined, in both traditions, in terms of political domination and exclusive rights to the space.

There are many rules of interpersonal life that will never be agreed upon between the secular and religious communities of the Middle East. They cannot form the basis of a social contract. But there are many other rules that can be the basis of a social contract. These sacred rules of interpersonal engagement should have their counterparts in secular constructs and contracts that all would agree to abide by on sacred ground, with religious obligations having their counterpart in secular formulations of civil rights. One group would see job training and employment programs, for example, as a civil right and others as a social/spiritual obligation.

This contractual commitment to sacred space could form the basis for a multi-religious treaty and secular-religious treaty on the long-term hopes for and commitment toward the governing of the entire Holy Land region as sacred space. Now this would not satisfy those for whom its sacredness is only vouchsafed by exclusive ownership, nor those who want to go further in disallowing any behavior contrary to traditional Jewish law or Islamic Shari'ah, as they interpret these laws. In other words, it will not satisfy those with messianic anticipation of theocracy and absolute control. But it will go a very long way toward creating a new and integrated culture of the region that will do the one thing that rejectionist religious parties to the conflict need. It will acknowledge their claims as at least partially acceptable, it will give them the dignity of participation in the construction of public, civil society, and it could bring healing and strength to those who are caught in the middle of these cultural struggles.

This will also require a re-visioning among utopian visionaries in all camps for whom exclusive or coercive future visions take precedence over ethics. What I am suggesting involves a vision that will not appeal to everyone but will include enough religious people on all sides to sideline a violent monotheistic posture. It will offer an alternative vision of sacred space that does not require exclusive ownership to be religiously fulfilling.

The re-visioning of sacred space is only one challenge of the peacemaking process regarding land. The struggle for the same space *for living* is less symbolic but far more at the heart the conflict that has led to enormous injuries and losses on both sides. These losses suffered by struggle over land are complexified by imbalances and complications in the losses. Palestinians in the tens of thousands lost their actual homes. Jews were the clear victors over land. Jewish losses of home and family in Europe, with 90 percent of European Jewry annihilated, cannot be blamed on Palestinians. And yet those losses are part and parcel of the struggle. These unfair asymmetries are a feature of countless inter-ethnic wars around the world, where one party pays for the injustices done to another by yet a third party, such as Bosnian Muslims paying the price, as the most defenseless and stateless party, for the destructions wrought on Serbians by others.

Thousands of years of determined independence from Christians cost the Jewish people very dearly in the final paroxysm of European anti-Semitism. A key element of that independence was the dream of returning to the land of Israel in the Messianic Era. Those losses make the need for land acute in the minds of millions of Jews. There are losses and needs here on all sides. Sephardi Jewry has a different set of losses that are related in a complicated way to an Arab world that was good to them in some ways and awful in others, as well as to the indignities of a biased Ashkenazi superstructure to Zionism and the State. Every group's losses here are tied to idealization of, nostalgia for, or memory of land. None of these losses admit of easy ways to overcome necessary losses through compromise.

Actual loss of life at specific locations is one critical way to think about the use of land to heal the past rather than perpetually mourn over it. Museums and memorials are critical to a community's capacity to cope with its past. Mourning over lost life is very related to lost land because for many people the land and life on the land are inextricably related. But land is so contested in this conflict that each and every effort at memorialization will be the subject of controversy. Nevertheless it is better that it be pursued anyway. The controversy could be utilized for constructive purposes.

I want to suggest that we consider the following *if and when there is a respite from the current stage of violent war*. Burying the dead, memorializing the dead, and mourning are gestures that are inherent in Abrahamic traditions. I suggest that religious people, leaders or lay people, jointly experiment with ways to lead their communities into an extended period of memorial and mourning over, very simply, the loss of life due to violence in this century that was experienced by each religious community for whatever reason, but especially when it was at the hands of the other groups.

This must be done in a way that each community shares in the memorialization with the other communities. There need to be numerous spaces created to remember, to acknowledge, to mourn, and to commit to a different path.

How would this be done? Key places where Palestinians have died violently at the hands of Jews, for whatever reason and without judgment or blame, would become places of joint mourning, memorial, and future commitments. There would be places and rituals in which the religious/cultural underpinnings of repentance and apology, such as are expressed by the institutions of *sulh* and *teshuva*, could be put into practice. Key places where Jews have died at the hands of Palestinians, for whatever reason and in whatever circumstances, would likewise become places of joint mourning, memorial, and future commitments.

These key places could include: Mahane Yehuda market in Jerusalem, for example, Ben Yehuda street, Netanya, Ma'a lot, Deir Yassin, the corridor of the forced march from Ramallah, Hebron's burial place of the Patriarchs and Matriarchs, *meor'at ha-makhpelah*, as well as the site of the Hebron Yeshiva in 1929, major places of battle in the wars, Al-Aqsa Mosque, key checkpoints, locations in Gaza, and numerous other locations in which either Jews or Palestinians died violently.

This process would have to occur over an extended period of time, and it would have to have an extensive bilateral basis. In other words, memorialization would have to take place in close bilateral proximity wherever possible, both in terms of time and space. It would be best if memorials that were close geographically were joined by simultaneous or near simultaneous ceremonies. Cemeteries where the victims are buried would be an equally suitable space of ceremony. The emotions will run high in these places, and we should be very prepared as to how to manage this well, and make this part of healing not an impediment.

To the degree to which each community is capable of expressing remorse for at least some of its actions, apology or requests for forgiveness at these sites where death occurred would be a major contribution to the healing process and the shift in relationship. However, my experience and that of others has suggested that this not be *de jure* or expected, but rather come naturally for those communities or individuals who are ready to do this.

The rituals and/or statements or prayers that would be appropriate in these places would have to depend completely on the parties themselves and what they deem appropriate. Minimally, however, there would have to be expressions of regret, if not acceptance of responsibility, as well as a commitment to a different future.

It is clearly the case that this process will invite or provoke backlash in a number of forms for which anyone in this work must be prepared. First of all, the actual violation of this sacred space and time by rejectionists will become a critical need of theirs, a way of remaining true to the dead. Memorials are or become contested spaces, as Jewish memorials in Europe have become, and, therefore, subject to desecration. Jewish graves around the world are periodically subject to desecration, for the mere memorials dedicated to the Jewish dead become an affront to anti-Semites or to those who, for religious reasons, feel that Jews should simply not exist. The dead have a way of heightening our conceptualization of life, and that is why cemeteries are such beautiful but vulnerable places.

A constructive approach to conflict resolution utilizes all pain and provocation to further the process of reconciliation. One of the more insidious causes of conflict is the illusion of non-conflict, and the burial of crime. Memorials bring all of this into sharp relief, both symbolically and historically. The very backlash against these memorializations is a good reminder to those who would become complacent and fall into the illusion that the work of peace, justice, reparation, and repentance is over simply because there is no overt violence.

Clearly readers who are used to conflict resolution as rationally determined processes of negotiation will be deeply uncomfortable with these suggestions. But their methods of approaching the conflict at hand have completely failed. It is not that negotiations are not crucial. It is rather that they are inadequate in terms of bringing the people to the point of trust and acceptance of peaceful solutions and necessary negotiations.

To do this one has to concentrate on deep human needs. It is hard, for example, for an outsider to understand that for many religious Jews, who have been rejectionists of the peace process, all hatred of Jews at the hands of Romans, Crusaders, Nazis, and Palestinians blurs into one bad dream to which they answer with the power of military might. In the case of *haredim*, they respond with the power of a supernatural narrative of history in which the gentiles will be punished collectively for their sins against God's people. This means that forging a relationship with gentiles in some new fashion must mean addressing all the deepest injuries of this century, and then some. There is no way around this. The same is true of many other conflicts, no matter how irrational this appears to outsiders. And it requires great patience from enemies for the obsessions and narcissisms of each group.

To Jews the excesses of Islamic extremism sweeping the globe are indicators of an enemy who can only be destroyed with brute force. It is certainly the case that many extremists in history could only be resisted with force. But it is also the case that millions join extremist alternatives when they have nothing to lose, when they feel like committing suicide anyway. It is amazing how many reports I receive from the field confirm those sentiments, especially among the young. Can this be combated successfully only through force, without any acknowledgment of legitimate grievances? Can it be effectively combated only in Oslo or Camp David? Did all the Palestinians who supported the bombers believe that they could prove to Israelis that they are not Nazis but merely fighting for their rights by turning Jewish children into charcoal at bus stops? None of this is rational, and much of it is suicidal. And it is only by focusing with a laser on human emotions, and the needs they express, that one can deter and discourage human insanity. To be sure, both sides have successfully proven with violence that they are here to stay. And negotiators have proven that there are formulae that may very well work. But no one has faced up to the overwhelming power of human emotions, to the way in which religion can intensify those emotions in astonishing ways, and that any way out of the current hell must seek to direct those emotions toward life and away from death.

A central strategy of this redirection of emotions is the language and frame of reference of familiar religious and cultural values. Whereas humiliation is a fundamental element of this dynamic of enemies, the range of practices in Judaism and Islam designed to affirm the dignity of the other should be utilized as a symbolic means of communication, as a way of counteracting the effects of repeated Arab defeats and daily humiliations. In parallel fashion, the way in which land has come to be seen as the only means of protection of life, and the only way to justify the death of loved ones, can be countered by shared mourning practices of both communities. These can provide religiously significant ways to deal with death other than through further killing or valuing land so much that it prevents rational problem solving and the division of scarce resources.

None of this implies that there are not very legitimate fears, grievances, and injustices. But it does suggest that that deep emotional way in which we human beings deal with such things can sometimes become maladaptive and self-destructive. Religious traditions know this well and deal with it not by suppressing human emotions through rationalistic pretense but by giving them healthy outlets through ethics and symbolic gestures and rituals. The combination of these practices, guided by wise students of religious traditions, together with future negotiation processes will, at the very least, make it harder to hijack religion to destroy rational negotiations. At best religion may provide creative middle positions of trust building, evidence of transformation, and interim pro-social measures that will grease the wheels of rational diplomacy, in addition to giving religious communities the respect that they deserve and need as their communities make fateful decisions.

If there is ever to be a two-state solution, with two democracies living side by side, it will not be because there is an end to religious fervor or strong emotions of attachment to the land. That is the sad fantasy of liberals. It will be because enough people on both sides have learned how to negotiate their religious dreams and emotions in new ways. It will be because they have come to value democracy among themselves and among their enemies as a reliable means to further the religious valuation of human life, for example, or of justice. It will be because they will adjust themselves to an intense love of the whole land that combines uneasily but necessarily with the religious pursuit of justice, compassion, and the abhorrence of the cardinal sins of the Biblical and Koranic stories, murder and theft.

Liberals will negotiate new realities in their way, businesspeople in another, and military analysts in still other ways. All ways are necessary for a durable peace. But the encouragement by all interested leaderships of pro-social gestures and behaviors that resonate emotionally with religious traditions is the only way that a large portion of the voting constituencies on either side of this conflict will trust a transition to two states or the equality of all citizens in Israel. They will have to witness and participate in this grand enterprise. I can think of no better forecasting mechanism than this enterprise to determine whether future peace agreements are reality or fantasy.

31

CATHOLIC PEACEMAKING, 1991–2005
The Legacy of Pope John Paul II

—Drew Christiansen

If the fall of the Berlin wall in 1989 marked the end of the Cold War, already by 1991 it was clear the world had entered a new era in international affairs distinguished by ethnic and religious warfare, humanitarian intervention, and new demands on international organizations. But not only that. The year 1991 also marked the beginning of a period of novel departures in Vatican diplomacy, deepening and broadening prior trends in the Catholic Church's teaching on war and peace.

Of course, both before and after 1991 Pope John Paul II was busy making history in international affairs—tutoring the Solidarity labor movement, contributing to the liberation of his native Poland and the end of communism in Eastern Europe, precipitating the fall of dictators and colonial regimes in oppressed countries where he made pilgrimage, and utilizing interfaith prayer and dialogue as means to oppose outbreaks of religiously inspired violence and the notion of a "clash of civilizations."[1] But in 1991 Cardinal Agostino Casaroli, the executor during the Cold War of Vatican *Ostpolitik*, retired.[2] Vatican foreign policy then fell under the direction of the Frenchman Archbishop Jean-Louis Tauran, who infused Vatican diplomacy with a new creative style, working closely with lay groups, like the Community of Sant'Egidio, and with bishops' conferences, like the U.S. Conference of Catholic Bishops (USCCB), to augment the Vatican's efforts.[3] Sant'Egidio is best known for its mediation leading to the end of civil war in Mozambique (1991), but was active in other troubled areas as well, including Kosovo and Algeria. USCCB was active in various conflicts in the former Yugoslavia, Guatemala, Haiti, Israel and Palestine, and Northern Ireland, and in campaigns against anti-personnel landmines and for international debt relief, among others. On these issues the conference worked with national episcopal conferences, nuncios (ambassadors) of the Holy See, and directly with the Vatican dicasteries (ministries).[4]

For the Holy See this period was a time of innovation in social teaching on international issues, too, with Pope John Paul II offering new teaching on themes like nonviolence and forgiveness in international politics and elaborating on some older ones like

* *The Review of Faith & International Affairs* 4, no. 2 (Fall 2006): 21–28.

the priority of international law and the need for international institutions. The Church's teaching on war also evolved, promoting humanitarian intervention and opposing the use of the just war tradition to legitimate preventive war.[5]

In the wake of this dynamic period of change and the inauguration of a new papacy in 2005, the time is ripe to do some stock-taking and evaluation of Catholic approaches to peacemaking that were prominent in the period 1991–2005. I will propose that the three most significant aspects of official Catholic peacemaking in this period were: (1) the articulation of a positive Catholic conception of peace and the development of new teaching on conflict with an accent on nonviolence; (2) an increased emphasis on international law and international institutions; and (3) the use of interreligious dialogue to counter violence and religious conflict.

A "Convoy Concept" of Peace:
From Just War to Justice and Nonviolence

Beginning with Pope John XXIII's landmark encyclical *Pacem in Terris* (1963), official Catholic teaching on peace has grown into a complex web of moral threads defining the positive dimensions of peace as more than "the absence of war."[6] For John XXIII, the substance of peace was the promotion, safeguarding, and defense of human rights; for Pope Paul VI it was socio-economic development, as in the famous dictum "If you want peace, work for justice" (*Populorum progressio*, 1968); and for John Paul II it was solidarity, understood as "the unswerving and persevering commitment to the common good" (*Sollicitudo rei socialis*, 1988), including both human rights and development.[7] In 1991 John Paul added nonviolence to this list, while continuing to promote development as an alternative to war (*Centesimus annus*), and finally in 2002, he added the element of forgiveness (World Day of Peace Message, "No Peace without Justice, No Justice without Forgiveness").

There are so many dimensions of this positive conception of peace that some may regard it as confused. I have found it helpful to say that the Catholic conception of peace is a "convoy concept," that is, a series of somewhat disparate but related requirements, like a series of ships in a convoy.[8] The image is helpful in that it indicates how different themes are parts of the one concept of peace. To be sure, these themes are not mutually exclusive, and conceptual boundaries do blur. In the field of socio-economic rights, for example, development overlaps with human rights. Still, while these goods are at times articulated in shifting, imprecise ways, by 2002 Catholic social teaching arrived at a rich, comprehensive, holistic conception of peace.

At the time of World War II, existing Catholic teaching approved of the just war doctrine as the exclusive basis of conscientious action in wartime. Since then Catholic teaching on war has evolved into a more complex view embracing both nonviolence and just war, placing both in the framework of a wider teaching on peace. Vatican II praised the witness of nonviolent resisters.[9] During the Cold War, John Paul II tutored and practiced nonviolence in confronting Poland's communist governments and their Soviet overlords. He later said, in his 1991 encyclical *Centesimus annus*, that he believed the lessons he learned then applied to international order. "May people learn to fight for justice without violence," he wrote, "renouncing class struggle in their internal disputes, and war in international ones[10]. . . . Just as the time has finally come when in individual states a system of private vendetta and reprisal has given way to the rule of law, so too a similar step forward is now urgently needed in the international system."[11]

Some question the consistency of this more complex teaching, saying that these two streams of tradition, nonviolence and just war, are incompatible. But the root of both positions in Catholic thought is the obligation to resist grave injustice.[12] The obligation exists whether one employs nonviolent means or legitimately uses force. Thus, the Catholic understanding of peace necessarily entails a defense of justice, and rejects passivity in the face of grave public injustice. In addition, the avoidance of war entails not just the prevention of conflict but alleviation of the conditions that lead to conflict. In his critique of war, Pope John Paul added:

> [A]t the root of war there are usually real and serious grievances: injustices suffered, legitimate aspirations frustrated, poverty and the exploitation of desperate people who see no possibility of improving their lot by peaceful means.[13]

Accordingly, John Paul, like his predecessor Paul VI, called for "a concerted worldwide effort to promote development."[14]

In their 1983 pastoral letter "The Challenge of Peace" the U.S. bishops identified nonviolence as a legitimate part of the Christian tradition. The letter advanced the teaching by articulating a common presumption against the use of force in both nonviolent and just war traditions.[15] Although conservative just-war theorists still resist the presumption against the use of force, this letter both represented and advanced the growing complexity of church teaching. Ten years later in the 1993 statement "The Harvest of Justice Is Sown in Peace," this process of growing complexity solidified when the bishops declared that nonviolence is the basic Christian response to injustice and that the legitimate use of force is essentially an exception—a last resort employed only when repeated attempts at nonviolent correction of injustice fail. In contrast to "The Challenge of Peace," which had legitimated nonviolence as a personal calling, "Harvest" stipulated it as a *prima facie* public obligation of government officials and citizens.[16]

Similarly, in their response to the terrorist attacks of September 11, 2001, the U.S. bishops affirmed the government's duty to defend the nation against terrorism but nonetheless urged extensive use of non-military resources to address "the roots of terrorism." "Stopping terrorism," they admonished, "must be a priority, but foreign policy cannot be wholly subsumed under this campaign."[17] It is becoming ever clearer that the government's duty to defend the public against terrorism cannot be separated from a broader range of policy concerns. In the Catholic vision of peace, resistance to evil must be accompanied by active peacemaking, understood as the defense of human rights, the promotion of development, the advance of justice, the increase of solidarity, and the strengthening of world order.

Going hand in hand with this elevation of nonviolence in Catholic thought has been an increasing skepticism about the efficacy of war and the probability of it ever really meeting just war criteria. Unlike Saint Augustine, who considered waging war an unavoidable responsibility of political authorities and one of the "necessities," as he called them, of sinful existence, modern Catholic social teaching has increasingly regarded war as an avoidable matter of policy. For instance, in January 2003, two months before the U.S. invasion of Iraq, in his annual address to the diplomatic corps accredited to the Vatican,

Pope John Paul II made clear his opposition to so-called wars of choice. "War," he said, "is never another means that one can employ for settling differences between nations. . . . [W]ar cannot be decided upon . . . except as the very last option and in accordance with very strict conditions."[18] At the time of the 1991 Persian Gulf War, he also publicized his reservations about war as a tool of policy:

> No, never again war, which destroys the lives of innocent people, teaches how to kill, throws into upheaval the lives even of those who do the killing, and leaves behind a trail of resentment and hatred, thus making it all the more difficult to find a solution of the very problems which provoked the war.[19]

For John Paul, war is always morally suspect, especially because it does not deliver the peace it promises. He summarized his view by writing of war as "the violence, which under the illusion of fighting evil, only makes it worse."[20]

The U.S. bishops have similarly doubted the usefulness of war. In their 1993 statement "The Harvest of Justice Is Sown in Peace," they expressed their conviction that under contemporary cultural conditions, it would be nearly impossible to wage a just war:

> Moral reflection on the use of force calls for a spirit of moderation rare in contemporary society. The increasing violence of our society, its growing insensitivity to the sacredness of life, and the glorification of the technology of destruction in popular culture could inevitably impair our society's ability to apply just war criteria honestly and effectively in time of crisis.[21]

They concluded, "Ten years after 'The Challenge of Peace,' given the neglect of the peaceable virtues and the destructiveness of today's weaponry, serious questions still remain about whether modern war in all its savagery can meet the hard tests set by the just war tradition."[22]

Following the attacks on the World Trade Center and the Pentagon, the bishops wrote in "Living with Faith and Hope after September 11": "Because of its terrible consequences, military force, even when justified and carefully executed, must be undertaken with a deep sense of regret."[23] Just a month before the 2003 invasion of Iraq, the conference judged that the impending war seemed to them, in light of the available evidence, not to satisfy the conditions for a just war.[24]

Along with skepticism about the use of force in international affairs has gone a greater stringency in the application of just-war norms. "The Challenge of Peace" ruled out nuclear fighting, the first use of nuclear weapons, and nuclear retaliation to a nuclear attack. It also expressed great skepticism about the use of battlefield nuclear weapons. "The Harvest of Justice Is Sown in Peace" questioned strategies of "overwhelming and decisive force," as declared and practiced in the first Gulf War, and it warned, "Efforts to reduce the risk to a nation's own forces must be limited by judgments of military necessity so as not to neglect the rights of civilians."[25] It also called for applications of ethical restraints to air power, particularly avoiding the bombardment of civilian infrastructure, a significant problem in the Gulf War and again in the intervention in Kosovo in 1999. Before the war with Iraq, both the Holy See and the USCCB vigorously opposed the notion of "preventive war" offered by the Bush administration as a justification for its campaign. And in 2005 "The Compendium of the Social Teaching of the Church" declared that "engaging in a preventive war without clear proof that an attack is imminent cannot fail to raise serious moral and juridical questions."[26]

In my view, the capstone of this trend from a presumption of just war to a priority of nonviolence and peacebuilding is Pope John Paul II's 2002 World Day of Peace Message, a response to the events of September 11 that introduced "forgiveness" as a necessary component in alleviating conflict and securing the peace, thereby adding forgiveness to the Catholic Church's "convoy concept" of holistic peace. Indeed, throughout his ministry John Paul sought forgiveness for the historic sins of the Church, and in the Day of Pardon in 2000, he prayed for forgiveness of sins committed in the name of the Church during the previous millennium.[27] The World Day of Peace message in 2002 was a continuation of this pattern, as it contended that forgiveness is a necessary condition of a just society. Societies, in addition to individuals, he argued, "are absolutely in need of forgiveness."[28] The stability of post-conflict societies and the steadiness of renewed social relationships, the pope argued, depend on forgiveness.

In short, the approach to conflict in contemporary Catholic teaching and in the papal ministry has evolved into a doctrine of resistance to evil with a priority on nonviolent means—a doctrine that must be applied in the context of a wider vision of peace, including forgiveness between antagonists.

International Law and International Institutions

World order is an often-overlooked component of the Catholic conception of peace. In fact, the biblical and theological sources of the Church's preoccupation with world order were underscored by "The Compendium of the Social Doctrine of the Church" (2005).[29] In addition, in "The Pastoral Constitution on the Church in the Modern World" the Second Vatican Council explained that the Church's promotion of world order stems from its belief in the fundamental unity of the human family and humanity's consequent communitarian vocation.[30] The Council defined the Church itself as a "sacrament or sign of intimate union with God and of the unity of all mankind" and declared that the promotion of unity is a primary service that the Church offers to the world.[31]

Over the last fifteen years, the exigencies of ethno-religious conflict, the legitimation of humanitarian intervention, the attenuation of sovereignty, and the advance of globalization and American unilateralism in the war on terror have all contributed to the Holy See's heightened insistence on international law and the strengthening of the United Nations. The most comprehensive statement on this matter was the 2004 World Day of Peace Message, "An Ever Timely Commitment: Teaching Peace," which devoted three sections (5–7) to international law and the international order. In this message Pope John Paul II criticized the assertive unilateralism widely associated with U.S. policy and he insisted that international law is a foundation of civilized life and that neglecting to keep agreements creates conflict. He wrote:

> The violation of this principle [the bindingness of international law] necessarily leads to a situation of illegality and consequently to friction and disputes which would not fail to have lasting negative repercussions. It is appropriate to recall this fundamental rule, especially at times when there is a temptation to appeal to the *law of force* rather than to the *force of law*.[32]

Pope John Paul noted that the breakdown of international legality led to the Second World War. Implicit is a warning that disregard of international law today, and particularly evasion of the provisions for collective security in Chapter VII of the United Nations' Charter, will lead to a new period of global violence. In that spirit, the pope supported renewal of the United Nations Organization, with the help of nongovernmental organizations and civic movements, to meet the demand for "a greater degree of international ordering."[33]

Religion, Violence, and Interreligious Dialogue

The third notable area of Catholic peacemaking in recent years is interreligious dialogue about religious violence. John Paul II led the way in inviting leaders of the world religions to denounce violence perpetrated in the name of religion.[34] As he declared to the diplomatic corps in 2003, "Killing in the name of God is an act of blasphemy and a perversion of religion."[35] The days of prayer for peace called by John Paul in Assisi in 1986, 1993, and 2002, and especially the latter two, were clear efforts to reject the accusation that religion is a source of violence; to build momentum among religious leaders for peacemaking; to contribute to the restoration of peace in the former Yugoslavia; and to respond to September 11 and the war on terror.[36] While these efforts, especially the interfaith meetings at Assisi, seem to have come into question under Pope Benedict XVI, there is no doubt that they are one of the most significant achievements of Pope John Paul II's papacy.

One country rent by conflict that received sustained, personal attention from John Paul was Lebanon.[37] Formed after World War II as a haven for Maronite Christians, Lebanon was an oasis of interreligious co-existence in the Middle East. But in 1970 the PLO took refuge there after its defeat in Jordan in the fighting of "Black December." The Palestinians became a state within a state, drawing with them Lebanon's Muslim population. In 1975 civil war broke out along sectarian lines and lasted fifteen years. Five years after the Taif agreements in 1989, which brought a cessation to hostilities, there was only an uneasy peace. John Paul hoped to secure religious comity and peace in the region, promote dialogue between Christians and Muslims, and strengthen religious freedom.[38]

In 1995, in anticipation of the synods that would prepare for the year 2000 Jubilee, John Paul summoned the Synod of Bishops in a Special Assembly for Lebanon, inviting observers from the Orthodox and Muslim communities. In May 1997, the pope himself visited Lebanon to deliver the apostolic exhortation, "New Hope for Lebanon," officially closing the synod.[39] John Paul turned his back on confessionalism, the basis of pre–Civil War political accommodation in Lebanon. He urged all parties to unite in claiming their citizenship of the one Lebanese state and in supporting democratic government. He strongly encouraged interreligious dialogue as a condition of peace and voiced his hope for "conviviality" among Lebanese as a model of interreligious harmony for the Middle East and the world. In the years following the pope's visit, Catholics coalesced politically with Sunni and Druze Muslims in the hope of preserving a secular, non-confessional Lebanese state. But the rise of Hezbollah, the growth of the Shi'ites as the largest Muslim group, and political interference from Syria impeded the achievement of Pope John Paul's vision of interreligious harmony.

Finally, the war on terror and especially the U.S. war in Iraq increased the need for interreligious dialogue, especially with Muslims.[40] In this context, a colloquium on the spiritual resources for peace, sponsored by the Pontifical Council for Inter-religious

Dialogue in 2003, identified interreligious dialogue itself as a tool for peacemaking. It also offered this summary understanding of the requirements of peacemaking:

> Opting for peace does not mean a passive acquiescence in evil or a compromising of principle. It demands an active struggle against hatred, oppression, and disunity, but not by using methods of violence. Building peace requires creative and courageous action. A commitment to peace is a labor of patience and perseverance. It involves as well a readiness to examine self-critically the relationship of our traditions to those social, economic, and political structures which are frequently agents of violence and injustice.[41]

Let this stand, too, as a summary of the direction of Catholic peacemaking in the last decade and a half, and particularly of the contribution of the late Pope John Paul II.

32

THE POTENTIAL FOR PEACEBUILDING IN ISLAM
Toward an Islamic Concept of Peace

—Hisham Soliman

In general, Islam has been at the center of socio-political debates following the tragic attacks of September 11, 2001. A flurry of research, mostly by non-Muslims, has been conducted since then to explore Islam and whether a call for violence is central to this faith. Some Muslim scholars have exerted parallel efforts as well. Most of the latter, however, were primarily apologetic in tone, adopting a defensive posture to counter the perceived attack on their religious identity in the wake of these events. As a result, most research has focused on studying the relationship between Islam and violence, which leaves the relationship between Islam and peace largely unexplored.[1] Confining the discussion to the relationship between Islam and violence legitimizes, rather than questions, the relationship. Broadening the horizon to include the relationship between Islam and peace is critical, as it has the advantage of shifting the debate on Islam into a dialogue between partners and equals rather than an interrogation in which Muslims feel compelled to defend their faith. This paper highlights the fact, usually overlooked by most of the literature, that Islam can be employed as a resource to build peace.[2] Highlighting the peaceful insights of Islam may both improve conditions in Muslim communities over the long term and provide them with a discourse while engaging in a dialogue with the other.

Uncovering the links between Islam and peace is not only important to redrawing the distorted image of Islam in the West, but also in helping peace studies grow as a discipline, a discipline that has been colored mostly by modern Western ideas.[3] As a field that is not confined in scope to a particular segment of humanity, it is important to diversify the resources of peace studies to cope with the diversity of the target population. With Muslims constituting more than one sixth of the world population and facing many challenges, it would be highly beneficial for scholars and practitioners in the field to become better equipped to deal with the problems Muslims face and to propose creative solutions grounded on Islamic values.

Journal of Religion, Conflict, and Peace 2, no. 2 (Spring 2009), http://www.religionconflictpeace.org/node/54.

Islam and Peace

The relationship between religion and peace in general is quite controversial. Some scholars, such as Asghar Ali Engineer, argue that Islam as a religion is all peace and does not allow for violence. On a wider scale, Engineer generally rejects drawing any integral relationship between any religion, including Islam, and violence. Rather, he sees violence as a social phenomenon that takes place as a result of certain negative conditions in specific societies where religion may be manipulated as a result.[4] More generally, other scholars, such as Scott Appleby, argue that although violence may not be integral to religion, religion retains a capacity for violence. This capacity, according to Appleby, results from the ambivalent nature of most of the sacred texts, which, as a result, allows for manipulating their interpretations in a way that can be used to legitimize violence.[5] What a religion teaches can, therefore, be different from how its followers hold it to be in practice, due to the influence of "self-justifying groups" such as religious or political institutions or cultural traits.[6] As a result, one cannot easily label a specific religion as either violence-prone or as a catalyst for peace. Rather, most religious interpretations have a capacity for both violence and peace. Against this backdrop, and against the vast literature developed on the relationship between Islam and violence, this paper argues for the necessity of uncovering an Islamic concept of peace, following the guidance that "the text . . . morally enrich[es] the reader, but only if the reader will morally enrich the text."[7]

To start with, linguistically, both *Islam* and *Salam/Silm* ("peace") are derived from the same root in Arabic, *s–l–m* (م ل س). Two words that share the same root in the Arabic language also share a relationship in meaning, that is, they carry the same meaning in essence while referring to different things at face value.[8] *Salam* was used in the Qur'an[9] basically to refer to: one of the attributes of *Allah*, or "God" in Arabic, the same as the God of Abraham, Moses, and Jesus;[10] staying away from the use of violence; and greeting people, as well as agreement among people. In the hadiths, *salam* carries some additional meanings, such as security from violence and corruption.[11]

The meaning of Islam then becomes "the peace of spirit that comes from submitting one's life to the will of God."

> But your god is One God: submit then your wills to Him (in Islam): and give thou the good news to those who humble themselves. To those whose hearts when Allah is mentioned, are filled with fear, who show patient perseverance over their afflictions, keep up regular prayer, and spend (in charity) out of what We (Allah) have bestowed upon them. (22:34-35)[12]

Consequently, "[after] adding the prefix MU to the root SLM," the meaning of the term Muslim becomes ". . . the one who has found peace of spirit in submitting his life to the will of God."[13]

Thus, the message of Islam is said to be one of peace for all humanity, as in Ayah 2:208, which says, "O ye who believe! Enter into Silm whole-heartedly," where *silm* was used to refer to Islam. That is why Engineer argues that this is an explicit invitation in sacred scripture for adopting peace as the path of believers.[14] This comes into line with the belief that humans were created originally in a state of harmony and peace.[15] Peace will also be the state of true believers in their final destination in the hereafter, *Dar-Al-Salam* ("House of Peace," referring to paradise).[16]

But Allah doth call to the Home of Peace: He doth guide whom He pleaseth to a way that is straight. (10:25)

The message of Islam, seen as a universal one, targets all human beings as *khalifat-o-Allah* or vicegerents of Allah on this earth, to worship Him and to prosper the earth and establish coexistent communities (*isti'maar*).[17] Consequently, the origins of Islam can be traced back to the existence of the first of human being, Adam, who was the first to submit and pray to Allah. In the same context, Islam is seen as a continuation of the preceding divine messages, notably those that came with Moses and Jesus.[18]

The same religion has He established for you as that which He enjoined on Noah—that which We have sent by inspiration to thee—and that which We enjoined on Abraham, Moses, and Jesus. (42:13)

Accordingly, Islam adopts a plural understanding of who is a believer. By presenting itself as a continuation of the previous Holy messages revealed through the apostles of Allah to humans, Islam incorporates them as part of the belief and faith:[19] "Then sent We our messengers in succession" (23:44).

Those who deny Allah and His messengers, and (those who) wish to separate Allah from His messengers, saying: "We believe in some but reject others": And (those who) wish to take a course midway, They are in truth (equally) unbelievers. (4:150–51)

That is, according to the teachings of Islam, Allah revealed His message to people on earth in stages, each building upon the previous one, with Islam the final one. And given that the Qur'an acknowledges that it does not present an exhaustive survey of all messengers who preceded the prophet Mohamed, anyone who claims himself to be a believer in Allah (God) and who does good and refrains from doing evil is perceived as part of the community of believers.

We did aforetime send messengers before thee: of them there are some whose story We have related to thee, and some whose story We have not related to thee. It was not (possible) for any messenger to bring a sign except by the leave of Allah: but when the Command of Allah issued, the matter was decided in truth and justice, and there perished, there and then those who stood on Falsehoods. (40:78)

And,

[Any] who believe in Allah and the Last Day, and work righteousness, shall have their reward with their Lord; on them shall be no fear, nor shall they grieve. (2:62)

No one is entitled to question the *Iman* (the authenticity of faith) of the followers of other faiths but Allah on the Day of Judgment.[20]

If Allah had so willed, He would have made you a single people, but (His plan is) to test you in what He hath given you: so strive as in a race in all virtues. (5:48)

This, according to Muslim thinker Jawdat Saeed, creates a foundation for togetherness and oneness in fate among all humans regardless of their religious affiliation, rather than sectarianism and ethno-centrism.[21] In other words, the universal message of Islam implies that there should be equal concern and care for the whole universe and not a sectarian approach to peace and justice that pays attention to the interests of a particular group only.

What follows will uncover some of the components of an Islamic concept of peace. The discussion will start by tackling the controversial meaning of the concept of jihad and how it relates to peace. A related topic is the Islamic understanding of nonviolence. Though these terms are seen as mutually exclusive, "nonviolence" has much resonance in both the teachings of Islam and the practices of some Muslims. The notions of justice and compassion and their relationship—or what is currently known as restorative justice—will then be presented as a primary component of this concept. My argument in this respect is that Islam, by integrating compassion (*rahma* or "forgiveness")[22] into the framework of its mechanisms of justice, creates a wide space for peace and reconciliation in the community. Principles for humanitarian work and the duty to work for peace will be highlighted as well, representing the motivation for concrete action for peace in Islam.

Jihad: A Tradition of Peace in Islam

Most religious traditions define peace in modern literature as "positive peace" (i.e., the presence of harmonious social relationships) or "negative peace" (i.e., the mere absence of war). Starting with the latter, Islam draws limits on the unjustified use of force in an endeavor to create societies where violence is absent under the normal conditions. On the other hand, the concept of positive peace in Islam comes through the configuration of a just society, which is ordered so that peace eventually prevails.[23] These two understandings of negative and positive peace, with greater value placed on the second, are always present in the teachings of the Qur'an and the hadiths of the prophet. It is the assignment of true believers to search for justice peacefully through jihad, the Arabic word for "struggle."[24]

There are many verses in the Qur'an that prefer peace to war and forgiveness to hatred.[25] This is evidenced by the fact that only some 60 verses out of 6,246 verses in the Qur'an deal with the rules of war and militarized jihad, while the rest deal with faith and moral issues.[26] However, the state of underdevelopment in which most of the Muslim world lives, following an extended period of oppressive colonialism, produced both ignorance and totalitarianism, which create the ideal setting for the rise of violence, violence that hijacked the Islamic concept of jihad.[27] "Military jihad" then became the label of jihad in Islam.[28]

One of the foundations of jihad in Islam is the hadith that says, "Jihad is the peak of Islam,"[29] which is usually misinterpreted as a call for violence in Islam. In fact, the aim of the hadith is to signify the importance of the spiritual struggle to establish justice and to build peace on this earth as a message of Islam. Al-Farabi (874–950), a renowned Muslim philosopher, maintained a clear distinction between "war" and "jihad" in his writings. War is only one form of jihad, which refers to military action. The true essence of jihad for al-Farabi is the internal struggle within one's soul between the forces of reason, on the one hand, and one's desires on the other, with the aim of the first to control or moderate the second so that virtue may prevail.[30] In other words, it can be said that there are two general forms of jihad: the "greater jihad," which is the inward effort to confront our lower nature; and the "lesser jihad," which has to do with the outward effort to fight injustices using military means.[31] It becomes important, however, for those who decide to engage themselves in the lesser jihad to first win the greater jihad themselves.[32] This is because peace with the inner self gained through the greater jihad would reflect itself externally in peace with other human beings and other creatures on this earth (ecological peace).[33] Hence, it can be argued that spiritual jihad is the basic form of jihad,[34] making "jihad . . . mercy, not a sword; and justice, not violence."[35]

More important is that the jihad for justice is grounded on the moral concept of responsibility to Allah. That is, before undertaking any action, each and every human being should pay attention to whether or not he or she is compliant with the orders of Allah.[36] It is reported that the prophet was once asked, "What is the best of Islam? He replied: jihad. And what is the best jihad? He replied: the *hijrah* (migration). Then he was asked what is the best hijra? He said from evil to good, or hijra to Allah, which is a life-long struggle."[37] Thus, if peace is the core message of Islam, and spiritual jihad is the way Muslims profess their faith, jihad then becomes the way Muslims work for peace. There-fore, jihad can be generally used to refer to peacemaking, and the Mujahid, the one who undertakes the mission of jihad, is a peacemaker.[38]

Greater jihad can take one of at least three forms. One is *jihad an-nafs* (spiritual jihad), which is an internal struggle against the lower nature of the human soul so as to do good and avoid evil. Another is word jihad, which is through the giving of *nasi'ha* (advice) and preaching against evil and injustice to all members of the community. It was reported that the Prophet recommended this form when the *nasi'ha* is directed to a tyrant ruler to urge him or her to stop injustices. A third form of jihad is the non-forceful jihad, nonviolent collective action geared toward fixing social problems, which will be investigated in more detail below.[39] Other forms include the struggle to learn, gain, and disseminate knowl-edge,[40] as well as to respect the structure of the family and to take care of the elders.[41] In fact, Islam has an intrinsic call for learning, evidenced by the fact that the first ayah revealed from the Qur'an was, "Proclaim! [or read!] in the name of thy Lord and Cher-isher, Who created" (96:1).

This does not neglect that the search for a just social order occasionally involves the use of military force for either its realization or its sustenance, defined here as the lesser jihad (*jihad al-qital*): "To those against whom war is made, permission is given (to fight), because they are wronged; and verily, Allah is most powerful for their aid" (22:39). This last type, erroneously depicted in Western media and most academic discourse as "holy war," is considered a "hated necessity."[42] It is a necessity in order to bring a state of injus-tice, such as oppression or prohibition from the practice of religion, to an end:

> Fighting (*qital*) is prescribed for you, and ye dislike it. But it is possible that ye dislike a thing which is good for you, and that ye love a thing which is bad for you. But Allah knoweth, and ye know not. (2:216)

Nevertheless, it is hated because it results in destruction of human lives, which are all equally sacred to Allah, the "Creator." This leaves no room for anyone to transgress against any of his or her fellow creatures, including not only human beings but also the ecology as well.[43] This is because human life is sacred, as are the resources that support it.[44] Destruc-tion or corruption (*fasad*) of the earth and its resources is seen as the worst of evils; rather, their development should be pursued in a just, compassionate manner.[45] That is why war is not permissible for its own sake, that is, to transgress or to terrorize:[46] "Fight in the cause of Allah those who fight you, but do not transgress limits; for Allah loveth not transgressors" (2:190).

The use of force in these cases can be justified only if: 1) the aim is a just cause; 2) no other means but war is available; 3) the war is conducted under the legitimate authority in the society (these constitute what is technically known as *jus ad bellum*, the justification for the war); and 4) the war is governed by the values of Islam (these constitute what is technically known as *jus in bello*, conduct during the war). This last criterion requires minimal use of force, prohibition of non-discriminatory killing, and maintaining the sanctity of the lives of non-warriors.[47] Given the increasing lethality of modern weapon systems, military jihad becomes more and more restricted. In addition, *jus in bello* does not allow fights against those who either have a peace treaty or are in the process of negotiating one with Muslims.[48] Thus, even when a war has to be waged, the rules that govern it minimize its destructive effects. The Qur'an, henceforth, orders the resort to peace once proposed by the other side:[49] "But if the enemy inclines towards peace, do thou (also) incline towards peace, and trust in Allah: for He is One that heareth and knoweth (all things)" (8:61).

In addition, there is a call in Islam to use the principle of deterrence, which guides Muslims to stay away from war. In the ayah cited below, it is one of the duties of the Muslim *umma* (community) to be always at the ready to deter its neighbors from transgression. And since Muslims are prohibited to transgress, the negative meaning of peace (the absence of war) therefore materializes.

> Against them make ready your strength to the utmost of your power, including steeds of war, to strike terror into (the hearts of) the enemies, of Allah and your enemies, and others besides, whom ye may not know, but whom Allah doth know. Whatever ye shall spend in the cause of Allah, shall be repaid unto you, and ye shall not be treated unjustly. (8:60)

In other words, peace is always displayed as the recommended state of life in the Qur'an, and its absence is portrayed negatively, except in the few cases qital is allowed as a temporary condition.[50] Since war is one way through which *fasad* (environmental destruction) takes place, it cannot be asserted as the way of true believers.[51] And those who transgress or initiate war in a way that contradicts the teachings mentioned above are sinful in Islam and are punished by the authorities for committing the crime of *hiraba* (equivalent to terrorism).[52] This is another way in which the emphasis is placed upon limiting the use of *jihad-al-qital*. As a strict exception, it does not become the norm.[53] The norm should be a never ending spiritual struggle, both within the self and with other creatures in the universe. Consequently, the principles mentioned hereafter can be considered as forms of the greater jihad for the cause of peace and justice in Islam.

Roots and Practices of Nonviolence in Islam

Generally speaking, opponents of nonviolence reject it as a form of passivity. This, however, is untrue, because nonviolence is a positive action using force that is not military in nature.[54] Nonviolence is very effective in terms of its capacity to coerce a challenged group by noncooperation and protest in a disciplined manner, complicating the functions of the group's normal systems.[55] In addition, nonviolence, compared to using armed force, reflects participation and inclusivity. Instead of a small part of the community working on behalf of all, the entire community collectively makes decisions within a framework of a nonviolent movement.[56] In Islam, as explained earlier, considering that the ultimate goal of the existence of humans on earth is to prosper through the creation of communities that interact peacefully, the way for accomplishing this is primarily through nonviolence. Once communities engage in violence, they will end up destroying the earth, themselves included, which contradicts the message of Islam.[57]

As a religion, Islam can be used to empower people for nonviolent action as part of its wide definition of jihad. These can be found in the moral-ethical and spiritual attitudes Islam requires its followers to abide by, among which are courage, discipline, and unity of purpose—all seen as fundamental to the success of a nonviolent action.[58] Some scholars, such as Chaiwat Satha-Anand, interpreted the five pillars of Islam[59] in terms of nonviolence. Witness to God (*Shahada*) is an implied expression of noncompliance to any power that contradicts the teaching of Islam and the rules of Islamic Law, creating room for civil disobedience. Prayers (*salat*) and pilgrimage (*hajj*) are performed in congregations. They are a portrait for equality among human beings. They also create a mental image of people gathering in the same place, which facilitates the mobilization of their collective power, crucial for nonviolence.[60] Given that the performance of these rituals is seen as a form of jihad to Allah, they imply discipline and commitment.[61]

Another foundation for nonviolence in Islam is proposed by Jawdat Saeed who sees in the story of Cain murdering Abel out of jealousy and hatred a great example on the necessity to use nonviolence. Saeed argues that the Qur'an showed in this story that there are two paths humans can pursue during their lives on this earth—the violent one represented by Cain the killer, and the nonviolent one symbolized by Abel the victim. With the Qur'an criminalizing the violent path, it becomes obvious that the path of the faithful should be that of nonviolence.[62]

An interesting application of nonviolence can be found in the notion of *hijrah*, the physical migration or withdrawal from the lands where there are injustices to other places where people can enjoy their freedoms.

> When angels take the souls of those who die in sin against their souls, they say: "In what (plight) were ye?" They reply: "Weak and oppressed were we in the earth." They say: "Was not the earth of Allah spacious enough for you to move yourselves away (From evil)?" Such men will find their abode in Hell, What an evil refuge! He who forsakes his home in the cause of Allah, finds in the earth many a refuge, wide and spacious." (4:97; 100)

The migrants are rewarded for doing this. "To those who leave their homes in the cause of Allah, after suffering oppression, We will assuredly give a goodly home in this world; but truly the reward of the Hereafter will be greater. If they only realized (this)" (16:41).

Two prominent incidents of hijrah took place in the early days of Islam. In the first, some Muslims migrated to Abyssinia from Mecca in the seventh century where they found safe refuge with the Christian King, Najashi, in 615 C.E. In the second, the prophet and most of the early Muslims migrated from Mecca to Medina[63] in 622 C.E. after enduring a decade of atrocious treatment by the Pagans of Mecca.[64] Hence, instead of repaying violence for violence, early Muslims managed to find other ways to remain true to their faith even if this led to migration, which sets the example for contemporary Muslims as well.

A more recent experience of nonviolence by Muslims can be found in the distinguished example of the Khuda-I Khidmatgar Movement (1929–1949) founded by the

Pashtun leader Khan Abdul Ghaffar Khan (1890–1988). The movement's main goal was raising awareness among community members of the necessity of renouncing violence. Incidents of violence, mutual retaliation, and extermination of possible competing leaders prevailed in the cruel mountainous frontier community. The British Army, controlling this then-Indian community, formed troops entirely of Pashtuns, known for their fierce valor in battle. But Khan's movement aimed at educating people in the effectiveness of nonviolent strikes and sit-ins in the battle against the oppressive local rulers who connived with the foreign colonizer.[65]

The movement had nearly 100,000 members. Each one was tested to determine the strength of his or her belief in the movement's principle of nonviolence and resolve not to resort to violence under any circumstances. Members, men and women equally, used to spend two hours each day to serve their communities. Khan believed nonviolence is supported by patience, calling it the weapon of the Prophet, strong enough that no police or army can stand against it. His focus on the centrality of the values of tolerance, amnesty, sacredness of human life and dignity in the teachings of the Prophet manifested his vision for confronting the outbreak of violence in his community, which he saw as the result of ignorance. He believed that jihad should be against those who carry the swords.[66] Notably, Khan managed to convince many community members of the necessity to change their current situation, which intensified his movement's impact on reshaping social relationships.[67]

Notions of Compassion and Forgiveness in Justice in Islam

The relationship between justice and peace in Islam is foundational. Engineer sees justice as the essence of peace in Islam. Peace in Islam is achieved through limiting the greed of people that motivates them to transgress the rights of their fellow human beings.[68] Rashied Omar highlights the understanding of justice in Islam, pointing to a justice-compassion typology in which both are viewed as ways to alleviate human suffering and build peace. In order for peace, then, to materialize, there should be a balance of both values, if not a dominance of compassion over justice.[69] This justice-compassion relationship manifests itself again in terms of the principle of *ist'imar* mentioned above. To keep humans committed to the goal of prospering on earth, they are held accountable for their actions (albeit in a just, merciful, manner)—particularly for acts of transgression on the rights of others.[70] Humans are presumably struggling all the time to do what is right and avoid what is wrong. Justice should not, therefore, be applied crudely to them for the sake of retribution. Instead, they should be encouraged to learn from their mistakes, which cannot be done except through a framework of compassion.[71] That is evidenced by the fact that only thirty ayahs in the Qur'an, out of more than 6,000, deal with crimes and punishment.[72]

In other words, this framework of compassion and justice finds its roots in the concept of *maslahat-al-umma*, or the collective interest of the community. It is in the interest of the community and all its members to reintegrate the transgressors and wrongdoers through forgiveness; it is in everyone's interest to restore or maintain the smooth interaction between victim and offender. Offenders should not be isolated or alienated from the community, as this would hurt both them and the community in the long run.[73] This understanding of the role of compassion and forgiveness in justice in Islam resembles that of restorative justice in the modern Western discourse, which aims to repair broken social relationships between offenders, victims, and their communities in order to establish "lasting peace through integration instead of lasting hurt."[74] This is evidenced by the fact that one of the words for justice in Arabic, *qist*, connotes "right relationship." That is, when injustices take place, fixing them means restoring right relationships.[75]

Restorative justice is usually seen as a counterpart of, and for some complementary to, retributive justice. Under retributive justice, punishment by the governing authorities is applied for the wrongdoing committed by a member of the community commensurate to the damage he or she caused to the social order through predetermined rules. In most cases, victims' voices are not listened to during the process, which also does not pay close attention to the social context of the crime. The offender and the victim are usually set apart as having no direct relationship in the justice process, which results in the alienation of the offender.[76] Instead of formulating crime as "breaking the law," it is defined within the restorative justice approach as "harm inflicted on the community and some of its members," negatively affecting their relationships. Humans, in their capacity as community members, become the focus of and actors in the justice process. Repairing the damaged relationships and restoring individuals is the desired outcome. Offenders are made to realize the offense committed against the victim and are encouraged to take accountability for it so as to repair the harm instead of merely accepting punishment for the crime. And it is in repairing this relationship that the community at large will benefit.[77] Victims are also heard when they have the opportunity to explain how they were harmed. In addition, restorative justice, through placing the crime in a social context, helps prevent its recurrence in the future by addressing its social roots, which becomes the responsibility of the society at large.[78]

That said, there is no parallel debate on retributive and restorative justice in Islamic discourse, except for one that took place between the Mu'tazili school of thought[79] and the mainstream legal (*fiqhi*) discourse in Islam. The Mu'tazilites were very legalistic in their perspective on justice, based on a literal interpretation of the ayah that says, "Then shall anyone who has done an atom's weight of good, see it! And anyone who has done an atom's weight of evil, shall see it" (99:7-8). That is why they argued that justice in Islam is retributive rather than restorative. Human beings are rational and are, thus, either rewarded for their good deeds or punished for their wrong doings with no place for forgiveness, as each and every individual is responsible for his or her own rational behavior.[80] In opposition, a famous religious scholar, Ibn Taymiyya (1263–1328), criticized this perspective and argued that in addition to retribution, compassion occupies a prominent place in the justice process. Consequently, it is important while believing that Allah is *Al-'Adil* (Just), judging and giving each of us our due, Allah is also *Al-Rahman* (Merciful).[81] Ibn Taymiyya supported his argument with some of the sayings of Prophet Muhammad (570–632), such as: "*Al Rahimoon* (Compassionates) receive mercy from Al-Rahman, show mercy to those on earth, you will receive mercy from Heaven" (i.e., from Allah). The prophet also confirmed the same meaning in a negative way when he said: "Those who do not show mercy will not receive it."

The ability to forgive is one way in which compassion, and therefore restoration, manifests itself in the Islamic mechanism of justice. The Qur'an records that one of the basic instructions to Muhammad is, "Hold to forgiveness; command what is right" (7:199), making forgiveness the core of the message of his prophethood. It is true that people can ask for punishment for those who offend them and there is no blame for them in a retributive manner; however, it is also stated that the highest reward goes to those who, even when they are justifiably angry, can forgive, as forgiveness yields a reward from Allah.

> Those who avoid the greater crimes and shameful deeds, and, when they are angry even then forgive." (42:37)

> If a person forgives and makes reconciliation, his reward is due from Allah. (42:40)

Most importantly in this context is that forgiveness is seen as an act of courageous will: "But indeed if any show patience and forgive, that would truly be an exercise of courageous will and resolution in the conduct of affairs" (42:43).

This has important implications for allowing forgiving people to think of what they do not as cowardice but as confirmation of their strength as human beings. It is vital that forgiveness is seen and felt as an empowering act. Islam, thus, has this characteristic of keeping the final decision to forgive or to avenge in the hands of the victim while encouraging the victim at the same time to keep the wider interest of the community in mind and not to be solely self-centered. This is because the infringements of the rights of people (*huquq an-nas*) cannot be forgiven except by the victims themselves, neither by Allah nor by the *qadi* (judge).[82] Emphasizing the involvement of the actor in the process, the institution of arbitration cannot act on behalf of the victims on its own. It, rather, plays its role in transforming retributive aspects of justice into restorative ones by stressing the importance of forgiveness and reminding the victims of alternatives available to them and then letting them decide.[83]

Tools for Humanitarian Work in Islam

This is another domain where jihad for peace and helping the poor and the needy manifests itself. Islam is generally believed to be a call for action inspired by its beliefs and the consideration that humans are social beings; Islam is, in other words, more than a mere practice of rituals.[84] The principle of "doing good and preventing evil" is thought of as the sixth pillar of Islam, due to the huge emphasis it got in the teachings of the prophet. It is important as well to convey that Islam is not just about negative action by staying away from evil; equally important is the undertaking of some positive action to do good and prohibit evil.[85] There are even penalties for those who do not undertake activities to help those at the bottom of the social pyramid, as in the hadith that says, "If a person dies of hunger in a community, then all the residents of that community have put themselves outside Allah's and the Prophet's protection."[86] Consequently it is a duty upon each and every Muslim to provide assistance, which is not confined to financial help, to those who need it.

In fact, one of the principles that inspire humanitarian work is also one of the pillars of the faith, *Zakat* (alms). It is held as mandatory on each and every capable Muslim to provide a certain portion of his or her net wealth every year to the poor and the needy.[87]

> It is righteousness to believe in Allah and the Last Day, and the Angels, and the Book, and the Messengers; to spend of your substance, out of love for Him, for your kin, for orphans, for the needy, for the wayfarer, for those who ask, and for the ransom of slaves;

to be steadfast in prayer, and practice regular charity; . . . Such are the people of truth, the Allah-fearing. (2:177)

And in their wealth and possessions (was remembered) the right of the (needy). (51:19)

Zakat is, thus, not just an act of good will on the part of the wealthy and the well off; but it becomes a social right of the poor in this wealth. It redistributes wealth in the community so as to decrease societal tensions that result from income gaps.[88]

Alms are for the poor and the needy, and those employed to administer the (funds); for those whose hearts have been (recently) reconciled (to Truth); for those in bondage and in debt; in the cause of Allah; and for the wayfarer. (9:60)

In this sense, Zakat aims at creating some sort of social justice and welfare system as well as helping people overcome their attachment to the pleasures of life.[89]

There is another basis, however voluntary, for acting in the social domain for the cause of Allah—*sadaqah* or "charity." The Arabic root of the word, *s-d-q* (ق د ص), refers to proving one's faith in a manner that not only has to do with one's relationship to Allah, but also one's relationship to people. In other words, doing the *sadaqah*, beyond the mandatory alms, is recommended and encompasses every good action a Muslim undertakes to help his community.[90] *Sadaqah*, here known as *kaffara*, is also recommended as one way in which Muslims can wipe out their pitfalls (*syie'at*) and to seek Allah's forgiveness. In this regard, the prophet was reported to have said, "Alms (referring to *sadaqah*) extinguish sins exactly as water extinguishes fire."[91]

A special form of *sadaqah* is the practice of *waqf Khairi* (endowments or charitable trusts) that were developed in the early days of Islam by religious scholars for the aim of serving the general interests of the Muslim community, motivated by a reward from Allah. *Waqf* is a *sadaqah* that "transcends time,"[92] inspired by the Prophet's hadith: "When a man dies his works stop bringing him a reward with the exception of three actions." These *awqaf* (plural of *waqf*) vary from financial grants to the provision of religious, educational, and other social service institutions that are dedicated by a member of the community (*waqif*), become public property, and are administered by trustees (*waliy*) appointed or elected to run it as decided by the *qadi* (judge) to whom they become accountable.[93]

Islam, Human Rights, and the Duty to Work for Peace

A loose set of international laws governing human rights based on the United Nations convention, the Universal Declaration on Human Rights (UDHR), and other specialized treaties, has been growing into a substantial code of basic human rights.[94] In 1984 a major step was taken in this regard by issuing a declaration by the United Nations General Assembly on the right of humans to peace as a framework to enjoy and practice other codified human rights, echoing earlier human rights treaties and mechanisms.[95] This declaration, however, was not legally binding on UN member countries; albeit, the extensive efforts over the last two decades by several organizations, such as UNESCO and many nongovernmental organizations, to develop and disseminate the ideas of a culture of peace with tolerance and nonviolence as its main pillars, are making it possible to talk about a human right to peace.[96] Nevertheless, the international human rights community, mostly

Western in outlook, is primarily concerned with political, cultural, and economic rights, with little attention to the notion of duty as a tool by which respect and protection of these rights will be realized.

The case for human rights in Islam in fact is compelling, as human rights are a mechanism to secure the dignity of all human beings and other creatures.[97] However, Islam's approach to human rights is not fully on terms with its Western counterpart. For example, between east and west there is no inclusive list of what exactly are the human rights. At the same time, both paradigms share the same inspired goal—the improvement of the way in which humans lead their lives on this earth.[98] Rights in Islam in general are codified in a categorical manner that expands to include the rights necessary for the perfection of one's self, reason, life, family, and property.[99] These rights are to be enjoyed by each and every human being, regardless of differences, all being the sons of Adam, the creatures of Allah:[100]

> O mankind! We created you from a single (pair) of a male and a female, and made you into nations and tribes, that ye may know each other (not that ye may despise (each other). Verily the most honoured of you in the sight of Allah is (he who is) the most righteous of you. (49:13)

Nevertheless, the idea of rights (*huquq*) in Islam combines with its counterpart, duties (*wagibat*). Hence, in order to enjoy our rights, we have to undertake parallel duties or responsibilities.[101] This emphasis on responsibilities stems from seeing human beings as part of a social setting in which they do not live alone.[102] Thus, it should be emphasized that enjoying rights implies the undertaking of some duties in a community of relationships, where relationships cannot be one-sided.[103] This web of relationships among diverse creatures of Allah is, therefore, the framework within which human rights and responsibilities are observed by each and every one.[104] Being followers of "a faith of peace," Muslims are required as well to act peace through showing mercy and forgiveness for their fellow human beings and the environment.[105] As has been highlighted above, it is important to acknowledge the right of people to live in peace for the sake of perfecting their selves—reason and life, family and property. Then, it follows that a duty to work for peace arises and becomes binding on each and every Muslim. In other words, it is important for Muslims in their jihad for the perfection of their souls and lives, not only to incorporate their right to live in peace, but also to acknowledge their duty for its realization.

Concluding Thoughts

These insights on the work for peace in Islam, of course, are not exhaustive by any means. They are, rather, suggestive. It is an invitation for the creativity of Muslims to transform the world in which they live into a more just, peaceful, and energetic one. It follows that the principles and values outlined above are not exclusive or separate from each other. They do interact and may even collapse onto each other. For example, these components can all fit together under the title of the greater jihad, as it is the motivation of all good work in Islam. They are also not peculiar to Islam alone, but they lie at its intersection with many of the great value systems present in our world.

That being said, however, most of these are theoretical principles that unfortunately lack genuine application in many contemporary Muslim societies.[106] While Muslims struggle all the time to excel in their attempts to follow in the path of Allah, the way in which they interpret His laws is still bound in social, historical, and political realities.[107] The absence of peace in Muslim communities is the outcome of the oppressive conditions under which they have lived over the last two centuries, especially conditions of colonization, underdevelopment, and authoritarian rule.[108] In addition, the religious institution is usually co-opted by the political institution, which leads to an interpretation of religious teachings that protects the interests of these institutions, even if they contradict the intended message of the sacred text.[109] With a lack of alternatives and a widespread state of frustration among many members of their communities, extremism finds a fertile ground to grow and intolerance becomes the norm.[110] Jihad is seen primarily through the carrying of arms, next to which spiritual strife is considered secondary. Retributive justice gets excessive emphasis, while compassion diminishes.[111]

Nevertheless, it is always crucial to recall that the absence of these—and other—theoretical principles from practice does not mean they do not exist. It is important for Muslims, therefore, to try to move beyond the narrow understanding of their religion, toward a wider one, where the whole universe becomes the center of attention,[112] and to go beyond the mere performance of rituals of the faith to live by its ethics and spirit.[113] It is of supreme importance for Muslims to engage in such values in order to improve their conditions, dependent on their own intellect and motivated by their own faith. It is Muslims who, when deviating from peace—the path of Islam—should work hard to return back to it.[114] If they do not hold firm to the basics of their beliefs, their doctrine will not count for much.[115] This is because it is according to their actions that the image of Islam is constructed. "Allah does not change a people's lot unless they change what is in their hearts" (13:11).

— Section VI —

RELIGION, GLOBALIZATION, AND TRANSNATIONALISM

33

JIHAD VS. MCWORLD

—Benjamin Barber

Just beyond the horizon of current events lie two possible political futures—both bleak, neither democratic. The first is a retribalization of large swaths of humankind by war and bloodshed: a threatened Lebanonization of national states in which culture is pitted against culture, people against people, tribe against tribe—a Jihad in the name of a hundred narrowly conceived faiths against every kind of interdependence, every kind of artificial social cooperation and civic mutuality. The second is being borne in on us by the onrush of economic and ecological forces that demand integration and uniformity and that mesmerize the world with fast music, fast computers, and fast food—with MTV, Macintosh, and McDonald's, pressing nations into one commercially homogenous global network: one McWorld tied together by technology, ecology, communications, and commerce. The planet is falling precipitantly apart *and* coming reluctantly together at the very same moment.

These two tendencies are sometimes visible in the same countries at the same instant: thus Yugoslavia, clamoring just recently to join the New Europe, is exploding into fragments; India is trying to live up to its reputation as the world's largest integral democracy while powerful new fundamentalist parties like the Hindu nationalist Bharatiya Janata Party, along with nationalist assassins, are imperiling its hard-won unity. States are breaking up or joining up: the Soviet Union has disappeared almost overnight, its parts forming new unions with one another or with like-minded nationalities in neighboring states. The old interwar national state based on territory and political sovereignty looks to be a mere transitional development.

The tendencies of what I am here calling the forces of Jihad and the forces of McWorld operate it with equal strength in opposite directions, the one driven by parochial hatreds, the other by universalizing markets, the one re-creating ancient subnational and ethnic borders from within, the other making national borders porous from without. They have one thing in common: neither offers much hope to citizens looking for practical ways to govern themselves democratically. If the global future is to pit Jihad's centrifugal whirlwind

* *The Atlantic Monthly* 269, no. 3 (March 1992): 53–65.

against McWorld's centripetal black hole, the outcome is unlikely to be democratic—or so I will argue.

McWorld, or the Globalization of Politics

Four imperatives make up the dynamics of McWorld: a market imperative, a resource imperative, an information-technology imperative, and an ecological imperative. By shrinking the world and diminishing the salience of national borders, these imperatives have in combination achieved a considerable victory over factiousness and particularism, and not least of all over their most virulent traditional form—nationalism. It is the realists who are now Europeans, the utopians who dream nostalgically of a resurgent England or Germany, perhaps even a resurgent Wales or Saxony. Yesterday's wishful cry for one world has yielded to the reality of McWorld.

The market imperative. Marxist and Leninist theories of imperialism assumed that the quest for ever-expanding markets would in time compel nation-based capitalist economies to push against national boundaries in search of an international economic imperium. Whatever else has happened to the scientistic predictions of Marxism, in this domain they have proved farsighted. All national economies are now vulnerable to the inroads of larger, transnational markets within which trade is free, currencies are convertible, access to banking is open, and contracts are enforceable under law. In Europe, Asia, Africa, the South Pacific, and the Americas such markets are eroding national sovereignty and giving rise to entities—international banks, trade associations, transnational lobbies like OPEC and Greenpeace, world news services like CNN and the BBC, and multinational corporations that increasingly lack a meaningful national identity—that neither reflect nor respect nationhood as an organizing or regulative principle.

The market imperative has also reinforced the quest for international peace and stability, requisites of an efficient international economy. Markets are enemies of parochialism, isolation, fractiousness, war. Market psychology attenuates the psychology of ideological and religious cleavages and assumes a concord among producers and consumers—categories that ill fit narrowly conceived national or religious cultures. Shopping has little tolerance for blue laws, whether dictated by pub-closing British paternalism, Sabbath-observing Jewish Orthodox fundamentalism, or no-Sunday-liquor-sales Massachusetts puritanism. In the context of common markets, international law ceases to be a vision of justice and becomes a workaday framework for getting things done—enforcing contracts, ensuring that governments abide by deals, regulating trade and currency relations, and so forth.

Common markets demand a common language, as well as a common currency, and they produce common behaviors of the kind bred by cosmopolitan city life everywhere. Commercial pilots, computer programmers, international bankers, media specialists, oil riggers, entertainment celebrities, ecology experts, demographers, accountants, professors, athletes—these compose a new breed of men and women for whom religion, culture, and nationality can seem only marginal elements in a working identity. Although sociologists of everyday life will no doubt continue to distinguish a Japanese from an American mode, shopping has a common signature throughout the world. Cynics might even say that some of the recent revolutions in Eastern Europe have had as their true goal not liberty and the right to vote but well-paying jobs and the right to shop (although the vote is proving easier to acquire than consumer goods). The market imperative is, then, plenty powerful; but, notwithstanding some of the claims made for "democratic capitalism," it is not identical with the democratic imperative.

The resource imperative. Democrats once dreamed of societies whose political autonomy rested firmly on economic independence. The Athenians idealized what they called autarky, and tried for a while to create a way of life simple and austere enough to make the polis genuinely self-sufficient. To be free meant to be independent of any other community or polis. Not even the Athenians were able to achieve autarky, however: human nature, it turns out, is dependency. By the time of Pericles, Athenian politics was inextricably bound up with a flowering empire held together by naval power and commerce—an empire that, even as it appeared to enhance Athenian might, ate away at Athenian independence and autarky. Master and slave, it turned out, were bound together by mutual insufficiency.

The dream of autarky briefly engrossed nineteenth-century America as well, for the underpopulated, endlessly bountiful land, the cornucopia of natural resources, and the natural barriers of a continent walled in by two great seas led many to believe that America could be a world unto itself. Given this past, it has been harder for Americans than for most to accept the inevitability of interdependence. But the rapid depletion of resources even in a country like ours, where they once seemed inexhaustible, and the maldistribution of arable soil and mineral resources on the planet, leave even the wealthiest societies ever more resource-dependent and many other nations in permanently desperate straits.

Every nation, it turns out, needs something another nation has; some nations have almost nothing they need.

The information-technology imperative. Enlightenment science and the technologies derived from it are inherently universalizing. They entail a quest for descriptive principles of general application, a search for universal solutions to particular problems, and an unswerving embrace of objectivity and impartiality.

Scientific progress embodies and depends on open communication, a common discourse rooted in rationality, collaboration, and an easy and regular flow and exchange of information. Such ideals can be hypocritical covers for power-mongering by elites, and they may be shown to be wanting in many other ways, but they are entailed by the very idea of science and they make science and globalization practical allies.

Business, banking, and commerce all depend on information flow and are facilitated by new communication technologies. The hardware of these technologies tends to be systemic and integrated—computer, television, cable, satellite, laser, fiber-optic, and microchip technologies combining to create a vast interactive communications and information network that can potentially give every person on earth access to every other person, and make every datum, every byte, available to every set of eyes. If the automobile was, as George Ball once said (when he gave his blessing to a Fiat factory in the Soviet Union during the Cold War), "an ideology on four wheels," then electronic telecommunication and information systems are an ideology at 186,000 miles per second—which makes for a very small planet in a very big hurry. Individual cultures speak particular languages; commerce and science increasingly speak English; the whole world speaks logarithms and binary mathematics.

Moreover, the pursuit of science and technology asks for, even compels, open societies. Satellite footprints do not respect national borders; telephone wires penetrate the most closed societies. With photocopying and then fax machines having infiltrated Soviet universities and *samizdat* literary circles in the eighties, and computer modems having multiplied like rabbits in communism's bureaucratic warrens thereafter, *glasnost* could not be far behind. In their social requisites, secrecy and science are enemies.

The new technology's software is perhaps even more globalizing than its hardware. The information arm of international commerce's sprawling body reaches out and touches distinct nations and parochial cultures, and gives them a common face chiseled in Hollywood, on Madison Avenue, and in Silicon Valley. Throughout the 1980s one of the most-watched television programs in South Africa was *The Cosby Show*. The demise of apartheid was already in production. Exhibitors at the 1991 Cannes film festival expressed growing anxiety over the "homogenization" and "Americanization" of the global film industry when, for the third year running, American films dominated the awards ceremonies. America has dominated the world's popular culture for much longer, and much more decisively. In November of 1991 Switzerland's once insular culture boasted best-seller lists featuring *Terminator 2* as the No. 1 movie, *Scarlett* as the No. 1 book, and Prince's *Diamonds and Pearls* as the No. 1 record album. No wonder the Japanese are buying Hollywood film studios even faster than Americans are buying Japanese television sets. This kind of software supremacy may in the long term be far more important than hardware superiority, because culture has become more potent than armaments. What is the power of the Pentagon compared with Disneyland? Can the Sixth Fleet keep up with CNN? McDonald's in Moscow and Coke in China will do more to create a global culture than military colonization ever could. It is less the goods than the brand names that do the work, for they convey life-style images that alter perception and challenge behavior. They make up the seductive software of McWorld's common (at times much too common) soul.

Yet in all this high-tech commercial world there is nothing that looks particularly democratic. It lends itself to surveillance as well as liberty, to new forms of manipulation and covert control as well as new kinds of participation, to skewed, unjust market outcomes as well as greater productivity. The consumer society and the open society are not quite synonymous. Capitalism and democracy have a relationship, but it is something less than a marriage. An efficient free market after all requires that consumers be free to vote their dollars on competing goods, not that citizens be free to vote their values and beliefs on competing political candidates and programs. The free market flourished in junta-run Chile, in military-governed Taiwan and Korea, and, earlier, in a variety of autocratic European empires as well as their colonial possessions.

The ecological imperative. The impact of globalization on ecology is a cliché even to world leaders who ignore it. We know well enough that the German forests can be destroyed by Swiss and Italians driving gas-guzzlers fueled by leaded gas. We also know that the planet can be asphyxiated by greenhouse gases because Brazilian farmers want to be part of the twentieth century and are burning down tropical rain forests to clear a little land to plough, and because Indonesians make a living out of converting their lush jungle into toothpicks for fastidious Japanese diners, upsetting the delicate oxygen balance and in effect puncturing our global lungs. Yet this ecological consciousness has meant not only greater awareness but also greater inequality, as modernized nations try to slam the door behind them, saying to developing nations, "The world cannot afford *your* modernization; ours has wrung it dry!"

Each of the four imperatives just cited is transnational, transideological, and transcultural. Each applies impartially to Catholics, Jews, Muslims, Hindus, and Buddhists; to democrats and totalitarians; to capitalists and socialists. The Enlightenment dream of a universal rational society has to a remarkable degree been realized—but in a form that is commercialized, homogenized, depoliticized, bureaucratized, and, of course, radically incomplete, for the movement toward McWorld is in competition with forces of global breakdown, national dissolution, and centrifugal corruption. These forces, working in the opposite direction, are the essence of what I call Jihad.

Jihad, or the Lebanonization of the World

OPEC, the World Bank, the United Nations, the International Red Cross, the multinational corporation . . . there are scores of institutions that reflect globalization. But they often appear as ineffective reactors to the world's real actors: national states and, to an ever greater degree, subnational factions in permanent rebellion against uniformity and integration—even the kind represented by universal law and justice. The headlines feature these players regularly: they are cultures, not countries; parts, not wholes; sects, not religions; rebellious factions and dissenting minorities at war not just with globalism but with the traditional nation-state. Kurds, Basques, Puerto Ricans, Ossetians, East Timoreans, Quebecois, the Catholics of Northern Ireland, Abkhasians, Kurile Islander Japanese, the Zulus of Inkatha, Catalonians, Tamils, and, of course, Palestinians—people without countries, inhabiting nations not their own, seeking smaller worlds within borders that will seal them off from modernity.

A powerful irony is at work here. Nationalism was once a force of integration and unification, a movement aimed at bringing together disparate clans, tribes, and cultural fragments under new, assimilationist flags. But as Ortega y Gasset noted more than sixty years ago, having won its victories, nationalism changed its strategy. In the 1920s, and again today, it is more often a reactionary and divisive force, pulverizing the very nations it once helped cement together. The force that creates nations is "inclusive," Ortega wrote in *The Revolt of the Masses*. "In periods of consolidation, nationalism has a positive value, and is a lofty standard. But in Europe everything is more than consolidated, and nationalism is nothing but a mania. . . ."

This mania has left the post–Cold War world smoldering with hot wars; the international scene is little more unified than it was at the end of the Great War, in Ortega's own time. There were more than thirty wars in progress last year, most of them ethnic, racial, tribal, or religious in character, and the list of unsafe regions doesn't seem to be getting any shorter. Some new world order!

The aim of many of these small-scale wars is to redraw boundaries, to implode states and resecure parochial identities: to escape McWorld's dully insistent imperatives. The mood is that of Jihad: war not as an instrument of policy but as an emblem of identity, an expression of community, an end in itself. Even where there is no shooting war, there is fractiousness, secession, and the quest for ever smaller communities. Add to the list of dangerous countries those at risk: In Switzerland and Spain, Jurassian and Basque separatists still argue the virtues of ancient identities, sometimes in the language of bombs. Hyperdisintegration in the former Soviet Union may well continue unabated—not just a Ukraine independent from the Soviet Union but a Bessarabian Ukraine independent from the Ukrainian republic; not just Russia severed from the defunct union but Tatarstan severed from Russia. Yugoslavia makes even the disunited, ex-Soviet, nonsocialist republics that were once the Soviet Union look integrated, its sectarian fatherlands springing up within factional motherlands like weeds within weeds within weeds. Kurdish independence would threaten the territorial integrity of four Middle Eastern nations. Well before the current cataclysm Soviet Georgia made a claim for autonomy from the Soviet Union, only to be faced with its Ossetians (164,000 in a republic of 5.5 million) demanding their own self-determination within Georgia. The Abkhasian minority in Georgia has followed suit. Even the good will established by Canada's once promising Meech Lake protocols is in danger, with Francophone Quebec again threatening the dissolution of the federation. In South Africa the emergence from apartheid was hardly achieved when friction between Inkatha's Zulus and the African National Congress's tribally identified members threatened to replace Europeans' racism with an indigenous tribal war. After thirty years of attempted integration using the colonial language (English) as a unifier, Nigeria is now playing with the idea of linguistic multiculturalism—which could mean the cultural breakup of the nation into hundreds of tribal fragments. Even Saddam Hussein has benefited from the threat of internal Jihad, having used renewed tribal and religious warfare to turn last season's mortal enemies into reluctant allies of an Iraqi nationhood that he nearly destroyed.

The passing of communism has torn away the thin veneer of internationalism (workers of the world unite!) to reveal ethnic prejudices that are not only ugly and deep-seated but increasingly murderous. Europe's old scourge, anti-Semitism, is back with a vengeance, but it is only one of many antagonisms. It appears all too easy to throw the historical gears into reverse and pass from a Communist dictatorship back into a tribal state.

Among the tribes, religion is also a battlefield. ("Jihad" is a rich word whose generic meaning is "struggle"—usually the struggle of the soul to avert evil. Strictly applied to religious war, it is used only in reference to battles where the faith is under assault, or battles against a government that denies the practice of Islam. My use here is rhetorical, but does follow both journalistic practice and history.) Remember the Thirty Years War? Whatever forms of Enlightenment universalism might once have come to grace such historically related forms of monotheism as Judaism, Christianity, and Islam, in many of their modern incarnations they are parochial rather than cosmopolitan, angry rather than loving, proselytizing rather than ecumenical, zealous rather than rationalist, sectarian rather than deistic, ethnocentric rather than universalizing. As a result, like the new forms of hypernationalism, the new expressions of religious fundamentalism are fractious and pulverizing, never integrating. This is religion as the Crusaders knew it: a battle to the death for souls that if not saved will be forever lost.

The atmospherics of Jihad have resulted in a breakdown of civility in the name of identity, of comity in the name of community. International relations have sometimes taken on the aspect of gang war—cultural turf battles featuring tribal factions that were supposed to be sublimated as integral parts of large national, economic, postcolonial, and constitutional entities.

The Darkening Future of Democracy

These rather melodramatic tableaux vivants do not tell the whole story, however. For all their defects, Jihad and McWorld have their attractions. Yet, to repeat and insist, the

attractions are unrelated to democracy. Neither McWorld nor Jihad is remotely democratic in impulse. Neither needs democracy; neither promotes democracy.

McWorld does manage to look pretty seductive in a world obsessed with Jihad. It
delivers peace, prosperity, and relative unity—if at the cost of independence, community,
and identity (which is generally based on difference). The primary political values required
by the global market are order and tranquility, and freedom—as in the phrases "free trade,"
"free press," and "free love." Human rights are needed to a degree, but not citizenship or
participation—and no more social justice and equality than are necessary to promote
efficient economic production and consumption. Multinational corporations sometimes
seem to prefer doing business with local oligarchs, inasmuch as they can take confidence
from dealing with the boss on all crucial matters. Despots who slaughter their own populations are no problem, so long as they leave markets in place and refrain from making war
on their neighbors (Saddam Hussein's fatal mistake). In trading partners, predictability is
of more value than justice.

The Eastern European revolutions that seemed to arise out of concern for global democratic values quickly deteriorated into a stampede in the general direction of free markets
and their ubiquitous, television-promoted shopping malls. East Germany's Neues Forum,
that courageous gathering of intellectuals, students, and workers which overturned the
Stalinist regime in Berlin in 1989, lasted only six months in Germany's mini-version of
McWorld. Then it gave way to money and markets and monopolies from the West. By the
time of the first all-German elections, it could scarcely manage to secure three percent of
the vote. Elsewhere there is growing evidence that *glasnost* will go and *perestroika*—defined
as privatization and an opening of markets to Western bidders—will stay. So understand-
ably anxious are the new rulers of Eastern Europe and whatever entities are forged from
the residues of the Soviet Union to gain access to credit and markets and technology—
McWorld's flourishing new currencies—that they have shown themselves willing to trade
away democratic prospects in pursuit of them: not just old totalitarian ideologies and
command-economy production models but some possible indigenous experiments with a
third way between capitalism and socialism, such as economic cooperatives and employee
stock-ownership plans, both of which have their ardent supporters in the East.

Jihad delivers a different set of virtues: a vibrant local identity, a sense of community, and solidarity among kinsmen, neighbors, and countrymen, narrowly conceived.
But it also guarantees parochialism and is grounded in exclusion. Solidarity is secured
through war against outsiders. And solidarity often means obedience to a hierarchy in
governance, fanaticism in beliefs, and the obliteration of individual selves in the name of
the group. Deference to leaders and intolerance toward outsiders (and toward "enemies
within") are hallmarks of tribalism—hardly the attitudes required for the cultivation of
new democratic women and men capable of governing themselves. Where new democratic experiments have been conducted in retribalizing societies, in both Europe and the
Third World, the result has often been anarchy, repression, persecution, and the coming of new, noncommunist forms of very old kinds of despotism. During the past year,
Havel's velvet revolution in Czechoslovakia was imperiled by partisans of "Czechland"
and of Slovakia as independent entities. India seemed little less rent by Sikh, Hindu,
Muslim, and Tamil infighting than it was immediately after the British pulled out, more
than forty years ago.

To the extent that either McWorld or Jihad has a *natural* politics, it has turned out to be more of an antipolitics. For McWorld, it is the antipolitics of globalism: bureaucratic, technocratic, and meritocratic, focused (as Marx predicted it would be) on the administration of things—with people, however, among the chief things to be administered. In its politico-economic imperatives McWorld has been guided by laissez-faire market principles that privilege efficiency, productivity, and beneficence at the expense of civic liberty and self-government.

For Jihad, the antipolitics of tribalization has been explicitly antidemocratic: one-party dictatorship, government by military junta, theocratic fundamentalism—often associated with a version of the *Fuhrerprinzip* that empowers an individual to rule on behalf of a people. Even the government of India, struggling for decades to model democracy for a people who will soon number a billion, longs for great leaders; and for every Mahatma Gandhi, Indira Gandhi, or Rajiv Gandhi taken from them by zealous assassins, the Indians appear to seek a replacement who will deliver them from the lengthy travail of their freedom.

The Confederal Option

How can democracy be secured and spread in a world whose primary tendencies are at best indifferent to it (McWorld) and at worst deeply antithetical to it (Jihad)? My guess is that globalization will eventually vanquish retribalization. The ethos of material "civilization" has not yet encountered an obstacle it has been unable to thrust aside. Ortega may have grasped in the 1920s a clue to our own future in the coming millennium.

> Everyone sees the need of a new principle of life. But as always happens in similar crises—some people attempt to save the situation by an artificial intensification of the very principle which has led to decay. This is the meaning of the "nationalist" outburst of recent years . . . things have always gone that way. The last flare, the longest; the last sigh, the deepest. On the very eve of their disappearance there is an intensification of frontiers—military and economic.

Jihad may be a last deep sigh before the eternal yawn of McWorld. On the other hand, Ortega was not exactly prescient; his prophecy of peace and internationalism came just before blitzkrieg, world war, and the Holocaust tore the old order to bits. Yet democracy is how we remonstrate with reality, the rebuke our aspirations offer to history. And if retribalization is inhospitable to democracy, there is nonetheless a form of democratic government that can accommodate parochialism and communitarianism, one that can even save them from their defects and make them more tolerant and participatory: decentralized participatory democracy. And if McWorld is indifferent to democracy, there is nonetheless a form of democratic government that suits global markets passably well—representative government in its federal or, better still, confederal variation.

With its concern for accountability, the protection of minorities, and the universal rule of law, a confederalized representative system would serve the political needs of McWorld as well as oligarchic bureaucratism or meritocratic elitism is currently doing. As we are already beginning to see, many nations may survive in the long term only as confederations that afford local regions smaller than "nations" extensive jurisdiction. Recommended reading for democrats of the twenty-first century is not the U.S. Constitution or the French Declaration of Rights of Man and Citizen but the Articles of Confederation, that suddenly pertinent document that stitched together the thirteen American colonies into what then seemed a too loose confederation of independent states but now appears a new form of political realism, as veterans of Yeltsin's new Russia and the new Europe created at Maastricht will attest.

By the same token, the participatory and direct form of democracy that engages citizens in civic activity and civic judgment and goes well beyond just voting and accountability—the system I have called "strong democracy"—suits the political needs of decentralized communities as well as theocratic and nationalist party dictatorships have done. Local neighborhoods need not be democratic, but they can be. Real democracy has flourished in diminutive settings: the spirit of liberty, Tocqueville said, is local. Participatory democracy, if not naturally apposite to tribalism, has an undeniable attractiveness under conditions of parochialism.

Democracy in any of these variations will, however, continue to be obstructed by the undemocratic and antidemocratic trends toward uniformitarian globalism and intolerant retribalization which I have portrayed here. For democracy to persist in our brave new McWorld, we will have to commit acts of conscious political will—a possibility, but hardly a probability, under these conditions. Political will requires much more than the quick fix of the transfer of institutions. Like technology transfer, institution transfer rests on foolish assumptions about a uniform world of the kind that once fired the imagination of colonial administrators. Spread English justice to the colonies by exporting wigs. Let an East Indian trading company act as the vanguard to Britain's free parliamentary institutions. Today's well-intentioned quick-fixers in the National Endowment for Democracy and the Kennedy School of Government, in the unions and foundations and universities zealously nurturing contacts in Eastern Europe and the Third World, are hoping to democratize by long distance. Post Bulgaria a parliament by first-class mail. FedEx the Bill of Rights to Sri Lanka. Cable Cambodia some common law.

Yet Eastern Europe has already demonstrated that importing free political parties, parliaments, and presses cannot establish a democratic civil society; imposing a free market may even have the opposite effect. Democracy grows from the bottom up and cannot be imposed from the top down. Civil society has to be built from the inside out. The institutional superstructure comes last. Poland may become democratic, but then again it may heed the Pope, and prefer to found its politics on its Catholicism, with uncertain consequences for democracy. Bulgaria may become democratic, but it may prefer tribal war. The former Soviet Union may become a democratic confederation, or it may just grow into an anarchic and weak conglomeration of markets for other nations' goods and services.

Democrats need to seek out indigenous democratic impulses. There is always a desire for self-government, always some expression of participation, accountability, consent, and representation, even in traditional hierarchical societies. These need to be identified, tapped, modified, and incorporated into new democratic practices with an indigenous flavor. The tortoises among the democratizers may ultimately outlive or outpace the hares, for they will have the time and patience to explore conditions along the way, and to adapt their gait to changing circumstances. Tragically, democracy in a hurry often looks something like France in 1794 or China in 1989.

It certainly seems possible that the most attractive democratic ideal in the face of the brutal realities of Jihad and the dull realities of McWorld will be a confederal union of semi-autonomous communities smaller than nation-states, tied together into regional economic associations and markets larger than nation-states—participatory and self-determining in local matters at the bottom, representative and accountable at the top. The nation-state would play a diminished role, and sovereignty would lose some of its political potency. The Green movement adage "Think globally, act locally" would actually come to describe the conduct of politics.

This vision reflects only an ideal, however—one that is not terribly likely to be realized. Freedom, Jean-Jacques Rousseau once wrote, is a food easy to eat but hard to digest. Still, democracy has always played itself out against the odds. And democracy remains both a form of coherence as binding as McWorld and a secular faith potentially as inspiriting as Jihad.

34

RELIGION AND GLOBALIZATION

—James Kurth

G lobalization is often described as a process: steadily progressing over time, pervasively spreading over space, and clearly inevitable in its development. But globalization is also a revolution, one of the most profound revolutions the world has ever known. Indeed, globalization is the first truly world revolution.

All revolutions disrupt the traditions and customs of a people. Indeed, they threaten a people's very security, safety, and even identity. The world revolution that is globalization in some measure threatens the security of every people on the globe.

Insecurity, Ideology, and Theology

When peoples have had their security threatened in the past, they have responded, even reacted, and these responses and reactions have had great and even grave consequences for the peoples around them. In the nineteenth century, the insecurities produced by the French and the Industrial Revolutions resulted in the ideologies of nationalism and socialism. In the twentieth century, the insecurities produced by defeats in the First World War resulted in the ideologies of Soviet communism and German National Socialism. Ideological responses to deep insecurities were characteristic of a particular era, however. This was the modern era, when the Enlightenment and secularization made secular worldviews and their ideologies seem the natural and logical way to interpret what was happening in the world around oneself.

In other eras—until the eighteenth century in Europe and America and until the twentieth century in much of the rest of the world—the responses to deep insecurities were not ideological, but rather theological or religious. This was the case in early modern Europe, when the commercial revolution and the European expansion into the New World (a still earlier stage on the path to globalization) created insecurities that were addressed by the Protestant Reformation and the Catholic Counterreformation. But it was also the case in much of the pre-modern world for millennia reaching back to the origins of civilizations. Indeed, the origins of such diverse and enduring religions as Christianity, Islam, and

* Templeton Lectures on Religion and World Affairs, FPRI Wire, May 1999.

Buddhism (the "world religions") can be interpreted as responses and reactions to the deep insecurities produced by radical social disruptions.

But now, at the end of the twentieth century (and at the beginning of the third millennium), we are not only in the globalization revolution, but also in the post-modern era. What will be the responses of peoples in this new era to the deep insecurities produced by globalization? Is it possible they then may be more theological and religious than ideological and secular?

Three Perspectives on Religion

There are three paradigms or perspectives from which one may view the role of religion in the globalization process: (1) the modernist, (2) the post-modernist, and (3) the pre-modernist.

The Modernist Perspective

The modernist perspective will seem the most familiar. It is the perspective of most intellectuals and academics.

The modernist perspective has had a particular and peculiar view of secularization. Beginning with the Enlightenment, modernists have entertained the prospect that all secularizations would eventually look alike; the different religions would all end up as the same secular and "rational" philosophy. This prospect seemed natural enough during the eighteenth and nineteenth centuries, when the only prominent secularization was that of Christianity. But even at that time, it should have been clear that secularized Protestantism was different from secularized Catholicism, and that there were even differences among the secularized Protestant denominations themselves.

In the simplest version of the modernist view, Enlightenment and secularization progressively spreads from the educated elite to other people as well, from the center of society to the periphery. If any religious communities should remain, they are composed of marginal people—marginal geographically, economically, or ethnically. Religious communities are almost like social fossils.

On occasion, of course, these fossils may come into conflict with each other, or with the enlightened center and the secular groups of a society. In doing so, they bring bizarre and atavistic conflicts into an otherwise modern, secular, and rational world. Leading contemporary examples have been Northern Ireland (1960s–1990s), Lebanon (1970s–1990s), Yugoslavia (1990s), Sri Lanka (1980s–1990s), and Kashmir (1940s–1990s). Many modernists would also add Evangelical Christians in the United States (1980s–1990s). But, from the modernist perspective, these religious conflicts are peripheral in space, temporary in time, and marginal in importance: In the end, secularization, which is now massively reinforced by globalization, will eliminate these fossils and conflicts.

At a somewhat more sophisticated level, the modernist perspective sees religion revivals as sometimes being a reaction to the Enlightenment and modernization. Entire societies, including their elites and not just their marginal groups, are judged by modernists to be reacting to modernization, as being irrational, unreasoning, "fundamentalist." Leading contemporary examples have been the Islamic revolution in Iran (1970s–1990s) and the Hindu revival in India (1990s). Here too, however, the religious reaction of peripheral countries is seen as being of secondary, temporary, and marginal importance, even if on a larger scale and for a longer duration than is the case with the religious reaction of marginal groups. Again, the view is that, in the end, secularization—now massively reinforced by globalization—will convert even these fundamentalist societies.

It is important to note, however, that revivalist Islam and even revivalist Hinduism have not been just reactions to the successes of modern, secular ideologies and projects. In reality, they have been responses to their failures—to the failures of Arab nationalism and socialism and of Iranian nationalism and secularism, in the case of revivalist Islam, and to the failures of Indian socialism and secularism, in the case of revivalist Hinduism. It is interesting that, even as the failures of the Arab, Iranian, and Indian secular ideologies were becoming evident in the 1970s or 1980s, none of the Western professional—and secular—experts on these regions predicted the religious revivals.

At a still more sophisticated level, the modernist perspective sees religion as sometimes being a reform of distortions of the Enlightenment and modernization. The now-common version of the modernist perspective sees free markets and liberal democracy to be the culmination of Enlightenment values. Accordingly, it sees both communism and right-wing authoritarianism as distortions of the Enlightenment. From this perspective, it is not surprising that there would arise opposition to communism and to right-wing authoritarianism and that some of this opposition could come from religious communities.

Thus, in the 1980s modernist proponents of the free market and liberal democracy acknowledged and even applauded the opposition of the Roman Catholic Church to the communist regime in Poland. And they could especially applaud the Solidarity movement, which, although largely Roman Catholic in membership and inspiration, was also a labor union. Similarly, in the 1990s they have applauded the opposition of the Tibetan Buddhists to the communist regime in China. In the opposite direction, in the 1980s the modernist proponents of the free market and liberal democracy applauded the opposition of the Roman Catholic Church to the right-wing authoritarian regimes in Latin America and the Philippines. And they could especially applaud the Liberation Theology movement, which, although based upon Roman Catholic theology, also exalted the idea of human liberation. Similarly, in the 1960s they applauded the opposition of the Vietnamese Buddhists to the authoritarian regime in South Vietnam.

All of these religious organizations and movements have been praised as useful corrections to distorted modernization. But from the modernist perspective, the prospect and ideal is that they too will disappear after they have performed their proper—and temporary—role. Indeed, now that Soviet communism and Latin-American right-wing authoritarianism have disappeared, most modernists wish that the Roman Catholic Church, indeed all churches, would disappear too.

It is important to note, however, what religious opposition movements have not been praised by modernists. In communist countries, including China and Vietnam, these have been Evangelical Christians ("Christian fundamentalists"). In right-wing authoritarian countries, such as the Shah's Iran and Egypt, these have been revivalist Muslims ("Islamic fundamentalists"). In other words, for modernists, the ultimate enemy is religious fundamentalism.

It is again important to note, however, that most of these religious opposition movements have been reactions to the failures of modern, secular ideologies and projects. These failures have been particularly spectacular in the cases of Soviet communism and

Latin-American right-wing authoritarianism. But again none of the Western professional and secular experts on these regimes predicted the strength of the religious opposition.

The Post-Modernist Perspective

The post-Enlightenment, post-modernist perspective joins with the Enlightenment, modernist one in rejecting traditional, pre-modern religions. But this perspective also rejects the Enlightenment, modernist values of rationalism, empiricism, and science, along with the Enlightenment, modernist structures of capitalism, bureaucracy, and even liberalism. The core value of post-modernism is expressive individualism.

The post-modernist perspective can include "spiritual experiences," but only those without religious (in the original sense of "binding") constraints. The New Age movement can be interpreted as the ideal, typical post-modernist spiritual expression. Post-modernists are also drawn to superficial, Americanized versions of certain Eastern religions, especially "lite" Buddhism and Hinduism. They are also drawn to an Americanized version of nature worship, a sort of neo-paganism.

For the most part, however, post-modernism is largely hyper-secularism, and it joins modernism in predicting, and eagerly anticipating, the disappearance of traditional religions. Globalization, by breaking up and dissolving every traditional, local, and national structure, will bring about the universal triumph of expressive individualism.

The Pre-Modernist Perspective

There is an alternative perspective, one which is post-modern in its occurrence but which is pre-modern in its sensibility. It is best represented and articulated by the Roman Catholic Church, especially by Pope John Paul II. The Pope's understanding obviously has drawn from his experiences with Poland, but it encompasses events in other countries as well.

From this pre-modernist perspective, many of the great modern, secular ideologies had manifestly failed by the 1970s–1980s. This was true of Soviet communism, Arab nationalism and socialism, and the nationalism and modernization project of the Shah's Iran. All of these were ideologies, even idolatries, of the state.

When the ideology's failure became manifest, however, the really effective opposition to it and to the state that it exalted did not develop among the secular sections of society, such as intellectuals, professionals, and managers. Rather, the only effective opposition movement developed among religious believers. It was only in the organized religious communities that there could be found large numbers of people willing to sacrifice their individual security for the greater movement. It was their religious faith and the religious community that supported it that gave these believers the commitment and the courage to persist in their opposition.

Even where secularization has occurred, the result has not been a homogeneous, or commonly shared, secular philosophy but rather a variety of different secularizations. Each religion has secularized in its own distinctive way, which has resulted in its own distinctive secular outcome. This suggests that even if globalization brings about more secularization, it will not soon bring about one common, global worldview.

The U.S. as the Leading Power in Globalization and Secularization

In the past two decades, secularization has been accelerated and accentuated by global-ization. This process has been led by the United States. Now "the sole superpower," "the high-technology economy," and "the universal nation," the United States has vigorously and consistently supported the revolution of globalization. It has done so by systemati-cally pressing to remove any national barriers to the free movement of capital, goods, and services. It has done so through the great international, now global, financial institutions, especially the International Monetary Fund (IMF), the World Bank, and the World Trade Organization (WTO). And it has done so because it has the political, economic, and mili-tary power to get its way. The triumphalist United States, which has reached the heights of being the sole superpower at the culmination of the "American Century" and at the end of the modern era, now seeks to lead the world into the globalized economy and the post-modern era.

The principle sources of resistance to globalization and to the grand project of the United States have become several of the great religions. Especially strong in their resis-tance have been revivalist Islam and a developing neo-Confucianism, known for promot-ing "Asian values." Also resistant have been revivalist Hinduism and Eastern Orthodoxy. The great religions correctly see the globalization led by the United States to be closely connected with secularization and therefore to be a threat to themselves.

The Protestant Rejection of Hierarchy and Community

The American role in international affairs has been, and continues to be, shaped by the Protestant origins of the United States. But the Protestantism that has shaped American foreign policy over two centuries has not been the original Protestant (especially Reformed) religion, but a series of successive, secularizing departures from it on a down-sliding scale. I will refer to this descending scale as the Protestant declension. We are now at the end point of this declension, and the Protestantism that shapes America's global role today is a peculiar heresy of the original religion. It is not the Protestant Reformation but what might be called the Protestant Deformation. In the 1990s, with the United States left as the sole superpower, this Protestant Deformation is at its greatest, now global, influence. But because it is such a peculiar religion, and indeed is correctly seen as a fundamental and fatal threat by all the other religions, its pervasive sway is generating intense resistance and international conflict.

All religions are unique, but Protestantism is more unique than all the others. No other religion is so critical of hierarchy and community, or of the traditions and customs that go with them. Indeed, most other religions are based upon both hierarchy and com-munity (in addition to Roman Catholicism, also Eastern Orthodoxy, Islam, Hinduism, Confucianism, and even, to a degree, Buddhism). At its doctrinal base, however, Protes-tantism is anti-hierarchy and anti-community.

The removal of hierarchy and community, traditions and customs—of any earthly intermediaries between the individual and God—strips away, at least for the most impor-tant purposes, any local, parochial, cultural, or national characteristics of the believer. In principle, grace, faith, and salvation can be received by anyone in the world; they are truly universal or catholic, in the original sense of the latter term. The Protestant reformers saw the vast variety of cultures and nations through a universal perspective, one that was even more universal than that of the Roman Catholic Church.

The Protestant Spread into Secular Life: The American Creed

In the three centuries after the Reformation, this Protestant rejection of hierarchy and community in regard to salvation spread to their rejection in regard to other domains of life as well. Some Protestant churches, particularly Reformed ones, rejected hierarchy and community in regard to church governance and local traditions. This was especially the case in the new United States, where the conjunction of the open frontier and the disestablishment of state churches enabled the flourishing of new unstructured and unconstraining denominations.

By the beginning of the nineteenth century, the Protestant rejection of hierarchy and community had spread to important arenas of temporal or secular life. Again, this was especially the case in the new United States. In the economic arena, the elimination of hierarchy (monopoly or oligopoly) and community (guilds or trade restrictions) meant the establishment of the free market. In the political arena, the elimination of hierarchy (monarchy or aristocracy) and community (traditions and customs) meant the establishment of liberal democracy.

The Protestant Reformation was giving birth to what by the early twentieth century would become the American Creed. The fundamental elements of that secular creed were free markets and equal opportunity; free elections and liberal democracy; and constitutionalism and the rule of law.

The American Creed definitely did not include as elements hierarchy, community, tradition, and custom. Although the American Creed was not itself Protestant, it was clearly the product of a Protestant culture and was a sort of secularized version of Protestantism.

The Culmination of Secularized Protestantism: Universal Human Rights

The final stage in the Protestant declension has been reached only in the last generation. In the 1970s, American political and intellectual elites began to promote the notion of universal human rights as a fundamental goal of American foreign policy. The American Creed was replaced by the universal conception of human rights or, more accurately, the elements of the American Creed were carried to a logical conclusion and to a universal extent.

In this new ideology, human rights are thus seen as the rights of individuals. The individual's rights are independent of any hierarchy or community, traditions or customs, in which that individual might be situated. This means that human rights are applicable to any individual, anywhere in the world, i.e., they are universal, and not merely communal or national. There is thus a close logical connection between the rights of the individual and the universality of those rights. Individual rights are universal rights, and universal rights are individual rights.

Numerous social analysts have noted that the United States has become in the past two decades a new kind of political society, what has been called "the republic of choice." It is characterized by the "rights revolution" in law, "freedom of choice" in politics, "consumer sovereignty" in economics, "question authority" in attitudes, and "expressive individualism" in ideology. In regard to spiritual life, one manifestation of this new mentality is "New Age."

The ideology of expressive individualism thus reaches into all aspects of society; it is a total philosophy. The result appears to be totally opposite from the totalitarianism of the state, but it is a sort of totalitarianism of the self. Both totalitarianisms are relentless in breaking down intermediate bodies and mediating institutions that stand between the individual and the highest powers or the widest forces. With the totalitarianism of the state, the highest powers are the authorities of the nation state; with the totalitarianism of the self, the widest forces are the agencies of the global economy.

Expressive individualism—with its contempt for and protest against all hierarchies, communities, traditions, and customs—represents the logical conclusion and the ultimate extreme of the secularization of the Protestant religion. The Holy Trinity of original Protestantism, the Supreme Being of later Unitarianism, and the American nation of the American Creed have all been dethroned and replaced by the imperial self. The long declension of the Protestant Reformation has reached its end point in the Protestant Deformation. The Protestant Deformation is a Protestantism without God, a reformation against all forms. The foreign policy of the republic of choice, of the Protestant deformation, is universal human rights.

As has been discussed by Samuel Huntington, this universalist and individualist project of the United States has generated resentment and resistance in societies whose religious traditions are different from the Christianity of the West. Huntington has called this "the clash of civilizations,"—a struggle between "the West and the rest." There has been almost no resistance in those nations with a Protestant tradition. There has been some resistance in those with a Roman Catholic tradition. The greatest resistance has come from those countries with an Islamic or a Confucian tradition.

We cannot now know the outcome of this "clash of civilizations," this struggle between the West and the rest, between the Protestant deformation and the skeins of the other great religions. But the ultimate answer may lie in the character of the Protestant deformation itself.

The Protestant Reformation was a prime movement in the making of the modern era. Almost five hundred years later, the Protestant deformation is a prime movement in the making of the post-modern era. Through its rejections, Reformed Protestantism was the most unique of all religions. Today the Protestant deformation seeks the end of all religions, or rather it seeks to replace the worship of God with the expression of the self.

The Protestant Reformation brought into being early nation states, such as the Netherlands and Britain, which became leading great powers of the modern era. The most Reformed Protestant of all nations was the United States, and it became the greatest of all great powers as well. Much of the power of the United States can be traced to the energy, efficacy, and organization that was a legacy of its Reformed Protestantism. However, the Protestant deformation, because of its universalist and individualist creed, seeks the end of all nation states, including any American one, and to replace loyalty to America with gratification of oneself. It relentlessly undermines the authority of the United States, the superpower which promotes that creed throughout the world.

In his *The Decline and Fall of the Roman Empire*, Edward Gibbon once wrote that the Roman Empire spread the Christian religion throughout the ancient world, but that the Christian religion then undermined the Roman Empire. In our own time, it seems, the American empire is spreading the Protestant deformation throughout the modern world, but the Protestant deformation is beginning to undermine the American empire itself.

35

TRANSNATIONAL RELIGIOUS ACTORS AND INTERNATIONAL POLITICS

—Jeffrey Haynes

The final two decades of the twentieth century were an era of fundamental global political, social, and economic changes, often associated with the multifaceted processes known collectively as "globalization." A rubric for varied phenomena, the concept of globalization interrelates multiple levels of analysis. McGrew suggests that globalization amounts to the product of myriad "linkages and interconnections between the states and societies which make up the modern world system."[1] There was not only the consolidation of a truly global economy and, some would argue, the gradual emergence of a "global culture," but also a number of fundamental political developments, including the steady, if uneven, advance of democracy to many parts of the world. In addition, there were myriad examples of the political involvement of religion, leading the U.S. commentator George Weigel to claim that there was a global religious revitalization, or, as he put it: the "unsecularization of the world."[2]

Weigel did not mean to imply that this was "only" an *apolitical* re-spiritualization; rather it was one linked to the interaction of religion and politics, facilitated by the processes of globalization and encouraged by the communications revolution. Beyer suggests that we now live in "a globalizing social reality, one in which previously effective barriers to communication no longer exist."[3] The development of transnational religious communities was greatly enhanced by ease of interpersonal and inter-group communications, helping to spread their message and to link up with like-minded groups across state boundaries.[4] If Weigel is right and there are political connotations to the "unsecularization of the world," it should be possible to judge the nature and substance of cross-border interactions between religious actors, especially of the world religions, such as Islam and Christianity, with their widespread, transnational networks.

I start from the premise that globalization is likely to facilitate the growth of transnational networks of religious actors which, feeding off each other's ideas and perhaps aiding each other with funds, form bodies whose main priority is the well-being and advance of their transnational religious community. In this article I want to examine the phenomenon

* *Third World Quarterly* 22, no. 2 (2001): 143–58.

of transnational religious actors and assess the claim that their activities undermine state sovereignty. In this context, I focus upon the Roman Catholic Church and the Organisation of the Islamic Conference.

States and Transnational Religion in Historical Context

To answer the question: to what extent have transnational religious interactions undermined state sovereignty?, we need, first, to ascertain what state sovereignty *is*. Bealey defines sovereignty as "a claim to authority, originally by sovereign monarchs, but by states since the Treaty of Westphalia in 1648. A state becomes sovereign when other states recognise it as such."[5] In Bealey's view the concept of sovereignty refers to states' independence from overt interference by other *states*; no mention is made of non-state bodies.

The absence of focus on religious bodies when discussing the concept of sovereignty is not unexpected given the history of the past 400 years in Western Europe. Earlier, Islam had expanded from its Arabian heartland in westerly, easterly, southerly, and northern directions for nearly a millennium. As a consequence vast territories in Africa and Asia and smaller areas of Europe (parts of the Balkans and much of the Iberian peninsula) came under Muslim control. However, unable to deal with the emergence of centralized Christian polities, the demise of the Islamic European empire was swift, a consequence of the rise of centralized European states with superior firepower and organizational skills. In sum, Islam, a religious, social, and cultural system, grew to become a global religion via the growth of a transnational religious community.

Christendom is another historic example of a transnational religious society. During mediaeval times, "Christendom" referred to a generalized conception among Christians of being subject to universal norms and laws derived from the word of God. Later, and contemporaneous with the demise of Islam as a major cultural force in Europe, expansion of Europeans to non-European areas facilitated the growth of a transnational Christian community, albeit one divided by differing interpretations of Christianity. The transborder spread of Christianity was facilitated by the search for gold in the Americas by sundry Spanish and Portuguese "explorers." This led, in the early sixteenth century, to the establishment of the "New World" of various European-administered colonies; contemporaneously, territory was also grabbed in the Caribbean and in Asia by Europeans. Inextricably linked to European expansion was the spread of Christianity, which became a major component of an emerging web of global interactions. Later, however, the public role of religion became increasingly marginal to political outcomes as secular states rose to prominence from the seventeenth century onwards. Since the Treaty of Westphalia in 1648 (which ended the religious wars in Europe between Catholics and Protestants) the history of the development of the global state system has largely been the history of clashing nationalisms, with each national group aiming for its own state and with religio-derived ideologies very much secondary.

In sum, Christian and Muslim transnational religious communities predated the emergence of centralized secular states. Before the seventeenth century, religious interactions were pivotal to the emergence of an international system. Both Christianity and Islam grew to become world religions, conveying their associated civilizations around the world via colonization, conquest, and the expansion of global trade. Contending religious beliefs were the chief motor of international conflicts, the main threat to peace and security. However, the political importance of religion in international politics became increasingly negligible from the seventeenth century, re-emerging as politically important only in the late twentieth century, encouraged by globalization and the accompanying communications revolution.

Transnational Civil Society

International relations theory has long been premised on the centrality of the state to global interactions. However, from the early 1970s, fuelled by a recognition that some non-state actors—such as the Organisation of Petroleum Exporting Countries—were simply too politically important to be ignored, states were not *automatically* seen as the primary actor in international politics. The growth of transnational relations from this time also pointed to the political and economic significance of various non-state actors, independent of state control, such as transnational corporations and international organizations of miscellaneous kinds. From this time, some analysts began to see the international system as an aggregate of different issue areas, such as trade, finance, energy, human rights, democracy, and ecology, where domestic and international policy processes merged. Management of growing global interdependencies was understood to be carried out via processes of bargaining, negotiation, and consensus-seeking among both state and non-state actors, rather than through expressions of military force. Order was maintained not by a traditional mechanism—the "balance of power"—but as a consequence of consensual acceptance of common values, norms, and international law. In other words, from the 1970s global political processes were seen not only to involve states but also non-state actors.

With the demise of the Cold War in the late 1980s, a new model for understanding the direction of global events emerged, sometimes known as the "cosmopolitan worldview," which placed groups of individuals—rather than states—at the center of analysis.[6] In particular, the cosmopolitan model emphasized the importance of international nongovernmental organizations (INGOs)—whose numbers had grown from just over 2,000 in 1972 to more than 5,000 two decades later—to international political outcomes. In particular, it saw the primacy of the state in international politics strongly challenged by the growth of transnational civil societies.

From a domestic perspective, the main concern of civil society—the group of nonstate organizations, interest groups, and associations such as trade unions, professional associations, further and higher education students, churches and other religious bodies, and the media—is often said to be to maintain a check on the power of the state. To what does the concept of transnational civil society refer? Transnational civil society is defined by Lipschutz as "the self-conscious constructions of networks of knowledge and action, by decentred, local actors, that cross the reified boundaries of space as though they were not there."[7] Unlike domestic civil society, transnational civil society is not *territorially* fixed. Rather it is a field of action whose boundaries can change to suit the requirements of new issues and changing circumstances. Transnational civil society is concerned to cultivate regular, expanding interactions across national boundaries when at least one actor is a nonstate agent or does not operate on behalf of a national government or an intergovernmental organization. The sum of such transnational interactions are networks ("civil societies") that cut across national societies, developing linkages between groups in different states.

To Attina, "social transnationalism" defines itself by the multiple linkages between individuals and groups in different societies that are tied by a shared concern for certain issues. Every country, regardless of how conventionally powerful it is, is penetrated by external actors and forces, helping to create what Attina calls the "international social layer," that is, the contacts between groups in different societies that underpin the formal world of supposedly independent states. What he calls "transnational citizen groups" form dedicated cross-border sociopolitical communities pursuing shared goals. But

> transnationalism is not just a matter of individuals and masses who feel conscious of being primary international subjects as they are entitled to civil, political, economic, social, and cultural right by positive international law. In the world system these subjects form the international social layer which claims primacy over the diplomatic layer [that is, states and their institutional order]. Today the chances of social transnationalism reside in INGOs whose members cross states and assert "panhuman" interests such as the promotion of human rights, environmental ecology, [and] international development co-operation.[8]

We might also add religion to the range of "pan-human" interests that Attina identifies. This leads to an interesting question: to what extent, if at all, do transnational religious interactions threaten state sovereignty?

Transnational Religious Actors and State Sovereignty

The theoretical literature on transnationalism has devoted little concentrated attention to religious phenomena. This is probably because transnational linkages and penetration have usually been studied in the international relations literature primarily to assess their impact on questions of political and economic security. The conventional security bias of much of the transnational literature helps explain the lack of references to religious actors. Until recently, with the rise of radical Islam, religious actors were widely regarded as remote from the central questions that affect states in international politics. The explanation for this relative neglect lies in a key assumption embedded in the social sciences. One presupposition, especially evident in theories of modernization and political development, was that the future of the integrated nation-state lay in secular participatory politics. The assumption was that nation-building would be illserved by allegedly "obscurantist" beliefs—such as religion—as secular leaders emerged politically dominant in place of previously powerful religious ones. The implication was that, in order successfully to build nation-states, political leaders would have to remain as neutral as possible from the entanglements of particularist claims, including those derived from religion. The connotation was that politics must be separated from religion (and ethnicity) so as to avoid dogmatism and encourage tolerance among citizens. As decades of apparently unstoppable movement towards increasingly secular societies in Western and other "modernized" parts of the world suggested, over time religion and piety became ever more private matters. The consequence was that religion was relegated to the category of a problem that must not be allowed to intrude on the search for national unity and political stability.

How, then, to explain the recent re-emergence of religious actors with political goals? There is no doubt that religion and religious movements can directly affect the internal politics of states and thus qualify state power, as conventionally understood. For example, North American Evangelical Protestants made a considerable religious and political impact in Guatemala in the 1980s. The outcome was that the Catholic Church there lost a great deal of its traditional institutional importance. Tacit, albeit often unstable, alliances formed between Evangelical Protestants and assorted conservative politicians who shared a goal: to destroy the competitive and socially progressive politics that Catholic liberation theology activists had striven to encourage from the 1960s and 1970s.[9]

Another example comes from Africa. Just as, in the 1980s, American fundamentalist Christians had aided and abetted "anti-communist" forces in Latin America,[10] contemporaneously in southern Africa right-wing Christians worked to aid rebel movements like Renamo and Unita, whose conflicts with their governments were portrayed to the outside world as a battle against "communism." During the Cold War the USA was particularly concerned to control perceived Soviet expansion in Africa. Christian fundamentalists were concerned to confront Satan (that is, communism) and to "win souls for Christ." It is by no means clear, however, that their efforts were coordinated or funded by the U.S. government or one of its agencies. Nevertheless, one of the clearest examples of the dual religious and anti-communist role of American Christian fundamentalists comes from southern Africa. In 1988 the Mugabe government curtailed proselytizing among Mozambican refugees in Zimbabwe by U.S. groups, such as Jimmy Swaggart Ministries, World Vision International, and Compassion Ministries. All were suspected of close links with Renamo. Suspicions appeared to be confirmed when a South African, Peter Hammond, of Front Line Fellowship and six American missionaries of the Christian Emergency Relief Teams (CERT) were captured in Tete province by Frelimo soldiers in late 1989.

Front Line Fellowship was founded on a South African military base in Namibia, allegedly by soldiers who wanted to take Bibles into Angola on their raids; in other words, they were soldier-missionaries, virulently anti-communist, mostly drawn from the (former Rhodesian) Selous Scouts and Five Recce, the South African Special Forces unit which ran Renamo. A local Zimbabwean church, Shekinah Ministries, associated with an American Christian evangelist, Gordon Lindsay, was discovered aiding the Renamo guerrillas in Mozambique in 1987, while in neighboring Angola the counterproductive nature of the MPLA government's anti-religion policy was evidenced in the Ovimbundu highlands and to the Southeast, where "a resistant Church of Christ in the Bush developed in tandem with UNITA."[11] The overall point is that various right-wing Christian individuals and groups worked to aid their anti-communist allies in Mozambique and Angola during the civil wars. However, this does not seem to have been a campaign involving either the hierarchies of the churches themselves or the government of the USA. In sum, these examples highlight the importance of various transnational religious organizations with political goals in Central America and southern Africa during the 1980s.

To pursue this theme further, I focus in the next section on the Roman Catholic Church as an example of a religious transnational community and examine its impact on state sovereignty. Following that, I turn to an assessment of the transnational political importance of the Organisation of the Islamic Conference.

The Political Significance of the Roman Catholic Church as a Transnational Religious Actor

Until recently, the Roman Catholic Church was widely seen as an "uncompromising opponent of liberalism and democracy."[12] During the 1920s and 1930s the Church had dealt with the rise of various manifestations of fascism in Europe by giving it at least tacit support. After World War II the Church enjoyed a close relationship with avowedly conservative Christian Democrat parties in Western Europe, as the latter sought to defeat socialism (and those generally advocating socially progressive measures) electorally. It was not until the Second Vatican Council of 1962–65 (known as Vatican II) that the Pope and other senior Catholic figures began publicly to express a concern with human rights and democracy issues.[13] This expression of papal interest came during a momentous period for world politics: the transition from colonial to post-colonial rule in Africa and the aftermath of decolonization in Asia. It was also the period of the rise of liberation theology in Latin America. But it was not necessarily the case that ordinary Catholics from such "Third World" regions were forcing the issue against the wishes of the Church's senior figures: in fact, it was often the case that Catholic officials in both Latin America and Africa were strongly opposed to the socially progressive articulations emanating from Vatican II, and, at least initially, did little or nothing concrete to further their progress.[14]

The emergence of an institutional Catholic concern with issues of social justice from the 1960s was followed, in the 1980s and 1990s, by a period of momentous change at the global level, a shift from the "old" order to a new global one; and the Catholic Church was important in these changes. For example, the Church was heavily involved in the breakdown of communism in Eastern Europe. Despite the communist system's policy of "cultural strangulation" towards religion, with the aim of choking off its social importance, the Catholic Church was a highly significant actor in the emblematic case of fundamental political reforms in Poland.[15] In this, a transnational element was crucial, notably in the part played by the Vatican and Pope John Paul II. Encouraged by the Pope's expressions of support, Polish Catholicism increasingly represented both a counter-culture and an alternative social space to the official ideology and channels. This led in 1980 to the creation of the Solidarity movement, which articulated and expressed Catholic social ethics as a counter-statement of those of communism. This reflected not only a significant convergence between national and religious identity in Poland, but also, just as importantly, symbolized the failure of a communist (secular) identity fundamentally to implant itself in the hearts and minds of most Poles, a people whose cultural heritage was firmly based in Christian traditions. Thus the Christian heritage and traditions were a vital resource in helping create and then sustain resistance not only in Poland but in Eastern Europe more widely.

A second example of the Church's transnational political involvement comes from Africa. The Catholic Church is by far the largest in the region, with around 100 million baptized followers. In other words, nearly one-fifth of Africans claim to be Catholics— about 10% of the global total. The Church's well developed institutional structure under the leadership of the Pope makes it, in effect, a transnational edifice with centralized control, a factor that facilitated its recent role in the forefront of Africa's democratic changes. It should be noted, however, that its role in this regard was not restricted to Africa alone. Witte observes that "twenty-four of the thirty-two new democracies born since 1973 are predominantly Roman Catholic in confession," including those in Brazil, Chile, the Philippines, South Korea, Poland, Hungary, Lithuania, and various countries in Central America.[16]

Senior Roman Catholic figures in, *inter alia*, Benin, Congo-Brazzaville, Togo, Gabon, and Zaire (now the Democratic Republic of the Congo) were centrally involved in processes of democratization in their countries, to the extent that they were chosen to chair their country's national democracy conferences.[17] The aim of the latter was to reach consensus between government and opposition over the democratic way forward. The involvement of senior African Catholics in democratization followed the Pope's encyclical of January 1991 (*Redemptoris Missio*) which was centrally concerned with the Church's duty to help "relieve poverty, counter political oppression and defend human rights." Why were leaders of the national Catholic churches chosen to chair national democratization conferences? The short answer is that, despite such figures' often close personal relations with their countries' authoritarian governments, in popular perceptions they were representatives of an important organization that was not perceived as being in thrall to the government. This was in part because the churches' independent financial positions enabled them to provide welfare—including, educational, health, and developmental programs—to the acclaim of numerous ordinary people.

It might seem, on the face of it, that the Catholic Church's involvement in both the anti-Communist revolution in Poland and in the pro-democracy events in Africa was a clear example of a religious organization seeking to undermine state sovereignty. However, I suggest that, in both cases, the Church's role should be seen *not* as symptomatic of a desire to undermine state sovereignty but rather primarily as a reflection of processes of growing globalization and nationalization which increasingly affected the Church. The background was that to validate its claims to *catholicity* (that is, universality) the institutional Roman Catholic Church and its leader had to try to resolve two sets of tensions: the first was related to its role as a religious establishment, that is, involving conflict between the Roman, the national, and the increasingly global character of the Church. The second concerned the strain between, on the one hand, national particularities—for example, of the Church in Poland—and the claimed *universality* of Catholic doctrinal principles and moral norms. The importance of both sets of tensions was exacerbated by processes of globalization which propelled these issues on to national and international agendas.

Looking at Catholicism globally throughout the twentieth century and particularly since the 1960s, three interrelated processes in dynamic tension with one another are apparent. First, over time, as a consequence of its transnational growth, there was a global strengthening of papal supremacy, Vatican administrative centralization, and the Romanization of Catholicism. One of the most important indications of this process was Vatican II and its result: an ensuing, general *aggiornamento* (liberalization), producing not only a pronounced trend towards administrative and doctrinal centralization but also a homogenization and globalization of Catholic culture at the elite level throughout the Catholic world.

Second, and occurring simultaneously with the process of Vatican centralization and Romanization of Catholicism, was a parallel process of the internationalization of Roman administrative structures and of globalization of Catholicism as a set of religious norms and practices. This reflected a twentieth-century trend: by the 1960s the Roman Catholic Church was no longer principally a Roman and European institution. This was because the number of Catholics had grown globally—from around 600 million in 1960 to nearly one billion by the mid-1990s—with a clear shift in the Catholic population from Europe to North and South America and, more generally, from North to South. As a consequence, the nature of the episcopal and administrative cadres of the Church also underwent modification. The First Vatican Council (1869–70) had been a mainly European event—albeit with 49 prelates from the USA, comprising one-tenth of the assembled bishops; by Vatican II, a century later, Europeans did not form a majority of the 2,500 bishops who attended. They came from practically all parts of the world, with 10 percent—228 individual bishops—coming from Asian and African countries. This was the consequence of three developments: decolonization, growth in numbers of African and Asian Catholics, and the indigenization of national churches. The result of the Church's extra-European geographical emphasis was clear: the internationalization of Catholicism after the middle of the twentieth century, no longer inevitably centered on Rome. Instead, there emerged numerous, geographically dispersed, centers of Catholicism, a development helping to facilitate the growth of transnational Catholic networks and exchanges of all kinds. Crisscrossing nations and world regions, they often bypassed Rome.

Third, there was a process of "nationalization," that is, a centralization of Catholic churches, at the national level. After Vatican II, national conferences of bishops were institutionalized in many countries, an evolution which reinforced the dynamics of a process of nationalization that earlier had been carried out primarily by different forms of Catholic Action, lay groups that sought to mobilize ordinary Catholics to defend and promote the interests of the Church in the post–World War II era, a time widely perceived as an increasingly hostile, modernized, above all, *secular* environment. The political mobilization of Catholicism was orientated towards putting pressure on the state, either to resist disestablishment or to counteract state-orientated secularist movements and parties, especially, and obviously, socialist- or communist-orientated ones. However, the Catholic recognition of the principle of religious freedom, together with the Church's gradual change of attitude towards the modern secular environment—increasingly it came to accept developments linked to modernization, including a trend in many countries towards societal secularization—served to facilitate significant fundamental transformation of national Catholic churches. They ceased being or aspiring to be state-compulsory institutions and evolved into free religious institutions linked to civil societies. One consequence was that Catholic churches came to dissociate themselves from and entered into conflict with authoritarian regimes, for example, in Poland, in various African countries and throughout much of Latin America. As already noted, this voluntary "disestablishment" of Catholicism permitted the Church to play a key role in recent transitions to democracy throughout the Catholic world.

Conclusion

Traditionally, the position and attitude of the Catholic Church towards political regimes was that of neutrality towards all forms of government. That is, government was seen as "legitimate": if its policies did not systematically infringe the corporate rights of the Church—to religious freedom and to the exercise of its functions—the Church would not question its general legitimacy. However, as the examples of the Church's recent political involvement in, *inter alia*, Poland and Africa suggest, the Church's view of what comprised a "legitimate" government has undergone a significant change in recent years. Increasingly, its view was grounded in a recognition that a "legitimate" government had responsibilities to its citizens: to afford them a clear measure of democracy and a satisfactory array of human rights. In other words, modern forms of democracy were necessary types of polity based normatively on universalist principles of individual freedom and individual rights.

The combination of globalization, nationalization, secular involvement, and voluntary disestablishment led the Catholic Church to a significant change of orientation, both within and between countries. National churches ceased viewing themselves as "integrative community cults" of the nation-state, and instead adopted new transnational global identities permitting them to confront the state. As already noted, among the most significant developments of recent decades was the crisis of absolute principles of state sovereignty and *raison d'état* and the increasingly pronounced global dynamics of democratization. Developments became focused in the decades after the 1970s, and were illustrated by the collapse of the system of socialist states; the (perhaps temporary?) global defeat of national security doctrines; the crisis of the established principle of non-interference in the internal affairs of states; the general disavowal of state-led models of economic development and modernization; and the new dynamics of civil society formation—both intra-societally and globally. The transnational Catholic regime reacted to the new challenges by playing a crucial role both in the revitalization of particular civil societies as well as in the emergence of an identifiable Catholic transnational civil society. In sum, the Catholic Church, which resisted so long the emergence of the modern system of nation-states, responded successfully to the opportunities offered by the crisis of territorial state sovereignty and by the expansion of cross-border civil society, and emerged stronger than before. However, its ability to deal with various crises was not linked to a challenge to state sovereignty.

The Organisation of the Islamic Conference: The Spearhead of Transnational Islam?

I have argued that Catholic sociopolitical involvement, both within and between countries, has been a notable development in recent years. Paralleling this has been a similar process involving Muslims in many parts of the world, especially the Middle East. Should we understand the growth of transnational Islam as the result of similar processes—that is, globalization, nationalization, secular involvement, and voluntary disestablishment—to those that led the Catholic Church to a significant change of orientation from nation-state to civil society, both within and between countries?

What Is the Organisation of the Islamic Conference?

It is sometimes suggested that, rather like the Roman Catholic Church, the Organisation of the Islamic Conference (OIC) is a body that seeks to extend the growth and influence of a certain religion at the global level. The OIC was established by the agreement of the participants of Muslim Heads of State at Rabat, Morocco, in 1969. The first conference was convened at Jeddah, Saudi Arabia, in 1970. A relatively unstructured organization, the body's main institutions is the Conference of Foreign Ministers, although a conference of members' heads of state is held every three years. There is also a Committee for Economic and Trade Cooperation (COMEC), as well as a Secretariat with Political, Cultural, Administrative and Financial divisions , each headed by a deputy secretary general. Various other bodies have been established within the organization, including the International Islamic Press Agency (1972), the Islamic Development Bank (1975), the Islamic Broadcasting Organisation (1975), and the Islamic Solidarity Fund (1977). The OIC has also set up various *ad hoc* bodies to deal with specific issues, including a "contact group" on the

Kashmir question and "an assistance mobilization group" charged with generating aid for Bosnia-Herzegovina (a predominantly Muslim state but not a full OIC member).

For Sardar, the OIC has

> [the] ability to bring all the nations of the Muslim world, even those who have openly declared war on each other, under one roof, and to promote cooperation and communication between Muslim people that has not been possible in recent history. Moreover, it has the potential of becoming a powerful institution capable of articulating Muslim anger and aspiration with clarity and force. . . . The creation of the OIC . . . indicates that the movement of a return to Islamic roots is a transnational phenomenon.[18]

The suggestion is that the purpose of the OIC is to promote Islamic solidarity and strengthen cooperation among member states in the social, cultural, scientific, political, and economic fields.

By the late 1990s, 30 years after its founding, the OIC had 53 members. Although the idea of an organization for coordinating and consolidating the interests of Islamic states originated in 1969 and meetings of the Conference have regularly been held since the 1970s, the OIC only began to attract much Western attention from the early 1980s, following the Islamic revolution in Iran. From the perspective of some Western observers, the OIC encourages "Islamic fundamentalism" and, as a result, is a serious threat to Western security. Huntington claimed that, after the Cold War, potentially coordinated by the OIC, Muslim-majority countries were poised *en masse* to enter into a period of conflict with the West.[19] The U.S. government put much effort into opposing radical Islamic groups as they appeared to threaten the stability of friendly regional states in the Middle East, and tried to isolate "rogue states" such as Libya and Iraq. The governments of such countries, it argued, were committed to state terrorism and might seek to use the OIC as a vehicle for their aspirations.

There is a fundamental flaw in the perception that the OIC is an important institutional sponsor of radical Islamic groups: its members are frequently at each other's throats. Much attention in the Conference since 1980 has been focused on wars involving member countries, including, *inter alia*, those between Iran and Iraq, the Iraqi invasion of Kuwait, and the conflict in Afghanistan. Such was the lack of concord between OIC members that the sixth summit, held in Dakar, Senegal in December 1991, was attended by fewer than half of the members' heads of state. This not only reflected the Conference's longstanding ineffectiveness but also continued cleavages within the Islamic community. Discord between the OIC's members led to fears that the organization would fade from the international political scene because of its failure to generate genuine Islamic solidarity.

By the mid-1990s the OIC was concerned about the global image of Islam. The 1994 summit sought to create a code of conduct regarding terrorism and religious extremism in order to try to deal with the "misconceptions" that had associated Islam with violence in some Western minds. Among other things, OIC governments agreed not to allow their territories to be used for terrorist activities. In addition, none of them would support "morally or financially" any Muslim "terrorists" opposed to member governments. However, with states such as Iran and Sudan (both charged with supporting extremist Islamic groups in other nations) signing the OIC statement, some observers described the document as a "face-saving" measure that masked continuing deep divisions on the issue. The point is that the OIC has never managed to function as an organization with clear goals because of divisions between member states. Some among the latter have sought to cultivate transnational links with radical Islamic groups primarily as a means to further their own influence; but this is old fashioned *realpolitik* rather than an aspect of a campaign coordinated by the Conference.

The chief rivals for superiority in the OIC have been Iran and Saudi Arabia, states that have used some of their oil wealth to try aggressively to expand international influence. Post-revolutionary Iran developed two linked foreign policy objectives: first, to proselytize its Shi'ite version of Islam and, second, to increase state influence in what its government perceives as a Western—especially American-dominated—international system. Iran's government was linked with radical Shi'ite groups, for example, in Lebanon, Bahrain, and Iraq, while also seeking to develop links with other radical Muslims in parts of Africa, especially Nigeria. During the 1980s Iran's diplomatic representatives in Lagos were accused of distributing posters of the late Ayatollah Khomeini and radical Islamic literature which the chief Imam of Lagos Central mosque, Ibrahim Laidi, criticized as perilous for the religious peace of the country. The Nigerian government also criticized the activities of some Iranian embassy staff who, it claimed, tried to introduce what it referred to as fundamentalist and revolutionary doctrines in order to "corrupt" Nigerian Islamic culture and forms of worship.[20] The Iranian attempt to target Nigeria in order to help it achieve its foreign policy objectives should be seen in the context of its rivalry with Saudi Arabia.

The Iranian government wished to create pockets of influence in Africa as the first step in a campaign to achieve a much higher profile in the region than hitherto. In February 1986 Iran's spiritual leader, Sayyid Ali Khamenei, stated that Iran "will survive, defend and protect our revolution and help others in the same cause of Islam to establish the rule of God wherever they are in the world."[21] A symptom of Iran's growing influence in Africa was exemplified by its close alliance with the Islamic rulers of Sudan. Saudi Arabia, on the other hand, the latter's main ally until the 1990–91 Gulf War, lost much of its influence there following its friendship with the USA. Saudi Arabia, like Iran, utilized Islam as a foreign policy tool—when it suited it. During Ethiopia's civil war, Saudi Arabia's support for the Eritreans remained constant despite the leadership of the main guerrilla groups passing from Muslims to Marxist-Leninists and Christians in the mid-1980s. What this brief discussion of the foreign policies of Iran and Saudi Arabia in sub-Saharan Africa has shown is that both states use religion to help them to pursue goals, targeting putative allies among local Muslims to help them.

In conclusion, both Iran and Saudi Arabia pursue Islamic-orientated foreign policies with religious objectives which underpin national interest goals. However, their role as *agents provocateurs* in the eruption of Islamically inspired social protest is a complex one. On the one hand, there are often localized reasons behind the outbreak of Islamic opposition, perhaps economically or ethnically inspired, while, on the other, there are also often foreign interests at work among the already disaffected. Two decades of strong oil revenues gave various states, including Iran and Saudi Arabia, the financial ability to prosecute aggressive foreign policies in which a separation of political, diplomatic and religious goals was difficult to make. Iran's biggest drawback—that it is predominantly a Shi'ite country when most African Muslims are Sunni—was partially offset for some African Muslim radicals—for example, in Nigeria—by its *bona fide* revolutionary credentials. Some ambitious

African Muslim radicals allowed themselves to be seduced by Iran's revolutionary message for two reasons: it gave them an immediately recognizable radical program for their own societies' politically marginalized and alienated; and, second, it offered such Muslim radicals a political platform from which to launch attacks on incumbent Muslim elites associated with the championing of an often unwelcome religious orthodoxy and social conservatism. Saudi Arabia's concerns, on the other hand, were less revolutionary in orientation: to aid alternative groups of Muslims to build a Saudi-style Islamic state by stages over time.[22]

This suggests that the rise of radical Islam was not in response to encouragement from the OIC but the culmination of decades of Western hegemony and accompanying modernization, encouraged by a small Westernized elite. From the 1960s, throughout the Muslim world, secular-orientated governments sought to impose Western rather than Islamic values. Via such ruling elites secularism, socialism, and nationalism all made inroads, while traditional forms of community and civility were undermined. But by the early 1970s this form of modernization was in crisis, leading to social and cultural dysfunctions and, in many cases, fast declining state legitimacy. The official response to growing popular discontent was slow to emerge and, when it did, it primarily took the form of attempted economic reforms, rather than those rooted in sociopolitical or cultural changes. In many countries, popular demands for change stemmed from a rapidly growing recourse to Islamic values and teachings that sought to fill the vacuum left by vacuous attempts to modernize using the Western template. And, as the state's ability to deliver development faded as a result of economic contractions, popular Islamic organizations stepped in, providing welfare, education, and health care which the state could or would no longer provide.

The Islamic revival was generated primarily in an urban setting among technical, professional, as well as clerical strata. The key issue was: what could Islam do for Muslims in the modern world? Could it rescue them from decline, purify society, and combat both internal and external forces of corruption? For many Islamic radicals the triumphant moment was the Iranian Revolution of 1979. This epochal event enabled political and religious authority in Iran to enforce shari'a law as the law of the land, to pursue social justice and roll back Western economic and cultural influence. Despite Western fears, while the Iranian success widely energized Islamic radicals in the Middle East and elsewhere, there was no general revolutionary wave. Instead, Muslim majority states typically responded to the radical Islamic threat by a variable mixture of state-controlled re-Islamicization, reform, and coercion. In response, a popular radical Islamic movement began to emphasize local social struggles. The aim was re-Islamicization "from below," focusing on the requirement for personal and social behavior to be "authentic," in line with tradition. Violence was not eschewed, if judged necessary for a community's "purification." Individual movements focused within countries were supported by the development of transnational networks difficult for states to control, resulting in a condition of endemic instability within many societies.

An interesting example comes from Algeria. There was much Western paranoia in the early 1990s as it appeared that Algeria was about to be taken over by radical Muslims. This fear led the governments of France and the USA to support a successful military *coup d'état* in early 1992 which prevented this outcome. The assumption was that if the radical

Muslims achieved power they would summarily close down Algeria's newly refreshed democratic institutions and political system as they had done in Iran. Following the coup, the main Islamist organizations were banned, and thousands of their leaders and supporters incarcerated. A civil war followed, during which an estimated 100,000 people died.

While the political rise of radical Islam in Algeria had domestic roots, it was undoubtedly strengthened by financial support from patrons such as the government of Saudi Arabia. In addition, there were the mobilizing experiences of Algerian *mujahidin*, who had served in Afghanistan during the anti-USSR war of the 1980s and, on returning home, were no longer content to put up with what was regarded as un-Islamic government. There was also a large cadre of (mostly secondary) school teachers from Egypt working in Algeria. Presumably influenced by the ideas of the Egyptian Muslim Brotherhood or its radical offshoots, they were thought to have introduced similar radical ideas to Algerian youth. These transnational links were not, however, supported by OIC member states; rather, they were transnational popular movements whose struggles were primarily against their own rulers rather than against the West *per se*.

This development was not new. Since the beginning of Islam over 1,000 years ago, Muslim critics of the status quo have periodically emerged in opposition to what they perceive as unjust rule. Contemporary Islamic radicals are the most recent example, characterizing themselves as the "just" involved in struggle against the "unjust." The dichotomy between "just" and "unjust" in the promotion of social change throughout Islamic history parallels the historic tension in the West between "state" and "civil society." The implication is that the "unjust" inhabit the state while the "just" look in from the outside, aching to reform the corrupt system. Historically, the goal of the Islamically "just" has been to form popular consultative mechanisms in line with the idea that Muslim rulers are open to popular pressure and would seek to settle problems brought by their subjects. This concept—*shura* (consultation)—should not be equated with the Western notion of popular sovereignty, because in Islam sovereignty resides with God alone. Instead, *shura* is a way of ensuring unanimity within the community of Muslims, "which allows for no legitimate minority position. The goal of the 'just' is an Islamically based society."[23]

The point is that the rise of radical Islam within numerous countries is primarily a result of the failure of modernization to deliver on its promises. Etienne and Tozy argue that Islamic resurgence carries within it "the disillusionment with progress and the disenchantments of the first 20 years of independence."[24] Faced with state power which seeks to destroy or control the former communitarian structures and to replace them with an idea of a national citizenry based on the link between state and individual, popular (as opposed to state-controlled) Islam emerges as a vehicle of political aspirations. The Muslim awakening should be seen primarily in relation to its *domestic* capacity to oppose the state: "It is primarily in civil society that one sees Islam at work."[25]

Conclusion

I earlier posed the following question: should we understand the growth of transnational Islamic groups as the result of similar processes—globalization, nationalization, secular involvement, and voluntary establishment—that led the Catholic Church to a significant change of orientation from nation-state to civil society, both within and between countries? The global Muslim community, the *umma*, is a good example of a transnational civil society (the Roman Catholic Church is another), which, containing within it the seeds of both domination and dissent, has responded to pressures from globalization and nationalization. Shared beliefs, relating especially to culture, sentiments, and identity, link Muslims, but they are fundamentally divided by various doctrinal issues, especially the schism between Sunni and Shi'a interpretations of the faith. While the rise of radical Islam was stimulated by the Iranian revolution, the fact that it was a Shi'a revolution meant that it was often difficult for Sunnis to relate to it. On the other hand, a combination of poor government, growing unemployment, and generalized social crisis encouraged radical Islamic movements throughout the Muslim world to the extent that, in some cases, although they exist in a Sunni country, they nevertheless may look to Shi'a Iran for support and guidance. The failure of the OIC to provide leadership not only reflects this division within Islam but considerably undermines the extent to which the OIC is a threat to state sovereignty.

Like Islam, the Roman Catholic Church has developed extensive transnational links which have important ramifications for the development of local and interstate religious-political cultures. Global networks of religious activists exist who communicate with each other, feed off each other's ideas, collectively develop religious ideologies with political significance, perhaps aid each other with funds, and, in effect, form transnational groups whose main intellectual referent derives from religious dogma which is of much greater relevance to them than the traditional ideological mobilizers, such as nationalism, communism, fascism, or liberal democracy. Their goal is the creation of communities of believers where God's will is supreme and temporal government downgraded or replaced. Over the last few decades, interpersonal communications have been greatly facilitated by the mass use of the telegraph, telephone, personal computer, email, and fax machine. This communications revolution helped stimulate a globalization of ideas which governments could not control, such as the importance of human rights and democracy. Like Islamic radicals, the Catholic Church was influential in some national contexts in helping undermine the hegemony of authoritarian governments but this should not be seen as a more general threat to state sovereignty.

36

TRANSNATIONAL RELIGIOUS CONNECTIONS

—Robert Wuthnow and Stephen Offutt

Scholars increasingly observe that religion in the United States cannot be understood by considering only the United States. This observation has arisen from several rather disparate lines of inquiry: theoretical arguments about globalization, studies of immigrant congregations, surveys about Americans' attitudes toward the world and the world's attitude toward America, discussions of global Christianity, and missiological research, among others. From these various perspectives, religion is increasingly viewed as a transnational phenomenon. Although it exists in local communities and is distinctively influenced by a national cultural and political context, it has connections with the wider world and is influenced by these relations. Transnational religious connections consist of actual flows of people, goods, services, and information across national boundaries. They are facilitated by transnational organizations and by broader trends in the global political economy.

The aim of this essay is to bring the insights of these diverse literatures into closer conversation with one another and thus to offer a framework for considering the varieties of transnational religious connections. Researchers have quite appropriately focused on specific ways of thinking about transnationalism, both in studies of religion and about other topics. For instance, it is helpful to examine immigrant communities to learn what they bring to American religion from their countries of origin or in other instances to show that they retain closer ties with those places than was possible for earlier waves of immigrants. It is equally appropriate to examine cross border traffic, remittances, and short-term mission trips, or to examine the shifting demographics of the world's Christian or Muslim populations. We miss seeing the larger picture and the relationships among these various processes, though, by considering each in isolation from the others.

A significant strand of scholarship on religion that spans national borders concentrates on diasporas, immigrants and refugees, residents of cosmopolitan cities, border towns, displaced workers, and traders. Evidence of transnationalism shows up among Cambodians in Vietnam, Senegalese in Italy, Central Americans in Houston, Portuguese in Boston, Muslims in Paris, Haitians in Harlem, Christians in China, Chinese in Calcutta,

* *Sociology of Religion* 69, no. 2 (2008): 209–32.

Moroccans in Rotterdam, and so on.[1] Not surprisingly, the people living in these communities often have mixed loyalties and a religious identity that transcends local boundaries. But, oddly enough, hardly any of this work includes the vast majority of congregations in which the U.S. population participates. Much of the literature on those organizations and their members suggests that they are oriented almost exclusively to the needs and interests of local communities (or are heavily nationalistic). Thus, one of the more popular interpretations of *global* Christianity in recent years suggests that churches in the southern hemisphere are flourishing entirely on their own.[2] In this view, there is a complete disconnect between congregations in the United States and the rest of the world.

But obviously this interpretation deviates from common sense. People who are not themselves recent immigrants or located in diasporic border towns are also influenced by globalization. They watch CNN, travel, visit friends and relatives in other countries, work for multinational corporations, and purchase goods from abroad. They live in a world in which transnationalism is very much present. If they are not themselves immigrants, they are increasingly involved in an economy based on transnational flows of labor and capital. They more easily travel abroad and communicate with friends and family in other countries than people did in the past. They receive instant news from around the world, and they often contribute to international relief organizations. With relative ease, they can talk to people in other countries who speak their language, converse about having shopped at Wal-Mart, and for sake of variety listen to "world music" or read imported books. Surely the religious organizations to which they belong are somehow involved in these transnational processes.

We focus on the activities of churches and church members in the United States that cross U.S. borders and, where possible, situate these activities in relation to information about religious practices in other countries. Our approach follows the literature on globalization that treats transnationalism as flows of people, goods, information, and other resources across national boundaries.[3] Flows that have been of interest in this literature include trade, foreign investment, capital, migration, telephone calls, remittances, music, pornography, protest networks, terrorist networks, and tourism.[4] In much of this literature, the more readily quantifiable flows have been examined not only descriptively but also with an eye toward understanding their consequences for a broad range of social phenomena, such as economic development, inequality, the authority of nation-states, and the structure of cities.[5] However, in the case of transnational religious connections, as with many other aspects of globalization, few of the descriptive questions have been fully addressed. This is especially evident when the complexity of these flows is recognized. Not only is it necessary to take account of different kinds (e.g., people, information), but also to consider their location (many are transnational, but few are truly global) and duration, as well as such aspects as speed, scope of societal involvement, and mode of organization.[6]

In emphasizing flows, our approach differs from that of studies in which transnationalism is taken to exist only if people develop an alternative sense of themselves as being citizens of no particular country or attach primary loyalty to a religious community that exists in several countries or engage in business activities that cause them to live and work on two sides of a border over a long period of time.[7] We understand that scholars investigating other topics have sometimes felt it necessary to define transnationalism in these ways. But for our purposes, a broader definition is essential in the same way it is for understanding the flows of people, goods, information, and resources in other spheres affected by globalization.

Any discussion of transnational religious connections must begin by acknowledging that relations of this kind have been around for a long time. Itinerant Buddhist monks in China and Japan, Spanish and Portuguese priests in South America, and the churching of North America by European immigrants are familiar examples. An early example that illustrates U.S. influences overseas is the American Board of Commissioners of Foreign Missions. It was founded in 1810 by Congregationalists and Presbyterians, and by 1835 had distributed 90 million pages of religious tracts, opened 63 overseas mission stations with 311 staff members, and initiated 474 schools for upwards of 80,000 pupils.[8] Religion is transnational because human flows so often transcend arbitrary political demarcations, but also because religious teachings frequently encourage geographic expansion.

If transnational ties are not new, they have become more pronounced and of greater interest in recent decades. Technological innovations have facilitated such connections in the past. London Missionary Society founder William Carey wrote in 1792 that the invention of the mariner's compass was key to the rising missionary movement. This is no less the case at present with email, the Internet, faster aviation, and cheaper shipping making it easier to communicate and travel. The United States—which ranked fourth overall in a recent ranking of countries on measures of globalization[9]—is increasingly connected with other countries through trade, migration, international investment, and technology. These linkages frequently facilitate religious connections as well.

We proceed as follows. First, we discuss transnational religious connections that can be conceptualized as flows of people, considering migration involving change of residence, but also more transitory connections that are increasingly important. Second, we discuss transnational religious connections that involve flows of goods, services, information, money, and other material resources. Finally, we discuss changing aspects of the global political economy that shape these other connections and constitute transnational influences on local and national religious communities.

The empirical information and examples we provide are mostly concerned with the religious connections between the United States and other countries, but include some research conducted in other countries. Besides published research, we draw on new results from the Religion and Global Issues Survey, conducted by Wuthnow in 2005 among a representative national sample of 2,231 active church members in the United States, supplemented with approximately 300 qualitative interviews with clergy and lay leaders of international organizations.[10] In addition, we draw some information from qualitative interviews conducted by Offutt in South Africa and El Salvador in which questions were included about connections to U.S. churches.[11]

Caveats

Two presuppositions guide the argument of this paper. First, the United States is a dominant player within the current international political and economic system, and continues to be a prolific producer and exporter of religion, especially of Christianity.[12] Our findings suggest that this situation will not change in the near future, as recent decades have witnessed significant increases in both the mechanisms by which the U.S. exports religion and the volume of religious actors and artifacts that flow through those mechanisms. Second, today's greatest religious dynamism can be found in the so-called "Global South." Evangelical Pentecostalism is flourishing in Africa, Asia, and Latin America, and various forms of Islam are also growing rapidly. The Catholic Church continues to grow apace, and new developments in Hinduism and Buddhism are making waves in India, Bangladesh, China and elsewhere.

These two global dynamics—the continuing role of the United States in the transnational spread of religion and the religious dynamism of the Global South—do not operate in isolation from one another. South-South (as well as North-South) transnational religious connections often bear the mark of U.S. influence. Consider, for instance, the Nigerian who attends a Bible College in South Africa, and is taught there by an American professor. Or the evangelical Honduran who, while on a business trip to El Salvador, relaxes in the evening with a book by Atlanta-based pastor John Maxwell. It is also true that religious communities in the United States are increasingly on the receiving end of religious transmissions originating in Asia, Latin America, and Africa. These newer influences join older foreign influences on the United States, such as missionaries reporting from the field to their sending churches.[13]

Unlike economic transactions, transnational religious connections cannot be summarized in numeric indices. Much of the relevant information is either qualitative or limited in scope. Our impression from examining this information is that the extent of transnational activity among U.S. religious organizations is probably greater than many observers may have assumed on the basis of previous research. For instance, one study found that only eight percent of Americans attend congregations that sponsor or participate in "programs explicitly mentioning beneficiaries outside the United States, including Crop Walk," and another concluded that only 11 percent of Americans had given time or money to support "international programs" through a religious venue.[14] The evidence we discuss points to significantly higher levels of involvement. In any case, these transnational activities need to be considered alongside the more commonly discussed evidence about congregations' and individuals' local activities and personal religious concerns.

We recognize that flows, networks, and connections are but one way in which religious transnationalism can be conceived. A different approach, for instance, stresses what might be termed transnational identity, such as people identifying themselves as global citizens rather than as members of a particular nation, or organizations promoting an idea of world culture or deterritorialized identity.[15] Our argument is that these shifts toward a transnational or global identity are often rooted in concrete instances of people moving across national boundaries, sending resources across borders, and developing organizations to administer such linkages. Thus, our emphasis is on connections rather than identity.

Our interest in conceptualizing transnational religious connections is especially motivated by the influential thinking that has taken place in recent years about global Christianity.[16] Attention has been drawn to the important fact that the majority of the world's Christian population is located in Africa, Latin America, and other parts of the developing world, rather than in the United States and Western Europe. Much discussion has followed about the apparent vitality of indigenous churches in the Global South and what this recentering may imply about churches in the Global North. However, we have been surprised that relatively little attention has been paid to the continuing—and in some instances, increasing—linkages between churches in the two hemispheres. As Christianity grows in developing countries, these linkages deserve more attention.

Flows of People

People who cross national borders to live, work, or travel in other countries constitute one important kind of transnational connection that often has a religious dimension. Immigration has received considerable attention because of its role in the formation of new ethnically defined religious congregations. People flows also include full-time religious workers, short-term volunteers, and tourists.

Migration

The past several decades have witnessed historic movements of people across borders. Between 1965, when immigration laws changed, and 2000, an estimated 22 million people immigrated legally to the United States and between seven and ten million more may have come as undocumented workers. The impact of immigration was especially evident among young adults where the proportion of men in their twenties who were non-citizens or naturalized citizens grew from four percent in 1970 to 18 percent in 2000.[17]

Migration to the United States is part of a larger global phenomenon. Immigrants to Britain made up 7.5 percent of the population in 2000, and the resulting religious diversity is challenging some to recast Britain's national identity as one of overlapping spiritual identities.[18] France's immigrant population in 2000 was 11 percent, and has brought Islam decisively into the French context.[19] Across the Middle East and Asia, city-states and select countries are being completely reshaped through migration. For instance, 58 percent of those living in Kuwait, 40 percent in Bahrain and Hong Kong, and 66 percent in Macao are immigrants. Although South Africa's foreign-born population of three to five percent appears to be more modest,[20] 41 percent of Botswanans and 54 percent of Mozambiquans in 2000 said their parents worked in South Africa, reflecting labor cycles that have long characterized economic life in Southern Africa.[21] Meanwhile, sending countries are also being restructured. At least 17 countries in the developing world experienced at least two percent annual population losses in the 1990s.[22] Even countries that continue to grow are affected by a still more quickly growing diaspora. El Salvador's population, for example, is about seven million, but an estimated 3.2 million more Salvadorans now live outside the country, with roughly 2.5 million of those living in the United States.

Immigrants not only add to the religious diversity of host societies, but also forge connections between societies. These ties emerge organically, but can generally be classified as connections between immigrants and their home country, immigrants and non-immigrants, or immigrants of different countries. Churches become intimately involved in the transnational ties of their congregants, and over time help to institutionalize and routinize these connections. Levitt[23] notes three strategies used by churches in this endeavor—extended, negotiated, and recreated—and the different types of religious organizations that most often employ them (Catholic, Protestant, and Hindu, respectively). The level of diversity between transnational patterns is, however, somewhat limited because immigrant churches of all stripes, as Ebaugh and Chafetz[24] point out, tend toward the "de facto Congregationalism" adopted by religious communities in America.[25]

The ties between immigrants and their home countries often allow them to participate in two communities simultaneously. Levitt[26] has shown that immigrants frequently make return trips to their countries of origin, maintain dual residences, and even participate in elections in more than one country. Remittances tend to be dominated by flows from host to sending countries, but forms of media flow freely in both directions, including newspapers, movies, television shows, radio programs, phone calls, email, and videos. Wuthnow's New Elites Project[27]—a study of 200 well-established, occupationally successful first-and second-generation immigrants from 35 countries—finds similar evidence of continuing transnational interaction despite these immigrants' successful assimilation into more general cultural norms within the United States. For instance, 73 percent had personally visited siblings or other immediate family members who lived outside the United States at least once a year. There is also ample evidence of the role played by transnational networks prior to their becoming permanent U.S. residents: 43 percent had previously worked in another country, 78 percent knew someone in the U.S. who helped them find a job or get settled, and 67 percent had studied abroad. In all of these ways, immigrants create and maintain ties to their countries of origin.

Besides these direct transnational ties, immigrants interact with other immigrants and with non-immigrants, often in churches. This is one way in which the impact of transnational ties extends beyond immigrant communities into the wider society. In Wuthnow's Global Issues Survey, eight percent of active U.S. church members were immigrants, but 74 percent of members attended congregations in which recent immigrants were present. Qualitative information shows that the presence of immigrants has various effects, both formal and informal, such as initiating special Bible study groups for non-English speakers and spinning off start-up ministries in predominantly immigrant neighborhoods. In addition, the presence of a few recent immigrants sometimes helps in initiating partnerships with churches in other countries and humanitarian programs. There are also increasing instances of congregations drawing together immigrants from different countries—sometimes from the same region and with the same language,[28] and sometimes from multiple continents (as in the case of a Philadelphia church in which members come from China, India, Kenya, and several Latin American countries).

Religious Workers

Professional and other full-time religious workers who go from one country to live and work in another country—i.e., *missionaries*—continue to be an important kind of transnational religious connection. Although casual observers often argue that the missionary era is over,[29] figures collected by Protestant mission agencies and denominations in 2001 show that there were 42,787 U.S. citizens working full-time as missionaries in other countries, representing an increase of approximately 16 percent over the previous decade, and significantly higher than the comparable number in the 1950s at the often assumed height of overseas missionary endeavors. Among Catholics, as of 2004, 111 American-born diocesan priests and 1,420 American-born religious priests were serving abroad. Unlike the upward trend among U.S. Protestant missionaries working abroad, this figure was approximately one-sixth the number of Catholic clergy who had served abroad in 1968. Instead, the number of foreign-born priests serving in the United States appears to be growing, judging from the fact that, in 2005, 16 percent of all U.S. priests and 27 percent of those recently ordained were foreign-born.[30]

While the large majority of religious workers in most countries are indigenous, foreign religious workers create important transnational linkages. According to the most comprehensive source for *global* Christian statistics, eight percent of full-time Christian workers worldwide in 2000 were non-citizens.[31] Non-citizens comprised nine percent of all Christian workers in Asia, 11 percent in Africa, 16 percent in Oceania, and 23 percent in Latin America, but only six percent in Europe and two percent in North America. Differences between poorer and richer parts of the world were also evident in the fact that the ratio of foreign religious workers received to religious workers sent abroad was 5.2 in Africa, 2.6 in Latin America, 2.4 in Asia, and 1.9 in Oceania, whereas it was 0.5 for Europe and 0.3 for North America.

Comparable data for other religions are unavailable; however, one estimate counted 141,630 Islamic *da'wah* groups (propagators of the faith) engaged in foreign missions worldwide.[32] As another example, hundreds of Turkish imams can now be found in Germany, the vast majority of whom are funded by the Turkish government and typically serve four year terms before returning to their own country.[33] In the United Kingdom, estimates suggest that 90 percent of the country's 2,000 imams have been trained abroad, many at schools funded by Saudi Arabia.[34]

Modern mission mobilization among Christian organizations involved transnational cooperation from the start, especially between agencies in the United States and England. These partnerships continued and broadened through such endeavors as the Lausanne Committee for World Evangelization and other international mission conferences in the twentieth century.[35] Among U.S. agencies, mission programs have long been centrally coordinated by denominational and interdenominational boards. This pattern continues. For instance, the International Mission Board of the Southern Baptist Convention had a budget of $283 million in 2005 and supported more than 5,000 full-time foreign missionaries—a five-fold increase since 1955. The support staff in Richmond, Virginia, consists of 500 full-time employees. The board is also responsible for training and deploying approximately 30,000 short-term volunteers. Through its missionaries and volunteers, the board claims approximately 600,000 baptisms annually worldwide and assists in the work of nearly 100,000 overseas churches.

Transnational missionary efforts are also widely supported by local congregations. In the Global Issues Survey, 74 percent of U.S. church members said their congregation supported a missionary working in another country during the past year. On average, four in ten said their congregation has a committee that focuses on overseas missions or other international programs, and one in five reported that his or her congregation had a full-time staff member with special responsibility for overseas missions and other global ministries.

Short-Term Volunteers

Increasingly, people go from one country to another as amateur volunteers for what have come to be called short-term mission trips. Although hard numbers are difficult to find, an estimate from the Global Issues Survey is that 1.6 million U.S. church goers participate in short-term mission trips to other countries each year. The median length of time abroad, not counting travel is eight days, meaning that short-term volunteers contribute approximately 30,000 person-years to U.S. mission efforts abroad—about one-fourth the amount provided by professional missionaries. The dollar value of this effort, using rates established by Independent Sector, is approximately $1.1 billion. At an average cost of at least $1,000 per trip, transportation conservatively totals at least another $1.6 billion.

Forty-four percent of those surveyed said their congregation sent a group abroad in the past year to do short-term missions or relief work. An indication that the numbers of people involved in short-term missions has probably increased is that only two percent of those who had been teenagers during the 1950s, 1960s, or 1970s said they had gone to another country on a short-term mission trip while in high school, whereas this proportion increased to five percent among those who had been teenagers in the 1990s and 12 percent among those who had been teenagers since the 1990s. Although short-term mission trips are primarily a U.S. phenomenon, Offutt's research uncovered teams originating in El Salvador that had visited Kosovo, Equatorial Guinea, Honduras, Niger, Nicaragua, and Vietnam. Teams originating in South Africa had gone to Greece, France, India, Lesotho, Malawi, Mozambique, Poland, and Thailand. These short-term trips are generally facilitated by preexisting transnational ties. For instance, in one case, a middle class Salvadoran immigrated to New Mexico and joined a church, which subsequently sent a team to the immigrant's previous church in San Salvador. In other cases, denominations provide a transnational link, often through congregation-to-congregation partnerships. Nongovernmental humanitarian organizations and campus-to-campus ties are also important facilitators.

When teams arrive at their destination, they engage in a wide variety of activities. Several of the churches we studied near the U.S.-Mexico border enlisted volunteer teams to collect building materials in the United States and assemble them in Mexico with local help. A congregation in Atlanta was fairly typical in sending a team to Africa for a week to investigate organizations with which the congregation would partner over a period of years to provide financial assistance. Teams of medical professionals volunteer at health clinics; groups of teachers volunteer at schools. Still other groups put on puppet shows for children, engage in evangelistic ministries, and distribute food and clothing to communities in need.

Long-term transnational connections may or may not result from short-term mission trips. Some medical professionals, for instance, serve in as many parts of the world as possible, and so view a trip to a specific location as a one time event. In other cases, return visits flow out of relationships that form across cultures. For example, a Seattle-based group first visited El Salvador to help build a house and to upgrade a local NGO's computer systems. A year later, one of the team members moved to El Salvador to assist the NGO in different ways. The other team members communicate regularly and visit El Salvador about once a year.

Religious Transnationalism in Other Fields

People travel internationally and live temporarily in other countries for leisure and work-related activities that may have nothing to do with religion, and yet insofar as they are religious people, their religious beliefs and practices are sometimes involved. By narrow definitions of transnationalism that restrict its meaning to long-term, identity-changing social relationships, these ephemeral contacts may not matter. And yet an understanding of *flows* of people across borders must include such contacts and must also include the possibility that they do broaden horizons and facilitate other kinds of exchange. In the Global Issues Survey nearly two-thirds (62 percent) of active church members said they had traveled or lived in another country—a figure that of course includes short-distance visits to Canada or Mexico.[36] One in seven (14 percent) had lived in another country for at least a year. More than four in ten (43 percent) had friends or relatives who lived outside the United States. Among church members currently working, 37 percent said they routinely interact with people from other countries at work. Transnational contacts of these kinds generally do not result in discussions about religion. And yet, 10 to 15 percent of Americans do talk about religion with people from other religious traditions who have grown up in other countries, and, not surprisingly, Americans who have traveled abroad are more likely to have participated in diverse worship services.[37]

Congregations are one of the places in which transnational contacts occur. In the Global Issues Survey, 48 percent said their congregation had hosted a guest speaker from another country in the past year. Colleges and universities are another. In 2004 the number of foreign students enrolled at American universities totaled more than 572,000, up from only 179,000 in 1975. Denominations, seminaries, and parachurch organizations are yet another source, hosting international conferences and study-abroad opportunities. One example is the triennial Urbana Missions Conference, which attracted 23,000 college-age participants in 2006. Another is Passion, a multi-day Christian music and worship fest that drew a similar number of young people to Atlanta in 2007.

Pilgrimages represent another critical component of transnational religious activity. Among Muslims, the annual *hajj* is a prominent example, drawing approximately 2.5 million visitors to Mecca each year, including an estimated 10,000 from the United States.[38] American Hindus are among the more than 100,000 pilgrims who travel annually to Kashmir to see a symbol of Lord Shiva, one of Hinduism's three most revered gods, and are said to be increasingly represented among pilgrims to large "Hindu theme parks" in India.[39] Hindus, Buddhists, Jains, and Bonpo believers all consider Mount Kailas in Tibet to be a place for pilgrimage at least once in their lifetimes, and come from all over the globe to circle its base.[40] For American Christians and Jews, visits to Israel frequently have meaning as religious pilgrimages. Overall, tourism to Israel (from all countries) grew from just over one million in 1990 to 2.4 million in 2000, declined to 862,000 in 2002 after the 9/11 attacks, and thereafter rose to 1.8 million in 2006.[41] Organizations such as Taglit-Birthright Israel, Hillel, the Catholic Pilgrimage Center, the World Religious Travel Association, local congregations, and commercial travel agencies are examples of organizations that facilitate pilgrimages.

Business and professional personnel increasingly travel internationally as the global economy expands, and in some instances also use these contacts to forge religious ties.[42] Offutt's research in Central America and Africa finds numerous examples. For instance, a Salvadoran visiting a plant in Honduras announces that he is an evangelical Christian and that he is interested in a potential project because he thinks it could honor and glorify God. The plant manager responds that he shares the Salvadoran's faith, and is excited about the partnership for the same reason. A South African commodities trader believes that "there are a lot of people in darkness," and he consequently tries to share his faith through his business interactions, which often cross national borders. Other examples include the international business leaders known as "boss Christians" in China,[43] and so-called "great commission companies," such as Pura Vida Coffee and Gateway Telecommunications.[44] Religious actors also create ties in diplomatic venues. For example, a South African Christian lawyer told Offutt she believes that God has called her to fight for social justice, and she does this by representing South Africa in committees at the United Nations and on women's issues in the Democratic Republic of Congo. She uses transnational connections, including contacts at American universities and in Washington, as resources.

Flows of Resources

Besides flows of people, transnational religious connections consist of exchanges of money, knowledge, information, and other goods and services between religious communities or between donors in one country and recipients in another. The cost of training, transporting, and maintaining religious workers abroad implies a transnational investment of resources. Others include remittances, funds for religious personnel and programs, humanitarian efforts, and flows of religious products and information.

Remittance

Global statistics for 2002, the most recent year available, shows that migrants sent nearly $80 billion home to developing countries. In Mexico alone, remittances from people working abroad totaled $9.8 billion, approximately twice the value of the country's annual agricultural exports.[45] In El Salvador, remittances totaled nearly $2.8 billion in 2005 and an estimated 22 percent of households in El Salvador receive remittances.

   Remittances primarily benefit family members, but in turn sometimes expand the possibilities for religious congregations to hire staff and run programs. Kurien's[46] research among Indian workers in the Middle East shows how remittances affect Christian, Muslim, and Hindu communities in India. Levitt's[47] research provides examples of remittances facilitating the activities of congregations in the Dominican Republic and Ireland. An example from Offutt's work in El Salvador also shows how churches benefit from remittances. Mario Gonzalez, the senior pastor of the Christian Community of Faith and Adoration estimates that all of his 150 members have relatives living in the U.S., and that 80 percent receive remittances. The church worships in a rented space in Zacamil, a lower middle class sector of San Salvador. Remittances enable the very simple lifestyle to which the members aspire. Gonzalez encourages members to tithe remittances just as they would income, and he estimated that 20 percent of them do. As it seeks to purchase a lot and erect a new church building, the added tithes from remittances will certainly help.

Religious Funding

Financial support of religious organizations and personnel in other countries represents another significant flow of resources. Studies of religious congregations in poor countries appropriately emphasize the role of indigenous leaders and local participation, and yet may underestimate the role of external funding in arguing that overseas missionaries are not involved. In 2001, approximately 65,000 non-U.S. citizens and foreign nationals were working in other countries under full financial sponsorship by a Protestant U.S. agency. Though small compared to the likely number of clergy supported through local funding, this number was larger by nearly half than the number of U.S. foreign missionaries. In total, U.S. Protestant churches contributed more than $3.7 billion for overseas ministries, an after-inflation increase of 45 percent over the previous decade.[48]

Whether the labor value of short-term volunteers represents an actual financial contribution can be questioned on grounds that these volunteers also consume time and resources from their hosts and may only be replacing local labor in areas where unemployment is already high. However, short-term volunteers sometimes provide financial assistance as well. For instance, a study of four U.S. teams of high school students working with Peruvian churches showed that the 89 volunteers contributed a total of more than $25,000 in cash toward church construction and repair.[49]

Humanitarian Aid

Congregations and denominations are significantly involved in international humanitarian aid. A national poll released on January 13, 2005 showed that 36 percent of the U.S. public claimed to have donated money to their churches for tsunami victims.[50] The Southern Baptist Convention collected $16 million, United Methodists took in more than $6 million, the United Church of Christ contributed more than $3 million, and the Evangelical Lutheran Church in America raised $2.5 million. Catholic Relief Services alone accounted for $114 million.

In the Global Issues Survey, 76 percent of active church members said they had personally given money in the past year for international relief or hunger projects. The same percentage said their congregation had an offering in the past year to raise money for overseas hunger or relief programs. In more than 80 percent of these congregations, there had been more than one such offering in the past year. The survey also showed that 29 percent belonged to congregations that had helped support a refugee or refugee family within the past year. Qualitative interviews with pastors and lay leaders suggested that congregations usually contribute in rather small ways to humanitarian efforts. This impression is reinforced by the survey in which 70 percent of respondents said they gave less than $500 total to religious organizations during the year and, of these, the majority either did not know or assumed the amount they had given to help people in other countries was less than $100.

Individual donations, though, comprise only part of what U.S. religious organizations contribute to international humanitarian aid. Data collected in 1981 showed that many of the largest nonprofit humanitarian organizations were religious—for example, Catholic Relief Services, World Vision, Church World Service, and the Adventist Development and Relief Agency—and that some of these organizations were receiving substantial revenue from government grants and contracts.[51] By 2003, judging from IRS 990 forms, inflation-adjusted budgets of the top 25 faith-based international aid organizations had grown 134 percent, reaching a total of $2.3 billion. Among the largest, Catholic Relief Services received 74 percent of its support from government sources. Church World Service, World Relief, the Adventist Development and Relief Agency, and World Vision received 64 percent, 50 percent, 46 percent, and 37 percent, respectively. Besides government funding, private philanthropy, such as that of the Arthur S. DeMoss Foundation, the DeVos Foundation, and the Maclellan Foundation, also played a significant role.

Religious Products and Information

One of the more important transnational flows of religious information is the production and distribution of Bibles. In 2006, approximately 24 million Bibles were distributed worldwide by United Bible Societies, a transnational organization that began in 1946 and currently includes offices in 120 countries. Bibles are printed in local languages and support is raised through local congregations. However, the effort also represents a significant investment of U.S. resources. The American Bible Society's 2006 IRS 990 form shows assets of $493.8 million and total expenses of $82.6 million, of which $37.7 million was for "overseas outreach."

Another example is the Jesus Project, a film about the life of Jesus produced and distributed by U.S.-based Campus Crusade for Christ. From the project's inception in 1979 through 2005, an estimated 42 million videocassettes (as well as 13 million audiocassettes) were distributed.[52] The material has been translated into 1,000 different languages, and the organization claims it has reached six billion people in 105 countries.

A third example is the leadership literature produced by John C. Maxwell.[53] Maxwell, an Atlanta-based speaker and author, appears regularly on bestseller lists such as *The New York Times* and *BusinessWeek*. He is aggressively reaching out around the globe, touring 12 countries in Latin America in 2006. In El Salvador he spoke to over 1,000 business and religious leaders before meeting with the country's President, Tony Saca. In 2007 Maxwell spoke to senior executives and ministry leaders in South Africa. His books are prominently displayed in Christian book stores throughout El Salvador and South Africa. When an assistant pastor in a Salvadoran megachurch of 15,000 was asked by Offutt which American authors he trusted, his first response was "John Maxwell."

Other religious products also facilitate a sense of a single faith community across borders. The second generation Swadhyayees (a Hindu movement) that Levitt studied watch videotapes (with English subtitles) of lectures by their leader. The Swadhyaya headquarters now has a unit that spends its days mailing these out around the world. Likewise in Pakistan, Farhat Hashmi, a female religious scholar who is very popular with middle-class Pakistani women, is spreading her word through audiotapes, video, and books; she is gaining increasing visibility throughout South Asia and the Middle East.[54]

The Global Political Economy

Besides the flows of people and resources that connect religious communities transnationally, religion is shaped indirectly by global economic and political relations. These economic and political relations are part of the globalization process and typically involve new market relations, rising opportunities for some and declining opportunities for others, trade agreements, and diplomatic relations. The impact of these changing dynamics of the global political economy on local religious communities is often profound. A good example of these indirect influences was the integration of northern Brazil into the global economy through the construction of the Belem-Brasilia highway and the subsequent growth of iron, timber, ranching, and hydroelectric power generation. As subsistence farmers and agricultural workers displaced from rural areas, Belem's migrant population swelled and the shantytown population increased four- to eightfold. Pentecostal churches grew rapidly in these neighborhoods, attracting domestic servants, security guards, janitors, day laborers, and the unemployed. Without healthcare or traditional family networks, people were especially drawn to the healing services the churches offered.[55] In other areas, Pentecostal and evangelical churches have grown among different social strata.[56] The point is that even religious developments led by indigenous clergy and in highly specific local settings are often shaped by transnational influences. Although a full treatment of these influences cannot be attempted here, they can be illustrated by mentioning several of the most pervasive aspects of globalization.

Trade and Communication

People in different parts of the world are increasingly connected through international trade and communication. As a share of Gross Domestic Product, international trade rose during the 1990s among 67 countries for which records were kept and declined among only 14, according to the World Bank.[57] During the same period, the United Nations tracked 1,885 changes in national regulations and found that 94 percent liberalized the flow of international trade (ww.uctad.org). International telephone traffic, as measured by minutes U.S. residents spent talking internationally, increased by 500 percent between 1990 and 2004.[58] The Internet, email, and satellite links to newspapers and cable television stations have also encouraged greater awareness of people and events beyond national borders. In the Global Issues Survey, 75 percent said they watched news about other parts of the world on television at least once a week, a quarter read about international news at least once a week, and four in ten obtained information about foreign events at least once a week from the Internet.

In our 300 qualitative interviews among U.S. clergy and laity, we found numerous examples of religious practices being influenced by international trade and communication. Liturgical prayers focused on late breaking news in some instances and included prayer requests received overnight from missionaries in others. A church in South Carolina started a relief project in Africa after one of its members returned there from a business trip. A lay leader in Massachusetts became interested in working with the International Justice Mission after hearing about human trafficking on a visit to Thailand. An immigrant church in Philadelphia keeps in close contact with family members in Nigeria through email.

Equality and Inequality

Free markets and increasing international trade have affected national economies nearly everywhere, bringing rising economic opportunities for some and reinforcing poverty for others. Between 1987 and 1998, the share of the world's population living in extreme poverty fell from 28 percent to 23 percent, with most of this decline occurring in China and India, while the number of poor people living in Africa increased.[59] Income inequality within developing countries appears to have declined in some cases and risen in others. Other measures of development, such as expansion of primary schooling and reductions in child mortality rates, show only modest gains during the recent period of globalization.[60]

Ethnographic studies suggest that religious communities have responded in complex ways to these shifting economic realities. Chesnut's[61] research in northern Brazil illustrates Pentecostalism's appeal to people in declining strata, while other research in southern Brazil suggests a different kind of Pentecostalism emerging among the rising middle class. Research among evangelicals in Ghana shows teachings that give hope and legitimacy to people with increasing economic aspirations but at the same time warn against the dangers of consumer gratification.[62] In China, studies variously suggest that business leaders with expanding profits from international trade are involved in bankrolling new Christian churches, that the rising urban middle class is both drawn to prosperity gospel preaching and increasingly secular, that the Korean expatriate community is growing and deeply religious, that the Chinese government is more tolerant of religion in some areas and better able to suppress it in others, and that rural poverty is a source of growing spiritualism and syncretic folk religious practices.[63] All of these developments are influenced by changes in the global economy.

Democracy

The democratic revolution that has affected many parts of the world since the end of the colonial era has been a transnational movement both in spreading ideas about democracy from one society to the next and in creating new political agreements (such as the European Union) that include multiple nations. As a significant feature of its foreign policy during and after the Cold War, the United States has sought to encourage democratic regimes at least in parts of the world where it was in the nation's interests to do so. One aspect of U.S. policy that dealt specifically with religion has been its attempts to promote international religious freedom as part of a broader agenda of extending human rights.

Although the implications of this democratic revolution for religion vary, three broad implications can be identified. First, democratic regimes have opened doors for foreign religious workers in many instances. Russia, other parts of Eastern Europe and central Asia, Uganda, and Indonesia are examples. Second, reactions against democratization, perceived as a Westernizing and secularizing influence, have emerged in Burma, Algeria, and some parts of the Middle East, effectively reducing opportunities for foreign religious workers. And third, questions about religious pluralism and the rights of religious minority groups have risen in importance as repressive regimes have disappeared and as smaller religious communities have acquired the right to speak on their own behalf.

Cultural Influences

Transnational religious connections are also influenced by the spread of common symbols and narratives. They do not displace local traditions, but they do reflect the power of rich countries to influence global culture. The fact that so many speak English has made long- and short-term mission work easier. English is the first language of only 375 million people, but is a second language for another 375 million people as a result of colonial histories and migration, and it is estimated to be part of the repertoire of another 750 million people who have felt the need to learn English as a second language. Consumer culture is another influence. In 2000, for instance, the global market for films was estimated at one trillion dollars, of which American content comprised slightly more than half.[64] Of the ten top-grossing films at the international box office, all originated in the United States. Although it is unclear how widespread these cultural influences may be, writers point to numerous anecdotal examples, such as "Amazonian Indians wearing Nike sneakers, denizens of the Southern Sahara purchasing Texaco baseball caps, and Palestinian youths proudly displaying their Chicago Bulls sweatshirts in downtown Ramallah."[65]

Local religious organizations are influenced by these messages, sometimes incorporating them and often warning followers against them.[66]

Conclusion

Globalization has been described as a culturally homogenizing force, spreading a mono-culture of fast food items and Western-style entertainment, and as an equalizing dynamic that reduces poverty. Both claims are disputed by scholars who argue that globalization actually facilitates diversity and perhaps increases income disparities. What is not disputed is the fact that some countries are much richer and more powerful than others. Global inequality is thus a significant reality for understanding transnational religious connections. It means that many of these connections are asymmetric.

For example, the 155 million Christians living in Brazil and the 192 million Christians living in the United States give an appearance that the two countries are nearly equivalent in religious demographics, but there are notable differences. In the United States the average Christian enjoys an annual income of $26,980, whereas the annual income of Christians in Brazil is $3,640. Not surprisingly, Christian organizations are much more numerous and better supported in the United States than in Brazil. Brazil has more than twice as many Catholics as the United States, but the United States has more than twice as many Catholic parishes as Brazil and the ratio of priests to parishioners is six times higher in the United States than in Brazil.[67] Overall, U.S. Catholic and Protestant churches take in approximately nine times more money annually than churches in Brazil. The point is not to diminish the importance of indigenous churches in Brazil, many of which have experienced explosive growth in recent decades, but that churches in the United States have enormous capacity to support programs both at home and abroad.

These asymmetries notwithstanding, symmetric links and counter-flows are also evident. For example, Pentecostal missionaries and telecasts from the United States to Brazil are now reversed through programming from the Universal Church of the Kingdom of God in Brazil, which is reproduced for the New York City Spanish language media market.[68] Similarly, black gospel music once imported in Ghana from the United States is more recently joined by holy hip hop music from Ghana being popular in Atlanta. Symmetry is encouraged by norms of reciprocity, by rising interest in cultural diversity, and in some instances by contact with visitors from rich countries conferring prestige on pastors and lay leaders in poor countries.

Although it is easiest to chart bilateral connections, multilateral ties are evident in both old and new forms. The Catholic Church, the Anglican Communion, and international meetings of Presbyterians or Baptists illustrate the older forms in which interaction among representatives from a number of countries was encouraged through formal assemblies and conferences. Newer forms appear to be less centrally organized and operate through congregations, personal ties, and short-term visits. For instance, in our qualitative interviews we found an independent evangelical church in the Midwest that sponsored a mission team from Belfast to work in Africa and one from Africa to work in Latin America. The aim is to promote cross-cultural learning.

Counter flows and multilateral connections are not ahistorical. Rather, they exist in the world created by the flows, counter flows, and multilateral connections that went before them. The culture that flowed through these connections yesterday is often repackaged and sent on again, picking up the local flavors of each stop in its transnational journey. Cultural echoes often reverberate back through the transnational connections to the senders, influencing those communities yet again, while the cultural artifacts go on to new places and take on unanticipated forms. In a remote section of Papua New Guinea that had never been missionized, Robbins[69] observed apocalyptic rumors of Christ's imminent return that betrayed a remarkable awareness of the wider world. The European Union was thought to be a harbinger of a world government, turmoil in the Middle East signaled the end times, a new world order was in the making, and Satan was behind the universal product code and the spread of ATM machines. Further investigation traced the rumors through local networks among the villagers and their pastor to several outside sources, including a New Zealand–based evangelist who had become popular in Papua New Guinea and who, in turn, had been heavily influenced by the American writer Hal Lindsey, author of the bestselling *Late Great Planet Earth*.

Clearly, the existence and probable increase of transnational religious connections poses new opportunities and challenges for scholars of religion. Besides chronicling the existence of these connections, future studies will need to consider the organizational mechanisms through which they are refracted, the ways in which easier travel and communication increase the chances of local congregations in different parts of the world supporting one another and working cooperatively, and how these possibilities affect local congregations and their choice of partners. As with other relationships involving power differences, those between religious organizations in rich and poor countries merit special consideration.

37

EUROPEAN POLITICS GETS OLD-TIME RELIGION

—Timothy A. Byrnes

In the late 1970s I spent a year as an "occasional student" at a British university. I was asked repeatedly during that year to explain, if not defend, the tense race relations that existed then (and exist now) in the United States. I offered the standard explanations, running from the legacies of slavery to the unfortunately blunt racism of some of my compatriots. But I always detected in the bewilderment of my British friends a sort of "Can we all get along" simplicity. And I also detected a bit of smugness—an assumption that they, and *their* compatriots, were above such prejudice.

I did not say it aloud very often, but I also knew that a big part of the explanation for racial tensions in my country was the racial diversity that characterized the American social landscape, and the races' proximity to one another. Part of the reason that the races did not get along very well in my country was that in the United States we had different races to *not* get along with. On the other side of the Atlantic, British homogeneity had bred British complacency in this regard. To be sure, there was more than a little self-deception in that complacency: Britain in the 1970s was already home to large immigrant populations that were undoing that homogeneity and challenging traditional notions of what it meant to be "British." But it took the Brixton riots, which broke out a few years after I left England, to shatter that complacency—and to demonstrate to me, and most of my British friends, that diversity can breed discord in London just as easily as it can in Los Angeles.

I have been thinking of those long-ago conversations recently as I have confronted another set of questions, this time concerning religion rather than race, and this time involving the United States and Europe writ large, rather than America and Britain alone. These days Americans are being challenged by their European counterparts—implicitly, at least, and sometimes quite explicitly—to defend, or explain, how a religious zealot like George W. Bush, with such a simplistic worldview, could become president of the United States; or, to take an even more recent example, how a provincial creationist like former Arkansas Governor Mike Huckabee could have emerged, at least temporarily, as a serious contender for the presidential nomination of the Republican Party.

* *Current History* (March 2008): 126–32.

These challenges indicate a deep divide between Europe and the United States concerning the assumptions people hold about religion and about religion's proper role in public life. Even Bush's staunchest opponents in America are not as startled as European observers are by the president's openly religious rhetoric, or by his evangelical view of the world and of international relations. Americans are more accustomed than are Europeans to hearing people, including politicians, talk this way. President Bush may be particularly clear in the degree to which he defines his own suppositions in religious terms, and in how he portrays the history of his nation as being driven and ordained by God. But many Americans continue to define their lives and their communities in just these terms. And even those who no longer do so are nevertheless more accustomed to being confronted by religious worldviews—and to facing the politically charged conflicts between such worldviews—than most Europeans are.

Yet today this distinction between the United States and Europe is rapidly blurring. This is happening not because the French, the Dutch, or the British are about to adopt American levels of religious belief or religious practice. Rather, it is happening because the reintroduction of religious diversity into European society—through the immigration of Muslims and the expansion of the European Union—is also reintroducing religion, and religiously motivated conflicts, to European politics.

Most of these conflicts concern the role of religion per se in a modern polity, and pit religious believers against defenders of a secular status quo. But some conflicts might also in time come to involve political contestation *between* adherents of diverse religious traditions. Large-scale Muslim migration into Europe, for example, may be having the remarkable effect of fanning and reigniting what Peter Katzenstein has called the "glimmering embers" of European Christianity, at least in political terms.

At the very least, close and sustained contact with religious "outsiders," in what is assumed to be a post-Christian Europe, is reviving old beliefs about European history and political development, beliefs that depend on Christianity for their vocabulary and institutional underpinnings. Indeed, today's debates over the role of religion in European politics could lead to forms of religiously charged political contestation that would make concerns about Huckabee's views on evolution seem rather mild in comparison.

The Migration Effect

Two factors are increasing the religious diversity of Europe and reintroducing religion to European politics. The first is the presence of up to 20 million Muslims within the EU's member states. While there is no doubt these Muslims are living in Europe, there is a lot of doubt as to whether they are actually *Europeans*. Are they hyphenated, marginalized, permanent visitors of some kind? Or do they constitute an organic element of the European population that—like other parts of the population—gets to assert its own identity within Europe, and gets to participate in the complex, ever-evolving process of defining what it means to be European?

The suburbs of Paris are home to large concentrations of Muslims. Amsterdam, before too much longer, will be a majority Muslim city. German society has been profoundly transformed by generations of Turkish *gastarbeiter* (guest workers) who somehow neglected to ever return "home." Europe, and its relationship to secularism, look a bit different when the designation "European" is granted to these residents of the continent.

It is fascinating that the same "Europe" that was defined for so long in explicitly religious terms as "Christendom" is now being defined by many Europeans in equally exclusive terms as a-religious, and perhaps even anti-religious. Europe is secular, the argument goes; so if Muslim populations are going to be accepted into European society and politics, they will have to accommodate themselves to the fundamentally secular worldview at the heart of European self-definition.

Two immediate responses can be made to this argument. The first is to point out just how recent a phenomenon this European devotion to secularism actually is. History did not end in 1648 with the Peace of Westphalia any more than it did in 1989 with the fall of European communism. Indeed, religion and religious categorizations remained, well into the twentieth century, central features of European political organization and crucial points of European political cleavage.

The second necessary response to the argument that secularism is the nonnegotiable heart of European political identity is to point out that this concept of secularism is a bit more complicated and variable than many Europeans imagine it to be. As José Casanova noted in his indispensable book *Public Religions in the Modern World*, secularism has at least two very separate meanings that are often inappropriately conflated as if they were the same thing, or as if one necessarily led to the other. The basic process of secularization as "the modern autonomous differentiation of the secular and religious spheres," to quote Casanova, does indeed constitute a central component of modern governance and social organization, certainly in the European context. But the idea that this institutional differentiation of the sacred from the secular will necessarily lead to the decline of religious belief and religious observance (the heart of the so-called modernization theory) was, according to Casanova, little more than a self-fulfilling prophecy promoted by European sociologists.

This latter definition of secularism, he argues, is decidedly not a necessary characteristic of "modern" politics and society outside of Europe. On the contrary, ample evidence suggests that religion can endure and even thrive within modernity, and that religion can intersect with, and participate in, political processes in "the modern world." Seen in this light, religion's estrangement from the political realm in Europe may not be a historically inevitable destination of modernization, but rather a time-specific phenomenon that will not necessarily be characteristic of Europe for the indefinite future. Again, though, it matters in this regard what counts as Europe, and who counts as European.

The Islamic Challenge

To be sure, secularism in the sense of institutional separation is a well-established feature of democratic governance in Europe, and European Muslims can fairly be expected to abandon any theocratic expectations that they may have brought with them to the continent. But part of the challenge that domestic Islam is posing to European secularism is that Islam does not recognize the distinction between the sacred and the profane in the same way that (at least modern) Christianity does. For this reason, Muslims in Europe will, as their numbers increase in both absolute and relative terms, continue to push the boundaries of "acceptable" religious politics on issues as varied as education, foreign policy, and the role of women in European societies.

This does not mean that we have a string of European Khomeinis to look forward to, or that secular Europe will give way to the much-feared "Eurabia." But it does mean that, short of draconian limitations on political participation by Europe's Muslims, non-Muslim Europeans can expect renewed public debate concerning the relationship between the secular principle and democratic governance, and concerning the appropriate role of religious belief in defining and articulating political interest.

How this debate will be framed and conducted in the long run is very difficult to predict at the moment. Consumers of a growing literature featuring titles like *While Europe Slept*, *The Last Days of Europe*, and *The Suicide of Reason* can be forgiven for not looking forward to this future with much confidence or enthusiasm. But alongside books like these, more hopeful scenarios have been imagined, some by Muslims such as Abdullahi An-Na'im, who has called for a worldwide "Islamic Reformation," and, in a different way, Bassam Tibi, who has insisted on the development of what he calls "Euro-Islam."

What should not be demanded, or at least not expected, is that Muslims abandon their religion wholesale; or that they accept the idea that religious belief should not inform their approaches to politics and policy. It would probably be a vain hope in any case to expect even those Muslims who acknowledge the differentiation of the sacred from the profane in institutional terms to also adopt the worldview of, say, a lapsed Dutch Catholic or a ceremonial British Anglican. Such a demand, moreover, would run the risk of violating the very liberal principles it would purport to uphold. What is so liberal, after all, about insisting that Muslims—or anyone else for that matter—renounce their religious beliefs in order to be accepted into liberal society?

Not So Secular

There is nothing very surprising about the prediction that European politics will, in the future, feature debates over the relationship between political worldviews defined by Islam and the secularist status quo. We are seeing this emerging already in all sorts of ways and places; the dynamic is sure to continue and to deepen. What is perhaps a bit surprising, and maybe even speculative, is my claim that the status quo itself may prove less secular than many of its advocates suppose. One of the results of the Islamic challenge to European secularism has been the revelation that some secularism in fact masks Christian assumptions and practices that are so deeply ingrained in European society as to go unnoticed until outsiders challenge them. Put another way, the "problem" with Europe's Muslims is not only that they believe something, as against a cultural requirement to believe nothing, but also that they believe particular things that do not fit with reflexive assumptions that persist across the continent.

No, European Christians have not been secretly attending mass in a catacomb somewhere, hidden from the dictates of secularism. But policies such as public funding of sectarian schools in Britain, or public financing of church operations in Germany, were devised quite obviously with Christian communities in mind. These policies as a result, in ways subtle and not so subtle, put Muslims at an institutional disadvantage in terms of gaining access to government funding. Yet, when Muslims call for reform of such policies to create a more level playing field—to pursue their own piece of the public pie—they face significant political opposition.

The problem, moreover, extends well beyond government programs and benefits. Consider a December 2007 speech by French President Nicolas Sarkozy, in Rome of all places, in which he suggested that "the roots of France are mainly Christian." France, he declared, is "looking for spirituality, values, and hope," and "needs convinced Catholics who are not afraid to affirm what they are and what they believe." The speech included all sorts of caveats and frequent reaffirmations of France's continued commitment to what Sarkozy called a "*positive laïcité*." But it was also larded with celebratory quotations from papal works. Indeed, its tone was so religious that it occasioned a cartoon in *Le Monde* depicting Sarkozy as a bishop. Tellingly, the cartoon also featured a chagrined President Bush complaining to the pope that the French president was "stealing my job."

Perhaps we should not make too much of one speech. Sarkozy is Sarkozy, after all, and part of his intention in Rome was undoubtedly to provoke and incite back in Paris. Still, France is often cited as among the most secular countries in the world, and it has long maintained a taboo against public approbation of religion's cultural and political role. Yet here was the president making a claim of civilizational identity for his French homeland, and defining that identity, at least in part, in unmistakably religious terms.

Sarkozy's speech takes on even more significance in light of the political context in which it was delivered. These were the words of a president who has practically reveled in his dismissal of the grievances of mostly Islamic protesters in the outskirts of Paris and other French cities, and who has left no ambiguity in his strenuous opposition to the prospect of Turkish membership in the EU. Sarkozy's rhetoric may be a long, long way from the traditional and troubling assertion that "to be a Pole is to be a Catholic" (this particular eastern formulation has not migrated west with expansion), but his words might not be so distant from the claim, often heard in America, that the United States is in some foundational and irreversible way a "Christian nation."

These considerations raise the important and interesting question of the degree to which widespread social conflict in contemporary Europe has anything to do with religion or religious identity in the first place. Just as we might easily deny that the troubles in Northern Ireland are about the primacy of the papacy or the nature of the sacraments, so we might easily dismiss an argument that the social marginalization of so many European Muslims has occurred *because* they are Muslims. Surely, much of this marginalization and the political conflict that arises out of it is attributable to factors such as class and race, and is related to the unfortunate circumstances in which migrants and their families find themselves all over the world.

But just because other explanations are available to account for political conflict associated with a religious minority does not necessarily mean that the conflict has *nothing* to do with the minority's religion. It will be important to observe carefully in the future the extent to which social dynamics in cities like Paris, Amsterdam, and Berlin are defined in religious terms, even obliquely.

Funda Müjde, a Dutch actress of Turkish descent, has noted a telling change in rhetoric associated with a series of religiously charged political developments in the Netherlands. In *Murder in Amsterdam*, Ian Buruma's 2006 book about a Muslim radical's slaying of the filmmaker Theo Van Gogh, Funda was quoted as saying that, in 2000, "I was called 'a filthy Turk.'" After 2001, it was "filthy foreigner." More recently, it was "filthy Muslim." Perhaps there was more expressed in that anti-Islamic epithet than a commitment to the separation of church and state.

The Turkish Question

The second factor that is reintroducing religious diversity to Europe, and thereby introducing the potential for renewed religious conflict to European politics, is the enlargement of the EU. Just as with Islamic migration, an important ramification of enlargement is the simple fact that it expands the universe of people who get to be counted as Europeans. Even given the emerging religious conflicts in the EU's western nations, "Europe" itself continues to seem more secular if it is defined as encompassing Paris, Amsterdam, and Berlin but not Warsaw, Belgrade, or certainly Istanbul.

Turkey is the central challenge in this regard, of course. If Turkey joins "Europe" through accession to the EU, then we should not expect the processes of "Europeanization" to move in only one direction. Europe would be changed by swallowing Turkey, just as Turkey would doubtless be changed by adapting itself to Europe. And this is presumably why so many Europeans, including the French Sarkozy and the German Benedict XVI (at least until he was chastened by controversy over his criticism of Islam), have been so opposed to the idea.

There are, of course, all sorts of reasons to resist taking in a struggling democracy of 70 million souls on Europe's eastern periphery, and many of the reasons have nothing to do with Islam. Still, when former French President Valéry Giscard d'Estaing says that the Turks cannot "join Europe" because they are not "Europeans," do we have to accept at face value that his continental designation has *nothing* to do with religious categorizations?

The conflicts associated with Turkish membership are multifaceted. On one hand, some political leaders are making a straightforward defense of secularism against a perceived sectarian challenge. They see Turkey—and its ostensibly moderate Islamist government—as a Trojan horse for a much more destabilizing form of religious politics. On the other hand, the challenges accompanying Turkey's application to the EU have led at least some Europeans to a reconsideration of their "Christian heritage" and to a renewed appreciation for the Christian Democratic roots of the European integration project from the very beginning.

The relationship between religion and politics is always a two-way street. Of course religion seeks to influence politics, and that is the pathway that causes so much concern among secularists in Europe and elsewhere. But religion, and the way that religion articulates itself, are also profoundly affected by their interaction with political institutions and political processes. Secularists in the West, for example, fear Turkish Islamism, no matter how "moderate" Prime Minister Recep Tayyip Erdoğan insists that it is. Yet, from Erdoğan's point of view, Turkish membership in the EU, with all of the union's secular assumptions and liberal protections, offers a pathway to a more secure Islamic political engagement inside Turkey. For the current government in Ankara, the relevant threat is not secularism or liberalism in Brussels and Paris. Instead, it is the commitment to secularism in Turkey itself, which might be used to justify the suspension of democracy by Kemalist elements in the Turkish military and political elite.

Similarly, Turkey's accession to the EU could offer Europeans a pathway to the political domestication of European Islam through its association with "liberal" democracy in Ankara, supported by broader democratic (and incidentally secular) political forces across the continent. Stranger things have happened. Consider how Roman Catholics were perceived in the United States not so long ago—how much of a threat they supposedly posed to American democracy—until the combined effects of the Second Vatican Council and the Kennedy presidency allowed a kind of reformed U.S. Catholicism to assimilate itself into the mainstream of American public life.

Churches at the Table

Meanwhile, the effects of EU enlargement on the role of religion in Europe go well beyond Turkey. States like Poland, which have already joined the union, bring with them a deep historical connection to a religious tradition and religious identity. Poles, of course, resent the idea that they have "joined Europe," or that they are undergoing something called "Europeanization." Yes, the Polish state has had to adapt its institutions to the dictates of EU conditionality; and, yes, Poland's post-communist governments have had to accede to the thousands of pages of accumulated EU laws. But Poles, in their political culture and historical mythology, continue to see their nation as the heart of Europe, as one of the central places where European identity was originally defined. What is more, Poles throughout their history have defined this special role in constructing Europe in explicitly religious terms. This "bulwark of Christianity," this "Christ of Nations," is now once again a full partner in the community of European nations. And it has taken its seat at the European table with its religion still displayed prominently on its sleeve.

It is possible to argue, of course, that "Europeanization" will work its "modernizing" magic, and that Polish Catholicism will in time go the way of the French or the Dutch versions (insofar as they have actually gone). The Polish pope repeatedly voiced precisely this concern, and this is one of the reasons that the Catholic-nationalist movement surrounding Father Tadeusz Rydzyk's Radio Maryja has opposed Poland's EU membership all along. Still, I would caution against facile predictions about the trajectory of secularization in Poland.

Indicators of decreasing religious practice in Poland do not mean that Poles have accepted the equation that modern equals irreligious, any more than many demonstrably "modern" Americans have. In the 1960s, the Catholic philosopher Michael Novak famously tried to capture the enduring strength of ethnic diversity in the United States by reference to what he called the "unmeltable ethnics." The Poles may or may not be unmeltably "Catholic," especially across generations. But "Europe," in all its complexity, now includes *Catholic Poland*, the country that has given Europe Pope John Paul II and the twin Polish leaders Jaroslaw and Lech Kaczynski. It was the Poles, not surprisingly, who were among the strongest supporters of the eventually unsuccessful effort to include an "invocation to God" in the doomed European constitution. And we can be fairly confident that the Poles will continue to insist on having their own distinctive say in future debates concerning the scope and meaning of the European project. The Poles are once again, in every sense of the term, Europeans.

The ties between religion and nation may be even stronger in an "Orthodox" place like Serbia than they are in a "Catholic" place like Poland, if that is possible. Were Serbia to join the EU, the Serbs would bring to Brussels yet another religious tradition and yet another deeply ingrained religious identity. The consequences of such a development could be far-reaching: Orthodox churches tend to play a prominent role in the institutional lives of individual states; Greece (and/or "Constantinople") could become the center of a kind of Orthodox commonwealth within the broader European community; and relations between "Europe" and Russia might well be affected.

But Orthodox religion's most significant effect on European enlargement might be as a drag on the process of enlargement itself. No, 2008 is not 1054. We are not talking about a renewal of the Great Schism. In Serbia and in other Orthodox settings, however, some politically significant elements are quite hesitant about the prospect of undergoing "Europeanization." Having just recaptured national sovereignty, and therefore autonomy for their churches, many Orthodox religious leaders, and many political leaders in Orthodox countries, are less than enthusiastic about surrendering hard-earned institutional gains to a political collectivity that was founded, after all, according to the dictates of the Treaty of Rome.

Transnational Religion

The expansion of the EU, along with the growth in Europe's domestic Islamic populations, is not only reintroducing religious diversity into the European context as it also reformulates what—and who—gets to count as "European." The truly epoch-making process of European integration is affecting the role of religion in European life in another important way. It is not just that individual nations are bringing to Brussels deeply seated religious traditions and well-defined religious identities; it is also that the very fact of integration will require religious leaders and religious communities to participate at a new (or actually renewed) level of political contestation. As European integration creates fundamental shifts in the continent's political structure, religious actors (like all politically relevant actors) will have to re-adapt, relearn, and retarget their political efforts vis-à-vis not only national but also supranational institutions and processes. An increasingly transnational Europe will raise the political profile of transnational religion.

It should be noted that this adaptive relationship between political structure and religious politics is a virtually universal phenomenon. The political role of the Catholic Church under the Roman Empire was nothing like the role of the church in the modern territorial state system. Islamic politics under the caliphate was completely distinct from Islamic politics under Western colonialism. And the role of the Orthodox churches was transformed utterly by the breakup of the Ottoman Empire, then by the establishment of Communist Yugoslavia, and then by the creation of the post-Yugoslav states in the Balkans.

I would take this argument one step further and say that meaningful political participation by a religious community in a given set of political structures is at least in part determined by the degree to which that community's own institutional imperatives match those of the political circumstances at hand. Thus, in an era of continental integration, religious traditions that are themselves transnational in character and structure will find it easier to make their way to Brussels, and to have their voices heard in the politics of "Europe," than those that are not.

The Orthodox churches, for example, have close theological ties with each other and are, in fact, devoted to a particular kind of transnational universality. But the defining concept of autocephaly, and the very close organic ties between church and nation in the Orthodox tradition, render these churches, in a certain way, out of step with the structural trends of contemporary European politics. This does not mean that Orthodoxy will not play a role in European politics. But that role will be primarily as an obstacle to further European integration.

Roman Catholicism, on the other hand, is almost perfectly suited in structural terms for participation in the new European politics. Paradigmatically transnational itself, the Catholic Church is not only comfortable participating at the level of "Europe" (Catholic bishops already have their own Eurocratic secretariat in Brussels) but is also anxious to reclaim its traditional role of defining what Europe is in historical and cultural terms. Listening to the last two popes—one a Pole and the other a German—one could be forgiven for thinking that they have envisioned Europe's integration as the re-inauguration of a kind of neo-Christendom. This is largely a papal pipe dream, of course. Pope John Paul II's hope for a new evangelization, running from east to west, was surely a vain one. Nevertheless, the Catholic Church is structurally prepared to participate in European politics in the future, and church leaders will have much to say about how this politics ought to be defined and advanced.

Islam is probably the most interesting of all in this regard. With its clear delineation of the Muslim people as a single *umma* (community), and its historic discomfort with the notion of individual state autonomy, Islam is at least as well situated structurally as Catholicism is for participation in transnational politics. Of course, Islam is a much less hierarchical religious tradition than Catholicism is. And the problem in the European context is that, in comparison with Catholic spokesmen, leaders of the Islamic faith are far less able to offer an account of European history, or a definition of European identity, that places them at the center of the story. Islam has been "the Other" against which "Europe" has defined itself for centuries, and this is likely to be the role that Islam will play in Europe's foreseeable future. Even so, the challenge Islam poses to European secularism will continue to put religion back on the agenda of European politics.

Exceptional Europe

In the near term, religion in the political arena may continue to be seen as a mostly peripheral force to be resisted by stalwart defenders of the secular status quo. Nevertheless, it seems eminently plausible that the role of religion in European politics could also grow more sectarian—and therefore more volatile—in the foreseeable future. The effort to reject Muslim inroads is leading more Europeans to rediscover their continent's "Christian heritage" and to reemphasize the dependence of European political life on what Americans have long called, with an exquisite lack of specificity, "Christian values." A debate is brewing in Europe about the question of "Europe's" borders, and about who gets to define the meaning of the designation "European." In the context of such a debate, invocations of religious designations and categorizations are bound to grow louder and more fractious.

For many years, devotees of modernization theory dismissed the United States as a deviant case—an undeniably modern but demonstrably religious polity in a secularizing era. But, as Casanova has reminded us, it was never the United States that was the exception to the rule; it was Europe. The precipitous decline of religious practice and the thoroughgoing relegation of religion to the margins of politics made Europe the aberrant secular case in an otherwise religious world. Now, as migration and integration continue to expand the definitions of what it means to be European, an increasingly diverse "Europe" is likely to see religion increasingly mixing with its politics. Why is this the case? Because that is what religion does. *Religion mixes with politics.* Everywhere.

RELIGION AND ECONOMIC DEVELOPMENT

38

MAX WEBER IS ALIVE AND WELL, AND LIVING IN GUATEMALA
The Protestant Ethic Today

—Peter L. Berger

Max Weber's essay, *The Protestant Ethic and the Spirit of Capitalism*, must surely be the most discussed piece of writing in the history of social science.[1] It has been the ship that launched a thousand dissertations, and it has created a cottage industry of exegesis. Needless to say, this is quite a tribute to Weber's intellectual stature. It indicates the continued relevance of Weber's analysis regarding the correlation of the Protestant ethic and economic development. A century after Weber's essay, Protestantism has changed dramatically. To what extent is this correlation still evident around the globe today?

It seems to me that there are four equally valid approaches to discussing the impact of *The Protestant Ethic*.

1. The obvious first approach is to explore the validity of Weber's historical argument: Did Protestantism really play the role he assigned to it in the genesis of modern capitalism? This question has occupied several cohorts of historians, from R. H. Tawney on.

2. Second, the essay can be placed within the overall context of Weber's opus, especially if one sees this opus, at least in part, as a debate with the ghost of Karl Marx. One can ask, "Just what is the role of ideas in processes of social change?" (In Marxist terms, if you will, this is the question about the relation of "superstructure" and "substructure," which preoccupied Gyorgy Lukacs and Antonio Gramsci, among others.)

3. Third, Weber's treatment of the Protestant ethic can be seen as a key element of a sociologically inspired philosophy of history, especially in terms of the unintended and unanticipated consequences of action.

4. And finally, one can, with all due respect, leave all the preceding issues aside and instead make a more practical and empirical investigation of how Weber's notion of the Protestant ethic helps us understand developments in the world today.

In what follows here, I offer an overview and analysis vis-à-vis this latter line of inquiry. I will frame these reflections with a series of questions.

* *The Review of Faith & International Affairs* 8, no. 4 (Winter 2010): 3–9.

First, *what are the key traits of the Protestant Ethic?* The answer to this question turns on Weber's concept of "this-worldly asceticism." This concept delineates a distinct pattern of human behavior:

- a disciplined attitude to work (not just *hard* work, which one finds in many very un-Protestant places, but what Weber understood as the *rationalization* of work);
- an equally disciplined attitude to other spheres of social life, notably the family (Weber's notion of life-discipline);
- a deferral of instant consumption, resulting in saving and, eventually, capital accumulation and social mobility (what psychologists call "delayed gratification");
- and all of this in the context of a worldview relatively free of magic (Weber's "disenchantment of the world").

To this list of traits one should add two that Weber did not enlarge upon:

- a strong interest in the education of children (originally based on the Protestant insistence that the Bible should be read by everyone),
- and the propensity to create voluntary associations of non-elite people.

This last trait, of course, has not been characteristic of classical Protestantism, but gained enormous importance from what David Martin has called the "bourgeois Protestant axis" (Amsterdam-London-Boston)—the principle of voluntarism bred by Dutch sectarianism, English Nonconformity, and, most explosively, American denominationalism (the vast progeny of New England Congregationalism).[2]

Where is such a constellation of traits to be found today?[3] The obvious first place to explore the contemporary presence of the Protestant ethic is in Protestantism itself. However, we can't assume that all forms of Protestantism propagate the ethic to the same degree. As Weber himself pointed out, this ethic declines after it has had its effect in the early stages of modern economic development. Thus it is present only in a very attenuated form in, say, mainline Protestant denominations in contemporary America.

One must look rather at what is arguably the most dynamic religious movement in the world today—the wildfire expansion of Pentecostal Protestantism in Latin America, sub-Saharan Africa, parts of east and southeast Asia, and in pockets of marginalized people in the most unlikely places (as among European Gypsies and low castes in Nepal). The phenomenon is vast: There are some 250 million Pentecostals in the world today, and possibly many more; 50 million is the estimate for Latin America.[4]

How does the behavioral profile of these people compare with the seventeenth- and eighteenth-century Protestants discussed by Weber? And how does it relate to economic development? In my view, the attitudes and behavior of the new Pentecostals bear a striking resemblance to their Anglo-Saxon predecessors. This can be observed most readily in Latin America. (Hence the title of this paper. Guatemala has the highest concentration of Protestants in Latin America, and most of them are Pentecostal: about a quarter of the population countrywide, and about a third of the population in the capital area.) What takes place here is nothing less than a cultural revolution, sharply deviant from traditional Latin American patterns. This new culture is certainly "ascetic." It promotes personal discipline and honesty, proscribes alcohol and extra-marital sex, dismantles the *compadre* system (which is based on Catholic practice and, with its *fiestas* and other extravagant expenditures, discourages saving), and teaches ordinary people to create and run their own grassroots institutions.

Pentecostalism, moreover, fosters a culture that is radically opposed to classical *machismo*. Indeed, in many ways it is a women's movement: while most preachers are men, women are important missionaries and organizers. Even more important, women take on leadership roles within the family, "domesticating" their husbands (or, alternatively, kicking them out if they refuse to adhere to Protestant moral standards) and paying attention to the education of their children. Gender is a factor that was outside Weber's horizon, but it is critical to any analysis of the social and economic effects of Pentecostalism. It is also important by way of comparison with the effects of that other explosive religious movement of the contemporary era: resurgent Islam.

It should not be surprising that these patterns produce what I like to call a "comparative cultural advantage" in terms of social mobility and economic development. Where the macro-economy is in very bad shape (for example, in the northeast of Brazil), this advantage is more or less dormant. But where people with these characteristics have a real chance—as, for example, in Chile or in southern Brazil (Sao Paulo has been called the world capital of Pentecostalism)—one can observe a positive correlation with social mobility and with it a truly novel phenomenon in Latin America: a growing Protestant middle class, economically productive and increasingly assertive politically. Of course, Latin American Pentecostalism is not a monolithic phenomenon. There are strands which deviate from the Weberian concept (for example, groups that promote a so-called "wealth gospel" wherein God provides benefits to people who have to make little effort beyond having faith). But the overall picture fits neatly with Weber's description of the Protestant ethic and its effects.

Pentecostalism's power to advance the Protestant ethic is evident outside Latin America, too. In recent years the Institute on Culture, Religion, and World Affairs at Boston University (my home institution) and the Centre for Development and Enterprise (Johannesburg, South Africa) have collaborated on research on Pentecostalism in sub-Saharan Africa.[5] The findings thus far strongly suggest that Pentecostalism is having similar socioeconomic effects in Africa as in Latin America—this despite the fact that African Pentecostalism/neo-Pentecostalism sometimes takes very different forms than the Latin American varieties. Pentecostalism in Africa frequently intersects with an important phenomenon that has no real analogue in Latin America—the so-called African Independent Churches, which combine a charismatic Christianity with elements of traditional African religion.

More broadly, *are there analogues to the Protestant ethic among non-Protestant groups?* Some sociologists (myself included) have examined the question of whether there are "functional equivalents" of the Protestant ethic. An interesting case in this connection is that of eastern Asia. Some have wondered whether specific cultural elements have been a factor in the region's rapid ascendancy, and some have argued that the Confucian heritage may be such a factor. Confucianism has been important in all the countries of the region—first in Japan, the earliest and most dramatic case of a non-Western society successfully modernizing; and then in what used to be called "the Four Little Tigers" of South Korea, Taiwan, Hong Kong, and Singapore; and then in the economies of southeast Asia, in which ethnic Chinese minorities played a leading economic role. The so-called "post-Confucian hypothesis" proposed that the Confucian heritage fosters values and behavior similar in important ways to the Protestant ethic—disciplined lifestyles, frugality, soberness, a consuming interest in education, and, last but not least, a disdain for magic (that is, an Asian version of "disenchantment").

Weber, of course, had also discussed Confucianism at great length. He saw it as a case of this-worldly *non*-asceticism and thus not conducive to modern economic development. Weber studied the worldview and the institutions of the literary bureaucracy of imperial China, where his interpretation was in all likelihood valid. However, leaving aside Japan (where Confucian ideas combined with a martial ethic of very different antecedents), the ethnic Chinese "carriers" of the "economic miracle" were mostly people who had never read the Confucian classics and whose lifestyle was vastly different from that of the imperial Mandarins. Robert Bellah coined the term "bourgeois Confucianism" to describe this value system.[6] Others have suggested that the operative values here were not so much Confucian but rather rooted in Chinese folk religion—a highly pragmatic (if you will, "rational") worldview and practice which indeed provided the cultural matrix of "high" Confucianism.

Although the exact origins may be uncertain, it is quite clear that analogues to the Protestant ethic can indeed be found in eastern Asia and these may be looked upon as "functional equivalents." As the luster of the east-Asian economies has diminished somewhat in recent years, there has been less talk about the post-Confucian hypothesis (apparently Confucianism is not a sufficient antidote to potential bankruptcy). This does not change the fact that cultural factors must be taken into account when studying the amazing achievement of these societies, which moved large numbers of people from abject poverty to a reasonably comfortable level of living. Gordon Redding demonstrated this in his study of Overseas Chinese entrepreneurs and he has more recently enlarged the scope of his research to other groups in the region, notably in Japan and South Korea. He has also been exploring the cultural factors in the remarkable development of mainland China since the onset of its economic reforms.[7] The recent economic upsurge of mainland China demonstrates that the same cultural values, which animated the success stories of the Overseas Chinese and which were long suppressed in the mainland, can suddenly produce dramatic effects if the environment changes.

Sinologists have disagreed for a long time on whether Confucianism is to be understood as a religion or as an essentially secular system of ethics (non-Sinologist though I am, I favor the former view). In any case, the quest for analogues to the Protestant ethic will bring up both cases of other religious traditions and cases of clearly secular values.

If there is one religious tradition conventionally viewed as inimical to modern capitalism, it would be that of Iberian Catholicism. Yet out of its most conservative circles has come a movement, Opus Dei, which has played a crucial role in the move toward a market economy in Spain, and which may play a similar role in some other predominantly Catholic countries (such as the Philippines). Opus Dei originated in Spain in the 1920s and 1930s, allied to the most conservative wing of Spanish Catholicism. It was organized as a strictly hierarchical order, containing both priests and lay people, and had as its particular focus the penetration of political and economic elites. It propagated a rigorously ascetic, quasi-monastic lifestyle, and adherence to strict doctrinal orthodoxy. Yet at the same time its mission was conceived as taking place in the world, not confined to monasteries or other ecclesiastical institutions. In other words, it rather closely resembled Weber's concept of this-worldly asceticism and his famous description of Protestantism as having abolished the monasteries and turned the world into a monastery.[8]

From the beginning it was closely associated with the Franco regime. In the final years of this regime it attained great political prominence. Somewhere along the line its leadership decided that Spain should embark on a capitalist course. Opus Dei not only founded two prestigious business schools, but it used its influence within the government to induce market-friendly economic policies. Its religious mission in Spain has hardly been successful; in the wake of the Franco regime, Spain underwent a dramatic process of secularization, greatly weakening the status and influence of the Catholic Church. But the economic success of Opus Dei has been brilliant in that it set out to make Spain into a suburb of Fatima, but succeeded in making Spain into a suburb of Brussels.[9]

Beyond Catholicism, Islam also presents interesting questions regarding analogues to the Protestant ethic. Indeed, one of the most timely questions concerning the relation of culture and economic development is that of the compatibility of Islam with the latter and with democracy. A widely held view maintains that there is an inherent incompatibility. Even if that were so (which I tend to doubt), there is one significant twentieth-century example of the contrary: Indonesia, the largest predominantly Muslim nation in the world.[10]

To be sure, different religious traditions have different degrees of affinity with modern capitalism and modern democracy. And I would argue that the type of Protestantism represented by contemporary Pentecostalism has an exceptionally high affinity. This does not mean, however, that other traditions are under some ancient curse which prevents them from adapting to new circumstances. At times these adaptations are dramatic and surprising. Opus Dei is one such case. Another is that of Old Believers in Russia. This group is about as "reactionary" as can be in their religious character, yet it produced a surprising number of successful capitalist entrepreneurs since the nineteenth century.

Analogues to the Protestant ethic can also be found in other carriers of modern capitalist culture. A fertile area of research is that of the military in developing societies. In many of these societies the military is one important institution that fosters "this-worldly asceticism" in its members. Of course, the military can also be the locale of corruption and ruthless power manipulations. But where an honorable military ethos prevails, it is plausible to hypothesize that it may carry over into economic and political life.

All in all, I would propose that something like the Protestant ethic is a necessary though not sufficient causal factor if a population is to move successfully from poverty to a reasonably decent standard of living. This is true both for entire societies and for groups within a society that have been left behind, such as marginalized groups in America or Europe. The prescription for attitudes and behavior conducive to economic development in, say, Bangladesh is not essentially different from that in an inner-city slum in the United States. The "carriers," of course, will be very different in these different locations.

Here it is important to address two further questions—one about "vanguards" and one about "expiration dates." First, *how do "vanguards" impact an entire society?* It is not necessary for an entire population to evince the traits of this-worldly asceticism for development to take place. It often suffices if a highly active minority possesses these traits and serves as the vehicle for development. As development takes place, other groups, even if they do not share the same traits, will benefit. As they do so, their own culture will inevitably change.

The metaphor to describe this is not the much-maligned "trickle-down effect." Rather, it is the metaphor of the rising tide which lifts all ships. This lifting can be speedy and dramatic, as has been nicely shown by the economic success stories of eastern Asia.

Both historically and today, these "vanguard" minorities can be religious or non-religious. Examples of religiously defined vanguards can be found not only among Protestants (such as the Huguenot refugees who were invited into Prussia and were very instrumental in its ascendancy), but also Jews in Poland (also invited), Armenians in the Middle East, and Jains in India. The vanguards can also be ethnic, with Overseas Chinese being a prime example. And they can be Indian castes or sub-castes, such as the Marwaris, who originated in Gujarat and became successful entrepreneurs throughout India.

Naturally, all of this can create significant political problems. The visible economic success of minorities, while the majority is still left behind, is likely to create severe and potentially violent resentments. Inevitably, the benefits of economic development will not be equally distributed, and inequality is likely to increase sharply in the earlier stages of economic growth. It requires very skillful political leadership to control this looming turbulence, especially under democratic regimes where the rhetoric and the policies of populist redistribution are very tempting.

As for "expiration dates" of the ethic: *Does the Protestant ethic "wear out" after marked economic development?* A very intriguing question is whether the Protestant ethic, so important in the earlier stages of capitalism, continues to be important in later stages. Where capitalism is successful, the productivity of the economy increases enormously. Put simply, much less hard work and discipline are necessary to keep the economy going. Some individuals (again, a sort of "vanguard") continue to work very hard (though even they tend to be less ascetic in their lives outside the workplace), often for very large rewards. Most of the population, though, can afford to be much more relaxed. Not surprisingly, then, the general culture becomes much more hedonistic, permissive, even lazy. A French bestseller nicely expresses this attitude: *Bonjour, paresse* or "Hello, laziness" (an allusion to Francoise Sagan's famous novel, *Bonjour, tristesse*). What this suggests is that any constellation of attitudes and behavior should, in terms of its economic functionality, have attached to it an "expiration date," marking it valid until a certain level of GDP has been reached.

Still, attitudes and behavior seen as economically dysfunctional at one time may paradoxically become functional at a later time. A comparison of Japan and India is instructive in this regard. It has been plausibly argued that the modernization of Japan was animated by a sort of de-militarization of the *samurai* ethos, and indeed many of the early capitalist entrepreneurs were members of the samurai class forced to find new occupations after the Meiji regime dismantled the institutions of feudalism. Here was a "this-worldly asceticism" with a vengeance—iron discipline, rigorous devotion to the tasks at hand, frugal living, and total loyalty to one's superiors, with the loyalty transferred from one's feudal overlord to one's company.

As Japan first industrialized in the Meiji era, and as it recovered from the devastation of World War II, this was a highly functional ethic. It is much more doubtful whether it is still so today, when Japan has entered a post-industrial phase, with a largely knowledge-driven economy. Again not surprisingly, the culture has become more hedonistic, individualistic, and less respectful of all hierarchies. This change has been deplored by traditionalists, but arguably the change is not only tolerable but may actually be necessary in the new economy.

Consider also the much less driven, even dreamy culture of traditional India, which has been interpreted as a dysfunctional factor for the development of the Indian economy. Yet it is precisely these features that may be conducive to success in a knowledge-driven economy. The amazingly successful Indian computer industry can illustrate this point. Put differently, asceticism may be a sin (or a virtue) of youth.

If this argument is valid, it implies a poignant human drama: The children reject the values and the lifestyles of their parents, despite (or perhaps because of) the fact that the easier life of the children was made possible by the sacrifices of the parental generation. And this would be but a modern reiteration of an age-old phenomenon. As "hard" societies become "soft," there occurs an inter-generational cultural shift. Traditionalists will interpret the softness as deplorable decadence. And where the earlier hardness was of a martial character, the softness may make the society more vulnerable to aggression from peoples of hardier temperament.

Generations of historians have so understood the decline of Rome, and perhaps this applies even today as the societies of the West confront violent aggression by groups that are very hardy indeed. But the same logic may not apply to economic behavior. If left alone by outsiders, the lazy may indeed inherit the earth—or rather, that patch of earth which has been made prosperous by the ascetic efforts of earlier generations.

Conclusion

When discussing the correlation of the Protestant ethic and economic development, Weber used a German term—*wahlverwandschaft*—usually translated into English as "affinity." There is an affinity between Protestantism and early capitalism. There is an affinity between Pentecostalism today and modern economic development. But it is not necessarily a simple cause-effect relationship. There is an interactive dynamic between numerous causal factors in economic development, and the dynamic can change over time. One thing, however, is very clear: you cannot ignore the religious factor as you look at economic development. Indeed, religion plays an important role in social change around the world. Whether one likes this or not is a philosophical question about which social scientists (as social scientists) have little to say.

39

INSPIRING DEVELOPMENT IN FRAGILE STATES

—Seth Kaplan

Western development agencies are largely secular. Standard bearers of a rationalist and bureaucratic culture, such institutions see the job of promoting economic and political modernization as one that requires scientific objectivity, dispassionate analysis, and number crunching. Few agencies seriously contemplate the idea that religion—whether in the form of spirituality or of organized religion—could make a positive contribution to such decidedly earthly matters as economic development and state building.

Yet religion's potential to spur development is enormous, especially in the world's poorest, most fragile states. From the Congo to Pakistan, faith-based organizations (FBOs) are often the only locally organized groups working among the destitute, filling in for governments where they are too feeble to provide even basic schooling and health care. In recent years, some international development agencies have enlisted FBOs to deliver various services in impoverished communities. Such schemes, however, see FBOs merely as cogs in a distinctly Western, top-down approach to development. They ignore the potential of religion and indigenous institutions to play a greater role in repairing the societal fractures and government weaknesses that hold back struggling countries.

The Western development community views the concept of development too narrowly. Part of the problem is a misdiagnosis of the major causes of the dysfunction that plagues fragile states across Africa, the Middle East, and elsewhere. Agencies execute initiatives as if economic reform, elections, and administrative training alone could fix these countries' problems. Sociopolitical dynamics have been practically ignored. When it comes to development, building social cohesion, social capital, and the capacity for self-governance should be the starting point for any initiative—and few organizations are better equipped to reverse social atomization and catalyze local capacities for self-governance than FBOs.

* *The Review of Faith & International Affairs* 8, no. 4 (Winter 2010): 11–21.

How Religion Spurred Western Development

In Africa, the Middle East, and many parts of Asia and Latin America, religion and governance were closely intertwined before the European imperialists arrived, and a similar pattern has reemerged since the Europeans departed. Today, religion continues to exert a powerful influence on how individuals and communities in the developing world interact with each other and with their governments. "For most people of the 'South,'" concluded one Western scholar after working in the field for several years, "spirituality is integral to their understanding of the world and their place in it, and so it is central to the decisions that they make about their own and their communities' development."[1] Indeed, faith is such a key component of the social fabric in the developing world that "some languages do not even have a word for 'religion'; life is steeped in belief and belief is life itself."[2]

In the West, by contrast, the separation of church and state is generally considered to have been a milestone along the road to modernization and is still hailed as a cornerstone of the West's prosperity and democracy. But even Westerners acknowledge that religion was instrumental in helping spur the economic and political revolution that enabled first Europe and then North America to enjoy global predominance. As Max Weber famously argued in the early 20th century, the "Protestant ethic" and "the spirit of capitalism" went hand in hand. Weber and subsequent sociologists identified at least five ways in which faith encouraged development.[3]

First, certain types of Protestantism—notably, Calvinism—promoted capitalist development in Britain, Holland, Germany, and the United States because they indirectly reshaped social ethics and economic activities. Protestant teachings encouraged, among other things, planning, frugality, diligence, discipline, capital accumulation, risk taking, a commitment to one's secular vocation, and the pursuit of new ideas such as the sciences and technology.

Second, the organizational structure of some denominations instilled attitudes and taught skills that encouraged economic and political modernization. For instance, some congregations encouraged widespread lay participation in the management of their affairs and debate among members, a style sharply at odds with existing norms in the wider society at that time. Some groups promoted greater egalitarianism, with the Quakers even instituting approximate equality between women and men within their congregations.[4] Their practices created an autonomous social space within which even the poorest congregants counted as individuals and were expected to demonstrate initiative.[5] At the same time, the breakdown in the religious monopoly previously held by the Catholic Church promoted pluralism and a fierce competition in ideas. All these things would lead, in time, to a population clamoring for a freer political and economic climate.

Third, the Protestant emphasis on reading the Bible encouraged literacy and promoted the rapid diffusion of printing press technology across much of Europe. The resulting increase in human capital (the stock of skills and knowledge able to produce economic value) significantly contributed to economic prosperity.[6]

Fourth, Protestantism also played an important role in expanding trade and finance by how it built social capital, ensured the implementation of contracts, and expanded business networks. As Adam Smith noted, close-knit faith groups could enforce social norms; this encouraged repeated interactions among members, cooperation, and trust—all essential for expanding commerce and lending, especially in societies lacking state institutions able to guarantee contracts. Similarly, Jews historically enjoyed many advantages in businesses that depended on a delay between the delivery of a good and the payment for it—trade in small, portable, and valuable commodities such as diamonds, fine metals, and expensive dye-stuffs, and banking and money lending—because of how their religious communities were able to instill and enforce social discipline.[7]

Fifth and last, Protestant "enthusiasm" helped "break down, delegitimate, and otherwise weaken the hold of authoritarian political and social structures."[8] As even David Hume argued, "enthusiasm [is] not less or rather more contrary to [priestly power], than sound reason and philosophy."[9] This type of religion inspired an intense morality among believers, who committed themselves to virtuous behavior and campaigned against corruption in public office, thereby encouraging citizens to hold their leaders to higher standards. In the Nordic countries, reformist churches operated more or less democratically from the eighteenth century onward, setting the stage for later social and democratic change.[10]

This is not to say that Christianity did not also deter development (Catholicism's dictates against the study of the sciences, for instance, surely held back many countries), nor to argue that other factors, such as the Enlightenment, were unimportant to Europe's emergence from feudalism and obscurantism. However, at the very least, religious belief significantly influenced the capacity of societies to develop, encouraging it in those places that developed first and discouraging it in areas that developed later.

How Religion Spurs Development Today

Today, a variety of religions and denominations in different developing countries are effecting similar changes to those wrought by the spread of Protestantism in early modern Europe.

In most African, South Asian, Middle Eastern, and Latin American states, religious belief shapes not only moral and ethical outlooks but also political opinions on subjects such as the legitimacy of leaders and governments. Some Brazilian Pentecostal and African charismatic churches, for example, are transforming many of the values, skills, and activities of their members by emphasizing the importance of acquiring wealth, encouraging congregants—especially women—to play a much greater role in their communities, and teaching leadership and management skills. "The initial impact of Evangelical conversion [in Latin America and other parts of the developing world] occurs . . . as a major mutation of culture: restoration of the family, the rejection of *machismo*, the adoption of economic and work disciplines and new priorities," writes David Martin, a sociologist of religion. These churches create "an autonomous social space within which people may participate in the creation of a different kind of sub-society . . . those who count for little or nothing in the wider world find themselves addressed as persons able to display initiative and to be of consequence. . . . As these enclaves multiply, religious monopoly breaks down and pluralism develops."[11]

Whereas the government may barely exist outside a few main cities, faith networks (and traditional social groupings that have a strong religious component) may be deeply enmeshed in communities across a country, providing in some cases the most reliable form of security, justice, and support for the poor. These closely knit religious groups are often catalysts for the formation of robust social networks, which are the main storehouses of social capital in countries where society is heavily fragmented and the state is too weak to govern effectively. The more cohesive groups, such as the Mouride brotherhood (a large Islamic Sufi order found mostly in Senegal and the Gambia) and the Sikhs in India, have been able to leverage their spiritual networks to foster entrepreneurship, trade, and wealth creation in ways their states cannot.

Throughout the developing world, FBOs have a tangible and profound impact on the everyday activities of people underserved by their governments. FBOs are essential providers of education, health, humanitarian relief, and microfinance to hundreds of millions of people, substituting for absent governments across large swathes of the developing world. They range from large Western-based, faith-based development organizations such as Catholic Relief Services, World Vision, the American Jewish Joint Distribution Committee, and Islamic Relief to the much smaller locally based organizations typically centered on churches, temples, or mosques; on madrasas, seminaries, and other religious schools; or on informal groups such as those teaching the Gospel or the Quran in the plainest of settings. Local religious organizations account for the bulk of organized group activity in many places, provide the primary means of relief for families in crises, and even play major roles in economic endeavors. The World Bank's 2000 *Voices of the Poor* study confirmed that "in ratings of effectiveness in both urban and rural settings, religious organizations feature more prominently than any single type of state institution."[12]

The importance of these groups is especially palpable in the education and health sectors. They deliver, for example, half of all such services in sub-Saharan Africa, according to the World Bank.[13] In some places, such as parts of the Democratic Republic of the Congo (DRC) and Pakistan, churches and mosques have effectively replaced the state as the primary supplier of public goods. One study concluded that "the only significant reductions in HIV prevalence that have been recorded [in Uganda] are in contexts where the faith community took on a leadership role."[14]

In fact, given the loss of confidence in formal government institutions and the dearth of professional opportunities available in stagnant, unstable environments, many talented local people see FBOs as one of the best outlets for their ambitions and energies, producing a noticeable shift of entrepreneurial skills from politics and business to religious entities. Groups such as Sri Lanka's Buddhist Sarvodaya Shramadana Movement (Sarvodaya), Turkey's Muslim Gülen movement, and Latin America's Jesuit-based Fe y Alegría all play important roles helping societies develop.[15]

To be sure, religion can cause problems. It can inspire bloodshed (either by itself or in combination with other markers of identity), and it is a very effective recruiting sergeant for terrorism. The same characteristic that makes religious groups so useful in commerce—social cohesion—also makes them highly effective perpetrators of violence. Faith is also a major determinant of social exclusion in some countries, and thereby contributes to poverty, disempowerment, and conflict.

Some religious doctrines—such as those against usury and private enterprise, and those that deny the rights of women and members of lower castes—continue to be a major obstacle to economic and social progress in some parts of the world. And countries that actively discriminate against minority faiths, as in Saudi Arabia, or allow a religious hierarchy to monopolize the interpretation of political and economic laws, as in Iran, are similarly likely to hold back the establishment of the accountable institutions and block the creative thinking necessary for development.

All these obstacles to development, however, are overshadowed by religion's potential to play an important role in promoting a gradual transformation of the political and economic landscape in the poorest parts of the world. Indeed, faith plays such an outsized role in the lives of people in such places that finding ways to take advantage of its values, organizations, and capacities to catalyze and transform how groups of people behave and cooperate is one of the few ways to change the dynamics of development in fractured, dysfunctional countries.

At Arm's Length: FBOs and the Western Development Community

Western governments and Western-led multilateral institutions such as the World Bank have tried in recent years to better engage faith groups. James Wolfensohn, in particular, tried to increase cooperation with FBOs during his term as president of the World Bank, but resistance within the institution eventually limited the impact of his work to the creation of a small internal unit offering policy advice. European government agencies, such as the United Kingdom's Department for International Development (DFID) and the Dutch Ministry of Foreign Affairs, have launched research projects and conducted policy reviews on religion's role in development, but simultaneously have felt obliged to "specifically point out" that such programs "should not be taken to imply that they have themselves abandoned their secular nature and outlook," for fear of offending their citizens or their employees.[16] The Bush administration had no such qualms and tried to boost support for and cooperation with FBOs, but even in that case cultural blinders and political realities dictated that the great majority of contracts went to U.S.-based Christian bodies (just two Muslim groups received any grants or contracts between 2001 and 2005).[17]

Many religious groups feel excluded from aid programs. Muslim organizations, for example, "are not part of major humanitarian reform efforts; they often see themselves pushed aside. . . . When Western groups come to the Muslim world, they try to work only with secular organizations, not with grassroots religious organizations that are well-represented in the local communities." The broad secular bias has serious practical implications for programs. For instance, "women seeking international help are completely left out unless they are secular."[18]

"Typically, secular and governmental donors' willingness to contribute varies inversely with an organization's overtly religious behavior," concluded a study published by Georgetown University's Berkley Center for Religion, Peace, and World Affairs.[19] Similarly, a 2004 DFID-funded report concluded that the organization's "quasi-secular model of development and its focus on partnership with mainstream Christian development organizations are increasingly untenable in the post-Cold War and post-9/11 worlds."[20] Relationships between Western governments, aid agencies, multilateral organizations, and NGOs, on the one hand, and, on the other, the great majority of local faith groups—especially those working in the Islamic, Hindu, Sikh, Buddhist, and African religious traditions—remain severely limited, with cooperation generally restricted to a very narrow set of secular activities. There has been almost no attempt to engage faith groups in developing countries on their own terms or any attempt to take advantage of the unique capacities that these groups bring to the table.

Faith Networks: Catalysts for Development

Development agencies cannot make states function properly from the outside. International assistance may be necessary but it is never sufficient to establish governments that are legitimate and sustainable and that can provide the positive societal incentives necessary to jumpstart the development process. Instead, communities need to look for ways to take advantage of their own resources, capacities, and institutions if they are ever to advance.

While government is often weak in these countries, just as often religion is strong: it shapes values and develops skills, it is the primary means of association and of conflict management, and it offers a way to build social capital and to hold community leaders more accountable. As Gerrie ter Haar and Stephen Ellis explain:

> In many of Africa's poorest countries, effective, centralized bureaucracies hardly exist. . . .
> In countries of this type, power is, literally, dis-integrated. It becomes a matter of necessity
> rather than choice to consider how development could be enhanced by using the resources
> in society at large. Many of the communities or social networks that carry the burden of
> development have a religious form or convey religious ideas in some sense."[21]

In the Middle East, notes Bernard Lewis, "religion, or more precisely membership of a religious community, is the ultimate determinant of identity . . . the focus of loyalty and, not less important, the source of authority."[22] Islamic organizations have in many cases—and certainly in all the poorest communities—such legitimacy and constituency that it would be hard to effect substantial change without their participation. Indeed, various studies and symposia have concluded that there is enormous potential "in more purposeful efforts to associate development issues, practices, and organizations with Muslim traditions and actors."[23]

Enhancing FBOs and Other Homegrown Social Networks

The international community's development agenda focuses far too much on top-down state building, which overemphasizes the role of Western development agencies, foreign NGOs, and national government ministries in capital cities often geographically and culturally remote from most of the population. Building states from the bottom-up around local groups would likely produce a much more sustainable process, as it would enmesh the state in the surrounding society and make the state dependent on the capacities and loyalties of local peoples.

If Western development agencies opted to emphasize programs that help societies reform from within, those agencies would quickly discover the merits of investing more of their resources in faith groups (and other indigenous networks). For instance, training the spiritual and administrative leaders of FBOs—everyone from ministers and imams to school principals and the heads of waqf foundations—on management, economics, education, and social welfare would help their organizations take on larger projects, expand their services, and improve their operations. Similarly, assisting well-established groups in introducing (in partnership, perhaps, with NGOs or private companies) savings and loans schemes, sanitation and garbage-collection systems, and housing development cooperatives would speed the spread of such programs throughout the developing world. Helping faith networks provide services such as microlending and trade facilitation—services that require cohesive groups able to ensure member compliance with commitments—would open new opportunities for members to advance themselves. Measures that fostered greater cohesion—by improving internal governance, by expanding services, by helping codify norms and discipline regimes, and by creating stronger ties between members—would foster more "spiritual capital" (social capital created through religion), an invaluable resource in the low-trust environment common in fragile states.[24]

Greater financial and material aid from the international community would enable mosques, churches, and temples to expand the numbers of poor children who benefit from the schooling they provide. The consequent boost in levels of literacy would, in turn, enable the poor to participate more fully in social, political, and economic life; give developing economies a better chance of meeting the challenges of globalization; and improve many other development indicators. An expansion of faith-based education might be a mixed blessing in parts of the Muslim world, where local madrasas play a key role in delivering education but have been accused of spreading political fundamentalism. Since 9/11, many groups have encouraged madrasas to renounce extremism and introduce new subjects, including secular subjects, into their curricula. For instance, the International Center for Religion and Diplomacy (ICRD), based in Washington, D.C., has worked with leaders of Pakistani madrasas to promote peace and tolerance.[25] Such efforts should be expanded.

Religious networks also offer unique ways to enhance government accountability and performance. These networks shape values and behaviors—and could be urged to do more to persuade bureaucrats and businessmen to eschew corruption. A partnership of the major networks within a city or region could constitute a powerful lobby for bottom-up reform of state institutions and for greater accountability of officials. Such a partnership could gradually be extended to encompass other stakeholders with similar interests in government reform (such as companies, tribal chiefs, and non-religious NGOs).

Reorienting Western Development Organizations

In order to take advantage of the human resources embedded in religious networks, Western development organizations, donors, multilateral organizations, and NGOs must seek a closer—and more evenhanded—partnership with local communities and the faith groups that play such prominent roles within those communities. This will require major changes in how these organizations operate. Besides reconsidering how development actually occurs—and how this might affect their programs—they will also have to reevaluate "the secular gospel underpinning the development enterprise,"[26] and begin "taking seriously people's world-views and considering their potential for the development process as a whole."[27] Western organizations that treat religion and development as separate and even incompatible phenomena not only undermine their ability to be effective but also risk offending and alienating the people of the communities they wish to serve. This danger is especially acute in non-Christian environments, where local populations tend to equate "Western" with "Christian" and thus will regard any denial of the importance of their religion as a Christian slur.

International development organizations will also have to stop emphasizing the amount of aid they disburse and focus instead on ensuring that the financing they provide complements and reinforces local capacities and institutions rather than undermining or warping local arrangements. While such organizations may gain prestige from the size of their budgets, community building based on a large number of small organizations—and most of the FBOs that serve the poor are small—requires a delicate approach consisting of modest, carefully targeted investments that reinforce capacities without undermining internal coherence and accountability. Understanding the special needs of—and crafting the right strategy to partner with—the large number of small organizations in underdeveloped areas may even require the creation of a new, intermediary organization to bridge the large gulf between the large donors and multinational NGOs and the many small grassroots entities that need support.[28]

Of course, any undertaking that engages religion needs to be careful on a number of fronts. In particular, any activity that smacks of favoring one faith or denomination over another risks exacerbating, rather than healing, divisions. Assistance needs to be distributed in an evenhanded fashion, so that no religious community feels itself excluded from international largesse. The provision of assistance must also be handled very carefully when dealing with any organization that proselytizes, especially in a sectarian environment. The goal should be to ensure that aid is not used in any way to promote a specific religious or political viewpoint, and that where it is used to fund the delivery of services, those services are available without discrimination to everyone in a given area.

However, proselytizing is an integral part of most religions—especially among the world's largest faiths, Christianity and Islam—and avoiding such groups will prove impossible in some cases. Indeed, given that missionary organizations are especially active among the most deprived sectors of society, and often have a closer relationship with them (living modestly and sharing the same deprivations) than do other NGOs, development agencies should not want to steer absolutely clear of proselytizers. Taking full advantage of religious networks and FBOs to promote development will require partnerships with a much broader set of organizations. A more nuanced and flexible approach should be formulated that balances the need to ensure equal access to services with the need to expand the range of organizations that agencies engage.

A Proposal for a New Organization

While government agencies, multilateral agencies, and secular NGOs can enhance their ability to promote development by working with FBOs, they are unlikely to overcome all of their hesitancy about working with religious bodies. That problem would be mitigated if an organization was created by and for the FBOs themselves. Such an organization could pool the knowledge, experience, and skills of numerous FBOs from different faiths. Unlike most FBOs, this organization would not concentrate on delivering services, and unlike existing interfaith bodies such as the World Parliament of the Religions, Religions for Peace (WCRP), and United Religions Initiative (URI), it would not focus on conflict resolution. Instead, with the financial and material support of major foundations, development agencies, and leading religious organizations from all creeds and from both the rich and the poor worlds, this new organization could explore a broader agenda for using religion to catalyze development in fragile states.

To begin, the new organization could launch a series of ambitious research programs on all facets of the relationship between religion and development. Although some universities have recently begun to explore this field (see below), the traditional reluctance among economists and other academics to analyze faith's impact has only reinforced the tendency among development professionals to ignore religious belief and the role of FBOs in their own work.[29] As one DFID-funded report explained, there has been "widespread neglect of the role of religion in both mainstream academic analysis of people's lives and social relationships and in development theories and practice."[30] As a result, few aid specialists are familiar with the many faith networks that dominate the landscape of the poor—from Brazil's *favelas* to Pakistan's tribal areas—and thus do not incorporate such networks into their studies and plans.

The new organization's research programs would do more than catalog information. They would seek to understand how faith networks function, how they influence the values of believers, how they are led, how they are funded, how effective their services are, and how well they are able to mobilize and discipline their members. Researching how religious values and relationships affect attitudes toward business and modernization would help development specialists learn how to better engage local populations—and how to do so without unnecessarily and unwittingly undermining their traditional beliefs and norms. Discovering how the groups within a particular country or region relate to each other and to the government would create a clearer picture of their capacity to work together to improve governance and enhance social cohesion. Studying local social structures and identities, and the role of religion in influencing these, could generate ideas for bridging the deep divides that scar these societies. More specific studies could focus on, say, faith-based patterns of poverty and social exclusion, lessons learned by donors from their past engagement with faith groups, and the process by which religious organizations build social capital. The resulting databases, case studies, historical analyses, and interfaith comparisons would offer a rich assortment of information to help the wider development community and governments better engage these groups.

But this organization should aim to do more than just conduct research. It should also seek to fill an important gap in the development field by providing training, guidance, and support to faith networks in poor countries, both directly and in partnership with aid agencies and Western FBOs, such as Saddleback Church, which has developed and trained its own international network of pastors in recent years. And by working directly with Muslim, Hindu, and other religious philanthropists and FBOs, the new body would be well placed to encourage more private resources be directed toward development.

To some extent, the research arm of this new organization would complement the promising work now being undertaken in a handful of institutions. The University of Birmingham in the United Kingdom, for example, is in the middle of a five-year research program on religions and development funded by DFID.[31] Georgetown University has taken over much of the work originally performed under the auspices of the World Bank to establish a program on religion and global development.[32] The Institute of Social Studies in The Hague has set up a Knowledge Centre on Religion and Development.[33] Harvard University and Johns Hopkins University also have been active in this area. But with the possible exception of the Birmingham program, none of these projects is attempting to systematically analyze all the issues raised in this paper related to development and religion. Most have only a handful of researchers. And their output is limited to papers, conferences, and catalogs of activities, which reach only small audiences. In short, there is as yet no agency proactively conducting research across all faiths with the intention of seeking to turn that knowledge into programs that can reach the great majority of religious groups and leaders around the world.

Conclusion

How might this gap be filled? What would it take to launch the kind of organization that can pool the intellectual capacities of FBOs and explore a broad agenda for catalyzing development? An initial step in this direction would require considerable commitment but only modest resources. Indeed, just one leader might be able to accomplish much if blessed with the threefold ability to develop a coherent vision of such an organization, to inspire individuals to embrace that vision, and to cajole institutions to fund its realization. As a first step, this person could seek to persuade a handful of the major religious organizations operating in the developing world—such as Caritas Internationalis, World Vision, the Aga Khan Foundation, Sarvodaya, and the Gülen movement—to form a partnership to establish a new organization around a few research and training programs. Each of the founding partners might play a different role—one might provide funds, for instance, while another offers intellectual advice—to support the work of the organization's staff and leadership. Slowly but systematically, the organization could broaden its agenda, expand its team of researchers and trainers, and invite other FBOs to participate. Similarly, the number of countries and denominations served and the types of assistance offered to FBOs in developing countries could gradually be expanded. Within a few years, this new organization might begin to have a major impact not only on the capacities and ambitions of faith groups engaged in promoting development but also on how development is perceived and approached.

Such change in perceptions might well extend even to secular-minded Western development agencies, which are well aware that their past efforts at repairing fragile states have yielded few positive results. For instance, the World Bank's own Independent Evaluation Group, which reports on the organization's activities to its board of directors, concluded that "past international engagement with [fragile states] has failed to yield significant improvements, and donors and others continue to struggle with how best to assist [them]."[34] There is thus a potentially receptive audience for any organization that can demonstrate an effective method of helping fragile states.

As this article has argued, Western blueprints for development are only partially effective because development is not primarily a top-down process but rather is fundamentally an organic, bottom-up process driven by local capacities and social relationships. International action should first and foremost facilitate these local processes, leverage local capacities, and complement local actions so that local citizens can create governance systems appropriate to their histories, values, and societies. In fragile states, the most effective institutions and most potent capacities are often to be found not within formal state structures but within non-state groups, organizations, and networks. And, in many cases, the most important of these are religious in nature.

If the new, FBO-funded organization could demonstrate this, it might make believers out of even the most secular of development professionals.

40

NEW HOUSE RULES
Christianity, Economics, and Planetary Living

—Sallie McFague

Introduction

Is the environment a religious issue? Many do not think so. For most Americans, the problems with our deteriorating planet can be fixed by science, managed with new technology.[1]

Let us hope that this is so, that science and technology *can* solve the looming environmental crisis. But it may not be that simple. Lynn White's oft-quoted 1967 essay laid the blame for environmental deterioration at the feet of religion, specifically Christianity.[2] If Christianity has been capable of doing such immense damage, then surely the restoration of nature must also lie, at least in part, with Christianity. I believe it does, but also with other world religions as well as with education, government, economics—and science. The environmental crisis is a "planetary agenda," involving all people, all areas of expertise—and all religions.

This is the case because the environmental crisis is not a "problem" that any specialization can solve. Rather, it is about how we—all of us human beings and all other creatures—can live justly and sustainably on our planet. It is about the "house rules" that will enable us to do so. These house rules include attitudes as well as technologies, behaviors as well as science. They are what the *oikos*, the house we all share, demands that we think and do so there will be enough for everyone. The words for these house rules are "derivatives" of *oikos*—ecumenicity, ecology, and economics—facilitating the management of the resources of planet Earth so that all may thrive indefinitely.

How does religion, and specifically Christianity, fit into this picture? Christianity fits where all religions do: as a worldview supporting the house rules. It fits at the level of the deeply held and often largely unconscious assumptions about who we are in the scheme of things, and how we should act.[3] While "anthropology" is not the only concern of religions, it is a central one and, for the purposes of the ecological crisis, the one that may count the most.

* *Daedalus* 130, no. 4 (Fall 2001): 125–40.

This essay will make the case that Christianity—at least since the Protestant Reformation, and especially since the Enlightenment—has, through its individualistic view of
human life, implicitly and sometimes explicitly, supported a neoclassical economic paradigm and a consumer culture that has devastated the planet and widened the gap between
the rich and the poor.[4] It will also suggest that Christianity, given its oldest and deepest
anthropology, should support an alternative ecological model, one in which our well-being
is seen as interrelated and interdependent with the well-being of all other living things and
earth processes.[5]

Religions, and especially Christianity in Western culture, have a central role in forming who we think we are and what we have the right to do. It is the claim of this author that
an individualistic anthropology is presently supported in the West not only by Christianity
but also by government and the contemporary economic system.[6] When these three major
institutions—religion, government, and the economic system—present a united front, a
"sacred canopy" is cast over a society, validating the behavior of its people. It is difficult to
believe that science and technology alone can solve an ecological crisis supported by this
triumvirate, for these institutions as presently constituted legitimate human beings continuing to feel, think, and act in ways that are basically contrary to the conservation and
just distribution of the world's resources.

Neoclassical and Ecological Economics

Neoclassical and ecological economics offer two dramatically different anthropologies, with
different "house rules." The first model sees human beings on the planet as a collection of
individuals drawn together to benefit each other by fully exploiting natural resources. The
second model sees the planet as a community that survives and prospers only through the
interdependence of all its parts, human and nonhuman. The first model rests on assumptions from the eighteenth century: it sees human beings as individuals with rights and
responsibilities, and the world as a machine, a collection of individual parts that are only
externally related to one another. The second model rests on assumptions from postmodern
science: it sees human beings as conscious and radically dependent parts of a larger whole,
and the world as an organism, internally related in all its parts.

Both are models, interpretations, of the world and our place in it: neither is a description. This point must be underscored because the first model seems "natural"—indeed,
"inevitable" and "true"—to most middle-class Westerners, while the second model seems
novel, perhaps even utopian or fanciful. In fact, both come from the assumptions of different historical periods; both are world-pictures built on these assumptions, and each vies
for our agreement and loyalty.

We need to assess the "economy" of both models, their notions of the allocation of
scarce resources to family members, to determine which view of the "good life" is better.
In this essay, I suggest that the machine model is injurious to nature and to poor people,
while the organic model is healthier for the planet and all its inhabitants.

The reason economics is so important, why it is a religious and ecological issue, is that
it is not just a "matter of money"; rather, it is a matter of survival and flourishing. Economics is an issue of values. In making economic decisions, the "bottom line" is not the
only consideration. Many other values come into play, from the health of a community to
its recreational opportunities; from the beauty of other life-forms to our concern for their

well-being; from a desire to see our children fed and clothed to a sense of responsibility for the welfare of future generations.

Contemporary neoclassicists generally deny that economics is about values.[7] But this denial is questionable. The key feature of market capitalism is the allocation of scarce resources by means of decentralized markets: allocation occurs as the result of individual market transactions, each of which is guided by self-interest.[8] At the base of neoclassical economics is an anthropology: human beings are individuals motivated by self-interest. The value by which scarce resources are allocated, then, is the fulfillment of the self-interest of human beings. The assumption is that each will act to maximize his or her own interest, and by so doing will eventually benefit all—the so-called invisible hand of Adam Smith's classical theory.

But what of other values? Two key ones, if we have the economics of the entire planet in mind, are the just distribution of the earth's resources, and the capacity of the planet to sustain our use of its resources. However, these matters—distributive justice to the world's inhabitants, and the optimal scale of the human economy within the planet's economy—are considered "externalities" by neoclassical economics.[9] In other words, the issues of who benefits from an economic system and whether the planet can bear the system's burden are not part of neoclassical economics.

In sum, the worldview or basic assumption of neoclassical economics is surprisingly simple and straightforward: the crucial assumption is that human beings are self-interested individuals who, acting on this basis, will create a syndicate or corporation, even a global one, capable of benefiting all eventually. Hence, as long as the economy grows, individuals in a society will sooner or later participate in prosperity. These assumptions about human nature are scarcely value-neutral. They indicate a preference for a certain view of who we are and what the goal of human effort should be: the view of human nature is individualism and our goal is growth.

When we turn to the alternative ecological economic paradigm we see a different set of values. Ecological economics claims we cannot survive unless we acknowledge our profound dependence on one another and the earth. Human need is more basic than human greed: we are relational beings from the moment of our conception to our last breath. The well-being of the individual is inextricably connected to the well-being of the whole.

These two interpretations of who we are and where we fit in the world are almost opposites of each other. Neoclassical economics begins with the unconstrained allocation of resources to competing individuals, on the assumption that if everyone acts in this way, issues of fair distribution and sustainability will eventually work themselves out. Ecological economics begins with the health of the whole planet, on the assumption that only as it thrives now and in the future will its various parts, including human beings, thrive as well. In other words, ecological economics begins with sustainability and distributive justice, not with the allocation of resources among competing individuals. Before all else, the community must be able to survive (sustainability), which it can do only if all members have the use of resources (distributive justice). Then, within these parameters, the allocation of scarce resources among competing users can take place.

Ecological economics does not pretend to be value-free; its preference is evident— the well-being and sustainability of our household, planet Earth. Ecological economics is the management of a community's physical necessities for the benefit of all, a human enterprise that seeks to maximize the optimal functioning of the planet's gifts and services for all users. Ecological economics, then, is first of all a vision of how human beings *ought* to live on planet Earth in light of the perceived reality of *where* and *how* we live. We live in, with, and from the earth. This story of who we are is based on contemporary science, not on an eighteenth-century story about social reality.

Neoclassical or Ecological Economics: Which Is Good for Planet Earth?

Can neoclassical economics as currently understood sustain the planet? In the neoclassical economic view the "world" is a machine; presumably, then, when some parts give out they can be replaced with substitutes. If, for instance, our main ecological problem is nonrenewable resources (oil, coal, minerals, etc.), then human ingenuity might well fill in the gaps when they occur. Since the earth is considered an "externality" by neoclassical economics, then "good for the planet" can only mean good for human beings to use. Sustainability is not the major priority.

At the beginning of the new millennium, however, our planet faces more than the loss of nonrenewable resources. It also faces an accelerating loss of *renewable* resources, such as water, trees, fertile soil, clean air, fisheries, and biodiversity. If our planet is more like an organism than a machine, with all its parts interrelated and interdependent, then as its various parts lose vitality, it will, like any "body," become sick to the point of not functioning any longer. Unable to sustain itself, it will die.

This is called the synergism of planetary operation. When the various members of an ecosystem are healthy, they work together to provide innumerable "free services" that none could provide alone, and that we take for granted: materials production (food, fisheries, timber, genetic resources, medicines), biological control of pests and diseases, habitat and refuge, water supply and regulation, waste recycling and pollution control, educational and scientific resources, recreation.[10] These services are essential to our survival and well-being; they can continue only if we sustain them. This "list" of services should be seen as a "web": none of them can function alone; each of them depends on the others. These services are the "commons" that we hold in trust for future generations.

The most important services are not necessarily the most visible ones. For instance, in a forest it is not only the standing trees that are valuable, but also the fallen ones (the "nurse logs" on which new trees grow), the habitat the forest provides for birds and insects that pollinate crops and fight diseases, the plants that provide biodiversity for food and medicines, the forest canopy that breaks the force of winds, the roots that reduce soil erosion, and the photosynthesis of plants that helps stabilize the climate. The smallest providers—the insects, worms, spiders, fungi, algae, and bacteria—are critically important in creating a stable, sustainable home for humans and other creatures. If such a forest is clear-cut to harvest the tress, everything else goes as well. All these services disappear. A healthy ecosystem—complex and diverse in all its features, both large and small—is resilient, like a well-functioning body. A simplified, degraded nature, supporting single-species crops in ruined soil with inadequate water and violent weather events, results in a diminished environment for human beings as well. "The bottom line is that for humans to be healthy and resilient, nature must be too."[11]

As we have seen, nature becomes unhealthy gradually and in particular parts and places. But when particular aspects are degraded beyond a certain point, the destructive effects on the whole can be dramatic.

An excellent example of such negative synergism is global warming. I choose this example not only because it is among the top three planetary problems (the other two being loss of biodiversity and uncontrolled growth in human population and consumption), but also because it illustrates how these problems interact.

Global warming is the result of emissions from the burning of fossil fuels; this has occurred because of the size of the human population and also the high energy consumption of industrialized societies. Global warming affects not only human beings, but also plants and other animals. Since the weather is the largest and most sensitive system influencing the planet, its state is a barometer of the earth's health.

Middle-class Westerners produce three to five times more of the carbon dioxide largely responsible for global warming than do people living in developing countries.[12] Automobiles are the single greatest producer of carbon dioxide emissions, but a consumer lifestyle in general is the culprit. While other countries such as China and India may equal or surpass the West in greenhouse gas emissions in the future, Westerners have been the preachers of consumerism as the good life. We have not only produced the vast majority of emissions to date, but we export the ideology of consumerism around the world as the heartbeat of every nation's prosperity. Neoclassical economics, with its twin values of individual insatiability and economic growth, is the engine behind global warming.

It is the growing consensus among the world's weather experts that by the year 2050 we can expect a 2.5°C increase in the worldwide temperature, and that this increase will be due largely to human activity, especially the burning of fossil fuels.[13] The results are predicted to be devastating from a human point of view: desertification of the chief grain-producing lands, a growing scarcity of fresh water, loss of trees, flooding of coastal areas and islands, the spread of tropical diseases, an increase in violent weather events, a likely shortage of food, and so on. Global warming will change life as we know it and has already begun to do so. Through our consumer lifestyle we have triggered fearful, though still largely unknown, consequences for the most important and sensitive system within which we and everything else exist.

The prospect of global warming is not science fiction. According to projections made by our best scientists, the question is no longer "What if global warming comes?" but "How bad will it be?" At both the United Nations Conference on the Environment and Development in Rio in 1992 and at the follow-up conferences since, the industrial countries agreed in principle to stabilize and eventually cut back carbon dioxide emissions. However, little if any practical progress has been made, in large part because the neoclassical economic worldview is so dominant. In countries like the United States, there has been little public discussion of the consequences of consumerism. *All* of us are collaborators in this silence. We enjoy the consumer lifestyle; in fact, most of us are addicted to it, and, like addicts, we cheerfully live in a state of denial. But we need to overcome our denial. The prospect of global warming should disturb our complacency. Unless we change our ways, the future will be very grim. Global warming is the canary in the mine, whose death is a clue that our lifestyle goes outside the planet's house rules.

Christianity and the Ecological Economic Model

One way to change our ways is to begin to think differently about economics. In metaphorical terms, ecological economics invites us to picture ourselves not as isolated individuals but as housemates. The ecological model claims that housemates must abide by three main rules: take only your share, clean up after yourselves, and keep the house in good repair for future occupants. We do not own the house; we do not even rent it. It is loaned to us for our lifetime, with the proviso that we obey the above rules so that the house can feed, shelter, nurture, and delight those who move in after us. These rules are not laws that we can circumvent or disobey; they are the conditions of our harmonious coexistence, and they are constitutive of our happiness.

If we were to follow these rules, we would be living within a different vision of the good life, the abundant life, than the one that is current in our consumer culture and that is destroying the planet. We would begin to accept what ecological economist Robert Costanza calls our greatest calling:

> Probably the most challenging task facing humanity today is the creation of a shared vision of a sustainable and desirable society, one that can provide permanent prosperity within the biophysical constraints of the real world in a way that is fair and equitable to all of humanity, to other species, and to future generations.[14]

Now, given these two economic worldviews—the neoclassical and the ecological—which should Christianity support? Presently, Christianity is supporting the neoclassical economic paradigm to the degree that it does not speak against it and side publicly with the ecological view. Does this evident indifference matter? Yes, it does, if one accepts the assumption of this essay that worldviews matter. While there is no direct connection between believing and acting, thinking and doing, there is an implicit, deeper, and more insidious one: when a worldview seems "natural" and "inevitable," it becomes a secret source of our decisions and actions.

Moreover, a persuasive case can be made that there is an intrinsic connection between the ecological economic model and Christianity. Distributive justice and sustainability, as goals for planetary living, are pale reflections, but reflections nonetheless, of what Jesus meant by the kingdom of God.[15] Let us look at the vivid portrait of Jesus by New Testament scholar John Dominic Crossan.[16] "The open commensality [i.e., table] and radical egalitarianism of Jesus' Kingdom of God are more terrifying than anything we have ever imagined, and even if we can never accept it, we should not explain it away as something else."[17] For Jesus, the kingdom of God was epitomized by *everyone* being invited to the table; the kingdom is radically egalitarian at the level of satisfying bodily needs. Crossan regards the Parable of the Feast as central to understanding what Jesus means by the kingdom of God. This is a shocking story, trespassing society's boundaries of class, gender, status, and ethnicity—as its end result is inviting *all* to the feast. There are several versions of the story (Matt 22:1-13; Luke 14:15-24; Gospel of Thomas, 64), but in each one a prominent person invites a number of other people to a banquet, only to have them decline the invitation. One chooses instead to survey a land purchase, another to try out some new oxen, a third to attend a wedding. The frustrated host then tells his servants to go out into the streets of the city and bring whomever they can find to dinner: the poor, the maimed, the blind, the lame, the good, and the bad (the list varies in the three versions). The shocking implication is that everyone—*anyone*—is invited to share in God's bounty. As Crossan remarks, if beggars come to your door, you might give them food or even invite them into the kitchen for a meal, but you do not ask them to join the family in the dining room or invite them back on Saturday night for supper with your friends.[18] But that is exactly what happens in this story. The kingdom of God, according to this portrait of Jesus, is "more terrifying than anything we have imagined" because it demolishes all our carefully constructed boundaries between the worthy and the unworthy, and it does so at the most physical, bodily level.

For first-century Jews, the key boundary was purity laws: an observant Jewish man did not eat with the poor, with women, with the diseased, or with the "unrighteous." For us, the critical barrier is economic laws: we are not called to sustainable and just sharing of resources with the poor, the disadvantaged, the "lazy." To cross these barriers in both cultures is improper, not expected—in fact, shocking. And yet, in both cultures, the issue is the most basic bodily one: who is invited to share the food—in other words, who lives and who dies? In both cases, the answer is the same: everyone, regardless of status, is invited. This vision of God's will for the world does not specifically mention just, sustainable planetary living—but it is surely more in line with that worldview than it is with the blind satisfaction of individual consumer desires.

Unlike our first-century Mediterranean counterparts, North American middle-class Christians are not terrified by the unclean; but we are terrified by the poor. There are so many of them—billions! Surely we cannot be expected to share the planet's resources justly and sustainably with all of them. Yet the Jesus of the parable appears to disagree: he is not, it seems, interested so much in "religion," including his own, as in human well-being, beginning with the body: feeding the hungry and healing the suffering. Moreover, his message, according to Crossan, had less to do with what he did for others than with what others might do for their neighbors:

> The Kingdom of God was not, for Jesus, a divine monopoly exclusively bound to his own person. It began at the level of the body and appeared as a shared community of healing and eating—that is to say, of spiritual and physical resources available to each and all without distinctions, discrimination, or hierarchies. One entered the Kingdom as a way of life and anyone who could live it could bring it to others. It was not just words alone, or deeds alone, but both together as life-style.[19]

The body is the locus: how we treat needy bodies gives the clue to how a just society will be organized. It suggests that correct "table manners" are a sign of a just society, the kingdom of God. If one accepts this interpretation, then the "table" becomes not just the bread and wine of communion, but also the public meals of bread and fishes that one finds throughout Jesus' ministry.[20] At these events, all are invited to share in the food, whether it be meager or sumptuous. Were such an understanding of the Eucharist to infiltrate Christian churches today, it could be mind-changing—and maybe world-changing, too.

Is it also absurd, foolish, and utopian? Perhaps, but, as I have suggested, there appears to be a solid link, a degree of continuity, between this reconstruction of society—the kingdom of God—and what I have described as the ecological economic worldview. Perhaps just, sustainable planetary living is a foretaste, a glimmer, an inkling of the kingdom of God.

If this is the case, then for middle-class North American Christians it may well be that *sin* is refusing to acknowledge the link between the kingdom and the ecological economic worldview, explaining it away because of the consequences for our privileged lifestyle. Sustainability and the just distribution of resources are concerned with human and planetary well-being *for all*. This, I suggest, is the responsible interpretation of the Parable of the Feast for North American Christians today. By paying attention to those invited to the feast and those excluded, this interpretation demands that we look at the systemic structures separating the haves and the have-nots in our time. And it demands that we name these structures for what they are: evil. They are the collective forms of our "sin." They are the institutions, laws, and international bodies of market capitalism (often aided by the silence of the church) that allow a few to get richer while most become poorer.

Next Steps: A Christian Response to the Environmental Crisis

In order to dislodge the neoclassical economic worldview and Christianity's complicity with it, three steps are needed.

The first step is to become conscious of neoclassical economics as a model—not a description—of how to allocate scarce resources. There are other ways to live, other ways to divide things up, other goals for human beings to pursue. "Economics" is always necessary, but not necessarily neoclassical economics: ecological economics is an alternative.

The second step is to suggest some visions of the good life that are not consumer-dominated, visions that are just and sustainable. The good life is not necessarily the consumer life; rather, it could include providing the basic necessities for all, universal medical care and education, opportunities for creativity and meaningful work, time for family and friends, green spaces in cities, and wilderness for other creatures. We need to ask what *really* makes people happy, and which of these visions is most just to the world's inhabitants and most sustainable for the planet.

The third step is to rethink what a different worldview—the ecological economic one—would mean for the basic doctrines of Christianity: God and the world, Christ and salvation, human life and discipleship. While this last task is beyond the scope of this essay, I would like to end with a few brief comments about God and the world, because this is at the heart of who we think we are and what we should do. Since our interpretive context, the ecological economic model, is about the just and sustainable allocation of resources among all planetary users, the framework for speaking of God and the world becomes worldly well-being. To phrase it in terms of a gloss on Irenaeus of Lyons: "The glory of God is every creature fully alive." Dietrich Bonhoeffer called it "worldly Christianity": he said that God is neither a metaphysical abstraction nor the answer to gaps in our knowledge—God is neither in the sky nor on the fringes, but at "the center of the village," in the midst of life, both its pains and its joys.[21] An ecological economic model means an earthly God, an incarnate God, an immanental God.

The general outline of this theology is basically different from the theology implied by the neoclassical model of economics. A "worldly Christianity" entails a movement toward the earth: from the otherworldly to this world; from above to below; from a distant, external God to a near, immanental God; from soul to body; from individualism to community; from mechanistic to organic thinking; from spiritual salvation to holistic well-being; from anthropocentrism to cosmocentrism. The ecological model means a shift not from God to the world, but from a distant God related externally to the world to an embodied God who is the source of the world's life and fulfillment. The neoclassical economic model assumes that God, like the human being, is an individual—in fact, the superindividual who controls the world through laws of nature. This God is like a good mechanic who has produced a well-designed machine that operates efficiently. This God is present at the beginning (creation) and intervenes from time to time to influence personal and public history, but is otherwise absent from the world. An ecological theology, on the contrary, claims that God is radically present in the world, as close as the breath, the joy, and the suffering of every creature. The two views of God and the world, then, are very different: in the one, God's power is evident in God's distant control of the world; in the other, God's glory is manifest in God's total self-giving to the world.

In closing, I will note that these two pictures of God and the world suggest two different answers to the questions of who we are and what we should do. In the first, we are individuals responsible to a transcendent God who rewards or punishes according to our merits and God's mercy. In the second, we are beings in community living in the presence of God who is the power and love in everything that exists. In the first, we should do what is fair to other individuals while taking care of our own well-being. In the second, we should do what is necessary to work with God to create a just and sustainable planet, for only in that way will all flourish. This is the great work of the twenty-first century. Never before have we had to think of everyone and everything all together. We now know that if we are to survive and if our planet is to flourish, we will do so as a whole or not at all. But we do not have to do this alone: "the earth is the Lord's and all that is in it, the world, and those who live in it."[22]

41

ISLAM, GLOBALIZATION, AND ECONOMIC PERFORMANCE IN THE MIDDLE EAST

—Marcus Noland and Howard Pack

The Middle East is sitting on a demographic time bomb. According to the United Nations Development Program's (UNDP) *Arab Human Development Report 2002*, the population of the Arab region is expected to increase by about 25 percent between 2000 and 2010 and 50 to 60 percent by 2020. The latter figure represents an increase of as many as 150 million people, or more than two additional Egypts. Even under the UNDP's more conservative scenario, in 2020, Bahrain, Kuwait, Qatar, and the United Arab Emirates will be the only Arab countries with median ages above 30.

These figures suggest that the region as a whole will experience labor force growth greater than 3 percent for roughly the next 15 years. On current trends, according to an Arab League report, unemployment in the region could rise from 15 million to 50 million over this period. Under plausible assumptions about the rate of productivity growth and required investment levels, the economies of the region will have to maintain investment rates on the order of 30 percent of gross domestic product and income growth of 5 to 6 percent each year to absorb all this labor. It is a very tall order, and recent history is not reassuring.

Fragmentary data from the 1950s and more comprehensive data from the 1960s indicate that, measured either in terms of per capita income growth or what economists call "total factor productivity growth"—how much economic bang one gets for the buck—the performance of countries in the Middle East was markedly different from other developing countries. The region was superior to sub-Saharan Africa (the other region most profoundly marked by weak states and arbitrary boundaries), worse than East Asia, and comparable to Latin America and South Asia.

This pattern had changed by the 1980s, following a decade that witnessed an acceleration of inflation globally, the collapse of the Bretton Woods system of fixed exchange rates, two oil shocks, and a deceleration of income and productivity growth rates worldwide. The experience in the Middle East differed considerably among the region's countries, with those states relying on oil production rather than a more diversified economy suffering the

* *The SAIS Review* 24, no. 2 (Summer–Fall 2004): 105–16.

worst. During the 1980s, the region as a whole actually experienced negative growth in per capita income, although Egypt, Morocco, and Tunisia were notable exceptions. And while per capita incomes once again began to rise in the 1990s, it was at rates markedly slower than those experienced by Latin America and South Asia, not to mention East Asia.

Still, the failure to achieve rapid growth in order to absorb the rising number of labor force entrants could have dire implications. In a Zogby poll of Arab attitudes, Saudi males stand out as uniquely dissatisfied and pessimistic about their children's future.[1] Presumably these feelings are rooted in the reality of dwindling employment prospects, the 40-percent decline in per capita income from its peak in 1982, and the lack of political voice. Dissatisfaction and pessimism about the future are mildly correlated with age, education level, and access to the Internet, with the youngest and least advantaged sections of society having the bleakest appraisal of the future. And, of course, fifteen of the nineteen September 11 hijackers were Saudi males.

Islam Is Not the Issue

Recent years have seen a revival of the neo-Weberian correlation between economic prosperity and religious observance. In this new rendition, instead of Calvinism acting as an agent of economic advancement, Islam is cast as an inhibitor. For example, in one of the world's most widely circulated series of economic working papers, three professors at prominent U.S. and European institutions characterize Islam as being negatively associated "with attitudes that are conducive to growth," and on the basis of their analysis of World Values Survey data, they assert that among adherents to the world's major religions, Muslims are the most "anti-market."[2] Popular commentaries are less nuanced.

There is, of course, some surface plausibility to this notion: Muslims around the world are often resident in poor countries such as Bangladesh and Pakistan, though it is also the case that many live in Indonesia and Malaysia, largely Muslim nations which have relatively high income levels and growth rates. Islam is associated with distinct practices such as the prohibition on *riba*, the charging of interest, or the injunction to observe *zakat*, the paying of alms, which could serve as causal links between theological belief and economic performance. Yet attempts to rigorously assess the impact of these unique practices suggest that they have little, if any, impact on the accumulation and allocation of capital.[3]

Likewise, research has generally failed to uncover links between Islam and economic performance in the context of conventional growth models that emphasize such factors as macroeconomic stability and educational attainment. When one introduces into these standard growth models explanatory variables such the Muslim population share, the statistical results are not robust.[4] If anything, Islam appears to promote growth. This result is obtained whether the examination is of large cross-sections of countries over decades, smaller groups of countries for most of the twentieth century, or sub-national jurisdictions within multi-ethnic, multi-religious states with substantial Muslim populations.

These results hold even if one allows the size of the Muslim population to indirectly impact economic performance, for example, by affecting educational attainment or the degree of political stability. Muslim countries do not appear to systematically deviate from the norm in any observable way. Statistically speaking, the economic performance of Muslim countries equates with what economic fundamentals would suggest.

Popular Attitudes and Successful Globalization

If not Islam, then what explains the relative underperformance of the Middle East in recent decades? A litany of indicators documents the weakness of the region's linkages to the world economy: import tariffs average over 20 percent, most of the larger countries in the region are not members of the World Trade Organization (WTO), the region's share of world exports has fallen steadily, and as a whole it attracts roughly as much foreign direct investment as Sweden.

It is almost impossible to imagine the Middle East generating the rapid employment growth necessary to absorb new entrants to the labor force without a big expansion of international trade. Countries such as South Korea or Taiwan, which achieved sustained periods of economic growth at rates sufficient to cope with an increasing population, did so in the context of an outward-oriented development strategy. In the early 1960s, the level of per capita income in Egypt, South Korea, and Taiwan was virtually identical, but the latter two quickly pulled ahead, leaving Egypt a generation behind. Twenty-five years ago, each of these Asian countries already achieved exports of manufactures *ten times what Egypt has today*. And although Egypt has a population more than South Korea's and Taiwan's combined, the Asian countries export more manufactures in two days than Egypt does in an entire year.

Although it is theoretically possible that the authorities could manage domestic aggregate demand in such a way to generate balanced growth of this magnitude for a decade or more, it is highly unlikely that it is possible in practice. The domestic economy will almost invariably develop bottlenecks if the authorities try to push it down a balanced growth path with such rapidity for such a sustained a period of time. The problem is particularly acute if the small size of the domestic market hampers firms. It is difficult to imagine a large economy like Egypt successfully pulling this off; it is virtually impossible to conceive of smaller economies like Syria or Tunisia doing so.

In one sense, the comparison with South Korea and Taiwan may be unfair—it is possible to argue that the contemporaneous levels of income in the 1950s or 1960s in these countries reflected wartime disruption of the late 1940s and early 1950s and that underlying social capacity was actually quite high. Unlike Egypt, the Asian countries, in a sense, were in the process of returning to their long-run development trajectory rather than blazing new trails.[5]

Yet similar, though less dramatic, comparisons could be drawn with other countries. Today, taking the level of physical capital, human capital, arable land, and labor into account, the most relevant comparators to Egypt and Jordan may be the Philippines, Costa Rica, and Bangladesh. Even tiny Costa Rica, with a population roughly 5 percent of Egypt, exports more than twice as many manufactures as Egypt or Jordan. And Egypt and the other countries of the region will not be able to pick and choose their competitors. Whatever the lessons of history, they will have to compete against large, formidable rivals such as China and India in world markets.

Yet it is unlikely that the Middle East will even be able to compete successfully with China or India on the basis of low wages, as they are already multiples of those found in the Asian giants, let alone other countries in the region. The possible competitive advantage of the Middle East instead lies in its proximity to Europe and its ability to service the European market in a more timely fashion than competitors in Asia, Latin America, or sub-Saharan Africa. This means integration into cross-border supply chains in which there is a premium on reliability, flexibility, and fast delivery. But as noted in a recent World Bank publication, the nations of the region are conspicuously absent from international production networks.[6]

This close integration with producers beyond the region requires cross-border investment and frequent physical contact, which immediately raises issues relating to political risk, broadly defined to include not only expropriation but also the physical security of both facilities and personnel. In the extractive sector, the location of production is determined largely by geology—if the marginal cost of extraction is sufficiently low relative to the world price, someone will run the risk of producing from that location (though the case of Sudan should stand as a warning that the simple existence of mineral deposits is not a sufficient condition for this to hold).

The same does not hold for manufacturing or back-office type service-sector activities that are not location-specific. In this regard, the Middle East must compete with alternative locations in Asia, Africa, and Latin America, and the security risk could potentially prove to be a serious constraint. While the attacks against "off-shoring" of American white-collar jobs have mounted, the targets of concern have been countries such as India, China, the Philippines, and Mexico—not Syria or Egypt. (In this regard prospects might be better for the former French colonies of the Maghreb once the process of outsourcing white-collar tasks begins in earnest in Francophone Europe.) Another great fear in America today—terrorism—also plays a role, and although there have been occasional threats against foreign businesses and attacks on foreign tourists, most notably at Luxor in 1997, to date this does not appear to be a major problem.

Less dramatic than terrorist attacks, though perhaps more important for economic development, are public attitudes toward foreigners and globalization. The 2003 Pew Global Attitudes survey revealed a significant level of discomfort with globalization in the Middle East.[7] As indicated in Figure 1, the percentage responding positively to globalization varies across the Middle East, with the populations of Jordan and Egypt considerably less accepting of globalization than either other Arab countries or other regions of the world surveyed. Three of the many questions posed in the Pew poll have particularly high correlations with measures of risk in economic exchange, especially foreign direct investment that involves a local physical presence. The regional pattern of responses to these three issues—the necessity of closing large, inefficient factories; the need to protect their way of life against foreign influence; and desirability of societal acceptance of homosexuality—are displayed in Figures 2–4.[8] Relative to most respondents in the rest of the world, Arabs were less willing to close inefficient factories, more committed to protecting the local way of life, and less tolerant of homosexuality. The picture that emerges from the pattern of responses to the full set of Pew survey questions is of local populations that are relatively averse to change, instead favoring the maintenance of existing economic and social arrangements, especially if the forces of change are regarded as emanating from foreign or non-traditional sources.

Controlling for economic fundamentals, such as the level of per capita income, macroeconomic stability, and corporate taxes, across a broad sample of countries these responses have some explanatory power with respect to measures of interest such as levels of inward foreign direct investment. Although the precise channels of causality are ill-defined, it is

FIGURE 1
Opinion of Globalization (% who responded it is "good")

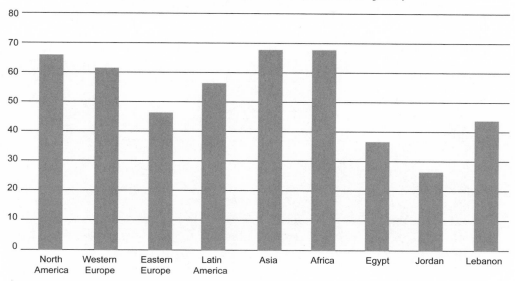

Source: Pew Research Center for the People and the Press, Pew Global Attitudes Project, 2002 and 2003.

FIGURE 2
Opinion on Closing Large Inefficient Factories
(% who responded "hardship but necessary")

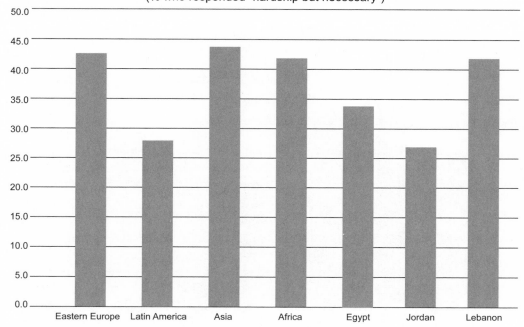

Source: Pew Research Center for the People and the Press, Pew Global Attitudes Project, 2002 and 2003.

FIGURE 3
Way of Life "Needs to be Protected against Foreign Influence"
(% of respondents who disagreed)

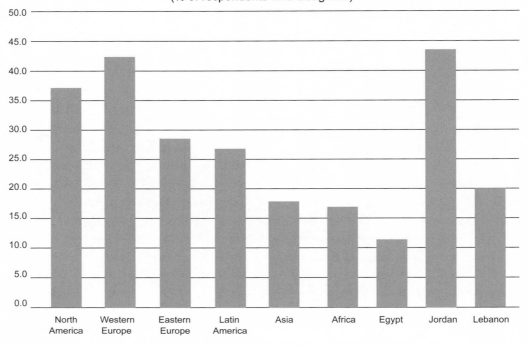

Source: Pew Research Center for the People and the Press, Pew Global Attitudes Project, 2002 and 2003.

FIGURE 4
"Homosexuality Should be Accepted by Society"
(% of respondents who agreed)

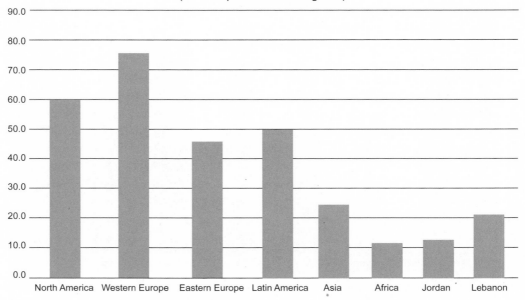

Source: Pew Research Center for the People and the Press, Pew Global Attitudes Project, 2002 and 2003.

plausible that the attitudes manifested in the survey responses are underpinning behaviors and practices that may impede successful globalization. The question about closing of factories could be interpreted as a straightforward question about the priority placed on efficiency. The questions about protecting against foreign influence and accepting homosexuality could be interpreted as capturing the extent of entry barriers to human capital from non-traditional sources.[9] So, for example, in a statistical sense, if Egyptian attitudes toward foreign influence were at the mean level of the least xenophobic countries of Latin America, Eastern Europe, and Sub-Saharan Africa, and Asia surveyed (Peru, Ukraine, Angola, and China, respectively), one would expect foreign direct investment (FDI) in Egypt to be almost 90 percent higher than it is. Likewise, if attitudes toward homosexuality in Jordan mimicked the most tolerant countries surveyed from Latin America (Argentina), Eastern Europe (the Czech Republic), Sub-Saharan Africa (South Africa), and Asia (the Philippines), FDI would be expected to be more than twice as high as it is today.

From this perspective, the attitudes revealed in the Pew survey are not auspicious. In a narrow sense, they reveal support for the current inward-oriented development strategy, which has been a relative failure, but at the same time, they may signal more profound levels of insecurity that could make successful globalization problematic. Given Egypt's labor abundance and proximity to Europe, an obvious potential market niche would be in the production of high-end garments, but fashion designers are known for their flamboyance if nothing else, and wholesale fashion buyers may rank second only to MTV producers in the their capacity to outrage traditional moral authorities. It is not clear that societies grappling with deep issues of self-definition and European fashion houses are necessarily a good fit.

Islam May Be Part of the Issue

The 2003 Pew survey also examined attitudes toward Islam and political life in a number of predominantly Muslim countries around the world, as well as several with large Muslim minorities, such as Nigeria and Tanzania. The poll revealed ubiquitous feelings of solidarity with co-religionists in the *umma* and widespread support for the notion that Islam was under threat, though the perceived sources of this threat were multiple and predominately reflected local concerns.

In this regard, concerns manifested through Islam may simply be one symptom of more complex social processes. Islam may matter, but not in the simple sense that belief in Allah dooms one to a low personal savings rate or that Islamic banking systems handicap financial efficiency. Instead, the implications of Islamic observance are more subtle. Today there are Muslim communities in the Middle East that are relatively discomfited by aspects of ongoing social change. To the extent that adherence to Islam is a significant component of personal and communal identity, Islamic belief will be one prism through which these developments are evaluated. This pattern of apprehension may be reinforced if Islam itself is regarded as being part of this contested terrain.

Yet the centrality of religious belief in this formative process should not be overstated. As revealed in the Zogby poll, religious orientation is generally only a secondary or tertiary source of personal identity in most Arab countries in the Middle East; rather, Arab ethnicity is the primary identifier. It is almost surely the case that feelings toward foreigners or homosexuals are derived from some admixture of religious teachings and prevailing cultural norms. Religious beliefs are but one input in a complex reaction to globalization.

Conclusion

Broadly speaking, the long-run economic performance of the Middle East appears neutral when viewed in comparison to other developing countries, and the concern expressed in some quarters about the impact of Islam on economic development would appear unwarranted. That said, there is serious cause for concern.

For reasons that are not fully understood, economic performance has slipped over the past quarter century or so relative to a broad set of comparators. This concern is made particularly acute by two ongoing developments, one external and one internal. The external source of worry relates to the successful ongoing globalization of China, India, and smaller rivals, which has created a more competitive global economic environment in which the Middle East must operate. The global marketplace simply embodies increasingly stringent competitive pressures and is less tolerant of substandard policies and practices than existed twenty or even ten years ago.

The internal pressure comes from demographics. The Middle East has entered a period in which its bulge generation is entering the labor force, and the imperative is to create jobs. It is almost impossible to imagine a sustained creation of employment opportunities on the needed scale without a successful process of globalization and cross-border economic integration.

This immediately raises difficult issues of sovereignty and cultural identity, and with them come obvious possibilities for self-reinforcing processes. The degree of insecurity in both economic and cultural dimensions presumably relates to actual economic performance, embodying possibilities of both virtuous and vicious circles. In this regard, the recent experiences of Saudi Arabia could be read as a cautionary tale: weak economic performance leading to pessimism about the future, accompanied by possibly counterproductive policy interventions, culminating in bouts of political extremism. It is not unreasonable to expect the exacerbation of this trend and its expansion into nearby states.

The good news is that to the extent that the Zogby poll accurately gauged regional attitudes, Saudi Arabia is the extreme case. Moreover, with fertility now dropping, the region may be well through the process of demographic transition, and as the size of the cohorts entering adulthood begins to shrink, there will be a concomitant diminution in the problems that all societies face in socializing young adult males. This process of absorbing a rapidly growing labor force, while prolonged, is self-terminating and not without end. Indeed, should the region manage to successfully surmount this challenge, it can look forward to a complementary period of "demographic dividend" as this generation enters its most productive working years—a phenomenon that contributed to the outstanding performance of East Asia over the past four decades. If the Middle East is able to cash in on this dividend, future pundits may praise the disciplined "Islamic ethic" as a contributor to development just as they today erroneously condemn it as an obstacle to growth.

42

DEVELOPMENT, RELIGION, AND WOMEN'S ROLES IN CONTEMPORARY SOCIETIES

—Katherine Marshall

Virtually every institution with international development as its focus pays tribute to the importance of women in their efforts. Strategy and vision statements promote the empowerment of women; education of girls is cited as a priority of priorities; and both the vulnerabilities and the potential power of the "girl child" are key elements in narratives about development. Transformation from traditional to modern societies requires new roles for women and girls and equality between women and men. Barack Obama noted this trend in his Cairo speech addressing majority-Muslim societies in June, 2009: "I am convinced that our daughters can contribute just as much to society as our sons. Our common prosperity will be advanced by allowing all humanity—men and women—to reach their full potential."[1]

There are, to be sure, variations in narrative and emphasis among the extraordinary array of actors and institutions that make up the development community. Many institutions contend that a "gender blind" approach is appropriate because in today's world equality means just that, and affirmative action toward women is no longer needed. Language and terminology has shifted, from Women in Development (old-fashioned WID) to Gender and Development (GAD); the change highlights that what is at issue is not favoring women but working with both men and women. (In some countries—Lesotho and Mongolia, for example—it is boys, not girls, who are disadvantaged.) Education may be the pivotal theme for one institution, reproductive rights for another, and economic empowerment the mantra in a third. A significant set of actors and observers notes that, despite fine rhetoric, efforts to prioritize the "engendering of development" are far from robust. But the development field has certainly seen a seismic shift over recent decades. The language of human rights and social justice is now interwoven with economic and social evidence that bolsters the claim that investing in women and girls is the right and the intelligent thing to do.

Bring religion[2] into the picture and the landscape quickly becomes more complicated. On the surface, it is not easy to discern marked differences in approach between religious

* *The Review of Faith & International Affairs* 8, no. 4 (Winter 2010): 35–42.

and non-religious development organizations. Strategy and vision statements from widely different faith-inspired organizations emphasize the importance of women's roles, and similar projects—microcredit, protecting girls in conflict zones, education, and so on—are part of the programmatic focus. Both secular and faith-inspired agencies' commitment to serve others often stems from a deep belief in universal human dignity.

Yet despite similar programming and a shared emphasis on dignity, when non-religious development specialists are challenged to take religion into account, religion's impact on women's roles is either explicitly or implicitly a concern. And for their part, many religious actors see common development models, especially those that highlight changing women's roles, as undermining traditional cultures and especially the family, which is seen as the pivotal institution for successful societies. Angry debates about the significance of reproductive health rights and what it means to protect adolescent girls cloud discussions about vital topics like HIV/AIDS and the trafficking of women and girls.

Religion and Development

The murky debates about gender, development, and religion take us swiftly to the much broader discussion about why religion matters for development work, why development matters for religion, and the implications for cooperation between religious and non-religious development actors.

Put simply, the development community has had patchy relationships with the vast array of religious institutions over most of the last six decades. Many faith-inspired institutions have harbored suspicions or reservations about non-religious development actors, portraying them as overly concerned with material gain and disrespectful of traditions and cultures. This is despite arguably shared concerns about the welfare of the world's poorest citizens and an underlying desire to right the injustices of the world. One illustration of the separation between religious and non-religious actors is the index to the lengthy and scholarly history of the World Bank's first 50 years, which has only one skimpy reference to religion.[3] When James D. Wolfensohn, then President of the World Bank, set out to bridge the gap in 1999 with a modest initiative devoted to dialogue (the World Faiths Development Dialogue[4]) a storm of controversy erupted. A hefty majority of the World Bank's 185 member countries voiced objections. Similar debates have divided other institutions, including specialized agencies of the United Nations, bilateral aid agencies, and many nongovernmental organizations, especially those focused on human rights. Despite what might seem compelling arguments that cooperation and partnership are logical and important, links between secular and faith-inspired development agencies have proved remarkably contentious.[5]

The arguments for linking development and religion stem in significant part from the large roles that faith-inspired organizations play in critical areas like health and education. Faith-inspired organizations, for example, are central players in addressing the AIDS pandemic. Religious roles range from direct service delivery (running schools and clinics) to mobilizing resources to advocacy to grappling with the ethical grounds for choices among strategies and honest management of programs.[6] Organizations like World Vision, Catholic Relief Services, Islamic Relief, and the Aga Khan Development Network are large and respected players. The reach of faith-inspired institutions is vast; these organizations are present in virtually every community and show stamina and continuity that stand in marked contrast to the (admittedly exaggerated) images of the "briefcase NGOs" who come and go with the vagaries of available funding.

There are various reasons for the continuing gap in religious and non-religious partnerships. There are remarkably limited data available about what faith-inspired institutions actually do and how well, and there are concerns about what motivations underlie religious institutions as they engage with development work. Are they truly motivated by an altruistic desire to help humankind or by a desire to win converts and shape beliefs and behaviors? While there is increasing awareness of the need to cooperate, in both religious and non-religious circles a patchy picture of research and action is still the reality.

Religion and Gender

It should go without saying that religion is an important factor shaping communities' norms and aspirations for women and girls.[7] The teachings and practices of different religions can be a catalyst to improve women's lives or they can be a source of conflict and inhibit change. Modernization and globalization challenge traditional norms in profound ways, including roles and behaviors that have strong religious elements.

Modernization's most significant social change is its effect on relationships between men and women. This social change challenges religious institutions as well as practices and beliefs. Relations between men and women affect every human being, each and every day. Obviously there are as many types of relationships as there are people, so sweeping generalizations are not helpful. But the contemporary norm of equality between men and women that is enshrined in the Universal Declaration of Human Rights and, more recently, in the year 2000 Millennium Declaration and Millennium Development Goals[8] is clear and explicit: even allowing for cultural diversity, women and men have equal rights in all spheres, including notably before the law and in education.

Issues and tensions from shifting gender roles spill over into development debates through a range of channels. The best known are debates regarding policies on reproduction. This category includes family planning, abortion, child marriage, female genital cutting (and male circumcision), and approaches to legal norms around sexual relations (adultery and polygamy, for example). Gender relations also spark human rights issues, affecting, for example, how societies address domestic violence, relationships among different religious groups in plural societies, norms of dress and behavior, and applicability of religiously-linked family law. Even areas that seem to be a universal norm, like education of girls, can spark tensions. These issues arise in many religious communities but, especially since 9/11, the Muslim faith's impact on women's roles has come into the spotlight. The Catholic Church, with its explicit prohibition on women becoming priests and with its distinctive views on reproductive health, also receives considerable attention.

To make sense of these development debates and religion's impact, the first step is to identify stereotypical perceptions and distinguish them from the more complex realities on the ground. Many current tensions between religious and non-religious development actors reflect simplistic mutual perceptions. Clarifying underlying and often dubious impressions can clear some undergrowth. Concerns and disagreements that have a real foundation can then be addressed in a more effective and civil fashion.

Stereotypes, Complex Realities, and Ethical Imperatives

One crude stereotype in non-religious circles is that religions are patriarchal and dominated by men who treat women as second class citizens. Traditional norms, reinforced by
religious leadership, block women's participation in the labor force, favor male over female
children, and turn a blind eye to abuse and harassment of women. An equally crude stereotype in religious circles paints feminists as anti-male and modern societies as homogenized,
with little respect for traditional family values including fidelity to marital partners.

These stereotypes run deep and wide. They shape and often inflame the approaches
and attitudes of many critics. They are of course informed by realities: cases of stoning of
girls accused of extramarital sex, horrific honor killings, and mounting divorce statistics
all reinforce images of irreconcilable differences between religious and secular ideals for
gender relations.

These crude stereotypes should be readily debunked, however, because the realities are
vastly more complex. Religious traditions and teachings vary widely in their treatment of
women, with some at the more progressive end where genuine equality is seen as progress.
Feminists and advocates of gender equality generally love their families and envision a
society where equality translates into equitable and lasting family and community bonds.
Wise religious leaders press to remove barriers that keep girls out of school and to fight
abuse and discrimination against women.

All sectors of the development world should approach these matters with greater depth
and respect. Basic development and religious literacy often helps advance the conversation
and allows the various actors to delve deeper into complex realities and ethical norms and
traditions. Actors should also understand the revolutionary and positive ideal that under-
pins development: that for the first time in human history all human beings can aspire to
develop their true potential, and that this ideal carries with it a new ethical imperative to
translate that aspiration into reality.

In what follows, I will briefly survey a range of areas where religion and gender intersect, each illustrating some reasons for tensions, areas for common ground, and potential
avenues for productive engagement.

Female Genital Cutting

Few issues raise the hackles of advocates for women and girls more than the practice of
female genital cutting (FGC). FGC, in widely varying forms, is often inflicted on very
young girls, is dangerous to their health, and has no discernible benefit whatsoever. The
practice is widespread, with an estimated 120 million women and girls affected. FGC has
proved stubbornly difficult to end.

Why is religion implicated? FGC is practiced across diverse societies, mostly but not
always in Muslim communities. It is commonly linked to cultural tradition, and religious
scholars at different levels and from different traditions have condemned the practice,
asserting that it has no basis in religious teachings or texts. But many women and men justify FGC as required by their religion and some religious leaders, especially at community
level, believe this to be true. Engaging religious leaders in a process designed to change
community norms has helped to end the practice in some places. Tostan, a Senegal-based
NGO widely admired for its thoughtful and effective work with communities in this and
other areas, attests to the effectiveness of this positive approach. By understanding what

drives mothers and fathers to cut their girls and persuading religious and community leaders that the practice is harmful and unnecessary, communities are encouraged to agree, together, to end the practice.

In short, a practice seen by many as intrinsically religious turns out not to be so. But because local religious leaders perceive it as a religious requirement, an approach that involves religion—from exploring theology to partnering with imams and pastors on the ground—can yield results.

Domestic Violence

Recent research and increased communication in modern societies have highlighted the extraordinary prevalence of domestic violence across widely differing social groups. Women are the most frequent victims of abuse, and it takes many forms. We now know that domestic violence is harmful and common. How often and effectively do religious leaders take a leading role in speaking out against it? The answer is decidedly mixed. Some religious leaders, for example Gunnar Stalsett, former Bishop of Oslo, are outspoken critics, setting an example of compassion and making the issue a priority for community change. But the more common reaction is to give it low priority, tacitly assuming that domestic violence is private, an embarrassing but accepted phenomenon. I have heard both men and women argue that the abused invited the treatment.

Domestic violence is an example of how, with better dissemination of facts and clearer examples of leadership by religious leaders, an ancient social ill could be more effectively addressed.

Missing Girls

Like FGC, another practice that is more "cultural" than "religious" is the wide preference of families for male offspring. Selective abortion, infanticide, and relative neglect of daughters have resulted in an extraordinary gap between the numbers of females that statistics suggest should exist and the demographic reality: over 100 million missing girls by some estimates. The preference for boys is stronger in some cultures, especially the Indian subcontinent and China, and is explained by economic factors as well as the higher intrinsic value placed on boys.

No religious tradition supports the practices that lead to missing girls (selective abortion, infanticide, and relative neglect of girl children), but passionate and effective advocacy for bringing about change is uncommon. Part of the challenge is that the practice is rarely visible; it is a genocide seen through statistics. Yet the practice is well known and increasingly discussed in public forums. If religious leaders and organizations, faith and interfaith, followed the lead of respected leaders like Sri Sri Ravi Shankar and Swami Agnivesh (who speak often and persuasively to the issue and, for example, have led marches focused on feticide), the pace of change would surely be far faster. The issue should offer the possibility of making common cause in public education at every level of society.

Rape as a Tool of War and Conflict

A horrifying dimension of contemporary conflicts, which involves non-combatants and ranges across widely dispersed areas, is the increasing use of rape as a tool of war. Darfur, eastern Democratic Republic of Congo, and the Balkans are places where countless thousands of women have been raped. Critics contend that religious leaders and institutions have rarely condemned this forcefully or demanded concerted action to arrest it. By not speaking out as forcefully as they might, religious communities are accused of condoning the practice or according it a low priority.

The reality is far more complex. In fact, Muslim leaders in the Balkans, interfaith groups in the case of Darfur, and the World Council of Churches in DRC, have mobilized their resources to speak out against all forms of violence in these conflict zones and in some cases to take direct action. Some religious communities and individuals, including for example extraordinarily courageous nuns who intervene at the risk of their lives in eastern DRC, set an example of forthright leadership, healing wounded women and standing between them and attackers. This may be a case where information is an issue: do religious leaders and communities have a sufficient appreciation for what is happening to women? Do they give it a high priority? Are there ways in which their prophetic voice and direct leadership might do more? These questions beg a more active partnership between military and civilian actors and secular and religious organizations to shine a light on violence and its impact on women.

Trafficking of Women and Girls

The exploitation of young girls, including through involuntary prostitution, is an ancient phenomenon. The mobility of contemporary societies has led to sharp increases in trafficking and far greater awareness of its patterns and effects. Anti-trafficking efforts have united widely different advocates, from left and right, secular and religious, in a desire to curb the traffic and to protect the girls and women who are caught in virtual slavery. Fighting sex trafficking is one of the issues that has encouraged evangelicals to become more engaged in international development advocacy and action. Legislation in the United States and UN treaties are examples of a renewed vigor in addressing the problem. Nicholas Kristof and Sheryl Wudon's recent book, *Half the Sky: Turning Oppression into Opportunity for Women Worldwide*,[9] is an example of shining more light on the topic and galvanizing interest and commitment to action. Trafficking is a topic whose ethical connotations engage religious communities at many levels, theological, social, and practical. In fact, it may be one of the best examples of cooperation between religious and non-religious actors in addressing a global issue.

Despite consensus for common action, complications do arise when it comes to tactics that entail, for example, cooperation with associations of prostitutes. However, most of those involved in fighting trafficking agree that the long-term solutions must look to improving prospects for families and especially girls, and thus must focus on economic development and education.

Family Planning

Demographic transition is an intrinsic part of modernization. With higher incomes, better education, and availability of family planning services, societies across the world have seen a reduction in the average number of children per couple. Spacing of children has important benefits for the health of mother and children; these benefits extend far into the life of the children (better educational performance, for example) and the family. Yet the topic of family planning has become embroiled in bitter debates, especially in the United States, to a point that considerable evidence suggests that discussion even of "natural" family planning has been driven underground.[10] A false assumption has taken hold that religious communities oppose family planning entirely. The well-known and fierce opposition of some religious communities to abortion and to the use of condoms as a public health tool, especially in fighting HIV and AIDS, has contributed to tensions.

Exploring attitudes among different religious communities and across different faiths (Muslim, Buddhist, Hindu, and Christian especially) reveals widespread support for child spacing as a practice beneficial to families and to women. Likewise, there is considerably more openness to family planning than the stereotypical assumption of opposition would suggest. Indeed religious communities, for example in Indonesia and Iran, have taken strong leadership roles in promoting family planning. Many Christian denominations support a range of family planning techniques. The Catholic Church's opposition to all but "natural" family planning stands out as distinct, yet Catholic health services support child spacing.

An investigation sponsored by USAID of religious attitudes towards family planning, undertaken by Georgetown University's Institute of Reproductive Health, is exploring different approaches and concerns in greater depth. Preliminary findings point to broad support for child spacing and family planning as beneficial to women and families. What is needed is more open dialogue about how different communities approach the topic and how that should translate into policy. Use of the term "population control" has had important negative effects, as have the largely U.S.-based debates that conflated family planning and abortion. Family planning offers two important lessons: first, terminology matters, and second, reframing the topic as centered on child spacing and family welfare can open the door to more fruitful dialogue.

Early Marriage

A powerful public health and human rights consensus supports action to raise the age at which young men and especially women marry. Younger brides—generally those younger than age 18—face health risks (as do their children) and early marriage curtails their opportunities for education in many if not most settings. Even where laws prohibit underage marriage, cultural traditions accept the practice and religious leaders are often those who advocate for marriage, as a way to protect young women who are seen as vulnerable to temptation if they are not married, and religious leaders actually perform the ceremony.

Addressing early marriage is an area where religious leaders and communities could and should play leading roles, acting positively to delay marriages as a matter of individual and social good. What is needed here is better information both about where early marriage is concentrated and about the rationales that are advanced for the practice and about the real disadvantages, for girls, their children, and families, of early and especially forced marriage. Campaigns by faith and interfaith alliances that link action to ensure that laws and norms on age of marriage are respected with concerted efforts to encourage girls to go to school, to succeed in their studies, and to stay in school through the secondary level could make a substantial difference.

AIDS: Abstinence, Fidelity, and Condoms

Perhaps no topic has pitted secular and religious communities so bitterly against one another than strategies to fight the HIV/AIDS pandemic. Attitudes towards women's roles

are a significant factor. HIV and AIDS afflict more women than men today, and disproportionately younger women than men. This highlights the vulnerability of women—as
adolescents in societies where respect for women's freedom of choice on all matters, including sex, is limited; as individuals with limited economic opportunities, making them prey
for "sugar daddies" who offer them an outlet; and as subservient wives within marriage.
The formula of abstinence plus fidelity favored by many religious organizations offers a
social ideal but not a practical response to real pressures facing millions. Against this backdrop, some religious voices present public health strategies that stress condom use and sex
education as encouraging immoral practices, while many AIDS advocates see opposition
to condoms and education as condemning millions to disease and death.

Experience suggests that the poisonous AIDS debates will not be readily resolved and
highlights how disagreements spill over into other development debates, sharpening pre-
conceptions and fueling tensions. A civil, reasoned debate that accepts the complexity of
local realities and works to advance strategies that are open to different approaches against
a backdrop of respect for each community's ethical norms seems the vital and obvious way
forward. Such dialogue is often possible at community and local levels, even on the most
contentious topics. Different groups agree explicitly or tacitly on de facto divisions of
responsibility that allow each to remain true to their ethical principles while assuring that
those they care for and about, for example unmarried mothers, are served. Such principled
compromise, however, seems more elusive in global forums. A practical consequence is
that initiatives like the Women, Faith, and Development Alliance (WFDA) avoid any
discussion of issues around reproductive health. This is an area of large and consequential
missed opportunities.

Conclusion

The list of topics outlined here illustrates the variety of development issues that involve
both gender and religion. It is, of course, not an exhaustive survey. There are many other
issues involving gender and religion, with important development dimensions, that merit
exploration. They include, for example, women's roles in religious peacebuilding and in
promoting good governance; here women's roles have received remarkably little recognition, reflecting the common phenomenon, heightened in many religious circles, of wom-
en's invisibility.

All issues at the intersection of religion, gender, and development deserve careful
research and purposeful attention and dialogue. When examined closely, each issue has
embedded within it both positive and negative dimensions: instances where long-standing
traditions that blend culture and theology contribute to unequal treatment of women, and
shining examples of strong leadership and a prophetic voice for change in translating ideals
for equality into practice. These issues also highlight the special sensitivities around gender,
as they so often demand changes in traditions at the level of personal and family behavior,
as part of the modernization process. Yet, at the most fundamental level, what is at stake is
the core principle of respect for human dignity and belief in human potential, principles
that are sacred to most religious traditions and that are also pivotal goals of human rights
and development.

— Section VIII —

RELIGION, DEMOCRACY, AND THE STATE

43

SEPARATION OF RELIGION AND STATE
IN THE TWENTY-FIRST CENTURY
Comparing the Middle East and Western Democracies

—Jonathan Fox and Shmuel Sandler

While religion has often been ignored as an important political factor, it is becoming increasingly clear that it plays a substantive role in world politics, both internationally and locally.[1] Fundamentalist movements, such as the religious right in the U.S. and the numerous Islamic movements in Islamic states, have had a significant impact on domestic politics. Many localized disputes with religious elements have had international implications due to the spread of conflict across borders and increasing international involvement in solving local disputes. They include conflicts in Israel, Chechnya, Afghanistan, Kashmir, and Sri Lanka. In addition, the international network of al-Qaeda has demonstrated the potential international impact of religious movements, though it is likely an extreme example.

This article reexamines the relationship between religion and politics using the recently compiled Religion and State (RAS) dataset, which is the most detailed data on the separation of religion and state. The focus here is on domestic politics, specifically the extent or lack of separation of religion and state in Western democracies and the Middle East.[2] The correlation between religion and democracy is examined implicitly through the comparison of the Middle East, the world's most autocratic region, with Western democracies, the most democratic states in the world.[3]

Theoretically, this study also asks whether the predictions of eighteenth- and nineteenth-century philosophers like Voltaire and Nietzsche that religion's influence on public life would decline in modern times have come true.[4] While many Western democracies like the U.S. have official separation of religion and state, others like Denmark and the U.K. have established religions. Some countries like Austria and Belgium give different official statuses to different religions, officially recognizing some but not others. Some European countries restrict minority religions. For instance, France and Germany restrict proselytizing. Also, every Western democracy other than the U.S. provides funds for religious education, and for most of them this funding includes religious education in public

* *Comparative Politics* 37, no. 3 (April 2005): 317–35.

schools. Is the U.S. model of separation of religion and state the norm for Western democracies or the exception?

In order to answer these issues, this study examines five aspects of the separation of religion and state: the structural relationship between religion and the state (the existence of an official religion or the legal position of religion within the state); the status of minority religions (restriction or banning of or provision of benefits to some religions but not others); discrimination against minority religions; regulation of the majority religion; and legislation of religion.

This five-pronged approach is used because the relationship between religion and the state is complex. While any one of these approaches is informative, it would be incomplete if examined individually. For example, both the U.K. and Iran have official state religions, yet the extent of separation of religion and state in these two states is clearly not similar. The official religion in the U.K. is to a great extent symbolic, while in Iran it is politically significant. The other measures help to account for this difference. Thus, examination of several aspects of the separation of religion and state should provide a clearer picture of the true impact of religion on domestic politics.

Religion and Democracy

There is no agreement on the link between religion and democracy. Many assume that the two are incompatible, yet many argue the opposite. Stepan notes that, when examining democracy outside the West, Western "analysts frequently assume that the separation of church and state is a core feature not only of Western democracy, but of democracy itself."[5] Rawls makes this argument in the form of the normative injunction that one must "take the truths of religion off the political agenda."[6]

This type of argument is rooted in modernization theory. This theory posits that factors inherent within the process of modernization, like literacy, economic development, urbanization, and advancements in science and technology, will lead to the demise of primordial factors in politics, including religion. While this theory was dominant in political science through the mid 1970s and in sociology through the mid 1990s, it has been increasingly called into question.[7] This type of argument also has its roots in U.S. thinking on liberal democracy, which emphasizes the importance of the separation of religion and state.[8]

Another strong trend posits that religious nationalism and liberalism are incompatible. For example, Juergensmeyer argues that religion and secular nationalism, which he defines as all Western secular ideologies including liberalism, fascism, communism, and socialism, are incompatible competitors for the minds of the people and for control of state institutions and apparatuses. Religion is experiencing a resurgence, especially in the Third World, because these secular nationalist ideologies have failed to provide the promised economic well-being and social justice and because they are perceived as having been imposed from the outside by the colonial West.[9]

There are also several types of arguments that posit that religion is not incompatible with democracy. First, Anthony Smith links many particular nationalist ideologies in democratic states to religious origins. These religiously inspired nationalisms include those of France, Greece, Ireland, the U.S., and the UK. Religious nationalism and democracy are, therefore, compatible.[10] Second, many Western European democracies have established churches and engage in a number of religious activities, especially support for religious education.[11] Third, Tocqueville argued that "successful political democracy will inevitably require moral instruction grounded in religious faith."[12] Fourth, religious groups often support democracy if they feel that they have a strategic interest in doing so. It has been argued that they did so in Belgium and a number of Catholic states.[13] Also, liberation theology, a movement among Catholics in Latin America, has precisely the goal of increasing democratic participation by the populace.[14]

A substantial number of studies also examine whether Islam is compatible with democracy. Those who say it is not make several arguments. First, Islam makes no separation between religion and state. Second, since Islamic law is the divinely decreed law of the land, there is no room for public participation in lawmaking. Third, not all citizens have the same rights. Non-Muslims are not accorded the same rights as Muslims, and women are not accorded the same rights as men.[15]

Many argue that Islam *can* be compatible with democracy. First, like other religions, there are diverse interpretations of Islam, many of which are compatible with democracy. These interpretations focus on Islamic principles like consultation, consensus, the equality of all men, the rule of law, and independent reasoning as a basis for Islamic democracy.[16] Second, while there are no democracies within the Arab world, about half of all Muslims live in democratic and semi-democratic states.[17] Third, Islamic parties have successfully used parliamentary systems to their benefit and even pushed for democratic reforms.[18] Fourth, while the doctrine of Islam may inhibit democracy, in practice there has rarely, if ever, been true unity between Islam and ruling regimes.[19]

Clearly, this vision of Islamic democracy does not include the separation of religion and state.[20] However, the impact of Islamic law on non-Muslims can be limited because "Islam recognizes the de facto separation of the strictly religious and the temporal realms of human activity."[21] Also, in theory Islam accepts differences in religious beliefs and recognizes that religious minorities have a right to live by their own laws.[22] It is clear that not all Muslims accept this reasoning.[23] But the many who do, and Europe's success in democratizing despite the authoritarian tendencies in Christianity, show that Islamic democracy is possible.

The few quantitative studies on the topic of religion and democracy have mixed results. For instance, studies of Islam and democracy have contradictory results. One found that Islam neither undermines nor supports democracy and human rights.[24] Others found Islamic and Middle Eastern states to be disproportionally autocratic.[25] Other studies have found that religiosity is correlated with individual authoritarian attitudes;[26] that many European states regulate religion;[27] that there is no correlation between democracy and abortion policy but that high religiosity and a Catholic state are both factors that strongly correlate with restrictive abortion policies;[28] and that the separation between religion and state is not influenced by whether a state is Catholic or Protestant.[29]

These studies all have at least one of two failings. First, they look only at the link between a particular religion and democracy. Second, they focus on only one or two aspects of the separation of religion and state in a limited context. This study is superior in that it focuses on two world regions and measures five aspects of the separation of religion and state. Furthermore, each of these measures is either a scale with several possible values or a composite of as many as thirty-three separate measures.

Research Design

This study uses the Religion and State (RAS) database. The project collects data on Western democracies and the Middle East and includes five variables for the year 2001 and one variable that combines them. It is important to emphasize that the RAS database focuses on official government structure, policies, institutions, practices, and laws rather than on civil society or religiosity within the population. While the correlation between these official and unofficial manifestations of religion is an interesting topic of inquiry, it is beyond the scope of this study. Also, for those countries with federal systems, the codings represent the behavior of the federal government unless a certain type of practice exists in the vast majority of local governments.[30]

The first variable, structural separation, measures the extent, if any, of incorporation of the church within governmental structure on the following scale.[31]

0   Hostile: Hostility and overt prosecution of all religions.

1   Inadvertent Insensitivity: Little distinction between regulation of religious and other types of institutions.

2   Separationist: Official separation of church and state and slight state hostility toward religion.

3   Accommodation: Official separation of church and state and benevolent or neutral state attitude toward religion in general.

4   Supportive: More or less equal state support of all religions.

5   Cooperation: State support (monetary or legal) of certain churches more than others without endorsing a particular church.

6   Civil religion: Without official endorsement of a religion, one religion as unofficial state civil religion.

7   More than one official state religion.

8   One official state religion.

The second variable measures whether the state restricts or bans minority religions as well as whether it gives preference to some religions over others on the following scale.

0   No other illegal religions and no significant restrictions on other religions.

1   No other illegal religions but practical limitations on some or all other religions or benefits to some religions not given to others due to some form of official recognition or status not given to all religions.

2   No other religions illegal but some or all other religions with legal limitations placed upon them.

3   Some other religions illegal.

4   All other religions illegal.

The third variable measures whether there is discrimination against minority religions based on sixteen individual factors, each of which is measured on the following scale.

0   Not significantly restricted for any.

1   The activity slightly restricted for some minorities.

2   The activity slightly restricted for most or all minorities or sharply restricted for some of them.

3   The activity prohibited or sharply restricted for most or all minorities.

The resulting variable ranges from zero to forty-eight. The specific factors are listed in Table 3 of the data analysis section below.[32]

The fourth variable measures whether the state regulates the majority religion based on eleven individual factors. Each of these factors is measured on the following scale:

0   No restrictions.
1   Slight restrictions, including practical restrictions.
2   Significant restrictions, including practical restrictions.
3   Illegal.

The resulting variable ranges from zero to thirty-three. The specific factors are listed in Table 3 of the data analysis section below.

The fifth variable measures whether the state legislates religious laws based on thirty-three types of religious laws that are listed in Table 4 of the data analysis section below. The resulting variable ranges from zero to thirty-three.

Finally, a combined separation of religion and state variable was constructed by rescaling all of the above five variables to measure from zero to twenty, then adding them to create a scale of zero to one hundred.[33]

The analysis of the data proceeds in four stages. First, the mean for each variable in the two regions is compared in order to establish the extent to which the regions in general differ. Second, each variable is examined in more detail in order to assess the extent and nature of separation of religion and state in each region. Third, the correlation between religion and democracy is examined for each region using two separate democracy variables. The first democracy variable is taken from the Polity dataset and measures democracy on a scale of -10 to 10. It is based on the structural and procedural aspects of democracy.[34] The second is a measure of 0 to 12 taken from the Freedom House project. It is based on the structural and procedural aspects of democracy as well as civil rights.[35] Finally, the correlation between specific denominations and separation of religion and state is examined in order to replicate the results of previous studies.

Data Analysis

The first test, shown in Table 1, compares the mean level of separation of religion and state in each region. Not surprisingly, the Middle East scores higher on all five variables. However, the results also show that all five types of religious involvement in government are present in at least some Western democracies.

The official role religion is given in a state is shown in Table 2. Not surprisingly, a large majority (84.2%) of Middle Eastern states have official religions, and the rest of them have strong state support for religion. More interestingly, 34.6 percent of Western democracies have one or more official religions, and an additional 46.2 percent strongly support one or more religions. Only 19.2 percent of Western democracies have full separation of religion and state on this measure.

TABLE 1

Mean Levels of Separation of Religion and State
in the Middle East and Western Democracies in 2001

		Religion Variables				
Region	*n*	Structural Separation of Religion & State	Restrictions on Minority Religions	Discrimination against Minority Religion	Regulation of Majority Region	Religious Legislation
Western Democracies	26	5.77	0.65	2.15	0.27	5.85
Catholics	13	5.38	0.77	1.69	0.38	5.46
Protestants	10	6.00	0.50	1.90	0.00	6.20
Middle East & N. Africa	19	7.63	2.21	13.32	5.37	17.42

The extent to which states restrict minority religions, also shown in Table 2, provides similar results. In the Middle East, 31.6 percent of states ban at least one religion, and the remaining states place legal or practical limitations on minority religions. While no Western democracies ban any religions, half do not give equal treatment to all religions.

As shown in Table 3, more Middle Eastern states engage in more types of discrimination against religious minorities than do Western democracies. All Middle Eastern states engage in at least some forms of religious discrimination. The most common forms of discrimination in the Middle East are restrictions on building or maintaining places

TABLE 2

Extent of Structural Separation of Religion and State and Restrictions on Minority
Religions in the Middle East and Western Democracies in 2001

	Percentage of States Which Fall into This Category Within	
Variable	Western Democracies	Middle East & North Africa
Separation of Religion and State		
Established religion	26.9%	84.2%
Multiple official religions	7.7%	0.0%
Civil religion	15.4%	10.5%
Cooperation	30.8%	5.3%
Supportive	0.0%	0.0%
Accommodation	15.4%	0.0%
Separationist	3.8%	0.0%
Inadvertent insensitivity	0.0%	0.0%
Hostile	0.0%	0.0%
Restrictions on Minority Religion		
All (minority) religions illegal	0.0%	5.3%
Some religions illegal	0.0%	26.3%
Legal limitations	19.2%	52.6%
Practical limitations or preferential treatment for some	30.8%	15.8%
None	50.0%	0.0%

of worship, bans on proselytizing, and bans on conversions away from Islam, all of which are practiced by a majority of Middle Eastern states.

In contrast, religious discrimination is less acute in Western democracies but by no means nonexistent. Of Western democracies, 61.5 percent engage in at least some religious discrimination. The most common forms of discrimination are the requirement of minority religions (as opposed to all religions) to register in order to have official status and limits on proselyting. However, neither of these individual practices is pursued by a majority of Western democracies.

The extent of the regulation of the majority religion, also shown in Table 3, presents a sharper contrast. While 89.5 percent of Middle Eastern states regulate Islam, only 15.4 percent of Western democracies regulate Christianity. The most common forms of government regulation of the majority religion in the Middle East are restrictions on speech by clergy, restrictions on religious parties, and the arrest, detention, or severe harassment of religious figures. These types of restrictions are those that a government afraid of a religious opposition to their rule might impose.

TABLE 3
Religious Discrimination against Minorities and Regulation of the Majority Religion in the Middle East and Western Democracies in 2001

Variable	Percentage of States Which Engage in This Type of Discrimination/Restriction	
	Western Democracies	Middle East & North Africa
Discrimination against Minorities		
Public observance	0.0%	42.1%
Building, repairing, or maintaining places of worship	15.4%	68.4%
Access to places of worship	7.7%	31.6%
Forced observance of religious laws of other group	3.8%	21.1%
Formal religious organizations	19.2%	36.8%
Running of religious schools and/or education	0.0%	31.6%
Arrest, continued detention, or severe harassment	11.5%	42.1%
Ability to make and/or obtain religious materials	0.0%	42.1%
Ability to write/publish/disseminate religious publications	11.5%	47.4%
Observance of religious laws concerning personal status	0.0%	26.3%
Ordination of and/or access to clergy	3.8%	26.3%
Conversion to minority religions	0.0%	68.4%
Forced conversions	0.0%	0.0%
Proselytizing	19.2%	89.5%
Must register to be legal or receive special tax status	38.5%	21.1%
Other restrictions	11.5%	21.1%
None of above discrimination	38.5%	0.0%

Cont. on next page

TABLE 3 (CONT.)

Religious Discrimination against Minorities

Variable	Percentage of States Which Engage in This Type of Discrimination/Restriction	
	Western Democracies	Middle East & North Africa
Restrictions on Majority Religion or All Religions		
Religious political parties	3.8%	68.4%
Arrest, continued detention, or severe harassment	0.0%	42.1%
Formal religious organizations other than political parties	0.0%	0.0%
Public observance	0.0%	0.0%
Public religious speech including sermons by clergy	0.0%	73.7%
Access to places of worship	0.0%	21.1%
Publication or dissemination of written religious material	3.8%	15.8%
People are arrested for religious activities	0.0%	11.5%
Religious public gatherings	0.0%	5.3%
Public display of religious symbols	7.7%	15.8%
Other restrictions	3.8%	5.3%
None of above restrictions	84.6%	10.5%

The extent of religious legislation, shown in Table 4, follows the pattern of the first three measures. It is more common in Middle Eastern states but still occurs often in Western democracies. All Middle Eastern states have religious laws on the books, and every type of religious law in the list exists in at least one Middle Eastern state with the exception of government collection of religious taxes. Furthermore, of the thirty-three items on the list, twenty exist in a majority of Middle Eastern states.

While religious legislation is less common in Western democracies, it is certainly present. No state except the U.S. (at the federal level) has no religious legislation on the books. All of them, again except the U.S., directly fund religious education. Though no other law is on the books for a majority of Western democracies, all but nine of the items on the list are legislated by at least one Western democracy. Belgium and the U.K. have the most religious legislation of Western democracies, each state with ten of the items present. Four of these items occur more often in Western democracies than in the Middle East.

The overall separation of religion and state in each individual state is shown in Table 5. As expected, this measure of religious influence on the state is much higher for Middle Eastern states, averaging almost fifty overall, than it is for Western democracies. Yet Western democracies still have an average of almost nineteen, much more than would be expected if separation of religion and state were an essential element of democracy. Furthermore, only the U.S. scores zero, and only Australia, Canada, and the Netherlands score below ten. Some, like Finland and Greece, score over thirty.

TABLE 4
Extent of Religious Legislation in the Middle East and Western Democracies in 2001

Type of Religious Legislation	Percentage of States Which Have This Type of Legislation	
	Western Democracies	Middle East & North Africa
Dietary laws	0.0%	78.9%
Restrictions or prohibitions on sale of alcoholic beverages	0.0%	63.2%
Personal status defined by clergy	3.8%	89.5%
Laws of inheritance defined by religion	0.0%	89.5%
Restrictions on conversions away from dominant religion	0.0%	78.9%
Restrictions on interfaith marriages	0.0%	89.5%
Restrictions on public dress	19.2%	78.9%
Blasphemy laws, or other religious restriction on speech	7.7%	100.0%
Censorship on grounds of being anti-religious	0.0%	78.9%
Mandatory closing of businesses during religious holidays	15.4%	26.3%
Other restrictions on activities during religious holidays	3.8%	21.1%
Religious education standard but optional in public schools	73.1%	10.5%
Mandatory religious education in public schools	3.8%	57.9%
Government funding of religious schools or education	96.2%	68.4%
Government funding of religious charitable organizations	34.6%	5.3%
Government collects taxes for religious organizations	50.0%	0.0%
Government positions, salaries, or other funding for clergy	38.5%	73.7%
Other funding for religious organizations or activities	7.7%	78.9%
Clergy/speeches in places of worship need govt. approval	0.0%	63.2%
Some clerical positions made by government appointment	23.1%	52.6%
Official government department for religious affairs	42.3%	84.2%
Certain government officials given official church position	15.4%	10.5%
Certain church officials given official government position	3.8%	10.5%
Some govt. officials must meet religious requirements	11.5%	52.6%

Cont. on next page

TABLE 4 (CONT.)

Extent of Religious Legislation in the Middle East and Western Democracies in 2001

Type of Religious Legislation	Percentage of States Which Have This Type of Legislation	
	Western Democracies	Middle East and North Africa
Religious courts with jurisdiction over some matters of law	3.8%	73.7%
Some seats in legislature/cabinet given along religious lines	3.8%	21.1%
Prohibitive restrictions on abortion	26.9%	78.9%
Presence of religious symbols on the state's flag	23.1%	36.8%
Religion listed on state identity cards	0.0%	31.6%
Religious orgs. must register with govt. for official status	42.3%	42.1%
Official govt. body monitoring "sects" or minority religions	30.8%	5.3%
Restrictions on women other than those listed above	0.0%	68.4%
Other religious prohibitions or practices that are mandatory	3.8%	21.1%
None of above legislation	3.8%	0.0%

In sum, while Western democracies have more separation of religion and state than the more autocratic states of the Middle East, there is clearly a significant amount of government involvement in religion in Western democracies. This conclusion raises the question whether there is a correlation between democracy and separation of religion and state, because, while the results show that separation of religion and state does not exist in the most democratic region of the world, this region has more separation of religion and state than the most autocratic region of the world, the Middle East. While it is possible that this difference is due to democracy, it is also possible that it is due to other cultural or historical factors since the two regions have significantly different cultures and histories.

To answer this question, the correlation between the religion and state variables and two measures of democracy for each of the two regions separately is examined (Table 6). The results show that there is some support for the argument that democracy is correlated with religion. With the Polity variable there is a correlation between democracy and state support of religion, but, as on the Polity variable all Western democracies save France score the same, this correlation has little significance. However, the Freedom House variable shows strong correlations between democracy and the lack of discrimination against minority religions, of banning of minority religions for both Western democracies and the Middle East, and of religious legislation in Western democracies. Nevertheless, there are many variables for which there are no strong correlations. While the results support the argument that democracies have more separation of religion and state than autocracies, the support is weak.

Finally, in order to replicate the results of previous studies, Table 1 examines the mean levels of separation of religion and state for different religious denominations. As almost

TABLE 5
Overall Separation of Religion and State in 2001

	Western Democracies				Middle East & North Africa	
Country	Combined Separation of Religion and State Score	Country	Combined Separation of Religion and State Score	Country	Combined Separation of Religion and State Score
Andorra	24.24	Italy	12.89	Algeria	52.16
Australia	2.42	Liechtenstein	27.42	Bahrain	41.44
Austria	24.14	Luxembourg	10.42	Egypt	59.85
Belgium	24.89	Malta	24.85	Iran	64.09
Canada	3.45	The Netherlands	2.42	Iraq	53.33
Cyprus	16.07	New Zealand	13.82	Israel	35.34
Denmark	25.27	Norway	25.68	Jordan	58.83
Finland	32.93	Portugal	20.03	Kuwait	42.42
France	15.72	Spain	27.11	Lebanon	21.94
Germany	19.74	Sweden	12.66	Libya	45.42
Greece	32.54	Switzerland	21.37	Morocco	47.50
Iceland	30.49	United Kingdom	27.48	Oman	45.45
Ireland	15.64	United States	0.00	Qatar	51.67
				Saudi Arabia	74.62
				Syria	42.80
				Tunisia	52.77
				Turkey	45.33
				UAE	51.86
				Yemen	43.03
		Average	18.99	Average	49.44

Significance (t-test) of difference between average for Western Democracies and the Middle East < .001.

TABLE 6
Correlations between Religion Variables and Democracy

Religion Variable	Western Democracies		Middle East & North Africa	
	Polity	Freedom House	Polity	Freedom House
Structural Separation	.416**	.018	−.272	.024
Other Religions Illegal	−.339	−.412**	−.058	−.433*
Restrictions on Minority Religions	−.236	−.456**	−.173	−.392*
Restrictions on Majority Religions	.094	−.017	−.047	−.289
Religious Legislation	−.018	−.387*	−. 202	−.265*

* = Significance (p-value) < .l.
** = Significance (p-value) < .05.

all of the Middle Eastern states examined here are Sunni Muslim, they are not reexamined; only Catholic and Protestant states among Western democracies are examined. The Greek Orthodox states of Greece and Cyprus and mixed Protestant and Catholic Switzerland are excluded. The results show little difference between the two. Protestant states score slightly higher on three measures, and Catholic states on two measures, with none of the difference statistically significant. These findings are consistent with previous studies.[36]

Discussion

First, on the question whether liberal democracy is compatible with religion, the majority of Western democratic states do not have anything near full separation of religion and state. Of them, 80.8 percent support some religions over others either officially or practically; half restrict at least one minority religion or give benefits to some religions and not others; 61.5 percent engage in some form of religious discrimination. Every Western democracy except the U.S. legislates at least some aspect of religion. The only type of religious practice eschewed by most Western democracies seems to be the regulation of the majority religion, and a minority (15.4 percent) of Western democracies also engage in this practice. Thus, it is fair to argue that religion can play a role in a liberal democracy. The only way to argue otherwise would be to say that there existed no liberal democracies among the Western democracies analyzed here in 2001, except perhaps the U.S.

While these findings may not be a complete surprise to specialists on Western Europe, their extent is likely to be unexpected. To those living in the U.S. who have little knowledge of politics outside of the U.S., they are likely to be astonishing. The U.S. is probably the only Western democratic state which, at least at the federal level as measured by the variables used in this study, has nearly complete separation of religion and state, scoring a zero on all five measures. Thus, U.S. democracy's strict adherence to separation of religion and state is the exception, not the rule.

This conclusion has an interesting implication for U.S. foreign policy. While many in the U.S. assume that the U.S. shares nearly identical values with regard to democracy with its Western European allies, this assumption is not completely true, at least with regard to the concept of separation of religion and state. It may also not be true of other values. If so, these differences in values can explain the many disagreements between the U.S. and Western Europe over a number of foreign policy issues.

However, is the U.S. really an exception? Most surveys show that the population in the U.S. is more religious than the populations of Western Europe.[37] Other survey data show strong support for prayer in public schools and government protection of the U.S. religious heritage.[38] Survey data also link religion in the U.S. to party affiliation and voting behavior.[39] Furthermore, religious issues like abortion have a continuing impact on U.S. politics. Religion is also important historically, as religious activists were key elements of the abolitionist movement, the early women's rights movement, and the civil rights movement.[40]

Hence it is clear that religious attitudes continue to influence the U.S. political agenda, but the United States' political regime seems to limit the ability of these attitudes to infringe on the constitutional separation of religion and state. This conclusion is not surprising, given that in Western democracies the structural separation of religion and state variable has a strong correlation of .495 (p = .1) with the religious legislation variable, but it is unrelated to the other religion variables. Thus, it can be said that the U.S. is the exception on two counts. First, it is the only Western democracy with nearly total separation of religion and state on the measures used here. Second, it has the most religious populace of the Western democracies.

This contrast between the structural and legal separation of religion and state in the U.S. and the importance of religion in civil society highlights the strengths and weaknesses of the RAS data. The data are the most detailed to date on the structural, legal, procedural, and policy aspects of religion's influence on the state. However, they do not account for civil society and informal aspects of religion's influence on the state. For instance, the role of influential individuals and lobby groups on policy is not included in this study. Neither is the collective influence of the many religious individuals on the political process through the various forms of participation available to citizens in a democracy. If these variables were to be measured, a task that is currently beyond the scope of the RAS project, it is likely that the U.S. would score higher than the majority of Western democracies. It would surely not score the lowest.

Another conclusion that can be drawn from this evidence is that a lack of separation of religion and state does not undermine a liberal democracy so long as religion is not an overly contentious issue. This conclusion can explain the lack of democracy in the Middle East. In Islamic states, like those of the Middle East, religion tends to be more contentious an issue than in non-Islamic states.[41] Furthermore, many of these states have religious minorities as well as differences of opinion within the Islamic majority as to what role Islam should play in government, not to mention different types of Islam. Given this overabundance of potential sources of religious tension, it is likely that any democracy in the Middle East without separation of religion and state would be undermined.

Algeria and Turkey are good examples. Algeria's civil war started with parliamentary elections that would have brought the FIS, an Islamic fundamentalist party, to power in 1992. Before the second round of elections could be completed, a military coup restored a secular government. In Turkey, also, the military has intervened repeatedly in order to prevent religious parties from taking over the government. In both cases the fear was that the religious parties would use democratic means to undermine democracy. However, recently the Justice and Development party, a Muslim party, has come to power in Turkey and advocates democratic rule.

Conclusion

Most Western democracies do not have full separation of religion and state. Only the U.S. has no government involvement in religion as measured by the variables used in this study. Liberal democracy is thus compatible with religion. The separation of religion and state in the U.S. seems to be the exception rather than the rule. These findings also show that the predictions of religion's demise by philosophers like Nietzsche and Voltaire were premature. These results apply to Western states, the part of the world where their predictions were most likely to come true.

Moreover, religious democracy, including Islamic democracy, is possible. Several hundred years ago Western nations were mostly authoritarian states with high levels of entanglement between religion and state. Today all Western nations other than the United States have some entanglement between religion and state and are nevertheless considered democratic. The same is possible for Islamic states. Christianity found a way to accommodate democracy, and Islam has within it doctrines that can be used to legitimize democracy. The true test will be the performance of Islamic political parties, like Turkey's Justice and Development party, which come into power through democratic means. However, it is important to remember that the existence of a potential for democracy within Islam does not mean that this potential will be realized. It is possible that Islam's more authoritarian interpretations will prevail.

This study creates more questions than it answers and provides a number of agendas for further research. First, to what extent are separation of religion and state and religiosity linked? Second, what other influence does religiosity have on the body politic, and what influence does the separation of religion and state, or their entanglement, have on other political and social phenomena? Cross-sectional studies have already linked other religious factors to various forms of conflict, including ethnic conflict,[42] international conflict,[43] and civil wars.[44] It is likely that separation of religion and state is linked to these and other political and social phenomena. Third, the nature of liberal democracies needs to be examined further. Does the coexistence of religion with so many of them mean that it is not incompatible with liberal democracy or that there exists a potential fifth column in the majority of Western democracies? Finally, since liberal democracies do not have full separation of religion and state, and some interpretations of Islam are compatible with democracy, is Islamic democracy truly possible? The data presented here, combined with other resources, provide a useful tool in answering these questions.

Appendix: Data Reliability

In order to test the reliability of the data presented here, we engaged in two procedures. First, backup codings were done for thirteen of the states by separate coders and compared to the original codings. Second, we compared the data to similar data collected by six other studies which are described below.

Backup Codings

Backup codings were done for Austria, Finland, France, Iceland, Malta, Spain, the U.K., Algeria, Iran, Iraq, Qatar, Saudi Arabia, and Turkey. Correlations between these codings and the original codings were extremely strong and significant and provide strong confirmation of the reliability of the codings. They were as follows: Structural Separation = .976 ($p < .001$); Restrictions on Minority Religions = perfect correlation; Discrimination against Minorities = .980 ($p < .001$); Restrictions on the Majority Religion = .959 ($p < .001$); and Religious Legislation = .997 ($p < .001$).

Chaves Data

Chaves collected data on eighteen Western democratic states in the late 1980s.[45] Two elements of these data are similar to the data collected here. First a variable measures whether a state had an official church in 1990. The data match this study's separation of state and religion variable except for Switzerland. Some of Switzerland's cantons have official religions, but this study codes only at the federal level. Second, twelve variables measure the presence of various types of religious legislation. These variables are added, resulting in a scale of zero to twelve. The correlation between the 1990 version of this study's religious legislation variables and that of Chaves is .818 (p < .001).

Fearon, Laitin, and Mecham Data

Fearon, Laitin, and Mecham coded information on the separation of religion and state for forty states that overlap with the states used here.[46] We compared several variables for the 1995 to 1999 period to the 1999 variables from this study. First, Fearon, Laitin, and Mecham's variable for official state religion matches the codings for this study. Second, the combination of two variables—whether the state gives added resources to any religion not available to others, and whether the state allows in general the free practice of religion— has a correlation of .712 (p < .001) with this study's variable for general restrictions on religion. Third, a variable that measures whether the state monitors or controls the activities of its religious elites had a correlation of .752 (p < .001) with the variable from this study that measures restrictions on the dominant religion. Fourth, a variable in Fearon, Laitin, and Mecham's data that measures whether the state regulates missionary activity has a correlation of .649 (p < .001) with this study's restrictions on proselyting variable. Finally, a variable in their data measures whether or not religious minorities suffer from religious discrimination has a correlation of .482 (p < .01) with this study's variable for religious discrimination. This relationship is not as strong as expected, because this study's sixteen specific measures of discrimination are more sensitive to discrimination than their data's more general measure.

Freedom House Data

Freedom House developed a seven-point scale for religious freedom based on restrictions on religious practices for a number of states, of which eighteen overlap with those in this study. This study's restrictions on religious minorities variable has a correlation of .887 (p < .001) with the Freedom House variable.[47]

World Christian Encyclopedia Data[48]

The data in the *World Christian Encyclopedia* focus on the treatment of Christians by the state and thus do not measure exactly the same thing as the variables in this study. However, three variables in the *World Christian Encyclopedia* are similar to the variables in this study. The *World Christian Encyclopedia* measures whether a state's "religion or philosophy" is religious. This variable has a correlation of .547 (p < .001) with this study's separation of religion and state variable. The difference is due to different definitions of separation of religion and state. As our variable matched up perfectly with the datasets of Chaves, and Fearon, Laitin, and Mecham, we have confidence that this study's coding is nevertheless accurate.

The *World Christian Encyclopedia* measures two variables that focus on the treatment of Christian minorities. Accordingly, it is only appropriate to compare them to the discrimination variable from this study in non-Christian, that is, Middle Eastern, states. The Christian safety index has a correlation of −.259 (p = .283) with this study's discrimination variable. While the direction of the correlation is as we would expect, the correlation is weak and insignificant. The *World Christian Encyclopedia* variable for suppression of

Christianity has a correlation of .298 (p = .216) with the religious discrimination variable. These weak correlations are likely due to the fact that the *World Christian Encyclopedia* variable measures something similar to but different from the variable used in this study.

State of the World Atlas Data

Two editions of the *State of the World Atlas* have data on religion and the state. The 1999 edition has two variables.[49] The first measures whether a state has none, one, or multiple official religions. It matches up with the separation of religion and state variable in all but nine of forty-two states in this study. The 1999 *World Atlas* also has a variable for religious tolerance that is scaled. It has a correlation of .634 (p < .001) with this study's variable for whether the state bans or limits minority religions. The 1995 *World Atlas* also contains two variables similar to ones in this study.[50] The first measures structural separation of religion and state but does not match up with the variable for this study on five of forty-one states. More interestingly, the variables from the 1995 and 1999 editions of the *World Atlas* do not match up with each other on nine of forty-one states for which both have data. This discrepancy calls into question the accuracy of the *World Atlas* data on the separation of religion and the state, as it is not even consistent across different volumes of the same publication. The second variable in the 1995 *World Atlas* measures whether states tolerate minority religions, but only for states with official religions. This variable has a correlation of .521 (p = .013) with this study's 1995 version of restrictions on minority religions.

Fox Data

Fox collected and tested data on ethnoreligious conflict that overlap with this study for twelve states.[51] We used the data from this study to collect a composite measure of religious discrimination using the eight measures that are common to both studies and compared it to the Fox data from 1995, the most recent year for which the Fox data are available. The correlation between the two is .865 (p < .001).

Conclusions

In all, there is strong evidence in favor of the reliability of these data. The backup and original codings are nearly identical. Also, the data from this study are compared to sixteen variables from six other studies. In twelve of these comparisons the correlation is strong and significant, and in an additional two the correlation is significant but of medium strength. Even those correlations that are not significant show that the variables from other studies are not inconsistent with the variables from this one. Overall, these results show considerable similarity between this study and others. Inconsistencies are explainable by different coding criteria. Based on these comparisons, there is considerable confidence in the reliability of the data presented here.

It should be noted that the data from this study, while similar to the data from the other studies listed here, are more detailed and usually cover more states and/or a broader section of the population of these states.

44

RETHINKING RELIGIOUS ESTABLISHMENT
AND LIBERAL DEMOCRACY
Lessons from Israel

—Steven V. Mazie

In the October 2003 issue of *The New York Review of Books*, Tony Judt declared the State of Israel an "anachronism." According to Judt, "the very idea of a Jewish state—a state in which Jews and the Jewish religion have exclusive privileges from which non-Jewish citizens are forever excluded—is rooted in another time and place."[1] Judt's proposed solution to the Israeli-Palestinian conflict, which effectively calls for the end of Israel as we know it, has its heart in a normative conception of the state that rejects any linkage between religion and constitution. Road map or no, Ariel Sharon or no, settlements or no, separation fence or no, Judt thinks Israel is illegitimate as a Jewish state *because* it is a Jewish state. Israel should abandon its illusory aspiration to be a "Jewish and democratic state" (as its basic legislation declares) and transform itself into a secular, democratic, bi-national state that embraces all the territory and all the people of historic Palestine.

According to this political philosophy, the traditional nation-state—based as it is on the ethnic or religious unity of a majority and some degree of discrimination against minorities—has no rightful place. Emerging in its stead, Judt writes, is cosmopolitan liberal democracy: "a world of individual rights, open frontiers, and international law." This trend leaves no room for nation-states like Israel—polities that promote a particular national character shaped by a particular religious tradition. Nor does it leave room for the development of other democracies in the Middle East which might entertain forms of religious establishment.

Despite its sweeping scope, the kernel of Judt's argument may resonate with an American audience: its logic is the logic of separating church from state. But even a cursory survey of comparative politics reveals a host of states that challenge his view: Costa Rica, Great Britain, Bahrain, and Denmark, for example, all maintain institutional or symbolic connections with a particular religion and yet provide various elements of liberal governance (including religious freedom for religious minorities) to their citizens. Israel is another prime example—a state which regards itself as both Jewish and as liberal-democratic. But

* *The Brandywine Review of Faith & International Affairs* 2, no. 2 (Fall 2004): 3–12.

is a Jewish and democratic state possible? Can *any* sort of religious establishment be reconciled with a liberal democratic framework?

As a theory of the social order emphasizing toleration, basic human rights, a democratic form of government, and the rule of law, liberalism is concerned above all with finding just institutional and social solutions to problems of pluralism. In this article, I argue that while connections between religion and state are often antithetical to liberal aims, they are not necessarily so. A Jewish and democratic state *is* possible: the challenge is to sort out which elements of establishment are compatible with liberal democracy and which are not. In what follows I draw few bright lines, but (borrowing from the lingo of American constitutional jurisprudence) I suggest three "levels of review" (and corresponding degrees of suspicion) with which various religion-state connections ought to be viewed: low/intermediate scrutiny, intermediate scrutiny, and strict scrutiny.

My argument builds on an NSF-funded research study in Israel, which included extensive interviews with diverse Israeli citizens concerning conceptual and practical matters related to their polity's religion-state arrangement. The insights into liberalism and religion developed here owe great debts to these respondents, some of whom I name (with pseudonyms) below. The guidelines I discuss may prove useful not only to the future of Israeli politics but to the development of new constitutional regimes in traditional societies such as Iraq and Afghanistan. Rethinking religious establishment is a matter of practical necessity: it is wildly unrealistic to expect today's traditional societies to abandon all vestiges of establishment overnight, when it took Americans several hundred years to even partially achieve this. With due reflection on the international diversity of religion in public life, it is apparent that the present-day American model may not be the one size that fits all.

Symbols, Holidays, and the Public Ethos: Low to Intermediate Scrutiny

Does liberalism demand that symbols marking the boundaries of a state's public ethos welcome all citizens equally? Does any degree of exclusiveness in religious symbolism constitute an intolerable "expressive harm" to the democratic citizen? Two contrasting views might be sketched that draw upon different interpretations of the nature and moral status of expressive harms committed by democratic nation-states:[2]

1. Liberal states must choose national symbols and holidays that are neutral or broad enough in meaning that all citizens can freely identify with them without compromising their core beliefs or values.
2. Liberal states need not worry about the effect of their symbolic speech on its citizens at all; those who identify with the symbols will do so, those who don't, won't; state expression can do no harm.

Many liberals sensitive to the expressive harms states are capable of inflicting might be inclined to choose the first option. In urging official state neutrality, this position extends the notion of equality as "equal concern and respect" (as defined by political philosopher Ronald Dworkin[3]) from its application in matters of distributive justice to symbolic questions of how a state represents itself to its citizens and to the world. A liberal state, on this view, has no business expressing an official connection with a single religion or ethnicity through symbols such as its flag or national anthem. The state, respecting the fact of pluralism, should choose unifying holidays (such as Thanksgiving in the United States) and neutral symbols (such as stripes) whose motifs cannot reasonably be rejected by any citizen.

Although this rubric for evaluating Israel's state symbols has initial appeal, it falters when we realize that expressive harms come in a range of intensities, not all of which can, or should, be avoided. More specifically, it fails to draw an important distinction between two quite different types of religion-state connections that fall under this category: what we might call *plural state affiliations* in which the state endorses one way but tolerates others (as in the examples of national holidays, languages, and calendars) and *exclusivist state affiliations* in which the state, in Hobbesian mode, consolidates all competing claims into a single product (e.g., national symbols such as flags, anthems, and emblems). In both cases the state is expressly siding with a particular religion and abandons any semblance of official neutrality.[4] But there is a significant difference between the two: Minority groups may, with appropriate legislative provisions, "opt out" of the *plural* state affiliations with religion and enjoy a parallel religious affiliation of their own. For example, although Saturday is the official day of rest in Israel, Muslims and Christians are not forced to partake in this weekly holiday or to abide by the restrictions on the opening of businesses that apply to Jews. Non-Jews may celebrate their own Sabbaths on Friday or Sunday, as is their custom. Likewise, although Hebrew is dominant in Israel, Arabic is an official (if underused) language as well.

As the name implies, though, *exclusivist* state affiliations are univocal and ask citizens to make a starker choice: to participate or not to participate. When it comes to a flag or an anthem, citizens can "take it or leave it": they can fly the flag or not, sing the national anthem or not, see themselves as represented in the symbols or not.[5] On these matters and with these media, the state does not permit alternate voices a say. There are no separate flags that non-Jewish Israelis may choose to fly, no alternative anthems (neither lyrics nor melody) that non-Jewish Israelis may choose to sing, no multiple official state emblems that non-Jewish Israelis may choose to design.[6] In these areas, the state not only links itself with a religious image, it claims a monopoly over that linkage. It not only endorses Judaism, we might say, it makes that endorsement exclusive and implicitly prohibits alternatives.

The distinction between exclusivist and plural religious affiliations, as patterns of my interviewees' responses convincingly suggest, entails a difference in their moral status as well. Arab and Jewish Israelis disagree sharply about the Jewish symbols associated with the state. Jews (with the exception of most Haredi, or ultra-Orthodox, Jews) broadly support the Star of David on the flag and the Zionist references in Hatikva, the national anthem, even if they sometimes do so with tepid voices, while many Arabs see these and other manifestations of the Jewish state as symbols of exclusion, discrimination, and alienation. There is much less disagreement, however, concerning what I have called plural public expressions of Judaism, such as kosher state kitchens and Sabbath and Jewish holiday celebrations: Jews and Arabs alike express varying levels of support (ranging from indifference to enthusiasm) for these elements of the public ethos.

Religious symbols of the plural type may constitute expressive harms in a liberal state, but these harms are seldom serious. When considered in light of their benefits, as my study's subjects (both Jewish and Arab) apparently did, non-coercive plural religious affiliations should not be seen as especially problematic from a liberal perspective. Kosher state kitchens do not restrict private eating habits; do not violate religious scruples of those who do not keep kosher; allow individuals of widely different religious backgrounds to eat together, perhaps stimulating greater social cohesion; and affirm the society's broadly defined Jewish ethos. Exclusivist affiliations, however, should be more suspicious from the perspective of liberalism. These affiliations—if not only exclusivist in nature but also exclusionary in effect—may provide no means for some citizens to view themselves as represented or as full and equal partners in a regime. As several of my Arab interviewees passionately argued, the Star of David and Hatikva don't just leave them cold. These exclusivist religious symbols, for Majjed and Youssef, Nadia and Omer, are "alienating" and "racist": they draw Arab citizens of Israel (nearly one of every five Israelis) out of the circle.

Few if any liberal democracies would pass the muster of a pure "neutralist" standard. The United Kingdom's flag features the intersection of three crosses: the red St. George's cross of England, the white St. Andrews's cross of Scotland, and the red (diagonal) St. Patrick's cross of Ireland. The Union Jack thus excludes not only the Welsh but all Britons who are not Protestant. By placing St. George's flag in the foreground, atop the others, the flag also communicates a political history of English domination over the other two kingdoms and implies a continuing symbolic claim to Ireland.[7] Even in some states with constitutionally mandated separation of church and state—France and Ukraine, to pick two—the seemingly neutral stripes of color carry religious meaning, or at least stem from religious sources.[8] Interestingly, one of the few states whose flag would arguably pass the most rigorous test of expressive harm is Costa Rica, a state that is officially (if benignly) linked to Catholicism.[9] On the neutralist interpretation, the very existence of Israel as a self-described Jewish state may constitute an impermissible expressive harm against its non-Jewish citizens. But this *reductio* equates, as the United Nations once did, Zionism with racism.[10]

Given the inescapability of non-neutrality, there is no reason to regard all exclusivist religious symbols—simply because they are religious—as proscribed by liberalism. To do so would transform liberalism into a doctrine denying independent states the moral right to even the most rudimentary form of political culture. It would thus give liberalism little traction in addressing solutions to problems in the real world. Yet the comments of the Arab interviewees in my study echo in our ears: every Arab interviewee except Muhammad expressed profound disagreement with Israel's state symbolism. Do their claims have any grounding within a theory of political liberalism?

Yes. But the claims of the Jewish subjects who approve of their flag and anthem— some of whom express feelings of deep attachment to these symbols—have a home within liberal theory as well. The challenge is how Israel might achieve what John Rawls (the twentieth century's leading political philosopher) terms a "proper patriotism" that reflects the Israeli majority's religio-national culture while also providing a society to which all of its citizens may stake a claim.[11] Neither of the two principles with which we began this section, then, is suitable. Contrary to the first, strict neutrality of symbols and culture is an unnecessary and futile aspiration of a liberal state. But contrary to the second principle, expressive harms do hurt; some hurt a lot. Liberal states must be mindful of the very real damage they can cause. Rejecting these extremes should lead us to a middle way: Liberal states need not be neutral and need not limit themselves to universally applicable symbols and holidays; they may, instead, specify symbols and festivals that refer to the history and aspirations of its majority even if minority groups find it difficult or impossible to relate to them, *provided that* the symbols do not connote a negative message about the minority group and minority groups may celebrate their own holidays, and rally around their own symbols, freely.

Funding Religion: Intermediate Scrutiny

If a complete separation of religious symbols and the state is not a requirement of liberal justice, what about the issue of funding for religious institutions and education? Should the state limit its affiliations with religion to certain non-problematic symbolic matters of national ethos, and maintain a hands-off stance with regard to religion in its budgets and expenditures? The United States, it might be said, takes this position. It has certain non-oppressive symbolic links with religion in general and with Christianity in particular—"In God We Trust," presidential prayer breakfasts, Christmas as a national holiday—but draws the line at government funding of religion. Occasional markers of affiliation, yes; dollars of support, no.[12]

In Israel, of course, the story is very different. Israel takes an active role in providing direct funds for religious education; for synagogues and ritual baths; for a Chief Rabbinate; for religious courts and local religious councils. Jews are the primary beneficiaries of this support, but Muslim and Christian groups enjoy support as well. Should liberal democracy tolerate such widespread government funding for religious services and institutions? Or ought it to insist on financial independence for religion—an unfettered market where religions rise or fall on the basis of the expressed intentions of individuals to take part and contribute? In answering these questions, contemporary liberals tend to take their cue from First Amendment jurisprudence in the United States. If something is prohibited by the Establishment Clause—or, in the event of an uncooperative Supreme Court majority, if something *ought to be read as* prohibited by the Establishment Clause—the reasoning goes, it must be illiberal.

But why, exactly, is this the case? Among the important considerations that should lead us to be wary of government funding of religion are risks of discriminatory allocation and entanglements between governmental and religious institutions that could sully church and state alike. In his frequently cited "Memorial and Remonstrance" (1785), James Madison raises fifteen points in opposition to a bill that would have established a tax to support teachers of Christianity—and, implicitly, propped up the Anglican church—in the Commonwealth of Virginia.[13] Of the fifteen arguments, we find two that employ slippery slope reasoning to warn that the Virginia assessment—while seemingly innocuous in itself—has dire logical consequences, including, ultimately, not only infringements on the cherished right of religious free exercise but the loss of *all* fundamental liberties. "It is proper to take alarm at the first experiment on our liberties," Madison admonishes. A three-pence tax to support churches might be a pittance, but it foretells doom for the republic. Once the principle that citizens may be taxed to subsidize religion gains legitimacy, there is no logical stopping point short of full ecclesiastical establishment.

The message becomes even more urgent in the second slippery slope argument Madison raises in paragraph 15, the final passage of the "Memorial and Remonstrance." Having argued that a church tax leads to establishment, and that establishment threatens religious free exercise, now he warns that the loss of the right to free exercise entails the loss of every fundamental right guaranteed by the nascent constitution. There are no third ways: either this bill to fund Virginia religious teachers' salaries through taxation is defeated, or the Bill of Rights and the structure of the U.S. government crumble. Religious liberty, as one of the rights most highly prized by the colonists, is the keystone to legitimate government.

Not even the most ardent activist for church-state separation today makes the case that spending three pennies of tax money on religion would bring us to the end of liberal democracy as we know it. None of the major U.S. advocacy groups policing separation, for example, rose up in opposition to the national prayer service held in the aftermath of the September 2001 terrorist attacks. None are mounting a serious campaign to end the tradition of taxpayer-funded clergy offering prayers before every session of the U.S. Congress. None wave "Separation Now" placards at presidential inaugurations, where ministers routinely invoke the name of God in praying for the nation's new leader.

There is good reason for even ardent separationists to pick their battles: sometimes the risks to religious liberty are negligible. The checks and balances of existing legislation and the legislative system, the judicial oversight of the Supreme Court, public opinion, lobbying groups, the constitutional text—any of these could serve as potential stopping points on a free-fall from innocent taxes to a tyrannical Christian state. Together, they constitute a fairly secure bulwark against the fundamental transformation of the United States from liberal democracy to theocracy.

In Israel, the slippery slope arguments are never heard. This is for an obvious and for a somewhat less obvious reason. First, it is silly to speak of the risks of a tax turning into an establishment in Israel, because there already *is* an establishment of sorts: Israel already is a Jewish state. Second, this establishment is, in itself, hardly an oppressive one for most Israelis. They have been in the belly of the beast, one might say, and it's not so bad. They don't worry about religious education funds leading to an odious outcome, despite the fact that they strongly disagree with some of the religious elements of their state as they know it. They denounce the rabbinical monopoly on marriage and divorce, for example (more on that below), but they do not associate this with state funding for religious institutions. When they complain that Haredim take more than they deserve—that the ultra-Orthodox Shas schools raid the public coffers to provide a longer school day, hot lunches, and free bus rides—Israelis remove the argument from the slippery slope, transferring it to a traditional public policy argument over the welfare state and distributive justice: who ought to get how much, and why. Their argument is not with the principle of state-funded religious education, but with specific policies and actual allocations the Knesset and government ministries provide.

Although advocacy groups such as Americans United for Separation of Church and State no longer stake their position on Madison's slippery slope arguments, they sometimes use similar rhetoric. They appropriate his "three pence" line not to warn of a theocratic apocalypse but to urge a quite different, much tamer, and conceptually muddled argument: the injustice of being forced to pay for something you don't agree with. Perhaps because of the change in circumstances between 1785 and today, and the implausibility that passage of, say, a faith-based charities bill (which may be ill advised for other reasons) would herald the collapse of freedom of religion, the separationists' argument is becoming increasingly banal. For example, Americans United for Separation of Church and State contends that, "Forcing taxpayers to subsidize religious institutions they may or may not believe in is no different from forcing them to put money in the collection plates of churches, synagogues and mosques."[14] Arguments of this structure have been used often in recent years in the United States to oppose state funding for various projects, both religious and non-religious. Former New York Mayor Rudolph Giuliani used it in his battle with the Brooklyn Museum of Art in the fall of 1999 over a controversial exhibit featuring a painting of the Virgin Mary decorated with elephant dung: "[T]o have the government subsidize something like that," he said, "is outrageous."[15] He repeatedly questioned the justice of forcing taxpayers to pay for an exhibit that, in his opinion, qualified as offense and not as art.

The answer to all arguments of this type is clear: individual taxpayers disagree with many different government expenditures for many different reasons. Doves might oppose high levels of military spending, libertarians may think not a dime should go to safety net programs like Medicaid—but taxpayers do not, and cannot, enjoy a line-item veto. Forcing someone to give a dollar to a religious institution in the pursuit of legitimate public policy goals is no different from forcing someone to put a dollar in Boeing's coffers to buy an F-14 fighter, or to send a dollar to Mexico for a government bailout.[16]

Consider now the case *for* government funding of religion that my Israeli interviewees advanced. It is a simple but powerful point: equality demands equal treatment of all people, whether religious or not. Israelis give financial support to religious education, says Naomi, "not because we want to . . . but because we are duty-bound." "The state," says Ronit, "must respect every [educational] stream and give it funding." Sectarian education, according to Tanya, "is a kind of special education" the state is fully justified in subsidizing. "If the state funds opera and supports football," Rotem claims, "then there is no reason why it shouldn't support religious education." "One of the rules of democracy," says Shmuel, "is that you give people the ability to live their own way. And if there are people who want to be religious that's fine and they are entitled to have their own budget."[17]

There is a curious feature of the justification for government funding of religion suggested in these quotes: None of the five interviewees cited in the previous paragraph is religious. Only one has attended a religious school, and all have sent or intend to send their children to secular schools. In addition, all of them express various degrees of disdain for religious Israelis, particularly Haredim, and have complaints about the ways in which some religious schools operate or take more than their fair share of funds. So the position in favor of government funding is not what some modern political scientists would think of as "rational," in the narrow sense of conducing to one's own ends. Nor is it rational in the wider sense that individuals take account of their families' and friends' welfare in their own utility calculations; many of Israel's secular Jews, we should recall, *hate* their Haredi brethren. No: the position seems to come from a sense of what counts as a fair allocation of state resources and thus is better described as *reasonable*—taking other people's interests as seriously as one's own interests and applying principles of justice in an even-handed manner.

A liberal state may decide to engage in funding for religious causes not in order to recognize that a particular religion is the true religion, and not to endorse particular religious practices or beliefs, but out of an objective concern for the things that citizens themselves happen to value. If something is important to a citizen, then, it is potentially important to the state as well—not because that something has innate value, or because the state itself finds value in it, but because a *citizen* ascribes value to it. A certain disinterested approval for citizens enjoying success in their life plans leads states to fund a range of activities, from health care to university studies, from sports programs and scientific research to art and music. There is no *a priori* reason why religion should not be added to this list.[18]

Vigilance is necessary whenever state funding of religious services is considered, however. Each such proposal should meet worthy objections with regard to the potential for discriminatory allocation, corruption, and abuse. There is little reason, however, to fear an uncontrollable slippery slope from "three pence" to theocracy. Providing additional state funds for faith-based charities will not turn the United States into a theocratic state that compels church attendance and launches an inquisition. Intermediate scrutiny is the appropriate standard in this case: if a government policy involving funding for religious institutions is thought to be closely linked to a significant (not simply legitimate) state interest, applied in an even-handed manner and in a way that takes seriously the interests of both religious and non-religious citizens, it may pass liberal muster.

Imposing Religion: Strict Scrutiny

In contrast to symbolic affiliations and financial ties between religion and state—which may at times be acceptable from the perspective of liberalism—direct links between political and ecclesiastical bodies that threaten individual rights are seldom, if ever, justifiable. In order to satisfy liberal demands, arrangements in this category must be necessary to serve a compelling state interest. They must be the only and best means available to solve a very urgent social problem.

The following are examples of religious affiliations that fit in this category: compulsory church attendance laws; the delegation of personal status issues such as marriage and divorce to religious courts; enforcement of religious gender roles (including dictates concerning dress, education, and work) in private or public; and forced tithing to a religious authority.[19] In short, this third category includes both coerced observance of religious commandments and systematic discrimination against nonbelievers or adherents of rival faiths. State policies which entail or cause these types of harms to individuals are extremely unlikely to be acceptable according to the principles of liberal democracy.

The principle of non-coercion is, on some accounts, the very heart of liberalism itself. As a theory that is built on the value of individual liberty—even as it arguably respects other values as well, such as cultural survival and national self-determination—liberalism ought to regard government policies that turn the state into the enforcement branch of any religion's commandments with the highest degree of suspicion. Individual citizens' basic human and civil rights—including rights of bodily integrity, equal treatment, legal due process, and political participation; and freedom of movement, occupation, speech, assembly, and religious exercise—are not subject to curtailment or control by any religious worldview. They are not to be denied by the state on the basis of a purely religious justification, nor are these rights to be delegated to religious authorities, in whose hands they are at risk of violation.

Still, in this category some questions are clearer than others. Subjecting citizens to violence or persecution on account of their religion; demanding the conversion of citizens to a particular religion; requiring or preventing attendance at a house of worship—all these are clear violations of liberalism's non-coercion principle and cannot be said to serve a legitimate, let alone a compelling, state interest. In John Rawls' philosophical terms, no suitably "public reason" could be summoned to justify any such impositions of the state on citizens' lives: the reason would have to rely solely on the *truth* of the religion in question, not a sense in which the proposal serves the general interest in a diverse polity. But other religiously motivated state infringements on liberty *could* be argued to have a legitimately public justification.

Take the question of Israel's millet system, according to which Jewish, Muslim, and Christian courts enjoy control over their respective religious communities in terms of many facets of family law. Among my Jewish interviewees, much consternation was voiced concerning the control that the rabbinical authorities wield over questions of marriage, divorce, and burial. The delegation of these personal status questions to the rabbinical authorities entails violations of fundamental human liberties including the right to marry and the right of free religious exercise. To be sure, arguments could be made that this arrangement is necessary either to ensure the continued existence of Israel as a Jewish state or to preserve the unity of the Jewish people as one nation—two values with a great deal of currency among all portions of Israel's Jewish population. Ultimately, however, these reasons fail to justify the policy.[20] The purported values, while legitimate, do not rise to the level of compelling state interests, given the very different senses in which different segments of the population regard "Israel as a Jewish state" and "Jews as a unified nation." There is too little agreement on the details of these values.

The assessment might be different, however, when considering the millet system as it applies to non-Jews. The Arab subjects I interviewed were divided on this question. Those opposing the power of Muslim and Christian religious courts over the faithful (and the not-so-faithful) in their respective communities cite the same reason Jews give for rejecting similar control by the rabbinate: the injustice of demanding religious action without consent. But several of the subjects (Muhammad and Omer) support the delegation of state authority to the Muslim and Christian courts on the grounds of religious autonomy. And indeed this is the justification Israel would offer for pursuing this policy. Toleration of minority religious cultures could be said to depend on giving each community a certain degree of control over its adherents. Without such authority, the communities may risk weakness, division, or even dissolution in a polity that is dominated by a single religio-national group. Empowering the minority religious leadership to lead, and to make rulings that apply to all members of the faith community, may be an effective way to keep the peace between the eighty percent Jewish majority and the twenty percent Arab minority.

Another admittedly contingent reason to keep the millet system for Muslim and Christian Arabs is this: it is the local tradition. First implemented by the Turks when Palestine was part of the Ottoman Empire, the system was adopted by the British after World War I and then by the Israelis in 1948. Consistency of policy has its virtues: it is what people are accustomed to, what they have come to rely on. It is on long deposit in the local bank of political ideas. So Israel's policy clearly pursues a compelling state interest—toleration of the religious minorities that comprise the Arab minority. And the means it employs toward this goal stem from local traditions and seem to be necessary: there are no obvious ways to rework the arrangement in ways that would satisfy the minority and keep the tenuous peace between Israeli Arabs and Israeli Jews. Still, the state may be able to provide exit options for individuals who want to marry outside the bounds of their religious authorities, thus preserving some measure of both group *and* individual autonomy.

Conclusion

The mistake of many general accounts of the relationship between liberal democracy and religion has been to regard *all* religious linkages with the state as coercion of religious practice or as religious discrimination—and thereby conclude that only a strict separation of religion and state will suit a liberal polity. But not all religion is oppressive. Not all is coercive. Some connections between religion and state express a partiality toward a particular tradition, help define a state's ethos, or aid individuals in living meaningful lives, while doing no harm or only minimal expressive harm to citizens affiliating with other traditions. Other matters involve state financial support for various kinds of religious institutions, including religious schools. These entail a higher risk of abuse and often lead to discrimination in favor of a majority religion. They should accordingly be subject to greater constraints than the purely symbolic elements of the first category, but—in light of the liberal value of impartial regard for all citizens' chosen ways of life—not ruled out of bounds entirely. Finally, affiliations between state and religion that require unwilling citizens to conform to certain religious beliefs or performances are particularly worrisome in any state worthy of the label "liberal democratic." These kinds of arrangements should nearly always be ruled out as violating individual rights—except, perhaps, when they serve less as a device for oppression than for group toleration and may be modified in favor of greater individual choice.

All religious infusions into politics should be regarded with some skepticism: on that point liberalism is instructive. The tragic history of attempts to integrate religion with state, from the wars of religion in sixteenth- and seventeenth-century Europe to the Islamic revolution in Iran to the repressive Taliban regime in Afghanistan, illustrates the profound dangers to life and liberty that can be associated with such a combination. Religious infusions in the state can indeed threaten liberal government. But liberals would be wise to consider these questions with a more nuanced, more contextual eye. In certain societies, and in particular ways, religion and constitution may legitimately, and even fruitfully, converge.

45

CHRISTIANITY AND DEMOCRACY
The Pioneering Protestants

—Robert D. Woodberry and Timothy S. Shah

"The authority of Christ," wrote the Scots Calvinist divine William Graham in 1768, "removes all civil distinctions, and all superiority founded upon such distinctions, in his kingdom. All are upon a level equally, as they shall soon be before the awful tribunal of the great Judge."[1] This stirring fusion of theology, eschatology, and politics not only characterizes Scottish Calvinism but also says much about the relationship between Protestantism and democracy. As an egalitarian religion profoundly opposed to hierarchy, Protestant Christianity would seem to enjoy a powerful affinity with democracy.

If the affinity between Protestantism and democracy is powerful, however, it is not automatic or uncomplicated. History and social science show that Protestantism has contributed to the development of democracy, yet they also show that the connections are often far from straightforward. After all, Protestantism has at times countenanced the establishment of brutal regimes and antidemocratic movements: The "righteous" dictatorship of Oliver Cromwell enjoyed the overwhelming support of English Puritans; the Dutch Reformed Church of South Africa theologized in defense of apartheid; and while some German Protestants (especially in the Confessing Church) fought Nazism, many others gave Hitler their warm backing. Recently, Protestant evangelicals in the Third World have lent their support to "godly" authoritarians such as former Zambian president Frederick Chiluba.

In other words, opposing hierarchy and liberating individual consciences in religion does not automatically make one a foe of authoritarianism and a friend of liberty in politics. In fact, some Protestants, including founding figures such as Martin Luther and John Calvin, favored authoritarian politics as a means of defending or extending the purity of Reformed doctrines and practices. As Michael Walzer argues, it was precisely a zeal for the comprehensive spiritual purification of society that led some Protestants—particularly Calvinists—to pursue a militant and authoritarian politics in seventeenth-century England, ending in Cromwell's Protectorate.[2] By the same token, hierarchical and communal

* *Journal of Democracy* 15, no. 2 (April 2004): 47–61.

religions—such as Roman Catholicism—do not automatically support a hierarchical or authoritarian politics.[3]

We argue that there is nonetheless compelling cross-national evidence of a causal association between Protestantism and democracy. At the same time, we emphasize that the association is not direct or automatic but mediated and contingent. Among the major mediating influences or mechanisms, we number: (1) the rise of religious pluralism and what Alfred Stepan terms the "twin tolerations"[4] or the mutual independence of church and state; (2) the development of democratic theory and practice; (3) civil society and independent associational life; (4) mass education; (5) printing and the origins of a public sphere; (6) economic development; and (7) the reduction of corruption. These mechanisms help to explain how and why Protestantism tends, on balance, to promote democracy and democratization over time.

Protestantism's contribution to democracy via such mediating mechanisms explains both the strength and the contingency of the relationship. These mechanisms *often* directly result from Protestant influences, and when present, *often* directly foster democratization. Yet "often" is different from "always." Various factors, including not only changing material conditions but also the complex interests and motives of Protestant actors themselves, may disrupt the positive relationship and cause Protestantism to have neutral or even negative effects on democracy.

When Luther in 1521 defied an imperial order to recant by insisting that "my conscience is captive to the Word of God," he stopped being the reformer of an old order and instead became the founder of a new stream of Christianity. He could flout the commands of popes, church councils, and emperors, but not those of his own individual conscience. Most Protestants follow his lead in a few large, defining ways. First, Protestants are Christians not in communion with Roman Catholicism or Orthodoxy. Second, they tend to believe that people can acquire saving faith only as they personally and individually appropriate God's Word. They thus tend to make the Bible (and particularly Paul's message of salvation by grace alone) the touchstone of faith and life, reject the independent salvific significance of most (if not all) sacraments, deny the necessary mediation of priests, and insist on the priesthood of all believers. Third, they tend toward separation and independence from ancient church structures and traditions as well as political authorities. The main reason for this is the important role of individual conscience. Because saving faith must be uncoerced and individual, it requires in practice a diversity of independent churches to satisfy the inevitable diversity of individual consciences.

The importance of Luther's latter-day descendants to democracy becomes clear from demography. Not only do Protestants presently constitute 13 percent of the world's population—about 800 million people—but since 1900 Protestantism has spread rapidly in Africa, Asia, and Latin America. According to the most extensive survey of religious demographics available, in 1900 about 2 percent of Africans were Protestant; by 2000 more than 27 percent were. In Latin America, the figures for those dates are 2.5 and 17 percent, while in Asia they are 0.5 and 5.5 percent.[5] Taking these three continents together, then, Protestants went from an average population share of just 1.66 percent in 1900 to a share of 16.5 percent in 2000—a stunning increase of almost 1,000 percent in just a hundred years. Much of the growth, moreover, has occurred quite recently, meaning since post–World War II decolonization across Africa and Asia, and since the historically Catholic countries of Latin America lifted restrictions on Protestant activities a few decades ago.[6]

To the extent that Protestantism facilitates democratic transitions, its recent and dramatic expansion may have important implications for many societies in the global South. Also of significance may be the reality that much of this intense recent growth has not been among older Protestant denominations, but rather among groups that are charismatic or Pentecostal in nature, and which may now be able to count as many as 400 million adherents across the whole of Asia, Africa, and Latin America. The full array of social and political effects that will flow from this remains a matter of disagreement and speculation even among experts.

Yet cross-national statistical research suggests a strong and consistent association between a society's proportion of Protestants and its level of political democracy. This association is consistent over time and across regions, and does not change with the application either of various statistical controls or of various ways to define and measure political democracy. Furthermore, Protestantism has a strong statistical association with the durability of democratic transitions. Neither the proportion of "nonreligious" people in the population nor the proportion of adherents of any other religious tradition seems to have a similar association with democracy.[7]

Some scholars, however, argue that the association between Protestantism and democracy is merely an association between European influence and democracy and, furthermore, that the original association between Protestantism and democracy in Europe is spurious. Perhaps preexisting social or economic conditions determined where Protestantism would emerge in Europe, and perhaps they—and not Protestantism—facilitated the later spread of democracy.

But the association between Protestantism and democracy is also found where Protestantism spread through later settlement or missionary activity. For example, a comparison across former colonies whose populations are mostly of European-settler stock reveals that democracy has fared better in historically Protestant-settler societies such as Canada, Australia, New Zealand, and the United States than it has in Catholic-settler societies such as Argentina, Chile, Costa Rica, and Uruguay. British colonialism may be a factor in these cases, but the pattern extends beyond European-settler colonies. Protestantism is associated with democracy outside of Europe and its daughter countries, so whatever causes the association must be portable.

Moreover, religious tradition remains a statistically significant predictor of democracy even when one controls for the identity of the former colonial power, the number of years when that power was in control, the number of years (if any) when that power was a democracy, the penetration of the English language, and the percentage of European descendants in the population. Thus, whatever causes the association seems to be distinct from European influence, British influence, or indirect exposure to democracy. Given the variety of regions in which the association between religious tradition and democracy can be observed, and the broad range of statistical controls used in previous analyses, an alternative explanation is more difficult to imagine.

Religious Pluralism and Democratic Theory

In identifying the mechanisms that explain why Protestantism has contributed to democracy, we begin with religious pluralism. Pluralism was built into the nature of Protestantism. From the beginning of the Reformation, the Protestant movement kept dividing in an endless ecclesial mitosis because it lacked a clear mechanism for settling doctrinal disagreement.[8] This pluralism fostered the "twin tolerations" that Alfred Stepan argues are essential to democracy—that is, the independence of the state from religious control and the independence of religion from state control.

First, as G. W. F. Hegel pointed out in 1821, the end of Catholic hegemony and the rise of religious pluralism facilitated state autonomy.[9] In societies with a significant Protestant presence, religious pluralism both made it harder for any single religious body to control state and society and gave the state a sharper incentive to exert its own autonomous control over the potentially destabilizing realm of religion. Eventually this made the rise of free government more feasible because states enjoyed an exclusive jurisdictional sway over their territories, a sway that could later be distributed democratically. The contrasting situation in predominantly Catholic societies underscores the importance of religious pluralism: In such societies, the state and the Catholic Church either combined to enforce repressive religiopolitical unity, or else fell into power struggles that reduced state autonomy and undermined the stability and liberality of democratic transitions.[10]

Second, Protestant pluralism helped to foster the other of Stepan's "twin tolerations," religious liberty. While Calvinists often took Old Testament Israel as the model for the ideal state and thus sometimes established theocracies, they also emphasized that true saving faith cannot be compelled by any earthly authority. So although a Calvinist such as Cromwell did not allow religious liberty in anything like the modern sense, he allowed more religious liberty than most of his secular, Catholic, or Anglican contemporaries. This relative freedom increased religious pluralism, as people formed new sects, and this increased pluralism in turn created greater pressure for religious liberty. For example, by the time Parliament restored the monarchy in 1660, Nonconformist sects had become too numerous to crush—a fact which impressed the young John Locke, causing him to revise his early absolutist views in favor of religious toleration. Eventually the sects forced the Crown to issue the Act of Toleration (1689). When transplanted to the New World, such sects (especially Baptists and Quakers) became major advocates of religious liberty in the colonies and the early American republic.

Beyond the Anglo-American world, the Protestant missionary movement played an important role in spreading religious liberty. Originally, the British banned missions in many colonial territories because officials feared that missionary activities would create turmoil and interfere with profits. But in 1813 Protestant missionary supporters forced the government to allow free access to all religious groups. The Protestant missions lobby also pressed for religious liberty in colonies of historically Catholic powers, but less successfully. Mission organizations collected international data on religious liberty and lobbied governments to insert religious-liberty clauses in international treaties, including the charter of the United Nations. This Protestant lobbying increased religious liberty in former British colonies and helped to spread it to other societies.

Moreover, Protestantism constituted one important source for early democratic theory. Robert A. Dahl rightly suggests that the antimonarchical and prorepublican thought of the English Puritans and Levellers arose from their understanding of Christianity.[11] Later, Calvinist families or schools produced many prominent democratic thinkers, including John Locke, James Madison, Alexander Hamilton, John Jay, and John Adams. Among other things, scholars argue that the Calvinist "societal covenant" inspired the "social contract";

that the doctrine of original sin helped to motivate the concern for checks and balances in the U.S. Constitution; and that belief in the inviolability of the individual conscience fueled the urge to limit state power. Even the Presbyterian form of church governance—in which ministers are subject to elders elected by congregations—influenced the organizational form of modern representative democracy.

The New Testament and the example of the early church also eased Protestant experimentation with democracy. Jesus said "my Kingdom is not of this world," and set up no political or legal system. The Apostle Paul declared that much of Jewish law does not apply to Christians. The lack of a mandatory political or legal model in the Bible permitted Protestants to develop their own. When Protestant beliefs in freedom and equality demanded a democratic politics, the Bible did not seem to stand in the way.

Civil Society and Mass Education

According to many scholars, a robust civil society is crucial for democracy. Here too, Protestants played a central role. As already noted, Protestant groups kept dividing, and not every denomination could be the state church. Governments generally discriminated against nonstate churches, which in turn drove such churches to fight for their own rights. This activism helped to establish the principle that organizations could exist outside state control—a principle that developed only later in societies with thinner nonstate religious sectors.

Moreover, because nonestablished churches received no money from the state, they needed to instill habits of voluntarism and giving in their congregants. The laypeople who ran religious organizations affiliated with these churches learned leadership skills, built wide geographical networks, and accumulated other resources helpful in organizing nongovernmental organizations and social movements. Nonstate churches were especially prominent in training women, then commonly excluded from much of life outside the home. In the early nineteenth century, Protestants from nonestablished churches were central to founding and supporting a plethora of voluntary organizations and social movements for causes such as combating slavery or alcohol use.

Michael Young has argued that modern social-movement organizations and tactics developed in the United States when the lay-focused revival movements of upstart sects such as the Methodists and the Baptists linked up with transnational organizations developed by Calvinists to promote missions and orthodoxy.[12] However, the 1820s and 1830s saw parallel social movements flower in England, the United States, and India—a phenomenon for which traditional state- or economy-centered explanations of the rise of such movements cannot account. What these politically and economically diverse areas had most saliently in common was the presence of activist Protestants from outside any state-sponsored church.

In fact, Protestant missions have been central to the development of organized civil society across much of the non-Western world. For instance, there is a clear link between Protestant missionary activity and the appearance of indigenous NGOs in India. Protestant missionaries tried to convert Hindus and to promulgate controversial social reforms such as outlawing widow-burning and improving the treatment of "untouchables." Both sorts of activity spurred Hindu groups to form in response. Such organizations were new in Indian history and later facilitated the development of the Indian National Congress and other anticolonialist, prodemocratic groups (as well as groups that advocate more problematic ideologies such as Hindu nationalism).

A similar pattern—Protestant activism followed by a local reaction imitating Protestant organizational forms in order to counter Protestant aims—can be traced throughout the histories of places as diverse as China, Egypt, Japan, Korea, Palestine, and Sri Lanka, to give a partial list. Protestant missionaries came to win souls and reform social customs, and both Christians and non-Christians organized in response. Religious competition among Christians, Muslims, Hindus, Jains, Sikhs, and Buddhists had gone on for centuries or even millennia across India, the Middle East, China, Japan, and elsewhere, yet no widespread budding of voluntary organizations happened in these lands until Protestant missionaries from nonestablished churches appeared on the scene.

Research also shows a consistent association between mass education and democracy. Mass education fosters democracy by increasing exposure to democratic ideals, promoting economic growth and the rise of a middle class, and dispersing influence beyond a small elite. Both historical and quantitative evidence suggests a close association between Protestantism and the spread of mass education, not least because of the Protestant emphasis on the need for all believers to read the Bible in their own languages. Calvinists especially made massive investments in education, building what today are many of the elite universities of the North Atlantic world. Lutheran Pietists first promulgated the ideal of universal literacy, and literacy campaigns spread rapidly through the Protestant world. Protestants started Sunday schools to teach reading to the poor, founded Bible and tract societies, and pressed governments to fund mass education.

Protestant missions were also central to expanding mass education outside the West, despite the resistance of local colonialists who feared the effects of widespread literacy among subject peoples. Other religious groups typically invested in mass education only when they had to compete with Protestants. Protestant missionaries lobbied so effectively that, for instance, British-run India had government-funded schools by 1813, twenty years before England did. Moreover, because the souls of all humans had equal value in the spiritual economy of the missionaries, they often provided the only formal education open to women and marginalized groups such as slaves, blacks in South Africa, or members of "untouchable" castes in India.

Areas of the non-Western world where Protestant missionaries had their strongest influence continue to have higher education rates. This is true both between countries and within countries. After statistical controls are applied to account for "Protestant missionaries per capita in 1925" and "percentage of the population evangelized by 1900," the impact of Gross Domestic Product on primary-education rates in non-Western societies disappears. To the extent that education fosters democracy, then, we would expect higher levels of democracy in areas with more Protestants and where Protestant missionaries had more influence.

Printing, Economic Development, and Corruption

While democratic theorists such as Jürgen Habermas and David Zaret emphasize the importance of printing for the development of a democratic public sphere, they underestimate or ignore the role of religion in facilitating this process.[13] Printing technology appeared in the West in the late 1400s. But the public debates that fostered a democratic public sphere in England did not develop until the mid-1600s—during the religious controversies surrounding the English Revolution. Similarly, in Germany religious controversies between Pietists and other Protestant groups spurred printing and lively public discourse before the coffee houses and salons of Habermas's account.

Because of the divisions within Protestantism and also because no one person or group had clear authority to decide theological questions, Protestantism spurred public religious debate and widespread printing more than other religious traditions. Protestants also believed that God's Word was uniquely available in the Bible, and that the Bible was translatable into vernacular languages without losing its core meaning. The mass literacy that Protestants promoted made widespread reading of petitions and newspapers possible and mass printing economically viable. While printing may have made possible the development of a public sphere, Protestantism not only promoted the early development and diffusion of such printing technologies as the steam press but also fostered the public theological debates that resulted in the emergence of a public sphere in Europe and North American.

Outside Western Europe and North America, the impact of Protestantism in spreading mass printing is especially clear. Protestant missionaries emphasized vernacular printing so that people could read the Bible in their own language. Wherever Protestant missionaries went, they rapidly gave local tongues a written form, translated the Bible into them, brought in printing presses, designed vernacular fonts, and began printing Bibles, tracts, textbooks, and even newspapers. Protestant missionaries often viewed newspapers as encouraging literacy, creating good will, and providing opportunities to discuss social reforms and religious issues. No other sizeable religious group placed comparable emphasis on literacy and the mass availability of religious texts. The Muslims of the Ottoman Empire, for example, had access to printing from 1493 onward, but made little use of it until spurred by Protestant missionary printing in the nineteenth century.

Like a vibrant public sphere, economic development and a large middle class are robust predictors of the level of political democracy and the durability of democratic transition, and Protestantism may have helped to promote both these predictors. Max Weber famously argues that Protestantism (particularly Calvinism) spurred the rise of modern capitalism. Others counter that this causal claim is spurious, and that both Protestantism and economic growth grew out of the same set of conditions in early-modern northwestern Europe. If this is so, however, one would not expect to see a robust association between Protestantism and economic development in non-European countries, where Protestantism is a transplant. Yet such an association exists.

Statistical research suggests that both in Africa and in other former colonies, areas with more Protestants have greater postcolonial economic-growth rates.[14] Ethnographic and statistical evidence also confirmed the association between Protestantism (or sometimes Christianity in general) and intergenerational improvements in the economic status of individuals—for example, in Latin America, New Guinea, Nigeria, Indonesia, and India. In Latin America, Protestantism has spread disproportionately among poor and marginalized people, yet Protestantism seems to foster moderate improvements in their incomes. Although Protestantism may not remove people's marginalized status, the children of Protestants tend to do better economically than other children in their original community. Protestantism may foster prosperity by reducing drinking and drug-taking, extramarital sex and child-bearing, and spending on communal festivals, while promoting education and a male sense of commitment to stable family life.

Protestantism seems to have fostered economic development even in societies where few people actually converted to Protestantism. This is because of the massive transfer of resources that accompanied the missionary movement, the impact that missionaries free of state affiliation had on moderating colonial abuses, and the changes that Protestant missionary presence induced in the behavior of other religious communities. Of course, Catholics also made major missionary efforts and transferred resources to colonies. But in historically Catholic countries and their colonies, Church-state pacts to bar religious competition also boosted state control and limited both resource transfers and the ability of Catholic missionaries to fight colonialist abuses.

Nonstate missionaries' reform campaigns also indirectly promoted economic development. Missionaries and their supporters were the main lobbyists for the immediate abolition of slavery and other forms of forced labor in the colonies, and were also often in the front rank of opposition to the officially sanctioned opium trade, the violent excesses of some colonial officials, and the tendency of European settlers to expropriate native lands. Because missionaries in historically Protestant colonies usually enjoyed more independence than their Catholic counterparts, the former could fight abuses more effectively. The British Empire banned slavery and forced labor earlier, punished abusive colonial officials more regularly, and on the whole managed to arrange more peaceful decolonization processes than did other European colonial powers—even when these were relatively democratic states such as France and Belgium. Historical evidence suggests that Protestant missionaries and their backers initiated these British reforms, which were not only generally humane but aided prosperity.

More than sheer altruism, of course, lay behind these efforts. Colonial abuses sowed anti-Western and hence anti-Christian resentment, as missionaries well knew. Other Europeans on the scene might know of abuses, but often benefited from them and had little incentive to expose them. Indigenous peoples had scant power to defend their own interests in the colonizing state. Missionaries—especially if they had political influence back home—were the main group with the means, motive, and opportunity to advance reform.

Moreover, Protestant competition seems to have spurred other religious groups to make "human-capital" investments in mass education and social services for the poor. Once Protestant groups initiated these services, other religious groups had to follow suit or risk losing congregants. This probably explains why former colonies of Catholic powers (which typically restricted Protestant activity) display historically lower levels of investment in schooling and social services, while non-Catholic-majority lands with histories of free religious competition usually feature Protestant and Catholic populations that boast similar levels of educational and economic attainment: In the latter type of society the Catholic Church had to invest while in the former it did not, and that has made a difference.

One way in which Protestantism contributes to both a vibrant public sphere and economic development is by reducing corruption. Scholarly research suggests that political corruption inhibits the emergence and survival of democracy by hampering social organization, undermining trust, and undercutting support for the political system. Corruption also indirectly hampers democracy by stifling economic development, increasing economic inequality, and restricting education. These findings hold for countries with different growth experiences, at different states of development, and using various indices of corruption.

Published statistical analyses universally find that societies with more Protestants are less corrupt and have more efficient governments. These results remain strong when scholars control for multiple factors, including economic development and democratic experience. They also hold for different regions of the world and for all societal subgroups scholars have tested so far: corruption by judges, policemen, politicians, and bureaucrats; elite corruption and street-level corruption. Even in the few cases where corruption data exist for the city or province level, areas with fewer Protestants per capita tend to be more corrupt. Other religious traditions do not seem to similarly reduce corruption or increase the efficiency of government.

Seymour Martin Lipset and Gabriel Lenz suggest that Protestantism minimizes corruption through an ethical mechanism. Other possible mechanisms include the reduction of resources controlled by church leaders (meaning less scope for clerical corruption), the creation of small face-to-face accountability groups that monitor individual behavior, and an organizational civil society that monitors government elites.[15]

Other Traditions and Newer Protestantisms

Our analysis suggests both that religion plays an important role in determining the political character of societies, and that religions other than Protestantism play a weaker role in promoting democracy—or may foster a different politics altogether. While the "democracy gap" between Protestantism and Catholicism is closing, this does not seem to be true of all other religious traditions. For example, quantitative research shows that predominantly Muslim societies are less democratic and have less durable democratic transitions. This is true across multiple regions and with multiple statistical controls. Claims that oil wealth allows elites to dodge democratization do not suffice, for majority-Muslim societies both with and without oil are consistently less democratic than their non-Muslim neighbors. Moreover, although the average Freedom House democracy score of non-Muslim societies has increased since the 1980s, the average democracy score of majority-Muslim societies has not.[16]

Yet just as the positive association between Protestantism and democracy is far from inevitable, so too is the observed negative association between Islam and that form of government. Religious traditions are multivocal; different groups and thinkers can and do interpret them differently in varying situations. Both Protestantism and Catholicism have shifted toward a stronger rapport with democracy over time, and other traditions—Islam included—may do so as well. To the extent that a religious tradition fosters the types of mediating mechanisms discussed above, it will be more likely to foster democracy. This is not to say that all the causal mechanisms enumerated above are prerequisites for democracy—a religious tradition that does not foster each and every one of them may still be compatible with liberal democracy. No religious tradition is either a necessary or sufficient cause of democratization, or an insuperable barrier to it.

Currently, newer strains of Protestantism—most often charismatic, evangelical, or Pentecostal—are growing rapidly across the global South. Will they, like older forms of Protestantism, exert a democratizing effect? Our analysis suggests the answer may depend on whether they foster the democracy-friendly mediating conditions enumerated above.

The ongoing paucity of democracy in Africa suggests at the very least that the impact of Protestantism is not immediate. Prior to 1900 there were very few Protestants and Catholics in Africa, but now many sub-Saharan African countries have Christian majorities. Although Catholic and Protestant leaders have condemned abuses by African governments and pressed for democracy, most African societies have poor democratic records. This also suggests that religious tradition is not the only factor that influences democracy; extreme poverty, a legacy of colonialist abuses, ethnic conflict, and other factors influence it as well. Moreover, religion may take generations to make its impact felt. The adoption of a new religious tradition does not instantly and completely transform all beliefs, practices, and social institutions. Change also takes resources. Protestants in poor countries may want universal literacy, but that will not pay for schools.

Nor is time the only issue. Some of Protestantism's contributions may be losing their distinctiveness as other religious traditions copy previously "Protestant" characteristics and as new forms of Protestantism—particularly Pentecostalism—develop and proliferate.

Over the past century, belief in mass education has spread well beyond Protestants. Increasingly, governments and other religious groups are willing to invest in it. Newer Protestant groups still advocate basic instruction, but the intensity of their stress on education does not match that of classical Calvinists. In many Pentecostal congregations, authority comes from spiritual gifts rather than higher study, making advanced schooling less important. Printing has also become widespread and commercially viable, so a distinction in print cultures between Protestant societies and others may disappear over time.

Some newer Protestant groups aggressively seek to insert religious symbols into the public sphere—such as declaring Zambia a "Christian nation" or organizing Christian prayers at government functions. This type of activity is of course not new and not unique to the global South. Moreover, such efforts are often designed more to serve evangelistic purposes than to restrict the religious liberty of others or to alter the character of the state. While Pentecostals and other evangelical Protestants may support particular policies or candidates based on their religious beliefs or even on putative special revelations, they lack an evangelical equivalent of Islamic shari'a to impose on society. The conviction that saving faith must come from within and cannot be compelled by the state is held firmly to by both the newer and the older Protestantisms. Structurally, the conditions for Protestants to impose a new "Christendom" do not exist because of the religious diversity that prevents them from forming new state churches remains. As other religious traditions permit religious liberty, Protestant distinctiveness on this question may erode. But it does not appear that the newer Protestants pose a threat to religious liberty.

Newer Protestant groups are still lay-supported voluntary organizations with weekly face-to-face meetings. They are likely to develop and promote organizations, skills, and resources among nonelite citizens and thus to foster civil society. In the long run, this should promote transitions to stable democratic government across the global South.

Where the newer Protestants may not be able to match their older counterparts or the Catholic Church is in the area of "speaking truth to power" and spurring rapid and overt regime change. The Catholic and Anglican churches, along with certain historic Protestant denominations, have a transnational presence and strong ties to Western societies that can offer resources, protection, and an identity that transcends sundry particularisms. Pastors of localized religious denominations are more vulnerable to both raw persecution and subtler pressures to make them trim religious principles with an eye to nearby realities. In addition, interviews with West African church leaders suggest that older denominations may be more adept "change agents" than their newer counterparts because the old-line groups have informational advantages—their church schools often count among their alumni many top government officials—that help church leaders know when to press an authoritarian regime and when to hold back.

Despite the consistent association between Protestantism and lower levels of corruption in cross-national statistical analysis, evidence from Africa and Latin America suggests that Protestantism is not a panacea. Over the past 75 years, Protestantism has spread rapidly—often among marginalized groups—in areas long troubled by high levels of corruption. Under these circumstances, some Protestants have arguably imitated more than firmly opposed dominant patterns of clientelist behavior. Concerns about corruption have regularly mobilized Protestants into politics and some Protestant politicians have vigorously fought corruption, but many vocally Protestant leaders (such as former president Kim Young-Sam of Korea) have fallen from grace precisely because of corruption in their administrations. While Protestants claim that such fallen politicians merely touted Protestant credentials to troll for votes, many new Protestant (and particularly Pentecostal) churches reproduce patron-client structures. Some also proclaim that God will materially bless those who give money to the church—a pattern that has often led to corruption.

Substantial evidence suggests that Protestantism still moderately increases the wealth of people who convert. The scale of change remains modest, however, and it may take considerable time before the changes are large enough to substantially alter a country's democratic potential.

Protestantism has played an important role in fostering and diffusing democracy. Over time the special association between Protestantism and democracy seems to be waning because other religious traditions are fostering many of the democracy-friendly, Protestant-aided social processes noted above. In addition, many new varieties of Protestantism have developed in the twentieth century. In particular, Pentecostal varieties have spread in Africa, Asia, and Latin America. Available evidence suggests that these new Protestant communities will on balance continue to foster democracy—although perhaps not as distinctively and dramatically as in previous generations.[17]

46

THE RISE OF "MUSLIM DEMOCRACY"

—Vali Nasr

Aspecter is haunting the Muslim world. This particular specter is not the malign and much-discussed spirit of fundamentalist extremism, nor yet the phantom hope known as liberal Islam. Instead, the specter that I have in mind is a third force, a hopeful if still somewhat ambiguous trend that I call—in a conscious evocation of the political tradition associated with the Christian Democratic parties of Europe—"Muslim Democracy."

The emergence and unfolding of Muslim Democracy as a "fact on the ground" over the last fifteen years has been impressive. This is so even though all its exponents have thus far eschewed that label[1] and even though the lion's share of scholarly and political attention has gone to the question of how to promote religious reform within Islam as a prelude to democratization.[2] Since the early 1990s, political openings in a number of Muslim-majority countries—all, admittedly, outside the Arab world—have seen Islamic-oriented (but non-Islamist) parties vying successfully for votes in Bangladesh, Indonesia, Malaysia, Pakistan (before its 1999 military coup), and Turkey.

Unlike Islamists, with their visions of rule by shari'a (Islamic law) or even a restored caliphate, Muslim Democrats view political life with a pragmatic eye. They reject or at least discount the classic Islamist claim that Islam commands the pursuit of a shari'a state, and their main goal tends to be the more mundane one of crafting viable electoral platforms and stable governing coalitions to serve individual and collective interests—Islamic as well as secular—within a democratic arena whose bounds they respect, win or lose. Islamists view democracy not as something deeply legitimate, but at best as a tool or tactic that may be useful in gaining the power to build an Islamic state. Muslim Democrats, by contrast, do not seek to enshrine Islam in politics, though they do wish to harness its potential to help them win votes.

The rise of the Muslim Democrats has begun the integration of Muslim religious values—drawn from Islam's teachings on ethics, morality, the family, rights, social relations, and commerce, for example—into political platforms designed to win regular democratic

Journal of Democracy 17, no. 2 (April 2005): 13–27.

elections. Challenges and setbacks will almost surely complicate the process, and the out-come is far from certain. Yet the ongoing dynamics of democratic consolidation, more than the promise of religious reform and ideological change, are likely to define the terms under which Islam and democracy interact in at least several Muslim-majority lands.

The past decade and a half has witnessed open electoral competition for legislative seats in Bangladesh (1991, 1996, and 2001); Indonesia (1999 and 2004); Malaysia (1995, 1999, and 2004); Pakistan (1990, 1993, and 1997); and Turkey (1995, 1999, and 2002). The length of this electoral era and the changes that it has set in train allow us to go beyond a "snapshot" of Muslim political preferences in order to track broader trends. Such trends suggest the shape of things to come among the political parties and platforms that will most likely dominate the strategic middle ground of politics in these Muslim-majority countries (or that, in the case of Pakistan, would dominate absent military intervention).

A brief rundown of results is suggestive. In Pakistan in 1997 the right-of-center but non-Islamist Pakistan Muslim League (PML) won 63 percent of the seats in parliament, marginalizing the Islamist party, Jamaat-e-Islami (JI). Similarly, in 2001 the Bangladesh Nationalist Party (BNP) captured 64 percent of the seats in parliament to sideline Bangla-desh's own JI. In Turkey in 2002 the Justice and Development Party (AKP)—a group with roots in the world of Islamism but which has always abjured such Islamist hallmarks as the demand for state enactment of shari'a—won 66 percent of the seats in parliament; voters had a clear Islamist alternative before them in the form of the Felicity Party, and turned it away with no seats. In Indonesia in 2004 a cluster of center-right Muslim parties, the National Mandate Party (PAN), National Awakening Party (PKB), United Development Party (PPP), plus Golkar (the old ruling party), won 53 percent of the seats, as compared to 8 percent for the Islamist Prosperous Justice Party (PKS). In Malaysia in 2004 the United Malays National Organization (UMNO) won 49.7 percent of the seats while the Islamic Party (PAS) managed to pick up only 3.2 percent.

Such results suggest that in these Muslim societies, the "vital center" of politics is likely to belong neither to secularist and leftist parties nor to Islamists. More likely to rule the strategic middle will be political forces that integrate Muslim values and moderate Islamic politics into broader right-of-center platforms that go beyond exclusively religious con-cerns. Such forces can appeal to a broad cross-section of voters and create a stable nexus between religious and secular drivers of electoral politics.

Muslim Democrats can begin from an Islamist point of departure, as is the case with Turkey's AKP, but may spring as well from nonreligious parties: Consider Pakistan's PML or Malaysia's UMNO. Not all those who have sought to stake a claim to the middle in Muslim politics have succeeded: In Pakistan, the military toppled the PML government of Prime Minister Nawaz Sharif. But the trend is clear, and so far seems to be a case of prac-tice outrunning theory. Muslim Democracy rests not on an abstract, carefully thought-out theological and ideological accommodation between Islam and democracy, but rather on a practical synthesis that is emerging in much of the Muslim world in response to the opportunities and demands created by the ballot box. Parties must make compromises and pragmatic decisions to maximize their own and their constituents' interests under democratic rules of the game.

In working more on the level of campaign-trail practice than of high theory, Muslim Democracy somewhat resembles Christian Democracy. The first Christian Democratic party was founded in southern Italy in 1919, decades before the theological rapprochement that the Catholic Church made with democracy around the time of the Second Vatican Council in the 1960s.

Liberalism and Consolidation

Muslim Democracy does not always flow from ideas of Islamic moderation, and it may not always act as a liberalizing force. In some cases, Muslim Democratic parties have backed Islamist demands for stricter moral and religious laws (Pakistan in the 1990s, Bangladesh since 2001) or sought to remove limits on Islamic schools (Turkey since 2002). Yet even such overtures to Islamism should be seen as strategic moves aimed at dominating the middle. The extent to which Muslim Democrats have backed the enforcement of Islamic law or restrictions on women and minorities has seemed to be less a matter of deep ideological conviction than of deals made to win votes in societies where conservative Islamic mores run strong.

The depth of commitment to liberal and secular values that democratic consolidation requires is a condition for Muslim Democracy's final success, not for its first emergence. As was the case with Christian Democracy in Europe, it is the imperative of competition inherent in democracy that will transform the unsecular tendencies of Muslim Democracy into long-term commitment to democratic values.[3]

Rather than arguing for changes in or fresh glosses on Islamic teaching as the path to democracy, Muslim Democrats are in the streets looking for votes and in the process are changing Islam's relation to politics. The shifts that Muslim Democracy will spark in Muslims' attitudes toward society and politics will come not from theoretical suppositions, but from political imperatives. The rise of Muslim Democracy suggests that political change will precede religious change.

Evidence now in from the Muslim world can help to identify the contours of Muslim Democracy, what it stands for, who supports it, and what factors have governed its evolution, its successes, and its failures. Muslim Democracy is a nascent force about which much remains to be learned.

Islamist ideology, which has dominated political debates from Malaysia to Morocco for a quarter-century, calls for the creation of a utopian Islamic state that notionally vests all sovereignty in God. This call is based on a narrow interpretation of Islamic law, and promotes an illiberal, authoritarian politics that leaves little room for civil liberties, cultural pluralism, the rights of women and minorities, and democracy. The Islamist surge since the Iranian Revolution of 1979 has led many to argue that well-organized and determined Islamists will use democratic reforms in Muslim-majority societies to seize power (probably through one-time elections) and impose theocracy. Democracy, the argument goes, should therefore wait until liberalization via ideological and religious reform can blunt the Islamist threat.

The assumption here has been that the key historical process which will lead to democracy in the Muslim world is an intellectual one, a moderation of the Islamist perspective, or more broadly, perhaps even an Islamic Reformation. While some reformists and moderates have been influential, more often than not their efforts have lagged behind the ground-level political realities that have been the growth medium of Muslim Democracy. It has not been intellectuals who have given shape to Muslim Democracy, but rather politicians such as Turkey's Recep Tayyip Erdoğan, Pakistan's Nawaz Sharif, and Malaysia's Anwar Ibrahim and Mahathir bin Mohamad. They are the ones grappling with key questions surrounding the interaction of Muslim values with democratic institutions, the nature of Muslims' voting behavior, the shape and location of an "Islamic" voter base, and the like.

One should also note that the rise of Muslim Democracy has occurred at the same time as a steady increase of religious consciousness within Muslim-majority societies.[4] The recent "greening" of Muslim societies, in other words, has led not to votes for Islamists but rather to something that looks at least somewhat like the early stages of Christian Democratic politicking in twentieth-century Western Europe. There are substantial differences, of course. Muslim Democracy, unlike Christian Democracy, cannot measure itself against an authoritatively expressed core of political and religious ideas that transcend national boundaries under the aegis of a centralized religious hierarchy such as the Vatican's. Muslim Democrats, not surprisingly, lack a clear, unified message. They seem instead like the inchoate offspring of various ad hoc alliances and pragmatic decisions made in particular political circumstances. Their provisional and experimental character, however, may be one of the reasons for their success: Free of heavy intellectual baggage, they can move nimbly with the changing tides of electoral circumstance. At the same time, the degree of commonality seen across Muslim Democratic movements in countries as far apart as Malaysia and Turkey underlines the likelihood that Muslim Democracy really is a major trend and not just a cluster of unrelated political accidents.

Still, the differences are important too. In each land, the Muslim Democratic experiment has proceeded more or less independently. In Turkey and Malaysia (as in precoup Pakistan), Muslim Democracy is a winning electoral formula that has yet to fully articulate a vision for governing (and it was failures of governance—especially rampant corruption—that helped set the stage for the Pakistani coup). In Indonesia, Muslim Democracy is less a platform and more a space wherein a number of parties are struggling to strike the right balance between secular politics and Muslim values. In Bangladesh, it is still only an ad hoc political alliance between right-of-center and Islamist parties that has captured the middle but has yet to resolve its own internal political and ideological differences.

Experiments with Muslim Democracy could eventually produce a more coherent political platform and Muslim political practice. What is notable at this stage is less what Muslim Democracy has said about Islam and more what has been achieved at the polls. The Muslim Democratic movements could become more like one another, or they could begin to take diverging paths. Muslim Democracy could prove an independent force for moderation within Islam, or it could come to seem a reflection rather than a shaper of society's religious values. For all these reasons, it will bear close scrutiny in the years ahead.

Key Factors

The rise of Muslim Democracy has depended on the interplay of several factors. First, Muslim Democracy has surfaced in countries where democracy emerged after the military formally withdrew from politics, but remained a powerful player de facto. (In Malaysia the military is not a political actor, but the ruling UMNO has played a similar role through its use of extensive authoritarian powers.) The gradual democratic openings in Turkey since 1983 and in Pakistan during the decade between the reigns of General Zia-ul-Haq (d. 1988) and General Musharraf (r. 1999–) were episodes in which the military shaped the opportunity structure in the democratic arena.

Military involvement in politics had three notable effects. First, it limited the Islamists' room to maneuver. Second, it gave all parties an incentive to avoid confronting the military while angling for advantage within the democratic process. Finally, the military's meddling in politics led to more elections, political realignments, and shifts in coalitions, accelerating and intensifying experimentation with new political formulas. Interestingly, the net effect of all this—a boost for Muslim Democracy—was the same in both Turkey, where the military strongly defended secularism, and Pakistan, where the military worked with Islamists. Turkey's Islamists learned to adopt pragmatic policies to avoid the generals' wrath, while Pakistan's right-of-center PML saw Muslim Democracy as the means to strengthen a frail system of elected civilian rule and the party's own standing within it.

Both the AKP and the PML sought to reduce military pressure on politics through a readiness to compromise with the generals as well as through efforts to build broader coalitions that the generals would hesitate to confront. The PML's success was one of the things that led the Pakistani military to stage its 1999 coup aimed at, among other things, stopping Muslim Democracy. The upshot, tellingly, has been that the seat share of Islamist parties in parliament has risen sharply from its negligible 1997 level of less than 1 percent to 20 percent in 2002. By removing the Nawaz Sharif government—and with it Muslim Democracy—General Musharraf has strengthened the Islamists, whether he meant to or not.[5]

While the Indonesian and Bangladeshi militaries have been more circumspect, each has also helped to nudge Islamists and right-of-center parties to explore Muslim Democracy. Malaysia is unique in that change there came not at military prompting, but from within the ruling party. In the 1980s, UMNO's control over national politics allowed it to restrain Islamists with one hand while using the other to reach out systematically to Muslim voters. The Malaysian case aside, it seems clear that Muslim Democracy is more likely to emerge when Islamist and democratic forces sense a common interest in protecting the democratic process from the military.

Second, Muslim Democracy has emerged in societies where the private sector matters. The less state-dependent and more integrated into the world economy a country's private sector is, the more likely is that country to see Muslim Democracy gain traction as a political force. Muslim Democracy, in short, needs the bourgeoisie, and the bourgeoisie needs Muslim Democracy. Muslim Democracy combines the religious values of the middle and lower-middle classes with policies that serve their economic interests.

In Turkey, the success of AKP's Muslim Democratic platform is less a triumph of religious piety over Kemalist secularism than of an independent bourgeoisie over a centralizing state. To understand the rise of Muslim Democracy in Turkey, one must consider the economic-liberalization policies of Prime Minister (later President) Turgut Özal (d. 1993) in the 1980s and the vibrant, independent private sector that they made possible. Similarly, Indonesia's Suharto regime in its later years mixed state support for moderate Islam with engagement in global trade. The same trend was evident in Malaysia, where the UMNO government combined economic globalization with promotion of a nationalist and moderate Muslim political platform that would support those economic policies. While Bangladesh and Pakistan lag behind Turkey, Indonesia, and Malaysia in terms of participation in global trade, they too boast robust private sectors that exert growing political influence. Yet the deeper involvement in the global economy and the greater independence of the Turkish, Indonesian, and Malaysian private sectors seem to correlate with the more Islamically moderate character of Muslim Democracy in those countries as compared to Pakistan or Bangladesh.

In addition to the military dynamic and the economic dynamic, a third motor of Muslim Democracy seems to be the existence of strong competition over votes. With no one party able easily to dominate the process, all parties feel pressed to act pragmatically. The presence of multiple parties with strong organizational structures and political legacies (some dating back earlier than the democratic opening) in turn fosters competition. Despite sustained bouts of military rule or one-party dominance in all these countries, multiparty politics has retained its vitality in each, and parties have bounced back as political processes have opened.

Regular competitive elections have both pushed religious parties toward pragmatism and pulled other parties into more diligent efforts to represent Muslim values. The net effect is to reward moderation. The game is to win the middle. This is the politics of what electoral experts call "the median voter," around whose position on the issue spectrum majorities cluster. Competition over the Muslim electorate means that non-Islamist groups can integrate those who vote based on Muslim values into broader platforms and wider coalitions than Islamists are capable of marshaling. In 1990s Malaysia, for instance, the UMNO successfully competed for the urban and middle-class Muslim vote and thwarted challenges by the Islamist PAS. At about the same time, the PML was doing much the same thing to the JI in Pakistan.

In Muslim-majority countries where the factors listed above do not exist or are weak, the prospects that Muslim Democracy will emerge are much lower. Yet even in such societies, the activities of Muslim Democrats elsewhere may prove relevant to local political discussions. In particular, if and when Muslim Democracy gains coherence, it will become readier for export to countries unable to produce it from scratch. Muslim Democracy can travel. In the 1990s, Pakistan's PML consciously sought to imitate Malaysia's UMNO. More recently, the rise of the Turkish AKP has been noted in Arab circles, secular, official, and Islamist alike. In Egypt, the Islamist Muslim Brotherhood has been keenly watching developments in Turkey, and some within Brotherhood ranks have begun taking measured steps toward the middle. In Algeria, it is the government that has been encouraging the Turkish model by trying to push the Islamic Salvation Front (FIS) to start acting more like the AKP.

The rise of Muslim Democracy suggests that the values of Muslims—which are not to be confused with the demands of Islamists—can interact with practical election strategies to play the main role in shaping political ideas and driving voter behavior.[6] In the end, Muslim Democracy represents the triumph of practice over theory, and perhaps of the political over the Islamic. The future of Muslim politics is likely to belong to those who can speak to Muslim values and ethics, but within the framework of political platforms fit to thrive in democratic settings.

After 1945, Christian Democracy sought to change Catholic attitudes toward democracy in order to channel religious values into mass politics.[7] Christian Democracy drew on Catholic identity, but also related it to social programs and welfare concerns. Christian Democrats provided the means for conservative religious values to find expression in secular politics. The rise of Christian Democracy reflected the desire of Church leaders to provide a voice for Catholic views in democracies, but it was also the result of strategic choices by political actors who saw opportunity in mobilizing religious values to further their political interests.[8]

Similar forces are now at work in some Muslim-majority countries, with ripple effects that will likely be felt throughout the Muslim world. Like the Catholic Church in the last century, Islamic-oriented parties are grasping the need to relate religious values to secular politics. As was also the case in Europe, secular parties and politicians are sensing the benefits of including appeals to religious values in their platforms. Thus Muslim Democracy, like Christian Democracy before it, is emerging as a political tendency that is strongly tied to both the democratic process and the use of direct appeals to the concerns of religious voters.

Limits and Potential

Considered together, the cases of Pakistan and Turkey point to the limits as well as the potential of Muslim Democracy. They help us to discern what is driving the rise of Muslim Democracy, what it stands for, whom it represents, and what challenges it faces. Ironically, Turkey has moved in a more liberal direction even though its Muslim Democratic party springs from Islamist roots, whereas in Pakistan the push toward Muslim Democracy that the non-Islamist PML began has been cut short by a military takeover. Economic factors figure prominently in both cases, and in both the military has played a large role, albeit with vast differences between one case and the other.

In Pakistan, 1988 saw a period of military rule come to a close with the mysterious midair death of General Zia, whose regime had mixed authoritarianism with Islamization. The main prodemocracy force at the time was the secular-leftist Pakistan People's Party (PPP). To limit PPP gains in the 1988 elections and guard their own interests, the departing generals cobbled together a PML-Islamist coalition called the Islamic Democratic Alliance (IJI).

Between 1988 and 1993, the power struggle between the PPP and the IJI plus the military's continued meddling transformed right-of-center politics into more than a tool for keeping civilian institutions weak. In 1990 the IJI won the elections after the military dismissed the PPP government. As the IJI's several parts, now secure in government, began to pursue their own respective agendas, the coalition frayed. The PML and the Islamists both began to sense a chance to dominate Pakistani politics as never before—under conditions of elected civilian rule. The PML moved first, distancing itself from both the generals and the Islamists (who remained close to each other) to wage the 1993 election campaign on its own with a platform that promised economic growth while placating nationalist and Muslim sensibilities. The latter strategy involved stealing such staples of Islamist rhetoric as the call for the enforcement of shari'a—although to please its more secular supporters the PML never did more than gesture at this goal.

Although the PPP wound up winning the October 1993 parliamentary elections, the PML's gambit succeeded at least in part. The party carried the Muslim vote and pushed JI to the margins with a dismal showing. This was the first time in the Muslim world that political maneuvering within a competitive electoral process had put a brake on Islamism. The next election, in 1997, only made the trend more evident as the PML returned to power with almost two-thirds of the seats in the National Assembly while the Islamists found themselves reduced to their smallest parliamentary contingent ever. To achieve this, the PML had cast itself simultaneously as a modern democratic party that was committed to the development of Pakistan and as the standard-bearer of Islamic identity—the latter a claim bolstered by the PML's success in taking over seats once held by avowed Islamists.[9] As is shaping up to be the case in Turkey today, it was the promise of Islamic legislation rather than its fulfillment that proved a sufficiently popular formula.

Between 1993 and 1999, the PML continued to push a mixture of business-friendly economic policies and nationalist-cum-Islamic appeals. Infrastructure development and globalization went hand-in-hand with a nuclear-weapons program, confrontations with India, and rhetorical support for Islamic legislation. Balancing the demands of the various constituencies at which these postures were severally aimed was the PML's challenge. Business interests supported peace with India, for instance, while nationalists and Islamists wanted a tougher stance. As the 1990s wore on, such tensions began to undermine the PML's appeal to its Muslim-minded voter base and gave the military angles to play against the party in advance of the 1999 coup.

It was the PML's very success, however, that set the stage for its fall. The generals began to worry that the party's strategy—which we can now see was a rough-and-ready version of Muslim Democracy—would actually succeed. There followed Musharraf's 1999 coup against Sharif and the systematic dismantling, under military tutelage, of the PML. When Musharraf allowed controlled elections to be held in 2002, Islamists did spectacularly well, rebounding all the way up to a best-ever 20 percent vote share. While Musharraf, especially since 9/11, has postured as Pakistan's sole bulwark against radical Islamist rule, a more accurate statement of the facts would say that the military did full-bore Islamism a huge favor by yanking the PML from power and stopping the country's uncertain yet real progress toward Muslim Democracy.

Turkish Trailblazers

In Turkey, the 1990s were a decade of struggle between Islamists and the military. Turkey's powerful military, unlike Pakistan's, did not support Islamist activism, and was restrained in its actions by its own commitment to democracy, economic reform, and European Union (EU) dictates regarding the rule of law.

The end of a bout of direct military rule in the early 1980s had opened the door for Islamists to enter politics. In 1987 Necmettin Erbakan organized the Welfare Party (RP) to marshal Islamist support among the lower and lower-middle classes as well as the booming independent private sector. By 1994 the RP was winning municipal races in Istanbul and Ankara. A year later, it took 22 percent of the vote in national parliamentary elections. In 1996 the RP formed a governing coalition with the secular True Path Party. Erbakan became prime minister of Atatürk's militantly secular Kemalist republic.

The Turkish military, long the fierce keeper of Kemalism's secular-nationalist flame, was not reconciled to an Islamist ascendancy. Beginning in early 1997, the generals launched what Cengiz Çandar has dubbed a "postmodern coup," manipulating the courts and the parliamentary process to upend Erbakan's government.[10] The RP found itself under a formal ban for transgressing the constitution's secularist red lines. Some of the party's activists tried to organize a new formation called the Virtue Party, but in 2001 that too was banned. Right-wing and especially nationalist parties stepped into the resulting gap by including appeals to traditional Muslim values in secular platforms. The lesson was not lost on Islamist politicians.

The military's politico-juridical strike against the Islamists split the Muslim-values bloc. In 2002 a group of younger Islamist politicians under Erdoğan—the onetime mayor of Istanbul who had just served a jail term on charges of inflaming religious passions—broke with Erbakan to form the AKP, leaving the Virtue Party's traditional-Islamist rump to rename itself the Felicity Party. The November 2002 elections were an AKP romp, as the party won a clear plurality of the popular vote and a huge majority of the seats in parliament.[11] Felicity won a scant 2.5 percent of the vote nationwide, well short of the 10 percent needed for parliamentary representation.

Many AKP members once belonged to the Welfare and Virtue parties. Yet there are also middle-class and lower-middle–class elements with no history of Islamist ties. In many ways, the AKP is less an extension of Welfare and Virtue than a reconstruction of the center-right, economically liberal Motherland Party (ANAP) of Turgut Özal, the architect of Turkey's bold plunge into democracy and the global economy in the 1980s.

More than two years into its rule, the AKP is still an electoral strategy in search of a governing agenda. It lacks a clear platform, much less a fully thought-out approach to the role of Islam in politics. And yet its experience so far is important in several respects. First, it is a case in which Islamist activists embraced a process of moderation and pragmatic change. Second, it highlights the factors that govern the rise of Muslim Democracy. Third, it gives us the best picture we have so far of what Muslim Democracy might become and what it might stand for. Then too, the AKP's case tells much about the tensions that inhere in the development of Muslim Democracy, the consolidation of its political position, and how it can contribute to the institutionalization of liberal democracy.

The AKP is the brainchild of Virtue Party moderates, led by Erdoğan, who concluded that Turkey's military would never allow an overtly Islamist party back into power, and—still more importantly—that the ban on Islamic parties was helping other right-of-center parties such as the Nationalist Action Party, which had come to hold nearly a quarter of the seats in parliament by 1999. Erdoğan and his colleagues realized that there was a robust base of Muslim-minded voters, and that the military would never allow an Islamist party to tap that base. Consequently, the AKP presented itself as a center-right party that appealed to Muslim values only indirectly, through the medium of more generically traditional values. By sublimating Muslim-minded politics into a broader appeal to traditional and conservative values in a society where the political center of gravity is on the center-right, the AKP was able to put together the wide support base that became the launching pad for its rocket ride to power in 2002.

Part of this skillfully executed effort involved crafting appeals that traveled across class lines. The AKP is popular in Istanbul and Ankara slums where Islamists have become known for their efficient management of social services such as law enforcement, sewage disposal, and trash pickup. The AKP watchword of "conservative democracy" (the phrase that Erdoğan prefers to "Muslim democracy," in part to allay military and EU fears that he might be a theocrat in a necktie[12]) also appeals to the "Anatolian tigers"—the pious and prosperous Muslims of the new private sector, whose "green capitalism" forms the basis of the independent bourgeoisie.[13] To keep those with more traditional Islamist leanings on board, the AKP is often more vociferous on secular matters (such as criticism of Israel) than on their purely religious concerns.

The Burdens and Limits of Power

The AKP must now master the challenge, common to all democratic parties, of balancing a set of divergent constituent demands within a single winning platform. Power and its responsibilities arguably make this harder. The urban poor like populist economics. The business community wants tightly managed fiscal and monetary policy that meets EU admissions standards.

Many AKP voters expect the party to tackle contentious symbolic issues such as the current ban on women's headscarves. With an eye on their conservative and nationalist supporters who do not necessarily favor overtly religious politics, AKP leaders shied away from the headscarf issue, and instead endorsed a bill that would criminalize adultery, for the former seems more like a purely "Islamic" issue while the latter can be called a matter of upholding "traditional values." Yet even here the AKP has faced problems: When the EU strongly objected to the adultery bill, the AKP quickly dropped it. The emphasis on "conservative" as distinguished from "Muslim" democracy in AKP parlance is also meant to help position the party as a potential partner for the Christian Democratic parties of the EU nations. What the AKP actually stands for, in short, is being worked out gradually as the limits of the possible become clearer. This degree of pragmatism sits uneasily with the AKP's highminded Islamic idealists (the party's very name in Turkish forms an acronym for "pure," "unsullied," or "honest"), but Erdoğan's personal popularity and the Islamic credentials of the party's founders have helped to bridge the gap.

Since taking office, the AKP has shown more interest in strengthening democracy than in delivering on the demands of its most Muslim-minded supporters. This approach may signal a shift from a state-centered to a society-centered perspective, from a strategy of struggling to capture state power on behalf of Islam to one of seeking to foster a civil society and a deeply rooted democratic order that together will embody Muslim values and limit state power.

This has meant serving the interests of private business, pursuing full EU membership, and deemphasizing the most Islamist aspects of the party's agenda—in other words, promising to create a space within which Muslim values can express themselves, but not pushing an Islamist legislative agenda. As it leads Turkey toward the EU, the AKP is now able credibly to present itself as the country's great champion of modernization—and as such has entered into a de facto competition with the military, which has long claimed that title for itself. In keeping with this, the AKP is increasingly engaging in the de facto promotion of what social theorists call "differentiation," as the party's actions, omissions, "body language," and actual language all seem to be recommending a distinction between the private practice of Islam (encouraged) and its public expression or imposition (approached shyly and with caution, if not abjured outright).

A strongly felt need to keep the military at bay no doubt underlies much of the AKP's strategy. Sensing this, the party's more pious supporters are giving it latitude as it avoids and postpones dealing with Islamic issues. The party also tells the faithful that a "soft" approach to Islam will ensure closer ties between Turkey and Europe. Europe alone has the capability to build institutional boundaries around the military and to protect Turkish democracy. Since liberal democracy is far more receptive to religious expression than is Kemalist secularism, Muslim-minded voters can see an interest in not pushing too hard for their favorite policies now, in hopes of strengthening Turkey's ties to Europe and with them Turkish liberal democracy. Although it is quite likely that Europe too will look unfavorably on drives for certain types of Islamic legislation, the EU will also perhaps do so somewhat less strenuously than will the Turkish military. And of course the Anatolian tigers and the rest of the AKP's private-sector base strongly favor closeness to Europe as a key to Turkey's hopes for prosperity.

As we have seen, the AKP currently has rather limited room for strategic choice, stuck as it is between its various groups of supporters, the Kemalist military and state establishment, and the Europeans. And yet that choice is pushing the party to define the middle in Turkish politics in terms of conservative values that embrace broader Islamic values and concerns, but which are not limited to narrow interpretations of Islamic law. Erdoğan's refusal to let the AKP be called a "Muslim" party bespeaks a large measure of sincerity as well as a dash of calculation.

Will the AKP's gambit succeed? Will the party prove itself able to establish a coherent definition of Muslim Democracy (with or without the actual name) that can channel a politics of Islamic concerns and aspirations into liberal-democratic channels? The answers will come not from the realm of theory and ideology, but from that of pragmatism and politics. Competitions for power—and the calculations to which these competitions give rise—are promoting continual and far-reaching change, regardless of whatever the AKP's original intentions may have been. In the ironic realm of history, even the winners often build other than they know. The result will be "secularization" as Martin Marty once defined it: "a complex set of radical religious changes, in which people act and think religiously in ways which differ from those of the past."[14] This is also the process that Stathis Kalyvas identifies in the development of European Christian Democracy, wherein unsecular political positions, once subjected to the pressures of competition, gradually adapted to the values and rules of democracy.

Turkey presents perhaps the most developed instance of Muslim Democracy, but the process is in evidence elsewhere as well. Even at this early stage it is clear that the sheer competitive logic inherent in open politics is driving Muslim Democracy forward, especially in places where gradual democratization has ensured the continuation of that competition through repeated elections. Established parties, a robust private sector, and an ongoing democratic process (even a rough and troubled one) are the ingredients that need to be in the mix if Muslim Democracy is to put down roots and blossom. Muslim Democracy offers the Muslim world the promise of moderation. As Islamists find themselves facing—or caught up in—the Muslim Democratic dynamic, they will find themselves increasingly facing the hard choice of changing or suffering marginalization.

For an example of what such change might look like, consider a recent *fatwa* (religious decree) that the Shi'ite Muslim Ayatollah Ali Sistani issued ahead of the 30 January 2005 elections in Iraq. Sistani sought to impress upon women their religious duty to vote even if their husbands forbade them to do so. Sistani is well known as a major backer of a unified Shi'ite-candidates' list. Evidently the imperative of notching a big win in the elections—more than any arguments about religious reform or women's rights—compelled the most senior Shi'ite religious leader in Iraq to advocate not only the enfranchisement of women, but even their right (or as Sistani would probably prefer to put it, their specific duty in this case) to disobey their husbands.[15]

Finally, it is Muslim Democracy—and not the creaky and brittle authoritarianisms by which the Muslim world is so beset—that offers the whole world its best hope for an effective bulwark against radical and violent Islamism.[16] Muslim Democracy provides a model for pragmatic change. That change will in turn be the harbinger, not the follower, of more liberal Islamic thought and practice.

47

PUBLIC THEOLOGY AND DEMOCRACY'S FUTURE

—Max L. Stackhouse

The defeat of fascism, the victory of anti-colonial movements, and the collapse of the Soviet Union in the late twentieth century made it appear possible that democracy would spread worldwide, accompanied by a fuller realization of human rights, a global economy that benefits more of the world's people, and a reduction of military threats to the world's security. That "end of history" view may yet prove to be the most probable global direction—some 120 nations adopted democratically oriented constitutions for the first time in the last half century. But there are many reasons to be concerned about the character of a democratic future. Some of the newly independent nations have become one-party states hovering on failure. Some Islamists have repudiated democracy altogether and advocate a return to caliphate governance under shari'a. Russia sometimes seems bound to resume a czarist model of centralized political control, and China is adamant in resisting democratic movements.

Moreover, some oppose the idea of human rights, one of the pillars of democracy, claiming that its implicit assumption—that humanity consists of autonomous individuals—is a modern secularist invention. Still others protest the currently emerging global economy, viewing it as a threat to sovereignty and a design of the rich to exploit the poor. And many fear endless attacks by shadowy, stateless terrorist networks or by ethnic factions, both of which challenge democratic prospects by inducing such a preoccupation with security that democratic freedoms are eroded.

In this situation, the world's most dynamic democracy and only superpower is expected to be not only the world's policeman, but also its godfather, bringing peace, prosperity, and democracy to Afghanistan and Iraq and solving every other problem that appears on the horizon, from Haiti to global warming to the AIDS crisis in sub-Saharan Africa. This charge could tempt the nation into a new imperialism. Even as the United States is criticized for not engaging the problems of the world, it is condemned for intervening everywhere and seducing the world's youth away from their own cultures.·

* Templeton Lectures on Religion and World Affairs, FPRI Wire, October 2004.

The deeper difficulty is that Americans do not have a clear moral or spiritual view of what we are about, of why we believe what we believe and do what we do. How can, should, or may we use our power, and why? And what is the source of that power?

Suppose that the U.S. succeeds in planting democracy throughout the world. One might see this as either cultural imperialism or a justifiable conversion of an unholy tyranny to a just system that corresponds to the deepest levels of human nature and the highest discernible sense of divine intent. That sense might of course simply be the reigning consensus among the currently powerful nations. Does that consensus have, or need, a deeper grounding, an ultimate source and norm of truth and justice that can guide how humanity ought to live?

Historically, advocates of democracy believed that it did. The late medieval "conciliarists" who displaced popes and overrode emperors thought so, as did the Reformers and the Puritans. We know that the deists and theists who advocated the Bill of Rights thought so. And the U.S. didn't hesitate to establish democratic regimes in Cuba and the Philippines at the end of the Spanish-American War, in Germany and Japan at the end of World War II, and in South Korea after the conflict there.

Is there in fact a basis for democracy that is deeper than the fact that it has apparently mostly worked better than other forms, at least in the West? How can we make the case for it today, especially with globalized media, technology, economy, culture, and religions that are beyond the control of any one government?

Critics regularly charge that America is an imperialist nation bent on ruling the world, ready to override other societies with its massive multinational corporations. No doubt some Americans have such interests, but most see their nation as rooted in "that order which we call freedom," with a mission to help others form open societies, adopt democratic values, and establish human rights in a flourishing economy. We have sometimes failed in this mission, but most agree on the mission.

However, religious leaders, theologians, political leaders, and commentators have failed to enunciate the basis for our mission, or identify ways to reform it when it goes wrong. Can we justly clarify what it is that makes us ready to send our young men and women to kill and die for democracy?

No civilization has yet endured that did not have a religious vision at its core. History is littered with the rubble of empires that fell as much by spiritual emptiness as by economic and military weakness or external pressure. But the enduring civilizations have had religious cores that touch the hearts and minds of the people, becoming the moral architecture to guide the leaders and evoke sacrificial commitments. These enable the societies' continual renewal. It is not that everyone agrees with the religious vision, or has to, but that there is a framework within which debate takes place.

One cannot imagine trying to understand the politics of China or India without reference to Confucianism or Hinduism, or the systems of government in Southeast Asia or the Middle East without understanding Buddhism or Islam, or what is going on in the EU without reference to the legacy of traditional Christendom (even if the EU's current advocates resist any reference to religion in its new constitution). Nor can we understand the U.S. without an awareness of Protestantism's historic influence—or of the failure of its mainline traditions to define the urgent social issues—and of the rise of Evangelicalism and Pentecostalism, on the one hand, and post–Vatican II Catholicism, on the other, as they seek to offer other perspectives on the ultimate issues. It is not the duty of religious organizations to make public policy, as some try to do, but it is their responsibility to seek to influence people's consciences so that their political decisions will be informed by moral and spiritual convictions.

Harvard professor Samuel Huntington has pointed out that many have tried to interpret the world as if religion were not central to societies and politics. But he argues that life cannot be understood exclusive of religious ideas, as they are incarnate in the dominant values of the culture. Indeed, Huntington speaks of the irrelevance of purely secular thought to contemporary politics, holding that politics is and must be religious:

> During the 20th century, a secular century, Lenin, Ataturk, Nehru, Ben Gurion, and the Shah (for instance) all defined the identity of their countries in the secular century's terms. That has changed, the Shah is gone, the Soviet Union is gone, and in its place is a Russia that in public statements identifies itself quite explicitly with Russian Orthodoxy. In Turkey, India, and Israel, major political movements are challenging the secular definition of identity. Politicians in many societies have found that religion either is crucial to maintaining their legitimacy as rulers or must be suppressed because it presents a challenge to that legitimacy.[1]

Societies do tend to have common features in the sense that we can study them comparatively and see how they similarly adapt to similar conditions and interests. Yet, societies develop differently because they are bent in different directions by distinctive religions; regulating convictions have become woven into cultural values.

Some of the regulating convictions that shape democracy become clear when we speak of human rights, which are affirmed by the vision behind democracy, notwithstanding our horrible record with regard to slavery and women's rights, and the betrayal of our own principles in wartime, from the early struggles with Native Americans to Abu Ghraib in 2004. Still, the conviction that humans have rights has prevailed again and again. Indeed, even in dark moments, prophetic voices have drawn on biblical roots to demand the recognition that each person is made in the image of God and thus has inalienable rights—even the criminal, the enemy, the heretic, the prisoner, and the terrorist.

As Michael Perry, one of the nation's leading authorities on law and morality, has put it, "some things should never be done to anyone; and some things should be done for everyone."[2] That is why the authors of America's Declaration of Independence and the UN's Declaration of Human Rights could appeal to biblical principles to advocate rights. They are "self-evident truths" that shape consciences, civilizations, and history. When one appeals to human rights in the face of tyranny, torture, servitude, arbitrary arrest, extortion, discrimination, or religious persecution, one has played a valid moral trump, and the people have the basis to demand a law code and to form judicial process as a recourse and remedy. The awareness of such principles gives hope for democratic vitality under just law.

A second feature of society that gives hope for democracy has to do with economic life. Capitalism is the most efficient and productive economic system yet to be devised, and it is sweeping the world. It improves the well-being of most people, including the poor. Not only parts of South America and the "little tigers" of East Asia, but also the two most populous nations of the world, India and China, have turned to versions of capitalism, making it likely that the World Bank and UN millennium goal of halving world poverty within ten years can be met. However, these same trends will also increase inequality. A great many are raised a little, and a substantial number are raised a good bit, but only a few are raised a great deal, widening the gap between the wealthy and the still struggling. A free society does not demand enforced equality of economic status, but it must work to equalize opportunity.

The formation of new middle classes and the rising aspirations of those who have grasped the lower rungs of the ladder increase the prospects for democracy. People with some financial means and even relative security are better able to educate their children, adopt new technologies, develop more stable lifestyles, and migrate out of dependency. They gain some command over their destinies, demand their freedom from restrictive constraints, and become more concerned about developing excellence in various areas of their lives—professional, educational, environmental, and institutional. They deal with others with greater integrity and seek to provide goods or services that make them contributing members of society.

But the formation of new middle classes does not guarantee democracy's development. Only some parts of the middle classes begin to extend economic opportunities, form communities of commitment, and exercise citizen participation. The prospect that the new middle classes will seek to extend democratic possibilities depends on their "calling." It is one thing to have a job and a career, it is quite another to see what one does in all the daily rounds of life as being under the scrutiny of a God who cares how we live and has purposes for our lives. Max Weber probably had it about right when he argued that this doctrine of vocation in the world played a distinctive role in bringing about the asceticism that generated the modern middle classes and its quest for excellence and professionalism.

Today's massive conversions to Pentecostalism in Latin America and Africa, and to Evangelicalism in Asia, replicate the earlier Reformation dynamics, though usually without the same doctrinal apparatus. This is also the case with the growth of parallel movements in America, in the "mega-churches" that puzzle the mainline churches that are declining in membership. Those given the opportunity to move toward the middle classes are questing for a new ordering of their lives, and these movements are drawing people into bonds of discipline and are often less tolerant of libertine lifestyles.

There are two key doctrinal points here that support democratic prospects: first, that humans are made in the image of God, and second, that God calls each person to live a godly life that is manifest in the development of excellence in all areas of worldly life. These doctrinal points are incarnate in the now public dynamics that are globalizing our world, one working through the attempt to articulate principles of justice, the other appearing in the forms of increased productivity and disciplined lifestyles. One aids democratic prospects from above, one from below. Both form a new middle.

I believe democracy does have a theological base, but a less direct one. It usually depends on a basically mechanical and statistical procedure whereby each person votes to determine leadership or policy. That procedure involves only two agents—individual votes, cumulatively tabulated, and the state, the organized body that manages the election and accepts its results. The Terrors of the French Revolution and of the Red Guard's Cultural Revolution remind us of the perils of the mobocracy into which mere populism can degenerate, while the fact that both Hitler and Stalin claimed to be elected reminds us of what statism can become.

If a democracy is to have an inner moral fiber, it must have several other things besides voters and the state, an independent legal system that recognizes the voters' human rights and civil liberties, and a free economic system. It must also have

- schools that teach critical thinking;
- media that provide information and inspiration from a range of perspectives;
- stable families that nurture responsible persons and inculcate moral habits and spiritual insight;
- political parties that voice the needs and hopes of the people and form the "loyal opposition" when they are not in power;
- voluntary associations that take up causes or perform services that need attention but are not the obvious duty of the government; and
- above all, independent religious communities able to treat both the political and social aspects of life from a transcendent point of view.

In short, a viable democracy depends on a division of powers not only within the government, but among the institutions outside state control in a viable civil society. This demands a separation of church and state, with the religious organizations providing an organized moral and spiritual center of loyalty that does not allow interests to be the only basis of politics.

Civil society is strongest where multiple religious institutions are well developed. Democracy as a political design was first mentioned in ancient Greece, but it did not flourish there: it fell every time it was tried to tyranny, mobocracy, plutocracy, or imperialism, for the character of ancient Greek religion could not sustain a moral core. Democracy only flourished after the church became a center of loyalty and began to form schools, hospitals, guilds, parties, and associations for fellowship and service, in what was a long and slow, but providential, process.

Other forms of democracy, most notably deriving from the French Revolution and influencing in various ways the German Enlightenment, the Russian Revolution, and the secular democrats of the Americas, renounced the idea that religion was a necessary part of democracy. Secular democrats attempted to establish a state-guided democracy based on what Rousseau called the "general will." Religion would be removed from public discourse, even prohibited from public display (as we have seen in the recent banning of the wearing of headscarves by Muslims and nuns, in schools and government offices).

This development was partly understandable, for there are forms of religious dogma that do not defend human rights and that inhibit economic development. And there are movements claiming roots in the Christian church that are anti-intellectual and sectarian. These groups hate pluralism and engender enclaves of self-righteous piety that worship a God who only condemns the world.

But their critique of bad religion banishes too much. The French Revolution yielded Napoleon, Germany's enlightened philosophers easily succumbed to fascism, the Soviet "people's democracy" fell to Bolshevism, and the secular populists of the Americas became prey of liberationist ideologies. As they say now in Latin America, the church opted for the oppressed, and the poor opted for Evangelicalism. Not only must religion be taken seriously, but also the kind of theology that is willing and able to touch the heart and address public issues must be seen as necessary for the future of democracy. A profound theology will press us toward a democracy ordered in a way that accords with God's law and purposes. That poses the critical issues.

All of us have a personal faith, a theology, a set of personal convictions about ultimate reality; and millions of people belong to some organized wing of their religious tradition. Each tradition has a distinctive way of defining the ideal political order. Some are more capable of supporting the conditions under which democracy flourishes than others. Most have some national or international religious body, or chief representatives, who periodically issue statements that have direct political implications—ethical issues framed by a theological tradition tend not to stay under the steeple.

Today, the debate about the morality of the Iraq war is very alive, with theological convictions about "just war" doctrines just below the surface. The question has arisen whether human rights are being compromised for the sake of security and national defense. The issue of the extent to which government should control corporations' ecological or outsourcing practices is also on the agenda, as well as the propriety of limiting abortion or stem-cell research. An open debate about these theologically laden issues is vital to democracy.

Public theology has the task of engaging in public dialogue on such ethical issues. The Judeo-Christian tradition offers two deeply rooted biblical themes that undergird the "principled pluralism" that presses society toward the kind of democracy that is the necessary supplement to the idea of the image of God, on which human rights rest, and to the idea of vocation, on which professional integrity rests. These are the recognition of sin and the possibility of covenant.

Recognizing sinfulness implies awareness that humans and their societies are all imperfect. Thus, every idealistic quest for harmony of all the parts will lead to pride and totalitarianism. The consolidation of power in the hands of the few tempts humanity to an arrogance that corrupts the powerful and either exploits or makes passive the rest. Accordingly, power must be distributed and thereby limited. If each sphere of civil society is well developed, the various spheres can correct one another or cooperate to reform the whole.

That cooperation invites the possibility of forming covenantal relationships. Daniel Elazar, one of the great scholarly gems of the last century, traced this idea through the West's history and documented how, from its roots in ancient Judaism, it was adopted and adapted by certain strands of Christianity and found resonance in many cultures, engendered a passion for a pluralistic democracy, and opposed both the hierarchical authoritarianism found in most classical cultures and the balkanizing atomism of modernity. The idea of covenant is based on the formation of communities of commitment for purposes that include but transcend our human material interests.

Christianity contributed to this concept the idea of love as the inner spirit of covenantal bonding. That is what forms character and reforms society in this life, even though perfection is impossible and forgiveness is necessary. Christians believe that this is what Christ manifest and what is working among us in all the spheres of common life. It is what gives us faith that, in spite of sin, evil will not prevail. Being realistic about sin and confident in the possibility of love allows Christians to believe that there is a moral and spiritual heart of a democratic society and political order.

If these theological motifs are, as I believe, already present deep within democratic life, they need to be made conscious for democracy to flourish and spread. A serious public theology will have to engage the great world religions to find out whether they have comparable concepts and prospects and where they may be able to adjust such motifs for the emerging global civil society. This is another area, for many the newest one, where our theology must be public.

48

PUBLIC RELIGION, DEMOCRACY PROMOTION, AND U.S. FOREIGN POLICY

—Thomas F. Farr

Disagreements over religion in the public square dominate U.S. domestic politics at the moment, but neither the left nor right has adequately addressed religion as an aspect of U.S. foreign policy. Some on both sides have an unhelpful view of Islam that could cripple American efforts to promote democracy in Muslim-majority countries.

The problem is this: even "moderate" Muslims fear that the secular democracy we are selling them is anti-Islam. This not only reduces our influence over political reform, it also plays into the hands of Islamist terrorists. Iraq's Grand Ayatollah Ali Sistani has said that U.S. sponsored secularism was "Iraq's gravest threat." Not surprisingly, Osama bin Laden has condemned as apostates anyone who seeks democracy, which he calls "the religion of unbelievers."

This kind of opposition to democracy has been exacerbated by decades of U.S. backing for secular authoritarian rulers who punished even peaceful public expressions of Islam. Some believe we are changing those failed policies, but the facts are troubling. Even if we do encourage serious reform in places like Egypt, Pakistan, or Saudi Arabia, U.S. foreign policy has no systematic strategy in place to overcome the presumption that democracy is anti-Islamic. For all its talk of "engaging Islam" the Department of State simply does not "do religion" in Muslim-majority societies. If anyone talks to the Iraqis on a regular basis about the relationship between religion and politics in an Islamic democracy, it's more likely to be a U.S. Marine than an American diplomat.

If Muslims do not get the religio-political balance right in places like Iraq, even successful elections are unlikely to produce enduring democracy. And if the fledging democracies we midwife in Muslim-majority contexts do not endure, if they collapse into civil war or are supplanted by radical Islamism, America's security will be plagued for the foreseeable future by a continuing stream of recruits to al Qaeda and other terrorist groups.

My 21 years in the Foreign Service left me with an abiding admiration for America's diplomats. But, truth be told, many would prefer a root canal in a foreign dentist's chair to a discussion on religion and politics with a Muslim leader. Often part of a secular elite

* *The Brandywine Review of Faith & International Affairs* 3, no. 1 (Spring 2005): 51–52.

that earnestly desires the privatization of religion, our diplomats are further handicapped by the absence of systematic training or any strategic context for discussing religion. This hands-off attitude was reflected in the 9/11 Commission Report, which simply punted on the issue of reconciling religion and democracy. "Lives guided by religious faith . . . represent no threat to us."[1] Case closed.

Some members of America's political class cling to a head-in-the-sand "secularization thesis" dominant among scholars of international relations. It holds that modernity necessitates the privatization of religion, if not its disappearance. Within democracies, religiosity will be relegated (if it survives at all) to the safe confines of churches, synagogues, and mosques, where it will not affect public policy.

Unfortunately, while most conservatives reject these views, many refuse to oppose their dominance in U.S. foreign policy, at least when it comes to Muslims. Most conservatives believe America's founding generation grounded U.S. democracy in religious freedom, not in order to ban religion from the public square but to ensure its flourishing as the very basis for public policy. They have fought, with limited success, against the tide of secularization to preserve a vital, religion-friendly democracy, based on the idea that all are created equal and endowed by God with inalienable rights.

But too many are unwilling to acknowledge and support Muslims who have a similar understanding of their own religion, and the political reform it can yield. Many are convinced that Islam is simply a launching pad for terrorism, too deeply flawed to warrant any latitude for its public manifestations. While there are certainly grounds for such fears, to allow them to paralyze U.S. efforts to promote democracy is foolish.

What can U.S. foreign policy do about all this? Part of the remedy is already in place at Foggy Bottom, but senior level leaders need to give it their personal support. In 1998 Congress passed a law requiring the State Department to advance religious freedom as a core element of U.S. foreign policy and established an office headed by an Ambassador-at-Large to spearhead the effort. In the pre-9/11 era, few of the law's sponsors saw it as a weapon in the war against terror, and many who talk about post-9/11 diplomacy seem unaware of its existence. The Ambassador and his staff have made significant strides, and have had an impact on, for example, the interim Iraqi constitution. But the office is still viewed within State as custodian of a special interest issue imposed by Congress, its subject utterly unconnected to the broader goals of U.S. foreign policy.

U.S. religious freedom policy can and should be employed as part of the nation's refurbished democracy project in Muslim-majority countries. American democracy was founded on religious freedom, defined not as the privatization of religion but its accommodation to the public square within carefully defined limits. America should provide models of democracy that will not ask Muslims to check their religion at the door, but will require them to elevate into politics those aspects of their faith that value human dignity and freedom. Our own nation's security depends on it.

— Section IX —

RELIGIOUS FREEDOM AND HUMAN RIGHTS

49

DEBATING INTERNATIONAL HUMAN RIGHTS
The "Middle Ground" for Religious Participants

—Paul A. Brink

While the assertion that religious believers have much to contribute to the world of international affairs is not new, the unique times in which we find ourselves lend particular urgency to the task of encouraging faith-based solutions to problems that secular modernity seems ill-equipped to address. Events of recent years have further undermined the already shaky confidence on the part of Western moderns that they have successfully understood the world. And as modernity's vision turns cloudy, more space has opened for the articulation of different visions of how religions, philosophies, and worldviews understand and engage the world around them.

While people of faith may find encouragement in this, there remains a great challenge, one that requires particular care and sensitivity. It is typically understudied and poorly considered, a problem that can result in great difficulties for those who are practitioners in the field, as well as for those trained to study the field as academics. The great challenge to which I refer is that of engaging in the international field in a way that does justice to the diversity of worldviews and commitments at play, but also in a way that does justice to one's *own* view.

The difficulty is particularly evident in the debate over the definition of human rights in national and international declarations and covenants. There continues to be a serious (and occasionally productive) debate on whether the notion of human rights is an inherently Western concept, that is, whether it is one that can be applied to other cultures only with difficulty. Even within the West, there are great debates concerning human rights, particularly concerning the manner in which they are justified philosophically (are they rooted in nature? God? something else?), their extent (political and civil? social and economic?), and where they might be located (individuals? groups? cultures?). Not surprisingly, the religious and philosophic views of the participants in such debates are typically implicated in the arguments made back and forth. How can we advocate for our own conception of universal rights in a way that is respectful of those who do not share our

* The Brandywine Review of Faith & International Affairs 1, no. 2 (Fall 2003): 13–20.

particular religious and philosophical foundations, yet not water down our views so much that we sacrifice our own integrity?

Believers do not want to be accused (especially in an age of "civilization conflict" and growing nervousness about American "empire") of imposing their religious or philosophical worldviews on others. But at the same time, no one wants to experience censorship or otherwise find oneself forced by conventions of liberalism to "translate" one's voice into a secular tongue. In other words, our challenge is one of finding ways for people of faith to speak and act in international relations—politically, respectfully—while at the same time keeping their "convictional particularities" intact.

In this essay I approach the issue from the perspective of a political theorist. Using as a starting point the work of political theorist John Rawls—the twentieth century's leading proponent of philosophical liberalism—I seek theoretical room, first within liberalism, but eventually outside it, for what I am calling "middle-ground" discourse. What is this middle ground? It is the space in principled public dialogue lying between "Thus saith the Lord"—type claims, on the one hand, and on the other hand situations where religious views must be pressed (awkwardly and artificially) into secular molds before they are granted legitimacy. To date, Western Christians have not been very successful at finding this middle ground, and part of the reason for this lack of success is that contemporary Western liberalism has not proven to be very supportive of it—indeed, it will occasionally go to great lengths to undermine it. Accordingly, my project is to do the reverse: I am seeking firm theoretical foundations for the middle ground, that is, a playing field respectful of both secular and religious worldviews.

The challenge of discerning a middle ground at the international level is acute, especially because of the profound and complex diversity of worldviews seeking to contribute to the dialogue. Defining its parameters is additionally difficult because the international arena is so devoid of authoritative institutions: legislatures, supreme courts, constitutions. Typically, when one considers the question domestically, within the context of American politics for example, one is drawn into debates concerning constitutional and legal restrictions—that we not establish a religion, and that we maintain things like freedom of speech and freedom of religion. However, the challenge that international politics represents can provide opportunities unavailable in the domestic sphere. Internationally, the lack of a strict constitutional or legal framework means that when we speak of restrictions on discourse, these tend to be moral and strategic in nature, rather than constitutional and legal. Debate shifts to questions of a significantly different nature, such as whether we are duly respecting Confucian values in our deliberations, whether people of faith from Islamic and Christian communities can come together as allies against strict secular worldviews, and so on. In this way, we may find that the international sphere can offer possibilities for the type of dialogue and decision-making that is all too rare domestically, coming closer in fact to what "politics," properly understood, is about.

A functioning middle ground is essential for a wide range of political goods, one of the most important of which at the international level is achieving a working agreement on human rights. As such, there is much that can be learned by looking closely at the real-world politics of producing the world's most venerable human rights document, the Universal Declaration of Human Rights. In what follows, I examine the negotiations within the United Nations Commission on Human Rights occasioned by the drafting of this seminal statement of basic rights, before moving to discuss broader implications for faith-based global engagement today.

Given the deep cultural and religious pluralism of the global public square, one might expect that any attempt by the nations of the world to proclaim together a "universal" declaration of human rights would be a project doomed to failure. How might agreement ever be achieved, given the diversity? Yet, we do have such an agreement—a document that has had extraordinary global influence and has come to possess tremendous moral authority. How can this be? How was it possible for people to agree, across all their other differences, about the rights people have? And given their philosophical, religious, and ideological differences, how did the delegates speak to one another out of their varying commitments? How close did the delegates come to finding the "middle ground"?

The Universal Declaration of Human Rights

At the time of the establishment of the United Nations, a number of countries and nongovernmental organizations made a significant attempt to entrench a strong human rights document in the UN Charter. Although that attempt failed, advocates were able to extract a commitment from the Great Powers to establish a Commission on Human Rights with the mandate to develop such a document. Under the leadership of the American delegate, the recently widowed Eleanor Roosevelt, the United Nations Commission on Human Rights began its deliberations in 1947.

Already in its first set of meetings, the Commission found itself paralyzed by foundational differences concerning the preamble to the Declaration, differences that immediately brought into sharp relief the philosophical and religious divisions within the Commission. The delegate from Lebanon, Charles Malik, summarized their difficulties well when he noted that "we are raising the fundamental question, what is man?"[1] Disagreements were not about matters of fact, or conflicts of interests, but the very nature of the person. "Is man merely a social being?" asked Malik. "Is he merely an animal? Is he merely an economic being?" Malik's own position, for example, emphasized the essential inviolability of individual conscience over against the state; his view was clearly informed by a religious vision of man and society, and he gave passionate, articulate, and well-reasoned accounts of that vision.

Malik's difficulty, however, was that the more he developed his argument—the more he added detail, the more he attempted to persuade others of his foundational reasons— the more he provoked his opponents. His conundrum was shared, not surprisingly, by others as well. The fact that delegates were able to give ever more detailed explanations for their views on human rights did not make their views more persuasive to those who held different philosophic and religious views. Rather, they only seemed false in greater detail.

The Yugoslavian delegate, Vladislav Ribnikar, for example, reacted quite strongly to Malik's position, proclaiming that human liberty cannot be found in opposition to state authority, but rather consists in "perfect harmony between the individual and the community." He charged that Malik's view of rights, stemming as it did from freedom of conscience and religious belief, would "only consider the rights favored by the ruling classes."[2] Notably, it was not only the late 1940s east-west divides that were causing problems. In their presentations, for example, the Americans and British typically spoke of the rights of the "individual," while the French, Indians, and others, including Malik, were uncomfortable with that term, preferring instead to speak of the rights of "persons," the better to capture the social nature of personhood, while also avoiding the Marxist variants.[3]

Attempts to sway the conversation away from ideological and philosophic disputes toward more pragmatic matters failed. Said one delegate to such an attempt by the Indian delegation: "Whatever you may say, Madam, must have ideological presuppositions, and no matter how much you might fight shy of them, they are there, and you either hide them or you are brave enough to bring them out into the open and see them and criticize them."[4] While this was true enough, it did not resolve the difficulty: the more that delegates brought their presuppositions into the open, the more distant seemed agreement. The debate appeared intractable.

Eventually, the Commission attempted what committees everywhere do with debates that seem intractable—it appointed a subcommittee, consisting of Roosevelt, Malik, Peng-chun Chang, the Chinese delegate, and John Humphrey, a Canadian representing the UN Secretariat. The debate continued, however. Consider Roosevelt's account of their first meeting:

> They arrived in the middle of a Sunday afternoon, so we would have plenty of time to work. It was decided that Dr. Humphrey would prepare the preliminary draft, and as we settled down over the teacups, one of them made a remark with philosophical implications, and a heated discussion ensued. Dr. Chang was a pluralist and held forth in charming fashion on the proposition that there is more than one kind of ultimate reality. The Declaration, he said, should reflect more than simply Western ideas and Dr. Humphrey would have to be eclectic in his approach. His remark, though addressed to Dr. Humphrey, was really directed at Dr. Malik, from whom it drew a prompt retort as he expounded at some length the philosophy of Thomas Aquinas. Dr. Humphrey joined enthusiastically in the discussion, and I remember that at one point Dr. Chang suggested that the Secretariat might well spend a few months studying the fundamentals of Confucianism![5]

As the philosophic debates invaded even the subcommittee's deliberations, the procedure ultimately adopted by the Commission was a two-stage process in which two people working individually did the bulk of the drafting of the text. This was then thoroughly debated by the drafting subcommittee and by the Commission, before going on to the Economic and Social Council and the General Assembly of the UN. Humphrey's initial draft resolved few of the foundational questions. In fact, many were amplified, as Humphrey included and affirmed both the political and civil rights familiar to the Anglo-French tradition, but also the economic and social rights found in the Soviet, Scandinavian, and some Latin American constitutions.

However, by the second draft, a "middle ground" began to come into view. The French delegate, René Cassin, committed himself to grounding both sets of rights in a way that was substantive but also acceptable to all the philosophical and religious viewpoints sitting around the table. In Cassin's own words, the challenge was one of developing a document "that did not require the Commission to take sides on the nature of man and society, or to become immured in metaphysical controversies, notably the conflict among spiritual, rationalist, and materialist doctrines on the origin of human rights."[6] Accordingly, Cassin had to reject the language found in many rights documents around the world, which then and now often contain explicitly philosophic or religious justifications bound to be controversial.

It was Cassin's skill in navigating this difficulty that made the Declaration successful. In his work, Cassin could take advantage of assistance from an unusual source—a new committee, the Committee on the Theoretical Bases of Human Rights, had recently been established by UNESCO. Essentially a committee of philosophers, it was chaired by E. H. Carr of Cambridge and included among its members Richard McKeon of the University of Chicago as well as the French social philosopher Jacques Maritain. The question that they set about to consider was how an agreement might be possible "among men who come from the four corners of the earth and who belong not only to different cultures and civilizations, but to different spiritual families and antagonistic schools of thought."[7] Towards this end, the group solicited input concerning the foundations of human rights from statesmen, scholars, philosophers, and religious leaders around the world: Aldous Huxley, Pierre Teilhard de Chardin, and Mohandas Gandhi, among others. Somewhat ironically, notes Mary Ann Glendon in her review, this committee of philosophers was coming to very practical conclusions at the same time that the Commission of politicians was bogged down in philosophical debate.[8]

A central finding of the committee was an affirmation from non-Western respondents that the sources of human rights were present in their traditions, although not expressed or justified in ways familiar to Westerners. Building upon these affirmations, the philosophers' committee was able to develop a list of principles common to all or most of the cultural and religious traditions surveyed, and they offered this agreement as sufficient to support something like a universal declaration of human rights.[9]

The committee was careful to emphasize that this agreement was not deep. In particular, justifications for these rights differed tremendously. Quoting the committee:

> The UNESCO Committee is convinced that the members of the United Nations share common convictions on which human rights depend, but it is further convinced that those common convictions are stated in terms of different philosophic principles on the background of divergent political and economic systems.[10]

Or, in Maritain's words, "we agree on these rights, *providing we are not asked why*. With the 'why,' the dispute begins."[11]

In particular, the committee noted numerous concerns regarding the predominant Western view that respect for rights must depend nearly exclusively upon notions of entitlement; many argued rather that rights be placed within a larger framework of duty or virtue or citizenship. However, strong disagreements such as this one were seen by the committee not as fatal flaws, but rather as signs of the agreement's widespread support. Again quoting Maritain, the agreement was "not on common speculative notions, but on common practical notions, not on the affirmation of the same conception of the world, man, and knowledge, but on the affirmation of the same set of convictions concerning action."[12] The common project could move forward without agreement on the reasons for it. Maritain acknowledged that this level of agreement was, in an important sense, unsatisfying, indeed "the last refuge of intellectual agreement among men." He continued, however, by asserting that this last refuge was "enough to undertake a great work. . . ."[13]

Cassin adopted this strategy in his revisions. Without adopting any one justification for human rights, and without excluding any, Cassin authored a document that he believed could enjoy universal support. To accomplish this, he introduced a number of new elements to Humphrey's draft: a new preamble, a number of introductory interpretative principles, and a novel organization of the various rights into logical categories. After a great deal of debate and some changes, Cassin's draft was approved by the Commission. After this point, there were several other important philosophical debates—concerning, for example, whether all human beings are in fact endowed with "reason and conscience,"[14] and also concerning the role of the state with respect to these rights—yet most of these were resolved following Cassin's model: seek agreement on the principle, without requiring agreement on the reasons why.

Toward a Theory of the Middle Ground

It is this approach to the fact of pluralism, described by the philosophers and adopted by Cassin, that is likely to be most helpful to us as we respond to the challenge of international relations introduced above. In the UN negotiation, respecting the plurality among the negotiating parties meant doing away with any requirement that all participants stick to the same script. Indeed, the single most important contributor to the success of the deliberations was that participants were not asked to accept a single account of the foundation of human rights. This was true in two respects, and both have implications for current debates.

First, no one was asked to "convert" to another view. After the first few meetings, a general recognition was reached that no one religious or philosophic view of human rights was going to "win out" over the others—pluralism was here to stay, even within the committee room. In the speech in which the Declaration was introduced to the General Assembly, Malik proclaimed this plurality of views as a strength, not a weakness; respecting the pluralism of foundations had resulted in a document built on a "firm international basis wherein no regional philosophy or way of life was permitted to prevail."[15]

Second, delegates were not asked to support a foundation for human rights that was somehow independent of all views in the room and therefore "neutral." This can be a tempting choice in situations of diversity; we might call it "the politics of abstraction," an attempt to create an abstract justification that is independent of any and all religious views, and that asks participants to confine their deliberations to those terms. In this series of negotiations, such an approach seems not to have been seriously considered, at least not explicitly.

Participants were free and in fact encouraged to support the text for whatever reasons they found persuasive, although they could not demand that others support the text for those same reasons. Nor were they required to keep silent about their motivating reasons simply because these were not shared. This was true not only during the drafting phase, but also in the debates in the Economic and Social Council and the UN General Assembly, both of which had to approve the Declaration in turn.

In the General Assembly debates, for instance, there were calls from numerous corners to introduce language in Article 1 declaring that human beings are endowed with reason and conscience "by God," thereby giving a theological foundation to the document. The Chinese delegate, P. C. Chang, argued against the proposal in order to ensure universal support. Significantly, however, he did not advocate establishing an alternative "secular" foundation—not even the words "by nature," which also had been proposed. On the contrary, he suggested that believers "could still find the idea of God" in the assertions that all human beings are born free and equal and endowed with reason and conscience.[16] A number of delegates were explicit in their concern to emphasize the relationship between the text and their religious views. With regard to the article concerning religious freedom, for example, the Muslim delegate from Pakistan, at that point the UN member with the largest Muslim population, declared that supporting the article "involved the honor of Islam," and, during the debates, cited and interpreted the Qur'an for the assembly, in support of his argument that faith could not be compelled.[17]

This, I argue, is a very different model of political decision-making than that to which we are accustomed, particularly in those countries indebted to the British version of liberal democracy. Ultimately, the political discussions that took place within the UN Commission were a variety of the politics of deep pluralism, a politics that demands only an agreement on some principles of respectful but candid coexistence—a constitutional bill of rights, if you will—but does not demand agreement on the reasons for supporting such constitutional principles. In fact, in this version of politics, there are potentially as many justifications for the principles as there are parties to the agreement. And notably, this plurality was not viewed as a weakness, but actually as a *virtue* of the agreement.

The contrast with American liberal democracy could not be greater. Indeed, most liberal democracies are quite concerned to reject such a model as that seen in the UN Commission. In the American context, the most important recent attempt to avoid it was led by political theorist John Rawls in his emphasis upon the use of "public reason" in political debate on important issues. This is the temptation to which I referred above, where participants are asked to confine their deliberations to reasons that can be justified upon a foundation purported to be "independent" of any controversial religious and philosophical views. There are many who still believe that constructive conversation can take place only when there is a common moral framework in which we find ourselves. Perhaps one of the most important lessons of the Commission's negotiations is that this argument does not hold up—it is contradicted both by theory and by experience.

What does this suggest for a search towards a "middle-ground theory"? It suggests, first, that the claims of those people who take their faith seriously in all areas of life, including in their engagement with global issues (people described by theorists such as Nancy Rosenblum as "integralists," Nicholas Wolterstorff as "religiously integrated," and me in other contexts as "seamless garment people")[18] demand certainly as great a respect internationally as they do domestically. Attempts to impose a liberal or other moral framework upon international dialogue are not only exclusive, but risk undermining the very democratic virtues we are trying to support. To restrict dialogue in this way is also spectacularly unwise, for to do so is to forsake the creative ideas and experiences that "integralists" may offer in our search for solutions to the vexing international problems we face.[19]

Finally, a theory of the middle ground will go further than articulating claims of inclusion. It will also entail obligations concerning the nature of that participation. As we consider these obligations—as we consider the ethics of open political engagement—we need to consider two different vantage points: that of the hearer and that of speaker.

From the perspective of the hearer, we must be careful not to insist upon certain modes of argument or reasoning as a condition for speaking with us. We are obligated to respect other parties as equal participants in the process; accordingly we cannot require other participants to borrow a language not their own to make their arguments. There can be no requirement that participants stick to a script, nor a requirement that people keep silent about their motivating reasons. In short, hearers are under an obligation to welcome reasons and arguments based in religious or philosophical views, and although they are under no obligation to agree with them, neither can they discount their political merits merely because they are premised on different grounds than their own.

From the perspective of the speaker, once it is clear that ideological diversity is acknowledged, there would seem to exist a corresponding obligation to speak, and to include one's motivating reasons if one chooses. Further to the goal of articulating middle ground reasons, the speaker should be willing to demonstrate how these motivating reasons have reference to the issue at hand—normally this will make strategic sense in any case. Note that this is not an obligation to make a religious contribution secular or freestanding or neutral or even understandable. Instead, we might speak of this as an obligation to specify what we see as the political implications of our philosophic or religious view.[20]

We might retain the terminology of "public reason" with regard to this obligation, although not in the Rawlsian sense. In the context of the UN Commission's deliberations, for example, there was no single conception of public reason—people could offer any reason that they themselves found persuasive. Rather, their reasons were public in that their *object* was public: the reasons people had for supporting the agreement were offered to the public at large, and they concerned an object of concern to the public—namely, a human rights document vitally concerned with matters of public justice.

From where do these obligations on the part of the speaker and the hearer stem? In the discussion of the Commission's negotiations, I identified as key to success the recognition (articulated most clearly by the philosophers' committee) to permit agreement on a text without demanding agreement on the reasons. But in fact there was a prior, probably implicit, agreement that was equally significant—the shared commitment to the political activity of negotiation itself. For the negotiations to come to fruition, there had to exist a commitment to work towards a text. There had to be a commitment to "the rules of the game." At the most basic level, this probably implied nothing more than agreeing to put aside the recourse to violence. But beyond that point, this meant agreeing to commit to the Commission's method of reaching agreement, which implied a commitment to the corollary principle: recognizing that others were going to support the text for reasons very different than one's own.[21]

The significance of these commitments is a willingness to operate by their terms, and a corresponding obligation to live up to them. The obligations of speaker and hearer are thus, in a sense, self-imposed: they are implied by the commitment to the process. But I think we might go further in this regard. We might also say that these obligations are imposed by the nature of "politics" itself as a sphere of normative discourse. The nature of political debate and decision-making itself will make demands upon faith-based participants—the other participants ought not to impose additional demands as a further condition for inclusion.

The fact of inclusion is highly significant; indeed, a determination that all parties have an equal opportunity to be genuine participants in the politics of international affairs (that is, on their own terms) is more just and ultimately more stabilizing than the search for religious, philosophic, or ideological uniformity among them. By moving toward a greater recognition of the plurality inherent in our social condition, in our politics, and in our reasons, we also move closer to a "middle ground" that preserves particularity even as it promotes public civility.

50

RELIGIOUS LIBERTY AND HUMAN DIGNITY
A Tale of Two Declarations

—Kevin J. Hasson

"We agree on these rights," Jacques Maritain once stated, "*providing we are not asked why.*"[1] He was referring to his work on the 1946 UNESCO Committee on the Theoretical Bases of Human Rights, but he might just as well have been referring to the American intellectual community today: We all agree that there is such a thing as human dignity (who would oppose it?), just so long as we do not have to say why. The "why" of human rights, however, is vitally important. For example, if human rights are widely said to follow from human dignity, then the contours of those rights must depend on the contours of that dignity. Change the basis or the scope of human dignity and the rights, so to speak, go all wrong. This article compares two human rights declarations, one that was unable to state an explicit basis for either rights or dignity, the United Nations' Universal Declaration of Human Rights ("Universal Declaration"),[2] and one that was prepared to argue for both, Vatican II's Declaration on Religious Freedom.[3]

I. Universal Declaration

In 1946 leading thinkers from around the world gathered under the auspices of the United Nations to determine whether a consensus on human rights could be achieved. They reached a limited one,[4] agreeing that such rights existed but not on how, in theory, to ground them.[5] As a result, when the Universal Declaration of Human Rights was promulgated two years later, its Preamble reflected this inability to achieve a consensus, by declaring that a "common understanding of these rights and freedoms, is of the greatest importance for the full realization of [the] pledge"[6] to respect human rights, then failing to explicitly define this "common understanding."[7]

Despite the inability of the Committee to establish a basis for human rights, the rise of totalitarianism made the United Nations' human rights project something of an emergency. After totalitarianism, it became necessary to defend, not merely *some* rights, *some* truths, or *some* moral principles, but the very existence of human rights, of truth, and of morality. Maritain and other thinkers knew it was critical to insist, at the moment of the

* *Harvard Journal of Law & Public Policy* 27, no. 1 (2003): 81–92.

founding of the United Nations, that there are rights—whatever their source—that must be recognized and respected in order to formulate "common principles of action."[8]

The drafters of the Universal Declaration were thus less concerned with attempting to create a theory underlying human rights than they were with the urgent task of agreeing together to protect those rights in practice,[9] leaving for another day a task they still thought vital, that of forging "a common understanding of these rights."[10]

While the Universal Declaration does not lay out a systematic grounding for human rights, it does hint at one. The Preamble implies that the fundamental error behind totalitarianism lies not in political theory, but rather in the human person. Because of a "disregard and contempt for human rights" at the heart of those "barbarous acts which have outraged the conscience of mankind," it was necessary to recognize "the inherent dignity and . . . the equal and inalienable rights of all members of the human family [as] the foundation of freedom, justice, and peace in the world."[11] This notion grounds the basis for justice in the idea of rights, which is somehow connected with "the inherent dignity" of the person. Consequently, it is not the nature of the state we are considering, but the nature of the human person.

The Preamble repeats this point, observing that in the United Nations Charter the member states "reaffirmed their faith in fundamental human rights, [and] in the dignity and worth of the human person,"[12] intertwining again the ideas of human rights and human dignity.

This connection between rights and dignity is no coincidence. As Professor Mary Ann Glendon observes, Maritain himself had insisted that if the future Declaration "were not to be a mere hodgepodge of ideas, it would need a tuning fork or 'key' according to which the rights could be harmonized. Everything depends, [Maritain] said, on 'the ultimate value whereon those rights depend and in terms of which they are integrated by mutual limitations.'"[13] In other words, if the Declaration could not appeal to an ultimate *source* of rights, it could, at least, appeal to an "ultimate value" that would make the document internally coherent. Professor Glendon has no trouble identifying that ultimate value, stating that [in] "the 'key' in which the various rights were to be 'harmonized,' the Universal Declaration belongs to a family of postwar rights instruments that accord their highest priority to human dignity."[14]

Therefore, human dignity is the "ultimate value" that gives coherence to human rights. But if rights somehow depend on dignity, where does dignity come from?

Once again, the Declaration does not specifically identify the roots of human dignity. Article I states that "[a]ll human beings are born free and equal in dignity and rights. They are endowed with reason and conscience and should act towards one another in a spirit of brotherhood."[15] The juxtaposition of freedom, dignity, and rights in the first sentence and reason and conscience in the second implies that human rights somehow follow from human dignity and human dignity follows from human rationality and conscience. Something about human intellect and conscience creates a duty to treat people in a certain way: in a spirit of brotherhood.

This is not just a throwaway line. It is because the drafters of the Universal Declaration believe that humans are naturally rational beings with consciences that they believe disputes may be settled peacefully. According to this logic, human beings give reasons for their actions, confessing to themselves and to one another that their actions are not random. Rather, their actions are based on premises that can be examined and judged by some standards outside of their own preferences. The Universal Declaration says humans possess a conscience that identifies these standards, meaning humans are capable of making moral distinctions, and are under some sort of normative obligation to seek out truth and make choices in accordance with it. The realities of intellect and conscience are what allow one person or society to bring normative obligations to the attention of any other person or society.

It is possible to aspire to resolving disputes through the use of persuasion rather than force only insofar as each individual's reason and conscience correspond to a single reality that all human beings share in common. This is why the Universal Declaration coherently claims in Article 28 that "[e]veryone is entitled to a social and international order in which the rights and freedoms set forth in this Declaration can be fully realized."[16] Without a common rationality and conscience to which all men and women may appeal—that is, a rationality and a conscience, grounded in common human reality itself, that transcend cultural boundaries—such a goal would not only be difficult to realize on a practical level, but, on a conceptual level, simply absurd.

The Declaration, positing the universality of intellect and conscience, envisions a world in which it is possible to call others to account for their behavior and to have a basis for human interactions outside the metric of brute force and power politics.

That seems to be the logic, as far as it goes. All this talk of dignity and conscience, however, hints of greater discoveries to be had. Can the dignity-conscience logic lead toward a theory of rights? There is reason for optimism. Almost twenty years after the United Nations' Universal Declaration, another declaration on human rights appeared. In 1965 the Second Vatican Council issued *Dignitatis Humanae*, its Declaration on Religious Freedom,[17] which made a similar but much more explicit argument about the relationship between human rights, human dignity, and human conscience.

II. *Dignitatis Humanae*

Vatican II's Declaration is a fitting counterpoint to the United Nations' Declaration because *Dignitatis Humanae* is not a purely religious document. Rather, the Council's argument for religious liberty as a fundamental human right proceeds along two tracks, one theological and one anthropological, a deliberate action that allowed the document to serve both as a source of doctrine for Catholics and, importantly, as a basis for dialogue with the world.[18] The resulting argument started from an understanding of human rights based in human dignity—and of human dignity based in the quintessentially human thirst for transcendence, which was a more explicit version of the personalist argument implied in the Universal Declaration.

The central inspiration behind *Dignitatis Humanae* is a point of view generally known as "personalism." Personalism is not so much a theory or a science of the person as it is an ethical stance, an attitude of living that treats oneself and others as subjects of rights. It is an attitude that sees *persons* as free individuals who are ordered toward participation with one another through the actions that they perform.[19] These actions affect those around us, and they also affect ourselves—when we act well, we become better *as persons*, and, when we act badly, we become worse, also *as persons*.

Dignitatis Humanae summarizes its argument as follows:

> It is in accordance with their dignity as persons—that is, beings endowed with reason and free will and therefore privileged to bear personal responsibility—that all men should be at once impelled by nature and also bound by a moral obligation to seek the truth, especially religious truth. They are also bound to adhere to the truth, once it is known, and to order their whole lives in accord with the demands of truth. However, men cannot discharge these obligations in a manner in keeping with their own nature unless they enjoy immunity from external coercion as well as psychological freedom. Therefore the right to religious freedom has its foundation not in the subjective disposition of the person, but in his very nature. In consequence, the right to this immunity continues to exist even in those who do not live up to their obligation of seeking the truth and adhering to it, and the exercise of this right is not to be impeded, provided that just public order be observed.[20]

This idea goes further than the United Nations' argument that reason and conscience provide the possibility of appealing to some common set of rights. It is an argument that reason and conscience actually demonstrate the basis for such rights.

Human dignity is said to follow from "reason and free will and therefore . . . personal responsibility."[21] That is, people have dignity because they are responsible for the choices they freely and knowingly make. This sense of responsibility is a universal experience, rooted in our very existence, that raises in us a series of questions, such as: Why am I here? What is the meaning of my life? And, most importantly, how do I daily choose how to act, what to value, what to avoid, who or what to love, in light of those prior questions? Our existence is thus a *project* to be fulfilled. We experience not only a freedom to mold our own lives, but also an obligation to mold our lives well as a condition for our own fulfillment. We realize that our choice of the goods we seek, and of the context within which we choose to seek them, commits us radically as persons. By freely seeking what is good (or evil) we become good (or evil) as persons.

This experience is inescapable. We can try to eschew reason and try to act randomly, but that results in being judged insane. Our capacity to reflect on our freedom and the necessity of choice forces us to face our responsibility, forcing us to face our deep need for knowledge about how to decide. We are confronted with a multiplicity of things that we *can* seek and actions we might take. While we all share certain basic needs and desires, there is virtually no limit to the ways in which these can be gratified or fulfilled, which poses even more questions: How do we order our individual desires, much less the multiplicity of human desires that coalesce and clash whenever human beings live together? How do we decide what to do, in the polling booth, or even just after rolling out of bed each morning? Because we humans are born with the necessity of choosing, we are also born with anxiety about choosing well, or to put it another way, with an innate thirst for discovering the truth about the good.

Furthermore, when we reflect on it, we consider the search for truth an adventure, not a chore. Truth is more than just information about other good things—it is a good thing itself. Mark Twain once defined a classic as "something that everybody wants to have read and nobody wants to read."[22] Truth is not like that for us. We do not just want to have learned it so we can get on with life. We enjoy discovering it. It is something that tastes good all by itself. Vatican II can say that we are "impelled by nature . . . to seek the truth";[23] it is itself a good thing that we naturally desire.

The Vatican Declaration adds that humans are "also bound by a moral obligation" to seek the truth.[24] And not only to seek it, but also to "adhere to the truth, once it is known," indeed "to order their whole lives in accord with the demands of truth."[25] Where do those requirements come from? The Vatican Declaration "professes its belief that it is upon the human conscience that these obligations fall and exert their binding force."[26] The document repeats the point later, stating that every person "has the duty . . . to seek the truth in matters religious."[27] The person "perceives and acknowledges" that duty "through the mediation of conscience."[28]

Conscience, in short, demands that our minds and hearts attend to their built-in hunger for the true and the good. It prods them along in their search for it—and then insists they embrace what they believe they have found. Conscience, of course, is neither omniscient nor infallible. Regardless, it must be obeyed if we are to keep our integrity. After all, conscience takes the truth, as we understand it, and applies it to concrete circumstances to judge what is good. To refuse to follow its judgment (even when it turns out to have been mistaken) is to consciously reject what we believe to be true and turn our back on what we believe to be good, which violates our nature, if nothing else. Consequently, we sense that we have betrayed ourselves when we yield to coercion and act contrary to our consciences.

Human dignity, therefore, is a result of an intelligence and free will that, by their very nature, impose on us a duty, which conscience enforces, as well as a hunger, to seek the truth. From that conception of dignity the Vatican Council finds it a short step to human rights, declaring that people have "the duty, *and therefore the right*, to seek the truth."[29] The Council elaborates:

> In all his activity a man is bound to follow his conscience. . . . It follows that he is not to be forced to act in a manner contrary to his conscience. Nor, on the other hand, is he to be restrained from acting in accordance with his conscience, especially in matters religious.[30]

While this particular argument focuses on the right to religious liberty, the dignity that it locates in human reason and freedom is broad enough to encompass the bases of the other, traditional human rights as well. A human person who is entitled to search freely for ultimate truth, and then to express publicly the results of that search, is surely entitled to freedom of speech, freedom from arbitrary arrest, from torture, etc. In short, intellect and conscience, which presumes free will, bestows dignity and gives rise to human rights.

Religious freedom, in this conception, is more than a social freedom or a matter of freedom of expression. It is the ultimate freedom, that of conscience and the freedom to seek and embrace the truth about the meaning and purpose of one's life. In short, at the foundation of the personalist vision lies religious freedom, not as a right, but as the foundation of the existence of any human right. Freedom of religious expression is the catalyst in any society to the awareness of the dignity of the human person and the most fundamental precondition for any intelligible discussion about human rights.

That idea is not very different from the language of the United Nations' Universal Declaration, which asserts that "human beings are born free and equal in dignity and rights. They are endowed with reason and conscience. . . ."[31] The Universal Declaration, recall, employs these concepts for a more limited purpose, using them to argue for the possibility of a worldwide forum for enforcement of the rights it enumerates (but doesn't yet theoretically ground). Nevertheless, in looking for the elusive "common understanding" of those rights, this language, on which international consensus has already been achieved, serves well as the foundation of a more profound argument—a personalist reading of the document itself. This foundation would likely make the case for human rights much clearer, more persuasive, and immune to the usual culturally relativist objections, since the personalist case for human rights draws on some of the most deeply-felt and universal human experiences and desires. Following this personalist view, we could agree on the rights—and we could even agree why.

In order to treat people as ends rather than means, we have to first see this core of dignity created by our shared and equal thirst for meaning, which can only be fulfilled to the extent that the person is free of coercion. Even those among us who seem at first glance to reject the existence of such absolute values as "truth" and "goodness," perhaps on the grounds that they seem not to be meaningful or that they seem to serve no purpose, will, on closer examination, usually be found to embrace them at a more profound level. Ultimate meaning, after all, is another way of saying absolute truth, just as ultimate value or purpose is another way of saying absolute goodness, and no one really wants to live a life ultimately devoid of meaning or purpose.

Religious freedom is not merely one of many rights, but the prototypical human right. The Vatican document locates the foundation of *all* human rights (not just religious rights) in the dignity of the human person and in what might be called the religious impulse: the way in which each man or woman experiences *a universal thirst for meaning and purpose in life*.

This theory of religious freedom brings coherence to what that right looks like in practice. With reason and conscience, and thus dignity, as the foundation of our theory of human rights, it becomes clear that religious liberty is a core right, against which there are three great threats: state-imposed atheism, state-imposed religion, and state-imposed secularism. These phenomena are useful to study because each demonstrates the importance and precise contours of the particular facet of religious liberty that it offends.

In the case of state-imposed atheism, the religious impulse is targeted for repression because it is considered both a source of illusion and a threat to the hegemony of the state. In an atheistic regime, religion is condemned because it is thought to be false. Perhaps more importantly, religious expression, especially in institutional form, is considered dangerous because it represents a source of authority that does not originate in, or otherwise depend upon, the state. The spiritual authority of religion, moreover, claims superiority to the temporal authority of the state.[32] Thus, religion offers a competing vantage point from which citizens may effectively critique and oppose government action.

Although this anthropology does not deny the religious nature of humanity, it errs in its evaluation by condemning rather than exalting that nature. On this view, the religious impulse certainly exists (or else there would be nothing systematically to repress), but that impulse *ought* to be repressed because it has no object in reality and precludes totalitarianism.

By contrast, where a state imposes one religion (or, less commonly, more than one), it affirms both the existence and value of the universal craving for God. Indeed, in a theocracy, satisfying that human need is deemed so urgent that the state will employ any means to that end. The stakes are so high—whether the fate of citizens' immortal souls, or the protection of society from corrosive forces—that the state considers itself justified in using force to exact religious observance.

But the conception of human nature implicit in this approach misunderstands the religious impulse. There is no exigency—spiritual, social, or otherwise—that warrants coercing religious belief or observance, by the sword or even by more subtle means. This is not because spiritual and social problems are unimportant, but because mandating religious adherence is not an effective remedy. In fact, enforced religion will only worsen those problems. Religion at gunpoint is merely the semblance of religion, not the real thing. Exacting such empty conformity neither vindicates our humanity nor promotes social harmony; even the overzealous state would be disappointed with this result. Indeed, theocracies *preclude* genuine adherence to whatever religion they enforce, because they squelch that freedom that is a necessary condition for authentic embrace of *any* religion. Religious coercion also commonly meets intense resistance, risking civil strife that would tatter the fabric of civil society. In short, if a government seeks to maximize the religious flourishing of its people, as well as the individual and collective goods attendant to that flourishing, mandatory observance will not achieve that result—freedom will.

But even where religious freedom is affirmed by the state, particularly in contemporary democracies, there remains the risk of state-imposed secularism. Although this is typically the result of well-intentioned but overzealous opposition to state-imposed religion, it is occasionally based on the same contempt for religion that animates state-imposed atheism. In either case, the nominal goal is government "neutrality" with respect to religion, but the effect is the banishment of religion from public life. The laudable institutional separation of church and state becomes the unworkable separation of anything religious from anything political. Thus, religious values must not inform any public moral debate, least of all any legislative action that might issue from such a debate. Though the state may not specifically target religion for suppression, the state remains free to act in callous disregard of it. Indeed, the "neutrality" of the state may be called into question if the state accommodates, or otherwise acts with sensitivity toward, religious expression.

Again, the problem with this approach is anthropological. "Neutrality" is understood to require the state to ignore the religious nature of humanity, to pretend it does not exist, rather than to acknowledge, accommodate, or promote it. But the human desire to seek the truth, and especially religious truth, cannot be overlooked, much less eliminated. Everyone is a religious thinker. Among a plethora of goods, every person must choose some ways of ordering them. Because we are human beings, not creatures of given instincts, to live we must act, and to act we must choose. By forcefully excluding certain criteria for ordering goods (personal, social, and political) as religious and therefore to be quarantined, the state uses its power to segregate, discriminate, and oppress those who find ultimate meaning in the service of God. Convictions derived from religious inquiry (including such inquiry that results in atheism, or humanism) unavoidably inform moral decision-making, which, in turn, unavoidably informs political decision-making. It is mere fiction that these intimately entwined aspects of human thought and social action can somehow be extricated from one another. Similarly, human beings will never cease to distinguish the sacred from the profane, and so will always require, to varying degrees, exceptions to ordinary rules of behavior for purposes of religious observance. In short, it is quite simply impossible to eliminate these hard-wired patterns of human being, whether for the sake of drawing a neat-and-tidy distinction between religion and politics, or for any other purpose. To ignore them is to base society on a lie, and a deforming lie at that.

By treating religious contributions to public debate as out-of-bounds or merely tolerable, the state needlessly deprives itself (and, in turn, the people it exists to serve) of the rich moral and political resources that so many religious traditions hold in stewardship for the benefit of all. In the same way, by failing to affirm the singular importance of religious observance in the lives of its citizens, and by insisting instead on regulating extraordinary and mundane behavior on the same terms, the state harms those religious communities and institutions that serve as the seedbeds of virtue. Thus, democracies that embrace religious freedom can avoid lapsing into state-imposed secularism by acknowledging that the presence of religion in public life is not merely inevitable, but invaluable.

Truth is a good that is *worthy of being sought in itself*. Philosophers have long considered the contemplation of truth as the goal not only of our intellectual activity, but also of our practical way of life. Religious leaders of all persuasions have seen in this goal the greatest achievement and fulfillment of the human person. Our own experience also tells us that we are most fulfilled when we act according to the truth about ourselves and our surroundings. The attainment of truth thus becomes an imperative for our own development as persons.

Human existence is thus a *project* to be completed.

51

ROMAN CATHOLICISM AND THE FAITH-BASED MOVEMENT FOR GLOBAL HUMAN RIGHTS

—Allen D. Hertzke

Beginning in the mid 1990s a new movement burst unexpectedly onto the international stage—a faith-based quest devoted to advancing human rights through the machinery of American foreign policy. This movement of unlikely allies passed a series of landmark congressional initiatives on international religious freedom, trafficking of women and children, atrocities in North Korea, and genocide in Sudan.

In 2005 movement leaders set their sights on an even more ambitious goal: legislation aimed at implementing comprehensive long-term strategies for ending dictatorships around the world. If true to form, this legislation will pass at the end of the 109th Congress, in 2006, rounding out a decade of lobbying achievements. This movement is filling a void in human rights advocacy, raising issues previously slighted—or insufficiently pressed—by secular groups, the foreign policy establishment, and the prestige press.

The catalyst for this movement was the campaign against global religious persecution, which united a broad spectrum of religious groups and resulted in the passage of the International Religious Freedom Act of 1998 (IRFA). Facing fierce opposition from the business community, the Clinton Administration, and foreign policy "realists," the legislation was given up for dead on more than one occasion. Its "miraculous" passage propelled the heady new religious alliance to attack other human rights abuses.

The Catholic Church was central in IRFA's passage, both in preparing the groundwork (long before the specific campaign) and providing pivotal lobbying resources during the legislative battle. Without understanding the Catholic Church's commitment to religious freedom, as articulated in the Vatican II declaration on religious liberty *Dignitatis Humanae*, we cannot appreciate how the religious community succeeded in erecting a new human rights architecture in American foreign policy.

From Resistance to Embrace

Central to the transformation of the Catholic Church's posture toward the world in the last century has been the concept of the dignity of the human person made in the image

* *The Review of Faith & International Affairs* 3, no. 3 (Winter 2005): 19–24.

and likeness of God. This idea, found in Pope Leo XIII's 1891 encyclical *Rerum Novarum* (which inaugurated modern Catholic social teaching), crystallized the Catholic Church's voice on social justice and provided the rationale for its ultimate embrace of democracy. Thus even before Vatican II, the Church was turning away from its earlier rejection of democratic governance. And like a great ocean liner that turns slowly but with enormous force in its new direction, the Catholic Church became a powerful engine of democratization in the last quarter of the twentieth century—promoting human rights and undermining the legitimacy of authoritarian regimes. As Samuel Huntington has documented, the third great wave of global democratization that began in 1975 in Iberia and continued through the collapse of communism in Eastern Europe was almost entirely a Catholic phenomenon.[1] From Latin America to the Philippines to Poland the Church played an active role in fostering human rights and democratic dissent.

Promotion of religious freedom was inextricably tied to this role, but in this case the Catholic Church's break from the past was more abrupt. As late as the 1950s the Church's official position was that since "error has no rights," Catholicism, as the true faith, should alone be sanctioned by the state. And the Church enforced that view on its priests and theologians. As Garry Wills recounts in painful detail, John Courtney Murray—who helped articulate the grounds for *Dignitatis Humanae* and served as a consultant in its drafting at Vatican II—was in the 1950s reproached, censored, and in some cases silenced as he sought to make the case for religious freedom, along with alternative forms of church-state relations and ecumenical understanding. He was even "dis-invited" to the first session of Vatican II. But with a Catholic in the White House it became untenable for the Church to resist beckoning the most celebrated American Catholic theologian to the historic meeting, and in the second session Murray creatively helped refashion Catholic teaching.[2]

But that is not the whole story, of course. Allied with Murray was one Bishop Wojtyla of Poland, whose experience defending the faith amidst the tyrannies of Nazism and Communism forged a fierce commitment to free churches as bulwarks of civil society and resistance to oppression. As one of the principal drafters of *Dignitatis Humanae*, the future Pope linked human dignity and conscience to the right of peoples to form churches and practice their faith free of government coercion.[3]

The election to the papacy of John Paul II was thus of momentous significance to our story, as the Pontiff literally became the globe's most visible promoter of religious freedom. Indeed, John Paul II placed religious freedom at the center of his vigorous defense of human rights. In a widely-cited speech before the Vatican diplomatic corps in 1996, the same year religious activists in the U.S. began mobilizing for congressional legislation, he sounded the clarion call against communist and militant Islamic regimes that "practice discrimination against Jews, Christians, and other religious groups, going even so far as to refuse them the right to meet in private for prayer." Placing such maltreatment in context, the Pope declared that "this is an intolerable and unjustifiable violation not only of all the norms of current international law, but of the most fundamental human freedom, that of practicing one's faith openly, which for human beings is their reason for living."[4] The Pope took action himself where possible, as when he named bishops for the Chinese church operating underground and in opposition to the state-sanctioned body.

The Pope also championed ecumenical efforts to document modern martyrdom in his eloquent apostolic letter, *Toward the Third Millennium* (*Tertio Millennio Adveniente*). There he noted that on the eve of the next millennium "the church has once again become a Church of martyrs," now a "common inheritance of Catholics, Orthodox, Anglicans, and Protestants." Many of these martyrs, he lamented, are "unknown soldiers" in God's cause. As much as possible, "their witness should not be lost to the Church." Local churches, therefore, "should do everything possible to ensure that the memory of those who have suffered martyrdom should be safeguarded, gathering the necessary documentation, a gesture that cannot fail to have an ecumenical character and expression." Though he argued that this would serve as the same kind of faith inspiration as the "martyrologium" of the first centuries, John Paul's call for documentation dovetailed with strategies of human rights advocates to shine the light on abuses.[5] By placing the powerful imprimatur of the Catholic Church on the side of the cause of religious freedom, the Pope helped invite activism by his priests and bishops and smoothed their ecumenical alliances.

The fact that the United States came to embrace religious freedom as a foreign policy aim seemed to bring the issue full circle, a fact not lost on the aging pontiff when he met with President George W. Bush in 2001. Unfortunately, when the head of the globe's largest religious institution met with the leader of its superpower on July 23, 2001, their discussion of religious freedom got submerged in the media's focus on the stem cell research controversy. But in fact the Pope had thanked the president for the nation's lead in making religious freedom a key foreign policy goal: "It is significant that the promotion of religious freedom continues to be an important goal of American foreign policy in the international community. I gladly express the appreciation of the whole Catholic Church for America's commitment in this regard."[6]

The Campaign for Congressional Legislation

With the Pope preparing the way, American Catholic veterans of human rights struggles—both leading bishops and staff at the U.S. Catholic Conference—became pivotal players in the faith-based alliance in the 1990s that pressed for religious freedom legislation.

As one of the most sweeping human rights statutes on the books, IRFA is drawing increasing attention from foreign capitals and embassies.[7] It designates an office at the State Department and an Ambassador-At-Large for International Religious Freedom. It mandates that State produce a comprehensive annual report on the status of religious freedom in every country around the world, which can set into motion presidential actions against violating nations. The law also authorizes an independent commission, with staff and budget, to recommend policies, monitor violations, and hold policy makers accountable for their response. Finally, it reaches into the daily routines of foreign policy by providing better training for diplomatic personnel and fostering their ongoing contacts with vulnerable religious communities on the ground.

But beyond its specific provisions, the law embodies the growing nexus of global church communities and American advocacy. In the ecology of human rights, the struggle for the International Religious Freedom Act shaped the environment for future initiatives. *Without IRFA, no Sudan Peace Act; without the religious advocacy coalition, no human trafficking law.* The religious freedom campaign thus represents a kind of liminal moment in the politics of human rights.[8]

Viewed as something of a miracle by partisans, the legislation was the product of an intense and sometimes bitter lobby campaign. Not only were corporate lobbyists opposed to legislation that might upset business arrangements with foreign countries, but religious partisans themselves were divided over how best the American government could respond to persecution around the world. Some religious leaders sought tough and visible action against persecuting countries; others wanted to employ the quiet routines of diplomacy. Those calling for tough action were comfortable with vigorous (even unilateral) American leadership; those stressing quiet diplomacy tended to favor multilateral approaches. In all the twists and turns of the legislative process this divide was manifest. It endures as a key feature of the continuing struggle over how America will respond to human rights abuses.

These competing visions often did not correspond to the conventional ideological categories of liberal versus conservative, or religious left versus evangelical right. Indeed, the 1998 struggle over which approach to take often involved *different camps of evangelicals* and their religious allies, unfortunately complete with recrimination and claims of bad faith. When we view these events from a greater distance—when we "get up on the balcony" and look down—we can see that this collective struggle produced legislation that blended aspects of both visions, encompassing the diversity of the American religious landscape.

The Catholic Response

In the midst of this unusual struggle to define America's response to religious oppression, Catholic leaders were positioned to play a unique role. In part this involved bringing the insights of *Dignitatis Humanae* into the debate. In 1996 testimony before Congress, Cardinal McCarrick of Washington, D.C., echoed the Pope's view that religious liberty is the "first freedom" because it is rooted in the God-given dignity of the human person's free will and conscience. Because of this understanding, McCarrick noted how the Church not only spoke out on behalf of Catholics, but challenged persecution against Jews in the Soviet Union, Buddhists in Vietnam, Muslims in Bosnia, evangelicals in China, and adherents of traditional African faiths in Sudan.[9]

The Catholic presence also came from such prominent human rights pioneers as Nina Shea, Director of the Center for Religious Freedom at Freedom House in Washington, D.C., whose story is instructive. A human rights lawyer, she took up the cause of religious persecution when she noticed that it was slighted by the major international rights groups. For over a decade she was a lonely public voice, sometimes even shunned by supposed champions of human rights on the Left.

A cradle Catholic, Shea attended parochial schools through high school, to which she attributes a sensitivity to religious freedom and human rights issues. After receiving her law degree in 1979, Shea worked for the International League for Human Rights, a global counterpart to the American Civil Liberties Union. As program director for the International League, Shea became involved in work documenting the atrocities of right-wing death squads during the civil war in El Salvador in the early 1980s. Well connected to liberal networks and human rights organizations, Shea found herself writing op-ed pieces in the *New York Times*, getting invited to give guest lectures at Harvard, and the like.[10]

That all changed when she turned her attention to abuses committed by the Marxist Sandinista government of Nicaragua, which led to condemnation of her in left-wing circles. Moreover, she discovered that concerns about religious oppression received short shrift from secular human rights groups. This experience of double standards and secular blinders motivated Shea to form a Catholic lay human rights organization devoted to religious freedom "for all creeds in all parts of the world." She ultimately merged this organization with Freedom House, the well established institute founded on the eve of the Second World War by Wendell Willkie and Eleanor Roosevelt to promote human rights and democracy. Under the auspices of Freedom House, Shea has carved a niche for herself as a key hub of religious freedom advocacy. Her Center for Religious Freedom co-sponsored the seminal 1996 conference in Washington, D.C., of evangelical, Jewish, and Catholic leaders announcing their call for American action against persecution, and she remains an ongoing participant in the implementation of IRFA as a member of the U.S. Commission on International Religious Freedom.

While the initial grass roots energy for the anti-persecution campaign came from the evangelical Protestant world—spurred on by the entrepreneurial efforts of others[11]—everyone knew that official Catholic endorsement was vital. Thus lobbyists for the U.S. Catholic Conference were key players in the legislative campaign, both because of the Church's record of defending human rights and its strategic position in American politics.

Not only is the Roman Catholic Church the largest religious institution in the nation with vast international connections, but its faithful are key swing voters. At the time of the campaign, Catholic Conference lobbyists and Bishops enjoyed access and strong credibility with key Democrats who would not have responded to an evangelical "Christian Right" campaign. The Catholic Church is also a large and complex organization that moves slowly and deliberately, thus its official endorsement provided a certain caché and credibility.

One advantage enjoyed by Catholic lobbyists was the long involvement of Catholic officials in international human rights and religious freedom work in Latin America, Eastern Europe, and elsewhere. Lobbyists for the Bishops have long felt that U.S. foreign policy neglected religious freedom. Thus they were immediately inclined to back legislation once certain concerns of theirs were addressed. When the U.S. Bishops Conference did endorse the House version of the legislation, as announced at the lobby kick-off meeting in February of 1998, critics had a harder time impugning the Act as a sop to the Christian Right. Because of its international connections, moreover, the Church "knew something," i.e., it had useful information to present about the problem and thus its concerns about religious persecution were hard to ignore.

A final role played by Catholic lobbyists was helping mediate among the religious partisans who often clashed rancorously over which approach to take in addressing the denial of religious rights. John Carr, the Church's Secretary for Social Development and World Peace, focused on "the people whose lives and rights are at risk" and remonstrated with the other partisans to get "beyond the personalities," to avoid imputations of bad will.[12]

Taken together, these diverse factors ensured a potent Catholic role in the new architecture for global human rights. Indeed, it is probably not an exaggeration to say, as one Catholic lobbyist did, that without Catholic Church backing religious freedom legislation was doomed.

Implementation and Beyond

It shall be the policy of the United States . . . to condemn violations of religious freedom, and to promote, and to assist other governments in the promotion of, the fundamental right to freedom of religion.

—International Religious Freedom Act[13]

The architecture built by IRFA has enhanced human rights attention in American foreign policy. A new State Department Office of International Religious Freedom, a unique
Ambassador-at-Large position, a vast annual reporting enterprise on the status of religious
freedom around the world, and an external watchdog entity (the U.S. Commission on
International Religious Freedom) not only highlight violations of religious freedom and
propose remedies but promote human rights more generally.

The Catholic presence in this enterprise has been manifest both in the State Department and in the U.S. Commission. For example, of the nine members on the Commission serving through 2006, three are prominent Catholics: Nina Shea; Reverend Ricardo
Ramirez, Bishop of Las Cruces, New Mexico; and Reverend Charles Chaput, Archbishop
of Denver. In addition, past commissioners have included Theodore Cardinal McCarrick,
Archbishop of Washington, D.C. (and member of the College of Cardinals), and Reverend William Francis Murphy, Bishop of Rockville Center, New York.

But perhaps the most intriguing Catholic influence came from the first director of the
State Department Office of International Religious Freedom, Thomas F. Farr, who served
from 1999 until his retirement in 2005. A veteran State Department official and Roman
Catholic, Farr was committed to the issue even before the legislation passed. Drawing
inspiration from Catholic social teaching, Farr staffed the work of Ambassadors Robert
Seiple and John Hanford. Part of his vision was to make religious concerns "part of the
wallpaper" of Foggy Bottom,[14] but along the way he helped produce uncharacteristically eloquent pleas from the "stodgy" State Department to defend "God-given" religious
freedom.

Though such pronouncements drew upon the American experience, there was an
unmistakable Catholic resonance as well. The introduction to the 2001 State Department
report, for example, asserted that the "inviolable and universal dignity of the human person" is "at the core of U.S. human rights policy abroad, including the policy of advocating
religious freedom."[15] That an official U.S. document articulated *Dignitatis Humanae*—the
dignity of the human person as mandating the right to seek transcendent truth and ultimate purpose—suggests the extent to which Catholic social teaching can inform America's
evolving human rights posture.

52

PATTERNS AND CONTEXTS OF RELIGIOUS FREEDOM AND PERSECUTION

—Paul Marshall

At the end of 1997, the former executive editor of the *New York Times*, A. M. Rosenthal, confessed, "Early this year I realized that in decades of reporting, writing, or assigning stories on human rights, I rarely touched on one of the most important. Political human rights, legal, civil and press rights, emphatically often; but the right to worship where and how God or conscience leads, almost never." While Rosenthal changed dramatically on this score, the pattern he describes is still widespread.

By religious persecution we should not mean human rights violations against "religious" persons. Since most people in the world have some religious identity, most human rights violations of any kind are against religious believers. Rather, we should focus on situations where a person's faith, or lack of it, is a component of the persecution or discrimination they suffer. Of course, there are few cases where religion is the only factor: religion is usually intertwined with ethnic, political, territorial, and economic concerns. Religious persecution occurs when some or all of the oppression that people suffer would not occur if they or their oppressors were of a different religion.

Why should we focus on this? Is suffering or death on religious grounds inherently worse than other suffering or death on other grounds? Surely not. Rather, it needs attention because it has been neglected by comparison with other human rights issues. Indeed, until very recently it has been the orphan child of the human rights movement.

Contemporary Patterns: Repression on the Rise

A world is difficult to summarize, but over the last ten years the majority of the most populated countries, such as China, India, Pakistan, Indonesia, and Nigeria, have shown an increase in religious oppression. China has always repressed religion, but it has cracked down even more harshly in the wake of Falun Gong's appearance in 1998. The government, mindful that religious groups have been a source of opposition throughout Chinese history, has also increased controls on unregistered Protestants and Catholics (the majority of Chinese Christians) as well as Tibetan Buddhists and Muslim Uighurs.

* *The Brandywine Review of Faith & International Affairs* 2, no. 3 (Winter 2004): 27–34.

In India, violent attacks on religious minorities increased after the Hindu-nationalist BJP came to power. It has portrayed non-Hindus as "foreigners" and openly advocated a Chinese model of church control.[1] In Pakistan, the government is still reluctant to rein in Islamic radicals intent on imposing Islamic shari'a law. The country's blasphemy laws, which carry the death penalty, are still used against religious minorities, including the Ahmadiyya (who are treated as heretics deserving of death).

Indonesia's welcome transition to democracy has been accompanied by religious violence. There are religiously oriented separatist movements in Islamic Aceh province and in predominantly Christian Irian Jaya. Many, largely Catholic, refugees from now independent East Timor still languish in the western half of the island. In Ambon, Christian/Muslim communal violence has been transformed into the slaughter of Christians by the influx of heavily armed "jihad lascar" warriors from elsewhere in the country. The death toll is in the thousands, with over a hundred thousand refugees. In Nigeria, most northern states have announced the institution of Islamic shari'a law. Fears among the Christian population that they will become second-class citizens have erupted in violence leaving over 10,000 dead since 2000.

Another important factor is the increasing saliency of religious elements in war-making. The fighting between Israel and the Palestinians has much more religious rhetoric and identification than in previous decades. The conflicts of the late 1980s, and more so the 1960s and 1970s, were characterized by nationalist rhetoric. Now the theme is defense of Islam and its holy places. The India-Pakistan struggle over Kashmir has always had religious elements. Indeed, India and Pakistan came into separate existence because of their different religions. But Kashmir, like Afghanistan and Iraq, has drawn militants from around the world and is portrayed as a holy war. Thankfully, the situation is now relatively stable, but we should remember that both countries have named their nuclear weapons after Hindu and Muslim heroes. The conflicts in Chechnya and the former Yugoslavia show the same religious radicalization.

Religion is also a hallmark of the world's most bloody, indeed genocidal, contemporary conflict. In Sudan a radical Islamic regime has sought to force its version of Islam on the whole country, including the predominantly Christian and animist south. Its tactics include slavery, forced conversion, and the bombing of schools, hospitals, and relief centers. Politically induced mass starvation has killed two million people in the last 15 years and, at five million, has produced a quarter of the world's displaced people. Now it pursues the same tactics in Darfur province.

None of this is to deny, of course, that there is also good news in some parts of the world. Latin America has become one of the most religiously free areas in the world. And, except for the former Yugoslavia, the countries of Eastern Europe have also become largely free. One great story of the last quarter century is the victory of freedom in the traditionally Catholic world. There are also many free countries in Africa, especially in the south, while several smaller Asian countries are also free. Nevertheless, the world is seeing the increasing political influence of authoritarian religion coupled with increasing religious repression.

While there are instances that do not fall into any clear pattern, most religious repression is now taking place in four contexts.[2]

1. Radical Islam

While historically Islam has often shown greater tolerance than its Christian counterparts, there are now, in addition to widespread international religiously based terrorism, intensifying attacks on religious minorities (mostly Christians but also Hindus and Buddhists) throughout the Islamic belt from Morocco to the Southern Philippines. There is direct state persecution in countries such as Saudi Arabia, where any non-Islamic or dissident Islamic religious expression is forbidden. Christian meetings are outlawed and worship services held anywhere other than the embassies of powerful countries are raided by the *mutawa*, the religious police. Any Saudi who seeks to leave Islam faces the real prospect of death. This is also true in some other Gulf States and in North Africa. In Mauritania, Iran, the Comoros Islands, and Sudan, it is part of the legal code.

In countries such as Pakistan, the threat often comes from vigilantes, with greater or lesser complicity from the government. In Iran there are strong indications that, apart from the persecution of the Baha'i, government death squads abetted the torture and assassination of Protestant leaders in the 1990s.

There is also widespread communal violence against minorities, often provoked by radical Islamicist leaders. This is true in Egypt, where the Coptic Church has been subject to church burnings and local massacres, such as the January 2000 murder of 21 Copts in the village of El Kosheh.[3] In Nigeria, thousands have been killed in mob violence prompted by northern state governments' attempts to impose shari'a law.[4] In Pakistan in 1997 one Christian town, Shantinagar, was virtually razed to the ground, and Ahmadiyya Muslims suffer similar treatment.

In Indonesia, which has long been a place of toleration among Muslims, Christians, and other minorities, there has been an epidemic of church burnings. As noted above, in Ambon, communal violence beginning in 1999 was transformed by the arrival of a private army of thousands of self-proclaimed jihad warriors. Their explicit goal is to kill or drive out the Christian majority in the area. In some cases, like Indonesia and Egypt, governments (and major Muslim groups) have opposed such attacks, though sometimes sporadically, and usually with little effect. In Algeria, Islamicist guerrillas opposed to the government have targeted the Muslim majority.

2. Communism and Post-Communism

The remaining Communist countries, or countries that still call themselves Communist, are China, Vietnam, Laos, North Korea, and Cuba. To these can be added countries such as Turkmenistan and Uzbekistan, that are nominally post-communist, but in which essentially the same regime has continued to hold power. In these countries, with the exception of North Korea, there may be relative freedom to worship in state controlled religious bodies, but any religious expression outside of these bodies is suppressed. In China, any religious group not registered with the state, and therefore under state authority, is illegal. Hence, the Roman Catholic Church is banned since it accepts an authority, the Pope, from outside of the country. Its priests and bishops have been imprisoned, while several hundred leaders of the Protestant underground church have also been jailed and sent to labor camps. Independent Buddhism, especially Tibetan Buddhism, has also been repressed.

Laos has a similar pattern, as does Vietnam, where the government has sought to control the major Buddhist groups, and has also been violently repressive of the rapidly growing churches among the tribal peoples. Turkmenistan and Uzbekistan also make it almost impossible for non-approved Muslim and Christian groups to have legal status, and then persecutes them as illegal. The situation in Cuba is similar, though the government often adjusts its policies when it can sense political gain. Reliable information on North Korea is hard to obtain but it appears almost every free religious expression is forbidden and viciously repressed and that the number of believers in labor camps and prisons is at least in the tens of thousands.

3. South Asian Religious/Ethnic Nationalism

Religious minorities also suffer at the hands of combined religious/ethnic nationalism, sometimes at the hands of the state, more commonly by communal violence. Violence and discrimination against minority religious groups is present in India, Nepal, Sri Lanka and Bhutan. In February 2002, up to 2,000 Muslims were killed in communal slaughter in Gujarat state, and religiously motivated attacks on Christians number in the hundreds per year. India also has "affirmative action" laws to ease the plight of the dalit, or "untouchables." While Hindus, Sikhs, and Buddhists are included under these laws, Christian untouchables (a majority of the 28 million Christians in India) are excluded.

In Burma the SLORC regime, lacking popular support, has tried to wrap itself in a cloak of Buddhism as part of its war against tribal minorities, especially the Rohingya Muslims in the west and the Karen and other tribes in the east, where Christians constitute a large proportion of the minorities. This campaign includes massacre, rape, forced labor, and the use of children to clear minefields.

4. Intra-Religious Repression

There are also intra-religious conflicts. In Eritrea, Protestants have been imprisoned and tortured by the state, often with the support of clergy of the Coptic Church. In the Mexican state of Chiapas, apart from conflicts with the Zapatista rebels, Protestant tribespeople (40 percent of the population) have been driven off their land and killed by local renegade "Catholic" leaders. In Afghanistan, thousands of Shi'ites were killed by the Taliban, who are Sunni. In Pakistan, there is ongoing strife between Sunni and Shi'ite Muslims.

In Russia there are repressive religion laws at the federal level, often backed by the Russian Orthodox Church, while local laws are often even more repressive. Similar patterns of discrimination against minority religious groups are present in Belarus. Meanwhile, several Western European countries, including Germany, Austria, Switzerland, Belgium, and France have become more controlling of what the majority regards as "sects" or "cults." Those targeted include the Unification Church, Scientologists, Hare Krishnas, and Christian Pentecostal groups.

These four contexts of religious suffering are not easily transformed, but neither should they be seen as inevitable. Like religious repression, religious freedom can be found in every area of the world. There are relatively free countries in every continent and of every religious background. There are no grounds for thinking that religious freedom is an exclusively Western desire or achievement. South Korea, Taiwan, Japan, South Africa, Botswana, Mali, and Namibia are freer than France and Belgium.

Some Third World tyrants and Western apologists elevate "Asian values" and "economic rights" as paramount, and then denigrate rights such as religious freedom as elitist

Western priorities, as quasi-luxuries to be advanced, if at all, only when basic food and shelter have been achieved. But such tyrants do not speak for their population. Asian countries such as South Korea and Taiwan, which have a background of grinding poverty, and Confucian traditions at least as strong as China and Vietnam, both value and successfully defend religious freedom, and desperately poor African countries do the same. Religious freedom is desired and often achieved throughout the world.

Overcoming Secular Myopia

Any effective response to the suffering caused by religious persecution must begin with a nuanced analysis of the variegated roles of religion around the world. Yet this is precisely what has most often been neglected in the study of human affairs. The essential point here is not whether one is personally religious but that, as an empirical fact, religion is a key element of politics throughout the world. For example, chronic armed conflict is geographically concentrated on the margins of the traditional religions. The Middle East, the southern Sahara, the Balkans, the Caucasus, Central Asia, and South Asia are where Islam, Christianity, Judaism, Buddhism, and Hinduism intersect. They are also the sites of most wars in the last 50 years. The issue is not *why* people fight, but *where* they fight. Again, religious factors are usually intertwined with ethnic, political, territorial, and economic ones. But, since religion is the most profound shaper of human culture, people at these boundaries often have different histories and different views of human life, and are more likely to oppose one another. Regardless of the varied reasons for conflict, these are the areas where conflict likely occurs. They are religious fault zones, and hence sites of political instability.

Yet the significance of religion in international affairs has long been ignored or underestimated, especially in academic and media circles. One reason for this comparative neglect is the prevalence in the Western world of what may be called "secular myopia," which can be described as "an inability even to see, much less understand, the role of religion in human life." This myopia is widespread amongst "the chattering classes." As Edward Luttwak notes, "Policymakers, diplomats, journalists, and scholars who are ready to over-interpret economic causality, who are apt to dissect social differentiations ever more finely, and who will minutely categorize political affiliations, are still in the habit of disregarding the role of religion, religious institutions, and religious motivations in explaining politics and conflict."[5]

This myopia can have painful consequences. One was U.S. ignorance of the views and power of the Ayatollah Khomeini's followers in the 1970s. Luttwak notes that there was only one proposal for the CIA to examine "the attitude and activities of the more prominent religious leaders" in Iran, and that even this proposal was vetoed as mere "sociology," intelligence-speak for irrelevant academic verbiage. Consequently, as the Shah's regime was collapsing about them, U.S. political analysts kept insisting that everything was fine. Following their training, they examined economic variables, class structure, and the military, and concluded that since these groups supported the Shah, he was safe. There were, of course, mullahs arousing Islamic sentiment, but analysts had been taught that such religious drives drew only on folk memories, were destined to disappear with "modernization," and were irrelevant to the real structures of political power. Parallel, though less striking, tales can be told of Vietnam, Bosnia, Lebanon, the Philippines, Nicaragua, India, Sudan, Indonesia, and the Middle East.

This neglect can come not only by ignoring particular trends, but also by redefining them.[6] For example, in September 2002, gunmen entered a Christian charity in Karachi, Pakistan, separated Christian from Muslim workers, and methodically shot seven Christians in the head. Although this massacre was the sixth in a series of attacks aimed at Christian targets in Pakistan, much of the media played down religion's role in favor of a secular storyline. The *New York Times* described the event as ending a lull in assaults on "Western targets" and suggested that the charity was chosen because it was not as well guarded as "foreign embassies and Western companies." It quoted a police official saying that the attack was designed to drive away "Western business." *Agence France-Presse* quoted a human-rights worker arguing that the violence was not against Christians but against those "striving for a tolerant society." (Then why not also kill the Muslims who, since they were working for a Christian charity, were almost certainly committed to a tolerant society?) *CNN International* reported that there "is no indication of a motive."

These comments are typical. After massacres at a Pakistani Christian school and hospital in August of that year, *Reuters* headlined its story, "Pakistan Attack Seen Aimed at West, Not Christians," while the *BBC* said, "The attack appears aimed at Western interests, rather than Pakistan's Christian minority." The *Associated Press* argued that the assaults were "directed against Western interests."

However, the people behind the attacks made their motives plain. Members of Lashkar-e-Jhangvi, the terrorist group claiming responsibility for an October 2001 massacre in a Christian church, said that "they planned to kill Christians" in revenge for Muslim deaths in Afghanistan. The men who claimed responsibility for attacking the school in August announced that they "killed the nonbelievers." Daniel Pearl, the *Wall Street Journal* reporter kidnapped in Pakistan in January 2002, was killed not only because he was a Westerner but also because he was Jewish, as his murderers made explicit.

There are also widespread tendencies to treat religion as a subset of ethnicity or psychology, or to treat it as the sublimation of drives which can really be explained by poverty, economic change, or the stresses of modernity. Of course these factors play a role; no part of human life is sealed off from any other. But all too often what we encounter is a priori methodological commitment to treat religion as secondary, as an evanescent and derivative phenomenon that can be explained, but never be used to explain.

Taking Religion Seriously

One major reason for deteriorating religious freedom is the increasing political influence of authoritarian religion. As noted, many Westerners wonder how this could possibly happen in our supposedly secular world. I will suggest some reasons below but, at one level, this fact needs no explanation. Human beings have fundamental beliefs about the world and these beliefs inevitably shape political life. As an empirical fact, religion is a key element of politics and human rights.

But why does religion in some contexts appear to be taking an authoritarian turn at this juncture in history? One reason is that, however we might define "globalization," it is penetrating deeply into traditional cultures. Traditional believers in Japan or Java did not in the past wonder about who they were. But now, through new communications and commodities, local identity becomes only one option in the bewildering menu of postmodern life. In order to be maintained, a traditional identity now needs to be *asserted*, not just organically assumed.

Another factor is changing generations of leaders. Immediate post-colonial political elites were shaped by conflict with, and education by, the colonial power, and adopted many of its beliefs and ways. For example, new leaders in India and Africa often adopted Fabian socialism, and similar patterns occurred in the Middle East. But succeeding generations, whether or not Western-educated, have grown up within their country and see less need to adopt Western ways.

Both these trends are exacerbated by the collapse of communism, ending the only major alternative to globalization. Consequently those distressed by the dominant directions of the world now look to their own country's and area's history and traditions, which of course are religious history and traditions.

One result is religious nationalism, whether heartfelt or contrived, wherein countries are defined increasingly by their religious inheritance. This typified the conflict between Serbs, Croats, and Bosnian Muslims. It is endemic in India, Sri Lanka, and Nepal. The Chinese government inveighs against "foreign" religions, while the clamor over so-called "Asian values" carries its faint echo.

Within the Islamic world, this religious nationalism is now being replaced by pan-Islamic motifs. In some places, such as Egypt and Malaysia, the focus is still mostly country-based, but loyalty to the Muslim world, the *umma*, is growing. It has become the major factor in the conflict between Israel and the Palestinians and, of course, in international terrorism from Chechnya to Indonesia.

Despite the claims of their proponents, these trends are not repristinations of previous religious patterns. In traditional societies there was little need to assert a religious identity, which is one reason that some of the more religiously free Muslim societies are monarchies such as Jordan and Morocco. But, in the modern world, religious identities are challenged and, hence, protagonists must rally their supporters. The result is that belief becomes more like ideology and the faithful become more like a movement. Religious differences are heightened and mobilized.

The point is this: to take religious freedom seriously, we must take religion seriously. Other countries do. In 1992 the Chinese press noted that "the church played an important role in the change" in Eastern Europe and the former Soviet Union and warned "if China does not want such a scene to be repeated in its land, it must strangle the baby while it is still in the manger." Chinese government documents implementing a crackdown on house churches have stated that one of their purposes is to prevent "the changes that occurred in the former Soviet Union and Eastern Europe."[7] *The Far East Economic Review*, in a 1997 cover story entitled "God Is Back," reported one Beijing official as saying "If God had the face of a seventy year old man, we wouldn't care if he was back. But he has the face of millions of twenty year olds, so we are worried."

I am not suggesting that religion, apart from other cultural, ethnic, economic, political, or strategic elements is the only or the key factor: societies are complex. But I am saying that it is equally absurd to examine a political order without attending to the role of religion. We need to deal consistently with religion as an important independent factor, and analyses that ignore religious dynamics should be inherently suspect. Similarly, discussions of human rights that neglect religious freedom and the role of religion in all human rights should be equally suspect.

Conclusion

The trends described earlier suggest that religious freedom, as well as human rights in general, will decrease in the short term. But history is not determined and political and other action can, at the least, alleviate some of these consequences. This will not happen, however, unless we take religious freedom, and religion itself, seriously at the international level.

Governments have many responsibilities, principal among them the protection of their citizens, but also the promotion of justice worldwide.[8] One part of this is the prevention and cessation of repression based on religion. In and of itself, such repression is no more worthy a cause than oppression based on racial or other grounds. Still, since it is a growing problem and has often been ignored or slighted, it does deserve special attention, albeit in ways that vary according to each cultural context: each country is different, and there is no blanket strategy for how this should be done.

Of course, while all human rights pressures make international relations realists nervous, religious repression and conflict carries the added burden of touching on very deep-seated commitments. Overt religious elements make conflicts intractable since compromises over religion are much harder than deals over land or water. But this concern all too often leads to silence about religious conflict even among those who recognize its influence. It is not named for fear that its mere mention conjures its existence.

However, religious conflict and religious repression will not go away simply because our elites, and often our media, are reluctant to speak of it. We can only address such conflict if we clearly and unsentimentally acknowledge it. This is a vital matter. Religious freedom is historically the first freedom in the growth of human rights and often has more to do with the growth of democracy than does a direct focus on political activity itself. If we intend to devise effective and enduring ways of helping those who suffer for their faith, we can no longer afford to be embarrassed by the discussion and analysis of "religion and politics" in polite company.

53

DOES THE HUMAN RIGHT TO FREEDOM OF CONSCIENCE, RELIGION, AND BELIEF HAVE SPECIAL STATUS?

—David Little

I. Introduction

Renewed controversy surrounds the status of Article 18, as it appears both in the Universal Declaration of Human Rights[1] and in the International Covenant of Civil and Political Rights (ICCPR),[2] because of the unanimous adoption by the United States Congress of the International Religious Freedom Act of 1998 (IRFA).[3] Considerable concern was expressed during the period of drafting and debate over that bill as to whether the United States, in embracing such legislation, intended to single out and give special priority to religious freedom.[4] By requiring the President and other U.S. officials to exert extra effort in support of the right of religious freedom around the world, does the legislation imply that that right has a higher—or at least different—status from other human rights?

While the United States is apparently trying to elevate this right, some other governments are urging extreme caution, if not opposition, to promoting religious freedom. These governments, and publicists sympathetic to their cause, fear that American policy, in its new-found exuberance, will ignore—and at times unfairly subvert—the particular historical experience of others and the delicate place religion occupies in each nation's peculiar identity. What religious freedom means in one national context may be altogether different from what it means in another.

In other words, religious freedom is just now the subject of intense international debate, usually described as a controversy over "cultural relativism," or what my colleague Samuel Huntington calls "the clash of civilizations."[5] The assumption of those espousing the relativist view is that the world is made up of distinct, self-contained, and conflicting units of culture or civilization. It is supposed to follow from this assumption that notions of human rights, including rights to religious freedom, vary according to culture and tradition. They are not readily translatable from one setting to another. This prompts a pointed question: How does the United States, which is only one country among many, have the authority, by means of IRFA or anything else, to impose on others its particular view of the meaning of religious freedom?

* *Brigham Young University Law Review* 2001, no. 2: 603–10.

In response, I want to raise and comment on two questions regarding the status of the right to freedom of conscience, religion, and belief. One is the status of that right within the corpus of international human rights as well as in Western history. This is essentially a descriptive, empirical matter. The second question concerns the status of this right from the perspective of world opinion. Here we are concerned with normative issues: whether the right to religious freedom is properly regarded as universally applicable in the same way that at least some other human rights are, such as prohibitions against extrajudicial killing, torture, enslavement, etc.

II. Legal and Historical Status of Religious Freedom

As to the relation of religious freedom to other human rights, it seems clear that existing human rights documents and recent international jurisprudence do give the right to religious freedom a certain kind of special status. The documents themselves elevate that right in some interesting ways. Recall that the right to religious freedom is, with some limitations, included among the nonderogable rights contained in Article 4 of the ICCPR. That fact itself suggests that freedom of conscience, religion, and belief is intended to be thought of as among the most sacred or most fundamental of the universally recognized human rights. Of course, it is not the only right so designated. Article 4 also stipulates that protections from racial, religious, gender, and other forms of discrimination, as well as the prohibition against arbitrary killing, torture, enslavement, etc., are also nonderogable.

To be sure, the limitations on the freedom to "manifest one's religion or belief" in regard to "public safety, order, health, or morals or the fundamental freedoms and rights of others," mentioned in paragraph 3 of Article 18 of the ICCPR, also obtain in Article 4. At the same time, recent authoritative interpretation of Article 18 by the Human Rights Committee attaches some important qualifications that narrow the application of paragraph 3.[6]

First, the freedom to hold or admit to any theistic, nontheistic, or atheistic belief or to refrain from holding or admitting to any such belief is, and remains, absolute. Governments and others are completely prohibited from compelling or punishing belief as such. "Manifestation" would appear to mean public advocacy or the expressing of belief in the form of overt behavior. Only activity of that sort is properly subject to limitation. Second, the state bears the burden of showing that any restrictions on religious freedom are "directly related and proportionate to the specific need on which they are predicated."[7] Third, the limitations clause may not be administered in a discriminatory fashion. That means that all fundamental beliefs must be treated without preference or prejudice. It also means that when authorities impose restrictions on the manifestation of religious or other basic beliefs by appealing to "morals," they must take into account "many social, philosophical, and religious traditions" and not rely on principles "deriving exclusively from a single tradition."[8] In short, the Human Rights Committee is aware of the possible abuses to which the limitations clause of Article 18 might be susceptible and sensibly moves to narrow the range of potential misuse.

Moreover, it is important to remember that Article 18 includes three discrete terms: "conscience," "religion," and "belief." We shall single out the idea of conscience presently, but, before doing that, let us emphasize another aspect of the *special status* that the Human Rights Committee extends to the right of freedom of conscience, religion, and belief.

According to the committee, "the [ICCPR] does not explicitly refer to a right of conscientious objection, but . . . such a right can be derived from Article 18, inasmuch as the obligation to use lethal force may seriously conflict with freedom of conscience and the right to manifest one's religion or belief."[9] This is a profound pronouncement for two reasons. First, some fundamental beliefs, even those enjoining otherwise illegal forms of behavior such as refraining from military conscription, are entitled, *as a matter of right*, to special deference. Second, the pronouncement incisively calls attention to the problematic character of the relation of force and fundamental belief. To be compelled against one's conscience, religion, or belief to use force in military service may reasonably appear as objectionable as employing force to compel belief itself. The arresting implication of the committee's opinion is that being forced against one's basic convictions to use force is a severe violation of the right of conscience, religion, and belief. (This special connection also serves, usefully, to narrow the range of actions exemptible on grounds of conscience, etc.)

Beyond these textual and jurisprudential references, there are additional historical reasons for assigning some kind of special status to religious freedom. Article 18, paragraph 2 of the ICCPR states that "No one shall be subject to coercion which would impair [one's] freedom to have or to adopt a religion or belief of [one's] choice." This implies an opposition between coercion and fundamental belief that lies deep within the Western tradition from which formulations of this sort have emerged. That opposition was highlighted by the twelfth century, when the age-old distinction between *forum internum* and *forum externum* took on new prominence and saliency in European life. At that time, the idea of an internal tribunal, understood as the conscience, was assigned special sovereignty and protection, as a matter of "natural right," over and against the external tribunal or civil authority.[10] The phrase "sovereignty of conscience" conveys the basic understanding that the civil authority is ultimately in business, so to speak, to defend and encourage the rights of conscience, religion, and belief. To be sure, these notions were subject, subsequently, to various and variable interpretations. Nevertheless, to conclude that the *forum externum* owes special deference and special forms of exemption to the *forum internum*, as has the Human Rights Committee, is perfectly consistent with the underlying assumptions. Indeed, one way to think about a crucial implication regarding the state's responsibility, namely, the enforcement of rights against murder, theft, libel, and other forms of arbitrary injury, is that such protection is a necessary condition for the exercise of conscience, religion, and belief. If individuals were not protected against violence and abuse of that sort, they would not be free—they would not enjoy the "sovereignty"—to pursue and work out the fundamental beliefs that make them who they are.

Incidentally, the whole idea of the sovereignty of conscience is very important in the formative period of United States history. The thoughts of individuals like Thomas Jefferson and James Madison eventually exerted considerable influence on existing human rights understanding. There is much to be said here. Let us be satisfied with an eloquent quotation from Jefferson: "[O]ur rulers can have no authority over such natural rights, only as we have submitted to them. The rights of conscience we never submitted, we could not submit."[11] It follows that to surrender to "our rulers" the "inalienable" rights of the internal forum would be tantamount to surrendering the core of the human personality.

III. Religious Freedom and World Opinion

Regarding the universal applicability of the right of conscience, religion, and belief, two things may be said. First, on inspection, we live in a world dominated not so much by a clash as by a confusion of civilizations. Contrary to the claims of cultural relativists and others that our world is divided up into distinct, self-contained, and conflicting units of culture or civilization, things are much more complicated and convoluted. In reality, there is no one Asian view, no one Islamic or European view, just as there is no one American view, of how rights, or anything else, ought to be interpreted and applied. Far from being unified and harmonious, cultures and civilizations are dynamic and fluid affairs, particularly under the influence of modern information technology. They are arenas of contention and controversy. Which version of "official culture" becomes dominant typically depends not on the result of informed and deliberative national consensus, but on the strength and influence of particular political and economic factions.

Ours is an age of nationalism where there is a strong impulse on the part of state authorities to ally themselves with one, often a majority, ethnoreligious group so as to create a national faith considered essential for political identity. The problem is that dissenters and minorities are left out. They are not treated according to the norms of nondiscrimination and freedom of conscience, religion, and belief enshrined in the human rights documents. On the contrary, they are regularly suppressed or punished as deviant and disloyal for no other reason than that they refuse to espouse or identify with the dominant faith.

This state of affairs explains the deficiencies of the cultural relativist position, as well as why the new emphasis on the freedom of conscience, religion, and belief is so relevant. Cultural relativists, in a word, have no place for minorities. A leading feature of modern international politics is the widespread existence of minorities. The radical problems they pose for dominant majorities readily defy and disprove the popular image of a world composed of monolithic, harmonious cultures or civilizations.

That is also why the right of religious freedom has such power throughout the world. Minorities recognize, in ways that majorities often do not, the urgency of protecting dissent and deviance. Therefore, minorities, and those who support them, frequently champion the rights of the dispossessed and disadvantaged, including the right to espouse and practice (within limits) the dictates of one's fundamental beliefs. In fact, there is new, compelling evidence that, among other things, human rights standards designed to protect the religious and cultural independence of minorities are beginning to have a positive effect.[12]

According to the recent findings of Gurr and associates, the "first and most basic" reason for the improvement of the treatment of minorities and the decline of ethnopolitical conflict worldwide is "the recognition and active protection of the rights of minority peoples: freedom from discrimination based on race, national origin, language, or religion, complemented by institutional means to protect and promote collective interests," implying "the right of national peoples to exercise some degree of autonomy within existing states to govern their own affairs."[13]

The second thing to be said on behalf of the universal applicability of the right to the freedom of conscience, religion, and belief is what we might call "the lesson of fascism." The fundamental reason the world embraced human rights after World War II was not because people suddenly became enamored of liberal philosophy or even because of the postwar dominance of the United States. The primary reason was the moral revulsion worldwide to the indisputable atrocities perpetrated in the name of fascism, in both its European *and* Asian versions.

A key feature of fascism was the direct assault on the right of conscience, religion, and belief. Those who, for whatever reason, questioned the national faith, who dissented from the collective myth, were automatically branded as subversives and thus became the fitting target of suppression and/or elimination. Their primary sin was *to fail to believe in* the theory of collective domination. The crucial part of the lesson of fascism is that it violated religious freedom along with the whole range of other rights now understood to be requisite for human fulfillment. Denial of the right of conscience, religion, or belief, it appears, seldom occurs in isolation.

IV. Conclusion

We may conclude both that the freedom of conscience, religion, and belief *does* enjoy a certain special status legally and historically and that it *ought* to enjoy such a status in the court of world opinion. At the same time, we should emphasize that the freedom of religion is part of a wider bundle of rights. To support freedom of conscience, religion, and belief requires the enforcement of rights against murder, torture, enslavement, and the whole host of other human rights that weave together into a fabric of protection essential to clothe human life with dignity. To single out and promote religious freedom in isolation from other human rights would be as mistaken as to deny the distinctive status of that right.

54

BALANCING RELIGIOUS FREEDOM
AND CULTURAL PRESERVATION

—José Casanova

Human rights, including the right to religious freedom, are presently in the process of becoming globalized. But, the fact that religious freedom is becoming a universal aspiration doesn't mean that religious freedom means necessarily everywhere the same thing. It may mean different things in different countries, and these different meanings may be in conflict with one another. Policies intended to implement international religious freedom may conflict with other cultures' understandings of religious freedom, and will be resisted accordingly.

Thankfully, there is also a growing global trend of mutual recognition of cultures. There is increasing awareness of the need, if we are going to live together peacefully and constructively in a shrinking world, for cultures to have a right to protect themselves from imperialist, or overly aggressive, attempts to change them. It is this awareness that allows a balance to be struck between the individual right of religious freedom, with its accompanying right to proselytize, and the communal right to preserve a culture. Importantly, to be most favorable, this balance calls for religious freedom implementation methods and proselytizing methods that are contextually specific.

Interestingly, only in the last 15 years has there been a major global movement, not only in the United States but elsewhere, to expand the principle of religious freedom. However, the principle itself is of course very old, being written into government documents during the inception of the American colonies, and later being included in the United States' Declaration of Independence and then in the first amendment of its Constitution. Around the same time, the principle took hold in France when the National Assembly proclaimed the Declaration of the Rights of Man and the Citizen. But even there we see already that the American Declaration and the French Declaration—the two key modern declarations of universal human rights principles—have been in tension for a very long time, as they articulated the right in distinct ways.

In addition to differences between cultures, changes within single cultures also complicate the promotion of human rights. For example, consider the Catholic Church, which

* *The Review of Faith & International Affairs* 6, no. 2 (Summer 2008): 13–15.

for 150 years attacked the Declaration of the Rights of Man and the Citizen for being against God, against the Church, and against dignity. And yet, in the last 40 years, the Catholic Church has become one of the global carriers of the principle of the sacred dignity of the human person. Cultures and religious confessional groups have dynamic conceptions of human rights; approaches to religious freedom that make simplistic assumptions about the static monolithic nature of certain groups will miss important opportunities, and can even be counterproductive.

An area where the complexity of the religious freedom issue comes into especially bold relief is cross-cultural religious proselytizing. I have witnessed these tensions first-hand many times. For example, for several years after the fall of the Berlin Wall I traveled regularly to Poland and Ukraine. The planes I flew on frequently also carried groups of enthusiastic American evangelicals intent on taking the gospel of Jesus Christ to the native inhabitants of these countries. As I interacted with and observed these missionaries, it became abundantly clear to me that they had no familiarity with the culture where they were going, and no idea what Eastern Christianity was. To these evangelicals, the people in Eastern Orthodox cultures could not be considered real Christians; these missionaries believed that, in order to be a Christian, one had to be specifically an evangelical Protestant. Most often, they didn't even know anything about the language; for instance, most had not bothered to learn that there is a difference between Ukrainian and Russian. Yet, they were convinced of their right to proselytize, sometimes very aggressively.

An extremely negative counter-reaction to Western proselytism occurred in Russia. Here, this process of culturally insensitive proselytizing led to an attempt by part of the Russian Orthodox Church to once again become allied with the Russian state. The Russian administration at that time eagerly became allied with the Russian church to protect its own control of society. What this episode illustrates is that while aggressive proselytizing in one cultural context, such as in the U.S., can be accepted as part of a healthy, robustly pluralistic civil society, in other cultural contexts it can have severe repercussions. To be sure, I am not saying that the current U.S. policy of promoting international religious freedom is outright culturally insensitive or imperialistic. I am only saying that in some contexts this is the way that it may be perceived. And, if it is perceived in this way, then it may have negative repercussions.

As mentioned above, the principle of individual religious freedom is in tension with another principle: the right of indigenous people to protect their culture from external pressure. This right, which the United Nations has recognized, is part of what I would call an emergent global denominationalism, a system of global society where religious groups respect others' religions, even as they defend and promote their own truth claims. This system would respect the right of cultural self-preservation not through crude instruments such as blasphemy laws and censorship regulations, but rather through a civil society that understands the need for cultural sensitivity. Global denominationalism would also defend the principle of individual religious freedom, which includes the right to conversion and the attendant right to evangelize, but would recognize that there are both appropriate and inappropriate ways to evangelize.

In an environment of global denominationalism, proselytizing groups would have appropriate amounts of respect for the religions of other cultures, and, because of the knowledge and the desire to not offend that comes with respect, they would thus adapt their proselytizing methods to be culturally specific. Mother Teresa is a great example of culturally contextualized evangelizing. She did not proselytize by explicitly trying to convert Hindus to Catholicism. She was just a witness of a Christian mission doing Christian work in India. This is a way of "proselytizing" that did not cause the negative reaction of groups in India who may have felt that overt proselytism was tied to Western imperialism.

What positive role can the United States play, then, in promoting international religious freedom during an era of globalization? Approaches that emphasize diplomacy and sanctions based ostensibly on standards of international law can be a part of the picture, but we must not underestimate the risk that such approaches will yield counterproductive results. Further, the United States doesn't have a very good record in recognizing the applicability of international law to itself. The United States sometimes claims that it should be above international law on various issues, which undermines the legitimacy of U.S. appeals to international law when it comes to human rights advocacy.

Rather than through foreign policy, the more effective long-term role for the U.S. in advancing international religious freedom may be through its example as a society. Indeed, we may even find here in the United States the chance to create the mother of global denominationalism. This is because the United States, being such a successful plural society for confessional groups, is already an approximate microcosm of the sought-for global system. A vivid illustration of the relative strength of respectful pluralism in contemporary U.S. society is what happened after Danish newspapers published cartoon caricatures of Islam. In Europe, many newspapers re-published these cartoons, notwithstanding the fact that these same newspapers would not think of publishing cartoons lampooning Christianity or stoking anti-Semitism. In the United States, by contrast, newspapers did not re-publish the Danish cartoons, voluntarily exercising restraint out of a simple recognition of the need for inter-religious respect.

Still, when we talk of denominationalism in the United States, we cannot forget that it also took a long time to be established. At first there was only denominationalism for the Protestants. Catholics were not accepted into the system and there were very serious attempts to force the Catholics to "Americanize," which is to say, "Protestantize." As a reaction, the Catholic Church tried to create a separate Catholic cultural structure through the school system and many other kinds of social structures that were separate from the hegemony of American Protestantism. Eventually, Catholicism was incorporated into a more inclusive vision of American "civil religion" that expanded the boundaries of respectful-yet-robust pluralism, an incorporation that has still allowed it to remain adequately autonomous. Eventually Judaism was similarly incorporated, and today of course we are in a context in which virtually all the world religions are being incorporated. The United States is thus uniquely positioned to act as a model through which to create a global denominationalism. We just need to remember that it will take time.

In conclusion, truly respectful religious freedom—the product of a creative tension and balance between individual religious freedom and communal religious pluralism—is becoming a universal aspiration. And it is transforming many of the world religions. It transformed Protestantism, then Catholicism, and it is transforming Islam, Hinduism, and Buddhism today. But we should be aware of the fact that, because cultural perceptions of religious freedom are different, this process may take different forms than the American evangelical Protestant one, and may unfold only over the course of several generations, not during the course of the next presidential administration.

55

SOUL WARS
New Battles, New Norms

—John Witte, Jr.

The problem of proselytism is one of the great ironies of the democratic revolution of the modern world. In the last four decades, more than 30 new democracies were born around the world. More than 150 major new national, regional, and international instruments on religious liberty were forged—many replete with generous protections of liberty of conscience and freedom of religious exercise, guarantees of religious pluralism, equality, and non-discrimination, and several other special protections and entitlements for religious individuals and religious groups.[1]

On the one hand, the modern human rights revolution has helped to catalyze a great awakening of religion around the globe. In regions newly committed to democracy and human rights, ancient faiths once driven underground by autocratic oppressors have sprung forth with new vigor. In the former Soviet bloc, for example, numerous Buddhist, Christian, Hindu, Jewish, Muslim, and other faiths have been awakened, alongside a host of exotic goddess, naturalist, and personality cults.[2] In post-colonial and post-revolutionary Africa, mainline religious groups have come to flourish in numerous conventional and inculturated forms, alongside a bewildering array of Traditional groups.[3] In Latin America, the human rights revolution has not only transformed long-standing Catholic and mainline Protestant communities but also triggered the explosion of numerous new evangelical, Pentecostal, and Traditional movements.[4] Many parts of the world have seen the prodigious rise of a host of new or newly minted faiths—Adventists, Baha'is, Hare Krishnas, Jehovah's Witnesses, Mormons, Scientologists, Unification Church members, among many others—some wielding ample material, political, and media power.[5] Religion today has become, in Susanne Rudolph's apt phrase, the latest "transnational variable."[6]

On the other hand, in parts of Russia, Eastern Europe, Africa, and Latin America, this human rights revolution has brought on something of a new war for souls between indigenous and foreign religious groups. With the political transformations of these regions, foreign religious groups were granted rights to enter these regions for the first time in decades. In the 1980s and 1990s, they came in increasing numbers to preach their faiths,

* *The Review of Faith & International Affairs* 5, no. 1 (Spring 2007): 13–19.

to offer their services, to convert new souls. Initially, local religious groups—Orthodox, Catholic, Protestant, Sunni, Shi'ite, and Traditional alike—welcomed these foreigners, particularly their foreign co-religionists with whom they had lost contact for many decades. Today, local religious groups have come to resent these foreign religions, particularly those from North America and Western Europe who assume a democratic human rights ethic. Local religious groups resent the participation in the marketplace of religious ideas that democracy assumes. They resent the toxic waves of materialism and individualism that democracy inflicts. They resent the massive expansion of religious pluralism that democracy encourages. They resent the extravagant forms of religious speech, press, and assembly that democracy protects.[7]

A new war for souls has thus broken out in these regions—a war to reclaim the traditional cultural and moral souls of these new societies and a war to retain adherence and adherents to the indigenous faiths. In part, this is a theological war—as rival religious communities have begun actively to demonize and defame each other and to gather themselves into ever more dogmatic and fundamentalist stands. The ecumenical spirit of the previous decades is giving way to sharp new forms of religious balkanization. In part, this is a legal war—as local religious groups have begun to conspire with their political leaders to adopt statutes and regulations restricting the constitutional rights of their foreign religious rivals. Beneath shiny constitutional veneers of religious freedom for all, and beneath unqualified ratification of international human rights instruments, several countries of late have passed firm new anti-proselytism laws, cult registration requirements, tightened visa controls, and various discriminatory restrictions on new or newly arrived religions.

Hence the modern problems of proselytism: How does the state balance one community's right to exercise and expand its faith versus another person's or community's right to be left alone to its own traditions? How does the state protect the juxtaposed rights claims of majority and minority religions, or of foreign and indigenous religions? How does the state craft a general rule to govern multiple theological understandings of conversion or change of religion? These are not new questions. They confronted the drafters of the international bill of rights from the very beginning. But some of the compromises of 1948 (the Universal Declaration of Human Rights) and 1966 (the International Covenant on Civil and Political Rights) have today begun to betray their limitations.

The Problem of Conversion

One side of the modern problem of proselytism is the problem of competing theological and legal understandings of conversion or change of religion.[8] For instance, how does a state craft a legal rule that at once respects and protects the sharply competing understandings of conversion among the "religions of the Book"—Judaism, Christianity, and Islam? Most Jews have difficult conversion into and out of the faith. Most Western Christians have easy conversion into and out of the faith. Most Muslims have easy conversion into the faith, but allow for no conversion out of it, at least for prominent members.[9] Whose rites get rights? Moreover, how does one craft a legal rule that respects Orthodox, Hindu, Jewish, or Traditional groups that tie religious identity not to voluntary choice, but to birth and caste, blood and soil, language and ethnicity, sites and sights of divinity?[10]

On the issue of conversion or change of religion, the major international human rights instruments largely accept the religious voluntarism common among libertarian and

Western Christian groups. The 1948 Universal Declaration of Human Rights includes an unequivocal guarantee: "Everyone has the right to freedom of thought, conscience, and religion; this right includes the right to change his religion or belief. . . ."[11] The 1966 International Covenant on Civil and Political Rights, the preparation of which was more highly contested on this issue, is a bit more tentative: "This right shall include freedom to have or adopt a religion or belief of his choice. . . ."[12] The 1981 Declaration on the Elimination of All Forms of Intolerance and of Discrimination Based on Religion or Belief repeated this same more tentative language. But the dispute over the right to conversion contributed greatly to the long delay in the production of this instrument, and to the number of dissenters to it.[13] The 1989 Vienna Concluding Document did not touch the issue at all, but simply confirmed "the freedom of the individual to profess or practice religion or belief" before turning to a robust rendition of religious group rights.[14] Today, the issue has become more divisive than ever as various soul wars have broken out, especially between and within Christian and Muslim communities around the globe.

"A page of history is worth a volume of logic," Oliver Wendell Holmes, Jr. once said.[15] And, on an intractable legal issue such as this, recollection might be more illuminating than ratiocination.

It is discomfiting, but enlightening, for Western Christians to remember that the right to enter and exit the religion of one's choice was born in the West only after centuries of cruel experience. To be sure, a number of the early Church Fathers considered the right to change religion as essential to the notion of liberty of conscience, and such sentiments have been repeated and glossed continuously over the centuries. But in practice the Christian Church largely ignored these sentiments for centuries. As the medieval Catholic Church refined its rights structures in the twelfth and thirteenth centuries, it also routinized its religious discrimination, reserving its harshest sanctions for heretics. The communicant faithful enjoyed full rights. Jews and Muslims enjoyed fewer rights, but full rights if they converted to Christianity. Heretics—those who voluntarily chose to leave the faith—enjoyed still fewer rights, and had little opportunity to recover them even after full confession. Indeed, at the height of the Inquisition in the fifteenth century, heretics faced not only severe restrictions on their persons, properties, and professions, but sometimes unspeakably cruel forms of torture and punishment.[16] Similarly, as the Lutheran, Calvinist, and Anglican Churches born of the Protestant Reformation routinized their establishments in the sixteenth and seventeenth centuries, they inflicted all manner of repressive civil and ecclesiastical censures on those who chose to deviate from established doctrine—including savage torture and execution in a number of instances.[17]

It was, in part, the recovery and elaboration of earlier patristic concepts of liberty of conscience as well as the slow expansion of new Protestant and Catholic theologies of religious voluntarism that helped to end this practice. But, it was also the new possibilities created by the frontier and by the colony that helped to forge the Western understanding of the right to change religion. Rather than stay at home and fight for one's faith, it became easier for the dissenter to move away quietly to the frontier, or later to the colony, to be alone with his conscience and his co-religionists. Rather than tie the heretic to the rack or the stake, it became easier for the establishment to banish him quickly from the community with a strict order not to return. Such pragmatic tempering of the treatment of heretics and dissenters eventually found theological justification. By the later sixteenth century, it became common in the West to read of the right, and the duty, of the religious dissenter to emigrate physically from the community whose faith he or she no longer shared.[18] In the course of the next century, this right of physical emigration from a religious community was slowly transformed into a general right of voluntary exit from a religious faith and community. Particularly American writers, many of whom had voluntarily left their European faiths and territories to gain their freedom, embraced the right to leave—to change their faith, to abandon their blood, soil, and confession, to reestablish their lives, beliefs, and identities afresh—as a veritable *sine qua non* of religious freedom.[19] This understanding of the right to choose and change religion—patristic, pragmatic, and Protestant in initial inspiration—has now become an almost universal feature of Western understandings of religious rights.

To tell this peculiar Western tale is not to resolve current legal conflicts over conversion. But it is to suggest that even hard and hardened religious traditions can and do change over time, in part out of pragmatism, in part out of fresh appeals to ancient principles long forgotten. Even those schools of jurisprudence within Shi'ite and Sunni communities that have been the sternest in their opposition to a right to conversion from the faith, do have resources in the Qur'an, in the early development of shari'a, and in the more benign policies of other contemporary Muslim communities, to rethink their theological positions.[20]

Moreover, the Western story suggests that there are half-way measures, at least in banishment and emigration, that help to blunt the worst tensions between a religious group's right to maintain its standards of entrance and exit and an individual's liberty of conscience to come and go. Not every heretic needs to be executed. Not every heretic needs to be indulged. It is one thing for a religious tradition to insist on observing its rules of heresy, when a mature adult, fully aware of the consequences of his or her choice, voluntarily enters a faith, and then later seeks to leave. In that case group religious rights must trump individual religious rights—with the limitation that the religious group has no right to violate, or to solicit violation of, the life and limb of the wayward member. It is quite another thing for a religious tradition to press the same charges of heresy against someone who was born into, married into, or coerced into the faith and now, upon opportunity for mature reflection, voluntarily chooses to leave. In that case, individual religious rights trump group religious rights.

Where a religious group exercises its trump by banishment or shunning and the apostate voluntarily chooses to return, he does so at his peril. He should find little protection in state law when subject to harsh religious sanctions—again, unless the religious group threatens or violates his or his family's life or limb. Where a religious individual exercises her trump by emigration, and the group chooses to pursue her, it does so at its peril. It should find little protection from state law when charged with tortious or criminal violations of the individual.

The Problem of Proselytism

The corollary to the problem of conversion is the problem of proselytism—of the efforts taken by individuals or groups to seek the conversion of another. On this issue the international human rights instruments provide somewhat more nuanced direction.[21]

Article 18 of the 1966 International Covenant on Civil and Political Rights protects a person's "freedom, individually or in community with others and in public or private, *to manifest his religion or belief in* worship, observance, practice, and *teaching.*"[22] But the same article allows such manifestation of religion to be subject to limitations that "are prescribed by law and are necessary to protect public safety, order, health, or morals, or the fundamental rights and freedoms of others."[23] It prohibits outright any "coercion" that would impair another's right "to have or adopt a religion or belief of his choice."[24] It also requires State parties and individuals to have "respect for the liberty of parents . . . to ensure the religious and moral education of their children in conformity with [the parents'] convictions"—a provision underscored and amplified in more recent instruments and cases on the rights of parents and children.[25]

Similarly, Article 19 of the same 1966 Covenant protects the "*freedom to seek, receive, and impart information and ideas of all kinds*, regardless of frontiers, either orally, in writing, or in print, in the form of art, or through any other media of his choice."[26] But Article 19, too, allows legal restrictions that are necessary for "respect of the rights and reputation of others; for the protection of national security or of public order (*ordre public*) or of public health or morals."[27] As a further limitation on the rights of religion and (religious) expression guaranteed in Articles 18 and 19, Article 26 of the 1966 Covenant prohibits any discrimination on grounds of religion. And Article 27 guarantees to religious minorities "the right to enjoy their own culture" and "to profess and practice their own religion."[28]

The literal language of the mandatory 1966 Covenant (and its amplification in more recent instruments and cases) certainly protects the general right to proselytize—understood as the right to "manifest," "teach," "express," and "impart" religious ideas for the sake, among other things, of seeking the conversion of another. The Covenant provides no protection for coercive proselytism. At minimum, this bars physical or material manipulation of the would-be convert, and in some contexts even more subtle forms of deception, enticement, and inducement to convert. The Covenant also casts serious suspicion on any proselytism among children or among adherents to minority religions. But, outside of these contexts, the religious expression inherent in proselytism is no more suspect than political, economic, artistic, or other forms of expression, and should, at minimum, enjoy the same rights protection.

Such rights to religion and religious expression are not absolute. The 1966 Covenant and its progeny allow for legal protections of "public safety, order, health, or morals," "national security" and "the rights and reputation of others," particularly minors and minorities. But all such legal restrictions on religious expression must always be imposed without discrimination against any religion, and with due regard for the general mandates of "necessity and proportionality"—the rough international analogues to the "compelling state interest" and "least restrictive alternative" prongs of the strict scrutiny test of American constitutional law. General "time, place, and manner" restrictions on all proselytizers that are necessary, proportionate, and applied without discrimination against any religion might thus well be apt. But categorical criminal bans on proselytism, or patently discriminatory licensing or registration provisions on proselytizing faiths, are *prima facie* a violation of the religious rights of the proselytizer—as has been clear in the United States since *Cantwell v. Connecticut* (1940)[29] and in the European community since *Kokkinakis v. Greece* (1993).[30]

To my mind, the preferred solution to the modern problem of proselytism is not so much further state restriction as further self-restraint on the part of both local and foreign religious groups. Again, the 1966 International Covenant on Civil and Political Rights provides some useful cues.

Article 27 of the Covenant reminds us of the special right of local religious groups, particularly minorities, "to enjoy their own culture, and to profess and practice their own religion." Such language might well empower and encourage vulnerable minority traditions to seek protection from aggressive and insensitive proselytism by missionary mavericks and "drive by" crusaders who have emerged with alacrity in the past two decades. It might even have supported a moratorium on proselytism for a few years in places like Russia so that local religions, even the majority Russian Orthodox Church, had some time to recover from nearly a century of harsh oppression that destroyed most of its clergy, seminaries, monasteries, literature, and icons. But Article 27 cannot permanently insulate local religious groups from interaction with other religions. No religious and cultural tradition can remain frozen. For local traditions to seek blanket protections against foreign proselytism, even while inevitably interacting with other dimensions of foreign cultures, is ultimately a self-defeating policy. It stands in sharp contrast to cardinal human rights principles of openness, development, and choice. Even more, it belies the very meaning of being a religious tradition. As Jaroslav Pelikan reminds us: "Tradition is the living faith of the dead; traditionalism is the dead faith of the living."[31]

Article 19 of the Covenant reminds us further that the right to expression, including religious expression, carries with it "special duties and responsibilities."[32] One such duty, it would seem, is to respect the religious dignity and autonomy of the other, and to expect the same respect for one's own dignity and autonomy. This is the heart of the Golden Rule. It encourages all parties, especially foreign proselytizing groups, to negotiate and adopt voluntary codes of conduct of restraint and respect of the other. This requires not only continued cultivation of interreligious dialogue and cooperation—the happy hallmarks of the modern ecumenical movement and of the growing emphasis on comparative religion and globalization in our seminaries. It also requires guidelines of prudence and restraint that every foreign mission board would do well to adopt and enforce: Proselytizers would do well to know and appreciate the history, culture, and language of the proselytizee; to deal honestly and respectfully with theological and liturgical differences; to respect and advocate the religious rights of all peoples; to be Good Samaritans as much as good preachers; and to proclaim their faith not only in word but also deed.[33] Moratoria on proselytism might provide temporary relief; but moderation by proselytizers and proselytizees is the more enduring course.

— Section X —

RELIGION AND THE FUTURE
OF U.S. FOREIGN POLICY

56

RELIGION AND INTERNATIONAL AFFAIRS

—Barry Rubin

For God doth know how many now in health
Shall drop their blood in approbation
Of what your reverence shall incite us to.
Therefore rake heed how you impawn our person,
How you awake our sleeping sword of war.

—William Shakespeare,
Henry V to the Archbishop of Canterbury
Henry V (Act l, Scene II)

United States foreign policy in recent decades has often misread the importance of religion as a factor in the national politics and international behavior of some countries
and regions. This has sometimes led to incorrect analysis and erroneous policy responses
that have proven quite costly. If previous experience is correctly evaluated, however, the
United States should be able to avoid potential future disasters.

The foundation of this problem is the generally accepted reading of European history that American political leaders, policymakers, and intellectuals have applied to Third
World realities, often in an uncritical manner. In this context, religion has been perceived
as a declining factor in world politics. There are three principal errors in this perception:

l. In modern times religion has increasingly been seen in the West as a theological
set of issues rather than as a profoundly political influence in public life. Having studied
the development of religion over the centuries and having been influenced, in particular,
by such events as the early Christian schisms, the Protestant Reformation, the Catholic
Counter Reformation, and the European wars of religion, some Western thinkers in the
past two centuries have come to believe that debate over theological questions is what

---

* Originally published in *The Washington Quarterly* 13, no. 2 (March 1990): 51–63, and republished in Douglas Johnston and Cynthia Sampson, eds., *Religion, the Missing Dimension of Statecraft* (Oxford: Oxford
University Press, 1994), 20–34.

makes religion political. For instance, disputes historically took place over the nature of Jesus or whether clergy should be allowed to marry. The example of the Medieval question of how many angels could stand on the head of a pin was used to ridicule the idea that religion is a key aspect of practical political disputes.

In many areas of the world, religion should be seen as a central political pillar maintaining the power of any ruler—a major pole in determining the people's loyalty—and as a key ingredient in determining a nation's stability or instability. In short, the issue is neither the content of a given religion nor one group's attempts to convert another group. Rather, religion plays its role as an important defining characteristic of politically contending communities. Yet, in the absence of a heated theological debate—or on the assumption by some modern Western scholars that such debates are trivial and abstracted from real considerations of power—religion as the prime communal identity has, until recently, been too often neglected.

2. The expectation that religion would inevitably decline in the process of Third World modernization was wrong. Noting the secularization process in most of the West during the eighteenth, nineteenth, and twentieth centuries, some observers have assumed that the rest of the world would follow the same pattern. It was expected that modern ideas, such as science, technology, secularism, and humanism, would overcome the religious concept of the universe that dominated premodern society. This position fails to comprehend several points that will be explored later in this chapter, including the fact that modern ideas came to many countries as imports, were often perceived as forcibly imposed or imperialistic, and, therefore, were viewed suspiciously and as being out of tune with the prevailing political culture.

3. The West—including the communist regimes—tended to misapply Marx's concept, accepted widely in some quarters of the Western intellectual tradition, that religion is the opiate of the masses. This concept was taken to mean that religion was a distraction from the important things of life and that the chance to improve one's existence in this world would obviate the need for a system that could only promise rewards in the world to come.

Marx himself and many others neglected the point that opiates are addictive. Heroin addicts usually can be weaned from their drug only by the use of methadone, an equally addictive drug that is dispensed by government authorities and that provides no "high." This is analogous to the role of comprehensive secular ideologies that revolutionary regimes often try to push onto the masses from above in lieu of religion. They must be imposed continually and bring relatively little satisfaction. Moreover, the substratum of religious belief often continues to exist underground, awaiting some opportunity to reassert itself as an ideology. Thus, Ayatollah Ruhollah Khomeini provided a better aphorism than Marx when he commented, "The masses are naturally drawn to religion."

Indeed, Marx's contemporary, Moses Hess, also understood far better than Marx the social function of religion. He used the word opium to denote a medicine rather than a drug:

> The people, as the Scriptures say, have to work in the sweat of their brows in order to maintain their lives of misery. . . . Such a people, we maintain, needs religion: it is as much a vital necessity for its broken heart as gin is vital for its empty stomach. There is no irony more cruel than that of those who demand from utterly desperate people to be

clear-headed and happy. . . . Religion can turn the miserable consciousness of enslavement into a bearable one by raising it to a state of absolute despair, in which there disappears any reaction against evil and with it pain disappears as well: just as opium does serve painful maladies.[1]

Strong Religions, Weak States

For several reasons, these points and the political importance of religion reverberate with special strength in Third World countries. First, the states of Africa, the Middle East, and Asia emerged to deal with modernity and industrialization in a way different from the West. Nationalism, for example, is largely a novel and foreign concept for these new states. Religion and clan (or ethnicity) were the primary, tightly entwined roots of ideology and loyalty in the long histories of their peoples. The nation-state is an existential notion that existed in practice before the concept was defined or accepted by the people. Moreover, religion has the form of an indigenous idea, developed or adapted through long internal practice. In contrast, nationalist, Marxist, humanist, and secularist ideas are imports that often are viewed with some suspicion, if not hostility.

Not having experienced a long period of communal fusion into a nation, these societies continue to see religion, clan, ethnicity, and other such factors as the markers of community identity. In the Middle East, national identification is still largely a function of religious affiliation. One's community is either Sunni or Shi'ite Muslim, Alawite, Druze, Christian (Roman Catholic, Maronite, Copt, Eastern Orthodox, or Greek Catholic), or Jewish.[2] Iran's Islamic revolution and Lebanon's civil war are only the most obvious and salient examples of this phenomenon that is present in many other situations. The Arab attitude toward the conflict with Israel is heavily conditioned by religion. Pakistan's raison d'être is its Islamic composition. Religion is also a fundamental political issue defining community in Sudan, India, Malaysia, Indonesia, and elsewhere. In sub-Saharan Africa, the Protestant and Catholic divisions often have manifested themselves along political lines as well.

Northern Ireland is a good example of a European society where religion remains the prime communal and, hence, political as well as ideological definition. Yet in formerly communist countries, the line of political community can run between believers and nonbelievers. Poland, where the Roman Catholic Church has been either the backbone of or inspiration for the opposition, is the clearest example. In places where Eastern Orthodox churches are hegemonic, like Romania, the long subordination of church to state makes that faith, both institutionally and ideologically, a weaker reed.

The disintegration of Yugoslavia provides several good examples of religion's importance as a definer of communal loyalties. The armed conflicts between Serbs, Croatians, and Bosnian Muslims are not wars of religion per se. Yet the durability of such intense hatreds among people who had so long lived side by side, spoken the same language, and practiced very similar cultures can only be explained by the different identities largely generated by being Eastern Orthodox, Catholic, or Muslim.

Religion played a role on several levels in the collapse of the USSR. Despite seven decades of communism, that country's society was in many ways far more traditional than those of the West. In addition, the USSR was still an empire, with religion one of the few ways—sometimes the only way—the distinct culture and history of national groups could be manifested. Communities were still defined largely by religion and by the language in which they practiced their faith. Ukrainians, Lithuanians, Jews, and others were distinguished by loyalty to their distinctive beliefs and practices, many of which had religious origins that had been so watered down during the communist era as to become more sentimental than ritual.

As for the Russians themselves, the eclipse of communism led to an upsurge in the Eastern Orthodox Church, which is still deeply rooted in their culture. Religion seems to be a central factor among conservative and right-wing nationalists, who are trying to build on Russian traditions to advocate a more chauvinistic foreign policy—including reestablishment of the USSR as a Russian empire—and a discriminatory attitude toward minority groups.

These points also hold true for the "Muslim" republics of the former Soviet Union, but in their case, speakers of Russian are often the victims of majority pressure. Religion's principal function is as a key element in the local ethnic revival—Azeri, Uzbek, Tajik, and others—which may be predominantly secular nationalist in political form. But there are also considerable Islamic fundamentalist movements encouraged by Iran. These groups could eventually take over one or several republics, considerably recasting the politics of the region.

Clearly, religion is playing a more important role throughout the former USSR. No area of the world illustrates more clearly the fallacy of past beliefs that religion would be a steadily declining influence in society.

In most of the countries discussed here, politics is characterized by communal divisions within nation-states. In largely homogeneous countries, however, religion can be a central factor in the dominant political culture.

To create a Third World Marxist cadre requires years of training, while Islamic fundamentalism, for instance, is easily grasped by far more people, regardless of their level of urban intellectual sophistication. On a related note, national elites are often more cosmopolitan, cynical, and worldly than the masses. They are more likely to have been educated overseas, to speak foreign languages, and to admire some aspects of Western culture. Like their counterparts abroad, they tend to have contempt for, or at least a lack of identification with, religion.

The admission of the masses into politics and the recruitment of huge numbers into a broadened elite of professionals, business people, military officers, government bureaucrats, and teachers are hallmarks of the modernization process. Yet these changes also give upward mobility to the religious sectors of the population that have greater loyalty to a more narrow, religiously defined community.

Thus the secret of the influence of religion in contemporary world politics is that the modernization process, rather than causing religion to weaken and disappear, often makes its public role stronger and a more necessary part of the process of state-building or revolutionary transformation. On a subnational level, religion underlies the definition of communities, each of which may contend for political power or some degree of autonomy. Consider, for example, the Muslims of the Philippines, whose guerrilla war against the central government has led them as far afield as Libya in order to obtain aid.

Given the lack of other strong social institutions, the church or mosque and their clerical hierarchies and laypeople come to play an important function. They define values, social goals, and foreign linkages, providing a base of support for the rulers or a foundation for the opposition. In Latin America, the role of the Catholic Church—or individual priests—on one side or the other of social and political issues has been of increasing importance, particularly because the Church is the social and intellectual center of the masses. In South Africa, Archbishop Desmond Tutu and other clerics have become political figures in their own right. The importance of religious institutions is further guaranteed because they and their personnel are usually relatively immune from repression.

Finally, religious structures are some of the strongest institutions in many Third World countries that generally have a weak state apparatus. As the most real and powerful arm of government, the armed forces of Third World countries are always a prime candidate for seizing control of the state. Religious institutions, however, have the greatest presence and, often, influence among the people. Thus, they are an alternative route to mobilization, having the capacity to provide the backbone for opposition to the authorities. In this context, several specific situations can be reexamined.

Lebanon

Lebanon's modern political system rested on an agreement among elites that divided power in a proportionate way. The following factors unhinged the compromise arrangement that had been enshrined in this National Pact: migration from rural areas to the cities, which brought together separate religious communities; demographic changes, which increased the proportion of Shi'ite Muslims to Maronite Christians; and new radical ideologies, which made groups believe they might be able to seize control of the whole country. Foreign interference, although important, was essentially secondary.

The theology and history of the various religious denominations in Lebanon had a great impact on their ideological orientations, operational characteristics, and foreign alliances. It is first necessary to introduce briefly the differences among the communities before explaining their significance for U.S. policymaking.

Sunni Muslims, as former rulers of Lebanon and the largest religious group in the Arab world, have considered themselves to be an aristocracy. They have looked down on the Shi'ites as poor, backward, and fated to follow Sunni leadership. Sunnis were also more likely to support pan-Arabism, believing it would reinforce their power.

Maronites, the politically dominant group in Lebanon, are not only Christians but also Catholics directly linked to the West. This factor made them allies of France when it ruled Lebanon, and later made France willing to reciprocate by supporting the Christians. Thus the Maronites see themselves as a besieged Western community in the Middle East whose interests are threatened by pan-Arab nationalism, and this idea is reinforced by their clergy.

Although Sunni Muslims and Maronites historically have been the two main forces in Lebanon, a third group, the Shi'ite Muslims, has become the largest single community there. In the past, the Shi'ites were uneducated, poor peasants living in Lebanon's neglected south. Then Shi'ites began migrating to the cities, where they gained higher level education and built communal self-consciousness. Charismatic clerics, notably the Lebanese Shi'ite founder of Amal, Musa al-Sadr, began to organize the Shi'ites in order to demand more rights. The Shi'ites' historic antagonism to the Sunnis began to reemerge. Theologically, the Sunnis were blamed for "stealing" in the seventh century the post of caliphate, the leadership of the Islamic state and religion, from the Shi'ite candidate, Ali, and from the family of the prophet Muhammad. Historically, Shi'ites have complained about Sunni oppression. Furthermore, the Shi'ites structurally were oriented more toward independent clerical leadership and charismatic leaders than were the Sunnis. Ideologically, the Shi'ites questioned the pan-Arabism that sought to unite the mainly Sunni Arab world under Sunni rule, providing over the decades little advantage for Lebanese Shi'ites.

Subsequent events made the Lebanese Shi'ite Muslims feel more distinct from Sunni Muslims. The Iranian revolution was the most important factor. The critical political issue was whether the Shi'ite community in Lebanon would see itself as being more Lebanese or more Shi'ite. In other words, would they identify themselves as a community within Lebanon seeking more rights or with Tehran's revolutionary Islamic fundamentalism so as to make Lebanon a Shi'ite-Islamic state? The former idea dominates the Amal faction; the latter is espoused by the Iran-backed group known as Hezbollah.

The Lebanese civil war, with the many shifts of alliances and advantages from its onset in 1975, has been essentially a battle among religiously defined communities, although they often divided into subfactions on other grounds. The maximal aim of each group—Maronite, Sunni, Shi'ite, and Druze—has been to dominate Lebanon; the minimal goal has been to achieve internal unity of the faction and to defend its own territory. The Syrians became the patrons of the Druze and of subfactions of the other three communities. During its 1982 invasion of Lebanon, Israel tried to consolidate the Maronites' grip on power. At that time, the United States became involved directly in Lebanon, but put too much stress on ideological factors. Some top policymakers in the United States viewed Christians as pro-Western moderates, saw Shi'ites as pro-Iranian fundamentalists, and mistakenly labeled the Syrians as Soviet surrogates. That analysis was too rigid and exaggerated Moscow's role. In fact, the main groups were primarily concerned with their own religio-political interests. Broader ideology or international alliances were distinctly secondary.

In this context, these same policymakers became preoccupied with the question of legitimacy of the government in Lebanon. Because Amin Gemayel was president and was battling Syrian forces, he was given U.S. support. This approach of supporting one beleaguered faction contrasts with the successful policy of the Eisenhower administration in 1958, when U.S. leverage forced Maronite concessions that reconciled the other groups, producing 17 years of relative stability and continued Maronite primacy.

In 1982 U.S. policymakers would have been far better advised to recognize the legitimacy of the concerns of other religious communities, build relations with those groups, and broker a compromise. Since many of those concerns derived from economic deprivation and lack of political power in addition to religion, compromise was possible. The old Sunni elite and Amal, along with their clerical supporters, would have been open to a deal. An accord might have included reducing Syrian influence, a larger share of power for Shi'ites (especially patronage and aid to south Lebanon), and Sunni reintegration into the government coalition.

Amal's faction, engaged in a struggle for hegemony with Hezbollah, would have welcomed aid in order to defeat its rivals and to bring material gains to the Shi'ite community. The conflict between Amal and Hezbollah for control of the Shi'ite community, which is the main source of anti-American terrorism, was fought as a theological battle in which both sides used religious justifications.[3] Still, the victory of Hezbollah and its radical fundamentalism was never inevitable because Amal offered equally valid theological arguments.

The Druze would have been harder for the United States to deal with—it was Druze artillery that shelled the U.S. Marines at the Beirut airport—but they, too, wanted a larger share of political participation. It is likely that Syria would have used its military power and influence over the Amal and Druze factions to try to block any United States–arranged pact. Still, given the central role of religion rather than ideology, such an effort might have succeeded and would have been preferable to the drift that led to the ensuing debacle and the deaths of so many U.S. citizens. The key then and now to Lebanon is to see its civil war not in ideological terms, but as a conflict with deep historical, social, and economic roots among groups that define themselves in religious terms.

Iran

Perhaps the best example of the centrality of religion as a factor in international affairs lies in the recent history of Iran. Lebanon's communal rivalries are religiously based, while Iran's ideology and movements manifest themselves through religious vocabulary and institutions.

The Iranian revolution was influenced and caused by a number of specifically Iranian factors. Some of these had implications for other countries. Religion, for example, was a major factor. Although Iran has a tradition of anticlericalism, clerics were highly respected and tended to be the most articulate and educated people who had regular contact with the masses. The clergy had accepted secret subsidies from the shah, Mohammad Reza Pahlavi; nonetheless, when his government came to be considered illegitimate, the clergy was the group least compromised by collaboration with or infiltration by the government.

The ideology of Iranian religious leaders embodied large elements of traditional thought and culture and provided the only completely developed alternative to Western, Marxist, and modernist worldviews. Moreover, the clergy, mosques, and religious schools enjoyed a certain immunity from repression that other groups such as students and merchants did not have.

Western observers, and particularly, the U.S. government, viewed religion in Iran under the shah as a weak and declining institution. As the Iranian people began to look for a source of identity during a period of turbulent change in the 1960s and 1970s, however, religion was being reinforced. Islam came to embody the country's ethos, filling a niche usually occupied by secular nationalism. In short, religion represented authenticity.

Just as religion was underestimated, so were its clerics. Although they were perceived as unworldly, naive ascetics, some of the Iranian clerics actually were shrewd, ruthless, worldly politicians. They were capable of maneuvering and mobilizing bases of support for themselves and were adept at propaganda.

In the Ayatollah Khomeini, the revolution had a charismatic, unbending man who used religion skillfully as a tool to manipulate power and who compared to Lenin as a compelling theorist and masterful leader. Khomeini's ideology was only one interpretation of Islam and of Shi'ite Islam, in particular. But it was one that lent itself to an extremist, xenophobic, and intolerant concept that became the governing ethos of Iran's Islamic republic.

The Iranian case raises a larger question about the difficulty that many members of the foreign policy community in the United States have in comprehending the role of religion in international affairs. Although religion is generally concerned with the problem of evil in the world, secular U.S. diplomatic thought is not. Holding that rational, national interests are the root of human and state motivation, many policymakers and diplomats have become incapable of understanding certain phenomena.

Motivated by transcendent beliefs, the religion-based ideology of Iranian and Lebanese Shi'ite fundamentalism obeys rules different from the materialism-based system of thought that dominates U.S. policymaking. Consequently, inaccurate assessments are often made of how such religiopolitical forces will behave.

With regard to Iran, the United States deemed it impossible that a fundamentalist government would take power; inconceivable that Khomeini would mean what he said; unexpected that Tehran would seize U.S. diplomats as hostages; unbelievable that Iran would continue a war with Iraq long after the battle was counterproductive; and irrational that Khomeini would call for the murder of author Salman Rushdie at the moment Iran needed Western investment for reconstruction. In addition to shortcomings of analysis— or even when analysis is reasonably accurate—policymakers face the even more difficult problem of how to deal with such situations.

The strategic, economic, and political factors that would seem to rule out the course Iran has taken during the last decade may eventually triumph. Tehran finally did release the American hostages and end the war. In any given crisis, however, the country's ideology will produce different decisions. Pragmatic choices regarding the hostages and the war were made in order to keep the Islamic government in power, enabling it to carry out its programs on every other front.

Failing to understand this principle, the administration of Jimmy Carter underestimated the radicalism of the Iranian revolution and then tried to overcome Iranian suspicion and antagonism by offering minimal concessions. Similarly, the administration of Ronald Reagan believed Tehran would be moved by appeals to its *realpolitik* interests. It thought that Iran must be either pro-West or pro-Soviet, while Tehran's religiously based ideology made it see the world in totally different terms. U.S. efforts in Iran failed completely, with resulting embarrassment and political costs.

The type of problem inherent in the Iranian case has broader importance. The West has often assumed that religion is shed in order to form national self-consciousness. As argued here, however, in the Third World, nation-state nationalism often is nonexistent and the state apparatus is relatively weak. In such areas, religion can be the strong institution that provides a central element in the building of a popular and national identity.

The type of religion in a region also must be understood. Politicized Christianity tends toward some form of Western ideology that may be pro-capitalist or, in the case of liberation theology, neo-Marxist. Islam, however, provides an alternative view of the world, institutional structure, and set of goals.

Fundamentalism and International Relations

The anti-Americanism of radical Islamic fundamentalism does not result from some mistaken U.S. policy or from a resolvable misunderstanding. In general, Islamic fundamentalists seek to take over Muslim countries in order to revolutionize their societies. If the United States opposes such objectives—and U.S. national interests make this inevitable— then the two forces are going to be adversaries.

It is a mistake, however, to assume that radical Islamic fundamentalism will inevitably win, just as it is a mistake to assume that all Muslims are "fundamentalists." Most individuals turning back to Islam prefer the religion's traditional form. Revolutionary fundamentalist Islam is a deviationist movement, and some of its key ideas are unacceptable to truly orthodox believers. In Sunni countries, radical fundamentalists are also anticlerical—at odds with a clergy that largely supports the incumbent government. Although it could be argued, for example, that Khomeini was in line with Islamic doctrine when he called for Rushdie's murder, a dozen other Muslim states found well-grounded doctrinal rationales for ignoring him.

Heterogeneous religious populations greatly affect the stability and foreign policy of many Middle Eastern countries. Islamic fundamentalism poses a major threat to Israel, from both its Arab citizens and residents of the occupied territories. In addition, small, ultraorthodox Jewish religious parties often hold the balance of power between the larger blocs in Israeli politics. Any understanding of Israeli policy and the Arab-Israeli peace process requires an appreciation of the depth of Israel's concern about the Islamic fundamentalist determination to destroy it and the role of Jewish religious parties in the movement to create West Bank settlements. The main opposition to the PLO and the peace accord comes from the Palestinian Islamic group Hamas.

The majority of Syrians are Sunni Muslims, but the ruling establishment is overwhelmingly Alawite. In Syria, Sunnis look down on Alawites, not even considering them Muslims. This religious antagonism is at the center of the internal power struggle in Syria and is a major motive for Syria's hard-line foreign policy. In order to forge domestic unity and prove themselves good Arabs and Muslims, the Alawites try to be the most steadfast in fighting Israel and U.S. "imperialism." This reason, among others, is why past U.S. efforts to draw Syria into Arab-Israeli peace talks or to appease Syria in Lebanon (especially in 1982–84) were doomed. Iraq's Saddam Hussein followed the same pattern. Only by understanding these religiopolitical issues to the fullest extent possible can U.S. policy deal effectively with religiously influenced states or with fundamentalist movements.

Religious Challenges in the Former Eastern Bloc

Religion is not just a problem or issue for the West. Religious worldviews and institutions were a central force challenging Marxist-Leninist governments in the Soviet Union and Eastern Europe. The Orthodox churches in the Soviet Union, on the other hand, were purely national bodies long subordinated to the state and as such were far less likely, or were structurally unable, to develop as opposition centers than was the self-ruling, internationalist Catholic church. Nevertheless, a revived religious consciousness played some role in the Russian dissident movements leading to the collapse of communism and the Soviet Union. The real question as one looks to the future is whether the broad-scale revival of Russian Orthodoxy will be used by forces favoring a nationalist, chauvinistic political vision.

In the former Soviet Union, an impressive blending of religion and nationalism was evident in the Jewish, Catholic, and Muslim communities. For instance, a revival of Jewish and Zionist sentiment, leading to a large-scale emigration movement, became a major issue in U.S.-Soviet relations. The activity of Lithuanian, Estonian, Latvian, and Armenian church groups was an important factor in promoting effective internal nationalist movements in their respective countries. In the Central Asian states that emerged from the Soviet Union, the growing Muslim population, with the potential appeal of Islamic sentiments in both fundamentalist and nationalist versions, will be a potential threat to regional stability in the next two decades. Evangelical Protestant groups that preach an extra-state loyalty may have a smaller but interesting effect as well.

These changes will challenge U.S. foreign policy in a number of ways, posing such questions as the following: How will an internal upsurge in religion affect Russia's stability and foreign policy? Will religious movements undermine Russia, or will they ultimately strengthen civil society there? Is a Russian nationalist movement going to produce an aggressive expansionism as did Marxism-Leninism?

A sort of limited and imperfect rehearsal of the challenge took place in Poland when the Catholic church and the Catholic-oriented Solidarity trade union, with aid from Polish-born Pope John Paul II, forced the Polish government to grant them a major share in decision making. The dramatic changes included holding the first free elections in the history of any communist government. Even in Poland, some U.S. policymakers tended to underestimate the power of the church as a political factor.

Religion and Opposition Movements

In other major crisis areas, religion has also played a central role in shaping opposition movements. Christian churches have become leading institutions and often the motivating philosophy in a number of countries, particularly in Central America, but also in the Philippines, South Korea, and South Africa.

During the struggle against the government of Ferdinand Marcos in the Philippines, the Catholic Church, led by Cardinal Jaime Sin, was a vanguard element. By underestimating the staying power and broad base of the church-based opposition movement, the top levels of the Reagan administration almost fell into a major foreign policy disaster. The mistake was their failure to understand that the church and allied forces provided a strong doctrine and alternative to communist elements. Fortunately, a number of mid-level officials at the departments of State and Defense and at the Central Intelligence Agency had a better understanding of the situation and were able to persuade their superiors that the anti-Marcos forces represented a powerful and moderate grouping that the United States should not oppose. Otherwise, to get rid of Marcos, the church and moderates might have been driven to support the Marxist-Leninist New People's Army.

Events in Nicaragua were similar to those in the Philippines, except that in Nicaragua the moderates were driven to support the radicals. In 1978–79 the powerful, centrist Catholic Church hierarchy was in the forefront of opposition to the government of General Anastasio Somoza. Despairing of success in overthrowing Somoza, the church turned to the Marxist-Leninist Sandinistas, whose armed struggle seemed the key to victory, instead of heading up a more moderate coalition.

The Sandinistas' victory posed a major problem for U.S. policy. Their success resulted, in part, from Washington's failure to listen to the Church's warnings of revolution and to work more with it and from U.S. underestimation of the Nicaraguan clerical and lay forces of Christian Democratic orientation. In this connection, many of the Sandinistas had religious backgrounds, and several of the movement's key leaders were priests. In general, as many, or more, contemporary Latin American revolutionary Marxists have come from Christian backgrounds as from the ranks of pro-Moscow communist parties. Especially now that the former Soviet Union does not seem an attractive model, people are motivated to support revolution through the religious view of injustice, with the vision of building a better world. Throughout Latin America, more and more leftists and those willing to engage in armed struggle have traveled this ideological path.

In contrast, Catholicism does not necessarily take this same path. In El Salvador, Archbishop Oscar Romero became the most respected political figure during the 1970s, before being gunned down by a right-wing death squad. He was a leader in demanding reform and democracy, criticizing both the military and the Marxist guerrilla groups. The Catholic Church, involved in a number of grassroots efforts to organize peasants, often collided with the extreme right. Priests and nuns were threatened, sometimes killed, or forced to leave the country. The Right's justification for these attacks was that the clerics were playing a political role, which was true. The Christian Democratic Party, which led the country during most of the 1980s, was religiously motivated in its philosophy and links.

Similarly, the church became the main public force in Sandinista-ruled Nicaragua, criticizing government policies and calling for a compromise settlement with the opposition. The Managua government, unable to repress the church itself, tried to create an alternative, state directed Catholic infrastructure, but the effort met with little success. The Sandinistas tried to woo Pope John Paul II but failed when his visit to the country ended with his being heckled by a Sandinista-organized crowd. Church opposition subsequently played a major role in the fall of the Sandinistas in the free elections of 1990.

Whether moderate or radical, theological thinking is a central force in Latin America, and its influence in politics is likely to increase in the coming years. United States foreign policy must study the trends, comprehend the stands and demands, analyze the effect on stability, and identify reformist and revolutionary religious elements in Latin America and throughout the world.

Why have Catholic bishops, priests, and nuns come to play such an important political role in nationalist, revolutionary, or pro-democratic movements? A number of factors can be cited:

- The Catholic Church's leaders and property are relatively inviolate. Although individuals may be slain or attacked by death squads, governments are loathe to court international disfavor and to risk alienating hundreds or thousands of believers by directly confronting the Catholic Church.

- Catholicism's international links as a movement and its connection with the Vatican in Rome make it easier to mobilize international support and more difficult for a government to dominate it. The pope always names cardinals and bishops, which allows him to choose candidates from the opposition, if he wishes.

- The Catholic Church's discipline is a powerful force that makes it a de facto political party. Its cadres are dedicated and often highly educated. The institution controls schools, radio stations, lay organizations, property, and, of great importance, its own finances.

- Catholicism has a distinct ideology, of which an important component is social justice, although the latter may be emphasized or deemphasized, depending on the Vatican and on local leadership. No matter what the government preaches, however, the church presents a fully realized, alternative worldview.

- In Pope John Paul II, the Catholic Church has a strong, charismatic leader who, in spite of opposing neo-Marxist liberation theology, is a firm supporter of democracy and activism. To this end, he is influenced deeply by his own experience in Poland and by his direct support of the Solidarity movement.

• Catholics compose the great majority of people everywhere in Latin America and form a very large bloc in several dozen countries throughout Africa and Asia.

Lacking some of these advantages, Protestant denominations have had less political influence. Their divisions among sects and philosophies, along with a looser internal organization, weaken their unity. Protestant groups still remain a minority in Latin America, but there are some signs that evangelical sects will play an important, conservative role in the future.

In parts of Africa and Asia, Catholicism and Protestantism have become new sources of identity that provide a basis for political communities. These definitions at times have supplemented kinship and ethnic distinctions, welding several smaller groups into a federated arrangement. In southern Nigeria and southern Sudan, for example, Christian affiliations were set off against the Muslim affiliations in the northern parts of those countries and became prime ingredients in the civil wars there. In Nigeria, riots on religious matters annually kill from 50 to 100 people—hundreds of lives were lost in 1992—and it is possible that Islamic fundamentalist movements will become politically important in that country.

In large areas of West Africa, deepening Christian and Muslim commitments are already influencing foreign alignments. The conversion from Christianity to Islam of Gabon's President Omar Bongo was motivated, at least in part, by the lure of aid from the Muslim world. The late Cote d'Ivoire President Félix Houphouët-Boigny built the world's largest church in his home village to strengthen Christianity in his country. His personal religious beliefs probably enhanced his links with the West.

In contrast, a relatively recent influx of Christianity in other societies brings with it new ideas about political alternatives and activism. South Korea provides a good example because Christian groups of all denominations were the main forces of the ultimately successful struggle for democracy there.

Finally, South Africa is a particularly interesting case in which religion characterized the formation of both the moderate and radical opposition to the existing system of government. Ministers and bishops, Archbishop Desmond Tutu being the best known among them, have led much of the black opposition movement. Within the African National Congress (ANC), a strong, Christian religious orientation has been the main competitor of Marxist-Leninist ideology and the principal restraint against using terrorism as a tactic. In the dominant white Afrikaner community as well, the Dutch Reformed church has been a central ideological and political force with both pro- and antiapartheid wings. Traditionally, the church had been a mainstay in justifying white rule and a pillar of the ruling National Party. In recent years, however, with the exception of certain hard-core elements, it has basically challenged the system and aligned itself with the antiapartheid movement. The success of a peaceful settlement of the conflict in South Africa will intertwine with the future role of these theological institutions and with their influence on the political contenders. To understand or influence the outcome, U.S. policy must be attuned closely to these factors.

Conclusion

For several decades, the prevailing school of thought underlying U.S. foreign policy has assumed that religion would be a declining factor in the life of states and in international affairs. However, experience has shown and projections indicate that the exact opposite is increasingly true. To neglect religious institutions and thinking would be to render incomprehensible some of the key issues and crises in the world today.

As more and more people become urbanized, educated, and politicized, they will search more consciously and systematically for identity and ideology. Prescribed status and customs increasingly will come under question, and religion will be enhanced as an answer to problems. In many Third World countries, disappointment with the postindependence course of events and the discrediting of radical and Marxist philosophies may result in religiously based or influenced political viewpoints filling the vacuum.

A number of possible outcomes may affect U.S. interests. The triumph of radical Islamic fundamentalism could destroy alliances and create new crises. Such a scenario would result not from the strength of existing fundamentalist movements, but from a breakdown of current structures, socioeconomic deterioration, and despair about lack of progress.

The political manifestations of Christianity and of Catholicism, in particular, have changed from a major force against change into a factor favoring the attainment of democracy and social justice through reformist or revolutionary means. Moreover, the Catholic Church has proved to be the one organized institution that has survived years of communist rule, having an almost instantaneous mass appeal.

A few decades ago, the highest foreign commitment of the United States went to a little country called South Vietnam led by President Ngo Dinh Diem. United States citizens were startled to see Buddhist monks burning themselves in graphic protest against the Diem regime, but these events proved to be the starting point for public opposition to the official U.S. engagement in Vietnam and to the instability that would overthrow Diem and help destabilize his successors.

More recently, (a) a religiously inspired revolution in Iran unexpectedly took power and followed an unpredictable course, (b) U.S. military forces suffered their single largest loss since Vietnam from a fundamentalist car bomber in Beirut, and (c) Christian-led movements brought democracy to the Philippines and South Korea—all of which posed issues for quick and difficult decision making by U.S. policymakers. No stronger argument could be made for the centrality of religion in international affairs than this graphic experience.

57

FAITH AND DIPLOMACY

—Madeleine Albright

"This would be the best of all possible worlds if there were no religion in it!!" So wrote John Adams to Thomas Jefferson. The quotation, well known to proselytizing atheists, appears differently when placed in context. The full passage reads:

> Twenty times in the course of my late reading have I been on the point of breaking out, "This would be the best of all possible worlds if there were no religion in it!!" But in this exclamation I would have been . . . fanatical. . . . Without religion this world would be something not fit to be mentioned in polite company, I mean hell.

In his song "Imagine," John Lennon urged us to dream of a world free of religious doctrines. For many nonbelievers, religion is not the solution to anything. For centuries, they argue, people have been making each other miserable in the name of God. Studies indicate that wars with a religious component last longer and are fought more savagely than other conflicts. As the acerbic liberal columnist I. F. Stone observed, "Too many throats have been cut in God's name through the ages, and God has enlisted in too many wars. War for sport or plunder has never been as bad as war waged because one man's belief was theoretically 'irreconcilable' with another."

The fault in such logic is that, although we know what a globe plagued by religious strife is like, we do not know what it would be like to live in a world where religious faith is absent. We have, however, had clues from Lenin, Stalin, Mao Zedong, and, I would also argue, the Nazis, who conjured up a soulless Christianity that denied and defamed the Jewish roots of that faith. It is easy to blame religion—or, more fairly, what some people do in the name of religion—for all our troubles, but that is too simple. Religion is a powerful force, but its impact depends entirely on what it inspires people to do. The challenge for policymakers is to harness the unifying potential of faith, while containing its capacity to divide. This requires, at a minimum, that we see spiritual matters as a subject worth studying. Too often, as the Catholic theologian Bryan Hehir notes, "there is an assumption

* Madeleine Albright, *The Mighty and the Almighty: Reflections on God, America, and World Affairs* (New York: HarperCollins, 2006), 65–78.

that you do not have to understand religion in order to understand the world. You need to understand politics, strategy, economics, and law, but you do not need to understand religion. If you look at standard textbooks of international relations or the way we organize our foreign ministry, there's no place where a sophisticated understanding of religion as a public force in the world is dealt with."

To anticipate events rather than merely respond to them, American diplomats will need to take Hehir's advice and think more expansively about the role of religion in foreign policy and about their own need for expertise. They should develop the ability to recognize where and how religious beliefs contribute to conflicts and when religious principles might be invoked to ease strife. They should also reorient our foreign policy institutions to take fully into account the immense power of religion to influence how people think, feel, and act. The signs of such influence are all around us in the lives of people of many different faiths. By way of illustration, I offer three stories.

In 1981 I visited Poland; it was during the second year of the uprising by the Solidarity movement against the communist government. I had long studied central and eastern Europe, where, for decades, very little had changed. Now the entire region was awakening, as from a deep slumber. A large part of the reason was that Pope John Paul II had earlier returned for the first time to Poland, his native land. Formerly Karol Wojtyla, a teacher, priest, and bishop of Kraków, the pope exemplified the pervasive role that religion had played in the history of Poland. While communist leaders in Warsaw dictated what Poles could do, parish priests in every corner of the country still spoke to what Poles believed. The government, alarmed by the prospect of the pope's pilgrimage, sent a memorandum to schoolteachers identifying John Paul II as "our enemy" and warning of the dangers posed by "his uncommon skills and great sense of humor." The authorities nevertheless made a tactical mistake by allowing church officials to organize the visit, giving them a chance to schedule a series of direct contacts between the "people's pope" and the pope's people.

One of the titles of the bishop of Rome is *pontifex maximus*, or "greatest bridge-builder." In Poland, John Paul II helped construct a bridge that would ultimately restore the connection between Europe's East and West. For bricks, he used words carefully chosen to expose the void at the heart of the communist system, arguing that if people were to fulfill their responsibility to live according to moral principles, they must first have the right to do so. He made plain his conviction that the totalitarian regime could not survive if Poles had the courage to withhold their cooperation. Above all, he urged his countrymen not to be afraid—a simple request with enormous impact. Slowly at first, but with gathering momentum, the pope's listeners drew strength from one another. No longer were they separated into small, controllable groups; the communists' obsession with isolating dangerous ideas had met its match. Standing amid huge crowds, the listeners recognized in each other once again the qualities that made them proud to be Polish—faith in God and a willingness to run risks for freedom. The pope's visits—for he made more than one—sparked a revolution of the spirit that liberated Poland, brought down the Berlin Wall, reunited Europe, and transformed the face of the world.

The pope helped the people of Poland to overcome their fear. Bob Seiple, who served with me in the State Department as the first American Ambassador-at-Large for International Religious Freedom, tells a second story, this one about overcoming hate. It concerns Mary, a young Lebanese woman he encountered while working as the head of World

Vision, a Christian relief and development agency. In the 1980s, Lebanon had been the scene of a destructive and multisided civil war. Mary lived in a mostly Christian village; and when a Muslim militia invaded it, everyone fled. Mary tripped on a root, plunging face-first to the ground. As she scrambled to her knees, a young man of no more than twenty pressed the barrel of a pistol into the side of her head and demanded, "Renounce the cross or die." Mary did not flinch. "I was born a Christian," she said. "I will die a Christian." The pistol fired, propelling a bullet through Mary's neck and spine. Remorselessly, the militiaman carved a cross on her chest with his bayonet, then left her to die.

The following day, the militia returned and prepared to occupy the village. As they carted off the dead, a few of them came across Mary, still alive but unable to move; she was paralyzed. Instead of finishing her off, the militiamen improvised a stretcher out of wood and cloth and took her to a hospital. Seiple continues:

> And I'm talking to Mary, sitting across from her, and I said, "Mary, this makes absolutely no sense. These are people who tried to kill you. Why in the world would they take you to the hospital the next day?"
>
> She says, "You know, sometimes bad people are taught to do good things."
>
> And I said, "Mary, how do you feel about the person who pulled the trigger? Here you are, an Arab woman in a land twice occupied at that time—the Israelis in the south, the Syrians every place else—strapped to a wheelchair, held hostage by your own body, a ward of the state for the rest of your life. How do you feel about the guy who pulled the trigger?"
>
> She said, "I have forgiven him."
>
> "Mary, how in the world could you forgive him?"
>
> "Well, I forgave him because my God forgave me. It's as simple as that."

In Seiple's view, there are two lessons in this story. The first is that there are people who are willing to die—and kill—for their faith. This was true thousands of years ago and is no less true today. The second lesson is that religion at its best teaches forgiveness and reconciliation, not only when those acts are relatively easy but also when they are almost unbelievably difficult. (Mary, I need hardly add, is a more forgiving person than most—including me.)

The third story involves a boy with haunted eyes whom I met on a blisteringly hot afternoon in December 1997 during my first trip to Africa as secretary of state. The youngster looked about five years old and spoke softly, in a voice drained of emotion. He told me that, two weeks earlier, the small village where his family lived had been attacked. His mother had thrown him to the ground, shielding him with her body. When it was quiet, he wriggled his way out from under her and looked. His mother was dead. The bodies of other women were nearby, more than a dozen, drenched in blood. The boy then heard an infant crying; it was his sister, lying among the corpses. He gathered the baby into his arms and started walking. For hours, as the youngster stumbled along over hills and rocks, the infant wailed. Eventually they came to a place where the boy knew from experience that they would be welcomed and kept safe.

That place was Gulu, a town in a remote part of northern Uganda. World Vision ran the camp and hospital there—a haven for local villagers, who were being terrorized by an outlaw militia group. During the previous decade, an estimated 8,000 children had been kidnapped; most were presumed dead. Boys who survived and did not escape were impressed into rebel units; girls were taken as servants or "wives."

Camp officials blamed rebel leaders who had twisted religion into something grotesque. The tragedy had begun in 1986, when a change in government threatened the privileges of a previously dominant tribe, the Acholi. Fear is a powerful motivator, and the Acholi feared retribution for the many abuses they had committed while in power. A potential savior arrived in the unlikely form of a thirty-year-old woman, Alice Auma, who said that she was able to commune with spirits—a rare but by no means unique claim in her culture. She told her companions that she had been possessed by a deceased Italian military officer who had instructed her to organize an army and retake Kampala, the Ugandan capital. Once victory was achieved, commanded the spirit, the Acholi should cleanse themselves by seeking forgiveness. Auma's sacred campaign was launched but lacked the military clout to match its supernatural inspiration. After some initial successes, the movement—armed only with sticks, stones, and voodoo dolls—was crushed. Auma, her mind no longer host to the Italian officer, found refuge across the border in Kenya.

That would have ended the story had not Joseph Kony, Auma's nephew, decided to take up the cause of holy war. Piecing together a small force from various rebel groups, he assembled what came to be known as the Lord's Resistance Army (LRA). From 1987 on, the LRA has attacked villagers throughout the region, also targeting local governments and aid workers. Because Kony finds adults hard to control and reluctant to enlist, he kidnaps children as a means of procuring troops. Once captured, the children are forced to obey or be put to death; and obedience demands a willingness to kill anyone, including one another. Discipline is administered in the form of beatings, lashings, and amputations predicated on their leader's reading of the Old Testament. The LRA's professed goal is to overthrow the Ugandan government and replace it with one based on the Ten Commandments—or actually ten plus one. The eleventh, added by Kony to restrict the movements of adversaries, is "Thou shalt not ride a bicycle."

Itself a product of fear, the LRA has survived twenty years by instilling fear in others. The Ugandan government has veered between efforts to make peace with the LRA and efforts to destroy it, but officials lack the resources to protect those living in the vicinity of the rebel force. That task has been left to World Vision and similar groups whose resources are also limited, as I saw during my tour of the camp in Gulu. The surroundings reminded me of pictures I had seen of the Crimean War. The camp hospital smelled of disinfectant and human waste. Ancient IVs dripped. Mosquitoes were buzzing everywhere. There were hundreds of patients, most of them children, many covered with welts and scars, some missing a limb. I met a group of teenage girls sitting on mattresses, braiding each other's hair. They looked as if they belonged in junior high school, yet several were already mothers, their babies sired by LRA rapists. "Even if you are a very young girl," said one, who was wearing a Mickey Mouse T-shirt, "you would be given to a man who was the age of my father."

As I started to leave, a young man came up to me holding an infant. "This is the girl that little boy brought to us, his little sister. Her name is Charity." As I cradled the tiny orphan, I was told that the girl had been named for one of the volunteers at the mission. There were many such volunteers. It was a place filled with terrible suffering but also a resilient joy. Patients and volunteers laughed, sang, played games, and cared for each other. The Italian doctor who ran the facility had been in Gulu for more than twenty years. What a contrast between the faith that manifests itself in such love and the twisted fantasies pursued by the LRA.[1]

One insight that is present in these stories and often in religious faith more generally is that we share a kinship with one another, however distant it may sometimes seem; we are all created in the image of God. This in turn places upon us a responsibility to our neighbors. That principle provides both a solid foundation for religion and a respectable basis for organizing the affairs of secular society. What complicates matters is that religion can be interpreted in ways that exclude large numbers of people from any claim to kinship. Those truly imbued with religious faith—such as Pope John Paul II, Bob Seiple's Mary, and the volunteers in Gulu—may affirm "We are all God's children"; but others may follow their convictions to a more argumentative conclusion—"I am right, you are wrong, go to hell!"

When I appeared on a panel with the Jewish writer and thinker Elie Wiesel, a survivor of the Holocaust, he recalled how a group of scholars had once been asked to name the unhappiest character in the Bible. Some said Job, because of the trials he endured. Some said Moses, because he was denied entry to the promised land. Some said the Virgin Mary, because she witnessed the death of her son. The best answer, Wiesel suggested, might in fact be God, because of the sorrow caused by people fighting, killing, and abusing each other in His name.

This is why so many practitioners of foreign policy—including me—have sought to separate religion from world politics, to liberate logic from beliefs that transcend logic. It is, after all, hard enough to divide land between two groups on the basis of legal or economic equity; it is far harder if one or both claim that the land in question was given to them by God. But religious motivations do not disappear simply because they are not mentioned; more often they lie dormant only to rise up again at the least convenient moment. As our experience in Iran reflected, the United States has not always understood this well enough. To lead internationally, American policymakers must learn as much as possible about religion, and then incorporate that knowledge in their strategies. Bryan Hehir has compared this challenge to brain surgery—a necessary task, but fatal if not done well.

In any conflict, reconciliation becomes possible when the antagonists cease dehumanizing each other and begin instead to see a bit of themselves in their enemy. That is why it is a standard negotiating technique to ask each side to stand in the shoes of the other. Often this is not as difficult as it might seem. The very fact that adversaries have been fighting over the same issue or prize can furnish a common ground. For centuries, Protestants and Catholics competed for religious ascendancy in Europe. That was a point of similarity: wanting to be number one. For even longer, Christians, Muslims, and Jews have pursued rival claims in Jerusalem; that, too, is a point of similarity—wanting to occupy the same space. In parts of Asia and Africa, Christians and Muslims are fighting, but they share a desire to worship freely and without fear. When people are pursuing the same goal, each side should be able to understand what motivates the other. To settle their differences, they need only find a formula for sharing what both want—a tricky task, but one that can at least be addressed through an appeal to reason.

Not all conflicts lend themselves to this sort of negotiation. During World War II, the Axis and the Allies were fighting for two entirely different visions of the future. Today, Al Qaeda's lust for a war of vengeance fought with the tools of terror cannot be accommodated. Some differences are too great to be reconciled. In most situations, however, reconciliation will be eminently preferable to continued stalemate or war. But how is reconciliation achieved?

When participants in a conflict claim to be people of faith, a negotiator who has the credentials and the credibility to do so might wish to call their bluff. If the combatants argue the morality of their cause, how is that morality reflected in their actions? Are they allowing their religion to guide them or using it as a debating point to advance their interests? Has their faith instilled in them a sense of responsibility toward others or a sense of entitlement causing them to disregard the rights and views of everyone else?

If I were Secretary of State today, I would not seek to mediate disputes on the basis of religious principles any more than I would try to negotiate alone the more intricate details of a trade agreement or a pact on arms control. In each case, I would ask people more expert than I to begin the process of identifying key issues, exploring the possibilities, and suggesting a course of action. It might well be that my involvement, or the president's, would be necessary to close a deal, but the outlines would be drawn by those who know every nuance of the issues at hand. When I was Secretary of State, I had an entire bureau of economic experts I could turn to, and a cadre of experts on nonproliferation and arms control whose mastery of technical jargon earned them a nickname, "the priesthood." With the notable exception of Ambassador Seiple, I did not have similar expertise available for integrating religious principles into our efforts at diplomacy. Given the nature of today's world, knowledge of this type is essential.

If diplomacy is the art of persuading others to act as we would wish, effective foreign policy requires that we comprehend why others act as they do. Fortunately, the constitutional requirement that separates state from church in the United States does not also insist that the state be ignorant of the church, mosque, synagogue, pagoda, and temple. In the future, no American ambassador should be assigned to a country where religious feelings are strong unless he or she has a deep understanding of the faiths commonly practiced there. Ambassadors and their representatives, wherever they are assigned, should establish relationships with local religious leaders. The State Department should hire or train a core of specialists in religion to be deployed both in Washington and in key embassies overseas.

In 1994 the Center for Strategic and International Studies published *Religion, the Missing Dimension of Statecraft*. The book makes a compelling case for recognizing the role of religion in affecting political behavior and for using spiritual tools to help resolve conflicts. Douglas Johnston, the book's coauthor, subsequently formed the International Center for Religion and Diplomacy (ICRD), which has continued to study what it calls "faith-based diplomacy" while also playing an important mediating role in Sudan and establishing useful relationships in Kashmir, Pakistan, and Iran. Johnston, a former naval officer and senior official in the Defense Department, believes that, ordinarily, everyone of influence in a given situation is not necessarily bad, and those who are bad aren't bad all the time. He argues that a faith-based mediator has means that a conventional diplomat lacks, including prayers, fasting, forgiveness, repentance, and the inspiration of scripture.

The ICRD is not alone in its efforts. After leaving the State Department, Bob Seiple founded the Institute for Global Engagement, which is working to improve the climate for religious liberty in such volatile nations as Uzbekistan and Laos. The institute's mantra is, "Know your faith at its deepest and richest best, and enough about your neighbor's faith to respect it."

While in office, I had occasion to work closely with the Community of Sant'Egidio, a lay movement that began in Rome in the 1960s, inspired by the Second Vatican Council of Pope John XXIII. Over a period of years, Sant'Egidio successfully brokered negotiations ending a long and bloody civil war in Mozambique. It has also played a constructive role in, among other places, Kosovo, Algeria, Burundi, and Congo. The community sees prayer, service to the poor, ecumenism, and dialogue as the building blocks of interreligious cooperation and problem solving.

Numerous other faith-based organizations, representing every major religion, are in operation. They are most effective when they function cooperatively, pooling their resources and finding areas in which to specialize. Some are most skilled at mediation; others are best at helping former combatants readjust to civilian life. Still others emphasize prevention, addressing a problem before it can explode into violence. Many are experts in economic development or building democracy, both insurance policies against war. Together, these activists have more resources, more skilled personnel, a longer attention span, more experience, more dedication, and more success in fostering reconciliation than any government.

The most famous example of faith-based peacemaking was orchestrated by President Jimmy Carter at Camp David in 1978. Most observers acknowledge that the peace agreement between Egypt and Israel would never have come about if not for Carter's ability to understand and appeal to the deep religious convictions of President Sadat and Prime Minister Begin. I recently asked the former president how policymakers should think about religion as part of the foreign policy puzzle. He told me that it is not possible to separate what people feel and believe in the spiritual realm from what they will do as a matter of public policy. "This is an opportunity," he argued, "because the basic elements of the major religious faiths are so similar—humility, justice, and peace." He said that in the unofficial diplomacy he is often asked to conduct through the Carter Center, one of the first aspects he investigates is whether the parties to a dispute represent the same faith. He said it is often simpler to deal with people of completely different faiths than with those who share a religion but disagree about how it should be interpreted. As a moderate Baptist, Carter said he found it less complicated to have a conversation with a Catholic than with a Baptist fundamentalist; with the Catholic it was easier simply to accept the differences and not feel obliged to argue about them.

When I broached this same subject with Bill Clinton, he stressed two points. First, religious leaders can help to validate a peace process before, during, and after negotiations; through dialogue and public statements, they can make peace easier to achieve and sustain. Second, persuading people of different faiths to work cooperatively requires separating what is debatable in scripture from what is not. "If you're dealing with people who profess faith," he said, "they must believe there is a Creator; if they believe that, they should agree that God created everyone. This takes them from the specific to the universal. Once they acknowledge their common humanity, it becomes harder to kill each other; then compromise becomes easier because they've admitted that they are dealing with people like themselves, not some kind of Satan or subhuman species."

Faith-based diplomacy can be a useful tool of foreign policy. I am not arguing, however, that it can replace traditional diplomacy. Often the protagonists in a political drama are immune to, or deeply suspicious of, appeals made on religious or moral grounds. But if we do not expect miracles, little is lost in making the attempt. The resurgence of religious feeling will continue to influence world events. American policymakers cannot afford to ignore this; on balance they should welcome it. Religion at its best can reinforce the core values necessary for people from different cultures to live in some degree of harmony; we should make the most of that possibility.

58

RELIGION AND AMERICAN FOREIGN POLICY

—Jack Miles

The 11 September attacks put religion on the American agenda in a new and urgent way. More narrowly, 11 September would seem to have put the Muslim religion on the agenda in the form of Islamist terrorism. Yet the Bush administration has declared war not on Islamist terrorism but on terrorism *tout court*. To be sure, it may be tactically wise for the administration to mention Islam only in passing and speak instead, as Attorney General John Ashcroft did on 19 February 2002, of freedom as a sacred cause transcending religious division:

> This is not a conflict based in religion. It is a conflict between those who believe that God grants us choice and those who seek to impose their choices on us. It is a conflict between inspiration and imposition; the way of peace and the way of destruction and chaos. It is a conflict between good and evil. And as President Bush has reminded us, we know that God is not neutral between the two.[1]

But it would seem essential for the administration to reckon at least privately with the fact that its enemy defines the war, to quote Osama bin Laden in late September 2001, as "Islam's battle in this era against the new Christian-Jewish crusade led by the big crusader Bush under the flag of the cross."[2]

To put this difference another way, the American "war on terrorism" clearly does not entail any action against the Tamil Tigers of Sri Lanka, the ETA of Basque Spain, the Real IRA of Northern Ireland, or any other non-Islamic form of terrorism. De facto, it is only Islamic terrorism that threatens the United States, and the American government has acted accordingly. But can this uniquely threatening form of terrorism be effectively engaged without engaging the terrorists' declared motivation?

A serious effort to understand the religious dimensions of the Islamist attacks must begin, paradoxically, with the history of religious warfare among Christians. After the Peace of Westphalia in 1648, religion virtually ceased to be a motive for warfare across national borders in the Christian West, despite continuing intense religious differences

* *Survival* 46, no. 1 (2004): 23–37.

and severe religious persecution within national borders. After Jan Sobieski's defeat of the Ottoman Turks at the gates of Vienna in 1683, Christian-Muslim warfare faded as well—at least warfare of a sort that might rally Christians across national lines.

From the Muslim side, this marked the beginning of a long and humiliating retreat that did not, however, entail any conceptual break with religious war corresponding to Westphalia's famous *Cuius regio eius religio* ("the sovereign determines the religion"). When Christian Russia took over Muslim Central Asia; when Christian Britain took over Muslim South Asia; when Christian Bulgaria, Serbia, and Greece took over the Muslim Balkans; when Christian France took over Muslim North Africa; and so down the long list, these defeats were still construed on the Muslim side as defeats for Islam in an unfinished war of religion. Then were laid the foundations for an immense historic misunderstanding that has continued to the present moment, for in Western eyes these victories were not construed as victories for Christianity but rather as victories for the affected nations as nations. Think, for example, of Lord Byron dying for Greece: Byron would not have died for Christianity. When a more-than-nationalist agenda was admitted during the nineteenth century, it was "civilization" or, at most, "Christian civilization" rather than mere Christianity. True, the Western powers continued to swathe themselves in explicitly Christian imagery at moments of national solemnity down to the end of the First World War (anyone who doubts this should visit the recently restored mosaics in the Gedächtniskirche on the Kaiserwilhelmstrasse in Berlin). Yet it matters that even in that very war, Germany was demonized as "the Hun"—as cultural barbarian, in other words, rather than as religious infidel. This shift matters because as the Western powers projected their own ever more secular nationalism upon the rest of the world, they assumed that if a counterattack were ever to come from defeated Turks, Arabs, or Punjabis, it would come in the name of a nation rather than of a religion.

But this is not what happened. Al-Qaeda is a Muslim power but not a nation. That point can scarcely be stated too often or too emphatically. Its key support comes not from Arab governments, which fear it for good reason, but from a widespread, albeit thin, stratum of Muslim society. Terrorism may be equally immoral as practiced by a religious sect like al-Qaeda, by a criminal cartel like the Mafia, and by an irredentist movement like the ETA, but it is not equally threatening in all three cases. But the working assumption of this essay is that such differences do indeed matter.

In *A Peace to End All Peace*, David Fromkin blames much of the instability of the modern Middle East on British and French overestimation of Arab nationalism and underestimation of Muslim religiosity.[3] The comparable error in our day would be to assume that there must be government sponsors of al-Qaeda, so that to eliminate one is to eliminate the other. That assumption reflects an a priori disbelief that a religion, relying only on its own social resources, can ever generate a grave challenge to a world power. But religion can do that. It has done it before. It can do it again.

The sweet dream of American political thought—reborn in each generation, it seems—is that cultural factors like religion will shrink into insignificance as blessed pragmatism finally comes into its own. After the fall of the Soviet Union, many were eager to go beyond religion and announce that even secular ideology would no longer be a cause for war. But something close to the polar opposite has now occurred. The West is confronted with an extra-national, religiously self-defined entity with something ominously like a nation's power to make war.

Al-Qaeda is a novelty because it is a throwback. It is not that the West has never faced anything like it before. It is just that the West has not faced such a thing for a very long time—not, in fact, since before the United States came into political existence. Novelties sometimes fade quickly, but we cannot yet know whether this one will do so. Communism remained ideologically and militarily potent for the better part of a century. All we know of Islamist terrorism at this point is that its end is not in sight.

Given a virulent challenge of potentially long duration, how is the United States to respond? If religion constitutes all or much of al-Qaeda's reason for attacking the United States, should the United States call attention to this religious motive in framing its continuing campaign against al-Qaeda? How much, if anything at all, should the United States say about al-Qaeda's claim to be, in effect, the only true form of Islam? Need we care how many accept that claim? Is a dismissive phrase enough, or will a more extended refutation and a counter-campaign eventually prove necessary? Just as important, how much, at such a juncture, should the United States say to the world about how religion is handled under the American Constitution and how, specifically, the Constitution affects the status of Christianity and Judaism, the numerically dominant American religions?

In a 2002 interview in *New Perspectives Quarterly*, Samuel P. Huntington described al-Qaeda as an "extensive, transnational terrorist network."[4] Huntington had pointedly observed to the interviewer, Nathan Gardels, that Osama bin Laden is an outlaw expelled from his own country, Saudi Arabia, and later Sudan. The Taliban, which supported him, was recognized by only three of 53 Muslim countries in the world. All Muslim governments except Iraq—but including Sudan and Iran—condemned his 11 September terrorist attacks. Most Muslim governments were at least acquiescent in the U.S. strategy to respond militarily in Afghanistan.

Huntington went on, however, to note that despite widespread official condemnation, bin Laden had extensive popular support in the Muslim and, especially, the Arab world and that "just as he sought to rally Muslims by declaring war on the West, he gave back to the West its sense of common identity in defending itself."[5]

Huntington was quite right in this assertion. Paradoxically, 11 September was a stroke that simultaneously split apart the Muslim *umma* and knit together the Western international community, weakening the one and strengthening the other, much against the intentions of the suicidal hijackers themselves. Eighteen months later, unfortunately, the invasion and occupation of Iraq have had the opposite effect, splitting apart the West and knitting together the *umma*, at least temporarily.

"Appropriately," Huntington said to Gardels, endorsing the Bush administration's first counter-terrorist efforts, "the U.S. thinks of its response not as war on Islam, but as a war between an extensive, transnational terrorist network and the civilized world." But rather than engage the state of Islam as in any way a policy issue in itself, Huntington—resisting repeated invitations from Gardels—was content to regard Islamically motivated terrorism as simply intolerance intensified. In this, he was altogether typical of his profession. But as the 11 September attack mushrooms before our eyes into a global conflict in which Huntington's "extensive, transnational terrorist network" invokes Islam in every engagement, the profession's understandable reluctance to "talk religion" seems increasingly ill-considered.

The Bush administration's response to 11 September, like Huntington's response to Gardels, is much in the American grain. Americans, by and large, would surely have been made exceedingly uncomfortable by a president who saw fit to take sides in a Muslim debate, sorting out the ideological underpinnings of Islam as differently understood by mainstream Islam and by al-Qaeda.

And yet if the outcome of a contest between contending Muslim ideologies or theologies bears heavily on whether or not there will be continuing traumatically violent attacks on the United States, then does this contest not merit a good deal of American attention, even at the level of policy? At a comparable moment in the struggle with militant communism, the American foreign-policy establishment certainly did not hesitate to engage its opponent intellectually. It was judged crucial in the 1950s to distinguish carefully and publicly between democratic socialism as practiced by several of America's most important allies and undemocratic socialism as practiced by the Soviet Union. Had that distinction not been made, some of our friends might have thought themselves our enemies, and our enemy would not have understood the basis for our enmity. Numbing as the Cold War "theology" may seem in retrospect, it had much to do at the time with winning an international battle for hearts and minds. Now, the rallying of Muslim allies and the isolation of the Islamist enemy would seem to call for an analogous effort, particularly so if the enemy can only be isolated by close police cooperation with Muslim countries. Granting that the making of theological distinctions is not a task that falls exclusively or even principally to the U.S. president, it may nonetheless be an urgent task and properly part of any American diplomatic response to the Islamist threat.

Where should such an intellectual engagement begin? The term "Islamism" has been coined to refer to an Islam reformed or, perhaps better, mobilized to function as a superior ideological and sociological alternative to communism, capitalism, nationalism, and such other -isms as have attracted modern Muslims. In his recent book *Terror and Liberalism*, Paul Berman sees the Egyptian Quranic scholar Sayyid Qutb as at once the Calvin of this Muslim reformation and the Marx of its attempt to transform Islam into a totalitarian ideology. Berman proposes that while responding militarily to al-Qaeda and its ilk, the West, and above all, the United States, must respond ideologically to Sayyid Qutb and his ilk. But this, in turn, means taking Qutb and the inner intellectual drama of Islam itself with a new seriousness.

Qutb reads the intellectual history of the world as a drama in which, in effect, Jews, Christians, and Muslims are the only actors of consequence. Secular modernity is simply Christian error writ large. The Western divorce of science from faith, the core flaw of modernity as he understands it, continues and exaggerates Christianity's earlier, fateful sundering of body from spirit. Muslims would not suffer from this essentially Christian spiritual disease—this "hideous schizophrenia," as Qutb calls it—if Western imperialism had not infected them with it. The promise of Qutb's Islamism, then, is, in the first instance, the liberation of a Muslim spiritual recovery and, in the second, a counter-imperialism or jihad that will rescue the rest of the world from the *jahiliya* or ignorance of expansionist secularism.

Qutb gives bold Muslim expression, Berman says, to something "that every thinking person can recognize, if only vaguely—the feeling that human nature and modern life are somehow at odds." Perhaps Qutb can be ignored as deviant and ultimately marginal, though his thinking has venerable Muslim precedent. But if Qutb's way of engaging this modern dilemma and al-Qaeda's way of applying his ideas threaten to become dominant within the Muslim world, then the challenge—not just within that world but also within ours—must be to formulate and propagate a better response to the same dilemma. And who is to do this? Berman writes:

> The followers of Qutb speak, in their wild fashion, of enormous human problems, and they urge one another to death and to murder. But the enemies of these people speak of what? The political leaders speak of United Nations resolutions, of unilateralism, of multilateralism, of weapons inspectors, of coercion and non-coercion. This is no answer to the terrorists. The terrorists speak insanely of deep things. The anti-terrorists had better speak sanely of equally deep things. Presidents will not do this. Presidents will dispatch armies, or decline to dispatch armies, for better and for worse. But who will speak of the sacred and the secular, of the physical world and the spiritual world? . . . Philosophers and religious leaders will have to do this on their own. Are they doing so? Armies are in motion, but are the philosophers and religious leaders, the liberal thinkers, likewise in motion? There is something to worry about here, an aspect of the war that liberal society seems to have trouble understanding—one more worry, on top of all the others, and possibly the greatest worry of all.[6]

One knows whereof Berman speaks. Everything has been said, to quote a French sage, but nothing has been heard. The reservoir of available political thought in the West may be hugely impressive in the abstract, but it has not been tapped very well for anything approaching practical policy. In governmental relations between Western nations and nations of Muslim majority, whether nominally secular or floridly religious, religion has been passed over in the usual, agreed upon silence in favor of more mundane matters.

The trouble is that diplomatic relations are in this regard a poor representation of social relations, for a powerful stratum of Muslim society is evidently in the mood not just to talk tough about religion but also to join tough talk to lethal action. If what is called for after 11 September is a response that reaches societies and not just states, then introducing religion into policy discussion at the state level alone—difficult as that may be in itself—may not suffice.

A force that in the long run may have more impact on Muslim cultures than anything undertaken by the State Department is the experience and, tacitly, the example of Muslim subcultures flourishing in Western countries. The American Muslim subculture, though not the largest, may be the best integrated and most prosperous in the West, a fact that the State Department has recently and quite appropriately sought to advertise. But leadership from that quarter will take time to mature, even with more encouragement than it now receives.

Meanwhile, if a serious and mutually revealing kind of cultural exchange between the West and the Muslim *umma* is to be launched in the interest of a peaceful and mutually beneficial kind of coexistence, state auspices of any kind may not be the best auspices for it. Dissident Muslim intellectuals, to be sure, deserve in principle the same official welcome, shelter, and support that dissident Eastern European intellectuals deserved and received during the Cold War. Does anyone doubt that a line of intellectual descent can be drawn between Czeslaw Milosz's *The Captive Mind* in the 1950s and the Polish Solidarity movement in the 1980s? But unofficial auspices, or what is sometimes called public diplomacy, may be more promising at this point than official diplomacy. When Milosz defected, it was not the CIA but the University of California at Berkeley that provided him employment, and was it not better thus for the future of his dissent? It was not Milosz's ambition to go from the employ of one side in the Cold War to the employ of the other. Dissident Muslims typically offer a critique of both sides in the conflict that has now succeeded the Cold War. If their character as dissident *intellectuals* is to be respected, then what is called for is not simple recruitment but conversation in as many extra-governmental forums as possible.

It is instructive at such a juncture to recall that the most effective intellectual leaders during Eastern Europe's liberation from communism did not see themselves as mere dissidents. They were not communists, of course. But just as Gandhi called on his followers to be affirmatively Indian rather than to be merely and trivially anti-British, so Adam Michnik, Vaclav Havel, and others of their generation did not want their political agenda to be reduced to something so puny as anti-communism. In his new book *The Unconquerable World*, Jonathan Schell lays great stress on this Eastern European form of Gandhian *satyagraha*, quoting a famous saying of Jacek Kuron to Poland's Solidarity: "Don't burn down Party Committee Headquarters; found your own."[7]

The lesson of the "velvet revolutions" for the United States in its confrontation with Islamism is both cautionary and salutary. Though a larger accommodation of religion in American international policy may well facilitate a superior response to Islamism, the wrong *kind* of accommodation can only too easily degenerate into a response in kind. Wherever Islamist violence has emerged, it has tended, in the first instance, to provoke counter-violence and escalation.

Thus, in India, those who want to respond to Islamist terrorism originating in Pakistan by reasserting the secularity of the Indian state have steadily been losing power to Hindu religious nationalists of India's Bharatiya Janata Party (BJP). "Muslims are cancer to this country," BJP leader Bal Thackeray said in a speech quoted in a recent issue of *The New Yorker*; "Cancer is an incurable disease. Its only cure is operation. O Hindus, take weapons in your hands and remove this cancer from the roots!"[8]

In Israel-Palestine, the progressive Islamicization of the once-secular Palestinian liberation movement has prompted an attempt to turn Israel from a secular into a confessional state or, to coin a term, from a Jewish state into a "Judaist" one. After the 1967 Six Day War, David Ben Gurion, a secularist then out of power, favored giving the West Bank and the Gaza Strip back to the Palestinians. In June 2003, Ahuvial Nizri, a Judaist settled in the tiny West Bank outpost of Givat Assaf, told the *Los Angeles Times*: "We believe this land is ours. It's written in the Bible that it is ours, and it's hard to argue with the Bible."[9]

Bal Thackeray and Ahuvial Nizri have in common with Osama bin Laden that they believe themselves engaged in a religious war. As for the United States, consider the announcement in early 2003 of a special program at a Christian college near Los Angeles under the title "God vs. Allah: Who Will Win?" Topics to be discussed included the following:

- Was the war against terror predicted in the Bible, and who will win?
- Does the present conflict in the Middle East mean the end of the world is near?
- When will God make wars cease, as He has promised, and nations build ploughshares instead of swords?
- What do Bible prophecies, written thousands of years ago, say about Islam versus Christianity, and how that conflict will affect our lives and the lives of our loved ones?[10]

The Bush administration's careful abstention from any such inflammatory Christian rhetoric as well the president's own rare but still helpful gestures toward Muslim groups in the U.S. have to be balanced against diplomatically consequential Christian activism beyond the beltway. During the Ottoman era, the United States insisted upon and received from Istanbul a grant of extra-territoriality for Christian missions staffed by Americans. If most Americans have forgotten this partnership between the American state and the Gospel, it should not be assumed that Muslims living in the territory of the former Ottoman Empire have forgotten as well. Nor should it be assumed that Christian missions even today would not seek or accept such protection were it offered and at least one strategically placed American military officer would seem predisposed to offer it.

Lieutenant General William G. "Jerry" Boykin, Secretary of Defense Donald Rumsfeld's deputy undersecretary for intelligence, has told Christian groups around the United States—often speaking in uniform—that radical Muslims hate the United States "because we're a Christian nation . . . and the enemy is a guy named Satan." Of a 1993 confrontation with a Somali warlord, he once said "I knew that my god was a real god and his was an idol." The *Los Angeles Times* quotes "a top U.S. official . . . traveling in the Middle East when news of Boykin's remarks broke": "It was the worst day of my life. It confirmed [the Muslims'] conspiracy theory that the war on terrorism is really a war on Islam."[11]

The Bush administration has dissociated itself from Boykin's views only in the briefest and mildest terms, and he retains his highly sensitive position, one whose success would seem to depend on Muslim cooperation. Pentagon sources characterize him privately as "indispensable," and some of President Bush's right-wing Christian constituents have been vociferous in support of him. If his immunity is a clue, then what impends for American diplomacy may be an unholy identification of Christianity with American power at a moment when what is most called for is an emphatic distinction between the two in the context of a major new effort at public diplomacy.

Though the present moment, with American influence at a low ebb both in the West and in the Muslim *umma*, does not seem at all an apt one for such an effort, Americans would be ill-advised not to begin. On the one hand, the United States badly needs to infuse new vigor into its own practice of freedom of religion and its own commitment to the First Amendment. On the other, American international policy requires public and vigorous support for those abroad who favor the same combination of non-establishment and free exercise that Americans practice domestically.

"The problem is that we always want them to look like us," comments one CIA veteran with extensive experience in Afghanistan and the Middle East. "In all the countries I've lived in, I never saw one that could afford American democracy. We're going to have to get a lot smarter than to just say, 'Get a copy of the *Federalist Papers* and the Constitution, and you're going to be okay.'"[12] We do need to be smarter than that, and we need as well the saving grace of humility. "Power always thinks it has a great soul," John Adams wrote, "and vast views beyond the comprehension of the weak."[13] But when all such cautions have been registered, we must recognize that democracy is more like soccer than it is like American football: it is a world game. I vividly recall the polite but unmistakable indignation of Kim Dae Jung, years before he came to power, at the notion that his was an authoritarian culture that could not realistically aspire to democratic governance. If the question is how to respond effectively to the appeal of terrorist Islamism, we need to recall that other Muslims have ever been its first targets, for total control is the condition of its operation. Accordingly, no long-term offensive against its religiously motivated terrorism will be more effective in the long run than the promotion of freedom of religion in the very nations where it most actively recruits. Regrettably, the United States has yet to make a gesture comparable in its awareness of this dynamic to the Nobel committee's presentation of its Peace Prize to Iranian human-rights activist Shirin Ebadi.

Is it realistic to promote freedom of religion in Muslim countries? Well, realists predicted in 1975 that the Helsinki Accords would be violated, and the realists were right. But realism had its limits then, and it has them still. The various Helsinki Accords monitoring groups, despite their early ineffectiveness, were a seed well planted. They took root and became a kind of government-in-waiting as communism was inexorably overtaken by its own internal contradictions—a very Marxist outcome. Democracy in Eastern Europe is scarcely imaginable without the Helsinki Accords monitoring groups. May we not imagine, then, an Islamic equivalent of the Helsinki Conference? Imagine, if you will, a Sarajevo Conference on Muslim Pluralism.

The encouragement of free trade and free elections—which is to say, of the American model in commerce and politics—has long been unabashed American policy. American international policy has included no comparably unabashed encouragement of freedom of religion. Yet worldwide freedom of religion is arguably an even more pressing American national interest than free trade. The ideologues of al-Qaeda regard freedom of religion—that is, the separation of political from religious power—as the mother of all sins, the vice that enables all other vices. Accordingly, militant Islamism, acting in what it considers the defense of Islam and of virtue, has been prepared to take violent action to prevent the spread of this freedom, crushing Muslim diversity no less than religious diversity beyond Islam. The United States, even as it addresses such other legitimate Muslim grievances as injure the cause of peace, should make freedom of religion the first item on its diplomatic agenda—not a dream endlessly deferred but the most urgent and practical first order of business.

It is an oft-repeated truism that democratic capitalist states do not make war on other democratic capitalist states in the pursuit of political or economic power. This can be expanded to include religion: societies in which there is freedom of religion do not make religious war on other religiously free societies. It must be stressed, though, that the unit of comparison here is not the state but the society. But how does a state engage a society about the society's religion? State-to-state diplomacy, even as it touches upon religion, is well enough understood. Informal society-to-society diplomacy or "public diplomacy" is equally well understood; religious delegations undertaking people-to-people missions are increasingly familiar. But asymmetrical, state-to-society diplomacy with religious reform as its target is virtually without precedent in the modern West.

Whence the great difficulty that has attended the attempt of the Coalition Provisional Authority to reform Iraqi society by establishing for it, through the U.S.-backed Iraqi Governing Council, a political system that will safeguard the freedom of religion that Americans regard as *conditio sine qua non* for democracy. Grand Ayatollah Ali Sistani wants elections before a constitution is in place that would determine how elections should be conducted. His Shi'ite followers are the majority in Iraq; and to the extent that democracy equals majority rule, his demand on their behalf is for democracy. But the Sunni Arab minority rightly fears that its erstwhile Shi'ite victim is poised to become its oppressor, while Kurds, Christians, and Turkomens have comparable but even more intense fears of their own. Only in the Balkans did the fall of communism present challenges comparable to these; and the Balkans, where the fall of communism was anything but a velvet revolution, may be our best contemporary Western clue to how freedom of religion may arrive in Muslim countries that now lack it.

Yet, we may take heart that the Muslim world, at this point in time, may be almost as exhausted from internecine warfare as the West was just after the Thirty Years War. That grim and blood-drenched moment in Western history was, paradoxically, the moment when a great cultural liberation was accomplished in the West. Western freedom of religion may have been rationalized by the later brilliance of the Enlightenment, but the necessary condition for it was the misery that followed the West's wars of religion and the mood of revulsion and surfeit that these wars created.

By a similar paradox, the brutally lengthy religious wars that have wracked the Muslim world in recent decades in Afghanistan, in Algeria, in Saudi Arabia after the Shi'ite attack on Mecca in 1979, in Egypt after the Muslim Brotherhood's assassination of Anwar Sadat in 1981, in Iran after the Islamic revolution, in Iraq during the Sunni reprisals after the first Gulf War and elsewhere may have fostered a new readiness to find somehow a Muslim path to at least Muslim pluralism. This much and no more would already be a Muslim Westphalia. It can scarcely have escaped all Muslim notice that every one of these bloody conflicts has reflected the determination of some Muslims to establish a fusion of religious and political power at the expense of all other Muslims. Michael Scott Doran writes in *Foreign Affairs*:

> Radical Sunni Islamists hate Shi'ites more than any other group, including Jews and Christians. Al-Qaeda's basic credo minces no words on the subject: "We believe that the Shi'ite heretics are a sect of idolatry and apostasy, and that they are the most evil creatures under the heavens."[14]

Shi'ite radicals offer a matching hatred. Ayatollah Ruhollah Khomeini came to power calling for the overthrow of the House of Saud and an end to Wahhabi control over Mecca and Medina.

Muslim intellectuals never tire of pointing out that the Muslim past was more pluralist than is the Muslim present. Perhaps sheer exhaustion may do more than Western intervention to make the Muslim future more like that Muslim past. But might leadership for a revival and rationalization of pluralism emerge in part from Western Muslims protected and supported by Western non-Muslims?

It might do so if the Westerners keep their own history in mind, for the fatal dream of the restored caliphate closely matches another fatal and seemingly immortal dream that finally did die—namely, the Caesaro-Papist dream of the West in the various sword-and-cross forms it took over the centuries. Until the end of the Thirty Years War, it seemed that the West would die at its own hand rather than surrender this dream. But once the dream was in fact surrendered, it seemed a nightmare from which all had blessedly awakened. If al-Qaeda represents, in cultural terms, a return to the first decades of the seventeenth century, when its latter-day prophets were flourishing, then let us be bold enough to think ahead to the middle and the end of the seventeenth century as we imagine futures and conjure up diplomacies.

The West and the United States are not synonymous, a fact that Europe is recalling just now with a vengeance, and one that Americans have their own reasons to remember. And yet the American disestablishment of religion, coupled as it is to a guarantee that all religions may be freely exercised in that country, is the fruit of a common Western history, a matter that Kevin Phillips recently documented exhaustively in his book *The Cousins' Wars*.[15] Each Western nation, as each has differently uncoupled political power from religious authority, has a slightly different lesson to impart. Belgium, Canada, Germany, France, even, latterly, Northern Ireland—these and many others may rightly claim a turn at the podium. I would claim no more than this for the distinctive American way of dealing politically with religion but also no less.

The ultimate goal of an American international policy on religion must be to make all religions equally secure in every nation, thus to ensure that no nation shall (or need) threaten any other nation's religion or religions. This happy state of affairs must not only obtain, it must be *seen* to obtain, for perceived danger provokes war, while perceived security preserves peace. Support, then, must be rallied not just for the practice of the freedom of religion but also for the inculcation and public celebration of the practice. Freedom of religion is not the default position of culture any more than flight is the default position of an airplane. Freedom of religion, on the contrary, is a craft kept aloft in a culture only by constant and highly self-conscious maintenance. Government cannot do all the necessary work, but it can do some of it.

When the Egyptian novelist Naguib Mahfouz won the Nobel Prize for Literature in 1988, a Palestinian professor of modern Arabic and Hebrew literatures at Berkeley, Professor Muhammad Siddiq, commented in the *Los Angeles Times Book Review* that Mahfouz was not just the greatest but also the first novelist in the Arab world.[16] In the West, fiction as what W. H. Auden called "feigned history" occupies a midpoint between falsehood and truth—between fantasy or pure fabrication, on the one hand, and factual report, on the other. Siddiq was pointing out that Arab literature had only lately, in the person of Mahfouz, recognized this midpoint.

Siddiq's comment made sudden sense for me of the baffling accusations made by so many Muslims—not just Arab Muslims—that Salman Rushdie had told lies about Muhammad in his novel *The Satanic Verses*. Perhaps what was true of Arab culture was true to some extent of all Muslim culture. Western commentators as well as Rushdie himself, at first, had greeted this charge of outright mendacity with a shrug and a smile: "Come now, can a novel lie?" But on a mental map in which there is no middle kingdom between truth and fabrication, a story that is not—like a fable—a transparent and total invention must necessarily be a deceptive report, and its author cannot be other than an outright liar.

Secularity is, like fiction, a middle kingdom. It lies between religion and irreligion, between belief and unbelief. Those who occupy this middle kingdom may seem, to those who recognize no such realm, to be necessarily irreligious unbelievers—enemies of religion as Rushdie seemed an enemy of truth. Such thinking is personified by Sayyid Qutb. An effective counter-offensive against his kind of thinking will involve demonstrating that secular man, although free in principle to be an enemy of religion, is not inevitably such. Once secular society prohibits the prohibition of religion, which is what American society does through the "free exercise" clause of the First Amendment, not only is it not necessarily anti-religious, it is necessarily *not* anti-religious. The United States is proof that a secular state can govern without prejudice a vibrantly religious society. Our sworn opponent may not so much have rejected this truth as failed to grasp it in theory or observe it in practice.

If all diplomacy contains some element of pedagogy, it is on this point that the pedagogy of Western diplomacy ought just now to be concentrated. The United States with its colossal arsenal is, empirically, a threat to the world. No power so heavily armed can fail to be perceived as a threat. But not the threat that we are perceived to be in the Muslim world: we are not a religious threat. This is a point that American diplomacy, unofficial as well as official, must learn how to make, but Americans must first perhaps make this very point to themselves with a new insistence.

Islam and the West do not, in the end, divide the world between them. China is another world. So is India. Yet large as they are, India and China do not aspire to turn all the world's people into Indians or Chinese. Islam and the West—the Christian West and now the secular West—have historically had just such aspirations. Each aspires to be not a guest, not even an honored guest, at the multi-national banquet but alone in the role of host.

This being the case, if a reconception of the place of religion in American international policy can foster peace between these two historically aggressive actors alone, then the dividend in peace for the world as a whole may be large indeed.

59

METHODOLOGY, METRICS, AND MORAL IMPERATIVES IN RELIGIOUS FREEDOM DIPLOMACY

—Robert A. Seiple

The Laotian Ambassador was clearly uncomfortable. I had called him into my office at the State Department to demonstrate our concern over what appeared at the time to be an increasingly problematic human rights record, particularly in religious freedom. As the U.S. Ambassador-at-Large for International Religious Freedom, I felt it necessary to point out the requirements of our newly minted International Religious Freedom Act of 1998 (IRFA), the obligation the U.S. was putting on countries who were suppressing religious freedom, and the potential punishments that could be applied to a country if positive progress was not made.

The issue of punishment seemed to both frighten and confuse the Laotian Ambassador. He asked, "Why would this great country want to punish a poor little country like Laos?" I remember thinking to myself, "Because we can!" But this also produced a quiet rebuke as well. His question was legitimate, and Laos was indeed poor; born poor, and made poor by war, location (land-locked), and years of inept governance. Forty percent of Laotians were living below the poverty line, and illiteracy was higher than 70 percent.

To make matters worse, unexploded ordinance (leftover bombs from our so-called "Secret War" over Laos in the 1960s and 70s) was still claiming victims 30 years later, mostly children playing in the fields. America dropped more bombs on Laos during the Vietnam War than were dropped on Germany during four years of WWII. The cost to both countries was enormous, and over 400 unexplored crash sites in Laos continue to attest to this cost. Against that difficult context, the United States was asking the Laotian government to forgo their own agenda for their country, adopt ours, and make religious freedom their top priority, preferably demonstrating positive progress before the next annual State Department report.

I've now had ten years to reflect on that meeting. Three conclusions emerge that I will unpack further in this essay. First, "punishment" as a methodology has had a checkered career at best. It is part of the baggage of the past and rarely moves the human rights needle. Second, "promotion" of religious freedom has generated greater success, especially

* *The Review of Faith & International Affairs* 6, no. 2 (Summer 2008): 53–56.

when this methodology is linked with vested self-interest. Third, a collaborative effort combining public and private intervention is essential if progress is to be sustainable. This may mean that the State Department will need to outsource the moral imperative until such time as national interests and national values become one and the same.

Our Fascination with Punishment

At the first meeting of the newly formed U.S. Commission on International Religious Freedom (created by the IRFA), one of the commissioners poetically posed the question so critical to the rationale for the independent Commission: "Are we here to light a candle, or curse the darkness?" There were no takers so the commissioner answered his own question: "I guess we're here to curse the darkness." At that point, at least for the Commission, a methodological course was set: promoting religious freedom gave way to punishing bad behavior.

Inside the Beltway, punishment has always had its advocates. It is part of how Washington works. Rhetorical bombasts, self-righteous breast-beating, and other manifestations of testosterone wars sometimes carry the day in an environment where atmospherics determine reality. But the truth of the matter is this: such antics may work in Washington; they work in no other place on earth. Have China, Iran, Burma, and Sudan, for example, rushed to embrace religious freedom? These countries were the first to be put on the State Department list of "Countries of Particular Concern" (CPCs) 10 years ago. Unfortunately, there is no discernable evidence that they have adopted religious freedom.

The United States has never been shy when it comes to sanctions. We sanction more countries than any five other countries combined. By any measure, sanctions have been a blunt instrument, most especially ineffective when unilaterally applied. Why, when the evidence in terms of behavioral change is virtually nonexistent, do we focus so intensely on a punishment methodology? Sadly, my initial answer to the Laotian Ambassador's question carries some psychological credibility: "Because we can." Sanctions may not accomplish much, but they make us feel good, or at least powerful. Amongst the many things that the State Department Office of International Religious Freedom does, designating the yearly CPCs takes only about 10 percent of its time, yet attracts 90 percent of the external interest. Public hangings always attract a crowd. Indeed, yearly "List" additions, for some, are the metric for success.

On my first visit to Vietnam on behalf of this legislation, Pete Peterson (our first ambassador) introduced me this way: "Ambassador Seiple is here representing the International Religious Freedom Act, a bill designed to punish Vietnam." Not surprisingly, I became an instant enemy. It would take some time to build trust through the methodology of "promoting," rather than "punishing."

Finding Common Ground, Promoting Self-Interest

The primary role of the Office of International Religious Freedom is to promote religious freedom. "Promotion" is also the cornerstone concept in the Office's mission statement, which I wrote as the first Ambassador-at-Large to lead the Office. Once this is understood, it clarifies our methodology and produces results, as a closer look at Laos will reveal.

Historically, there is no reason that Laos should feel any desire to gravitate towards a U.S. agenda. While we came and went during the Vietnam War, Laos stayed and absorbed—everything from cluster bombs to Agent Orange. When Vietnam fell, Laos also fell, to a closed economy and a communist ideology. With the end of the war, there was no more use for the Ho Chi-Minh Trail. Sea lanes were now open between North and South Vietnam. Laos, as a staging area for the war, was no longer needed, and was soon forgotten. It seemed to me that threatening Laos with a CPC designation was nothing more than "piling on."

We decided on another approach. The message we sent was this: "We want to work with you, because we feel that an improved religious freedom record is essential to how you will be perceived by the global community." It was clear early on that security and trade would be the specific points of vested self-interest. In our conversations with the Lao, we always talked about religious freedom in the context of security. When the populace feels that the government has their best interest at heart, that populace is more loyal to the government. Loyalty brings stability. Stability allows for security. In this sense, religious freedom and security are two sides of the same coin.

Permanent, normalized trade relations (PNTR) were also a necessity if Laos was to make a dent in its poverty statistics. This took an unconscionably long time to produce, but during this period we were also creating a relationship of trust, an absolutely essential foundation for future progress. We stopped making threats and started offering invitations. After leaving the State Department, I stayed close to Lao officials and the U.S. Embassy in Vientiane. Through the Institute for Global Engagement, a religious freedom nonprofit I founded, we sponsored a high level Lao delegation visit to the United States. For 15 days we introduced the Lao to U.S. government officials, to religious pluralism, to American culture, and to the positive results of human freedoms. This proved to be a major turning point in bilateral relations. When the delegates returned home, for example, they spread out over Laos, visiting prisons where Lao were incarcerated because of faith issues. Thirty-four of 37 Christians were released from prison during the next two weeks.

In the next few years, two religious freedom conferences were held in Vientiane for government officials throughout Laos. I was asked to keynote both of them, and also was invited to talk about religious freedom at the Lao Foreign Affairs Institute. During this time, a Prime Minister's Decree for religious freedom was enacted, after consultation with a number of religious communities in Laos.

Unofficially, we also worked with the Lao Embassy in Washington. Special "Lao Days" were created, whereby the entire Embassy could come to my home on the Eastern Shore in Maryland for a day of boating, golf, fishing, and feasting. We flew the Lao flag on such days. The Ambassador whom I had once made extremely uncomfortable in my State Department office became a close family friend.

And religious freedom improved in Laos. In the 2004 Annual Report on International Religious Freedom issued by the State Department, there were two countries (and only two) noted for a marked improvement in religious freedom: Kazakhstan and Laos. Laos had made our agenda their own. In spite of the enormous challenges that faced Laos, the promotion of religious freedom—working together for a common good—captured their attention, earned their trust, and produced a result worthy of the highest expectations of our religious freedom legislation.

Outsourcing the Moral Imperative, or Track 1.5 Diplomacy

Laos has become a success. That is not to say that all problems have been resolved, but we can still point to this country with both pride and gratitude. In Vietnam, Laos' next door neighbor, the same careful attention to relationships has produced progress as well. So there are at least two countries that have come a long way in securing religious freedom. The question is: Why aren't there more?

First, the "promotion" methodology takes time. One cannot rush relational diplomacy. Annual reports, election cycles, five-year plans, and other self-imposed time constraints work against the kind of sustainable progress we all desire.

Second, the State Department has never been known for innovation. Every new thought is held hostage to a protracted clearance exercise. Multiple agendas sometimes suffocate new ideas. The wise Foreign Service employee restricts his/her agenda to a few items that have the best chance to be advanced during their tenure in the Department. Usually the tyranny of the urgent works against someone's longer term objectives.

Third, turnover is intentional. Diplomats are moved from place to place to avoid "clientitis." Celebrity players (appointed diplomats) also come and go relatively quickly. If a problem cannot be fixed in three years, it is often pushed to the back of an agenda. It is exceedingly rare for decision makers to "stay at the table" for over five years.

A new structure needs to be formalized. One of the major reasons for the Laotian success was a public (U.S. Embassy)–private (Institute for Global Engagement) collaboration that began with both entities essentially "on the same page." Each had similar motives, but different gifts. An Embassy relationship was essential. From timely briefings to good communication, from organizing key meetings to travel logistics, from initial ideas to after-action follow-up, the U.S. Embassy role was indispensable. From the nongovernmental side, the primary contribution was that one "face" would stay at the table until the desired outcome was assured. Rarely is the NGO motivated by legacy. Rarely is the NGO hindered or constrained by time. Most importantly, however, the private NGO only has one issue to represent. This was made very clear to me during my last visit to Laos. My final meeting was with Deputy Prime Minister Somsavat Lengsavad. We have known each other for a number of years. I have always found him to be helpful to our cause and a genuine friend. When we met in the large Foreign Ministry meeting room, he was all smiles. He immediately greeted me with the words, "My friend, welcome," followed by a big hug.

The U.S. Ambassador stood awkwardly to one side. She tried her best to look happy, but this kind of display clearly made her wince. I think I understand what was going on. I had been coming to Laos for 18 years, she for only three. More importantly, I only had one issue on my agenda, religious freedom, and things were going reasonably well. She had a dozen or more issues, and most of them were "issues" because they were not going well. I had an issue to celebrate. She had a dozen to fight over. But both of us understood the role of the other. This was a good collaboration because we were able to create a situation where one plus one equaled three—that is, we were considerably better off working together than each going a separate way. These kinds of collaborations need to be forged with great intentionality. They will produce results.

Regardless of how much we may want to see *realpolitik* and the moral imperative come together, we will suffer from time to time when national interests and national values are not one and the same. This creates inconsistency, and inconsistency is the Achilles' heel of human rights efforts. Good collaborative efforts, however, with the public and private sectors working at their best, will produce the greatest opportunity for memorable celebration in the future.

NOTES

1   Introduction

1   Edward Luttwak, "The Missing Dimension," in Douglas Johnston and Cynthia Sampson, eds., *Religion, the Missing Dimension of Statecraft* (Oxford: Oxford University Press, 1994).

2   Luttwak, "Missing Dimension," 9–10.

3   See Nikki R. Keddie, "Secularism and Its Discontents," *Daedalus* 132, no. 3 (Summer 2003): 14–30.

4   Luttwak, "Missing Dimension," 12.

5   Daniel Philpott, *Revolutions in Sovereignty: How Ideas Shaped Modern International Relations* (Princeton, N.J.: Princeton University Press, 2001), 9. The journals are *International Organization, International Studies Quarterly, World Politics,* and *International Security.*

6   See Jack Snyder, ed., *Religion and International Relations Theory* (New York: Columbia University Press, 2011).

7   Samuel Huntington, "The Clash of Civilizations?" *Foreign Affairs* 72, no. 3 (Summer 1993): 22–49.

8   Another issue that began to emerge was religion and development, as can be seen for instance in the 1998 founding of the World Faiths Development Dialogue. See http://berkleycenter.georgetown.edu/wfdd.

9   Johnston and Sampson, *Religion, the Missing Dimension of Statecraft.*

10   The International Center for Religion and Diplomacy (ICRD) works to resolve identity-based conflicts that exceed the reach of traditional diplomacy by incorporating religion as part of the solution. Typically, these conflicts take the form of ethnic disputes, tribal warfare, or religious hostilities. See www.icrd.org. See also the books published under ICRD auspices, such as Douglas M. Johnston, *Religion, Terror, and Error: U.S. Foreign Policy and the Challenge of Spiritual Engagement* (Westport, Conn.: Praeger, 2011) and Douglas M. Johnston, ed., *Faith-Based Diplomacy: Trumping Realpolitik* (New York: Oxford University Press, 2003).

11   The Institute for Global Engagement (IGE) is a "think-and-do-tank" that cultivates sustainable environments for religious freedom and equips people to exercise that freedom responsibly. See www.globalengage.org. See also IGE's quarterly journal, *The Review of Faith & International Affairs* (http://www.tandfonline.com/toc/rfia20/current) and the books published under IGE auspices, such as Chris Seiple, Dennis R. Hoover, and Pauletta Otis, eds., *Routledge Handbook of Religion and Security* (Oxford: Routledge, forthcoming); H. Knox Thames, Chris Seiple, and Amy Rowe, *International Religious Freedom Advocacy* (Waco, Tex.: Baylor University Press, 2009); Joshua T. White, *Pakistan's Islamist Frontier* (Arlington, Va.: Center on Faith & International Affairs, 2008); and Robert A. Seiple and Dennis R. Hoover, eds., *Religion & Security: The New Nexus in International Relations* (Lanham, Md.: Rowman & Littlefield, 2004).

12   World Vision is an international faith-based relief and development organization.

13 We list the following as just a few of the many examples: Center for World Religions, Diplomacy, & Conflict Resolution, George Mason University, founded in 2003; Center for the Study of Religion and Conflict, Arizona State University, founded in 2003; *The Review of Faith & International Affairs*, launched in 2003; Religion and International Affairs Initiative, Luce Foundation, launched in 2005; Religion and International Affairs Project, Social Science Research Council, started in 2005; Madeleine Albright's book, *The Mighty and the Almighty: Reflections on America, God, and World Affairs*, published by Harper-Collins in 2006; Berkley Center for Religion, Peace, and World Affairs, Georgetown University, founded in 2006; Religion and Foreign Policy Initiative, Council on Foreign Relations, started in 2006; Center for the Study of Democracy, Toleration, and Religion, Columbia University, founded in 2006.

14 Daniel Philpott, "The Challenge of September 11 to Secularism in International Relations," *World Politics* 55, no. 1 (October 2002): 68.

2 Taylor: The Meaning of Secularism

1   This essay is adapted from Charles Taylor, "The Polysemy of the Secular," *Social Research* 76, no. 4 (Winter 2009): 1143–66; and Charles Taylor, "Foreword. What Is Secularism?" in *Secularism, Religion and Multicultural Citizenship*, ed. Geoffrey Brahm Levey and Tariq Modood (Cambridge: Cambridge University Press, 2009), xi–xxii.

2   Rajeev Bhargava, "What Is Secularism For?" in *Secularism and Its Critics*, ed. Rajeev Bhargava (Delhi: Oxford University Press, 1998), 486–520 (see esp. 493–94 and 520 for "principled distance"); and Rajeev Bhargava, "The Distinctiveness of Indian Secularism," in *The Future of Secularism*, ed. T. N. Srinavasan (Delhi: Oxford University Press 2007), 20–58, esp. 39–41.

3   See, e.g., José Casanova, "Immigration and the New Religious Pluralism: A European Union-United States Comparison," in Levey and Modood, *Secularism, Religion and Multicultural Citizenship*, 139–63.

4   Andrew Koppelman, "Rawls and Habermas," private communication.

5   *Church of the Holy Trinity v. United States*, 143 U.S. 457 (1892), at 471.

6   See Article II at http://candst.tripod.com/nra.htm.

7   Christian Smith, *The Secular Revolution* (Berkeley: University of California Press, 2003). See also Tisa J. Wenger, "The God-in-the-Constitution Controversy: American Secularisms in Historical Perspective," in *Comparative Secularisms in a Global Age*, ed. Linell E. Cady and Elizabeth Shakman Hurd (New York: Palgrave Macmillan, 2010).

8   Marcel Gauchet, *La Religion dans la Démocratie* (Paris: Gallimard, 1998), 47–50.

9   I have discussed this relation in "Les Sources de l'Identité Moderne," in *Les Frontières de l'Identité: Modernité et Postmodernisme au Québec*, ed. Mikhaël Elbaz, Andrée Fortin, and Guy Laforest (Sainte-Foy: Presses de l'Université Laval, 1996), 347–64.

10 See Charles Taylor, *Modern Social Imaginaries* (Durham, N.C.: Duke University Press, 2004).

4 Philpott: The Challenge of September 11 to Secularism

*   The author wishes to thank the organizers of and participants in the conference, "The New Era in World Politics after September 11," at Princeton University, May 3, 2002, particularly Miguel Centeno for his valuable comments. An earlier version of the paper was also presented at the "Authority in Contention" conference of the Collective Behavior and Social Movements section of the American Sociological Association, University of Notre Dame, August 14, 2002, and at the Colloquium on Religion and History at the University of Notre Dame, September 18, 2002. The author also thanks Sohail Hashmi, John Owen, Eric Patterson, Andrew Moravcsik, Rashid Omar, Michael Francis, Paul Vasquez, Paul Marshall, A. James McAdams, John Carlson, and Nelson Gonzalez for helpful comments, and Colleen Gilg for excellent research assistance. All opinions herein are solely those of the author.

1   See Wilfred Cantwell Smith, *The Meaning and End of Religion* (San Francisco: Harper & Row, 1978); William Cavanaugh, "'A Fire Strong Enough to Consume the House': The Wars of Religion and the Rise of the State," *Modern Theology* 11 (October 1995); and Paul Griffiths, "The Very Idea of Religion," *First Things* 103 (May 2000).

2   I have been influenced here by Roy Clouser, *Knowing with the Heart: Religious Experience and Belief in God* (Downers Grove, Ill.: InterVarsity, 1999), esp. 11–42.

3   For an assessment of secularization, the concept, the phenomenon, and the literature, see Rodney Stark, "Secularization, R.I.P.," *Sociology of Religion* 60, no. 3 (1999).

4   Davie, "Believing without Belonging: Is This the Future of Religion in Britain?" *Social Compass* 37 (1990): 455–69.

5   Martin, *A General Theory of Secularization* (New York: Harper & Row, 1978), 69.

6   See Daniel Philpott, *Revolutions in Sovereignty: How Ideas Shaped Modern International Relations* (Princeton: Princeton University Press, 2001), 9. The journals are *International Organization, International Studies Quarterly, World Politics,* and *International Security.*

7   See *Orbis: A Journal of World Affairs* 42 (Spring 1998); and *Millennium: Journal of International Studies* 29, no. 3 (2000). In the *Millennium* collection, a particularly strong perspective of religion's role in the discipline and the practice of international relations is Scott M. Thomas, "Taking Religious and Cultural Pluralism Seriously: The Global Resurgence of Religion and the Transformation of International Society." See also the writings of Sohail Hashmi: Hashmi, "International Society and Its Islamic Malcontents," *Fletcher Forum* 20 (Winter–Spring 1996); idem, "Interpreting the Islamic Ethics of War and Peace," in Terry Nardin, ed., *The Ethics of War and Peace* (Princeton: Princeton University Press, 1996); idem, "Islamic Ethics in International Society," in David R. Mapel and Terry Nardin, eds., *International Society: Diverse Ethical Perspectives* (Princeton: Princeton University Press, 1998); Jonathan Fox, "Religion as an Overlooked Element in International Relations," *International Studies Review* 3, no. 3 (2001); *SAIS Review* 18 (Summer–Fall 1998); and Barry Rubin, "Religion and International Affairs," *Washington Quarterly* 13, no. 2 (1990).

8   See Huntington, *The Clash of Civilizations and the Remaking of World Order* (New York: Simon & Schuster, 1996); idem, "The Clash of Civilizations?" *Foreign Affairs* 72 (Summer 1993). The fact that Huntington's thesis was published in a semipopular journal (*Foreign Affairs*) and then by a trade press is indicative of how little attention international relations scholars in the field proper have accorded religion.

9   For scholarship that asserts the growing global role of religion in politics, see R. Scott Appleby, *The Ambivalence of the Sacred: Religion, Violence, and Reconciliation* (Lanham, Md.: Rowman and Littlefield, 2000); Fawaz A. Gerges, *America and Political Islam: Clash of Cultures or Clash of Interests* (Cambridge: Cambridge University Press, 1999); Shireen Hunter, *The Future of Islam and the West: Clash of Civilizations or Peaceful Coexistence?* (Westport, Conn.: Praeger, 1998); Peter L. Berger, *The Desecularization of the World: Resurgent Religion and World Politics* (Washington, D.C.: Eerdmans, 1999); Mark Juergensmeyer, *The New Cold War? Religious Nationalism Confronts the Secular State* (Berkeley: University of California Press, 1993); Gilles Kepel, *The Revenge of God: The Resurgence of Islam, Christianity, and Judaism in the Modern World* (University Park: Pennsylvania State University Press, 1994); Benjamin Barber, *Jihad vs. McWorld: How Globalism and Tribalism Are Reshaping the World* (New York: Times Books, 1995); Thomas L. Friedman, *The Lexus and the Olive Tree* (New York: Farrar, Straus, & Giroux, 1999); Susanne Rudolph and James Piscatori, *Transnational Religion and Fading States* (Boulder, Colo.: Westview Press, 1997); José Casanova, *Public Religions in the Modern World* (Chicago: University of Chicago Press, 1994); and the essays in R. Scott Appleby and Martin Marty, eds., *The Fundamentalist Project* (Chicago: University of Chicago Press, 1991, 1993, 1994, 1995). For an earlier exception to the general secularization of international relations scholarship, see also Adda Bozeman, *Politics and Culture in International History* (Princeton: Princeton University Press, 1960).

10 See J. R. Strayer, *The Medieval Origins of the Modern State* (Princeton: Princeton University Press, 1970); Susan Reynolds, *Kingdoms and Communities in Western Europe, 900–1300* (Oxford: Clarendon Press, 1984); Michael Wilks, *The Problem of Sovereignty in the Middle Ages* (Cambridge: Cambridge University Press, 1964); Walter Ullman, *Principles of Government and Politics in the Middle Ages* (New York: Barnes and Noble, 1966).

11 Jean Berenger, *History of the Habsburg Empire, 1273–1700* (London: Longman, 1994); Robert A. Kann, *A History of the Habsburg Empire* (Berkeley: University of California Press, 1974), 1–24; H. G. Koenigsberger, *Estates and Revolutions: Essays in Early Modern European History* (Ithaca, N.Y.: Cornell University Press, 1971).

12 Holsti, *Peace and War: Armed Conflicts and International Order, 1648–1989* (Cambridge: Cambridge University Press, 1991), 46–59.

13 The locus classicus for the concept of international society is Hedley Bull, *The Anarchical Society* (New York: Columbia University Press, 1977). For a good discussion of religious pluralism in international society, see Thomas, "Taking Religious and Cultural Pluralism Seriously," 819–24.

14 Quoted in David Maland, *Europe in the Seventeenth Century* (London: Macmillan, 1966), 16.

15   "*Dignitatis Humanae* (Declaration on Religious Liberty)," in *Vatican Council II: The Conciliar and Post Conciliar Documents* (Northport, N.Y.: Costello Publishing, 1975).

16   For broadly material arguments, see Perry Anderson, *Lineages of the Absolutist State* (London: N.L.B., 1974); Brian Downing, *The Military Revolution and Political Change* (Princeton: Princeton University Press, 1992); Douglass C. North and R. P. Thomas, *The Rise of the Western World* (Cambridge: Cambridge University Press, 1973); Hendrik Spruyt, *The Sovereign State and Its Competitors* (Princeton: Princeton University Press, 1994); Charles Tilly, *Coercion, Capital, and European States, AD 990–1992* (Oxford: Basil Blackwell, 1992). For my argument that material explanations are insufficient and that Protestant ideas were a central cause, see Philpott, *Revolutions in Sovereignty*, 97–149.

17   More specifically, it was Protestants of the magisterial Reformation who took this course— Lutherans, Calvinists, the Church of England. In fact, the Reformation was a spate of diverse movements. Some, like the Anabaptists, separated themselves from temporal authority as far as they could.

18   See R. J. Vincent, *Nonintervention and International Order* (Princeton, N.J.: Princeton University Press, 1974).

19   See Stanley Hoffmann, "An American Social Science: International Relations," in *Janus and Minerva: Essays in the Theory and Practice of International Politics* (Boulder, Colo.: Westview Press, 1987).

20   See Friedrich Meinecke, *Machiavellianism: The Doctrine of Raison d'état and Its Place in Modern History* (Boulder, Colo.: Westview Press, 1984).

21   See Waltz, *Theory of International Politics* (Lexington, Mass.: Addison-Wesley, 1979). Michael Doyle explains the similarity between Waltz and Hobbes, both "structural" realists, in Michael Doyle, *Ways of War and Peace* (New York: W. W. Norton, 1997), 111–36. On Hobbes, see also a section of an essay by Stanley Hoffmann on Rousseau; Hoffmann, "Rousseau on War and Peace," in Hoffman, "American Social Science," 25–36.

22   Doyle, *Ways of War and Peace*, 93–110.

23   For an excellent recent study of Morgenthau's early influences and intellectual formation, see Christoph Frei, *Hans J. Morgenthau: An Intellectual Biography* (Baton Rouge: Louisiana State University Press, 2001), 98–102.

24   Niccolò Machiavelli, *The Prince and the Discourses* (New York: Modern Library, 1950).

25   Reinhold Niebuhr, *The Irony of American History* (New York: Charles Scribner's Sons, 1952); idem, *Christian Realism and Political Problems* (New York: Charles Scribner's Sons, 1953).

26   See Jack Donnelly, "Twentieth-Century Realism," in Terry Nardin and David Mapel, eds., *Traditions of International Ethics* (Cambridge: Cambridge University Press, 1992); Steven Forde, "Classical Realism," in Terry Nardin and David Mapel, eds., *Traditions of International Ethics* (Cambridge: Cambridge University Press, 1992).

27   Waltz, *Theory of International Politics.*

28   See Doyle, *Ways of War and Peace*, 205–311; and Arnold Wolfers and Laurence Martin, *The Anglo-American Tradition: Readings from Thomas More to Woodrow Wilson* (New Haven: Yale University Press, 1956).

29   See Peter J. Katzenstein, ed., *The Culture of National Security: Norms and Identity in World Politics* (New York: Columbia University Press, 1996).

30   For a survey description of the ambitions of the secularization thesis, see Stark, "Secularization, R.I.P."

31   Berger, *Desecularization of the World*, 2.

32   Stark, "Secularization, R.I.P.," 253–60.

33   On this trend, see Casanova, *Public Religions.*

34   James Turner Johnson, "Jihad and Just War," *First Things* (June–July 2002).

35   See, for instance, Fouad Ajami, "What the Muslim World Is Watching," *New York Times Magazine*, November 18, 2001. See also Zogby International's "Impressions of America" poll of April 11, 2002.

36   Hashmi, "International Society and Its Islamic Malcontents," 21.

37   Hashmi, "Interpreting the Islamic Ethics," 223–24.

38   Hashmi, "International Society and Its Islamic Malcontents," 17.

39   Michael Scott Doran, "Somebody Else's Civil War: Ideology, Rage, and the Assault on America," in Gideon Rose and James F. Hoge, Jr., eds., *How Did This Happen? Terrorism and the New War* (New York: Council on Foreign Relations, 2001), 34.

40   Hashmi, "Interpreting the Islamic Ethics," 223.

41   Karen Armstrong, *The Battle for God: A History of Fundamentalism* (New York: Ballantine Books, 2000), 236–38.

42 Armstrong, *Battle for God*, 220–23; Bassam Tibi, *The Challenge of Fundamentalism: Political Islam and the New World Order* (Berkeley: University of California Press, 1998), 58; Russell Watson, "An Army of Eternal Victims," *Newsweek*, March 15, 1993, 2.

43 Karen Armstrong, *Islam: A Short History* (New York: Modern Library, 2000), 170.

44 William E. Shepard, *Sayyid Qutb and Islamic Activism: A Translation and Critical Analysis of Social Justice in Islam* (New York: Brill, 1996), xl.

45 Armstrong, *Battle for God*, 241.

46 Said Amir Arjomand, "Unity and Diversity in Islamic Fundamentalism," in Martin Marty and R. Scott Appleby, eds., *Fundamentalisms Comprehended* (Chicago: University of Chicago Press, 1995), 184.

47 For more on Qutb's thought, see Tibi, *Challenge of Fundamentalism*, 56–63; Armstrong, *Battle for God*, 238–44; Shepard, *Sayyid Qutb*, ix–lv; Ahmad S. Mousalli, *Radical Islamic Fundamentalism: The Ideological and Political Discourse of Sayyid Qutb* (Beirut: American University of Beirut, 1992); Kepel, *Revenge of God*, 18–22.

48 Tibi, *Challenge of Fundamentalism*, 138, 152.

49 Tibi, *Challenge of Fundamentalism*, 144–46.

50 Tibi, *Challenge of Fundamentalism*, 101, 140–46.

51 Tibi, *Challenge of Fundamentalism*, 55.

52 Kepel, *Revenge of God*, 20.

53 Arjomand, "Unity and Diversity," 185–86.

54 Roy, "Afghanistan: An Islamic War of Resistance," in Martin Marty and R. Scott Appleby, eds., *Fundamentalisms and the State*, no. 3 (Chicago: University of Chicago Press, 1993); idem, *Islam and Resistance in Afghanistan* (Cambridge: Cambridge University Press, 1990).

55 Doran, "Somebody Else's Civil War," 33–43.

56 Paul L. Williams, *Al Qaeda: Brotherhood of Terror* (Parsippany, N.J.: Alpha Books, 2002), 76, 78.

57 Peter L. Bergen, *Holy War, Inc.: Inside the Secret World of Osama Bin Laden* (New York: Free Press, 2001), 196.

58 The most prominent constructivist work is Alexander Wendt, *Social Theory of International Politics* (Cambridge: Cambridge University Press, 1999). See also the collection in Katzenstein, *Culture of National Security*.

59 Margaret Keck and Kathryn Sikkink, *Activists beyond Borders: Advocacy Networks in International Politics* (Ithaca, N.Y.: Cornell University Press, 1998).

60 The locus classicus here is Bull, *Anarchical Society*.

61 See Geoffrey Garrett and Barry R. Weingast, "Ideas, Interests, and Institutions: Constructing the European Community's Internal Market," in Judith Goldstein and Robert O. Keohane, eds., *Ideas and Foreign Policy: Beliefs, Institutions, and Political Change* (Ithaca, N.Y.: Cornell University Press, 1993).

5   *Hackett: Rethinking the Role of Religion in Changing Public Spheres*

*   My thanks go to Bob Dowd, Predrag Klasnja, Rashied Omar, Philip Ostien, and Charles H. Reynolds for their helpful comments and suggestions on an earlier version of this essay which appears in *Comparative Perspectives on Shari'ah in Nigeria* (Philip Ostien et al. eds., 2005). The writing of this essay was also greatly facilitated by the staff and resources at the Joan B. Kroc Institute for International Peace Studies at the University of Notre Dame, where I was a Visiting Rockefeller Fellow from 2003 to 2004.

1   R. Scott Appleby, "Retrieving the Missing Dimension of Statecraft: Religious Faith in the Service of Peacebuilding," in *Faith-Based Diplomacy: Trumping Realpolitik*, ed. Douglas Johnston (New York: Oxford University Press, 2003), 231.

2   Robert A. Seiple, "Why Brandywine Review?" *The Brandywine Review of Faith & International Affairs*, 1, no. 1 (Spring 2003): 1.

3   See, e.g., Daniel H. Levine, "The News about Religion in Latin America," in *Religion on the International News Agenda*, ed. Mark Silk (Hartford, Conn.: Pew Program on Religion and the News Media and the Leonard E. Greenberg Center for the Study of Religion in Public Life, Trinity College, 2000), 122.

4   Migrant populations and religious revivalism are openly challenging the Western paradigm of the secular state and privatized, individualized religion in post-colonial states, as well as in the United States. See, e.g., Dale F. Eickelman and Jon W. Anderson, "Redefining Muslim Publics," in *New Media in the Muslim*

World, ed. Dale F. Eickelman and Jon W. Anderson (Indianapolis: Indiana University Press, 1999), 1 (stating that much of the public sphere is "[s]ituated outside formal state control").

5   Talal Asad, *Formations of the Secular: Christianity, Islam, Modernity* (Palo Alto, Calif.: Stanford University Press, 2003), 1.

6   Many would rightly argue that these debates about religion in the public sphere cannot be understood in isolation from religion-state relations and constitutional and international human rights perspectives; the literature in this area now abounds. See, e.g., John Anderson, *Religious Liberty in Transitional Societies: The Politics of Religion* (New York: Cambridge University Press, 2003); W. Cole Durham, Jr., "Perspectives on Religious Liberty: A Comparative Framework," in *Religious Human Rights in Global Perspective: Legal Perspectives*, ed. Johan D. van der Vyver and John Witte, Jr. (Boston: M. Nijhoff, 1996); Carolyn Evans, *Freedom of Religion under the European Convention on Human Rights* (New York: Oxford University Press, 2001); Malcolm D. Evans, "Religion, Law and Human Rights: Locating the Debate," in *Law and Religion in Contemporary Society*, ed. Peter W. Edge and Graham Harvey (Surrey, UK: Ashgate Pub Ltd, 2000); Tore Lindholm et al., eds., *Facilitating Freedom of Religion or Belief: A Deskbook* (Leiden, The Netherlands: M. Nijhoff, 2004); Derek H. Davis and Gerhard Beiser, eds., *International Perspectives on Freedom and Equality of Religious Belief* (Waco, Tex.: J.M. Dawson Institute of Church-State Studies, 2002); James T. Richardson, ed., *Regulating Religion: Case Studies from Around the Globe* (New York: Kluwer Academic/Plenum Publishers, 2004). For additional resources, see Religion and Law Research Consortium, http://www.religlaw.org (last visited March 22, 2005); Center for the Interdisciplinary Study of Religion, http://www.law.emory.edu/cisr/ (last visited March 22, 2005); *Journal of Law and Religion*, available at http://www.hamline.edu/law/jlr/index.html (last visited March 22, 2005); "Human Rights and Freedom of Religion or Belief Links," in University of Minnesota Human Rights Library, http://www1.umn.edu/humanrts/links/religion.html (last visited March 22, 2005).

7   On the plight of religious minorities in particular, see Pete G. Danchin and Elizabeth A. Cole, eds., *Protecting the Human Rights of Religious Minorities in Eastern Europe* (New York: Columbia University Press, 2002).

8   E.g., scholars and observers missed the religious roots of the civil rights movement in the United States and misread the surge of the Iranian revolution. Levine, "News about Religion," 122.

9   Samuel P. Huntington, "The Clash of Civilizations?" *Foreign Affairs* (Summer 1993): 22; see also Samuel P. Huntington, *The Clash of Civilizations and the Remaking of World Order* (New York: Simon & Schuster, 1996). See also Huntington's latest work, Samuel P. Huntington, *Who Are We? The Challenges to America's National Identity* (New York: Simon & Schuster, 2004), on the erosion of America's Anglo-Protestant culture by the problems of massive immigration, bilingualism, multiculturalism, etc.

10   Robert D. Kaplan, "Looking the World in the Eye," *Atlantic Monthly* (December 2001): 68. For a critique by eminent scholars of Islam regarding Huntington's suggestion that Islam and the West were on a collision course, see Emran Qureshi and Michael A. Sells, eds., *The New Crusades: Constructing the Muslim Enemy* (New York: Columbia University Press, 2003). See also Akeel Bilgrami, "The Clash Within Civilizations," *Daedalus: Journal of the American Academy of Arts and Sciences* (Summer 2003): 88.

11   Huntington, "The Clash of Civilizations?" 22.

12   See Daniel Philpott, "The Challenge of September 11th to Secularism in International Relations," *World Politics* (October 2002): 66, for a discussion of this body of literature. Of particular note is "Religion and International Relations," *Millennium: Journal of International Studies* 3 (2000). See also Jonathan Fox and Shmuel Sandler, *Bringing Religion into International Relations* (New York: Palgrave Macmillan, 2004).

13   Douglas Johnston and Cynthia Sampson, eds., *Religion, the Missing Dimension of Statecraft* (New York: Oxford University Press, 1995).

14   José Casanova, *Public Religions in the Modern World* (Chicago: University of Chicago Press, 1994).

15   Additional key works in this area are Roland Robertson, *Globalization: Social Theory and Global Culture* (London: Sage, 1992); Susanne Hoeber Rudolph and James Piscatori, eds., *Transnational Religion and Fading States* (Boulder, Colo.: Westview Press, 1997); and Peter Beyer, "The Modern Emergence of Religions and a Global Social System for Religion," *International Sociology* 13 (1998): 151. See also Stephen Ellis and Gerrie ter Haar, *Worlds of Power: Religious Thought and Political Practice in Africa* (New York: Oxford University Press, 2004) (arguing that religious and spiritual beliefs persist and flourish amidst the vagaries of social and political life).

16   Hent de Vries, *Religion and Violence: Philosophical Perspectives from Kant to Derrida* (Baltimore: Johns Hopkins University Press, 2001), 19.

17   Manuel Castells, *The Power of Identity* (Malden, Mass.: Blackwell, 1997), 10–11.

18   Castells, *Power of Identity*, 11.

19   Castells, *Power of Identity*.

20   Castells, *Power of Identity*, 65–67.

21   Peter van der Veer prefers to designate these movements as "religious nationalisms," since many of them "articulate discourse on the religious community with discourse on the nation." Peter van der Veer, "The Victim's Tale: Memory and Forgetting in the Story of Violence," in *Violence, Identity and Self-Determination*, ed. Hent de Vries and Samuel Weber (Palo Alto, Calif.: Stanford University Press, 1997), 186, 195.

22   Castells, *Power of Identity*, 25; Chidi Anselm Odinkalu, "Back to the Future: The Imperative of Prioritizing for the Protection of Human Rights in Africa," *Journal of African Law* 47 (2003): 15 (tracing the "pathologies of suffering, conflict and systematic violations of human rights that Africa has suffered" back to colonial patterns of exclusion and ethnic discrimination). See also van der Veer, "Victim's Tale."

23   Philip Jenkins, "The Next Christianity," *Atlantic Monthly* (October 2002): 54.

24   R. Scott Appleby, *The Ambivalence of the Sacred: Religion, Violence, and Reconciliation* (Lanham, Md.: Rowman & Littlefield, 1999). The phrase, ambivalence of the sacred, refers to the idea that religion can serve as a vehicle for either violence or peace. Appleby, *Ambivalence of the Sacred*.

25   Abdullah A. An-Na'im, "Consciousness of Vulnerability," in *A Human Rights Message* 16 (1998).

26   For instance, on the Hardback Non-Fiction list for March 9, 2005, one could find *Secrets & Mysteries of the World* by Sylvia Browne, a self-proclaimed psychic who tries to explain the inexplicable, and *God's Politics* by Jim Wallis, an evangelical Christian who argues that Democrats must "take back the faith" and not allow conservative Republicans to hijack the Bible. At the top of the Hardcover Advice list was *Your Best Life Now* by Joel Osteen, who advocates a faith-based approach to living with enthusiasm. This was closely followed by *The Purpose-Driven Life* by Rick Warren, who seeks to find the meaning of life through God.

27   Karen Armstrong, *The Battle for God* (New York: Alfred A. Knopf, 2000); Karen Armstrong, *A History of God: The 4000-Year Quest of Judaism, Christianity and Islam* (New York: Knopf, 1993).

28   Stephen L. Carter, *The Culture of Disbelief: How American Law and Politics Trivialize Religious Devotion* (New York: Basic Books, 1993).

29   See Franklin Foer, "The Stephen Carter Moment: Will the Provocative Yale Law Prof. Save Us from Our Culture of Disbelief?" Beliefnet, http://www.beliefnet.com/story/50/story_5093_1.html (last visited March 22, 2005) (reviewing Stephen L. Carter, *God's Name in Vain: The Wrongs and Rights of Religion in Politics* [New York: Basic Books, 2000]).

30   Carter, *Culture of Disbelief*.

31   Carter, *God's Name in Vain*.

32   Carter, *God's Name in Vain*, 4.

33   Carter, *God's Name in Vain*. In a similar vein, Paul Gifford, ed., *The Christian Churches and the Democratisation of Africa* (New York: E.J. Brill, 1995), critically examines the contribution of the African churches in several countries to the processes of democratization.

34   Carter, *Culture of Disbelief*, 7.

35   Russell T. McCutcheon, *Critics Not Caretakers: Redescribing the Public Study of Religion* (Albany: State University of New York Press, 2001), 131.

36   Kenneth R. Craycraft, Jr., *The American Myth of Religious Freedom* (Dallas: Spence Publishing, 1999), 156–57.

37   Appleby, *Ambivalence of the Sacred*; Jayne Seminare Docherty, *Learning Lessons from Waco: When the Parties Bring Their Gods to the Negotiation Table* (New York: Syracuse University Press, 2001); Cynthia Sampson and John Paul Lederach, eds., *From the Ground Up: Mennonite Contributions to International Peacebuilding* (New York: Oxford University Press, 2000); Marc Gopin, *Between Eden and Armageddon: The Future of World Religions, Violence, and Peacemaking* (New York: Oxford University Press, 2000); see also John L. Esposito, *Unholy War: Terror in the Name of God* (New York: Oxford University Press, 2002); Mark Juergensmeyer, *Terror in the Mind of God: The Global Rise of Religious Violence* (Berkeley: University of California Press, 2003).

38   Johnston, *Faith-Based Diplomacy*.

39   Johnston, *Faith-Based Diplomacy*, 3.

40   Johnston, *Faith-Based Diplomacy*, 5–6.

41   Seiple, "Why Brandywine Review?" 1.

42   Brian Cox and Daniel Philpott, "Faith-Based Diplomacy: An Ancient Idea Newly Emergent," *The Brandywine Review of Faith & International Affairs*, 1, no. 2 (Fall 2003): 31.

43   The International Center for Religion and Diplomacy, http://www.icrd.org (last visited March 13, 2005).

44   The International Center for Religion and Diplomacy, *Mission*, http://www.icrd.org/about.html (last visited March 22, 2005).

45   Tanenbaum Center for Interreligious Understanding, http://www.tanenbaum.org (last visited March 6, 2004).

46   PeaceMakers International, Inc., http://www.peacemakers.net (last visited March 6, 2004).

47   The Joan B. Kroc Institute for International Peace Studies, Program on Religion, Conflict and Peacebuilding, http://kroc.nd.edu/research/religion.html (last visited March 6, 2004).

48   See also U.N. Educ., Sci. & Cultural Org. [UNESCO], *Interreligious Dialogue*, http://portal.unesco.org/culture/en/ev.phpURL_ID=11680&URL_DO=DO_TOPIC&URL_SECTION=201.html (last visited March 22, 2005).

49   John Witte, Jr., *The New Freedom of Public Religion*, Editorial Opinion, Center for the Interdisciplinary Study of Religion, Emory University, http://www.law.emory.edu/cisr/pressreleases/Editorialjohnwitte.htm (last visited March 25, 2005). On the Supreme Court's treatment of religion, see Winnifred Fallers Sullivan, *Paying the Words Extra: Religious Discourse in the Supreme Court of the United States* (Cambridge, Mass.: Harvard University Press, 1994).

50   Letter from Thomas Jefferson to the Danbury Baptist Association of Connecticut (January 1, 1802), available at http://www.usconstitution.net/jeffwall.html.

51   On the growing tendency of the Supreme Court to favor equal treatment of religion with other forms of expression and activity, see Derek H. Davis, "A Commentary on the Supreme Court's 'Equal Treatment' Doctrine as the New Constitutional Paradigm for Protecting Religious Liberty," *Journal of Church & State* 46 (2004): 717–38.

52   Witte, *New Freedom of Public Religion*.

53   Witte, *New Freedom of Public Religion*.

54   Dennis R. Hoover, "Charitable Choice and the New Religious Center," *Religion in the News* (Spring 2000), available at http://www.trincoll.edu/depts/csrpl/RINVol3No1/charitable_choice_2000.htm; see also Stephen P. Brown, *Trumping Religion: The New Christian Right, the Free Speech Clause, and the Courts* (Tuscaloosa: University of Alabama Press, 2004).

55   See Mark Silk, "From the Editor: A Different Spiritual Politics," *Religion in the News* (Summer 1999), available at http://www.trincoll.edu/depts/csrpl/RINVol2No2/spiritualpolitics.htm.

56   International Religious Freedom Act of 1998, Pub. L. No. 105-292, 112 Stat. 2787 (1998); see also U.S. Dep't of State, *International Religious Freedom*, http://www.state.gov/g/drl/irf/ (last visited March 25, 2005); Allen Hertzke, *Freeing God's Children: The Unlikely Alliance for Global Human Rights* (Lanham, Md.: Rowman & Littlefield, 2004).

57   U.S. Department of State, *International Religious Freedom*.

58   Rosalind I. J. Hackett, Mark Silk, and Dennis R. Hoover, eds., *Religious Persecution as a U.S. Policy Issue* (Hartford, Conn.: Trinity College, 2000); T. Jeremy Gunn, "American Exceptionalism and Globalist Double Standards: A More Balanced Alternative," *Columbia Journal of Transnational Law* 41 (2002): 137; T. Jeremy Gunn, "A Preliminary Response to Criticisms of the International Religious Freedom Act of 1998," *Brigham Young University Law Review* (2000): 841; Eugenia Relaño Pastor, "U.S. International Religious Freedom Act of 1998: A European Perspective," *Brigham Young University Law Review* (2005): 711.

59   See, e.g., "Alan Cooperman, Openly Religious, to a Point," *Washington Post*, September 16, 2004, A01, available at http://www.washingtonpost.com/wp-dyn/articles/A24634-2004Sep15.html.

60   See, e.g., Jane Lampman, "New Scrutiny of Role of Religion in Bush's Policies," *The Christian Science Monitor*, March 17, 2003, http://www.csmonitor.com/2003/0317/p01s01-uspo.html.

61   Lampman, "New Scrutiny of Role of Religion."

62   See, e.g., Stephen Carter et al., "Roundtable on Religion in Politics," *Tikkun Magazine* (November–December 2000): 24.

63   This is well evidenced in the publication *Religion in the News* from the Leonard E. Greenberg Center for the Study of Religion in Public Life, Trinity College, Hartford, Conn., available at http://www.trincoll.edu/depts/csrpl/RIN.htm (last visited August 25, 2005).

64   William E. Connolly, *Why I Am Not a Secularist* (Minneapolis: University of Minnesota Press, 1999).

65 Connolly, *Why I Am Not a Secularist*, 19.

66 Connolly, *Why I Am Not a Secularist*, 23.

67 See Jeffrey Stout, *Democracy and Tradition* (Princeton, N.J.: Princeton University Press, 2004).

68 Stout, *Democracy and Tradition*, vi.

69 Stout, *Democracy and Tradition*, 4–6. For a thoughtful review, see David Reidy, "Speaking for the State," in *Soundings* (2005). See also the debate on this topic between two distinguished philosophers, Robert Audi and Nicholas Wolterstorff, *Religion in the Public Square: The Place of Religious Convictions in Political Debate* (Lanham, Md.: Rowman & Littlefield, 1997).

70 Paul J. Weithman, *Religion and the Obligations of Citizenship* (New York: Cambridge University Press, 2002); Weithman, ed., *Religion and Contemporary Liberalism* (Indiana: Notre Dame Press, 1997).

71 Weithman, *Religion and the Obligations of Citizenship*; Weithman, *Religion and Contemporary Liberalism*, 2.

72 Weithman, *Religion and the Obligations of Citizenship*, 2.

73 Weithman, *Religion and the Obligations of Citizenship*.

74 Weithman, *Religion and the Obligations of Citizenship*.

75 Weithman, *Religion and the Obligations of Citizenship*.

76 Weithman, *Religion and the Obligations of Citizenship*, 3.

77 Weithman, *Religion and the Obligations of Citizenship*.

78 Weithman, *Religion and the Obligations of Citizenship*, 5; see also Mark Chaves et al., "Does Government Funding Suppress Nonprofits' Political Activities?" *American Sociological Review* 69 (2004): 292.

79 *Daedalus: Journal of the American Academy of Arts and Sciences* (Summer 2003).

80 Martin Marty, "Our Religio-secular World," *Daedalus: Journal of the American Academy of Arts and Sciences* (Summer 2003): 42.

81 Asad, *Formations of the Secular*. For a review, see Robert W. Hefner, *Rethinking Religion and the Modern*, H-Net Reviews, H-Gender-MidEast, March 2004, http://www.h-net.org/reviews/showrev.cgi?path=89361083559676 (reviewing Asad, *Formations of the Secular*).

82 Asad, *Formations of the Secular*, 17.

83 Asad, *Formations of the Secular*, 205.

84 Asad, *Formations of the Secular*. These ideas developed in Western Europe in tandem with the formation of the modern state. In the final chapter of the book, "Reconfigurations of Law and Ethics in Colonial Egypt," Asad probingly examines how the secular was thought about and absorbed in Egyptian culture prior to its ascendance to a modern state. He finds that the reconfigurations of law, religion, and ethics in colonial Egypt created new social spaces in which secularism could grow. Asad, *Formations of the Secular*, 208.

85 Asad, *Formations of the Secular*, 255.

86 Asad, *Formations of the Secular*, 194.

87 Asad, *Formations of the Secular*, 200.

88 Asad, *Formations of the Secular*, 199.

89 Nikki R. Keddie, "Secularism and Its Discontents," *Daedalus: Journal of the American Academy of Arts and Sciences* (Summer 2003): 14.

90 Keddie, "Secularism and Its Discontents," 15.

91 Keddie, "Secularism and Its Discontents," 15–16.

92 Keddie, "Secularism and Its Discontents," 18.

93 Keddie, "Secularism and Its Discontents," 25.

94 See David Westerlund, "Secularism, Civil Religion or Islam: Islamic Revivalism and the National Question in Nigeria," in *Religion, State and Society in Contemporary Africa: Nigeria, Sudan, South Africa, Zaire, and Mozambique*, ed. Austin Metumara Ahanotu (New York: Peter Lang, 1992).

95 Keddie, "Secularism and Its Discontents," 25.

96 Keddie, "Secularism and Its Discontents," 28; see also Richard Francis Gombrich and Gananath Obeyesekere, *Buddhism Transformed: Religious Change in Sri Lanka* (Princeton, N.J.: Princeton University Press, 1988); Mark Juergensmeyer, *The New Cold War? Religious Nationalism Confronts the Secular State* (Berkeley: University of California Press, 1993); Stanley Jeyaraja Tambiah, *Buddhism Betrayed? Religion, Politics, and Violence in Sri Lanka* (Chicago: University of Chicago Press, 1992).

97 Keddie, "Secularism and Its Discontents," 28.

98 See, e.g., Sebastian Kim, *In Search of Identity: Debates on Religious Conversion in India* (New York: Oxford University Press, 2003); T. N. Madan, ed., *Modern Myths, Locked Minds: Secularism and Fundamentalism*

in India (New York: Oxford University Press, 1997); Rajeev Bhargava, ed., *Secularism and Its Critics* (New York: Oxford University Press, 1998).

99 Keddie, "Secularism and Its Discontents," 28.

100 See Madhu Kishwar, *Religion at the Service of Nationalism and Other Essays* (New York: Oxford University Press, 1998); A.G. Noorani, *The RSS and the BJP: A Division of Labor* (2000).

101 E.g., Neera Chandhoke, *Beyond Secularism: The Rights of Religious Minorities* (Oxford: Oxford University Press, 1999); James Massey, *Minorities and Religious Freedom in a Democracy* (New Delhi: Manohar, 2003).

102 See, e.g., Abdullahi A. An-Na'im, "The Synergy and Interdependence of Human Rights, Religion and Secularism," *Polylog: Forum for Intercultural Philosophy* 3 (2001): 13, available at http://them.polylog.org/3/faa-en.htm; "Consciousness of Vulnerability," in *A Human Rights Message*, ed. Government of Sweden (1998): 16–19.

103 See Simeon O. Ilesanmi, *Religious Pluralism and the Nigerian State* (Athens: Ohio University Center for International Studies, 1997); Simeon O. Ilesanmi, "The Myth of a Secular State: A Study of Religious Politics with Historical Illustrations," *Islam & Christian-Muslim Relations* 6 (1995): 105–17.

104 Levine, "News about Religion," 135. The three presidential candidates in the December 2003 elections in Guatemala reflected this plurality: one was a Catholic, another was an evangelical Protestant, and the third was a priest of the Mayan indigenous religion.

105 Levine, "News about Religion," 123–24.

106 Levine, "News about Religion," 135.

107 Levine, "News about Religion."

108 Levine, "News about Religion," 136.

109 Johan D. van der Vyver, "Constitutional Perspectives of Church-State Relations in South Africa," *Brigham Young University Law Review* (1999): 635–72.

110 Rosalind I. J. Hackett, "Mediated Religion in South Africa: Balancing Air-time and Rights Claims," in *Media, Religion and the Public Sphere*, ed. Birgit Meyer and Annelies Moors (Indianapolis: Indiana University Press, 2005).

111 See Abdulkader Tayob and Wolfram Weisse, eds., *Religion and Politics in South Africa: From Apartheid to Democracy* (New York: Waxmann Publishing, 1998); J. W. de Gruchy and S. Martin, eds., *Religion and the Reconstruction of Civil Society* (South Africa: Unisa Press, 1995); David Chidester et al., eds., *Religion in Public Education: Options for a New South Africa* (Cape Town: UCT Press, 1994); H. Christina Steyn, "The Role of Multi-religious Education in the Transformation of South African Society," in *Religion and Social Transformation in Southern Africa*, ed. Thomas G. Walsh and Frank Kaufmann (St. Paul, Minn.: Paragon House, 1999), 131–42. Similarly, Professor Abdelfattah Amor, the former Special Rapporteur of the Sub-Commission on Freedom of Religion and Belief of the United Nations Commission on Human Rights, has launched meetings and publications since 1995—several organized by the Oslo Coalition on Freedom of Religion and Belief—to explore the role of school education in relation to religious tolerance and intolerance. See U.N. High Commissioner for Human Rights, *Interim Report Prepared by Abdelfattah Amor, Special Rapporteur of the Commission on Human Rights on Freedom of Religion or Belief*, U.N. GAOR, 58th Sess., Annex, Agenda Item 119(b), U.N. Doc. A/58/296 (Aug. 19, 2003), available at http://www.unhchr.ch/huridocda/huridoca.nsf/0/DFDC01ED0062E4C8C1256DB1004EB2C8/$File/N0347258.doc?OpenElement; see also Lena Larsen and Ingvild T. Plesner, eds., *Teaching for Tolerance and Freedom of Religion or Belief* (2002); The Oslo Coalition on Freedom of Religion and Belief, *Teaching for Tolerance for Freedom of Religion or Belief*, http://www.oslocoalition.org/html/project_school_education/index.html (last visited March 25, 2005).

112 ZAR.co.za, Statistics, http://zar.co.za/stats.htm (last visited on March 25, 2005). This is a promotional website providing general statistics and information about South Africa.

113 Katherine Pratt Ewing, "Legislating Religious Freedom: Muslim Challenges to the Relationship between Church and State in Germany and France," in *Engaging Cultural Differences: The Multicultural Challenge in Liberal Democracies*, ed. Richard Shweder et al. (New York: Russell Sage Foundation, 2002), 63–80; see also An-Na'im, "Synergy and Interdependence."

114 See, e.g., Richardson, *Regulating Religion*; Symposium, *Freedom of Religion or Belief in the OSCE Region: Challenges to Law and Practice, Concluding Seminar Statement by the Moderator* (June 28, 2001), available at http://www.osce.org/documents/odihr/2001/06/1523_en.pdf.

115 Thomas Robbins, "Combating 'Cults' and 'Brainwashing' in the United States and Western Europe: A Comment on Richardson and Introvigne's Report," *Journal for the Scientific Study of Religion* 40 (2001): 73.

116 Mastafa Malik, "A Woman's Head Scarf, a Continent's Discomfort," *Washington Post*, March 13, 2005, B02.

117 "France Awaits Headscarves Report," *BBC News*, http://news.bbc.co.uk/1/hi/world/europe/3307995.stm (last visited March 25, 2005). For a comparative analysis, see T. Jeremy Gunn, "Under God But Not the Scarf: The Founding Myths of Religious Freedom in the United States and Laïcité in France," *Journal of Church & State* 46 (2004): 7.

118 Human Rights Without Frontiers International contends that the overt or covert denial of the rights of religious minorities should be part of the test for admission to the European Union. See generally Human Rights Without Frontiers Int'l, http://www.hrwf.net (last visited March 25, 2005); see also Igor Rotar, "Kyrgyzstan: Chinese Pressure Achieves Falun Gong Deregulation," *Forum 18 News Service*, March 22, 2005, http://www.forum18.org/Archive.php?article_id=529.

119 See Brian Barry, *Culture and Equality: An Egalitarian Critique of Multiculturalism* (Cambridge, Mass.: Harvard University Press, 2001); Bhikhu Parekh, *Rethinking Multiculturalism: Cultural Diversity and Political Theory* (Cambridge, Mass.: Harvard University Press, 2002); Winnifred Fallers Sullivan, *The Impossibility of Religious Freedom* (Princeton, N.J.: Princeton University Press, 2005). See generally Rosalind I. J. Hackett and Winnifred Fallers Sullivan, "Law and Human Rights," *Culture & Religion* (March 2005).

120 Terrence Murray, "Europe Debates God's Place in New Constitution," *The Christian Science Monitor*, April 10, 2003, available at http://www.csmonitor.com/2003/0410/p07s01-woeu.html.

121 See Doris Buss and Didi Herman, *Globalizing Family Values: The Christian Right in International Politics* (Minneapolis: University of Minnesota Press, 2003).

122 Martha C. Nussbaum, *Women and Human Development: The Capabilities Approach* (New York: Cambridge University Press, 2000). Cf. Rosalind I. J. Hackett, "Is Religion Good News or Bad News for Women? Martha Nussbaum's Creative Solution to Conflicting Rights," *Soundings* (Fall/Winter 2002): 615–25. See also Bahia Tahzib-Lie, "Applying a Gender Perspective in the Area of the Right to Freedom of Religion or Belief," *Brigham Young University Law Review* (2000): 967–88.

123 See Bill Moyers, *Genesis and the Millennium: An Essay On Religious Pluralism in the Twenty-first Century, Including Eight Ecumenical Responses* (Waco, Tex.: J.M. Dawson Institute of Church-State Studies, 2000).

124 Compare Jean Bethke Elshtain's rejection of "liberal monism" for postulating a "single vocabulary of political discussion." Jean Bethke Elshtain, "Against Liberal Monism," *Daedalus: Journal of the American Academy of Arts and Sciences* (Summer 2003): 78.

125 See Shweder et al., *Engaging Cultural Difference*.

126 Richard E. Wentz, *The Culture of Religious Pluralism* (Boulder, Colo.: Westview Press, 1998), 118.

127 Hoeber Rudolph and Piscatori, *Transnational Religion and Fading States*, 8.

128 Hoeber Rudolph and Piscatori, *Transnational Religion and Fading States*.

129 Asad, *Formations of the Secular*, 179–80.

130 Massimo Introvigne and James T. Richardson, "Western Europe, Postmodernity, and the Shadow of the French Revolution: A Response to Soper and Robbins," *Journal for the Scientific Study of Religion* 40 (2001): 182.

131 Rosalind I. J. Hackett, "Discourses of Demonization in Africa and Beyond," *Diogenes* 50, no. 3 (2003): 61–75.

132 See R. Scott Appleby et al., *Strong Religion: The Rise of Fundamentalisms Around the World* (Chicago: University of Chicago Press, 2003).

9   Hoover: Unrealistic Realism

1 Salvator Mundi, "Tea Leaves, Global Politics," *The Economist*, February 23, 2002.

2 Hardy Green, "The Business Week Best-Seller List," *Business Week*, April 1, 2002.

3 Paul Rosenberg, "Narrow Viewpoint Hampers Rhetoric," *Denver Post*, March 3, 2002.

4 Ken Ringle, "Oracle of a New World Disorder," *Washington Post*, February 21, 2002.

5 See Allen D. Hertzke, *Representing God in Washington: The Role of Religious Lobbies in the American Polity* (Knoxville: University of Tennessee Press, 1988); *Wise as Serpents, Innocent as Doves: American Mennonites Engage Washington* (Knoxville: University of Tennessee Press, 1996).

6   Douglas Johnston and Cynthia Sampson, eds., *Religion, the Missing Dimension of Statecraft* (New York: Oxford University Press, 1994).

7   See R. Scott Appleby, *The Ambivalence of the Sacred: Religion, Violence, and Reconciliation* (Lanham, Md.: Rowman & Littlefield, 2000); David Smock, ed., *Private Peacemaking: Peacemaking Projects of Nonprofit Organizations* (Peaceworks, May 1998); John Paul Lederach, *Building Peace: Sustainable Reconciliation in Divided Societies* (Washington, D.C.: USIP, 1997).

8   Glen Stassen, ed., *Just Peacemaking* (Cleveland: Pilgrim Press, 1998), 4.

9   Brian C. Anderson, "Warrior Politics," *National Review* 54, no. 3 (February 2002): 46–48.

10 Robert Kagan, "The Return of Cheap Pessimism," *The New Republic*, April 10, 2000, 32.

11 Jonathan Chaplin, "Staring Power in the Face: Time for a Global Debate on U.S. Power," *Public Justice Report*, April 25, 2002, 8–9.

12 See the debate between James Skillen, "U.S. Shortsightedness on the ICC," *Capital Commentary*, July 15, 2002, and Richard John Neuhaus, "The Public Square," *First Things* (November 2002): 81–82.

13 George F. Kennan, "Foreign Policy and Christian Conscience," *Atlantic Monthly* 203, no. 5 (May 1959): 44–49.

14 Thomas L. Friedman, "The American Idol," *The New York Times*, November 6, 2002.

11   Niebuhr: Augustine's Political Realism

1   *De Trin.*, 15.22.

2   *De Civ. Dei*, 14.5.

3   *De Civ. Dei*, 19.7.

4   *De Civ. Dei.*

5   *De Civ. Dei*, 19.5.

6   *De Civ. Dei*, 19.21.

7   *De Civ. Dei*, 19.15.

8   Sermon cccliv, ix, 9.

9   Sermon ccxiii, vii, 7.

10 *Comm. on Ps.* cxi, 9.

11 *Comm. on Ps.* cxx, 3.

12 *Comm. on Ps.* cxxxvi, 3, 4.

12   Rees: "Really Existing" Scriptures

1   George Monbiot, "America Is a Religion," *The Guardian*, July 29, 2003, www.guardian.co.uk/coment/story/0,3604,1007741,00.html.

2   The notion of "Empire" is used as an interpretive lens in both biblical and political studies. For an example of the former see Richard Horsley, ed., *Paul and Empire: Religion and Power in Roman Society* (Harrisburg, Pa.: Trinity Press International, 1997); for the latter see Michael Hardt and Antonio Negri, *Empire* (Cambridge, Mass.: Harvard University Press, 2000) and the useful critique by Tarak Barkawi and Mark Laffey, "Retrieving the Imperial: Empire and International Relations," *Millennium: Journal of International Studies* 31. no. 1 (2002): 109–27. For an analysis of the attempt to forge a *Pax Americana* see Chalmers Johnson, *The Sorrows of Empire: Militarism, Secrecy and the End of the Republic* (New York: Metropolitan, 2004).

3   Richard Bauckham, *The Bible in Politics* (Louisville, Ky.: Westminster John Knox, 1989), 4

4   Clifford Geertz, "Which Way to Mecca? Part II," *The New York Review of Books*, July 3, 2003, 36.

5   Scott Thomas, "Taking Religious and Cultural Pluralism Seriously: The Global Resurgence of Religion and the Transformation of International Society," *Millennium: Journal of International Studies*, 29, no. 3 (2000): 815–41.

6   Amartya Sen, "Democracy and Its Global Roots," *The New Republic*, October 6, 2003, 29–30.

7   Edward Said, "The Clash of Ignorance," *The Nation*, October 22, 2001 (www.thenation.com, downloaded November 10, 2001). The essay critiques Samuel P. Huntington's thesis on the "Clash of Civilizations" in light of the events of the attacks upon Washington and New York on September 11, 2001.

8   Andrew Linklater, *The Transformation of Political Community: Ethical Foundations of a Post-Westphalian Era* (Cambridge: Polity, 1998).

9   Editor's note, "Forum on *The Transformation of Political Community*," *Review of International Studies* no. 25 (1999): 139.

10 On the need to rediscover religion in international relations scholarship see Daniel Philpott, "The Challenge of September 11 to Secularism in International Relations," *World Politics* 55 (October 2002): 66–95.

11 Jean Bethke Elshtain, "Really Existing Communities," *Review of International Studies* no. 25 (1999): 143.

12 Elshtain, "Really Existing Communities," 143.

13 Hasan Hanafi, "Alternative Conceptions of Civil Society: A Reflective Islamic Approach," in S. Chambers and W. Kymlicka, eds., *Alternative Conceptions of Civil Society* (Princeton, N.J.: Princeton University Press, 2002), 173.

14 Brian Cox and Daniel Philpott, "Faith-Based Diplomacy: An Ancient Idea Newly Emergent," *The Brandywine Review of Faith & International Affairs* 1, no. 2 (Fall 2003): 32.

15 Thomas, "Taking Religious and Cultural Pluralism Seriously," 823.

16 Stanley Hauerwas, *The Peaceable Kingdom* (Notre Dame, Ind.: University of Notre Dame Press, 1983), 77.

17 On the uniqueness of Christian polity see Stanley Hauerwas and William Willimon, *Resident Alien: Life in the Christian Colony* (Nashville, Tenn.: Abingdon, 1989, 1991). For an incisive critique of Hauerwas' position as anti-political see Oliver O'Donovan, *The Desire of the Nations: Rediscovering the Roots of Political Theology* (Cambridge: Cambridge University Press, 1996), 4–12.

18 Clodovis Boff, *Theology and Praxis: Epistemological Foundation* (New York: Orbis, 1987), 63.

19 Elshtain, "Really Existing Communities," 144. On the argument for "symbolic and concrete" forms of political authority in Christian political theology see O'Donovan, *Desire of the Nations*, 25.

20 The subtext of national security against Islamic terrorists must also be recognized.

21 Jonathan Sacks, *The Politics of Hope* (London: Random House, 1997), 55.

22 John Keane, *Civil Society: Old Images, New Visions* (Oxford: Blackwell, 1998), 53–54.

23 Keane, *Civil Society*, 53.

24 See, e.g., John A. Rees, *Ideology, Interpretation and Romans 13:1-7: A Reading in Political Hermeneutics* (unpublished manuscript, 2003).

25 Walter Wink, *The Powers That Be: Theology for a New Millennium* (New York: Doubleday, 1998), 32, emphasis in original.

26 Martin Krygier, *Between Fear and Hope: Hybrid Thoughts on Public Values* (Sydney: ABC Books, 1997), 106.

27 Krygier, *Between Fear and Hope*, 101.

28 Sohail H. Hashmi, "Islamic Ethics in International Society" in S. H. Hashmi, ed., *Islamic Political Ethics: Civil Society, Pluralism, and Conflict* (Princeton, N.J.: Princeton University Press, 2002), 149.

29 Hashmi, "Islamic Ethics," 150–51.

30 Hashmi, "Islamic Ethics," 152.

31 Hashmi, "Islamic Ethics," 152.

32 Hashmi, "Islamic Ethics," 153.

33 Hasan Hanafi in Chambers and Kymlicka, *Alternative Conceptions*, 171–89.

34 Salman Rushdie, "Ghandi, Now," in S. Rushdie, *Step Across This Line. Collected Non-Fiction 1992–2002* (London: Jonathan Cape, 2000), 184.

35 Karen Armstrong, "In Defence of Khomeini," *AFR Review*, October 20, 2000, 1, 2, 11.

36 Olivier Roy, "Islamists in Power," in M. Kramer, ed., *The Islamism Debate* (Tel Aviv: Tel Aviv University 1997), 72.

37 Armstrong, "In Defence of Khomeini," 11.

38 Robert Hillman, "Endgame in Tehran," *AFR Review*, February 13, 2004, 3; Ed O'Loughlin, "A Love of Cash Unites Bickering Hardliners," *Sydney Morning Herald*, February 28–29, 2004, 22.

39 H. E. Chehabi, "Religion and Politics in Iran: How Theocratic Is the Islamic Republic?" *Daedalus* (Summer 1991): 87.

40 Avishai Margalit, *The Decent Society*, trans. N. Goldblum (Cambridge, Mass.: Harvard University Press, 1996). Ignatieff quotation on the back cover, originally from the *Times Literary Supplement*.

41 Sacks, *Politics of Hope*, 55–65.

42 Sacks, *Politics of Hope*, 55.

43 Sacks, *Politics of Hope*, 58.

44 Sacks, *Politics of Hope*, 58.

45 Sacks, *Politics of Hope*, 59.

46 Sacks, *Politics of Hope*, 61, 62.

47 Sacks, *Politics of Hope*, 64.

48 Sacks, *Politics of Hope*, 57.

49 J. R. Gibbins and B. Reimer, *The Politics of Postmodernity: An Introduction to Contemporary Politics and Culture* (London: Sage, 1999), 115.

50 Keane, *Civil Society*, 28.

51 Keane, *Civil Society*, 28–31. Keane cites several works including R. Ghannouchi, "The Participation of Islamists in a Non-Islamic Government," in A. Tamimi, ed., *Power Sharing Islam?* (London: Liberty Publications, 1993).

52 Abdou Filali-Ansary, "Islam and Liberal Democracy: The Challenge of Secularization," *Journal of Democracy* 7, no. 2 (1996): 77; see 76–80; see also Robin Wright, "Islam and Liberal Democracy: Two Visions of Reformation," *Journal of Democracy* 7, no. 2 (1996): 64–75.

13 *Thomas: Isaiah's Vision of Human Security*

1 Martin Wight, "God in History," sermon preached in Great St. Mary's Church, Cambridge, February 4, 1951 (unpublished MS, LSE Archive).

2 Inis L. Claude, Jr., *Swords into Plowshares: The Problems and Progress of International Organization*, 3rd ed. (New York: Random House, 1964).

3 Daniel Berrigan, *Isaiah: Spirit of Courage, Gift of Tears* (Minneapolis, Minn.: Fortress Press, 1998).

4 Brevard S. Childs, *The Struggle to Understand Isaiah as Christian Scripture* (Grand Rapids: Eerdmans, 2004); John F. A. Sawyer, *The Fifth Gospel: Isaiah in the History of Christianity* (Cambridge: Cambridge University Press, 1998).

5 Michael G. Cartwright, "Biblical Argument in International Ethics," in Terry Nardin and David R. Mapel, eds., *Traditions of International Ethics* (Cambridge: Cambridge University Press, 1992), 270–96.

6 John N. Oswalt, *The Book of Isaiah, Chapters 1–39*, New International Commentary on the Old Testament (Grand Rapids: Eerdmans, 1986), 4.

7 Terry C. Muck, "General Editor's Preface," in John N. Oswalt, *Isaiah*, The NIV Application Commentary (Grand Rapids: Zondervan, 2003), 11–12.

8 Adam Watson, "Scope and Definitions," in Adam Watson, *The Evolution of International Society* (London: Routledge, 1992), 13–18; Martin Wight, "De Systematibus Civitatum," in Martin Wight, *Systems of States*, introduction by Hedley Bull (Leicester: University of Leicester Press, 1977), 21–46.

9 John Galtung, *Peace by Peaceful Means: Peace and Conflict, Development and Civilization* (Oslo: International Peace Research Institute, 1996); Arie M. Kacowicz, *Pluralistic Security Communities and "Negative Peace" in the Third World* (Working Paper Series on Regional Security, Global Studies Research Program, University of Wisconsin–Madison, 1994).

10 Jeanne A. K. Hey, ed., *Small States in World Politics: Explaining Foreign Policy Behavior* (Boulder, Colo.: Lynne Rienner, 2003).

11 Walter Brueggemann, *Theology of the Old Testament: Testimony, Dispute, Advocacy* (Minneapolis, Minn.: Fortress, 1997), 521.

12 On the interpretive tension between Kings 18:14-16 and Isaiah 36–38, see Christopher R. Seitz, *Isaiah 1–39* (Louisville, Ky.: Westminster John Knox, 1993), 13–15, 242–60.

13 B. Uffenheimer, "Isaiah's and Micah's Approaches to Policy and History," in Henning Graf Reventlow, Y. Hoffman, and B. Uffenheimer, eds., *Politics and Theopolitics in the Bible and Postbiblical Literature, Journal for the Study of the Old Testament*, Supplement Series 171 (Sheffield, UK: JSOT Press, 1994), 176–88.

14 Seitz, *Isaiah 1–39*, 76.

15 Scott M. Thomas, *The Global Resurgence of Religion and the Transformation of International Relations* (New York: Palgrave Macmillan, 2005).

16 Similarly, Archbishop Desmond Tutu, on a recent series on the BBC World Service, "Who Runs Your World," responded in the same way Isaiah did—it is God's world, *regardless of what we think we see happening in world politics*.

17 See John Barton, "Virtue in the Bible," in John Barton, *Understanding Old Testament Ethics* (Louisville, Ky.: Westminster John Knox, 2003), 65–74.

18   Chalmers Johnson, *Blowback: The Costs and Consequences of American Empire* (New York: Holt, 2004).

19   Edmund Pincoffs, "Quandary Ethics," in Stanley Hauerwas and Alasdair MacIntyre, eds., *Revisions: Changing Perspectives in Moral Philosophy* (South Bend, Ind.: University of Notre Dame Press, 1983), 92–112.

20   When Prime Minister David Ben-Gurion presented his first government of the newly formed state of Israel to the Knesset he insisted, "Our activities and policy are not guided by economic considerations alone, but by a political and social vision that we have inherited from our prophets and imbibed from the heritage of our greatest sages and teachers of our own day." The state would foster these values, he said, "as the way . . . to educate youth and forge the image of the Jewish nation that is true to its ancient source of the vision of the End of Days." Tom Segev, *1949: The First Israelis* (New York: Holt, 1986; new preface, 1998), x.

21   Alexander Wendt, *Social Theory of International Politics* (Cambridge: Cambridge University Press, 1999); Maja Zehfuss, *Constructivism in International Relations: The Politics of Reality* (Cambridge: Cambridge University Press, 2002).

22   Robert Cooper, *The Breaking of Nations: Order and Chaos in the Twenty-First Century* (London: Atlantic Books, 2003).

23   Walter Brueggemann, *Isaiah 1–39* (Louisville, Ky.: Westminster John Knox, 1998), 65.

24   Otto Kaiser, *Isaiah 1–12: A Commentary* (London: SCM Press, 1972), 89.

25   Walter Brueggemann, *An Introduction to the Old Testament: The Canon and Christian Imagination* (Louisville, Ky.: Westminster John Knox, 2003), 161.

26   Brevard S. Childs, *Isaiah*, The Old Testament Library (Louisville, Ky.: Westminster John Knox, 2001), 30–31.

27   Rabbi Michael Goldberg quotes from the Talmud, Avot 1:1, "Moses received Torah from Sinai, and he passed it on to Joshua, Joshua to the elders, the elders to the prophets, and the prophets passed it on to the men of the Great Assembly [who] said: 'Raise up many disciples . . . ,'" in "Discipleship: Basing One Life on Another—It's Not What You Know, It's Who You Know," in Stanley Hauerwas, Nancy Murphy, and Mark Nation, eds., *Theology without Foundations: Religious Practice & the Future of Theological Truth* (Nashville, Tenn.: Abingdon, 1994), 289–304.

28   Barry Buzan, *People, States & Fear: An Agenda for International Security Studies in the Post–Cold War Era* (London: Harvester Wheatsheaf, 1991).

29   "New Dimensions of Human Security," *Human Development Report* (New York: UN Development Programme, 1994); *Human Security Now* (New York: Commission on Human Security, 2003); S. Neil MacFarlane and Yuen Foong Khong, *Human Security and the UN: A Critical History*, UN Intellectual History Project Series (Bloomington: Indiana University Press, 2006).

30   Kaiser, *Isaiah 1–12*, 40–42.

31   Kaiser, *Isaiah 1–12*, 42.

32   I. W. Zartman, ed., *Collapsed States: The Disintegration and Restoration of Legitimate Authority* (Boulder, Colo.: Lynne Rienner, 1995).

33   Kaiser, *Isaiah 1–12*, 20.

34   Robert Putnam, *Bowling Alone: The Collapse and Revival of American Community* (New York: Simon & Schuster, 2000), 340.

35   Kaiser, *Isaiah 1–12*, 42.

36   Kenneth Boulding, *Stable Peace* (Austin: University of Texas Press, 1979); Arie M. Kacowicz, Yaacov Bar Siman Tov, et al., *Stable Peace among Nations* (Lanham, Md.: Rowan & Littlefield, 2000); James E. Goodby, Piet Buwalda, and Dimitrii Trenin, *Strategy for Stable Peace: Towards a Euroatlantic Security Community* (Washington, D.C.: U.S. Institute for Peace Press, 2002).

37   Gerhard von Rad, *Old Testament Theology*, vol. 1 (New York: Harper & Row, 1962), 130, 372.

38   Walter Brueggemann, *Peace* (Understanding Biblical Themes) (St. Louis, Mo.: Chalice Press, 2001).

39   Nigel Bigger, *Burying the Past: Making Peace and Doing Justice after Civil Conflict*, 2nd ed. (Washington, D.C.: Georgetown University Press, 2003); Jean Bethke Elshtain, "Politics and Forgiveness," in Leroy S. Rouner, ed., *Religion, Politics, and Peace* (Notre Dame, Ind.: University of Notre Dame Press, 1999), 32–47; Andrew Rigby, *Justice and Reconciliation: After the Violence* (Boulder, Colo.: Lynne Rienner, 2001).

40   Priscilla B. Hayner, *Unspeakable Truths: Facing the Challenge of Truth Commissions* (London: Taylor & Francis, 2002).

17 Williams and Weigel: War and Statecraft

1   The original version of this article was delivered as a lecture to the Royal Institute for International Affairs.

19 Kelsay: The New Jihad and Islamic Tradition

1   See partial transcript at www.memri.org, Special Dispatch Series, entry number 400, from which I quote.
2   See www.observer.co.uk/worldview/story/0,11581,845725,00.html.
3   My translation.

20 Juergensmeyer: Terror Mandated by God

1   Noam Friedman, quoted in Marjorie Miller, "Israeli Opens Fire in Hebron Market," *Los Angeles Times*, January 2, 1997.
2   Mark Juergensmeyer, *The New Cold War? Religious Nationalism Confronts the Secular State* (Berkeley: University of California Press, 1993).
3   For other works in what might be called an emerging field of "comparative cultural studies of terrorism" see James Aho, *The Politics of Righteousness: Idaho Christian Patriotism* (Seattle: University of Washington Press, 1990); Jeffrey Kaplan, "The Context of American Millenarian Revolutionary Theology: The Case of the 'Identity Christian' Church of Israel," *Terrorism and Political Violence* 5, no. 1 (Spring 1993): 30–82, and idem, "Right Wing Violence in North America," in Tore Bjørgo, ed., *Terror from the Extreme Right* (London: Frank Cass, 1995), 44–95; Cynthia Keppley Mahmood, *Fighting for Faith and Nation: Dialogues with Sikh Militants* (University Park: University of Pennsylvania Press, 1997); Ehud Sprinzak, *The Ascendance of Israel's Radical Right* (New York: Oxford University Press, 1991); and Paul Steinberg and Annamarie Oliver, *Rehearsals for a Happy Death: The Testimonies of Hamas Suicide Bombers* (New York: Oxford University Press, 1997). See also the articles of Robin Wright, who writes for the *Los Angeles Times* and such journals such as *Foreign Affairs*, and has written several books on Iran including *In the Name of God: The Khomeini Decade* (New York: Simon & Schuster, 1989).
4   I expand on this distinction between ethnic religious nationalism and ideological religious nationalism in my article, "The World-Wide Rise of Religious Nationalism," *Columbia Journal of International Affairs* 50, no. 1 (Summer 1996): 1–20.
5   Interview with Jun'ichi Kamata, former public affairs officer for the Tokyo headquarters of Aum Shinrikyo, Tokyo, January 12, 1996.
6   Interview with Jun'ichi Kamata.
7   Shoko Asahara, *Disaster Approaches the Land of the Rising Sun: Shoko Asahara's Apocalyptic Predictions* (Tokyo: Aum Publishing, 1995), 190 (translated and edited by Aum Translation Committee).
8   Asahara, *Disaster Approaches*, 190.
9   Sheik Omar Abd al-Rahman, quoted in Kim Murphy, *Los Angeles Times*, March 5, 1993.
10   Bruce Hoffman, *"Holy Terror": The Implications of Terrorism Motivated by a Religious Imperative* (Santa Monica, Calif.: RAND, 1993), 13. See also Mark Hosenball, "Another Holy War, Waged on American Soil: Al-Fuqra, a Muslim Sect with a Dangerous Agenda," *Newsweek*, February 28, 1995, 29–31.
11   Clifford Geertz, "Centers, Kings, and Charisma: Reflections on the Symbolics of Power," in Joseph Ben-David and Terry Nichols Clark, eds., *Culture and Its Creators: Essays in Honor of Edward Shils* (Chicago: University of Chicago Press, 1977); this essay is reprinted in Clifford Geertz, *Local Knowledge: Further Essays in Interpretive Anthropology* (New York: Basic Books, 1983), 121–46.
12   Geertz, "Centers, Kings, and Charisma," 151.
13   Juergensmeyer, *The New Cold War?* 11–25.
14   Jürgen Habermas, "Modernity—An Incomplete Project," reprinted in Paul Rabinow and William M. Sullivan, eds., *Interpretive Social Science: A Second Look* (Berkeley: University of California Press, 1987), 148.

21 Huntington: The Clash of Civilizations?

1   Murray Weidenbaum, *Greater China: The Next Economic Superpower?* Contemporary Issues, Series 57 (St. Louis, Mo.: Washington University Center for the Study of American Business, February 1993), 2–3.

2   Bernard Lewis, "The Roots of Muslim Rage," *The Atlantic Monthly* 266 (September 1990): 60; *Time*, June 15, 1992, 24–28.

3   Archie Roosevelt, *For Lust of Knowing* (Boston: Little, Brown, 1988), 332–33.

4   Almost invariably Western leaders claim they are acting on behalf of "the world community." One minor lapse occurred during the run-up to the Gulf War. In an interview on "Good Morning America," December 21, 1990, British Prime Minister John Major referred to the actions "the West" was taking against Saddam Hussein. He quickly corrected himself and subsequently referred to "the world community." He was, however, right when he erred.

5   Harry C. Triandis, *The New York Times*, December 25, 1990, 41, and "Cross-Cultural Studies of Individualism and Collectivism," *Nebraska Symposium on Motivation* 37 (1989): 41–133.

6   Kishore Mahbubani, "The West and the Rest," *The National Interest* (Summer 1992): 3–13.

7   Sergei Stankevich, "Russia in Search of Itself," *The National Interest* (Summer 1992): 47–51; Daniel Schneider, "A Russian Movement Rejects Western Tilt," *Christian Science Monitor*, February 5, 1993, 5–7.

8   Owen Harries has pointed out that Australia is trying (unwisely in his view) to become a torn country in reverse. Although it has been a full member not only of the West but also of the ABCA military and intelligence core of the West, its current leaders are in effect proposing that it defect from the West, redefine itself as an Asian country, and cultivate close ties with its neighbors. Australia's future, they argue, is with the dynamic economies of East Asia. But, as I have suggested, close economic cooperation normally requires a common cultural base. In addition, none of the three conditions necessary for a torn country to join another civilization is likely to exist in Australia's case.

22   *Rubenstein and Crocker: Challenging Huntington*

1   Samuel P. Huntington, "The Clash of Civilizations?" *Foreign Affairs* 72, no. 3 (Summer 1993): 21–49.

2   Samuel P. Huntington, "If Not Civilizations, What? Paradigms of the Post–Cold War World," *Foreign Affairs* 72, no. 5 (November–December 1993): 190.

3   John Burton, ed., *Conflict: Basic Human Needs* (New York: St. Martin's Press, 1990).

23   *Seiple: Memo to the State*

1   Gerard F. Powers, "Religion, Conflict, and Prospects for Peace in Bosnia, Croatia, and Yugoslavia," in Paul Mojzes, ed., *Religion and the War in Bosnia* (Atlanta: Scholars Press, 1998), 245.

24   *Jenkins: The Politics of Persecuted Religious Minorities*

1   Neera Chandhoke, *Beyond Secularism: The Rights of Religious Minorities* (New Delhi: Oxford University Press, 1999).

2   Mario Apostolov, *Religious Minorities, Nation States, and Security: Five Cases from the Balkans and the Eastern Mediterranean* (Burlington, Vt.: Ashgate, 2001).

3   Yitzhak Nakash, *The Shi'is of Iraq* (Princeton, N.J.: Princeton University Press, 1994).

4   Christopher W. Marsh, *The Family of Love in English Society, 1550–1630* (Cambridge: Cambridge University Press, 1994).

5   See Paul B. Henze, *Islam in the Caucasus: The Example of Chechnya* (Santa Monica, Calif.: RAND, 1995); Anssi Kullberg, "The Sufi Resistance," *The Eurasian Politician*, October 2003, http://www.cc.jyu.fi/~aphamala/pe/2003/tsets-2.htm (January 10, 2004).

6   See Ofra Bengio and Gabriel Ben-Dor, eds., *Minorities and the State in the Arab World* (Boulder, Colo.: Lynne Rienner, 1999); Malise Ruthven, *Islam in the World*, 2nd ed. (New York: Oxford University Press, 2000).

7   See Amandeep Singh Madra and Parmjit Singh, *Warrior Saints: Three Centuries of the Sikh Military Tradition* (London: I.B. Tauris in association with The Sikh Foundation, 1999); Mark Juergensmeyer, *Terror in the Mind of God: The Global Rise of Religious Violence*, 3rd ed. (Berkeley: University of California Press, 2003).

8   See Stuart Hall, "Tam Recalls His Proud Days with the Real Tartan Army," *icLanarkshire*, http://iclanarkshire.icnetwork.co.uk/news/localnews/rutherglen/content_objectid=12660341_method=full_siteid=50144_headline=-Tam-recalls-his-proud-days-with-the-Real-Tartan-Army-name_page.html (January 10, 2004).

9   See Matti Moosa, *The Maronites in History* (Syracuse, N.Y.: Syracuse University Press, 1986); Mordechai Nisan, *Minorities in the Middle East*, 2nd ed. (Jefferson, N.C.: McFarland, 2002).

10   See Hillel Schwartz, *The French Prophets: The History of a Millenarian Group in Eighteenth-Century England* (Berkeley: University of California Press, 1979); Clarke Garrett, *Spirit Possession and Popular Religion: From the Camisards to the Shakers* (Baltimore, Md.: Johns Hopkins University Press, 1987). A classic analysis is found in Norman Cohn, *The Pursuit of the Millennium: Revolutionary Millenarians and Mystical Anarchists of the Middle Ages*, rev. and expanded ed. (New York: Oxford University Press, 1970).

11   John Bossy, *The English Catholic Community, 1570–1850* (New York: Oxford University Press, 1976).

12   See Juan R. I. Cole and Nikki R. Keddie, eds., *Shi'ism and Social Protest* (New Haven, Conn.: Yale University Press, 1986); Juan Cole, *Sacred Space and Holy War: The Politics, Culture and History of Shi'ite Islam* (London: I.B. Tauris, 2002).

13   The speech is very widely available: see for instance http://www.irelandsown.net/ppearse2.html.

14   See Joyce Pettigrew, ed., *Martyrdom and National Resistance Movements: Essays on Asia and Europe* (Amsterdam: VU University Press for Centre for Asian Studies, 1997); Juergensmeyer, *Terror in the Mind of God*. For a Christian variant of this tradition, see Anna L. Peterson, *Martyrdom and the Politics of Religion: Progressive Catholicism in El Salvador's Civil War* (Albany: State University of New York Press, 1997).

15   Elaine Pagels, *The Gnostic Gospels* (New York: Vintage Books, 1989).

16   Robert Hugh Benson, *Come Rack! Come Rope!* (London: Hutchinson, 1912).

17   Seán Farrell Moran, *Patrick Pearse and the Politics of Redemption: The Mind of the Easter Rising, 1916* (Washington, D.C.: Catholic University of America Press, 1994). Compare Norman Davies, *Heart of Europe: The Past in Poland's Present* (New York: Oxford University Press, 2001).

18   See Bossy, *The English Catholic Community*.

25   Grim: Religious Freedom

1   See "World Publics Welcome Global Trade—But Not Immigration," Pew Global Attitudes Project, October 4, 2007, http://pewglobal.org/reports/pdf/258topline.pdf. Question wording: "How important is it to you to live in a country where you can practice your religion freely? Is it very important, somewhat important, not too important or not at all important?" Countries covered: *The Americas:* Argentina, Bolivia, Brazil, Chile, Mexico, Peru, Venezuela; *Eastern Europe:* Bulgaria, Czech Republic, Poland, Russia, Slovakia, Ukraine; *Middle East:* Egypt, Jordan, Kuwait, Lebanon, Morocco, Palestinian territories, Turkey; *Asia:* Bangladesh, India, Indonesia, Malaysia, Pakistan; *Africa:* Ethiopia, Ghana, Ivory Coast, Kenya, Mali, Nigeria, Senegal, South Africa, Tanzania, Uganda. The question was not asked in Western Europe.

2   Brian J. Grim and Roger Finke, "International Religion Indexes: Government Regulation, Government Favoritism, and Social Regulation of Religion," *Interdisciplinary Journal of Research on Religion* (2006). See data on religious abuse and displacement coded from the State Department International Religious Freedom reports at www.thearda.com.

3   See Brian J. Grim and Roger Finke, "Religious Persecution in Cross-National Context: Clashing Civilizations or Regulated Religious Economies?" *American Sociological Review* 72, no. 4 (2007): 633–58; and Brian J. Grim, "God's Economy: Religious Freedom and Socio-Economic Well-being," in Paul Marshall, ed., *Religious Freedom in the World* (Lanham, Md.: Rowman & Littlefield, 2008), 42–47.

4   CIA Factbook estimates.

5   "Responsible" freedom means that freedoms should be used responsibly for the good of people; otherwise, anarchy and exploitation of the weak can result. Specifically, religious freedom does not give license to cause harm or exploit others.

6   Correlations between the Hudson Institute's Religious Freedom Score and the other measures reported by Grim, "God's Economy," are all statistically significant at $p < .001$, two-tailed, and are as follows: Freedom House civil liberty index (.862); Freedom House political liberty index (.822); Reporters Without Borders press freedom index (.804); Heritage Foundation economic freedom index (.743); and the longevity of democracy index (.646).

7   See Amartya K. Sen, *Development as Freedom* (New York: Knopf, 1999) and Amartya K. Sen, *Rationality and Freedom* (Cambridge, Mass.: Belknap Press of Harvard University, 2002).

8   Correlations between the Hudson Institute's Religious Freedom Score and the other measures reported by Grim, "God's Economy," had the correlation signs reversed in this analysis to reflect correlation with religious freedom rather than restricted freedom; the correlations are statistically significant at $p < .05$,

two-tailed (or better), and are as follows: Military Expenditure as a percentage of GDP in 2005 (−.3); Armed Conflict since 1988 (−.3); Seats in parliament held by women (.3); percentage of females reenrolled in tertiary schools, 2002/2003 (.6); female earned income (.6); male earned income (.5); gross domestic product (.3); human development index (.5); physicians per 100,000 people (.3); infant deaths per 1,000 (−.4); underweight children (−.3).

9   See Rodney Stark and Roger Finke, *Acts of Faith: Explaining the Human Side of Religion* (Berkeley: University of California Press, 2000) and Roger Finke and Rodney Stark, *The Churching of America 1776–2005: Winners and Losers in Our Religious Economy* (New Brunswick, N.J.: Rutgers University Press, 2005).

10 Grim, "God's Economy."

11 A new initiative studying spiritual capital is funded by the John Templeton Foundation (http://www.templeton.org/funding_areas/core_themes/spiritual_capital/); for papers offering an analysis of religion from a "religious economies" perspective, see http://www.religionomics.com/.

12 See Edward C. Green, "Faith-Based Organizations: Contributions to HIV Prevention" (Washington, D.C.: USAID, 2003).

13 See Harold G. Koenig, Michael E. McCullough, and David B. Larson, *Handbook of Religion and Health* (New York: Oxford University Press, 2000).

14 For example, the growth of newcomer evangelical groups in Catholic areas has been argued to promote gender equality. See Christian Smith and Joshua Prokopy, eds., *Latin American Religion in Motion* (New York: Routledge, 1999).

15 See Eric M. Uslaner, "Religion and Civic Engagement in Canada and the United States," *Journal for the Scientific Study of Religion* 41, no. 2 (June 2002): 239–54, and Corwin Smidt, "Religion and Civic Engagement: A Comparative Analysis," *Annals of the American Academy of Political and Social Science* 565 (September 1999): 176–92.

16 Harvard sociologist Robert Putnam notes that diversity without activities aimed at integrating divergent groups can divide societies, but that activities such as proselytism and inter-religious marriage (both dependent on religious freedom) help social identities to become permeable and thus better integrate people into societies. See Robert E. Putnam, "E Pluribus Unum: Diversity and Community in the Twenty-First Century: The 2006 Johan Skytte Prize Lecture," *Scandinavian Political Studies* 30, no. 2 (June 2007): 137–74.

17 Some claim that the religious competition that resulted from the Reformation kept the Catholic Church from remaining a medieval religion. For a discussion of the controversies surrounding interpretations of the impact of the Reformation on religion, see Philip S. Gorski, "Historicizing the Secularization Debate: Church, State, and Society in Late Medieval and Early Modern Europe, ca. 1300 to 1700," *American Sociological Review* 65 (2000): 138–67. Also, without competition, the Russian Orthodox Church easily became a tool of the Czars; see Adamantia Pollis, "Eastern Orthodoxy and Human Rights," *Human Rights Quarterly* 15, no. 2 (May 1993): 339–56.

18 My analysis of data from Penn State's ARDA on restrictions to conversion in 196 countries shows that having no restrictions on conversions is significantly correlated (at least at p < .05, two-tailed) with economic freedom (.3), civil liberties (.6), political rights (.5), and press freedom (.5). They also relate to democracy (.4) and lower levels of armed conflict (.3). They correlate with higher income for females (.2), presence of females in legislatures (.5), higher percentages of female professional (.5), higher gender empowerment (.5), more expenditures on public health (.2), fewer people living below the poverty line (.3), and lower percent of GDP spent on the military (.5).

19 The social restriction of religious freedom can be thought of as the gap between the value people place on living in a country with religious freedom for their own religion versus freedom for other religions. A recent survey by the Pew Forum on Religion & Public Life of populations in 10 countries from Asia, the Americas, and Africa found an average gap of 14 percentage points across the countries. For details see http://pewforum.org/publications/surveys/pentecostals-06.pdf.

20 Although these effects of social restrictions on religious freedom often play themselves out at the local or provincial level, they also play out at the trans-national level. For example, on September 11, 2001, the world was introduced to the power of asymmetrical religion-related warfare, where religiously motivated non-state actors rained down violence upon thousands. 9/11 shows how the actions of religiously motivated social actors—many of whom came from Saudi Arabia, where religious freedom does not

exist—lead to higher worldwide government restrictions of religion-related groups (rightly and wrongly) suspected of being like or related to Al Qaeda. As documented by the State Department, the pressures to reduce religious freedom for the sake of security are real and growing in many countries today, representing a globalized version of the religious violence cycle.

21   See Vincent Y. C. Shih, *The Taiping Ideology: Its Sources, Interpretations, and Influences* (Seattle: University of Washington Press, 1967).

22   See William I. Brustein, *Roots of Hate: Anti-Semitism in Europe before the Holocaust* (Cambridge: Cambridge University Press, 2003). Also see Hannah Arendt, *Eichmann in Jerusalem: A Report on the Banality of Evil* (New York: Viking, 1963).

23   In the *ASR* piece, "violence" is termed "persecution," and is defined as the abuse or displacement of people due to religion.

24   Peter Berger, "Religion in a Globalizing World," Pew Forum presentation, Key West, Florida, December 4, 2006, http://pewforum.org/events/?EventID=136.

25   N. J. Demerath III, *Crossing the Gods: Worldly Religions and Worldly Politics* (New Brunswick, N.J.: Rutgers University Press, 2002), 124.

26 Carlson and Correa: How Shall We Study Religion and Conflict?

1   Martin E. Marty, "The Economist on Religion," *Sightings*, November 11, 2007.

2   Charles Kimball, *When Religion Becomes Evil* (San Francisco: HarperCollins, 2002); Bruce Lincoln, *Holy Terrors: Thinking About Religion after September 11*, 2nd ed. (Chicago: University of Chicago Press, 2006); and Jessica Stern, *Terror in the Name of God: Why Religious Militants Kill* (New York: Ecco, 2003).

3   Sam Harris, *The End of Faith: Religion, Terror, and the Future of Reason* (New York: Norton, 2004); Christopher Hitchens, *God Is Not Great: How Religion Poisons Everything* (New York: Twelve/Hachette, 2007); and Richard Dawkins, *The God Delusion* (New York: Houghton Mifflin, 2006).

4   For example, R. Scott Appleby, *The Ambivalence of the Sacred: Religion, Violence, and Reconciliation* (Lanham, Md.: Rowman & Littlefield, 2000) and Mark Juergensmeyer, *Terror in the Mind of God: The Global Rise of Religious Violence* (Berkeley: University of California Press, 2000).

5   See Philip Jenkins' global Christianity trilogy including *God's Continent: Christianity, Islam, and Europe's Religious Crisis* (New York: Oxford University Press, 2007).

6   David Brooks, "Kicking the Secularist Habit," *Atlantic Monthly*, February 24, 2003.

7   Stephen R. Prothero, *Religious Literacy: What Every American Needs to Know—and Doesn't* (San Francisco: HarperSanFrancisco, 2007).

8   Todd Kerstetter, *God's Country, Uncle Sam's Land: Faith and Conflict in the American West* (Urbana: University of Illinois Press, 2006).

9   Raymond Bingham, "Bridging the Religious Divide," *Parameters* (Autumn 2006): 50–66.

10   Daniel Philpott, *Revolutions in Sovereignty: How Ideas Shaped Modern International Relations* (Princeton, N.J.: Princeton University Press, 2001); Susanne Hoeber Rudolph and Joseph Piscatori, eds., *Transnational Religion and Fading States* (Boulder, Colo.: Westview Press, 1997); Elizabeth Hurd, *The Politics of Secularization in International Relations* (Princeton, N.J.: Princeton University Press, 2007); and Joshua Mitchell, *Not by Reason Alone: Religion, History, and Identity in Early Modern Political Thought* (Chicago: University of Chicago Press, 1996).

11   Madeleine Albright, *The Mighty and the Almighty: Reflections on America, God, and World Affairs* (New York: HarperCollins, 2006).

12   Douglas Johnston, ed., *Faith-Based Diplomacy: Trumping Realpolitik* (New York: Oxford University Press, 2003).

13   More established programs—such as those sponsored by the Pew Forum on Religion and Public Life, the Center for Religion and Public Life, Ethics and Public Policy Center, the International Center for Religion and Diplomacy, and the Institute for Global Engagement—must not be overlooked.

14   A few of which include the Center for the Study of Religion and Conflict (Arizona State University), the Joan B. Kroc Institute for International Peace Studies (University of Notre Dame), and the Berkley Center for Religion, Peace, and World Affairs (Georgetown University).

15   This is a recurring theme in Martin E. Marty and R. Scott Appleby's five-volume work on "fundamentalism," which includes *Fundamentalisms and the State: Remaking Polities, Economies, and Militance* (Chicago: University of Chicago Press, 1993).

16 Pew Research Center and the Pew Forum on Religion and Public Life, "Many Americans Uneasy with Mix of Religion and Politics," August 24, 2006.

17 Linell E. Cady, "Categories, Conflicts, Conundrums: Reflections on the Religion/Secular Divide," in Peter French and Jason Short, eds., *War and Border Crossings: Ethics When Cultures Clash* (Lanham, Md.: Rowman & Littlefield, 2005).

18 This working notion of "religion and conflict" may strike some as too broad or ambivalent. It captures, however, important cultural dimensions that "religion and violence" or "religion and politics" exclude. Yet these sometimes distinct categories share common features (e.g., relational dynamics between fundamentalism and secularism) that "religion and conflict" would seek to address. Others may object that the study of religion is the study of conflict. While no doubt true, not all intra- or inter-religious conflict assumes a strong public, violent, or global character.

19 Paul Ramsey, *The Just War: Force and Political Responsibility* (New York: Scribner, 1968); Michael Walzer, *Just and Unjust Wars: A Moral Argument with Historical Illustrations* (New York: Basic, 1977), and *Arguing About War* (New Haven, Conn.: Yale University Press, 2004); James Turner Johnson, *Just War Tradition and the Restraint of War: A Moral and Historical Inquiry* (Princeton, N.J.: Princeton University Press, 1981); United States Conference of Catholic Bishops, *The Challenge of Peace: God's Promise and Our Response: A Pastoral Letter on War and Peace* (Washington, D.C.: United States Catholic Conference, 1983); Richard B. Miller, *Interpretations of Conflict: Ethics, Pacifism, and the Just-War Tradition* (Chicago: University of Chicago Press, 1991); and Charles Reed and David Ryall, eds., *The Price of Peace: Just War in the Twenty-First Century* (Cambridge: Cambridge University Press, 2007).

20 Colm McKeogh, *The Political Realism of Reinhold Niebuhr: A Pragmatic Approach to Just War* (New York: St. Martin's Press, 1997); Ronald H. Stone, *Prophetic Realism: Beyond Militarism and Pacifism in an Age of Terror* (New York: T&T Clark, 2005); and Anatol Lieven and John Hulsman, *Ethical Realism: A Vision for America's Role in the World* (New York: Pantheon Books, 2006).

21 John Kelsay, *Arguing the Just War in Islam* (Cambridge, Mass.: Harvard University Press, 2007); Khaled Abou El Fadl, *Violence and Rebellion in Islamic Law* (Cambridge: Cambridge University Press, 2006); and Sohail H. Hashmi, ed., *Islamic Political Ethics: Civil Society, Pluralism, and Conflict* (Princeton, N.J.: Princeton University Press, 2002).

22 Terry Nardin, ed., *The Ethics of War and Peace: Religious and Secular Perspectives* (Princeton, N.J.: Princeton University Press, 1996); Richard Sorabji and David Rodin, eds., *The Ethics of War: Shared Problems in Different Traditions* (Burlington, Vt.: Ashgate, 2006); R. Joseph Hoffmann, ed., *The Just War and Jihad: Violence in Judaism, Christianity, and Islam* (Amherst, N.Y.: Prometheus, 2006); James Turner Johnson and John Kelsay, *Cross, Crescent, and Sword: The Justification and Limitation of War in Western and Islamic Tradition* (New York: Greenwood Press, 1990); and James Turner Johnson, *The Holy War Idea in Western and Islamic Traditions* (University Park: Pennsylvania State University Press, 1997).

23 John D. Carlson and Erik C. Owens, eds., *The Sacred and the Sovereign: Religion and International Politics* (Washington, D.C.: Georgetown University Press, 2003); Jonathan Fox and Shmuel Sandler, *Bringing Religion into International Relations* (New York: Palgrave Macmillan, 2004); Ted Gerard Jelen and Clyde Wilcox, eds., *Religion and Politics in Comparative Perspective: The One, the Few, and the Many* (Cambridge: Cambridge University Press, 2002); Pippa Norris and Ronald Inglehart, *Sacred and Secular: Religion and Politics Worldwide* (Cambridge: Cambridge University Press, 2004); Fabio Petito and Pavlos Hatzopoulos, eds., *Religion in International Relations: The Return from Exile* (New York: Palgrave Macmillan, 2003); and Scott M. Thomas, *The Global Resurgence of Religion and the Transformation of International Relations: The Struggle for the Soul of the Twenty-First Century* (New York: Palgrave Macmillan, 2005).

24 Robert A. Seiple and Dennis R. Hoover, eds., *Religion & Security: The New Nexus in International Relations* (Lanham, Md.: Rowman & Littlefield, 2004) and Thomas F. Farr, *World of Faith and Freedom: Why International Religious Liberty Is Vital to American National Security* (Oxford: Oxford University Press, 2008).

25 Douglas Johnston, *Faith-Based Diplomacy*; Douglas Johnston and Cynthia Sampson, eds., *Religion, the Missing Dimension of Statecraft* (New York: Oxford University Press, 1994).

26 Larry Diamond, Marc F. Plattner, and Philip J. Costopoulos, eds., *World Religions and Democracy* (Baltimore: Johns Hopkins University Press, 2005); Martha C. Nussbaum, *The Clash Within: Democracy, Religious Violence, and India's Future* (Cambridge, Mass.: Harvard University Press, 2007); and Noah Feldman, *After Jihad: America and the Struggle for Islamic Democracy* (New York: Farrar, Straus & Giroux, 2003).

27   René Girard, *The Scapegoat* (Baltimore: Johns Hopkins University Press, 1986) and *Violence and the Sacred* (Baltimore: Johns Hopkins University Press, 1977); Juergensmeyer, *Terror in the Mind of God*; William T. Cavanaugh, "Sins of Omission: What 'Religion and Violence' Arguments Ignore," *The Hedgehog Review* 6, no. 1 (Spring 2004): 34–50; J. Harold Ellens, ed., *The Destructive Power of Religion: Violence in Judaism, Christianity, and Islam*, 4 vols. (Westport, Conn.: Praeger, 2004). See also Regina M. Schwartz, *The Curse of Cain: The Violent Legacy of Monotheism* (Chicago: University of Chicago Press, 1997); Hector Avalos, *Fighting Words: The Origins of Religious Violence* (Amherst, N.Y.: Prometheus, 2005); and works by Charles Kimball, Bruce Lincoln, and Jessica Stern. There are also extensive works dedicated to religious violence in specific regional settings.

28   Richard John Neuhaus, *The Naked Public Square: Religion and Democracy in America* (Grand Rapids: Eerdmans, 1984); Robert N. Bellah, *Habits of the Heart: Individualism and Commitment in American Life* (Berkeley: University of California Press, 1985); and James Davison Hunter, *Culture Wars: The Struggle to Define America* (New York: Basic, 1991).

29   John Rawls, *Political Liberalism* (New York: Columbia University Press, 1996); Richard Rorty, "Religion as a Conversation-Stopper," in *Philosophy and Social Hope* (London: Penguin, 1999), 168–74 and "Religion in the Public Square: A Reconsideration," *Journal of Religious Ethics* 31, no. 1 (Spring 2003): 141–49.

30   Stephen L. Carter, *The Culture of Disbelief: How American Law and Politics Trivialize Religious Devotion* (New York: Anchor, 1993); Michael J. Perry, *Religion in Politics: Constitutional and Moral Perspectives* (New York: Oxford University Press, 1997); and Jeffrey Stout, *Democracy and Tradition* (Princeton, N.J.: Princeton University Press, 2004).

31   John Paul Lederach, *The Moral Imagination: The Art and Soul of Building Peace* (New York: Oxford University Press, 2004) and *Building Peace: Sustainable Reconciliation in Divided Societies* (Washington, D.C.: U.S. Institute of Peace, 1997); Marc Gopin, *Holy War, Holy Peace: How Religion Can Bring Peace to the Middle East* (New York: Oxford University Press, 2002) and *Between Eden and Armageddon: The Future of World Religions, Violence and Peacemaking* (New York: Oxford University Press, 2000); and Appleby, *Ambivalence of the Sacred*.

32   John W. de Gruchy, *Reconciliation: Restoring Justice* (Minneapolis, Minn.: Fortress Press, 2002) and *Donald W. Shriver, An Ethic for Enemies: Forgiveness in Politics* (New York: Oxford University Press, 1995).

33   Jonathan Z. Smith, *Imagining Religion: From Babylon to Jonestown* (Chicago: University of Chicago Press, 1982); Russell McCutcheon, *Manufacturing Religion: The Discourse on Sui Generis Religion and the Politics of Nostalgia* (New York: Oxford University Press, 1997); and Tomoko Masuzawa, *The Invention of World Religions or, How European Universalism Was Preserved in the Language of Pluralism* (Chicago: University of Chicago Press, 2005). Some scholars observe that overgeneralization about religion obscures underlying forms of political and cultural domination on the part of those with authority distinguish religion from non-religion. For example, David Chidester argues that colonizers' recognition of native African religions (or not) worked to further the aims of the colonizers, *Savage Systems: Colonialism and Comparative Religion in Southern Africa* (Charlottesville: University of Virginia Press, 1996). See also Talal Asad, *Genealogies of Religion: Discipline and Reasons of Power in Christianity and Islam* (London: Johns Hopkins University Press, 1993).

34   Hitchens, *God Is Not Great*; Harris, *End of Faith*.

35   Juergensmeyer, *Terror in the Mind of God*; idem, "Review Essay: Thinking about Religion after September 11," *Journal of the American Academy of Religion* 72, no. 1 (March 2004): 221–34.

36   Jonathan Riley-Smith, *The Crusades: A History*, 2nd ed. (New Haven, Conn.: Yale University Press, 2005) and Christopher Tyerman, *Fighting for Christendom: Holy War and the Crusades* (New York: Oxford University Press, 2004).

37   Michael Scheuer, *Imperial Hubris: Why the West Is Losing the War on Terror* (Washington, D.C.: Potomac Books, 2005).

38   Appleby, *Ambivalence of the Sacred*.

39   Cavanaugh, "Sins of Omission." See also Janet Jakobsen, "Is Secularism Less Violent Than Religion?" in Elizabeth A. Castelli and Janet R. Jakobsen, eds., *Interventions: Activists and Academics Respond to Violence* (New York: Palgrave Macmillan, 2004), 53–70.

40   James Turner Johnson observes important moral distinctions between *bellum*, involving public use of force reserved to the state's effort to protect its citizens, and *duellum*, or private acts of force by those not charged with the protection of the community, *Just War Tradition*, 44–49.

41   Hannah Arendt, *On Violence* (New York: HBJ/Harcourt Brace, 1970).

42   Martin Luther King's famous "Letter from Birmingham Jail" elaborates this point.

28   *Cox and Philpott: Faith-Based Diplomacy*

1   This article was the product of a CFIA Task Force on Faith-Based Diplomacy. The Task Force members were: Brian Cox, Daniel Philpott, Darin Hamlin, Thomas F. Farr, Katie E. Johnson, Diana Barnes, Scott Thomas, and Nell Bolton.

2   Joseph Montville, "Transnationalism and the Role of Track-Two Diplomacy," in *Approaches to Peace: An Intellectual Map*, ed. W. Scott Thompson and Kenneth M. Jensen (Washington, D.C.: United States Institute of Peace, 1991).

3   R. Scott Appleby, *The Ambivalence of the Sacred: Religion, Violence, and Reconciliation* (Lanham, Md.: Rowman & Littlefield, 2000), 10–13.

4   See Appleby, *Ambivalence of the Sacred*; Marc Gopin, *Between Eden and Armageddon: The Future of World Religions, Violence, and Peacemaking* (Oxford: Oxford University Press, 2000); John Paul Lederach, *Building Peace: Sustainable Reconciliation in Divided Societies* (Washington, D.C.: United States Institute of Peace, 1997).

5   Douglas Johnston, *Faith-Based Diplomacy: Trumping Realpolitik* (Oxford: Oxford University Press, 2003).

6   Other principles can also be included, as should the familiarly liberal democratic ones that our participants stressed.

7   Appleby, *Ambivalence of the Sacred*, 245–80.

8   Lederach, *Building Peace*, 38–55.

9   To clarify, Jammu and Kashmir is a state of India, consisting of three sub-regions, Kashmir (often called the "Kashmir Valley"), Jammu, and Ladakh. The Kashmir Valley is a Muslim majority area, Jammu a Hindu majority area, and Ladakh is divided evenly between Muslims and Hindus. The term "Kashmir" is often used generically to mean either the entire State of Jammu and Kashmir or else the even larger region that is disputed by India and Pakistan, straddling the Line of Control that de facto divides the sovereign states of India and Pakistan. Thus far we have used "Kashmir" in these more generic senses.

10   Gopin, *Between Eden and Armageddon*, 172.

29   *Johnston: Military Chaplains*

1   This team, which was led by the International Center for Religion and Diplomacy (ICRD), included Richard Ruffin, then Executive Director of Moral Rearmament USA; Donald Shriver, President Emeritus of Union Theological Seminary; Joseph Montville, then Director of the Preventive Diplomacy Program at the Center for Strategic and International Studies; and Douglas Johnston, President of ICRD.

2   The "line community" includes those personnel in the military chain of command who are directly responsible for the war-fighting function. Other responsibilities that do not contribute directly to the combat mission, such as chaplains, lawyers, physicians, or civil engineers are considered to be in the "staff" (as opposed to "line") component.

3   Even among those chaplains who are volunteers, it is essential to recognize and accommodate through training the fact that chaplains are not trained negotiators; nor do they typically speak the language or qualify as cultural experts wherever they are stationed. Finally, despite the fact that chaplains have a basic ability to interact with clergy of different faiths, not every volunteer will be temperamentally suited to engage local religious leaders.

4   Douglas M. Johnston, "We Neglect Religion at Our Peril," *United States Naval Institute Proceedings* 128 (January 2002): 50–52.

5   John Boardman, Jasper Griffin, and Oswyn Murray, eds., *The Oxford Illustrated History of the Roman World* (New York: Oxford University Press, 1986), 420.

6   Daniel B. Jorgensen, *Air Force Chaplains: Volume 1—The Service of Chaplains to Army Air Units 1917–1946* (Washington, D.C.: Superintendent of Documents, U.S. Government Printing Office, 1961), 5.

7   "Adhémar of Monteil," *Encyclopedia Britannica* (2009), www.britannica.com.

8   Thomas F. Madden, *The New Concise History of the Crusades* (Lanham, Md.: Rowman & Littlefield, 2005), 31.

9   David S. Bachrach, "The Medieval Chaplain and His Duties," in *The Sword of the Lord: Military Chaplains from the First to the Twenty-First Century*, ed. Doris L. Bergen (Notre Dame, Ind.: University of Notre Dame Press, 2004), 69–70.

10 Bergen, *Sword of the Lord*, 7–8.

11 William Jackson Johnstone, *George Washington, the Christian* (New York: Abingdon, 1919), 69.

12 Johnstone, *George Washington*, 217–18.

13 Derek Davis, *Religion and the Continental Congress, 1774–1789* (New York: Oxford University Press, 2000), 80.

14 John W. Brinsfield, "The Army Chaplaincy and World Religions: From Individual Ministries to Chaplain Corps Doctrine," *The Army Chaplaincy* (Winter–Spring 2009): 17.

15 Herbert L. Bergsma, *Chaplains with Marines in Vietnam, 1962–1971* (Washington, D.C.: History and Museums Division Headquarters, 1985), 151.

16 Based on their position and training, chaplains are better suited to serving as "bridge builders" rather than negotiators.

17 "Military Chaplains as Peace Builders: Embracing Indigenous Religions in Stability Operations," a report published by the U.S. Army Peacekeeping and Stability Operations Institute, concluded after analyzing competing categories of personnel that chaplains were the staff element best suited for religious leader engagement based on their training, skills, credentials (in the eyes of the local population), and accessibility to the combatant commander. In essence, the multi-faith experiences of military chaplains coupled with their considerable interpersonal skills are attributes that make them particularly well suited to the complex challenges of religious engagement.

18 *JP 1-05: Religious Affairs in Joint Operations* (Joint Chiefs of Staff, 2009), III-5.

19 A good example cited by Commander George Adams in the 2006 USIP publication, "Chaplains as Liaisons with Religious Leaders" was a collaborative effort by Army chaplain Eric Eliason (with the 1st Battalion, 19th Special Forces Group) and Afghan elders and imams to renovate twenty-six mosques—an initiative that both discredited Taliban and al-Qaeda propaganda and won the trust of the local population. USIP, *Peaceworks* no. 56 (2006): 9.

20 The 2009 International Military Chief of Chaplains Conference held in Cape Town, South Africa, February 1–6, 2009.

21 Chaplain (LCOL) Ira C. Houck III, "Strategic Religious Engagement for Peacebuilding" (USAWC Civilian Research Project, U.S. Army War College, 2009), 15, 20; http://www.dtic.mil.

22 Exacerbating this problem is the fact that the personal religious perspective of the commander often dictates how the chaplain is utilized. Or, taking it even further (and as expressed by one senior Army chaplain), "personal prejudice against religion among commanders is shameful but real." Chester Lanious, e-mail to author, June 8, 2009.

23 Paul R. Wrigley, "The Impact of Religious Belief in the Theatre of Operations," *Naval War College Review* (Spring 1996), www.dtic.mil.

24 Maj. Gen. Douglas L. Carver, "From the Chief," *The Army Chaplaincy* (Winter/Spring 2009): 1. Ideally, it would also be desirable to develop a future chaplain capacity relating to justice, human rights, religious tolerance, ethical engagement, and religious freedom.

25 Indicative of the challenge that awaits is the December 2007 study by Auburn University's Center for the Study of Theological Education in which 2,300 seminary graduates were asked to rank 14 areas of study in order of relevance to their professional life and work. "World religions" was ranked 13. Holly Lebowitz Rossi, "Many Mansions," *Sojourners Magazine* 37, no. 9 (September/October 2008): 34

26 The Army is currently moving in this direction, having just added a special skill identifier (SSI) for world religion experts based on graduate level education on the subject.

27 Dr. Pauletta Otis, e-mail to author, June 1, 2009.

28 U.S. Navy Chaplain (Commander) George Adams, "Chaplains as Liaisons with Religious Leaders: Lessons from Iraq and Afghanistan," *Peaceworks* no. 56 (2006). This article provides a rich source of anecdotes illustrating a wide range of effective chaplain involvements in Iraq and Afghanistan.

29 Based on interview with the chaplain involved, who wished to remain anonymous. Also verified independently with other sources by the author.

30 Interview with the chaplain involved.

31 John Proctor, "A Short History of Religious Leader Engagement Operations in Operation Iraqi Freedom" (a paper presented at the 19th Expeditionary Sustainment Command, Korea, 2008), 3.

32   U.S. Army Chaplain (Lieutenant Colonel) Scottie Lloyd, "USAWC Strategy Research Project, Chaplain Contact with Local Religious Leaders: A Strategic Support," Project submitted to U.S. Army War College (March 2005), 6; www.dtic.mil.

33   Canadian National Defense, *Called to Serve: A Strategy for the Canadian Forces Chaplaincy* (Canada: February 2008), 5.

34   William S. Lee, Christopher Burke, and Zonna Crayne, "Military Chaplains as Peace Builders: Embracing Indigenous Religions in Stability Operations," *The Cadre Papers* no. 20 (Maxwell Air Force Base, Ala.: Air University Press, 2004), 21.

35   Lee, Burke, and Crayne, "Military Chaplains," 23.

36   Lee, Burke, and Crayne, "Military Chaplains," 16.

37   John W. Kiser, "An Algerian Microcosm: Monks, Muslims, and the Zeal of Bitterness," *Cisterian Studies Quarterly* 38, no. 3 (2003): 353.

30   *Gopin: Religion as Destroyer and Creator of Peace*

1   *The New York Times*, January 5, 2001, A6.

2   Marc Gopin, "Share Jerusalem or Battle Forever," *Boston Sunday Globe*, Focus Section, September 24, 2000.

3   See *Sahih Bukhari*, Book 2:39, "Narrated by Al-Bara' (bin 'Azib): When the Prophet came to Medina, he stayed first with his grandfathers or maternal uncles from Ansar. He offered his prayers facing Baitul-Maqdis (Jerusalem) for sixteen or seventeen months, but he wished that he could pray facing the Ka'ba (at Mecca)." See also Book 4:147. Jerusalem is sometimes referred to as *Ilya*, the ancient Roman name, and sometimes as *bait al maqdis*, depending on the context. Most important is that sometimes it is referred to both as Temple and *bait maqdis*. See *Sahi Muslim*, Book 1: 0309, "It is narrated on the authority of Anas b. Malik that the Messenger of Allah (may peace be upon him) said: I was brought al-Buraq who is an animal white and long, larger than a donkey but smaller than a mule, who would place his hoof a distance equal to the range of version. I mounted it and came to the Temple (Bait Maqdis in Jerusalem), then tethered it to the ring used by the prophets. I entered the mosque and prayed two rak'ahs in it, and then came out and Gabriel brought me a vessel of wine and a vessel of milk. I chose the milk, and Gabriel said: You have chosen the natural thing. Then he took me to heaven." The ancient Jewish word for the two temples, one destroyed in 586 B.C.E. and the second destroyed in 70 C.E., is *bet ha-miqdash*, which is the exact cognate of the term used in the *hadith*. It means literally "the house of holiness," or "the sanctified house." There is no doubt that Mohammed, at least according to the classical Islamic sources, made a clear connection between this sacred spot and its Jewish spiritual origins. This is one more example of how the politicization of religion, or the modern fundamentalist turn in religion, is only sometimes a return to original, intolerant sources. Often it is a distortion of classical sources for contemporary political agendas.

4   The latter, by the way, does not require Jewish residence in Hebron, though it would be wonderful and restorative if the original Jewish community, destroyed by the 1929 riots, were welcomed back as honored guests, as opposed to the belligerent force of radicals there now. The key to inter-religious peace ultimately must be access and respect, not domination by one party or the other. Similarly, the impossibility of all Palestinian refugees returning to Israel is evident to both sides. But many restorative gestures and welcomes home for some of them are possible. It would be a wonderful opportunity for bilateral healing, if on the same day that the Hebron Palestinian community made gestures to the survivors of the 1929 Jewish community that a Jewish community inside Israel welcomed back the survivors of original residents of a nearby Palestinian community. It would be especially effective if it were accompanied by gestures at the Cave of the Patriarchs and Matriarchs, which was in parallel to a rededication of a mosque inside Israel. These are not pipe dreams. They do require long periods of cultivation, extensive financial support so that talented people can work on this exclusively, and support from leaders who at least get out of the way of these developing relationships.

5   Psalm 15, for example. Clearly this would involve building moral sources and precedents from all the Abrahamic traditions, but, in terms of the Temple Mount, Judaism and Islam. In Islam, there are laws governing sacred spaces as well. See, for example, *Sahih Muslim Book 7: Kitab al-hajj*, #3153-3154, which involve the declaration of Mecca and Medina as sacred, and the prohibition against cutting trees there or killing the animals.

6   Psalm 15:1.

31 Christiansen: Catholic Peacemaking, 1991–2005

* This article is an expanded version of a talk prepared for a meeting of the Catholic Peacebuilding Network, Chicago, Ill., April 19–20, 2006.

1 For the role of John Paul II in the ending of communist rule in his native Poland, see Geoffrey Garton Ash, *The Magic Lantern: The Revolution of 1989 Witnessed in Warsaw, Budapest, Berlin and Prague* (Vintage, 1990) and George Weigel, *The Final Revolution: The Resistance Church and the Collapse of Communism* (Oxford, 1992). For a detailed account of John Paul's personal influence on the defense of human rights and the liberation of one colonized people, the East Timorese, see Arnold Kohen, *From the Place of the Dead: The Epic Struggle of Bishop Belo of East Timor*, introduction by the Dalai Lama (St. Martin's, 1999). Other examples of John Paul's engagement in situations of conflict may be found in *Libano: Faccio Mio L'Appello di un Popula: Interveni di Giovanni Paolo II gennaio 1989–aprile 1990*, Quaderni de "L'Osservatore Romano," no. 13, ed. Mario Agnes (Vatican, 1990); *John Paul II for Peace in the Middle East, War in the Gulf: Gleanings from the Pages of "L'Osservatore Romano,"* Quaderni de "L'Osservatore Romano," no. 16, ed. Mario Agnes (Vatican, 1992); *La crisi iugolsava*, Quaderni de "l'Osservatore Romano," ed. Mario Agnes, no. 19 (Vatican, 1992); and *Assisi 1993, Giovanni Paolo II per la pace in Bosnia ed Erzegovina*, Quaderni de "l'Osservatore Romano," no. 21, ed. Mario Agnes (Vatican, 1993).

2 My entry "The Vatican" in the *Encyclopedia of Politics and Religion*, rev. ed. (Congressional Quarterly Press, forthcoming), provides a general description of the Vatican's role in international politics. On the Vatican's *Ostpolitik* (i.e., its policy toward Communist Eastern Europe) prior to 1989, see Eric O. Hanson, *The Catholic Church in World Politics* (Princeton, 1987), chap. 6, "Catholic Poland and *Ostpolitik*," 197–233.

3 One area of conflict in which there was close cooperation between the USCC (later USCCB) and the Holy See was the Holy Land. In 1996, e.g., USCC helped disseminate specially prepared documents on the future of Jerusalem, and in 1998 facilitated the organization of European, Canadian, and American bishops' conferences to support the church in the Holy Land. In 2001 that group began annual meetings of presidents of episcopal conferences in Jerusalem and elsewhere in the Holy Land to express solidarity with the church there.

4 The Holy See is the official name applied to the Catholic Church, and specifically to the pope and the Roman curia (the pope's administrative arm), in international affairs. For an interpretative survey of the role of the Holy See in world politics prior to 1988, see Hanson, *The Catholic Church in World Politics*; Andre Dupuy, *Pope John Paul II and the Challenge of Papal Diplomacy: Anthology (1978–2003)* (Pontifical Council for Justice and Peace/New York, Paths to Peace Foundation, 2004); and Bernard J. O'Connor, *Papal Diplomacy: John Paul II and the Culture of Peace* (Saint Augustine, 2005). This last volume includes the pope's annual addresses to the diplomatic corps up to 2003 in their entirety. The addresses provide a handy year-by-year summary of the international concerns of the Holy See. Also see *John Paul II and the Family of Peoples: The Holy Father to the Diplomatic Corps (1978–2002)* (Pontifical Council for Justice and Peace, 2002) and *Ways of Peace: Papal Messages for the World Days of Peace (1968–86)* (Pontifical Council for Justice and Peace, 1986). More recent statements for the World Day of Peace may be found at the Vatican website: http://www.vatican.va/holy_father/messages/peace.

5 For a summary of the Church's position on humanitarian intervention, see *The Compendium of the Social Doctrine of the Church* (Pontifical Council for Justice and Peace/United States Conference of Catholic Bishops, 2005), nos. 504–6. Preventive war is treated below. (N.B. References to the documents of Catholic social teaching are commonly made to enumerated sections or paragraphs in the text rather than to pages.)

6 On *Pacem in Terris*, see my "Commentary on *Pacem in Terris*" in Kenneth Himes et al., eds., *Catholic Social Teaching: Commentaries and Interpretations* (Georgetown, 2005), 217–43. On the positive Catholic conception of peace, see National Conference of Catholic Bishops, "The Challenge of Peace: God's Promise and Our Response" (USCC, 1983), nos. 68–69. I trace the concept further in a talk for a panel on Catholic peacemaking for the United States Institute of Peace in "Catholic Peacemaking: From *Pacem in Terris* to *Centesimus annus*." The talk was reported in detail by David Smock in "Catholic Contributions to International Peace," USIP Special Report 69 (April 2001).

7 For the principal documents of contemporary Catholic social teaching, see David J. O'Brien and Thomas W. Shannon, eds., *Catholic Social Thought: The Documentary Heritage* (Maryknoll, 1995).

8 On the idea of a "convoy concept," see David Braybrooke, *Three Tests for Democracy: Personal Rights, Human Welfare, Collective Preferences* (Random House, 1968), 92.

9   "*Gaudium et Spes* (The Pastoral Constitution on the Church in the Modern World)," no. 78, in *Catholic Social Thought*.

10 *Centesimus annus* (On the Hundredth Anniversary of *Rerum Novarum*) in *Catholic Social Thought*, no. 23.

11 *Centesimus annus*, no. 52.

12 See Vatican Council II, *Gaudium et spes*, no. 78, in *Catholic Social Thought*.

13 *Centesimus annus*, no. 52.

14 *Centesimus annus*.

15 "The Challenge of Peace: God's Promise and Our Response," no. 71.

16 United States Conference of Catholic Bishops, "The Harvest of Justice Is Sown in Peace" (United States Conference of Catholic Bishops, 2001), 12.

17 For the bishops' response to September 11, see http://www.usccb.org/sdwp/sept11.

18 Address to the Diplomatic Corps, January 13, 2003, no. 4, in *Papal Diplomacy*.

19 *Centesimus annus,* no. 52.

20 *Centesimus annus*, no. 25.

21 United States Conference of Catholic Bishops, "Harvest of Justice," 15.

22 United States Conference of Catholic Bishops, "Harvest of Justice," 16.

23 See http://www.usccb.org/sdwp/sept11.

24 Bishop Wilton D. Gregory, President, United States Conference of Catholic Bishops, "Statement on Iraq," February 26, 2003: "Based on the facts that are known, it is difficult to justify resort to war against Iraq, lacking clear and adequate evidence of an imminent attack of a grave nature or Iraq's involvement in the terrorist attacks of September 11. With the Holy See and many religious leaders throughout the world, we believe that resort to war would not meet the strict conditions in Catholic teaching for the use of military force."

25 United States Conference of Catholic Bishops, "Harvest of Justice," 12.

26 *Compendium*, no. 501.

27 On John Paul's ministry of forgiveness, see Luigi Accattoli, *When A Pope Asks Forgiveness: The Mea Culpas of John Paul II*, trans. Jordan Ammann, O. P. (Pauline, 1998).

28 See http://www.vatican.va/holy_father/john_paul_i_mes_20011211_world_day_for _peace_en.html.

29 *Compendium*, nos. 428–32.

30 For the foundational theological themes of the unity of the human family and the consequent communitarian nature of the human vocation, see *Gauidum et Spes*, nos. 23–32 and 42. The last identifies "the promotion of unity" in the world community as one of the principal ways in which the Church serves the world.

31 Vatican Council II, *Lumen Gentium* ("The Dogmatic Constitution on the Church") no. 1, in the *Documents of Vatican II*, general editor Walter Abbott, S. J. (America Press, 1966). On the service of the world through the promotion of unity in the human family, see "The Pastoral Constitution on the Church in the Modern World," no. 42, in *Catholic Social Thought*.

32 World Day of Peace Message, 2004.

33 World Day of Peace Message.

34 Some commentators have perceived a difference of attitude to interreligious dialogue on Pope Benedict XVI's part in his re-assignment of the President of the Pontifical Council for Interreligious Dialogue, Archbishop Michael Fitzgerald, to be nuncio in Egypt and the merging of the council with one dedicated to culture. But see John Borelli, "From Tiber to Nile," *The Tablet*, April 8, 2006, 10–11.

35 Address to the Diplomatic Corps, January 10, 2002, no. 3, in *Papal Diplomacy*.

36 For materials from the first Assisi meeting, see the *Bulletin of the Secretariat for Non-Christians* 22, no. 1 (1987). For use of the Assisi meetings on behalf of peace in the former Yugoslavia, see *Assisi 1993*, also cited in n. 2 above.

37 On the church's role in post–civil war Lebanon, see Carole H. Dagher, *Bring Down the Walls: Lebanon's Post-War Challenge* (St. Martin's, 2000).

38 For regional views of Christian-Muslim dialogue, see "Ensemble Devant Dieu Pour Le Bien de la Personne et de la Socieite: La coexistence entre musulmans et chretiens dans le monde arabe," Third Pastoral Letter of the Catholic Patriarchs of the Middle East (General Secretariat of the Council of Patriarchs of the East [Bkerke, Lebanon] 1994); and Sixth Pastoral Letter of the Patriarchs of the East, "Ensemble pour l'avenir" in "Pour qu'ils aient la vie et qu'ils l'aient en abondance," Acts of the 1st Congress of Catholic

Patriarchs and Bishops of the East (General Secretariat of the Council of Patriarchs [Bkerke, Lebanon], 1999), 426–27.

39   "La Nouvelle Espérance pour le Liban" (Vatican, 1997).

40   On Catholic-Muslim dialogue in general, see Michael L. Fitzgerald and John Borelli, *Interfaith Dialogue: A Catholic View*, Part II: *Christian Muslim Relations* (SPCK, 2006), 85–162. Pope John Paul's efforts in opposing the war in Iraq led to the recognition by leading Muslim clerics that the U.S.-led effort was not a Christian or "crusader" war against Islam.

41   Final Declaration of Participants in the Symposium on "The Spiritual Resource of the Religions for Peace," Rome, January, 16–18 2003. See Vatican website: http://vatican.va/roman_curia/pontifical_councils/ interreligious_dialogue/rc_pc_interlg_doc_20020311_religions-peace_en.html.

32   Soliman: *The Potential for Peacebuilding in Islam*

1   Albert B. Randall, *Theologies of War and Peace among Jews, Christians, and Muslims* (New York: Edwin Mellen Press, 1998), 25. This was evidenced by searching the Library of Congress online catalog; around 10,000 items resulted from looking for the available literature on "Islam" and "violence," while barely one tenth of that number resulted from searching under "Islam" and "peace" or "Islam" and "nonviolence."

2   Robert C. Johansen, "Radical Islam and Nonviolence: A Case Study of Religious Empowerment and Constraint among Pashtuns," *Journal of Peace Research* 34, no. 1 (1997): 67.

3   Abdul Aziz Said, Nathan C. Funk, and Ayse S. Kadayifci, "Introduction," in *Peace and Conflict Resolution in Islam: Precept and Practice*, edited by Abdul Aziz Said, Nathan C. Funk, and Ayse S. Kadayifci (Lanham, Md.: University Press of America, 2001), 1–26.

4   Asghar Ali Engineer, "On the Concept of Compassion in Islam," http://www.andromeda.rutgers .edu/~rtavakol/engineer/compassion.htm, accessed on 28 March 2007.

5   R. Scott Appleby, *The Ambivalence of the Sacred: Religion, Violence and Reconciliation* (New York: Carnegie Commission on Preventing Deadly Conflict, 2000), 25.

6   Randall, *Theologies of War*, 289–90.

7   Khaled Abou El Fadl, *The Place of Tolerance in Islam*, edited by Joshua Cohen and Ian Lague (Princeton, N.J.: Beacon Press, 2002), 15.

8   Mahmoud Zaki Naguib, *Ro'ya Islamia* (Cairo: Egyptian Public Book House, 1995), 24 (Arabic).

9   The Qur'an, the literal word of God and the primary source of teaching in Islam, is revealed (*wahy* in Arabic) to Prophet Mohammed from Allah through Gabriel (an angel) to guide humans. It is composed of 114 suras (chapters), each constituting of a number of ayahs (verses), compiled in the Mushaf, the name of the book containing the Qur'an. The words and deeds of Prophet Mohammed are considered the second source of religious teachings in Islam, transmitted by his companions and the scholars after them in the form of *hadiths* (short sayings).

10   Khaled M. Abou El Fadl, *The Great Theft: Wrestling Islam from the Extremists* (New York: HarperCollins, 2005), 115.

11   Sheikh Mohamed El-Gharawi, *As-Salam fil-Qur'an wa Al-Hadith* (Beirut: Dar el Adwaa', 1990), 28–34 (Arabic).

12   English interpretations of the ayahs of the Qur'an are by Abdullah Yusuf Ali, as downloaded from: http:// www.soundvision.com/info/~qu7ran/search.asp?sura=&transtable=yusufali&ayah=&Submit=Search& word=justice&offset=0.

13   Randall, *Theologies of War*, 300.

14   Asghar Ali Engineer, "The Concept of Peace in Islam," http://www.dawoodi-bohras.com/perspective/ islam_peace.htm, accessed on 19 April 2007.

15   Abdel-Aziz Said and Nathan C. Funk, "Peace in Islam: An Ecology of the Spirit," in *Islam and Ecology—A Bestowed Trust*, edited by Richard C. Foltz, Frederick Mathewson Denny, and Haji Baharuddin Azizan (Boston: Harvard University Press, 2003), 155–83.

16   Randall, *Theologies of War*, 404–5.

17   Roger Boase, "Ecumenical Islam: A Muslim Response to Religious Pluralism," in *Islam and Global Dialogue: Religious Pluralism and the Pursuit of Peace*, edited by Roger Boase (London: Ashgate, 2005), 251–52.

18 Roger Garaudy, "Human Rights and Islam: Foundation, Tradition, Violation," in *The Ethics of World Religions and Human Rights*, edited by Hans Kung and Jurgen Moltmann (Philadelphia: Trinity Press International, 1990), 46.

19 Mahmoud M. Ayoub, *Islam: Faith and Practice* (Ontario: Open Press, 1989), 26.

20 Murad Wilfrid Hofmann, "Religious Pluralism and Islam in a Polarized World," in Boase, *Islam and Global Dialogue*, 238.

21 Jawdat Saeed, "Law, Religion, and the Prophetic Method of Social Change," trans. Afra Jalabi, *Journal of Law and Religion* 15, nos. 1–2 (2000–2001): 93.

22 Mohammed Abu-Nimer, *Nonviolence and Peacebuilding in Islam: Theory and Practice* (Gainesville: University Press of Florida, 2003), 68.

23 John Kelsay, *Islam and War: A Study in Comparative Ethics* (Louisville, Ky.: Westminster John Knox, 1993), 29.

24 Kelsay, *Islam and War*, 30.

25 Randall, *Theologies of War*, 292.

26 Mohamed Fathi Osman, "God Is the All-Peace, the All-Merciful," in *Beyond Violence: Religious Sources of Social Transformation in Judaism, Christianity, and Islam*, edited by James L. Heft (New York: Fordham University Press, 2004), 68.

27 Osman, "God Is the All-Peace," 69.

28 Randall, *Theologies of War*, 289.

29 Translation from the original Arabic text is done by the author unless cited.

30 Joshua Parens, *An Islamic Philosophy of Virtuous Religions: Introducing Alfarabi* (Albany: State University of New York Press, 2006), 64–65.

31 Rabia Terri Harris, "Nonviolence in Islam: The Alternative Community Tradition," in *Subverting Hatred: The Challenge of Nonviolence in Religious Traditions*, edited by Daniel L. Smith-Christopher (New York: Orbis Books, 2007), 96.

32 Harris, "Nonviolence in Islam," 107.

33 Boase, "Ecumenical Islam," 257.

34 Randall, *Theologies of War*, 401–2.

35 Nissim Rejwan, *The Many Faces of Islam: Perspectives on a Resurgent Civilization* (Gainesville: University Press of Florida, 2000), 27.

36 Kelsay, *Islam and War*, 32–33.

37 Ayoub, *Islam*, 49–50.

38 Randall, *Theologies of War*, 359.

39 Randall, *Theologies of War*, 318–19.

40 Mohamed Abdel Hamed Mohamed, *Al-Sufia wa-l-jihad fi sabil Allah* (Alexandria: Dar Al-Wafaa'), 29–30 (Arabic).

41 Ali Gom'aa, *Al-Jihad fil-Islam* (Cairo: Nahdet Misr, 2005), 15 (Arabic).

42 Randall, *Theologies of War*, 322.

43 Osman, "God Is the All-Peace," 59.

44 Abu-Nimer, *Nonviolence and Peacebuilding*, 59.

45 El Fadl, *Great Theft*, 130.

46 Randall, *Theologies of War*, 323–24.

47 Kelsay, *Islam and War*, 35–36.

48 Randall, *Theologies of War*, 351–52.

49 Osman, "God Is the All-Peace," 62–63.

50 El Fadl, *Great Theft*, 237.

51 El Fadl, *Great Theft*, 238.

52 El Fadl, *Great Theft*, 242–43.

53 El Fadl, *Great Theft*, 237.

54 Abu-Nimer, *Nonviolence and Peacebuilding*, 54.

55 David Cortright, *Gandhi and Beyond: Nonviolence in the Age of Terrorism* (Boulder, Colo.: Paradigm, 2006), 122, 127.

56 Diana Francis, *Rethinking War and Peace* (London: Pluto Press, 2004), 117.

57 Abu-Nimer, *Nonviolence and Peacebuilding*, 39.

58 Karim D. Crow, "Islamic Peaceful Action (al-Jihad al-Silmi): Nonviolent Approach to Justice and Peace in Islamic Societies," *Capitol Journal on Culture and Society* 12, no. 1 (2001–2002): 149–50.

59 The five pillars of Islam are the rituals Muslims are required to adopt, which are: witness to Allah; prayer; alms giving; fasting during the lunar month of Ramadan; and pilgrimage to Mecca.

60 Chaiwat Satha-Anand (Qader Muheideen), "The Nonviolent Crescent: Eight Theses on Muslim Nonviolent Actions," in Islam and Nonviolence, edited by Glenn D. Paige, Chaiwat Satha-Anand (Qader Muheideen), and Sara Gilliatt (Honolulu: Center for Global Nonviolence Planning Project, Matsunaga Institute for Peace, University of Hawai'i, 1993), 22.

61 Ayoub, *Islam*, 116.

62 Saeed, "Law, Religion, and the Prophetic Method," 124–25.

63 The names of two cities in Arabia. The first, Mecca, is a sacred place for Muslims and it is where the message of Islam originally started. The second, Medina, is where the prophet spent the rest of his life after migration from Mecca as he gained the support of its people.

64 Crow, "Islamic Peaceful Action," 152.

65 Mohammad Shahabuddin, "Learning from the Past: Role of Religion in Peacebuilding," *Journal of International Affairs* 8, nos. 1–2 (2004): 70.

66 Shahabuddin, "Learning from the Past," 71.

67 Johansen, "Radical Islam," 59.

68 Asghar Ali Engineer, "On Developing a Theology of Peace in Islam," http://www.andromeda.rutgers.edu/~rtavakol/engineer/theology.htm, accessed on 28 March 2007.

69 Rashied A. Omar, "Towards a Peace Service in Islam," in *Peace Services in the Abrahamic Traditions* (The Netherlands: The International Fellowship of Reconciliation, 2006), 51–52.

70 Muhammad Abu-Laila, "Islam and Peace," *Islamic Quarterly* 35, no. 1 (1991): 61.

71 Majid Khadduri, *The Islamic Conception of Justice* (Baltimore: Johns Hopkins University Press, 1984), 8.

72 Nawal H. Ammar, "Restorative Justice in Islam: Theory and Practice," in *The Spiritual Roots of Restorative Justice*, edited by Michael L. Hadley (New York: State University of New York Press, 2001), 166.

73 Khadduri, *Islamic Conception of Justice*, 137.

74 Michael C. Braswell and J. Gold, "Peacemaking, Justice, and Ethics," in *Justice, Crime, and Ethics*, edited by Michael C. Braswell, Belinda R. McCarthy, and Bernard J. McCarthy (Cincinnati, Ohio: Anderson LexisNexis, 2002), 31.

75 Daniel Philpott, "What Religion Brings to the Politics of Transitional Justice," *Journal of International Affairs* 61, no. 1 (2007): 98.

76 Lisa Schirch, "Linking Human Rights and Conflict Transformation: A Peacebuilding Framework," in *Human Rights and Conflict: Exploring the Links between Rights, Law, and Peacebuilding*, edited by Jeffrey Helsing and Julie Mertus (Washington, D.C.: U.S. Institute of Peace Press, 2006), 80–82.

77 Howard Zehr, "Restorative Justice: The Concept," *Corrections Today* 59, no. 7 (1997): 68.

78 Mohsen Rahami, "Islamic Restorative Traditions and Their Reflections in the Post Revolutionary Criminal Justice System of Iran," *European Journal of Crime, Criminal Law, and Criminal Justice* 15, no. 2 (2007): 227–28.

79 This school is the rationalist school of thought in Islamic jurisprudence, and its main argument is that humans were created to be able to understand good and evil objectively using reason, and that justice is accorded upon this objective knowledge. See Abu-Nimer, *Nonviolence and Peacebuilding*, 64.

80 Jon Hoover, "The Justice of God and the Best of All Possible Worlds: The Theodicy of Ibn Taymiyya," *Theological Review* 27, no. 2 (2006): 58.

81 Hoover, "Justice of God," 68–69.

82 Khaled Abou El Fadl, "The Human Rights Commitment in Modern Islam," in *Human Rights and Responsibilities in the World Religions*, edited by Joseph Runzo, Nancy M. Martin, and Arvind Sharma (Oxford: Oneworld Publications, 2003), 334.

83 Ammar, "Restorative Justice in Islam," 172.

84 Ayoub, *Islam*, 126.

85 El Fadl, *Great Theft*, 122.

86 Jamal Krafess, "The Influence of Muslim Religion in Humanitarian Aid," *International Review of the Red Cross* 87, no. 858 (2005): 328.

87 Krafess, "Influence of Muslim Religion," 327.

88   Garaudy, "Human Rights and Islam," 53.

89   Ayoub, *Islam*, 134.

90   Krafess, "Influence of Muslim Religion," 329.

91   Krafess, "Influence of Muslim Religion," 329.

92   Krafess, "Influence of Muslim Religion," 332.

93   Monica M. Gaudiosi, "The Influence of the Islamic Law of WAQF on the Development of the Trust in England: The Case of Merton College," *University of Pennsylvania Law Review* 136, no. 4 (1988): 1233–34.

94   El Fadl, "Human Rights Commitment," 312.

95   Douglas Roche, *The Human Right to Peace* (Ottawa: Novalis, 2003), 123.

96   Roche, *Human Right to Peace*, 122.

97   Jack Donnelly, "Human Rights and Human Dignity: An Analytic Critique of Non-Western Conceptions of Human Rights," *American Political Science Review* 76, no. 2 (1982): 303.

98   El Fadl, "Human Rights Commitment," 311.

99   El Fadl, *Great Theft*, 187–88.

100 Abdul A'la Mawdudi, *Human Rights in Islam* (London: The Islamic Foundation, 1980), 15–16.

101 El Fadl, *Great Theft*, 186–87.

102 Joseph Runzo, "Secular Rights and Religious Responsibilities," in Runzo, Martin, and Sharma, *Human Rights and Responsibilities*, 15.

103 Runzo, "Secular Rights and Religious Responsibilities," 15–16.

104 El Fadl, "Human Rights Commitment," 329.

105 El Fadl, *Great Theft*, 234–35.

106 Ammar, "Restorative Justice in Islam," 178.

107 El Fadl, "Human Rights Commitment," 325–26.

108 Omar, "Towards a Peace Service in Islam," 51–52.

109 Garaudy, "Human Rights and Islam," 46.

110 Ronald Lukens-Bull, *A Peaceful Jihad: Negotiating Identity and Modernity in Muslim Java* (New York: Palgrave Macmillan, 2005), 123.

111 Omar, "Towards a Peace Service in Islam," 51.

112 Chandra Muzaffar, *Rights, Religion and Reform: Enhancing Human Dignity through Spiritual and Moral Transformation* (London: Routledge Curzon, 2002), 188–89.

113 Muzaffar, *Rights, Religion and Reform*, 249.

114 Randall, *Theologies of War*, 420.

115 Boase, "Ecumenical Islam," 260.

35   *Haynes: Transnational Religious Actors and International Politics*

1   A. McGrew, "Conceptualising Global Politics," in A. McGrew and P. Lewis, eds., *Global Politics* (Cambridge: Polity, 1992), 23.

2   Weigel, quoted in S. Huntington, "The Clash of Civilizations?" *Foreign Affairs* 72, no. 3 (1993): 26.

3   P. Beyer, *Religion and Globalization* (London: Sage, 1994), 1.

4   S. Rudolph and J. Piscatori, eds., *Transnational Religion and Fading States* (Boulder, Colo.: Westview, 1997); J. Piscatori, "Religious Transnationalism and Global Order, with Particular Consideration of Islam," in J. Esposito and M. Watson, eds., *Religion and Global Order* (Cardiff: University of Wales Press, 2000).

5   F. Bealey, *The Blackwell Dictionary of Political Science* (Oxford: Blackwell, 1999), 306.

6   C. Bretherton, "Universal Human Rights," in C. Bretherton and G. Ponton, eds., *Global Politics. An Introduction* (Oxford: Blackwell, 1996), 243–68.

7   R. Lipschutz, "Reconstructing World Politics: The Emergence of Global Civil Society," *Millennium* 21, no. 3 (1992): 390.

8   F. Attina, "The Study of International Relations in Italy," in H. Dyer and L. Mangasarian, eds., *The Study of International Relations: The State of the Art* (London: Macmillan, 1989), 350–51.

9   J. Haynes, *Religion in Global Politics* (London: Longman, 1998), 56–59.

10   M. d'Antonio, *Fall from Grace. The Failed Crusade of the Christian Right* (London: Deutsch, 1990).

11   J. Haynes, *Religion and Politics in Africa* (London: Zed, 1996), 91.

12   D. Rueschemeyer, E. Stephens, and J. Stephens, *Capitalist Development and Democracy* (Cambridge: Polity, 1992), 281.

13   A. Hastings, *A History of African Christianity, 1950–75* (Cambridge: Cambridge University Press, 1979), 173.

14   J. G. Vaillancourt, *Papal Power. A Study of Vatican Control over Lay Catholic Elites* (Berkeley: University of California Press, 1980).

15   Haynes, *Religion in Global Politics*, 93–94.

16   J. Witte, Jr., "Introduction," in Witte, ed., *Christianity and Democracy in Global Context* (Boulder, Colo.: Westview, 1993), 11.

17   P. Gifford, "Some Recent Developments in African Christianity," *African Affairs* 93, no. 373 (1994): 513–34.

18   Z. Sardar, *Islamic Futures. The Shape of Ideas to Come* (London: Mansell, 1985), 51–52.

19   Huntington, "Clash of Civilizations?"

20   Haynes, *Religion in Global Politics*, 221.

21   *Sunday Triumph* (Lagos), February 23, 1986.

22   J. Haynes, *Religion in Third World Politics* (Buckingham: Open University Press, 1993), 122–44.

23   S. Dorr, "Democratization in the Middle East," in R. Slater, B. Schutz, and S. Dorr, eds., *Global Transformation and the Third World* (Boulder, Colo.: Lynne Rienner, 1993), 151.

24   B. Etienne and M. Tozy, "Le glissement des obligations islamiques vers le phénomène associatif à Casablanca," in Centre de Recherches et d'Etudes sur les Sociétés Mediterranéennes, *Les Maghreb Musulman en 1979* (Paris: CNRS), 251, quoted in C. Coulon, *Les Musulmans et le Pouvoir en Afrique Noire* (Paris: Karthala, 1983), 48.

25   Coulon, *Les Musulmans et le Pouvoir en Afrique Noire*, 49.

36   *Wuthnow and Offutt: Transnational Religious Connections*

*   Support was provided by the Lilly Endowment. The authors are grateful to Peggy Levitt, Wendy Cadge, David Yamane, and an anonymous reviewer for comments on an earlier draft.

1   See John Bowen, "Does French Islam Have Borders? Dilemmas of Domestication in a Global Religious Field," *American Anthropologist* 106 (2004): 43–55; Elizabeth McAlister, "The Madonna of 115th Street Revisited: Vodou and Haitian Catholicism in the Age of Transnationalism," in *Gatherings in Diaspora: Religious Communities and the New Immigration*, ed. R. S. Warner and J. G. Wittner (Philadelphia: Temple University Press, 1998), 123–60; Ellen Oxfield, *Blood, Sweat, and Mahjong: Family and Enterprise in an Overseas Chinese Community* (Ithaca, N.Y.: Cornell University Press, 1993); Helen Rose Ebaugh, "Religion across Borders: Transnational Religious Ties," *Asian Journal of Social Science* 32 (2004): 216–31; Bruno Riccio, "From 'Ethnic Group' to 'Transnational Community'? Senegalese Migrants' Ambivalent Experiences and Multiple Trajectories," *Journal of Ethnic and Migration Studies* 27 (2001): 583–99; Miwa Hirono, "Framing Interaction: Transnational Religious Actors and Ethnic Communities in China," Working Paper, Australian National University, Research School of Pacific and Asian Studies (2004); Oscar Salemink, "Transnational Religious Networks and Protestant Conversion among the Hmong in Northern Vietnam," Working Paper, University of Amsterdam, Faculty of Cultural Anthropology and Sociology (2006).

2   See Philip Jenkins, *The Next Christendom: The Coming of Global Christianity* (New York: Oxford University Press, 2002).

3   See Richard B. Freeman, "People Flows in Globalization," *Journal of Economic Perspectives* 20 (2006): 145–70; Ulf Hannerz, *Transnational Connections: Culture, People, Places* (London: Routledge, 2006); Douglas Kellner, "Theorizing Globalization," *Sociological Theory* 20 (2002): 285–305; Manfred B. Steger, *Globalization: A Very Short Introduction* (New York: Oxford University Press 2003); United Nations, *Human Development Report* (New York: United Nations, 2004).

4   See Victor Asal, Brian Nussbaum, and D. William Harrington, "Terrorism as Transnational Advocacy: An Organizational and Tactical Examination," *Studies in Conflict & Terrorism* 30 (2007): 15–39; Donatella Della Porta, Massimillano Andretta, Lorenzo Mosca, and Herbert Reiter, *Globalization from Below: Transnational Activists and Protest Networks* (Minneapolis: University of Minnesota Press 2006); Rachel Harris, "Reggae on the Silk Road: The Globalization of Uyghur Pop," *China Quarterly* 183 (2005): 627–43; Anne-Mette Hjalager, "Stages in the Economic Globalization of Tourism," *Annals of Tourism Research* 34 (2007): 437–57; John Page and Sonia Plaza, "Migration Remittances and Development: A Review of Global Evidence," *Journal of African Economies* 15 (2006): 245–336; Risa Palm, "International

Telephone Calls: Global and Regional Patterns," *Urban Geography* 23 (2002): 750–70; Richard Rose-crance and Peter Thompson, "Trade, Foreign Investment, and Security," *Annual Review of Political Science* 6 (2003): 377–98; Carolyn E. Sachs, "Going Public: Networking Globally and Locally," *Rural Sociology* 72 (2007): 2–24; Joseph G. T. Salisbury and George A. Barnett, "The World System of International Monetary Flows: A Network Analysis," *Information Society* 15 (1999): 31–49; Barbara Stallings, "The Globalization of Capital Flows: Who Benefits?" *Annals of the American Academy of Political and Social Science* 610 (2007): 202–16; Sidney Tarrow, *The New Transnational Activism* (New York: Cambridge University Press, 2005); Matthew A. Zook, "Underground Globalization: Mapping the Space of Flows of the Internet Adult Industry," *Environment and Planning* A 35 (2003): 1261–86.

5   See Arthur S. Alderson and Jason Beckfield, "Power and Position in the World City System," *American Journal of Sociology* 109 (2004): 811–51; Henry John Farrell, "Regulating Information Flows: States, Private Actors, and E-commerce," *Annual Review of Political Science* 9 (2006): 353–74; Peter J. Marcotul-lio, "Globalisation, Urban Form and Environmental Conditions in Asia-Pacific Cities," *Urban Studies* 40 (2003): 219–47; Michael Allen Sacks, Marc J. Ventresca, and Brian Uzzi, "Global Institutions and Networks: Contingent Change in the Structure of World Trade Advantage, 1965–1980," *American Behavioral Scientist* 44 (2001): 1579–601; Moritz Schularick, "A Tale of Two 'Globalizations': Capital Flows from Rich to Poor in Two Eras of Global Finance," *International Journal of Finance & Economics* 11 (2006): 339–54; Ming Chang Tsai, "Does Globalization Affect Human Well-Being?" *Social Indicators Research* 81 (2007): 103–26.

6   See Steger, *Globalization: A Very Short Introduction*; Justin Rosenberg, *The Follies of Globalisation Theory* (London: Verso, 2000).

7   Among the approaches that take a different approach are treatments of religion and globalization that emphasize the theoretical implications of long-term modernization processes [See Peter Beyer, *Religion and Globalization* (Thousand Oaks, Calif.: Sage, 1994); Roland Robertson, *Globalization: Social Theory and Global Culture* (Thousand Oaks, Calif.: Sage, 1992)], and studies that consider transnationalism only in the context of immigrant communities that sit astride political borders to such an extent that they are neither here nor there [See Alejandro Portes, "Transnational Communities: Their Emergence and Significance in the Contemporary World-System," *Latin America in the World Economy*, ed. R. P. Korzeniewicz and W. C. Smith (Westport, Conn.: Greenwood Press, 1997), 151–68; Alejandro Portes, "Globalization from Below: The Rise of Transnational Communities," *The Ends of Globalization: Bringing Society Back In*, ed. D. Kalb, M. van der Land, and R. Staring (Boulder, Colo.: Rowman & Littlefield, 1999), 253–70; Alejandro Portes, Luis E. Guarnizo, and Patricia Landolt, "The Study of Transnationalism: Pitfalls and Promise of an Emergent Research Field," *Ethnic and Racial Studies* 22 (1999): 217–37].

8   See Rufus Anderson, *Memorial Volume of the First Fifty Years of the American Board of Commissioners for Foreign Missions* (Boston: ABCFM, 1861).

9   See A. T. Kearney, "The Global Top 20," *Foreign Policy* (November/December 2006): 74–81.

10 Conducted by Schulman, Ronca, and Bucuvalas, Inc., between January 19 and June 22, 2005, and consisting of approximately 200 fixed-response questions asked in 35 minute telephone interviews, including interviews in Spanish. Sampling was achieved through an random digit dialing (RDD) method, with screening asking how many adults age 18 or older in the household were "church members or attend church services at least once a month," after selecting the designated person within the household verifying that the respondent was in fact "a member of a church or attend religious services at least once a month." In all, 41 percent of the households contacted included an eligible church member by this criterion. The cooperation rate for the study was 68.4 percent and the response rate was 56.2 percent.

11 In all, Offutt conducted 118 interviews in 2006 and 2007 as part of his ethnographic research in the two countries.

12 See Mark Noll, "The American Contribution to World-Wide Evangelical Christianity in the Twentieth Century," Paper presented at International Conference on Evangelical Protestantism, Groupe de Sociologie des Religions et de la Laicite, Paris (2002); Fenggang Yang and Helen Rose Ebaugh, "Transformation of New Immigrant Religions and Their Global Implications," *American Sociological Review* 66 (2001): 269–88.

13 See Dana L. Robert, "The First Globalization: The Internationalization of the Protestant Missionary Movement between the World Wars," *International Bulletin of Missionary Research* 26 (2002): 50–66.

14 See Mark Chaves, *Congregations in America* (Cambridge, Mass.: Harvard University Press, 2004); John C. Green, "Evangelical Protestants and Civic Engagement: An Overview," in *A Public Faith: Evangelicals and Civic Engagement*, ed. M. Cromartie (Lanham, Md.: Rowman & Littlefield, 2003), 11–30.

15 Peggy Levitt, "Local-Level Global Religion: The Case of U.S.-Dominican Migration," *Journal of the Scientific Study of Religion* 3 (1998): 74–89; Peggy Levitt, "Between God, Ethnicity, and Country: An Approach to the Study of Transnational Religion," Working Paper, Princeton University, Center on Migration and Development (2001); Peggy Levitt, "Redefining the Boundaries of Belonging: The Institutional Character of Transnational Religious Life," *Sociology of Religion* 65 (2004): 1–18; Riva Kastoryano, *Negotiating Identities: States and Immigrants in France and Germany* (Princeton, N.J.: Princeton University Press, 2002); Riva Kastoryano, "Politization of Islam in Europe: Recognition and Human Rights," Working Paper, Georgetown University, Berkley Center for Religion, Peace, and World Affairs (2007).

16 See Jenkins, *The Next Christendom: The Coming of Global Christianity*.

17 See Robert Wuthnow, *After the Baby Boomers: How Twenty- and Thirty-somethings Are Shaping the Future of American Religion* (Princeton, N.J.: Princeton University Press, 2007).

18 See Ian Bradley, *Believing in Britain: The Spiritual Identity of "Britishness"* (New York: I.B. Tauris, 2007).

19 See John Bowen, *Why the French Don't Like Headscarves: Islam, the State, and Public Space* (Princeton, N.J.: Princeton University Press, 2007).

20 See Lawrence Schlemmer, "Immigrants in South Africa: Perceptions and Reality in Witbank, a Medium-Sized Industrial Town," *CDE Focus* (Johannesburg: Centre for Development and Enterprise, May 2006).

21 See Jonathan Crush, Vincent Williams, and Sally Peberdy, "Migration in Southern Africa: A Paper Prepared for the Policy Analysis and Research Programme of the Global Commission of International Migration" (Geneva: Global Commission on International Migration, 2005).

22 See United Nations, *Human Development Report*.

23 See Peggy Levitt, "Redefining the Boundaries of Belonging: The Institutional Character of Transnational Religious Life," 1–18.

24 See Helen Rose Ebaugh and Janet Saltzman Chafetz, "Structural Adaptations in Immigrant Congregations," *Sociology of Religion* 61 (2000): 135–53.

25 See R. Stephen Warner, "The Place of the Congregation in the American Religious Configuration," in *American Congregations* vol. 2, ed. J. P. Wind and J. W. Lewis (Chicago: University of Chicago Press, 1994), 54–99.

26 See Peggy Levitt, *God Needs No Passport* (New York: New Press, 2007).

27 See Robert Wuthnow, *American Mythos: Why Our Best Efforts to Be a Better Nation Fall Short* (Princeton, N.J.: Princeton University Press, 2006).

28 See Helen Rose Ebaugh and Janet Saltzman Chafetz, "Dilemmas of Language in Immigrant Congregations: The Tie That Binds or the Tower of Babel?" *Review of Religious Research* 41 (2000): 432–52; Ebaugh and Saltzman Chafetz, eds., *Religion across Borders: Transnational Immigrant Networks* (Walnut Creek, Calif.: AltaMira, 2002).

29 See Alex MacLeod, "A New Reformation Is Happening in Global Christianity," *Presbyterian Record* 128 (2004): 44–45; Uwe Siemon-Netto, "Surprise: Resilient Christianity," *World & I* 18 (2003): 29–31.

30 See Patricia Lefevere, "Study Looks at Foreign-Born Priests Serving in U.S.," *National Catholic Reporter* (February 2006), retrieved 17 December 2007 (http://findarticles.com/p/articles/mi_m1141/is_17_42/ai_n16107683).

31 See David B. Barrett and Todd M. Johnson, *World Christian Trends, AD 30–AD 2200: Interpreting the Annual Christian Megacensus* (Pasadena, Calif.: William Carey Library, 2001).

32 See Todd M. Johnson and David R. Scoggins, "Christian Missions and Islamic Da'wah: A Preliminary Quantitative Assessment," *International Bulletin of Missionary Research* 29 (2005): 8–11.

33 See James Gibbon, "Religion, Migrants, and the Turkish Government in Germany," Working Paper, Princeton University, Center for the Study of Religion (2006).

34 See Jytte Klausen, "Is There an Imam Problem?" *Prospect* 98 (May 2004), retrieved 17 December 2007 (http://www.prospect-magazme.co.uk/article_details.php?id=5945).

35 See Ralph D. Winter and Steven C. Hawthorne, *Perspectives on the World Christian Movement* (Pasadena, Calif.: William Carey Library, 1999).

36 This figure may be skewed by the fact that active church members tend to be better educated than the general public; nevertheless, among respondents who had not been to college, 41 percent reported having

traveled or lived outside the United States. In a previous national survey, 51 and 58 percent of regular church attenders and non-attenders, respectively, said they have traveled or lived outside the United States; among those who had, 11 percent of both groups had been to the Middle East and 17 and 20 percent, respectively, had been to India, China, Japan, or another part of Asia.

37 See Robert Wuthnow, *America and the Challenges of Religious Diversity* (Princeton, N.J.: Princeton University Press, 2005).

38 See Afzal Kahn, "American Muslims Perform Hajj, Celebrate Eid-ul Adha," *Current Issues* (January 2005), retrieved 17 December 2007 (http://usinfo.state.gov/xarchives/display.html?p=washfile-english&y=2005&m=January&x=20050121173803cpataruk0.6693384).

39 See David Rohde, "Braving Nature and Militants: Hindus Trek for a Peek at God's Icy Symbol," *The New York Times* (August 2002), retrieved 17 December 2007 (http://query.nytimes.com/gst/fullpage.html?res=9C01EED8133BF936A35 75BC0A9649C8B63&sec=&spon=); Prema Kurien, *A Place at the Multicultural Table: The Development of an American Hinduism* (New Brunswick, N.J.: Rutgers University Press, 2007).

40 See Alexander Henriksen, "Trekking Towards Enlightenment," *Geographical* 75, no. 11 (2003): 22–29.

41 Figures from annual reports by the United Nations' World Tourism Organization, online at www.world-tourism.org.

42 See Tetsunao Yamamori and Kenneth A. Eldred, *On Kingdom Business: Transforming Missions Through Entrepreneurial Strategies* (Wheaton, Ill.: Crossway, 2003).

43 See Chen Cunfu and Huang Tianhai, "The Emergence of a New Type of Christians in China Today," *Review of Religious Research* 46 (2004): 183–200.

44 See Steve Rundle and Tom Steffen, *Great Commission Companies* (Downers Grove, Ill.: InterVarsity, 2003).

45 See Kearney, "The Global Top 20," 74–81.

46 See Prema Kurien, *Kaleidoscopic Ethnicity: International Migration and the Reconstruction of Community Identities in India* (New Brunswick, N.J.: Rutgers University Press, 2002).

47 See Levitt, *God Needs No Passport*.

48 See Dotsey Welliver and Minnette Northcutt, *Mission Handbook, 2004–2006: U.S. and Canadian Protestant Ministries Overseas* (Wheaton, Ill.: Billy Graham Center, 2004).

49 See Robert J. Priest, "Peruvian Protestant Churches Seek Linking Social Capital," Working Paper, Trinity Evangelical Divinity School, Deerfield, Ill. (2007).

50 See www.pewresearchcenter.org.

51 See Brian H. Smith, *More Than Altruism: The Politics of Private Foreign Aid* (Princeton, N.J.: Princeton University Press, 1990).

52 According to the project's website (www.jesusfilm.org).

53 See John C. Maxwell, *The 21 Irrefutable Laws of Leadership* (Nashville: Thomas Nelson, 1998).

54 See Levitt, *God Needs No Passport*.

55 See R. Andrew Chesnut, *Born Again in Brazil: The Pentecostal Boom and the Pathogens of Poverty* (New Brunswick, N.J.: Rutgers University Press, 1997).

56 See David Martin, *Pentecostalism: The World Their Parish* (Oxford: Blackwell, 2002).

57 See www.worldbank.org.

58 See Kearney, "The Global Top 20," 74–81.

59 See David Dollar, "Globalization, Poverty, and Inequality," in *Globalization: What's New?* ed. M. M. Weinstein (New York: Columbia University Press, 2005), 96–428.

60 See Martin Ravallion, "The Debate on Globalization, Poverty and Inequality: Why Measurement Matters," World Bank Policy Research Working Paper No. 3038 (2003), retrieved 17 December 2007 (http://ssrn.com/abstract=636400).

61 See Chesnut, *Born Again in Brazil: The Pentecostal Boom and the Pathogens of Poverty*.

62 See Birgit Meyer, "Commodities and the Power of Prayer: Pentecostalist Attitudes Towards Consumption in Contemporary Ghana," *Development and Change* 29 (1998): 751–76.

63 See Jacqueline E. Wenger, "Official vs. Underground Protestant Churches in China: Challenges for Reconciliation and Social Influence," *Review of Religious Research* 46 (2004): 169–82; David Ownby, "China, Religion, and Human Rights: Social Change and State Response," Working Paper, Georgetown University, Berkley Center for Religion, Peace, and World Affairs (2007).

64 See Yasuki Hamano, "Building the Content Industry," *Japan Plus: Asia-Pacific Perspectives* (May 2004), retrieved 17 December 2007 (http://www.jijigaho.or.jp/old/app/0405/eng/sp12.html).

65 Steger, *Globalization: A Very Short Introduction*, 36.

66 See Meyer, "Commodities and the Power of Prayer: Pentecostalist Attitudes Towards Consumption in Contemporary Ghana," 751–76.

67 See Bryan T. Froehle and Mary L. Gautier, *Global Catholicism: Portrait of a World Church* (Maryknoll, N.Y.: Orbis, 2003).

68 See Cristina Mora, "Transnational Religious Organizations and the Production of 'Made for TV' Conversion Narratives in the U.S. and Brazil," Working Paper, Princeton University, Center for the Study of Religion (2007).

69 See Joel Robbins, *Becoming Sinners: Christianity and Moral Torment in a Papua New Guinea Society* (Berkeley: University of California Press, 2004).

38 Berger: Max Weber Is Alive and Well, and Living in Guatemala

1 This article is based on a conference paper presented at "The Norms, Beliefs, and Institutions of 21st Century Capitalism: Celebrating Max Weber's *The Protestant Ethic and the Spirit of Capitalism*," held October 8–9, 2005 at the Center for the Study of Economy & Society (www.economyandsociety.org) at Cornell University. See Max Weber, *The Protestant Ethic and the Spirit of Capitalism* (1904; repr., Oxford: Routledge, 2001).

2 See David Martin, "Integration und Fragmentierung: Religionsmuster in Europa," *Transit* 26 (Winter 2003–2004): 120–43.

3 Since its inception in 1985, the Institute on Culture, Religion, and World Affairs at Boston University has pursued questions related to religion and development in a series of projects in different parts of the world, beginning with two pioneering studies. The first, by David Martin, explored the colossal explosion of Pentecostalism in Latin America. This was first described in his book *Tongues of Fire: The Explosion of Protestantism in Latin America* (Oxford: Blackwell, 1990), and since then he and others have studied the phenomenon in other parts of the world. In the second study, Gordon Redding examined the values and lifestyles of Overseas Chinese entrepreneurs, reported on in his book *The Spirit of Chinese Capitalism* (Berlin: Walter de Gruyter, 1990).

4 See Martin, *Tongues of Fire*.

5 See the report, "Faith on the Move: Pentecostalism and its Potential Contribution to Development," Centre for Development and Enterprise, August 2008. This report and related resources are available online at http://www.cde.org.za/article.php?a_id=320.

6 See Robert Bellah, "Cultural Identity and Asian Modernization," in *Cultural Identity and Modernization in Asian Countries: Proceedings of Kokugakuin University Centennial Symposium*, 1093, available online at http://www2.kokugakuin.ac.jp/ijcc/wp/cimac/bellah.html (accessed August 12, 2010).

7 See generally Redding, *The Spirit of Chinese Capitalism*.

8 See Max Weber, *General Economic History* (1927; repr., Mineola, N.Y.: Dover, 2003).

9 My institute's study of Opus Dei was summarized by Joan Estruch in *Saints and Schemers: Opus Dei and Its Paradoxes* (New York: Oxford University Press, 1995).

10 My institute has conducted research on this question under the direction of Robert Hefner, as reported in his book, *Civil Islam: Muslims and Democratization in Indonesia* (Princeton, N.J.: Princeton University Press, 2000). Similar to Islam, some have alleged an incompatibility of Eastern Christian Orthodoxy with modern economic and political institutions. Christopher Marsh has been conducting a number of studies, some under the auspices of my institute, on religion in Communist and post-Communist Russia. See for example Marsh, "Counting One's Blessings: The Economic Values of Russian Orthodox Christians," in *Markets, Morals, and Religion*, ed. Jonathan B. Imber (New Brunswick, N.J.: Transaction, 2008), 179–90.

39 Kaplan: Inspiring Development in Fragile States

1 Kurt Alan Ver Beek, "Spirituality: A Development Taboo," in *Development and Culture*, ed. Deborah Eade (Oxford: Oxfam, 2002), 60.

2 Dennis de Jong, Jacob de Jonge, Piet Kuijper, David Renkema, Lisette van der Wel, and Louke van Wensveen, "Religion and Development Policy" (handout, Ministry of Foreign Affairs of The Netherlands and several development NGOs, Utrecht, 2008), 8.

3   Gerrie ter Haar and Stephen Ellis divide religious resources into four major categories—ideas, prac-
     tices, organization, and experiences—all of which can "produce knowledge that, in principle, could be
     beneficial to a community for development purposes." See ter Haar and Ellis, "The Role of Religion in
     Development: Towards a New Relationship between the European Union and Africa," *European Journal
     of Development Research* 18, no. 3 (September 2006): 356.

4   Charles Tilly, *Democracy* (Cambridge: Cambridge University Press, 2007), 31.

5   "Autonomous social spaces" is a phrase generally attributed to David Martin, who uses it often in his writ-
     ings on evangelical Christians. I find it equally useful in a historical context. See David Martin, *Tongues
     of Fire: The Explosion of Protestantism in Latin America* (Oxford: Blackwell, 1990).

6   Sascha O. Becker and Ludger Woessmann, "Was Weber Wrong? A Human Capital Theory of Protes-
     tant Economic History" (CESifo Working Paper Series no. 1987, IZA Discussion Paper no. 2886, May
     2007), available at http://ssrn.com/abstract=988031 (accessed May 1, 2009).

7   Barak D. Richman, "Community Enforcement of Informal Contracts: Jewish Diamond Merchants in
     New York" (Discussion Paper no. 384, John M. Olin Center for Law, Economics, and Business at Har-
     vard University, Cambridge, Mass., September 2002), 49–51.

8   Timothy Samuel Shah, "The Bible and the Ballot Box: Evangelicals and Democracy in the 'Global
     South,'" *SAIS Review* 24, no. 2 (Summer–Fall 2004): 128.

9   David Hume, "Of Superstition and Enthusiasm," in *Political Essays*, ed. Knud Haakonssen (Cambridge:
     Cambridge University Press, 1994), 47–48.

10   Tilly, *Democracy*, 30–31.

11   David Martin, "The Evangelical Upsurge and Its Political Implications," in *The Desecularization of the
     World*, ed. Peter L. Berger (Grand Rapids: William B. Eerdmans, 1999), 39, 41.

12   Deepa Narayan, Robert Chambers, Meera K. Shah, and Patti Petesch, *Voices of the Poor: Crying Out for
     Change* (Washington, D.C.: World Bank, 2000), 222.

13   James Wolfensohn, "Millennium Challenges for Faith and Development: New Partnerships to Reduce
     Poverty and Strengthen Conservation" (speech, Interfaith Conference of Metropolitan Washington, Trin-
     ity College, Washington, D.C., March 30, 2004).

14   Berkley Center for Religion, Peace, and World Affairs, *Faith-Inspired Organizations and Global Develop-
     ment Policy: U.S. and International Perspectives—"Mapping" Faith-Based Development Work in the United
     States, A Background Review* (Washington, D.C.: Georgetown University, April 9, 2007), 20.

15   See http://www.sarvodaya.org, http://en.fgulen.com, and http://www.feyalegria.org/ (accessed Septem-
     ber 30, 2010).

16   ter Haar and Ellis, "Role of Religion in Development," 364.

17   Farah Stockman, Michael Kranish, Peter S. Canellos, and Kevin Baron, "Bush Brings Faith to Foreign
     Aid: As Funding Rises, Christian Groups Deliver Help—with a Message," *Boston Globe*, October 8,
     2006.

18   Georgetown University Center for International and Regional Studies and Berkley Center for Religion,
     Peace, and World Affairs, "Global Development and Faith-Inspired Organizations in the Muslim World"
     (symposium, Doha, Qatar, December 17, 2007), http://berkleycenter.georgetown.edu/subprojects/the
     -muslim-world (accessed May 1, 2009).

19   Berkley Center, *Faith-Inspired Organizations and Global Development Policy*, 17.

20   Centre for Development Studies, University of Wales Swansea and the Department of Theology and
     Religious Studies, University of Wales Lampeter, *A Leap of Faith? DFID's Engagement with Faith-Based
     Organisations and the Role of Faith Groups in Poverty Reduction* (Final Report, Centre for Development
     Studies, University of Wales Swansea, December 17, 2004), v.

21   ter Haar and Ellis, "Role of Religion in Development," 362.

22   Bernard Lewis, *The Multiple Identities of the Middle East* (New York: Schocken Books, 1998), 15, 22.

23   Georgetown University Center for International and Regional Studies, "Global Development and Faith-
     Inspired Organizations."

24   For more on spiritual capital, see, among others, Peter Berger and Robert W. Hefner, "Spiritual Capital
     in Comparative Perspective" (paper, Spiritual Capital Research Program Planning Meeting, Philadelphia,
     March 2003), http://www.spiritualcapitalresearchprogram.com/research_articles.asp (accessed May 1,
     2009).

25 See United States Institute of Peace, "Promoting Peace and Tolerance through Madrasa Reform" (report and audio recording of a public meeting held in Washington, D.C., February 5, 2007), http://www.usip .org/events/promoting-peace-and-tolerance-through-madrasa-reform (accessed May 1, 2009).

26 Gerard Clarke, "Faith Matters: Development and the Complex World of Faith-Based Organisations" (paper, Development Studies Association annual conference, Milton Keynes, UK, September 7–9, 2005), 3.

27 ter Haar and Ellis, "Role of Religion in Development," 353.

28 Georgetown University Center for International and Regional Studies, "Global Development and Faith-Inspired Organizations."

29 "Development economics remains largely silent on the role of religion, largely maintaining a traditional approach of assuming religion away as part of 'society' or 'culture.'" Paul Jackson and Christiane Fleischer, "Religion and Economics: A Literature Review" (Research and Development Programme Working Paper 3, University of Birmingham, Birmingham, UK, 2007), 23. Although there has been "a vigorous interest in political science in examining the relationship between politics and religion . . . very little of the current output is focused on developing countries." Gurharpal Singh, Heather Marquette, and Namawu Alhassan Alolo, "Political Science, Religion, and Development: A Literature Review" (Research and Development Programme Working Paper 7, University of Birmingham, Birmingham, UK, 2007), 1.

30 Carole Rakodi, "Understanding the Roles of Religions in Development: The Approach of the RaD Programme" (Research and Development Programme Working Paper 9, University of Birmingham, Birmingham, UK, 2007), 10.

31 See http://www.rad.bham.ac.uk/index.php?section=1 (accessed May 1, 2009).

32 See http://berkleycenter.georgetown.edu/programs/127 (accessed May 1, 2009).

33 See http://www.iss.nl/ (accessed May 1, 2009).

34 World Bank Independent Evaluation Group, *Engaging with Fragile States: An IEG Review of World Bank Support to Low-Income Countries under Stress* (Washington, D.C.: World Bank, 2006), ix.

40 McFague: New House Rules

1 In a special issue of *Daedalus* entitled "The Liberation of the Environment," the lead essay, by Jesse Ausubel, opens with the claim that the liberator of the environment will be human culture, whose "most powerful tools are science and technology." *Daedalus* 125, no. 3 (Summer 1996): 1. The tone throughout the essay as well as others in the issue is optimistic, as Ausubel notes in closing by quoting the epitaph inscribed on the U.S. National Academy of Sciences in Washington, D.C.: "To science, pilot of industry, conqueror of diseases, multiplier of the harvest, explorer of the universe, revealer of nature's laws, eternal guide to truth." Ausubel, "Liberation of the Environment," 15.

2 Lynn White, Jr., "The Historical Roots of Our Ecological Crisis," *Science* 155 (March 10, 1967): 1203–7.

3 Marcus J. Borg describes this well: "A root image is a fundamental 'picture' of reality. Perhaps most often called a 'world-view,' it consists of our most taken-for-granted assumptions about what is possible. . . . Very importantly, a root image not only provides a model of reality, but also shapes our perception and our thinking, operating almost unconsciously within us as a dim background affecting all of our seeing and thinking. A root image thus functions as both an image and a lens: it is a picture of reality which becomes a lens through which we see reality." Marcus J. Borg, *Jesus in Contemporary Scholarship* (Valley Forge, Penn.: Trinity Press International, 1994), 127.

4 The literature on the neoclassical economic model and its alternative—what I am calling the ecological economic model—is large and growing. Some of the works I found most helpful are as follows: Lester R. Brown et al., *State of the World* annual reports (New York: W.W. Norton, 1984–); Robert Costanza et al., *An Introduction to Ecological Economics* (Boca Raton, Fla.: St. Lucie Press, 1997); David A. Crocker and Toby Linden, eds., *Ethics of Consumption: The Good Life, Justice, and Global Stewardship* (Lanham, Md.: Rowman & Littlefield, 1998); Herman E. Daly and John B. Cobb Jr., *For the Common Good: Redirecting the Economy Toward Community, the Environment, and a Sustainable Future*, 2nd ed. (Boston: Beacon Press, 1994); Herman E. Daly, *Beyond Growth: The Economics of Sustainable Development* (Boston: Beacon Press, 1996); Neva R. Goodwin, Frank Ackerman, and David Kirion, eds., *The Consumer Society* (Washington, D.C.: Island Press, 1997); Steven C. Hackett, *Environmental and Natural Resources Economics: Theory, Policy and the Sustainable Society* (Armonk, N.Y.: M. E. Sharpe, 1998); Larry L. Rasmussen, *Earth Community Earth Ethics* (Maryknoll, N.Y.: Orbis Books, 1996); Joerg Rieger, ed.,

Liberating the Future: God, Mammon, and Theology (Minneapolis, Minn.: Fortress Press, 1998); United Nations, *Human Development Report*, issued annually (New York: Oxford University Press, 1990–); Michael Zweig, ed., *Religion and Economic Justice* (Philadelphia: Temple University Press, 1991).

5   By the oldest and deepest anthropology, I am referring to what George Hendry calls the "cosmological" and "political" understandings of God and the world rather than the more recent and narrow "psychological" view. George Stuart Hendry, *Theology of Nature* (Philadelphia: Westminster Press, 1980), chap. 1. The latter, which supports individualism, has arisen in the last several hundred years; but the other two, one emphasizing the whole creation and the other the community of all human beings, are grounded in the Hebrew Scriptures as well as in the New Testament and early theology (esp. Irenaeus and Augustine).

6   The evidence supporting this claim would take considerable space to lay out. Suffice it to say here that both the born-again and New Age versions of popular religion do so; the Declaration of Independence's "life, liberty, and the pursuit of happiness" does; and Adam Smith's description of the human being as a creature of insatiable greed makes a significant contribution. All focus on the rights, desires, and needs of individuals.

7   Milton Friedman's distinction between "positive" and "normative" economics is typical: "Normative economics is speculative and personal, a matter of values and preferences that are beyond science. Economics as a science, as a tool for understanding and prediction, must be based solely on positive economics which 'is in principle independent of any particular ethical position or normative judgments.'" Milton Friedman, *Essays in Positive Economics* (Chicago: University of Chicago Press, 1953), 4.

8   Hackett, *Environmental and Natural Resources Economics*, 33.

9   See Daly, *Beyond Growth*, 50ff.

10   Janet N. Abramowitz, "Valuing Nature's Services," in *State of the World 1997*, ed. Lester R. Brown et al. (New York: W. W. Norton, 1977).

11   Abramowitz, "Valuing Nature's Services," 109.

12   Bangladesh, a country that may well be flooded through global warming, produces a yearly average of 183 kg of carbon dioxide per capita versus an average of 11,389 kg per capita in the industrialized countries. United Nations Development Programme, *Human Development Report 1998* (New York: Oxford University Press, 1988), 57.

13   *Intergovernmental Panel on Climate Change: Second Assessment-Climate Change 1995*, published by the world Meteorological Organization and the United Nations Environmental Programme. It should be noted that this report was the consensus of 2,500 weather scientists and was published without a dissenting minority report. Since that time, its results have been confirmed by recent studies.

14   Costanza et al., *An Introduction to Ecological Economics*, 179.

15   If all contemporary understandings of Christ should be grounded in historical judgments about Jesus of Nazareth—if there should be continuity between the Jesus of history and the Christ of faith—then we need to see if the ecological economic context is an appropriate one for interpreting Christ and Christian discipleship for the twenty-first century. I am not suggesting that a Christian's faith is based on the state of historical Jesus research at any particular time; nonetheless, Christianity has always claimed continuity with its founder. Recent research, which has moved out of narrow church contexts of interpretation to sociological, cultural, and political ones of first-century Mediterranean society, has reached a remarkable consensus on some broad outlines of Jesus' life: most notably, that he was a social revolutionary opposed to the structures of domination and domestication of his day. This consensus is expressed in different ways by New Testament scholars such as E. P Sanders, Burton Mack, Elisabeth Schüssler Fiorenza, Marcus Borg, John Dominic Crossan, and Richard Horsley. For an overview of the scholarship, see Borg, *Jesus in Contemporary Scholarship*.

16   John Dominic Crossan, *Jesus: A Revolutionary Biography* (San Francisco: HarperSanFrancisco, 1994).

17   Crossan, *Jesus*, 73–74.

18   Crossan, *Jesus*, 68.

19   Crossan, *Jesus*, 113–14.

20   See Crossan, *Jesus*, 79–81.

21   See letter of 30 April 1944 in Dietrich Bonhoeffer, *Letters and Papers from Prison* (London: Collins, 1960), 90ff.

22   Psalm 24:1.

41 Noland and Pack: Islam, Globalization, and Economic Performance in the Middle East

1   James Zogby, *What Arabs Think: Values, Beliefs, and Concerns* (Zogby International and The Arab Thought Foundation, 2002).
2   Luigi Guiso, Paola Sapienza, and Luigi Zingales, "People's Opium? Religion and Economic Activities," *NBER Working Paper* 9237 (Cambridge, Mass.: National Bureau of Economic Research, 2002).
3   Timur Kuran, *Islam and Mammon* (Princeton, N.J.: Princeton University Press, forthcoming).
4   Marcus Noland, "Religion, Culture, and Economic Performance," *Working Paper Series* 03-8 (Washington, D.C.: Institute for International Economics, 2003).
5   Marcus Noland and Howard Pack, *Industrial Policy in an Era of Globalization* (Washington, D.C.: Institute for International Economics, 2003).
6   World Bank, *Trade, Investment, and Development in the Middle East and North Africa* (2003).
7   "Views of a Changing World" (The Pew Research Center for the People and the Press, June 2003).
8   The country samples in Figures 1–4 differ slightly from figure to figure. Respondents in North America, Western Europe, and Japan were not asked about closing factories. The pollsters were not permitted to ask the question about homosexuality in Egypt.
9   The cross-national correlation of attitudes toward homosexuality and prosperity in particular echoes a similar relationship observed across metropolitan areas in the United States. Richard Florida, *The Rise of the Creative Class* (New York: Basic Books, 2002).

42 Marshall: Development, Religion, and Women's Roles

1   Barack Obama, "Remarks by the President on a New Beginning" (speech, Cairo University, Cairo, Egypt, June 4, 2009), available from http://www.whitehouse.gov/the_press_office/Remarks-by-the-President-at-Cairo-University-6-04-09/ (accessed September 12, 2010).
2   Terminology around faith and religion presents seemingly insoluble problems. This article uses religion and faith interchangeably to refer to the full array of faith-inspired organizations. These range from churches and congregations to social movements to faith-linked and inspired nongovernmental organizations.
3   See generally Devesh Kapur, John D. Lewis, and Richard Webb, *The World Bank: Its First Half Century* (Washington, D.C.: Brookings Institution, 1997).
4   See http://berkleycenter.georgetown.edu/wfdd for background on WFDD's history and current work (accessed September 12, 2010).
5   For an account of the debates and lines of arguments advanced, see Katherine Marshall, "Religion and Global Development: Intersecting Paths," in *Religious Pluralism, Globalization, and World Politics*, ed. Thomas Banchoff (New York: Oxford University Press, 2008), 195–228.
6   See the Berkley Center's website for reviews mapping faith work in different regions and exploring a range of development issues including shelter, governance and corruption, malaria, and tuberculosis: http://berkleycenter.georgetown.edu/programs/religion-and-global-development (accessed September 12, 2010).
7   A more detailed discussion, including a range of views from people involved in the debates, can be found in, Berkley Center for Religion, Peace, and World Affairs, *Challenges of Change: Faith, Gender, and Development* (Washington, D.C.: Georgetown University, 2008), available from http://repository.berkleycenter.georgetown.edu/080501BerkleyGender.pdf (accessed September 12, 2010).
8   For a quick sketch of the MDGs, see http://www.undp.org/mdg/basics.shtml (accessed September 12, 2010).
9   Nicholas Kristof and Sheryl Wudon, *Half the Sky: Turning Oppression into Opportunity for Women Worldwide* (New York: Knopf, 2009).
10 See, e.g., Douglas Huber, Evelyn Rong Yang, Judith Brown, and Richard Brown, *International Family Planning: Christian Actions and Attitudes* (McLean, Va.: Christian Connections in International Health, 2008), available from http://www.ccih.org/doclibrary/ccih_fp_survey_revised_031509_reduced_size.pdf (accessed September 12, 2010).

43 Fox and Sandler: Separation of Religion and State in the Twenty-First Century

* We would like to thank Robert Barro, Eliezer Don-Yehiyia, Ted R. Gurr, Pat James, Rachel McCleary, Shlomo Shpiro, and Bernard Susser, as well as *Comparative Politics'* anonymous reviewers, all of whom provided useful criticisms at some point in this project. We would also like to thank the research assistants who helped to collect the data, Aharon Etengoff, Dahlia Ganz Podolak, and Doni Schuman. This research was supported by the Israel Science Foundation (Grant 896/00). A copy of the data used in this study may be obtained by contacting Jonathan Fox at foxjon@mail.biu.ac.il.

1 Jonathan Fox, "Religion: An Oft Overlooked Element of International Studies," *International Studies Review* 3 (Fall 2001): 53–73.

2 For the purposes of this study, Western democracies include western Europe, the U.S., Canada, Australia, and New Zealand. The Middle East includes the Arab countries of the Middle East and North Africa, as well as Turkey, Israel, and Iran.

3 Keith Jaggers and Ted R. Gurr, "Tracking Democracy's Third Wave with the Polity III Data," *Journal of Peace Research* 32 (1995): 469–82.

4 For a full discussion of the predictions regarding religion, see Brian S. Turner, *Religion and Social Theory*, 2nd ed. (London: Sage, 1991).

5 Alfred Stepan, "Religion, Democracy, and the 'Twin Tolerations,'" *Journal of Democracy* 11 (2000): 40.

6 John Rawls, *Political Liberalism* (New York: Columbia University Press, 1993), 151.

7 For a more complete discussion of religion and modernization theory and its critics see Jonathan Fox, *Ethnoreligious Conflict in the Late 20th Century: A General Theory* (Lanham, Md.: Lexington Books, 2002), 31–64.

8 Fox, "Religion: An Oft Overlooked Element."

9 Mark Juergensmeyer, *The New Cold War?* (Berkeley: University of California Press, 1993). Similar arguments are made by Jeff Haynes, *Religion in Global Politics* (New York: Longman, 1998); and James Piscatori, "Accounting for Islamic Fundamentalisms," in Martin E. Marty and R. Scott Appleby, eds., *Accounting for Fundamentalisms: The Dynamic Character of Movements* (Chicago: University of Chicago Press, 1994), 361–63. T. K. Oommen, "Religious Nationalism and Democratic Polity: The Indian Case," *Sociology of Religion* 55 (1994): 455, applies this argument specifically to democracy.

10 Anthony D. Smith, "The Sacred Dimension of Nationalism," *Millennium* 29 (2000): 791–814.

11 Stepan, "Religion, Democracy," 41–42.

12 Hillel Fradkin, "Does Democracy Need Religion?" *Journal of Democracy* 11 (2000): 90–91.

13 Stathis N. Kalyvas, "Commitment Problems in Emerging Democracies: The Case of Religious Parties," *Comparative Politics* 22 (2000): 379–98; Stathis N. Kalyvas, "Democracy and Religious Politics: Evidence from Belgium," *Comparative Political Studies* 31 (1998): 292–320; Juan J. Linz, *Crisis, Breakdown, and Reequilibration* (Baltimore: Johns Hopkins University Press, 1978), 29.

14 Phillip Berryman, *Liberation Theology* (Philadelphia: Temple University Press, 1987); H. Mark Roelofs, "Liberation Theology: The Recovery of Biblical Radicalism," *American Political Science Review* 88 (1988): 549–66.

15 Stepan, "Religion, Democracy," 46–48; Katrina Dalacoura, "Unexceptional Politics? The Impact of Islam on International Relations," *Millennium* 29 (2000): 879; and Bernard Lewis, *Islam and the West* (Oxford: Oxford University Press, 1993), 96–98.

16 John L. Esposito and James P. Piscatori, "Democratization and Islam," *Middle East Journal* 45 (1991): 427–40; John L. Esposito and John O. Voll, "Islam and Democracy," *Humanities* 22 (2001): 22–26; Noah Feldman, "Muslim Democrats? Why Not!" *The Wall Street Journal*, April 8, 2003; Graham E. Fuller, "The Future of Political Islam," *Foreign Affairs* 81 (2002): 48–60.

17 Stepan, "Religion, Democracy," 48–49.

18 Esposito and Piscatori, "Democratization and Islam."

19 Haynes, *Religion in Global Politics*, 128–29.

20 Feldman, "Muslim Democrats?"

21 Abdulaziz Sachedina, "Religion and Global Affairs: Islamic Religion and Political Order," *SAIS Review* 18 (1998): 62.

22 Khaled A. El Fadal, "Muslims and Accessible Jurisprudence in Liberal Democracies: A Response to Edward B. Foley's Jurisprudence and Theology," *Fordham Law Review* 66 (1998): 1227–31.

23   Esposito and Piscatori, "Democratization and Islam"; Esposito and Voll, "Islam and Democracy"; Feldman, "Muslim Democrats?"

24   Daniel E. Price, "Islam and Human Rights: A Case of Deceptive First Appearances," *Journal for the Scientific Study of Religion* 41 (2002): 213–25.

25   Manus I. Midlarsky, "Democracy and Islam: Implications for Civilizational Conflict and the Democratic Peace," *International Studies Quarterly* 42 (1998): 458–511; Jonathan Fox, "Is Islam More Conflict Prone Than Other Religions? A Cross-Sectional Study of Ethnoreligious Conflict," *Nationalism and Ethnic Politics* 6 (Summer 2000): 1–23; Jonathan Fox, "Are Middle East Conflicts More Religious?" *Middle East Quarterly* 8 (Fall 2001): 31–40; Jaggers and Gurr, "Tracking Democracy's Third Wave."

26   Gary K. Leak and Brandy A. Randall, "Clarification of the Link between Right-Wing Authoritarianism and Religiousness: The Role of Religious Maturity," *Journal for the Scientific Study of Religion* 34 (1995): 245–52.

27   Mark Chaves and David E. Cann, "Religion, Pluralism and Religious Market Structure," *Rationality and Society* 4 (1992): 272–90.

28   Michael Minkenberg, "Religion and Public Policy: Institutional, Cultural, and Political Impact on the Shaping of Abortion Policies in Western Democracies," *Comparative Political Studies* 35 (2002): 221–47.

29   Minkenberg, "Religion and Public Policy."

30   For a full discussion of the sources and methodology used to collect the data, see Jonathan Fox and Shmuel Sandler, "Quantifying Religion: Toward Building More Effective Ways of Measuring Religious Influence on State-Level Behavior," *Journal of Church and State* 45 (2003): 559–88. For the results of backup codings as well as other tests of the data's accuracy, see the Appendix.

31   This scale was adopted from one developed by W. Cole Durham, Jr., "Perspectives on Religious Liberty: A Comparative Framework," in John D. van der Vyver and John Witte, Jr., eds., *Religious Human Rights in Global Perspective: Legal Perspectives* (Boston: Martinus Nijhoff, 1996), 1–44.

32   This list is adopted from a similar list developed by Jonathan Fox, "Religious Causes of Ethnic Discrimination," *International Studies Quarterly* 44 (September 2000): 423–50, with several additions.

33   For the purposes of this variable, the separation of religion and state variable was coded as zero for separationist and accommodationist regimes. Three was subtracted from all other categories. The resulting variable was rescaled from zero to twenty.

34   For more details on the Polity variable, see Jaggers and Gurr, "Tracking Democracy's Third Wave," and the project website at www.cidcm.umd.edu/inscr/polity.

35   While the Freedom House variable measures democracy on a scale of two to fourteen with two being the most democratic, we subtracted two so the scale would start at zero and inverted it so twelve would be the most democratic, making it easier to compare to the Polity measure. For more details on the variable, see the Freedom House website at www.freedomhouse.org.

36   Minkenberg, "Religion and Public Policy."

37   Robert A. Campbell and James E. Curtis, "Religious Involvement across Societies: Analysis for Alternative Measures in National Surveys," *Journal for the Scientific Study of Religion* 33 (1994): 215–29.

38   Mariana Servin-Gonzalez and Oscar Torres-Reyna, "Trends: Religion and Politics," *Public Opinion Quarterly* 63 (1999): 592–621.

39   Louis Bolee and Gerald De Maio, "Religious Outlook, Culture War Politics, and Antipathy toward Christian Fundamentalists," *Public Opinion Quarterly* 63 (1999): 29–61.

40   Horst Mewes, "Religion and Politics in American Democracy," in William Safran, ed., *The Secular and the Sacred: Nation, Religion, and Politics* (London: Frank Cass, 2002), 4–5.

41   Fox, "Is Islam More Conflict Prone?"

42   Fox, *Ethnoreligious Conflict*; Marta Reynal-Querol, "Ethnicity, Political Systems, and Civil Wars," *Journal of Conflict Resolution* 46 (2002): 29–54; and Rudolph J. Rummel, "Is Collective Violence Correlated with Social Pluralism?" *Journal of Peace Research* 34 (1997): 163–75.

43   Errol A. Henderson, "The Democratic Peace through the Lens of Culture, 1820–1989," *International Studies Quarterly* 42 (September 1998): 461–84.

44   Jonathan Fox, "Religion and State Failure: An Examination of the Extent and Magnitude of Religious Conflict from 1950 to 1996," *International Political Science Review* 25 (2004).

45   Chaves and Cann, "Religion, Pluralism."

46   James Fearon and David Laitin, "Ethnicity, Insurgency, and Civil War," *American Political Science Review* 97 (February 2002): 75–90.

47   For more information on the Freedom House data, see www.freedomhouse.org/religion.

48   These data can be found in D. B. Barret, G. T. Kurian, and T. M. Johnson, *World Christian Encyclopedia*, 2nd ed. (Oxford: Oxford University Press, 2001), 834–35.

49   Dan Smith, *The State of the World Atlas*, 6th ed. (London: Penguin, 1999).

50   Michael Kidron and Ronald Segal, *The State of the World Atlas*, 5th ed. (London: Penguin, 1995).

51   Fox, *Ethnoreligious Conflict*; Fox, "Religious Causes of Ethnic Discrimination."

44   Mazie: Rethinking Religious Establishment and Liberal Democracy

1   Tony Judt, "Israel: The Alternative," *The New York Review of Books* 50, no. 16 (October 23, 2003).

2   By an "expressive harm" I mean an injury inflicted through the communication of an idea (verbally or otherwise). An analysis and defense of the expressive interpretation of law, including applications to several constitutional questions in the United States, is found in Elizabeth S. Anderson and Richard H. Pildes, "Expressive Theories of Law: A General Restatement," *University of Pennsylvania Law Review* 148 (May 2000): 1503–75.

3   Ronald Dworkin, *Taking Rights Seriously* (Cambridge, Mass.: Harvard University Press, 1977), 180.

4   My use of the term "plural" is therefore a bit problematic. In some cases, as in Israel's designation of both Hebrew and Arabic as official languages, or its concurrent use of the Hebrew and Roman calendars, what I am calling plural state affiliations explicitly make provisions for multiplicity. In other cases, as in its Sabbath policies, Israel sets Judaism as the standard and allows alternatives or exemptions from that standard for members of other religions. In all cases, it may be said, Israel expresses a preference for Jews and Judaism over non-Jews and other religions and so is not "pluralist" in the strong sense of respecting each religion equally.

5   As some passages from the interviews show, choices may be somewhat more nuanced: Arabs might show some respect to the Israeli national anthem by standing (but not singing) as it is played; or they might show contempt for it by hoisting anti-Israel placards or shouting down those who choose to sing.

6   This exclusivism is not unique, of course, to states with religious motifs in their flags or anthems: every state represents itself with a single flag and a single official anthem.

7   See Flags of the World website, http://www.crwflags.com/fotw/flags/gb.html (August 4, 2004) and the British Government's website, http://www.royal.gov.uk/output/page398.asp (August 4, 2004).

8   France's blue, white, and red vertical stripes represent, respectively, Saint Martin, the Virgin Mary (to whom France was consecrated by Louis XIII in the seventeenth century), and Saint Denis (the patron saint of Paris). Ukraine's horizontal light blue and yellow stripes signify an affiliation with Christianity. For France, see Flags of the World website, http://www.crwflags.com/fotw/flags/fr.html (August 4, 2004); for Ukraine, see http://www.crwflags.com/fotw/flags/ua.html (August 4, 2004).

9   Costa Rica's flag has five horizontal stripes of red, white, and blue, thought to represent unifying ideals such as intellectualism, perseverance, happiness, wisdom, freedom, and generosity. See http://www .costarica.com/culture/national-symbols/national-flag.html (August 4, 2004).

10   The UN General Assembly adopted the "Zionism is racism" principle, Resolution 3379, on November 10, 1975. It rescinded it in December 1991. See text of the resolution on the Jewish Virtual Library website, http://www.us-israel.org/jsource/UN/unga3379.html (August 4, 2004). An attempt to pass a similar resolution (stating that the "Zionist movement . . . is based on racial superiority") at the August 2001 UN World Conference Against Racism in Durban, South Africa was unsuccessful.

11   John Rawls, *The Law of Peoples* (Cambridge, Mass.: Harvard University Press, 1999), 62.

12   This oversimplifies the matter: in the United States, religious organizations enjoy fire and police protection, not to mention tax-exempt status; they also receive government funds for a number of purposes, including charitable work. These benefits are provided, however, not as aids to religion but as secular goods.

13   See http://www.law.ou.edu/hist/remon.html (August 4, 2004).

14   Americans United for Separation of Church and State, "The Bush Faith-Based Initiative: Why It's Wrong," February 20, 2001.

15   Dan Barry and Carol Vogel, "Giuliani Vows to Cut Subsidy Over Art He Calls Offensive," *The New York Times*, September 23, 1999.

16   An apropos comic by political cartoonist Tom Tomorrow, author of the weekly "This Modern World": A penguin stands in an IRS office and declares: "I find our support of the Indonesian military highly offensive." The clerk replies: "I'm terribly sorry, sir. We'll replace your portion immediately!" See Salon. com website, http://www.salon.com/comics/tomo/1999/10/18/tomo/index.html (August 4, 2004).

17   Bhikhu Parekh draws out the argument: "Just as we should allow religious citizens to speak in a religious language, we should also find other ways of valuing their presence and encouraging their contribution to collective life. The state could give them a charitable status as it generally does in all liberal societies, contribute towards their upkeep as it does in Germany, Sweden, the Netherlands, Britain, and elsewhere, encourage them to undertake philanthropic activities, and so forth. It might be argued that public funds should not be used to support sectional interests. If that were so, no public authority would be justified in supporting or giving a charitable status to museums, art galleries, universities, and operas, spending public funds to rescue mountain climbers or those lost in dangerous expeditions, or providing designated areas to anglers and ramblers. We rightly want it to support these activities because they are valuable, are shared by sizable sections of citizens, and add to the richness of collective life. Religion belongs to this category." We might put the point more strongly, since many more people are involved in religion than in activities like mountain climbing. Bhikhu Parekh, "The Voice of Religion in Political Discourse," in *Religion, Politics and Peace*, ed. Leroy S. Rouner (Notre Dame, Ind.: University of Notre Dame Press, 1999), 77–78.

18   A libertarian opposing all redistributive taxation will argue that *none* of these ought to be on the list of state responsibilities. There is no libertarian argument, however, as to why religion is a special case that is particularly unsuited for government funding. My argument here is thus less with libertarians than with liberals who believe the state does have at least some role in providing basic resources to help its citizens pursue their own values and ideas of the good life.

19   Forced tithing differs from taxation to support religion, which can, as I argued above, be consistent with liberalism. The latter, I am assuming, supports even-handed distribution of state resources in ways determined by representative political institutions; its purpose is to serve the public at large. The former simply delivers private funds directly to the coffers of a church with no government control or oversight; it pursues its aim to prop up a single religion by subjecting citizens to religious law without their consent.

20   I provide a more detailed argument for this conclusion in my book [*Israel's Higher Law: Religion and Liberal Democracy in the Jewish State* (Lanham, Md.: Lexington Books, 2006)].

45   *Woodberry and Shah: Christianity and Democracy*

*   Robert D. Woodberry thanks the Louisville Institute General Grant, Lilly Endowment, for financial support. Both authors gratefully acknowledge the support of the Harvard Academy for International and Area Studies' "Religion in Global Politics" project, funded by the Smith Richardson Foundation and the Weatherhead Center for International Affairs.

1   Quoted in James E. Bradley, "The Religious Origins of Radical Politics in England, Scotland, and Ireland, 1662–1800," in James E. Bradley and D. K. Van Kley, eds., *Religion and Politics in Enlightenment Europe* (Notre Dame, Ind.: University of Notre Dame Press, 2001), 215.

2   Michael Walzer, *The Revolution of the Saints: A Study in the Origins of Radical Politics* (Cambridge, Mass.: Harvard University Press, 1965).

3   Samuel P. Huntington, *The Third Wave: Democratization in the Late Twentieth Century* (Norman: University of Oklahoma Press, 1991), 72–85.

4   Alfred Stepan, "Religion, Democracy, and the 'Twin Tolerations,'" *Journal of Democracy* 11 (October 2000): 37–57.

5   Figures are for the year 2000. We drew them from David B. Barrett, George T. Kurian, and Todd M. Johnson, eds., *World Christian Encyclopedia*, 2nd ed. (Oxford: Oxford University Press, 2001). To arrive at our figures, we combine the *Encyclopedia's* "Anglican," "historic European Protestant," and "independent" categories.

6   Paul E. Sigmund, ed., *Religious Freedom and Evangelization in Latin America: The Challenge of Religious Pluralism* (Maryknoll, N.Y.: Orbis, 1999). For global Protestant and particularly evangelical growth, see Donald Lewis, ed., *Christianity Re-Born: Evangelicalism's Global Expansion in the Twentieth Century* (Grand Rapids: Eerdmans, 2004).

7   Most of the arguments and citations for this and subsequent sections come from Robert D. Woodberry, "The Shadow of Empire: Christian Missions, Colonial Policy, and Democracy in Postcolonial Societies" (Ph.D. diss., University of North Carolina–Chapel Hill, 2004); and Robert D. Woodberry, "Religion and Democratization: Explaining a Robust Empirical Relationship" (paper, annual meeting of the Religious Research Association, Boston, November 5–7, 1999).

8   Daniel Philpott, *Revolutions in Sovereignty: How Ideas Shaped Modern International Relations* (Princeton, N.J.: Princeton University Press, 2001), 105.

9   G. W. F. Hegel, *Elements of the Philosophy of Right*, trans. Allen W. Wood (Cambridge: Cambridge University Press, 1991), 301–2.

10 For a discussion of the historically Catholic dynamic, see David Martin, *A General Theory of Secularization* (Oxford: Blackwell, 1978), 15–27, 36–54.

11 Robert A. Dahl, *Democracy and Its Critics* (New Haven, Conn.: Yale University Press, 1989), 32.

12 Michael Young, "Confessional Protest: The Religious Birth of U.S. Social Movements," *American Sociological Review* 67 (October 2002): 660–88.

13 David Zaret, "Petitions and the 'Invention' of Public Opinion in the English Revolution," *American Journal of Sociology* 101 (May 1996): 1497–1555; Jürgen Habermas, *The Structural Transformation of the Public Sphere* (Cambridge, Mass.: MIT Press, 1991). For religious printing's impact on newspapers and secular printing, see David Paul Nord, *Faith in Reading: Religious Publishing and the Birth of Mass Media in America* (New York: Oxford University Press, 2004).

14 Robin Grier, "The Effect of Religion on Economic Development: A Cross-National Study of 63 Former Colonies," *Kyklos* 50 (February 1997): 47–62.

15 Daniel Treisman, "The Causes of Corruption: A Cross-National Study," *Journal of Public Economics* 76 (June 2000): 399–457; and Seymour Martin Lipset and Gabriel S. Lenz, "Corruption, Culture, and Markets," in Lawrence E. Harrison and Samuel P. Huntington, eds., *Culture Matters: How Values Shape Human Progress* (New York: Basic, 2000), 112–24.

16 Christopher Clague, Suzanne Gleason, and Stephen Knack, "Determinants of Lasting Democracy in Poor Countries: Culture, Development, and Institutions," *Annals of the American Academy of Political and Social Science* 573 (January 2001): 16–41.

17 On the newer Protestant forms and democracy in the global South, see Paul Freston, *Evangelicals and Politics in Asia, Africa and Latin America* (Cambridge: Cambridge University Press, 2001) and Timothy S. Shah, "Evangelical Politics in the Third World: What's Next for the 'Next Christendom'?" *The Brandywine Review of Faith & International Affairs* 1 (Fall 2003): 21–30.

46   *Nasr: The Rise of "Muslim Democracy"*

1   After the November 2002 Turkish elections, some in the West began extolling the Justice and Development Party of Recep Tayyip Erdoğan as a group of "Muslim Democrats" not unlike the Christian Democrats. See, for example, Radwan A. Masmoudi, "A Victory for the Cause of Islamic Democracy: An American Muslim Analyzes the Surprise Election in Turkey," www.beliefnet.com/story/116/story_11673_1.html. While I plainly think that Masmoudi was on to something, I should note that Erdoğan himself has taken pains publicly to disown the "Muslim Democrat" label and to embrace the idea of "conservative democracy" instead. See Erdoğan's remarks in Vincent Boland, "Eastern Premise," *Financial Times* (London), December 3, 2004.

2   See John L. Esposito and John O. Voll, *Islam and Democracy* (New York: Oxford University Press, 1996); and Larry Diamond, Marc F. Plattner, and Daniel Brumberg, eds., *Islam and Democracy in the Middle East* (Baltimore: Johns Hopkins University Press, 2003).

3   Stathis Kalyvas, "Unsecular Politics and Religious Mobilization," in Thomas Kselman and Joseph Buttigieg, eds., *European Christian Democracy* (Notre Dame, Ind.: University of Notre Dame Press, 2003), 293–320.

4   Genevieve Abdo, *No God But God: Egypt and the Triumph of Islam* (New York: Oxford University Press, 2000); Hakan Yavuz, *Islamic Political Identity in Turkey* (New York: Oxford University Press, 2003); Bahtiar Effendy, *Islam and the State in Indonesia* (Athens: Ohio University Press, 2003); Seyyed Vali Reza Nasr, *Islamic Leviathan: Islam and the Making of State Power* (New York: Oxford University Press, 2001).

5   Vali Nasr, "Military Rule, Islamism, and Democracy in Pakistan," *Middle East Journal* 58 (Spring 2004): 195–209.

6   Saiful Mujani and R. William Liddle, "Politics, Islam, and Public Opinion," *Journal of Democracy* 15 (January 2004): 109–23.

7   José Casanova, *Public Religions in the Modern World* (Chicago: University of Chicago Press, 1994), 5–39.

8   Stathis Kalyvas, *The Rise of Christian Democracy in Europe* (Ithaca, N.Y.: Cornell University Press, 1996), 2–4.

9   As Nawaz Sharif once put it, he wanted to be "both the [Turkish Islamist leader Necmettin] Erbakan and the [economically modernizing Malaysian prime minister] Mahatir of Pakistan." Author's interview, Lahore, Pakistan, October 1997.

10   Cengiz Çandar, "Postmodern Darbe" (Postmodern coup), *Sabah* (Istanbul), June 28, 1997. See also Cengiz Çandar, "Redefining Turkey's Political Center," *Journal of Democracy* 10 (October 1999): 129–41.

11   Ziya Öniş and Fuat Keyman, "Turkey at the Polls: A New Path Emerges," *Journal of Democracy* 14 (April 2003): 95–107.

12   As Erdoğan put it to one interviewer, "[W]e are conservative democrats. . . . our notion of conservative democracy is to attach ourselves to the customs, traditions, and values of our society, which is based on the family. . . . This is a democratic issue, not a religious issue." Boland, "Eastern Premise."

13   Hakan Yavuz, "Opportunity Spaces, Identity, and Islamic Meaning in Turkey," in Quintan Wiktorowicz, ed., *Islamic Activism: A Social Movement Theory Approach* (Bloomington: Indiana University Press, 2004), 270–88.

14   Martin Marty, *The Modern Schism: Three Paths to the Secular* (New York: Harper & Row, 1969), 108.

15   This *fatwa*—apparently spoken rather than written—was reported from Baghdad by *Newsweek* correspondent Rod Nordland in a dispatch on the Iraqi elections dated January 30, 2005. Nordland wrote that "Sistani's *fatwa* ordered Shi'a women to vote, even if their husbands told them not to." See www.msnbc .msn.com/id/6887461/site/newsweek. Nordland and Babak Dehghanpisheh reported in a dispatch dated February 14, 2004 that every third candidate on the Shi'ite list that Sistani helped to create was a woman. See www.msnbc.msn.com/id/6920460/site/newsweek.

16   Alfred Stepan and Aqil Shah, "Pakistan's Real Bulwark," *Washington Post*, May 5, 2004, A29.

47 Stackhouse: Public Theology and Democracy's Future

1   Samuel Huntington, "Religion, Culture, and International Conflict after September 11," Ethics and Public Policy Center Conversations, June 17, 2002, www.eppc.org.

2   Michael Perry, *The Idea of Human Rights* (Oxford: Oxford University Press, 1998), 35.

48 Farr: Public Religion, Democracy Promotion, and U.S. Foreign Policy

*   Originally published under the title, "Public Religion, Secretary Rice, and U.S. Foreign Policy."

1   See http://www.9-11commission.gov/.

49 Brink: Debating International Human Rights

1   Charles Malik, quoted in Mary Ann Glendon, *A World Made New: Eleanor Roosevelt and the Universal Declaration of Human Rights* (New York: Random House, 2001), 39.

2   Quoted in Glendon, *World Made New*, 39.

3   Glendon, *World Made New*, 42.

4   Quoted in Glendon, *World Made New*, 41.

5   Quoted in Glendon, *World Made New*, 47.

6   Quoted in Glendon, *World Made New*, 68.

7   Jacques Maritain, *Man and the State* (Chicago: University of Chicago Press, 1951), 77.

8   Glendon, *World Made New*, 73.

9   For the committee's list of principles, see UNESCO Committee on the Theoretical Bases of Human Rights, "The Grounds of an International Declaration of Human Rights," in *Human Rights: Comments and Interpretations*, ed. UNESCO (London: Allan Wingate, 1949), 268–71.

10   UNESCO Committee on the Theoretical Bases of Human Rights, "Grounds of an International Declaration," 258–59.

11   Maritain, *Man and the State*, 77, emphasis in original.

12   Maritain, *Man and the State*, 77.

13 Maritain, *Man and the State*, 77.
14 Cf. Article 1 of the Universal Declaration of Human Rights.
15 Quoted in Glendon, *World Made New*, 165.
16 Quoted in Glendon, *World Made New*, 146.
17 Glendon, *World Made New*, 168.
18 Nancy L. Rosenblum, "Introduction," in *Obligations of Citizenship and Demands of Faith*, ed. Nancy L. Rosenblum (Princeton, N.J.: Princeton University Press, 2000), 15; Nicholas Wolterstorff, "Why We Should Reject What Liberalism Tells Us about Speaking and Acting in Public for Religious Reasons," in *Religion and Contemporary Liberalism*, ed. Paul J. Weithman (Notre Dame, Ind.: University of Notre Dame Press, 1997), 177; Paul A. Brink, "Negotiating a Plural Politics: Public Liberty, Public Reason, and the Duty of Civility" (paper, meeting of the American Political Science Association, Atlanta, 1999), 5.
19 At a more foundational level, to do so is also to misunderstand religion and religious belief. Scott M. Thomas has noted how the "political mythology of liberalism," in which liberalism and religious toleration developed together out of the destruction of the religious wars, has resulted not only in an underestimation of the significance of religious and cultural pluralism, but also in the imposition of a new concept of religion itself. See Scott M. Thomas, "Taking Religious and Cultural Pluralism Seriously: The Global Resurgence of Religion and the Transformation of International Society," *Millennium: Journal of International Studies* 29, no. 3 (2000): 815–41.
20 For a thoughtful discussion of how this articulation might proceed within a Christian framework, see Mark T. Mitchell, "A Theology of Engagement for the 'Newest Internationalists,'" *The Brandywine Review of Faith & International Affairs* 1, no. 1 (Spring 2003): 17–19.
21 It is important to note however that these rules, and particularly the less basic rules, although important, are not themselves beyond discussion and possible revision—theoretically, they are the product of an agreement that they be basic for the purposes of the negotiation.

50 Hasson: Religious Liberty and Human Dignity

1 Jacques Maritain, *Man and the State*, 4th ed. (Washington, D.C.: Catholic University of America Press, 1956), 77.
2 Universal Declaration of Human Rights, G.A. Res. 217A (III), U.N. Doc. A/810 (1948), 71.
3 *Vatican Council* (2nd: 1962–1965), "Declaration on Religious Freedom," reprinted in *The Sixteen Documents of Vatican II*, ed. Marianne Lorraine Trouvé, trans. N. C. W. C. (Boston: Pauline, 1999), 481.
4 The preamble consistently explicates the cooperation between Member Nations required to define the idea of human rights. See Universal Declaration of Human Rights, 72. ("The General Assembly [p]roclaims this Universal Declaration of Human Rights as a common standard of achievement for all peoples and all nations.")
5 See Universal Declaration of Human Rights; see also Mary Ann Glendon, "Reflections on the UDHR," *First Things* 82 (1998). ("Different understandings of the meanings of rights usually reflect divergent concepts of man and of society, which in turn cause those who hold those understandings to have different views of reality.")
6 Universal Declaration of Human Rights, 72.
7 See Universal Declaration of Human Rights, 71–72; see also Glendon, "Reflections," 24. ("The [drafter of the Declaration] tried to satisfy the Soviets by making clear that the new rights, like the old, are importantly related to human dignity. It met the English concerns by establishing that the new rights were different in kind, if not in importance, from traditional political and civil liberties. They are dependent on 'the organization and resources' of each state . . . in a way that, say, the right to be free of torture is not.")
8 Maritain, *Man and the State*, 78–79.
9 See Maritain, *Man and the State*; see also Universal Declaration of Human Rights, 71. ("[D]isregard and contempt for human rights have resulted in barbarous acts which have outraged the conscience of mankind, and the advent of a world in which human beings shall enjoy freedom of speech and belief and freedom from fear and want has been proclaimed as the highest aspiration of the common people.")
10 Universal Declaration of Human Rights, 72.
11 Universal Declaration of Human Rights, 71.
12 Universal Declaration of Human Rights, 72.
13 Glendon, "Reflections," 23.

14   Glendon, "Reflections," 24.

15   Universal Declaration of Human Rights, 72.

16   Universal Declaration of Human Rights, 76.

17   *Vatican Council* (2nd: 1962–1965), "Declaration," 481.

18   Douglas G. Bushman, "Introduction" to *Vatican Council* (2nd: 1962–1965), 483–85.

19   See Karol Wojtyla, "Personalizm tomistyczny," *Znak* 13 (1961): 664, translated in Karol Wojtyla, "Thomistic Personalism," in *Person and Community: Selected Essays*, ed. Andrew N. Woznicki, trans. Theresa Sandok (New York: Peter Lang, 1993), 165. ("Personalism is not primarily a theory of the person or a theoretical science of the person. Its meaning is largely practical and ethical: it is concerned with the person as a subject and an object of activity, as a subject of rights, etc.")

20   *Vatican Council* (2nd: 1962–1965), "Declaration," 493.

21   *Vatican Council* (2nd: 1962–1965), "Declaration."

22   Mark Twain, "The Disappearance of Literature, Speech Before the Nineteenth Century Club, Nov. 20, 1900" (quoting his friend, Professor Caleb Winchester), in *Samuel L. Clemens, Mark Twain Speaking*, ed. Paul Fatout (Iowa City: University of Iowa Press, 1976), 358–59.

23   *Vatican Council* (2nd: 1962–1965), "Declaration," 493.

24   *Vatican Council* (2nd: 1962–1965), "Declaration."

25   *Vatican Council* (2nd: 1962–1965), "Declaration."

26   *Vatican Council* (2nd: 1962–1965), "Declaration," 492.

27   *Vatican Council* (2nd: 1962–1965), "Declaration," 493.

28   *Vatican Council* (2nd: 1962–1965), "Declaration."

29   *Vatican Council* (2nd: 1962–1965), "Declaration," emphasis added.

30   *Vatican Council* (2nd: 1962–1965), "Declaration," 493–94.

31   Universal Declaration of Human Rights, 72.

32   Maritain, *Man and the State*, 153.

51   Hertzke: Roman Catholicism and the Faith-Based Movement for Global Human Rights

1   Samuel Huntington, *Third Wave: Democratization in the Late Twentieth Century* (Norman: University of Oklahoma Press, 1991).

2   Garry Wills, *Why I Am a Catholic* (Boston: Houghton Mifflin, 2002), 214–21.

3   George Weigel, *Witness to Hope: The Biography of John Paul II* (New York: Harper Perennial, 2001).

4   Pope John Paul II, "Annual Address to Diplomatic Corps," January 13, 1996, Vatican Information Service.

5   Pope John Paul II, "Tertio Millennio Adveniente: Toward the Third Millennium," Apostolic Letter, November 10, 1994.

6   Speech of Pope John Paul II, July 23, 2001.

7   For a good overview see T. Jeremy Gunn, "A Preliminary Response to Criticisms of the International Religious Freedom Act of 1998," *Brigham Young University Law Review* (September 2000): 841–66. For an example of the criticism see Peter Danchin, "U.S. Unilateralism and the International Protection of Religious Freedom: The Multilateral Alternative," *Columbia Journal of Transnational Law* 41 (2002).

8   Liminal is variously defined as the "threshold of a physiological or psychological response," or a subtle membrane separating states, or a threshold. *American Heritage College Dictionary* (Boston: Houghton, 1997). Because the 1998 legislation marked the threshold of a new era in human rights advocacy, but one barely discerned at the time, it represents a kind of liminal moment. Subsequent initiatives on Sudan, human trafficking, and North Korea especially show this.

9   Testimony of then Archbishop of Newark, Theodore E. McCarrick, before the Subcommittee on International Operations and Human Rights of the Committee on International Relations, U.S. House of Representatives, February 15, 1996, "Persecution of Christians Worldwide."

10   A good summary of her story is by Sheryl Henderson Blunt, "The Daniel of Religious Rights," *Christianity Today*, September 2005. Other material from this section comes from personal interviews.

11   I devote Chapter 5 of *Freeing God's Children* to the special role of Michael Horowitz in spurring the evangelical elite to action on religious persecution.

12   John Carr, interview by Allen Hertzke.

13 International Religious Freedom Act, Public Law 105-292, 22 USC 6401, signed into law October 27, 1998.

14 Tom Farr, interview by Allen Hertzke.

15 U.S. Department of State, *Annual Report on International Religious Freedom 2001* (Washington, D.C.: GPO, December 2001), Introduction. As the Director of the Office, Tom Farr was responsible for assembling the nation reports and helping draft the introduction. I strongly suspect that the Catholic language can be traced to his influence.

52 Marshall: Patterns and Contexts of Religious Freedom and Persecution

1 See Paul Marshall, *The Rise of Hindu Extremism* (Washington, D.C.: Freedom House, 2003).

2 Much of the survey material that follows is an updated summary of Paul Marshall, ed., *Religious Freedom in the World: A Global Survey of Freedom and Oppression* (Nashville, Tenn.: Broadman & Holman, 2000) and Paul Marshall, *Their Blood Cries Out* (Dallas: Word, 1997).

3 See Paul Marshall, *Massacre at the Millennium* (Washington, D.C.: Freedom House, 2000).

4 See Paul Marshall, *The Talibanization of Nigeria* (Washington, D.C.: Freedom House, 2001); *Egypt's Endangered Christians* (Washington, D.C.: Freedom House, 1999).

5 See Luttwak's "The Missing Dimension," in *Religion, the Missing Dimension of Statecraft*, ed. Douglas Johnston and Cynthia Sampson (Oxford: Oxford University Press, 1994).

6 See my "Motive for Massacre," *Wall Street Journal*, September 27, 2002.

7 From "Opinions Concerning the Implementation of the Special Class-Struggle Involving the Suppression of Catholic and Protestant Illegal Activities According to Law," Tong Xiang, Zhejiang province, February, 1997, available at Freedom House's Center for Religious Freedom.

8 On the question of the nature and task of government, see my *God and the Constitution: Christianity and American Politics* (Lanham, Md.: Rowman & Littlefield, 2002).

53 Little: Does the Human Right to Freedom of Conscience, Religion, and Belief Have Special Status?

1 See "Universal Declaration of Human Rights," G.A. Res. 217, U.N. GAOR, 3d Sess., U.N. Doc. A/810 (1948).

2 See "International Covenant on Civil and Political Rights," opened for signature December 16, 1966, 999 U.N.T.S. 171.

3 See "International Religious Freedom Act of 1998," 22 U.S.C. § 6401 et seq. (2000).

4 Because it is cumbersome to keep referring to "freedom of conscience, religion, and belief," the phrase "religious freedom" occasionally is used for shorthand. The other two ideas are decidedly implied. See note 9 (indicating why "freedom of thought," a term also included in Article 18, should be seen in a different light from the other three ideas).

5 See Samuel P. Huntington, *The Clash of Civilizations and the Remaking of the World Order* (New York: Simon & Schuster, 1996).

6 See "United Nations Human Rights Committee General Comment No. 22" (48), U.N. Human Rights Committee, PP 1, 2, 3, 8, U.N. Doc. CCPR/C/21/Rev.1/Add.4 (1993), reprinted in *Religion and Human Rights: Basic Documents*, ed. Tad Stahnke and J. Paul Martin (New York: Columbia University, Center for the Study of Human Rights, 1998), 92–95.

7 "United Nations Human Rights Committee General Comment No. 22," 8.

8 "United Nations Human Rights Committee General Comment No. 22."

9 "United Nations Human Rights Committee General Comment No. 22," 11. Notice that the committee here refers only to "conscience" or "religion or belief" in reference to a right to conscientious objection and not to "freedom of thought" (which is also mentioned in Article 18). It is unlikely that that omission is accidental. It would appear that "thought" is a much more inclusive category than "conscience, religion, and belief." The latter seems to refer to a quite narrow and select range of "thought," namely, certain fundamental convictions that occupy an especially important and potent place in the life of any individual. It is these, and not "thought" in general—however protected it may also be—that yields a special exemption like a right of conscientious objection.

10 See Brian Tierney, "Religious Rights: An Historical Perspective," in *Religious Human Rights in Global Perspective: Religious Perspectives*, ed. John Witte, Jr. and Johan D. van der Vyver (The Hague: Martinus Nijhoff, 1996), 17, 26–30.

11   Thomas Jefferson, "Notes on Virginia," in *The Life and Selected Writings of Thomas Jefferson*, ed. Adrienne Koch and William Peden (New York: Modern Library, 1944), 185, 274–75.

12   See, e.g., Ted Robert Gurr, *Peoples Versus States: Minorities at Risk in the New Century* (Washington, D.C.: United States Institute of Peace Press, 2000), 275. Gurr states: "The breakup of the international system into warring ethnic statelets, which many feared in the early 1990s, has been checked by more effective international and domestic strategies for managing ethnopolitical conflict. Relations between [ethnic] groups and states in heterogeneous societies changed in the 1990s in ways that suggest that a new regime governing minority-majority relations is under construction."

13   Gurr, *Peoples*, 278.

55   *Witte: Soul Wars*

1   For a good sampling of international and local legal documents on religious liberty, see Natan Lerner, *Religion, Beliefs, and International Human Rights* (Maryknoll, N.Y.: Orbis, 2000) and Tad Stahnke and J. Paul Martin, eds., *Religion and Human Rights: Basic Documents* (New York: Columbia University, Center for Study of Human Rights, 1998). For analysis, see Kevin Boyle and Juliet Sheen, *Freedom of Religion and Belief: A World Report* (London: Routledge, 1997) and Malcolm D. Evans, *Religious Liberty and International Law in Europe* (Cambridge: Cambridge University Press, 2004).

2   John Witte, Jr. and Michael Bourdeaux, eds., *Proselytism and Orthodoxy in Russia: The New War for Souls* (Maryknoll, N.Y.: Orbis, 1999).

3   Abdullahi Ahmed An-Na'im and Frances Deng, eds., *Human Rights in Africa: Cross-Cultural Perspectives* (Washington, D.C.: Brookings, 1990); Abdullahi Ahmed An-Na'im, ed., *Proselytization and Communal Self-Determination in Africa* (Maryknoll, N.Y.: Orbis, 1999); "Symposium: 'The Problem of Proselytism in Southern Africa: Legal and Theological Dimensions,'" *Emory International Law Review* 14 (2000): 491–1303.

4   Paul E. Sigmund, ed., *Religious Freedom and Evangelization in Latin America: Linking Pluralism and Democracy* (Maryknoll, N.Y.: Orbis, 1999).

5   H. Meldgaard and J. Aagaard, eds., *New Religious Movements in Europe* (Aarhus: Aarhus University Press, 1997); E. Barker and M. Warburg, eds., *New Religions and New Religiosity* (Aarhus: Aarhus University Press, 1998); Jonathan Luxmoore and Jolanta Babiuch-Luxmoore, "New Myths for Old: Proselytism and Transition in Post-Communist Europe," *Journal of Ecumenical Studies* 36, nos. 1–2 (Winter–Spring 1999): 43–64.

6   Susanne Hoeber Rudolph, "Introduction," in Susanne Hoeber Rudolph and James Piscatori, eds., *Transnational Religion and Fading States* (Boulder, Colo.: Westview, 1997), 6.

7   See sources in notes 2–4, and "Symposium: Pluralism, Proselytism and Nationalism in Eastern Europe," *Journal of Ecumenical Studies* 36, nos. 1–2 (Winter–Spring 1999): 1–286.

8   See the comprehensive study of Natan Lerner, "Proselytism, Change of Religion, and International Human Rights," *Emory International Law Review* 12 (1998): 477–561, updated in Lerner, *Religion, Beliefs*, 80–118, and more briefly Evans, *Religious Liberty*, 201ff., 221ff.; J. A. Walkate, "The Right of Everyone to Change his Religion or Belief," *Netherlands International Law Review* 2 (1983): 146–60.

9   See respectively, Joel A. Nichols, "Mission, Evangelism, and Proselytism in Christianity: Mainline Conceptions as Reflected in Church Documents," *Emory International Law Review* 12, no. 1 (1998): 563–650; David Novak, "Proselytism and Conversion in Judaism," in John Witte, Jr. and Richard C. Martin, eds., *Sharing the Book: Perspectives on the Rights and Wrongs of Proselytism* (Maryknoll, N.Y.: Orbis, 1999), 17–44; Donna E. Arzt, "The Treatment of Religious Dissidents under Classic and Contemporary Islamic Law," in John Witte, Jr. and Johan D. van der Vyver, eds., *Religious Human Rights in Global Perspective: Religious Perspectives* (Grand Rapids: Eerdmans, 2000), 387–453.

10   See, e.g., Michael J. Sandel, "Freedom of Conscience or Freedom of Choice," in James Davison Hunter and Os Guinness, eds., *Articles of Faith, Articles of Peace* (Washington, D.C.: Brookings, 1990), 74–92.

11   Article 18.

12   Article 18.1.

13   Article 1.1.

14   Principle 16.

15   *New York Trust Co. v. Eisner*, 256 U.S. 345, 349 (1921).

16 W. J. Sheils, ed., *Persecution and Toleration* (Oxford: Blackwell, 1984); James Parkes, *The Jew in the Medieval Community: A Study of His Political and Economic Situation*, 2nd ed. (New York: Hermon Press, 1976); Solomon Grayzel, *The Church and the Jews in the XIIIth Century* (Philadelphia: Dropsie College for Hebrew and Cognate Learning, 1933).

17 See sources and discussion in Noel B. Reynolds and W. Cole Durham, Jr., eds., *Religious Liberty in Western Thought* (Grand Rapids: Eerdmans, 1996).

18 The most famous formulation of the right, and duty, of the dissenter to emigrate peaceably from the territory whose religious establishment he or she cannot abide, comes in the Peace of Augsburg (1555), and its provisions are repeated in the Edict of Nantes (1598) and the Religious Peace of Westphalia (1648). See Sidney Z. Ehler and John B. Morrall, eds., *Church and State through the Centuries: A Collection of Historical Documents with Commentary* (London: Newman Press, 1954), 164–98.

19 Max L. Stackhouse and Deirdre King Hainsworth, "Deciding for God: The Right to Convert in Protestant Perspectives," in Witte and Martin, eds., *Sharing the Book*, 201–30 and further sources on the 19th century American experience in my *Religion and the American Constitutional Experiment: Essential Rights and Liberties* (Boulder, Colo.: Westview, 2000), 96–100.

20 Farid Esack, "Muslims Engaging the Other and *Humanum*," in Witte and Martin, eds., *Sharing the Book*, 118–44; Richard C. Martin, "Conversion to Islam by Invitation," in Witte and Martin, eds., *Sharing the Book*, 95–117; Arzt, "Treatment of Religious Dissidents"; Donna E. Arzt, "Jihad for Hearts and Minds," in Witte and Martin, eds., *Sharing the Book*, 79–94.

21 Lerner, *Religion, Beliefs*, 80–118; Tad Stahnke, "Proselytism and the Freedom to Change Religion in International Human Rights Law," *Brigham Young University Law Review* (1999): 251–350.

22 ICCPR, Article 18.1, emphasis added.

23 ICCPR, Article 18.3.

24 ICCPR, Article 18.2.

25 ICCPR, Article 18.4. See further Convention on the Rights of the Child (November 20, 1989), 28 I.L.M. 1448.

26 ICCPR, Article 19.2, emphasis added.

27 ICCPR, Article 19.3.

28 ICCPR, Article 27. See further Declaration on the Rights of Persons Belonging to National or Ethnic, Religious, and Linguistic Minorities, United Nations General Assembly Resolution 135 (December 18, 1992), Article 2.1, reprinted in Lerner, *Religion, Beliefs*, 140, and analyzed in Lerner, *Religion, Beliefs*, 33–35.

29 *Cantwell v. Connecticut*, 310 U.S. 296 (1940).

30 *Kokkinakis v. Greece*, 260-A Eur. Ct. H. R. (ser. A) 18.

31 Jaroslav Pelikan, *The Vindication of Tradition* (New Haven, Conn.: Yale University Press, 1984), 68.

32 ICCPR, Article 19.3.

33 See Anita Deyneka, "Guidelines for Foreign Missionaries in the Soviet Union," in Witte and Bourdeaux, eds., *Proselytism and Orthodoxy*, 331–40; and Lawrence A. Uzzell, "Guidelines for American Missionaries in Russia," in Witte and Bourdeaux, eds., *Proselytism and Orthodoxy*, 323–30.

56 Rubin: Religion and International Affairs

1 Shlomo Avineri, *Moses Hess: Prophet of Communism and Zionism* (New York: New York University Press, 1987), 102.

2 Approximately four-fifths of the world's Muslims are Sunni. Shi'ite Muslims comprise the majority of Iranians and sizable communities in Iraq, Lebanon, Bahrain, Kuwait, Pakistan, India, and elsewhere. Shi'ites argue that the post of caliph should have passed to Ali, the prophet Muhammad's son-in-law, and thus reject the line of Sunni caliphs, who ruled the Muslim world for several centuries after Muhammad's death in 632. Shi'ite Islam is characterized also by a more independent clergy and by the belief that 12 imams, beginning with Ali, exercise religious authority that is divinely guided and thus infallible. The Alawites, a sect that combines certain Christian and Islamic beliefs, are regarded as heretical Muslims by most Sunnis. Lieutenant General Hafiz al-Assad of Syria is an Alawite. The Druze are a breakaway Muslim sect centered in the mountains of Lebanon and Syria, which combines Shi'ite rites with some pre-Islamic elements of religion. Walid Jumblatt of Lebanon is one of the major hereditary leaders of the Druze. The Maronite Christians, a Roman Uniate sect, adhere to some Eastern rites but have submitted

to papal authority since 1736. Copts are members of the traditional Monophysite Christian church that originated and is centered principally in Egypt.

3   Martin Kramer, *Hezbollah's Version of the West* (Washington, D.C.: Washington Institute for Near East Policy, 1989), 21–22.

57 *Albright: Faith and Diplomacy*

1   In October 2005, the International Criminal Court issued arrest warrants for Joseph Kony and four other LRA leaders on the charge of crimes against humanity. The court does not, however, have any independent capacity to enforce those warrants.

58 *Miles: Religion and American Foreign Policy*

1   "Prepared remarks of Attorney General John Ashcroft, National Religious Broadcasters Convention, Nashville, Tennessee," February 19, 2002, http://www.usdoj.gov/ag/speeches/2002/021902religiousbroadcasters.htm.

2   Osama bin Laden statement, broadcast by Al Jazeera and reported by the Dubai bureau of the Associated Press on Monday, September 24, 2001.

3   David Fromkin, *A Peace to End All Peace: The Fall of the Ottoman Empire and the Creation of the Modern Middle East* (New York: Owl Books, 1989).

4   "Osama bin Laden Has Given Common Identity Back to the West," *New Perspectives Quarterly* (Winter 2002): 5–8.

5   "Osama bin Laden Has Given."

6   Paul Berman, "The Philosopher of Terror," *New York Times Magazine*, March 23, 2003. See also chapter 3, "In the Shade of the Koran," and chapter 4, "The Hideous Schizophrenia," in Paul Berman, *Terror and Liberalism* (New York: W. W. Norton, 2003) as well as chapter 2, "Ibn Taymiyya and His Children," in Daniel Benjamin and Steve Simon, *The Age of Sacred Terror* (New York: Random House, 2002). In sharp distinction from these views is Graham Fuller who sees Islamism as far more pluriform and pragmatic. He argues in *The Future of Political Islam* (New York: Palgrave Macmillan, 2003), 193, that "political Islam cannot properly be considered as an alternative to other ideologies such as democracy, fascism, socialism, liberalism, and communism. It cannot be put anywhere clearly on an ideological spectrum. It is far more useful to see it as a cultural variant, an alternative vocabulary in which to dress any one of these ideological trends. . . . Islamism is therefore not an ideology but a religious-cultural-political framework for engagement on issues that most concern politically engaged Muslims." For Fuller, a thinker like Sayyid Qutb represents one, but not the only, form that Islamism can take.

7   Jonathan Schell, *The Unconquerable World: Power, Nonviolence, and the Will of the People* (New York: Metropolitan Books/Henry Hold, 2003), 200.

8   Larissa MacFarquhar, "Letter from India. The Strongman," *The New Yorker*, May 26, 2003, 50–57.

9   Alissa J. Rubin, "Tiny Israeli Outposts Loom Large on Mideast Road Map," *Los Angeles Times*, June 6, 2003.

10   Chapman University, Orange, California, May 25, 2003. The program was promoted as "a special live edition of the popular talk-radio show, *Christian Questions*, with talk show host, Rick Suraci, of 980 AM WSUB, New London, Connecticut."

11   William M. Arkin, "A General Bind for Rumsfeld. What to Do When an Extremist Subordinate Is Also 'Indispensable'?" *Los Angeles Times*, October 26, 2003; Johanna Neuman, "Boykin Furor Bedevils President. Arab World Seethes at General's Linking Islam with Satan. And Bush's Response Angers His Base," *Los Angeles Times*, November 23, 2003.

12   The speaker is Milton A. Bearden, quoted in Susan Sachs, "How to Rig a Democracy," *The New York Times*, June 30, 2002.

13   Quoted by Jack Beatty, "In the Name of God," *The Atlantic Monthly*, March 5, 2003.

14   Michael Scott Doran, "The Saudi Paradox," *Foreign Affairs* (January–February 2004): 46.

15   Kevin Phillips, *The Cousins' Wars: Religion, Politics, & Triumph of Anglo-America* (New York: Basic Books, 1999).

16   Muhammad Siddiq, "Naguib Mahfouz and the Rise of the Arabic Novel," *Los Angeles Times*, November 27, 1988.

LIST OF CREDITS

Originally published in *St. Antony's International Review* (STAIR) 3, no. 2 (2008): 13–30. ©
2008 by *St. Antony's International Review*. Reprinted with permission of *St. Antony's International Review*.

R. SCOTT APPLEBY, "Religion and Global Affairs: Religious 'Militants for Peace.'"
Originally published in *The SAIS Review* 18, no. 2 (1998): 38–44. © 1998 The Johns Hopkins
University Press. Reprinted with permission of The Johns Hopkins University Press.

BRIAN COX and DANIEL PHILPOTT, "Faith-Based Diplomacy: An Ancient Idea Newly
Emergent."
Originally published in *The Brandywine Review of Faith & International Affairs* 1, no. 2 (Fall
2003): 31–40. Copyright © Institute for Global Engagement. *The Brandywine Review of Faith
& International Affairs* (now titled *The Review of Faith & International Affairs*) is available
online at: http://www.tandfonline.com/loi/rfia20.

DOUGLAS M. JOHNSTON, "Military Chaplains: Bridging Church and State."
Previously published as a chapter in Douglas M. Johnston, *Religion, Terror, and Error: U.S.
Foreign Policy and the Challenge of Spiritual Engagement* (Westport, Conn.: Praeger, 2011),
127–36. Copyright 2011 by Douglas M. Johnston, Jr. Reproduced with permission of ABC-
CLIO, LLC.

MARC GOPIN, "Religion as Destroyer and Creator of Peace: A Postmortem on Failed Peace
Processes."
Originally published on the website of the Center for World Religions, Diplomacy, & Conflict
Resolution at George Mason University, January 26, 2002, http://crdcgmu.wordpress.com/
research/. Reprinted with permission of the author.

DREW CHRISTIANSEN, "Catholic Peacemaking, 1991–2005: The Legacy of Pope John
Paul II."
Originally published in *The Review of Faith & International Affairs* 4, no. 2 (Fall 2006): 21–28.
Copyright © Institute for Global Engagement. *The Review of Faith & International Affairs* is
available online at: http://www.tandfonline.com/loi/rfia20.

HISHAM SOLIMAN, "The Potential for Peacebuilding in Islam: Toward an Islamic Concept
of Peace."
Originally published in the *Journal of Religion, Conflict, and Peace* 2, no. 2 (Spring 2009),
online at http://www.religionconflictpeace.org/node/54. Reprinted with the permission of the
author.

BENJAMIN BARBER, "Jihad vs. McWorld."
Originally published in *The Atlantic Monthly* 269, no. 3 (March 1992): 53–65, as an introduction to the book *Jihad vs. McWorld* (New York: Ballantine, 1996), a volume that discusses and
extends the themes of the original article. Reprinted with the permission of the author.

JAMES KURTH, "Religion and Globalization."
1998 Templeton Lecture on Religion and World Affairs. Originally published on FPRI Wire,
May 1999, http://www.fpri.org/fpriwire/0707.199905.kurth.religionglobalization.html. Also